HANDBOOK OF PERSONALITY ASSESSMENT

HANDBOOK OF PERSONALITY ASSESSMENT

HANDBOOK OF PERSONALITY ASSESSMENT

Irving B. Weiner
Roger L. Greene

John Wiley & Sons, Inc.

Published by John Wiley & Sons, Inc., Hoboken, New Jersey.
Published simultaneously in Canada.

Wiley Bicentennial Logo: Richard J. Pacifico

This publication is designed to provide accurate and authoritative information in regard to the subject matter covered. It is sold with the understanding that the publisher is not engaged in rendering professional services. If legal, accounting, medical, psychological or any other expert assistance is required, the services of a competent professional person should be sought.

Designations used by companies to distinguish their products are often claimed as trademarks. In all instances where John Wiley & Sons, Inc. is aware of a claim, the product names appear in initial capital or all capital letters. Readers, however, should contact the appropriate companies for more complete information regarding trademarks and registration.

For general information on our other products and services please contact our Customer Care Department within the United States at (800) 762-2974, outside the United States at (317) 572-3993 or fax (317) 572-4002.

Wiley also publishes its books in a variety of electronic formats. Some content that appears in print may not be available in electronic books. For more information about Wiley products, visit our web site at www.wiley.com.

Library of Congress Cataloging-in-Publication Data:

Weiner, Irving B.
    Handbook of personality assessment / Irving B. Weiner, Roger
    L. Greene.
      p.   cm.
    Includes index.
    ISBN 978-0-471-22881-3 (cloth : alk. paper)
 1. Personality assessment—Handbooks, manuals, etc.   I. Greene, Roger L.   II. Title.
    BF698.4.W45   2007
    155.2′8—dc22   2007016884
Printed in the United States of America.

10 9 8 7 6 5 4 3 2 1

In Memory of W. Grant Dahlstrom, John E. Exner Jr., and Jerry S. Wiggins

Contents

Preface ————————————————————————————

Personality assessment consists of procedures for identifying what people are like and how they are likely to think, feel, and act. By illuminating the nature of people and their disposition to conduct themselves in certain ways, personality assessment plays important roles in psychological science and practice. Measures of personality characteristics help researchers examine individual differences in response style, unravel the origins of distinctive behavior patterns, and map developmental paths to diverse types of life adaptation. Personality assessment helps practitioners discern an individual's frame of mind and behavioral tendencies. They can then use this information to reach relevant conclusions and make useful recommendations in a broad range of clinical, health care, forensic, educational, and organizational applications.

The personality characteristics that define the nature and dispositions of an individual can be assessed in several ways: (a) by conducting a diagnostic interview with the person; (b) by obtaining information about the person from historical records and from the reports of collateral persons who know the person well; (c) by observing the person's behavior; and (d) by administering to the person a battery of standardized personality assessment instruments.

The *Handbook of Personality Assessment* focuses on the last of these strategies—the assessment of personality functioning with standardized psychological tests. The text is addressed to two primary groups of readers: graduate students who are learning about personality assessment methods and issues, and professional psychologists who would like to refresh and update their familiarity with these methods and issues, or perhaps become acquainted with measures other than the ones they customarily use. To these ends, the chapters in this *Handbook* provide basic instruction in the administration, scoring, and interpretation of the most widely used multidimensional personality assessment instruments, and they also review and comment on contemporary clinical and research literature concerning the scientific status and practical applications of these measures.

Part I of the *Handbook* comprises chapters on four general considerations in personality assessment: its history, its procedural aspects, its psychometric foundations, and its ethical requirements. Chapter 1 (on history) relates the scientific and professional development of personality assessment as a field of study and practice, with attention to trends over time and issues of terminology. Chapter 2 (on the assessment process) discusses the purposes of personality assessment and issues connected with collecting and using assessment information, including management of the referral process, selection of a test battery, integration of assessment data from multiple sources, and utilization of computer programs in test administration, scoring, and interpretation. Chapter 3 (on psychometric foundations) reviews procedures for determining the reliability and validity of assessment methods and delineates broad issues in clinical decision making, including adequate allowance for bias and base rates. Chapter 4 (on ethical considerations) discusses each of 11 standards in the *Ethical Principles and Code of Conduct* of the American Psychological Association that have particular relevance to the personality assessment process.

Part II of the *Handbook* presents information about self-report personality inventories. Chapter 5 provides an overview of self-report inventories and the ways in which they resemble or differ from each other, including their item characteristics, their method of scale development, and their manner of determining test validity. The remaining chapters in Part II provide in-depth coverage of the most widely used and frequently studied personality assessment instruments of this kind. Chapter 6 addresses the Minnesota Multiphasic Personality Inventory-2™(MMPI-2);[1] Chapter 7, the Minnesota Multiphasic Personality Inventory—Adolescent™(MMPI-A);[2] Chapter 8, the Millon Clinical Multiaxial Inventory-III (MCMI-III); Chapter 9, the Personality Assessment Inventory (PAI); and Chapter 10, the NEO Personality Inventory—Revised (NEO-PI-R). These five chapters are organized according to a template consisting of each instrument's history, administration, scoring, validity assessment, interpretation, applications, and psychometric foundations.

Part III of the *Handbook* presents information about what have traditionally been called "projective" measures but, for reasons discussed in Chapter 1, can more appropriately be categorized as performance-based measures. Four chapters provide in-depth coverage of the most widely used performance-based methods of personality assessment. Chapter 11 addresses the Rorschach Inkblot Method (RIM); Chapter 12, the Thematic Apperception Test (TAT); Chapter 13, the Figure Drawing Methods, including the Draw-A-Person (DAP), House-Tree-Person (HTP), and Kinetic Family Drawing (KFD) tests; and Chapter 14, the Sentence Completion Methods, including the Rotter Incomplete Sentences Blank (RISB) and the Washington University Sentence Completion Test (WUSCT). The template for these four chapters consists of the nature, history, administration, scoring, interpretation, applications, and psychometric foundations of each of these measures.

Part IV of the *Handbook* provides sample interpretive reports generated by computer programs for the MMPI-2, MMPI-A, MCMI-III, PAI, NEO-PI-R, and RIM. These sample reports, which include profiles of the test scores on which the interpretive statements are based, illustrate the breadth and depth of the information that can be obtained from personality assessment instruments. The conclusions and recommendations suggested in these reports illustrate as well their potential for helping examiners provide useful diagnostic consultations. Readers, however, should attend to the limitations as well as the advantages of computer-based test interpretations; these are discussed in Chapter 2 and included in the caveats that accompany most computer-generated test reports.

---

[1]"MMPI-2," "Minnesota Multiphasic Personality Inventory-2," and "The Minnesota Report" are trademarks of the University of Minnesota.
[2]"MMPI-A," "Minnesota Multiphasic Personality Inventory—Adolescent," and "The Minnesota Report" are trademarks of the University of Minnesota.

We would like to acknowledge the valuable advice of the distinguished colleagues in personality assessment who reviewed chapter drafts for us and suggested how we might improve them. These collegial reviewers included Marvin Acklin, Robert Archer, James Butcher, James Choca, Paul Costa, Leonard Handler, Gregory Meyer, Leslie Morey, David Nichols, Paul Retzlaff, Barry Ritzler, David Steiner, Donald Viglione, and Jed Yalof. Three graduate students at Pacific Graduate School of Psychology also reviewed most of these chapters: Sarah Davis, Megan Holcomb, and Raazhan Rae-seebach. We also express our appreciation to the American Psychological Association, Caldwell Report, Pearson Assessments, and Psychological Assessment Resources, from whom we received permission to reprint copyrighted materials. We are indebted as well to our Wiley editors, Tracey Belmont and Lisa Gebo, whose guidance was of great help in our preparation of this text.

Irving B. Weiner
Roger L. Greene

About the Authors

Irving B. Weiner, PhD, is Clinical Professor of Psychiatry and Behavioral Medicine at the University of South Florida and former Director of Psychological Services at the University of South Florida Psychiatry Center in Tampa, Florida. He resides in Tampa and is in the practice of clinical and forensic psychology.

Dr. Weiner received his doctorate in clinical psychology from the University of Michigan in 1959. His positions since that time have included Professor of Psychiatry and Pediatrics and Head of the Division of Psychology at the University of Rochester Medical Center; Professor and Chair of the Department of Psychology at Case Western Reserve University; and Vice-President and Chief Academic Officer at the University of Denver and at Fairleigh Dickinson University. He is a Fellow of the American Psychological Association and of the Association for Psychological Science, a Diplomate of the American Board of Professional Psychology in both Clinical and Forensic Psychology, and a licensed psychologist in the state of Florida. He is President-elect of the Society of Clinical Psychology (APA Division 12), Past President of the International Rorschach Society, current President of the Society for Personality Assessment, and a recipient of the Society for Personality Assessment Distinguished Contribution Award. He served as editor of the *Journal of Personality Assessment* from 1985 to 1993 and as editor of *Rorschachiana: Yearbook of the International Rorschach Society* from 1990 to 1996. His writings include numerous articles and chapters and the following books:

Psychodiagnosis in Schizophrenia, 1966; republished ed., 1997
Psychological Disturbance in Adolescence, 1970; 2nd ed., 1992
Rorschach Handbook of Clinical and Research Applications, 1971
Child Development, 1972
Principles of Psychotherapy, 1975; 2nd ed., 1998
Clinical Methods in Psychology (Ed.), 1976; 2nd ed., 1983
Development of the Child, 1978
Child and Adolescent Psychopathology, 1982
Rorschach Assessment of Children and Adolescents, 1982; 2nd ed., 1995
Adolescence: A Developmental Transition, 1985; 2nd ed., 1995
Handbook of Forensic Psychology, (Ed.), 1987; 2nd ed., 1999; 3rd ed., 2006

Principles of Rorschach Interpretation, 1998; 2nd ed., 2003
Handbook of Psychology (12 vols.) (Editor-in-Chief), 2003
Adult Psychopathology Case Studies (Ed.), 2004

Roger L. Greene is a professor at Pacific Graduate School of Psychology in Palo Alto, California, where he served as Director of Clinical Training for twelve years. Dr. Greene has worked in a variety of clinical settings and with different types of patients in his clinical career. His particular area of interest clinically is the assessment and treatment of alcohol and drug abuse. He has written a number of texts and articles on the use of the MMPI-2. His most recent book, *The MMPI-2: An Interpretive Manual* (2nd ed.) was published in 2000. His books on the MMPI/MMPI-2 have been among the standard references for over two decades. He is a Fellow of Division 12 of APA and the Society for Personality Assessment. He has served on the Board of Trustees and as an Associate Editor of the *Journal of Personality Assessment* for the Society of Personality Assessment. His writings include numerous articles and chapters and the following books:

The MMPI: An Interpretive Manual, 1980
The MMPI-2/MMPI: An Interpretive Manual, 1991
Emerging Issues and Methods in Personality Assessment (Co-Ed.), 1997
The MMPI-2: An Interpretive Manual, 2000

Part I

BASIC CONSIDERATIONS

Chapter 1 ————————————————————

HISTORY OF PERSONALITY ASSESSMENT

Personality assessment, as studied and practiced today, has evolved from long-standing recognition that people differ from each other in how they think, feel, and act and are generally disposed to behave in particular ways. Awareness of individual differences among people is almost as old as civilization itself, and the great literature of the world, from the Greek tragedies to modern fiction, contains vivid descriptions of men and women with distinctive personality characteristics. (Was there ever a meaner person than Dickens's Scrooge, or a more decent person after he underwent a change of heart?) Literary depictions of distinctive personality patterns predated by far the emergence of psychology as a recognized field of study, and attention to individual differences was brought early into the beginnings of formal psychological science and practice.

The advent of formal psychological science is customarily dated to the establishment of Wundt's laboratory in Leipzig in 1879 (see Fuchs & Millar, 2003). In 1883, James McKeen Cattell began working for Wundt as a graduate assistant and asked permission to do a doctoral dissertation on individual differences in reaction time. Being a nomothetic scientist interested in psychological processes, Wundt tended to look at differences among people as bothersome error variance, but he nevertheless acceded to Cattell's request. This was the beginning of a distinguished career for Cattell, in which he pioneered mental testing, generated widespread scientific interest in measuring individual differences with psychological tests, and became regarded as the father of assessment psychology (see Weiner, 2003).

Formal practical applications of psychological assessment also began over 100 years ago, when Alfred Binet was asked in 1904 to help develop a method for identifying intellectually limited children in the Paris public schools who were in need of special attention. In collaboration with Theodore Simon, Binet drew on prior research he had done on the nature of intelligence to construct the Binet-Simon scales, which in their expanded English version later became the well-known Stanford-Binet Intelligence Scale.

The early assessments of mental functions in the tradition of Cattell and Binet had relatively little to do with determining how people are likely to think, feel, and act. It was not until the 2nd decade of the twentieth century that events ushered in formal psychological testing to address individual differences in psychological adjustment and personality style. Later on, in the 1930s and 1940s, personality assessment received considerable impetus from the emergence of personality as a discrete field of study in psychology, the expanded needs for mental health services to the military during World War II, and the post–World War II formal doctoral training and Veterans Administration programs in clinical psychology.

Following a heyday as the major focus of clinical psychology that extended to the late 1960s, personality assessment passed through an era of both shrinkage and growth that continues to the present time. This introductory chapter reviews these historical developments and concludes with some observations on the implications of idiographic and nomothetic perspectives in personality assessment and on alternative terminology for categorizing different types of personality assessment measures.

EARLY EVENTS

A seminal event in the history of applied personality assessment was the 1917 entry of the United States into World War I and the concerns it generated about the susceptibility of front-line soldiers to traumatic stress reactions (known then as "shell shock"). For help in identifying psychologically fragile draftees, the War Department turned to Robert Woodworth, a prominent experimental psychologist who had studied with Cattell. In response, Woodworth started working on a checklist of probable symptoms of psychological disturbance, to be answered "Yes" or "No" (e.g., "Are you happy most of the time?"). The intent was to use this checklist as a screening device to deselect emotionally unstable draftees.

As matters turned out, the war ended before Woodworth finished constructing his measure, and it was never used for its original purpose. Following the war, however, Woodworth wrote about his checklist in a 1919 journal article and then published the list as the Personal Data Sheet (Woodworth, 1919, 1920). The Personal Data Sheet found civilian use as a measure of adjustment, and it was the first formal self-report personality assessment questionnaire to become generally available. Woodworth's measure was limited in scope, providing only a single score for overall level of adjustment and no other information about personality characteristics. His Personal Data Sheet nevertheless served as a model for later generations of similar but more complex checklists.

The first noteworthy advance over Woodworth's unidimensional measure was a multidimensional self-report personality inventory published by Robert Bernreuter in 1931. The Bernreuter Personality Inventory comprised scales for several different personality characteristics, including neurotic tendencies, ascendance-submission, and introversion-extroversion. Highly respected and widely used in its day, Bernreuter's measure was the forerunner of many currently prominent multidimensional personality inventories, including the Minnesota Multiphasic Personality Inventory (MMPI), the Minnesota Multiphasic Personality Inventory—Adolescent (MMPI-A), the Millon Clinical Multiaxial Inventory (MCMI), the Personality Assessment Inventory (PAI), and the NEO-Personality Inventory (NEO-PI). The individual histories of these self-report inventories are discussed in Chapters 6 through 10.

A second significant event in the early history of formalized personality assessment was also contemporaneous with World War I, but unrelated to it. Hermann Rorschach, a Swiss psychiatrist working in a mental hospital, became interested in using reports of what patients saw in inkblots as indicators of their mental state and personal dispositions. Rorschach's experimental testing of several hundred nonpatients and patients with various disorders resulted in the 1921 publication of *Psychodiagnostics* (Rorschach, 1921/1942). In this book, Rorschach presented guidelines for administering, scoring, and interpreting responses to a set of 10 inkblots that has subsequently become known as the Rorschach

Inkblot Method (RIM). Chapter 11 elaborates Rorschach's personal history and the subsequent embellishment of his method by Rorschach practitioners who followed in his wake.

Although much more complex than Woodworth's checklist, Rorschach's inkblots were similarly intended more as a tool for identifying disorder than for describing personality. Rorschach's *Psychodiagnostics* is subtitled "A Diagnostic Test Based on Perception," and he explicitly stated about his measure: "It is to be understood that the test is primarily an aid to clinical diagnosis" (Rorschach, 1921/1942, p. 121). Nevertheless, Rorschach did posit numerous relationships between certain inkblot findings and particular personality characteristics, and later generations of Rorschach clinicians and scholars developed his method into a rich source of information about how people are likely to perceive events, experience emotion, manage stress, and relate to other people (see Chapter 11).

Rorschach's approach to assessing people differed markedly from the methods used by Woodworth and by other developers of self-report inventories for measuring personality. The self-report method asks people to describe themselves (e.g., "I am a very sociable person" answered as "True" or "False") and then infers fairly directly from this response some personality characteristic or behavioral tendency (e.g., being an outgoing person who enjoys being around other people, or a reclusive person who is more comfortable when alone than when in the company of others). Rorschach instead asked people to report what inkblots might be and then, from the manner in which they performed this task, inferred certain behavioral dispositions (e.g., taking their manner of responding to the color in the blots as a clue to whether they were likely to be reserved or excitable in expressing emotions).

Based on Rorschach's approach, other personality assessment measures were developed in which the critical data similarly comprised not what people said about themselves, but how they performed on various tasks. Along with the inkblot method, three similar methods are commonly used today: (1) asking people to make up stories about pictures, as exemplified by the Thematic Apperception Test (TAT) discussed in Chapter 12; (2) having people draw figures and tell stories about what they have drawn, as is done with the Draw-a-Person, House-Tree-Person, and Kinetic Family Drawing tests described in Chapter 13; and (3) asking people to extend words or phrases into complete sentences, as illustrated by the Rotter Incomplete Sentences Blank (RISB) and the Washington University Sentence Completion Test (WUSCT) presented in Chapter 14.

EMERGENCE OF PERSONALITY PSYCHOLOGY

Personality assessment received its next important impetus from the emergence in the 1930s of personality psychology as a discrete field of study. Prior to this time, as recounted by Barenbaum and Winter (2003; see also Winter & Barenbaum, 1999), numerous articles and books referring to "personality" had been published. However, just as the early methods of personality assessment stressed disorder and diagnosis rather than personality description, the early personality literature was more concerned with deviant traits and abnormal conditions than with the nature of people.

The psychoanalytic theory of personality formulated by Sigmund Freud (1916–1917/1963) and his followers during the first third of the twentieth century was a significant exception (see Bornstein, 2003; Westen & Gabbard, 1999). These psychoanalytic perspectives gained considerable popularity outside the academic community and greatly influenced psychological treatment methods, but they had little impact on what university faculty of the day believed or taught their students. When pre-1930 academic psychologists thought about personality processes, moreover, they tended to view them as subtopics within abnormal, social, or educational psychology, rather than as a separate field of study in their own right.

Personality psychology emerged from this restricted focus and subfield status with the contributions of two major figures in the history of psychology whose work emphasized the individual uniqueness of people. Gordon Allport (1937) and Henry Murray (1938) asserted in landmark books that people should be studied and understood not as an assemblage of unrelated traits, each to be examined separately, but instead with holistic attention to all the interactive facets of their unique life experiences that make people the distinctive individuals they are (see Hall, Lindzey, & Campbell, 1998, chaps. 6, 7). The Allport and Murray texts, together with a text by Stagner (1937), were the first three books devoted to broadly conceived personality theory, and the impact of these volumes was largely responsible for turning personality into a major field of psychology with its own literature, courses of study, and research programs.

Murray's contribution to energizing personality psychology held special significance for personality assessment, by virtue of his developing the TAT as his favored measure for exploring the individual experiences and perspectives of people (see Chapter 12). Progress in personality psychology also created new opportunities for using personality assessment measures in research studies. With increasing awareness of the possible contribution of personality factors to variations in whatever phenomena they were studying, investigators after the 1930s became more likely to include measures of personality characteristics among their procedures.

WORLD WAR II AND THE EXPANSION OF CLINICAL PSYCHOLOGY

Just as in World War I, the participation of the United States in World War II, beginning in December 1941, created urgent needs for psychological services. The Office of Strategic Services (OSS), which was the predecessor of the Central Intelligence Agency (CIA), asked Murray to help them select people who could function effectively in secret missions overseas. Murray brought his background in personality assessment to bear in creating and overseeing a selection process for this purpose. More than 5,000 candidates passed through Murray's evaluation program, which was staffed by approximately 50 professional persons, mostly psychologists, and encompassed just under 100 different psychological tests and behavioral measures. Following declassification of their work after the war, the OSS staff published a detailed description of its methods and reviewed how the selection program had contributed to the war effort (Office of Strategic Services Assessment Staff, 1948; see also Handler, 2001).

On a much larger scale than the OSS selection program, psychologists were brought into the armed forces during World War II to assist in providing diagnostic and treatment services for military personnel. These services included personality assessment instruments in widespread screening of inductees for possible mental or emotional disorder, much as had been planned but never fully implemented during World War I. In contrast, before

World War II ended, "Hardly a male adult of military potentiality within the United States escaped psychological testing" (Reisman, 1974, p. 271).

As the Second World War progressed, mounting psychological casualties required assigning an increasing number of psychologists to military hospitals. Continuing need for veterans' mental and other health services following the war led the Veterans Administration (VA) to create a vast hospital system in which large numbers of staff positions for psychologists became available. Faced with a shortage of psychologists to fill these positions, the VA established a clinical psychology training program that provided paid supervised clerkships for graduate students. As an additional response to pressing needs for trained psychologists, the United States Public Health Service developed a training grant program of financial support for clinical doctoral students and their university departments.

With a beckoning job market, paid training positions, and available financial aid for entering an interesting and challenging profession, a tidal wave of students sought admission to graduate training programs in clinical psychology in the late 1940s and early 1950s. Some universities had been awarding occasional doctorates in clinical psychology for many years, but few of them prior to 1946 had any prescribed educational program for becoming a doctoral level clinical psychologist. In 1944, recognizing the need for a structured curriculum and a set of educational requirements for the professional preparation of clinicians, the American Psychological Association (APA) appointed David Shakow to chair a committee charged with addressing the matter. Shakow's committee and a later APA Committee on Training in Clinical Psychology that he also chaired formulated guidelines for a multiyear doctoral program of course work, clinical experience, and scholarly engagement. Commonly referred to as the Shakow Report and published in 1947, these guidelines have continued to shape graduate education requirements in clinical psychology since that time (APA, 1947; Shakow, 1965).

Evolving as a profession with eager students, ample financial support, a structured curriculum, and a good job market, clinical psychology expanded rapidly in the post-World War II era, and personality assessment flourished along with it. Although clinical students also received training in psychotherapy, the identity of clinical psychology in those days was vested largely in psychological assessment. Assessment formed the core of training in clinical psychology, and most doctoral programs included substantial course requirements in psychological testing. Diagnostic consultation was what clinical psychologists did for the most part, and their services were sought primarily as consultants who alone among mental health professionals could bring data from standardized tests to bear in facilitating differential diagnosis and treatment planning. These and other aspects of the emergence of clinical psychology as a profession are elaborated by Reisman (1974), Routh (1994), and Routh and Reisman (2003).

TRENDS OVER TIME: SHRINKAGE AND GROWTH

The heyday of personality assessment as a central focus of clinical psychology extended from the post-World War II era to the late 1960s. The approximately 40 years since that time are usually regarded, with good reason, as an era of shrinkage in the field. Ironically, the post-1970 years were also a time of considerable growth in both scientific and professional aspects of personality assessment.

Years of Shrinkage

During the 1950s, when education in clinical psychology emphasized personality assessment and training programs usually included two or three required courses in testing, most graduate students were being trained in psychotherapy as well. In time, interest in conducting psychotherapy began to supplant diagnostic testing as a preferred career activity among clinical psychologists, and this development was hastened during the 1960s by the passage of certification and licensing laws that identified psychotherapy as a legitimate professional function of psychologists, independent of medical supervision (see Benjamin, DeLeon, Freedheim, & Vandenbos, 2003).

The 1960s was also a time when psychologists played leadership roles in advancing a wide variety of treatment modalities, including group and family therapy, behavioral methods, and community mental health approaches. With so much else for them to learn and do, clinical psychologists began to decrease the amount of time they devoted to mastering and practicing personality assessment. This shift in focus was spurred in part by the personal experience of many clinicians that newer roles offered more prestige, autonomy, and satisfaction than providing test results to be used by others in planning and providing treatment services.

Concurrently with these changes in the profession, the radical behavioral perspectives on psychology in the 1960s brought personality assessment under heavy scholarly attack. Leading social learning theorists like Mischel (1968/1996) and Peterson (1968) asserted in influential books that traditional personality assessment serves no useful purpose. There is no such thing as personality, according to these authors, and what people do is determined by the situations in which they find themselves, not by any abiding dispositions to behave in certain ways. Hence, they said, clinicians should stop trying to infer personality characteristics from test responses and concentrate instead on constructing test situations that provide representative samples of whatever behaviors are to be predicted.

From a much different theoretical perspective, humanistic psychologists around this time began to question the morality of using personality assessment instruments to classify people. These early humanistic perspectives on assessment derived mainly from the writings of Maslow (1962) and Rogers (1961), who contended that people can be understood only by learning how they experience themselves, and not by any external observations of what they say and do. From this humanistic perspective, moreover, classifying people according to personality traits or behavioral characteristics they share with other people was not only a waste of time, but also a dehumanizing procedure that strips people of their individual dignity and wrongfully presumes the right of one person to pass judgment on another.

Behaviorism and humanism challenged the pursuit of personality assessment in the 1960s not only directly, but also indirectly by derogating the entire field of personality psychology. As described by Carlson (1975), the negative perspectives that emerged from these sources contributed to a dark age for personality psychology, such that personality as an area of inquiry "virtually disappeared during the 1960s," largely due to "the burgeoning technology of behavior modification, and the celebrations of humanistic ideology" (p. 393).

This period of generally decreased interest in personality as an explanatory concept, combined with the expanded roles available to clinical psychologists and the behaviorist and humanistic labeling of personality assessment as irrelevant or improper, led many academic faculties to question the value of acquiring assessment skills. As a consequence, the utility of personality assessment was often neglected in doctoral programs, along with the unique significance of assessment in the professional identity of clinical psychologists. Frequently typifying this neglect were reduced course offerings in personality assessment, minimal requirements for assessment competency, and limited opportunities or encouragement for students to become involved in assessment-related research (see Butcher, 2006; Childs & Eyde, 2002; Exner & Erdberg, 2002; Weiner, 2003).

As the twentieth century drew to a close, personality assessment was attacked from a third direction—this time not for being behaviorally irrelevant or humanistically improper—but for being unnecessary and financially uneconomical. This line of attack emanated mainly from health care managers who alleged that the cost of personality assessment outweighs its benefits in planning and implementing appropriate interventions. These allegations were used as a basis for limiting or disallowing financial reimbursement for personality assessments, an action that caused assessment psychologists considerable concern about losing income and having either to curtail their practice or find referral sources outside the health care industry (see Acklin, 1996; Stout, 1997).

Years of Growth

Fortunately for the field of personality assessment, the aforementioned challenges to its relevance, propriety, and utility did not prove fatal. The behavioral emphasis exclusively on environmental contingencies ran out of steam in time, as did disavowal of persistent personality characteristics and limiting explanations of behavior to situational factors. Thoughtful theorists commented on the shallowness of denying that people are disposed to think, feel, and act in certain ways (see Epstein, 1979; Millon, 1984), and research findings documented broad consistencies in individual differences and the longitudinal stability of many personality characteristics (see Roberts & DelVecchio, 2000).

In the face of these developments, many prominent proponents of radical situationism, including Mischel, eventually modified their position in favor of an interactive perspective that allowed for "dispositional constructs" to influence the likelihood that a particular action will be evoked by particular external circumstances (e.g., Mischel, 1973; see also Wright & Mischel, 1987). Mischel has continued to allow a place for personality assessment in determining why people behave as they do, by acknowledging the stable individual differences among people and "the psychological invariance that distinctively characterizes an individual and that underlies the variations in the thoughts, feelings, and actions that occur across contexts and over time" (Mischel, 2004, p. 1).

This reversal in the earlier behaviorist view that traditional personality assessment serves no useful purpose was accompanied by a corresponding shift in the focus of behavioral assessment. Instead of being limited to situational observations of representative samples of behavior, recommended procedures for behavioral assessment began to include interviews and self-report inventories as well. Moreover, specialists in behavioral assessment turned some of their attention from environmental contingencies to aspects of cognitive style and the kinds of feelings, fantasies, expectations, and beliefs that people bring with them into situations (e.g., Ciminero, Calhoun, & Adams, 1977; Kendall & Hollon, 1981).

As for humanistic concerns about neglecting individuality, this criticism of personality assessment gradually gave way to recognizing that there is nothing inherently prejudicial in conducting psychological evaluations. Accurate assessment of a person's assets and limitations does not inevitably prove damaging to that individual, nor is there any necessary obstacle to psychological examiners paying just as much attention to how people differ from as well as resemble each other. To the contrary, great strides have been made by humanistic psychologists in developing assessment procedures that enhance rather than restrict attention to the unique needs of individuals. Notable among these enhancements are procedures for evaluating the implications of people's test responses and for molding the feedback of test findings into a therapeutic encounter for the person who has been examined (see Finn, 1996; Finn & Tonsager, 2002; Fischer, 1994, 2000).

Personality psychology as a field of study was rejuvenated along with personality assessment by the softening of the radical behaviorist position and the emergence of cognitive perspectives in psychology. No longer persuaded that psychological science should attend only to observable situational determinants of behavior and give no credence to inferred cross-situational characteristics of people, many researchers resumed studying individual consistencies in attitudes, motives, self-perceptions, and personality traits. As testimony to this renaissance in personality psychology, McAdams and Pals (2006) wrote, "Once an endangered scientific species, the concept of the personality *trait* now enjoys a privileged status among personality researchers and an increasingly prominent role in studies done in social, developmental, cultural, and clinical psychology" (p. 204).

With regard to the managed care allegations that personality assessment is neither useful nor economical, empirical evidence has indicated otherwise. An extensive literature documents the utility of properly conducted personality assessment in planning therapeutic interventions, monitoring their course, and enhancing their effectiveness. Moreover, follow-up findings have shown that appropriate applications of personality assessments in health care are likely to have the long-term effect of decreasing costs rather than adding to them (Butcher, 1997; Finn & Kamphuis, 2006; Kubiszyn et al., 2000; Maruish, 2004; Weiner, 2004).

Finally, of note, survey findings suggest that managed care has had less of a negative impact on personality assessment than was originally feared. A slight majority of survey respondents report a negative impact, but only small reductions in the percentage of cases in which they use personality assessment instruments, and less than a third report that managed care had a negative impact on their ability to diagnose clients accurately (Cashel, 2002). Other survey data indicate that managed care has been accompanied by only a slightly decreased frequency of comprehensive, multimethod personality assessments using full-length measures and that fewer than one-third (29%) of training directors of APA-approved doctoral programs believe that their training in psychological testing had been significantly affected by managed care (Belter & Piotrowski, 2001; Piotrowski, Belter, & Keller, 1998).

In describing the reversal of fortunes for personality assessment that began during the early 1980s, some authors noted that the bloom had never gone entirely off the psychodiagnostic rose (Millon, 1984; Weiner, 1983). Even with the expanding roles available to clinical psychologists, and despite challenges to the relevance and propriety of personality assessment, many personality assessors continued to find professional autonomy, respect, and satisfaction in functioning as expert consultants whose specialized skills could help resolve diagnostic dilemmas and point the way to effective interventions. As these expert diagnostic consultants discovered, there are many circumstances in which determining the kind of health care intervention likely to prove beneficial is a more challenging and prestigious activity than providing the intervention.

Having survived earlier challenges, personality assessment practice and research began to grow in the 1980s. A smaller percentage of clinical psychologists than before were involved in personality assessment and were devoting less of their time to it (i.e., the shrinkage). These percentage decreases were more than offset during the latter part of the twentieth century by sharply increasing numbers of doctoral level clinicians. Among these increased numbers of clinical psychologists, assessment remained the second most frequent service they provided in various settings, after psychotherapy, and survey respondents working in independent practice or in health care or government settings reported spending 15% to 23% of their time doing assessment (Phelps, Eisman, & Kohout, 1998).

In addition to growing along with the increasing numbers of clinical psychologists, personality assessment benefited from a post-1980 expansion of clinical psychology into diverse new settings that welcomed and appreciated psychological consultants. In health care, psychology's traditional focus on the diagnosis and treatment of mental disorders broadened to encompass assessment of personality characteristics associated with the origins and course of physical illness, adjustment to chronic disability, tolerance for medical and surgical procedures, and maintenance of a healthy lifestyle (see Boyer & Paharia, 2007; Friedman & Silver, 2007; James & Folen, 2005; Nezu, Nezu, & Geller, 2003; Sweet, Tovian, & Suchy, 2003). Psychologists became increasingly active in forensic, educational, and organizational settings in which personality evaluations could contribute to administrative decisions.

In the forensic area, personality test indications that a criminal defendant is out of touch with reality can be relevant to the court's determination of the person's competence or sanity, and personality characteristics that suggest psychic injury or that have implications for parental effectiveness can prove relevant in personal injury and child custody litigations (see Archer, 2006; Craig, 2005; Heilbrun, Marczyk, DeMatteo, & Mack-Allen, 2007; Ogloff & Douglas, 2003). In educational settings, personality assessment can help cast light on the needs and concerns of students showing conduct or learning problems (Braden, 2003). In organizational settings, personnel decisions related to fitness for duty or employee selection and promotion often hinge on personality characteristics that can be measured with psychological tests (see Borum, Super, & Rand, 2003; Hough & Furnham, 2003; Klimoski & Zukin, 2003). Whenever personality characteristics are relevant to decisions facing courts, schools, employers, or agencies of any kind, experts in assessing personality can make a valuable sometimes critical contribution. These practical applications of personality assessment are discussed further with respect to specific assessment instruments in Chapters 6 through 14 of this *Handbook*.

To summarize, a shrinkage in the prominence of personality assessment among the activities of clinical psychologists since the post-World War II era was accompanied by a substantial increase in the number of clinical psychologists. These increasing numbers, combined with expanded applications of personality assessment in diverse settings, generated consistent growth in the field beginning in the 1980s. As reflections of this growth, the membership of the Society for Personality Assessment doubled in size between 1980 and 2000, and a stable cadre of persons in both academic and practice positions identify themselves as assessment psychologists.

The growth and current vigor of assessment psychology is reflected as well in a burgeoning literature. In a review of published research articles on personality assessment measures over a 20-year period from 1974 to 1994, Butcher and Rouse (1996) found a higher annual rate of publication in the 1980s and 1990s than in the 1970s and concluded, "Research in clinical personality assessment continues to be carried out at a high rate" (p. 103). In 1980, just one major journal was devoted to personality assessment—the *Journal of Personality Assessment (JPA)*—with occasional articles on assessment topics appearing in the *Journal of Consulting and Clinical Psychology,* the *Journal of Clinical Psychology,* and *Professional Psychology.* The *JPA* has since been joined by the *European Journal of Psychological Assessment* in 1984, *Psychological Assessment* in 1989, and *Assessment* in 1994; assessment-related articles also appear in *Clinical Psychology: Science and Practice,* begun in 1994. Each of these journals has expanded in size over the past 10 years, and numerous articles from them, together with dozens of texts and handbooks concerning personality assessment issues and instruments, are cited throughout the chapters of this *Handbook.*

CONCLUDING COMMENTS

In concluding this brief history of personality assessment, some comments are in order concerning two matters that are relevant to the following chapters: (1) the distinction between *idiographic* and *nomothetic* approaches to personality assessment, and (2) choosing apt terminology for categorizing personality assessment measures.

Idiographic and Nomothetic Approaches to Personality Assessment

Psychologists have approached personality assessment from two different perspectives, commonly called the *idiographic* and the *nomothetic*. Idiographic perspectives reflect Cattell's previously mentioned interest in individual differences, which laid the groundwork for the field of assessment psychology. As delineated in the recommendations of Allport and Murray for using individual case studies as a way of understanding personality, idiographic assessment emphasizes ways in which people differ from each other and is focused on identifying each person's unique constellation of personality characteristics.

In contrast, nomothetic personality assessment emphasizes ways in which people resemble each other and is focused on personality characteristics and dimensions that are common to most people. Nomothetic perspectives can also be traced back to early twentieth-century research, when studies of traits and temperament were sufficiently numerous to warrant their being reviewed by Thurstone in 1916 and Allport in 1921. In short, then, nomothetic personality assessment is primarily process-focused, whereas idiographic personality assessment is primarily person-focused.

On the one hand, idiographic approaches to personality assessment have traditionally been more relevant to the purposes of practitioners than researchers. In clinical settings, practitioners conduct personality evaluations mainly to facilitate differential diagnosis and treatment planning for persons with psychological problems. To be effective and helpful in their work, clinical assessors must be closely attuned to the particular needs, capacities, and preferences of each person they examine. An examinee's resemblance to certain groups of people can provide useful information, as when a person being evaluated appears to be depressed. Nomothetically speaking, persons who are depressed are more likely than most people to commit suicide, which means that indications of depression are a risk factor in evaluating suicide potential. Yet the vast majority of people who become depressed do not take their own lives, which means idiographically speaking that clinicians evaluating a depressed person's likelihood of becoming suicidal must take into account numerous aspects of his or her particular mental state and environmental circumstances, aside from indications of depression (see Yufit, 2005).

Nomothetic assessment, on the other hand, serves mainly the purposes of researchers rather than practitioners. Personality researchers assess people to learn about the normal and abnormal course of personality development, the types of genetic dispositions and life experiences that give rise to particular traits and coping styles, and what kinds of people tend to behave in certain ways. Such nomothetic research yields probabilistic statements that expand basic knowledge of personality processes. For nomothetic assessors, individual differences and deviations from the average detract from the generalizability of whatever relationships are suggested by the data and from the universality of whatever principles they appear to identify.

These differences between idiographic and nomothetic approaches to personality assessment notwithstanding, every individual's personality always consists of some ways that differ from and others that resemble the ways of most people. Hence clinicians despite their idiographic focus need to have a good grasp of normative expectations to recognize whether and to what extent an examinee is showing unique characteristics. Conversely, psychological processes cannot be fully understood without some grasp of which individuals, for what reasons, and under what circumstances are likely to deviate from normative expectation. Hence researchers despite their nomothetic focus need to go beyond viewing exceptions to the rule as error variance and seek explanations for why the behavior of certain people in certain circumstances differs substantially from normative expectations.

Terminology for Categorizing Personality Assessment Measures

Woodworth's Personal Data Sheet and the similar measures that it prompted became commonly known as "self-report inventories," which is an informative and accurate way of categorizing them. As noted, however, Rorschach's approach to assessment differed from Woodworth's and could not be considered a self-report method. Instead of relying on relatively direct inferences from what people reported about themselves, Rorschach relied on making relatively indirect inferences from how people reported what inkblots might be. In an influential article published in 1939, Frank suggested that personality tests like the Rorschach, in which the stimuli and instructions are relatively unstructured, induce a person to "project upon that plastic field . . . his private world of personal meanings and feelings" (pp. 395–402). Frank's suggestion resulted in Rorschach's test, together with picture-story, figure drawing, and sentence completion tests, becoming referred to as *projective* methods.

Over time, it became common practice to differentiate the so-called projective methods from self-report inventories by referring to the latter as *objective* methods. This distinction between objective and projective measures is misleading because it implies that if one type of measure is objective (and hence scientific and dependable), the other type of measure must be subjective (and hence less scientific and dependable). In truth, self-report inventories are not entirely objective, nor are projective tests entirely subjective. Self-report items often involve subjectivity with respect to how persons being examined interpret them. Asked to answer "Yes" or "No" to statements like "I get angry sometimes" and "I am happy most of the time," examinees must determine for themselves the benchmarks for deciding how frequent "sometimes" and "most of the time" are, and what extent of ire or joy constitutes being "angry" or "happy."

As for the so-called projective measures, all of them involve some elements of objectivity in either their instructions or stimuli. In Rorschach testing, people are asked to indicate where in the inkblots they saw each of their percepts, which is an unambiguous instruction. Most of the TAT pictures have unambiguous stimulus elements, such as a clear depiction of a boy and a violin in Card 1, and the instructions for figure drawing and sentence completion methods are quite precise about what examinees are expected to do (e.g., draw a figure, complete these sentences), even though open-ended with respect to how they should do it. Ambiguity is thus a dimensional and not a categorical characteristic of personality assessment instruments, and none of them is totally objective or subjective. Self-report inventories and performance-based measures vary in ambiguity, and they differ among themselves as well as from each other in the extent to which the test stimuli and the examinee's task are ambiguous.

With these considerations in mind, many personality assessors have recommended replacing the self-report/objective and projective/subjective distinction with less valued-laden categorizations of personality assessment measures (see Meyer & Kurtz, 2006). As one generically accurate possibility, these two types of test could be referred to as being "relatively structured" or "relatively unstructured" measures. A more denotative distinction has been suggested by the Psychological Assessment Work Group (PAWG), a task force appointed by the Board of Professional Affairs of the American Psychological Association. In its final report concerning the utility of psychological assessment methods, the PAWG group separated tests into two groups: self-report instruments, which function on the basis of what people say about themselves, and performance-based measures, which are based on how examinees are observed to perform tasks that are set for them (Meyer et al., 2001).

In accord with the PAWG recommendation, the chapters that follow categorize personality assessment methods as self-report instruments or performance-based measures. This distinction has important implications for the personality assessment process, because self-report and performance-based methods have some potential advantages and limitations relative to each other. With respect to the advantages of self-report measures, the best way to learn something about people is usually to ask them about it. If you want to know if someone feels anxious, you ask, "Are you feeling anxious?" If you want to know if a person is using drugs, you ask, "Do you use drugs?" If you want to know if a person had a happy childhood, has ever been arrested, or is satisfied with his or her sex life, you ask. How people answer direct questions about such matters is more likely to provide definitive information than indirect impressions based how they perform certain tasks.

On the other hand, the information provided by self-report instruments is limited to what people are able and willing to say about themselves. What people can say about themselves depends on how fully aware they are of their own characteristics. What they are willing to say about themselves depends on how prepared they are to be open and truthful. Limited self-awareness or reluctance to disclose can detract from the dependability of the self-descriptions people provide when they are being interviewed or are filling out a self-report inventory. In a review of empirical findings concerning this potential shortcoming of self-reported assessments, Dunning, Heath, and Suls (2004) came to the following conclusion:

> The views people hold of themselves are often flawed. The correlation between those views and their objective behavior is often meager to modest, and people often claim to have valuable skills and desirable attributes to a degree that they do not. (p. 98)

Performance-based measures, because of the indirect methodology they employ, can often circumvent this limitation of self-report instruments. As a trade-off for sometimes generating less certain and more speculative inferences than a direct inquiry, the indirect approach is often more likely than self-report inventories to reveal personality characteristics that respondents do not fully recognize in themselves or are hesitant to admit when asked about them directly (see Bornstein, 1999; Greenwald et al., 2002; Schmulke & Egloff, 2005). In light of the relative advantages and limitations of self-report and performance-based assessment methods, many contemporary authors recommend an integrative approach to personality assessment that employs both kinds of measures (see Beutler & Groth-Marnat, 2003; Meyer et al., 2001; Weiner, 2005). The nature of these two types of test and the benefits of integrative personality assessment are discussed further in Chapter 2, which elaborates the personality assessment process.

REFERENCES

Acklin, M. W. (1996). Personality assessment and managed care. *Journal of Personality Assessment*, *66*, 194–201.

Allport, G. W. (1921). Personality and character. *Psychological Bulletin*, *18*, 441–455.

Allport, G. W. (1937). *Personality: A psychological interpretation*. New York: Holt.

American Psychological Association, Committee on Training in Clinical Psychology. (1947). Recommended graduate program in clinical psychology. *American Psychologist*, *2*, 539–558.

Archer, R. P. (Ed.). (2006). *Forensic uses of clinical assessment instruments*. Mahwah, NJ: Erlbaum.

Barenbaum, N. B., & Winter, D. G. (2003). Personality. In I. B. Weiner (Editor-in-Chief) & D. K. Freedheim (Vol. Ed.), *Handbook of psychology: Vol. 1. History of psychology* (pp. 177–293). Hoboken, NJ: Wiley.

Belter, R. W., & Piotrowski, C. (2001). Current status of doctoral-level training in psychological testing. *Journal of Clinical Psychology*, *57*, 717–726.

Benjamin, L. T., Jr., DeLeon, P. H., Freedheim, D. K., & Vandenbos, G. R. (2003). Psychology as a profession. In I. B. Weiner (Editor-in-Chief) & D. K. Freedheim (Vol. Ed.), *Handbook of psychology: Vol. 1. History of psychology* (pp. 37–45). Hoboken, NJ: Wiley.

Bernreuter, R. G. (1931). *The Personality Inventory*. Palo Alto, CA: Consulting Psychologists Press.

Beutler, L. E., & Groth-Marnat, G. (2003). *Integrative assessment of adult personality* (2nd ed.). New York: Guilford Press.

Bornstein, R. F. (1999). Criterion validity of objective and projective dependency tests: A meta-analytic assessment of behavioral prediction. *Psychological Assessment*, *11*, 48–57.

Bornstein, R. F. (2003). Psychodynamic models of personality. In I. B. Weiner (Editor-in-Chief), T. Millon, & M. J. Lerner (Vol. Eds.), *Handbook of psychology: Vol. 5. Personality and social psychology* (pp. 117–134). Hoboken, NJ: Wiley.

Borum, R., Super, J., & Rand, M. (2003). Forensic assessment for high-risk occupations. In I. B. Weiner (Editor-in-Chief) & A. M. Goldstein (Vol. Ed.), *Handbook of psychology: Vol. 11. Forensic psychology* (pp. 133–147). Hoboken, NJ: Wiley.

Boyer, B. A., & Paharia, I. (Eds.). (2007). *Comprehensive handbook of clinical health psychology.* Hoboken, NJ: Wiley.

Braden, J. P. (2003). Psychological assessment in school settings. In I. B. Weiner (Editor-in-Chief), J. R. Graham, & J. A. Naglieri (Vol. Eds.), *Handbook of psychology: Vol. 10. Assessment psychology* (pp. 261–290). Hoboken, NJ: Wiley.

Butcher, J. N. (Ed.). (1997). *Personality assessment in managed health care.* New York: Oxford University Press.

Butcher, J. N. (2006). Assessment in clinical psychology: A perspective on the past, present challenges, and future prospects. *Clinical Psychology: Science and Practice, 13,* 205–209.

Butcher, J. N., & Rouse, S. V. (1996). Personality: Individual differences and clinical assessment. *Annul Review of Psychology, 47,* 87–111.

Carlson, R. (1975). *Personality. Annual Review of Psychology, 26,* 393–414.

Cashel, M. L. (2002). Child and adolescent psychological assessment: Current clinical practices and the impact of managed care. *Professional Psychology, 33,* 446–453.

Childs, R., & Eyde, L. D. (2002). Assessment training in clinical psychology doctoral programs: What should we teach? What do we teach? *Journal of Personality Assessment, 78,* 130–144.

Ciminero, A. R., Calhoun, K. S., & Adams, H. E. (Eds.). (1977). *Handbook of behavioral assessment.* New York: Wiley.

Craig, R. J. (2005). *Personality-guided forensic psychology.* Washington, DC: American Psychological Association.

Dunning, D., Heath, C., & Suls, J. M. (2004). Flawed self-assessment implications for health, education, and the workplace. *Psychological Science in the Public Interest, 5,* 69–106.

Epstein, S. (1979). The stability of behavior: Pt I. On predicting most of the people much of the time. *Journal of Personality and Social Psychology, 37,* 1097–1126.

Exner, J. E., Jr., & Erdberg, P. (2002). Why use personality tests? A brief history and some comments. In J. N. Butcher (Ed.), *Clinical personality assessment* (2nd ed., pp. 7–12). New York: Oxford University Press.

Finn, S. E. (1996). Assessment feedback integrating MMPI-2 and Rorschach findings. *Journal of Personality Assessment, 67,* 543–557.

Finn, S. E., & Kamphuis, J. H. (2006). Therapeutic assessment with the MMPI-2. In J. N. Butcher (Ed.), *MMPI-2: A practitioner's guide* (pp. 165–191). Washington, DC: American Psychological Association.

Finn, S. E., & Tonsager, M. E. (2002). How therapeutic assessment became humanistic. *Humanistic Psychologist, 30,* 10–22.

Fischer, C. (1994). *Individualizing psychological assessment.* Hillsdale, NJ: Erlbaum.

Fischer, C. (2000). Collaborative, individualized assessment. *Journal of Personality Assessment, 74,* 2–14.

Frank, L. K. (1939). Projective methods for the study of personality. *Journal of Psychology, 8,* 543–557.

Freud, S. (1963). Introductory lectures on psychoanalysis. In J. Strachey & A. Tyson (Eds. & Trans.), *The standard edition of the complete psychological works of Sigmund Freud* (Vols. *XV* & *XVI*). London: Hogarth. (Original work published 1916–1917)

Friedman, H. S., & Silver, R. C. (Eds.). (2007). *The evolution of health psychology.* New York: Oxford University Press.

Fuchs, A. H., & Millar, K. S. (2003). Psychology as a science. In I. B. Weiner (Editor-in-Chief) & D. K Freedheim (Vol. Ed.), *Handbook of psychology: Vol. 1. History of psychology* (pp. 1–26). Hoboken, NJ: Wiley.

Greenwald, A. G., Banaji, M. R., Rudman, L. A., Farnham, S. D., Nosek, B. A., & Mellott, D. S. (2002). A unified theory of implicit attitudes, stereotypes, self-esteem, and self-concept. *Psychological Review, 109*, 3–25.

Hall, C. S., Lindzey, G., & Campbell, J. B. (1998). *Theories of personality* (4th ed.). New York: Wiley.

Handler, L. (2001). Assessment of men: Personality assessment goes to war by the Office of Strategic Services assessment staff. *Journal of Personality Assessment, 76*, 558–578.

Heilbrun, K., Marczyk, G., DeMatteo, D., & Mack-Allen, J. (2007). A principle-based approach to forensic mental health assessment: Utility and update. In A. M. Goldstein (Ed.), *Forensic psychology: Emerging topics and expanding roles* (pp. 45–72). Hoboken, NJ: Wiley.

Hough, L. M., & Furnham, A. (2003). Use of personality variables in work settings. In I. B. Weiner, (Editor-in-Chief), W. C. Borman, D. R. Ilgen, & R. J. Klimoski (Vol. Eds.), *Handbook of psychology: Vol. 12. Industrial and organizational psychology* (pp. 131–170). Hoboken, NJ: Wiley.

James, L. C., & Folen, R. A. (Eds.). (2005). *The primary health consultant: The next frontier for psychologists in hospitals and clinics*. Washington, DC: American Psychological Association.

Kendall, P. C., & Hollon, S. D. (Eds.). (1981). *Assessment strategies for cognitive-behavioral interventions*. New York: Academic Press.

Klimoski, R. J., & Zukin, L. R. (2003). Psychological assessment in industrial/organizational settings. In I. B. Weiner (Editor-in-Chief), J. R. Graham, & J. A. Naglieri (Vol. Eds.), *Handbook of psychology: Vol. 10. Assessment psychology* (pp. 317–344). Hoboken, NJ: Wiley.

Kubiszyn, T. W., Meyer, G. J., Finn, S. E., Eyde, L. D., Kay, G. G., Moreland, K. L., et al. (2000). Empirical support for psychological assessment in clinical health care settings. *Professional Psychology, 31*, 119–130.

Maruish, M. E. (2004). *The use of psychological testing for treatment planning and outcome assessment* (3rd ed.). Mahwah, NJ: Erlbaum.

Maslow, A. H. (1962). *Toward a psychology of being*. Princeton, NJ: Van Nostrand.

McAdams, D. P., & Pals, J. L. (2006). A new Big Five: Fundamental principles for an integrative science of personality. *American Psychologist, 61*, 204–217.

Meyer, G. J., Finn, S. E., Eyde, L. D., Kay, G. G., Moreland, K. L., Dies, R. R., et al. (2001). Psychological testing and psychological assessment: A review of evidence and issues. *American Psychologist, 56*, 128–165.

Meyer, G. J., & Kurtz, J. E. (2006). Advancing personality assessment terminology: Time to retire "objective" and "projective" as personality test descriptors. *Journal of Personality Assessment, 87*, 223–225.

Millon, T. (1984). On the renaissance of personality assessment and personality theory. *Journal of Personality Assessment, 48*, 450–466.

Mischel, W. (1973). Toward a cognitive social learning reconceptualization of personality. *Psychological Review, 80*, 252–283.

Mischel, W. (1996). *Personality and assessment*. Mahwah, NJ: Erlbaum. (Original work published 1968)

Mischel, W. (2004). Toward an integrative science of the person. *Annual Review of Psychology, 55*, 1–22.

Murray, H. A. (1938). *Explorations in personality*. New York: Oxford University Press.

Nezu, A. M., Nezu, C. M., & Geller, P. A. (Eds.). (2003). *Handbook of psychology: Vol. 9. Health psychology*. Hoboken, NJ: Wiley.

Office of Strategic Services Assessment Staff. (1948). *Assessment of men*. New York: Rinehart.

Ogloff, J. R. P., & Douglas, K. S. (2003). Psychological assessment in forensic settings. In I. B. Weiner (Editor-in-Chief), J. R. Graham, & J. A. Naglieri (Vol. Eds.), *Handbook of psychology: Vol. 10. Assessment psychology* (pp. 345–364). Hoboken, NJ: Wiley.

Peterson, D. R. (1968). *The clinical study of social behavior*. New York: Appleton-Century-Crofts.

Phelps, R., Eisman, E. J., & Kohout, J. (1998). Psychological practice and managed care: Results of the CAPP practitioner survey. *Professional Psychology*, *29*, 31–26.

Piotrowski, C., Belter, R. W., & Keller, J. W. (1998). The impact of "managed care" on the practice of psychological testing: Preliminary findings. *Journal of Personality Assessment*, *70*, 441–447.

Reisman, J. M. (1974). *A history of clinical psychology (Rev. ed.)*. New York: Wiley.

Roberts, B. W., & DelVecchio, W. F. (2000). The rank-order consistency of personality traits from childhood to old age: A quantitative review of longitudinal studies. *Psychological Bulletin*, *126*, 3–25.

Rogers, C. R. (1961). *On becoming a person*. Boston: Houghton-Mifflin.

Rorschach, H. (1942). *Psychodiagnostics: A diagnostic test based on perception*. Bern, Switzwerland: Hans Humber. (Original work published 1921)

Routh, D. K. (1994). *Clinical psychology since 1917: Science, practice, and organization*. New York: Plenum Press.

Routh, D. K., & Reisman, J. M. (2003). Clinical psychology. In I. B. Weiner (Editor-in-Chief) & D. K. Freedheim (Vol. Ed.), *Handbook of psychology: Vol. 1. History of psychology* (pp. 337–355). Hoboken, NJ: Wiley.

Schmulke, S. C., & Egloff, B. (2005). A latent state-trait analysis of implicit and explicit personality measures. *European Journal of Psychological Assessment*, *21*, 100–107.

Shakow, D. (1965). Seventeen years later: Clinical psychology in the light of the 1947 Committee on Training in Clinical Psychology report. *American Psychologist*, *20*, 353–362.

Stagner, R. (1937). *Psychology of personality*. New York: McGraw-Hill.

Stout, C. E. (Ed.). (1997). *Psychological assessment in managed care*. New York: Wiley.

Sweet, J. J., Tovian, S. M., & Suchy, Y. (2003). Psychological assessment in medical settings. In I. B. Weiner (Editor-in-Chief), J. R. Graham, & J. A. Naglieri (Vol. Eds.), *Handbook of psychology: Vol. 10. Assessment psychology* (pp. 291–316). Hoboken, NJ: Wiley.

Thurstone, L. O. (1916). Character and temperament. *Psychological Bulletin*, *13*, 384–388.

Weiner, I. B. (1983). The future of psychodiagnosis revisited. *Journal of Personality Assessment*, *47*, 451–461.

Weiner, I. B. (2003). Assessment psychology. In I. B. Weiner (Editor-in-Chief) & D. K Freedheim (Vol. Ed.), *Handbook of psychology: Vol. 1. History of psychology* (pp. 279–302). Hoboken, NJ: Wiley.

Weiner, I. B. (2004). Monitoring psychotherapy with performance-based measures of personality functioning. *Journal of Personality Assessment*, *83*, 322–330.

Weiner, I. B. (2005). Integrative personality assessment with self-report and performance-based measures. In S. Strack (Ed.), *Handbook of personality and psychopathology* (pp. 317–331). Hoboken, NJ: Wiley.

Westen, D., & Gabbard, G. O. (1999). Psychoanalytic approaches to personality. In L. A. Pervin & O. P. John (Eds.), *Handbook of personality* (2nd ed., pp. 57–101). New York: Guilford Press.

Winter, D. G., & Barenbaum, N. B. (1999). History of modern personality theory and research. In L. A. Pervin & O. P. John (Eds.), *Handbook of personality* (2nd ed., pp. 3–37). New York: Guilford Press.

Woodworth, R. S. (1919). Examination of emotional fitness for war. *Psychological Bulletin*, *15*, 59–60.

Woodworth, R. S. (1920). *Personal data sheet*. Chicago: Stoelting.

Wright, J. C., & Mischel, W. (1987). A conditional approach to dispositional constructs: The local predictability of social behavior. *Journal of Personality and Social Psychology*, *53*, 1159–1177.

Yufit, R. I. (2005). Assessing the vital balance in evaluating suicide potential. In R. I. Yufit & D. Lester (Eds.), *Assessment, treatment, and prevention of suicide behavior* (pp. 121–141). Hoboken, NJ: Wiley.

Chapter 2

THE PERSONALITY ASSESSMENT PROCESS

Personality assessment consists of procedures for identifying similarities and differences among people in their personal characteristics and capacities. The commonly used self-report inventories and performance-based measures described in this *Handbook* provide the cornerstone for contemporary personality assessment, although the implications of personality test findings must always be weighed in light of information from other sources as well. These other sources include interview responses, collateral reports, and historical documents that provide information about a person's prior experiences, sociocultural background, and current life circumstances.

Implied in this attention to multiple sources of information is an important distinction between *testing* and *assessment*. As customarily defined, personality testing refers to the use of psychological tests to identify an individual's personality characteristics, whereas personality assessment involves integrating many kinds of information into a set of personality-based conclusions and recommendations concerning a person who has been evaluated (American Educational Research Association [AERA], American Psychological Association, and National Council on Measurement in Education, 1999, chap. 12; Fernandez-Ballesteros, 1997; Matarazzo, 1990; Meyer et al., 2001).

Personality assessment serves several purposes in relation to many types of referral questions. The present chapter delineates these purposes and questions, and then discusses general aspects of preparing for and conducting personality assessments, interpreting personality assessment data, and reporting the implications of personality assessment findings. Although attention is paid to multiple sources of data, the discussion focuses primarily on using self-report inventories and performance-based measures to obtain information about an individual's personality characteristics.

PURPOSES OF PERSONALITY ASSESSMENT

Personality assessment derives its purposes from the relevance of personality characteristics to making decisions in clinical, health care, forensic, educational, and organizational settings. As noted in Chapter 1, clinical settings are the traditional and perhaps still the most common setting in which assessment psychologists conduct personality evaluations. Personality assessment in clinical settings is undertaken mainly to address questions of differential diagnosis and treatment planning. By clarifying the nature and extent of psychological disorder in persons being evaluated, personality assessment facilitates decisions about how best to provide treatment for them and monitor their progress in it.

Personality assessment also contributes to treatment planning and outcome evaluation by identifying individuals' personality strengths and weaknesses, their adaptive capacities and limitations, their preferred coping style, their underlying needs and concerns, and their attitudes toward themselves and other people. This information can help clinicians formulate treatment goals in psychotherapy and implement strategies for achieving these goals (see Beutler, Malik, Talebi, Fleming, & Moleiro, 2004; Butcher, 1997; Hurt, Reznikoff, & Clarkin, 1991; Lambert & Hawkins, 2004; Weiner, 2004).

As also noted in Chapter 1, personality assessment emerged in nontraditional clinical settings as psychologists began to play consultative roles in these settings. Personality assessment in health care settings can be helpful in identifying psychological aspects of physical illness, monitoring adaptation to chronic illness or disability, estimating tolerance for surgical procedures, and revealing the sources of an unhealthy lifestyle or poor compliance with prescribed treatment.

In forensic settings, personality test indications of mental impairment can contribute in criminal cases to determinations of competence and sanity. In civil cases, personality assessment findings related to psychological dysfunction or incapacity are often relevant in adjudicating personal injury and disability claims. In family law, personality test information about the personal qualities and psychological adjustment of children and their parents is commonly considered in mediating child custody and visitation rights.

In educational settings, the results of personality assessments can identify the need to provide counseling or special educational services for students with conduct or learning problems. In organizational settings, personality assessment can prove useful in evaluating candidates for employment or promotion, and test findings can help determine the fitness-for-duty of persons who have become psychologically impaired or who have behaved in ways that raised concern about their potential for violence. Publications describing these consultative contributions of personality assessors in clinical, health care, forensic, educational, and organizational settings are referenced in Chapter 1 (see p. 11), and Chapters 6 through 14 provide guidelines for applying specific personality assessment instruments in these diverse settings.

PREPARING FOR PERSONALITY ASSESSMENTS

In preparing to conduct a personality assessment, examiners should have clearly in mind the referral questions that are being asked and the kinds of conclusions and recommendations that will be responsive to these questions. Clarity about referral questions guide examiners in collecting appropriate assessment data and interpreting these data in a useful way. Adequate preparation for conducting a personality assessment thus consists of clarifying the referral questions and selecting a test battery, and it must include obtaining informed consent from the person who is to be examined.

Clarifying the Referral

Referral questions should inform personality assessors what the most relevant features of their test data are likely to be and the specific issues they should address in reporting their findings. Vague referrals call for clarification prior to beginning an evaluation. A clinical referral for "differential diagnosis" needs to state the alternative diagnostic possibilities being considered by the referring person (e.g., "bipolar disorder versus borderline personality disorder"), for examiners to know which personality test variables should receive particular attention. Similarly, a referral for "personality evaluation" needs to clarify why the evaluation is being requested (e.g., "to assist in treatment planning"), for examiners to know what personality characteristics would be important to emphasize in their report.

Some referrals may be unclear, not because they lack specificity, but because they concern matters with which the examiner is unfamiliar. In the first example just given, being adequately prepared to conduct a differential diagnosis assessment of bipolar and borderline personality disorder requires knowing what personality test variables are likely to discriminate between these two conditions. In the second example, adequate preparation would include being knowledgeable about the implications of various personality characteristics for treatment planning. Examiners who are not well-versed in the content of a referral question will have difficulty responding to it with sensible conclusions and useful recommendations unless they close this gap in their knowledge.

In the context of a personnel rather than a clinical evaluation, suppose an organization is seeking help in assessing candidates for a leadership position. Effectiveness in providing this help will depend in part on an examiner's awareness of personality characteristics that are likely to promote effective leadership, such as being energetic, decisive, assertive, self-confident, and reasonably unflappable (see Zaccaro, 2007). Familiarity with the relevance of these and other personality characteristics to leadership potential prepares examiners to focus on these characteristics in collecting, interpreting, and reporting assessment data in ways that facilitate the organization's selection process.

Implicit in the preceding examples is the additional necessity of clarifying whether a personality assessment is being requested for *clinical* or *administrative* purposes. In clinical assessments, psychologists are responsible to the person being examined, the person being examined is seeking some type of help, and the examination is intended to benefit this person and be responsive to the person's needs. Assessments for clinical purposes typify practice in clinical and health care settings, in which evaluations are geared to identifying and ameliorating psychological difficulties.

In administrative assessments, psychologists are responsible not to the people they examine, but to third parties who have requested the evaluation. To be sure, examiners are ethically obliged to treat administrative examinees fairly and with respect. Nevertheless, administrative evaluations are conducted for the benefit of the parties requesting them, not the person being examined, and the results may or may not meet this person's needs. Administrative purposes typically characterize assessments in forensic, educational, and organizational settings, in which psychologists are requested to help decide such matters as whether a prison inmate should be paroled, a student should be suspended from school, or a manager should be promoted to an executive position.

The difference between clinical and administrative assessments often affects the frame of mind in which people come for an examination. Most clinically referred persons appear voluntarily and hope to gain some benefit from being evaluated. Administratively referred persons have usually been mandated to appear and are fearful of negative consequences of the examination. Administratively referred persons can decline to be examined, but they usually appreciate that doing so can have a negative impact on decisions made about them by the referring party. Hence they appear, but they tend to be more anxious about being examined than clinically referred persons and more inclined to respond in a guarded manner. Determining in advance whether they will be conducting a clinical or an administrative evaluation helps examiners anticipate an examinee's test-taking attitudes and prepare for discussing with the person such matters as who will receive the results of the examination.

Selecting the Test Battery

Adequate preparation for conducting a personality assessment includes informed selection of assessment instruments to include in the test battery. Depending on the referral question, it may be helpful to administer certain unidimensional checklists and relatively brief questionnaires. Frequently used measures of these kinds, in alphabetical order, include the Beck Depression Inventory-II (BDI-II; Beck, Steer, & Brown, 1996), the Child Behavior Checklist (CBCL; Achenbach, 1992), the Eating Disorders Inventory-3 (EDI-3; Garner, 2004), the Michigan Alcoholism Screening Test (MAST; Selzer, 1971), the Psychopathy Checklist—Revised (PCL-R; Hare, 1990), the Reynolds Adolescent Depression Scale-2 (RADS-2; Reynolds, 2002), the State-Trait Anger Expression Inventory-2 (STAXI-2; Spielberger, 1998), the Suicide Probability Scale (SPS; Cull & Gill, 1988), and the Trauma Symptom Inventory (TSI; Briere, 1995).

In choosing among the multidimensional self-report and performance-based types of instruments discussed in Chapters 6 through 14, personality assessors can expect to enhance their evaluations by selecting at least one measure of each type. As mentioned in Chapter 1, self-report and performance-based instruments measure personality characteristics in different ways and at different levels of examinees' ability to recognize and willingness to acknowledge their own characteristics. For this reason, as elaborated next, self-report inventories are likely to be particularly sensitive to personality states, and performance-based measures are likely to be particularly sensitive to personality traits. Additionally, either type of instrument can yield data of questionable dependability, especially when people are being guarded or defensive in responding to them. A balanced test battery that includes both types of multidimensional measures cuts across these differences and also allows examiners to derive useful information from patterns of congruence and divergence between them (see Acklin, 2002).

Differential Sensitivity to Personality State and Traits

As indicated in Chapter 1, self-report inventories inquire fairly directly about such matters as what people think, how they feel, how they spend their time, and whether they are experiencing various symptoms of psychological disorder. These measures are accordingly well-suited to identifying personality states, explicit motives, and other characteristics that people customarily recognize in themselves. Moreover, because self-report inventory statements resemble the interview questions used to establish a formal diagnosis according to the *Diagnostic and Statistical Manual of Mental Disorders* (*DSM-IV-TR;* American Psychiatric Association, 2000), self-report inventories are especially helpful in determining the presence and severity of specific psychological disorders. Because they are so direct in asking people to describe themselves in specific terms, self-report measures may not shed much light on personality traits and behavioral dispositions that people do not fully recognize in themselves and are therefore unable to disclose.

Performance-based measures function quite differently in these respects. Because they are indirect and rarely ask people specific questions about themselves, they seldom provide much information about what people are thinking and feeling at the moment or about what symptoms they might be experiencing. By virtue of their relative lack of obvious content and by sampling how people deal with relatively unstructured tasks, performance-based measures commonly reveal traits, dispositions, underlying attitudes, and implicit motivations of which individuals are not fully cognizant.

Neither the particular sensitivity of self-report inventories to personality states and explicit motives, nor the particular sensitivity of personality-based measures to personality traits and implicit motives, constitutes an absolute distinction between these two types of assessment. Self-report data sometimes speak to an individual's abiding dispositions, and performance-based test data may help identify personality states and psychological disorders. There is nevertheless compelling conceptual basis and solid empirical support for expecting these two types of measures to tap different levels of conscious awareness and to be differentially sensitive to state and trait dimensions of personality functioning (see Aspendorf, Banse, & Mucke, 2002; Bornstein, 1999; McClelland, Koestner, & Weinberger, 1989; Weiner, 2005).

Differential Dependability of Obtained Data

People who are willing to disclose their personality characteristics ordinarily respond to testing in an honest and forthright manner and produce ample test protocols. Their responsiveness makes it possible to generate the full range of each measure's interpretive hypotheses and thereby enhances the dependability of the test data they provide. Reluctance to disclose information, on the other hand, leads examinees to approach testing in a guarded and defensive manner that limits what can be learned about them. Unwilling examinees may decline to answer certain questions on self-report inventories; they may give brief responses on performance-based measures; they may object to taking particular tests; or they may refuse to be tested at all. Each of these degrees of guardedness limits the test data that examiners can obtain, the number of interpretive inferences they can draw, and the confidence with which they can present their conclusions and recommendations.

People who are reluctant to reveal aspects of themselves are not necessarily difficult to examine. Despite their aversion to self-disclosure, unwilling examinees may intend to avoid appearing resistive, especially if they have been referred for administrative purposes, and they may for this reason go through the motions of cooperating with the test procedures, even to the point of being deferential and ingratiating. While being overtly cooperative, however, defensive examinees often compromise the dependability of the test data they produce by responding dishonestly or less fully than they could have done.

When reluctant examinees cooperate at least to the extent of not refusing to respond, self-report data tend to be more dependable than performance-based data for two reasons. First, each self-report item response is a complete response (e.g., a True/False answer or a scale rating). Unless they omit numerous items entirely, then, reluctant but cooperative examinees will give enough complete answers to generate all the scales and indices used in making interpretations. Second, most self-report inventories include validity scales that help to identify when the obtained data are misleading or untrustworthy.

By contrast, the open-ended format of performance-based measures allows people to be overtly cooperative while restricting the number and richness of their responses. As elaborated in Chapter 11, short Rorschach records that satisfy a validity criterion of containing at least 14 answers may still not be long enough to ensure the dependability of certain summary scores and indices. Even while producing Rorschach records with a great many responses, examinees are free to restrict each response to bland and unelaborated content that reveals very little about their personality characteristics. As for the other performance-based personality measures discussed in Chapters 12 through 14, examinees can, if they wish, tell brief and simplistic stories about pictures, draw vague and sketchy figures, and write banal and uninformative sentence completions. Although guardedness may be inferred in these circumstances, performance-based personality measures, with the exception of the 14-response Rorschach requirement, do not provide any quantitative scale indicators for the extent to which the test data may be undependable.

On the other hand, the indirect nature and lack of obvious item content in performance-based measures may, as noted in Chapter 1, help circumvent guardedness. People who are unwilling to admit their shortcomings or reluctant to report their difficulties may unwittingly provide clues to these shortcomings and difficulties in the way they deal with the relatively ambiguous test stimuli and unstructured task requirements of performance-based personality measures. The relative ambiguity and lack of structure in performance-based measures make it particularly difficult for guarded examinees to decide how to respond to them, which can account for their inadvertently disclosing more information about themselves on these measures than was their intent.

As a related difference in test method that can affect the openness of examinees and the dependability of the test data they produce, some people feel more comfortable in structured than in unstructured situations, and vice versa. Individuals who like to be told what to do, to know what is expected of them, and to conform to specific guidelines are more likely to be relaxed and cooperative when answering specific questions about themselves than when they are responding to an open-ended examination procedure consisting of relatively ambiguous test stimuli and vague instructions. Persons who resent authority and shun conformity, on the other hand, may resist being straight-jacketed by structured test items that have to be answered in certain ways and be more responsive when they are free to say as much or as little as they wish and to express themselves in their own words.

To summarize these implications of defensiveness for test dependability, self-report inventories are more likely than performance-based measures to elicit full protocols from guarded examinees, whereas performance-based measures are more likely than self-report inventories to reveal personality characteristics that guarded individuals would prefer not to disclose. Moreover in the examination of guarded or defensive examinees, dishonesty in self-report inventories, limited productivity in performance-based measures, and aversion either to highly structured or open-ended situations may limit the value of either instrument as a source of information about an individual's personality characteristics.

Congruence and Divergence between Tests

Because of the differences between self-report inventories and performance-based measures, their conjoint use enriches personality evaluations whether their findings are congruent or divergent. Congruent findings that identify the same or similar personality characteristics confirm that these characteristics are present and indicate further that these characteristics are recognized by the person who has been examined and are likely to be apparent in both relatively structured and relatively unstructured situations. Consistent indications from different types of tests that certain characteristics exist in a person, are recognized by that person, and are broadly manifest in that person's behavior increase the confidence and certainty with which examiners can draw conclusions and offer recommendations based on their test data.

As noted in Chapter 3, consistent indications of symptomatic or behavioral patterns across self-report inventories do not necessarily increase the likelihood that they are present. Because many inventories ask similar kinds of questions, agreement among them may often be redundant rather than confirmatory. It is when congruence emerges between different types of assessment instruments—as between self-report inventories and performance-based measures—that it is most likely to increase the certainty of inferences derived from the test data.

Divergent findings in conjoint personality assessments identify dissimilar characteristics and may even suggest contrary conclusions. In some instances of divergence, either self-report or performance-based test protocols may contain abundant evidence of psychological disturbance when the other type of test does not. As another possibility, a person's self-report or performance-based test protocol may indicate a marked degree of some personality state or trait that is only mildly or not at all suggested by the other type of test protocol. Divergent findings are not necessarily contradictory, nor do they signify that one of the data sets captures certain truth and the other data set gross error. Instead, both types of data show how people have chosen to respond in a test situation, and there is something to be learned from pondering why they have chosen seemingly different paths.

People whose performance-based test protocols suggest psychological disturbance, whereas their self-report protocols do not, may feel more comfortable in structured than unstructured situations and become upset or disorganized mainly in the latter. Conversely, disturbance appearing in self-report but not performance-based protocols may identify a person who functions more effectively in relatively open-ended than in highly prescribed situations. In this way, possible explanations for seemingly divergent findings—such as the differential impact of structure on how a person is likely to feel and behave—can add information that would not have emerged from a test battery consisting only of self-report or performance-based measures.

Finn (1996) has elaborated a similar formulation concerning the implications of test convergence and divergence for psychological disturbance, using the Minnesota Multiphasic Personality Inventory-2 (MMPI-2) and the Rorschach Inkblot Method (RIM), respectively, as examples of relatively structured and relatively unstructured instruments. For convergence, Finn suggested that if valid MMPI-2 and RIM protocols both show a low level of disturbance, this indicates a resilient individual with good stress tolerance who is experiencing little if any distress and can function well, even in unfamiliar and challenging situations. MMPI-2 and RIM protocols both showing a high level of disturbance would indicate a person who is experiencing considerable distress and having substantial difficulty coping adequately even in familiar and undemanding situations.

As for divergence, Finn (1996) suggested that persons showing minimal disturbance on the MMPI-2 but considerable disturbance on the RIM are likely to function adequately in relatively familiar and undemanding situations but struggle with underlying cognitive, affective, or interpersonal dysfunctions that surface primarily in unfamiliar and challenging situations. Finally, individuals with a high level of disturbance on the MMPI-2 and a low level of disturbance on the RIM are often intent on drawing attention to their problems and concerns while concealing or minimizing their actual ability to cope adequately with most situations.

In matters of differential sensitivity, differential dependability, and divergence, then, personality assessors should recognize that assessment instruments with dissimilar formats measure personality characteristics in different ways and with different emphases. Because of such method variance, a battery of tests with the potential to provide both congruent and divergent bits of information is more likely to paint an accurate and multidimensional picture of an individual's personality functioning than any single instrument. This observation flows from recommendations made many years ago by Campbell and Fiske (1959) for multimethod assessment in psychology, and it echoes the view of the American Psychological Association's Psychological Assessment Work Group mentioned in Chapter 1 that conjoint testing with both self-report and performance-based instruments is a procedure by which "practitioners have historically used the most efficient means at their disposal to maximize the validity of their judgments about individual clients" (Meyer et al., 2001, p. 150).

Obtaining Informed Consent

Prior to beginning a personality assessment, examiners are ethically and legally obliged to obtain informed consent from the person who is to be examined. As discussed further in Chapter 4, obtaining informed consent involves acquainting people with various aspects of the examination process and asking for their agreement to be tested under these conditions. Examiners will usually find it helpful to begin the consent process with a brief review of the referral they have received. Although people usually know by whom and for what reason they have been referred for an evaluation, assumptions in this and similar respects are ill-advised. An explicit summary of the referral avoids subsequent misunderstandings, especially for persons who are uncertain why testing has been recommended or required, or whose memory becomes faulty later on. Discussing the referral before asking for consent to be examined shows respect for examinees and eliminates examiner culpability should an examinee protest at some future point, "You never told me that."

An examiner doing a clinical evaluation might begin by saying, "As I think you know, Dr. Smith wanted you to see me for a personality evaluation that will give her additional information that will help in planning the treatment that will work best for you." For an administrative referral, this opening statement might take the form of, "As I think you know, the human resources manager in your company, Mr. Brown, asked to have you examined with respect to the problems that led to your being suspended from your job and to help determine if you're ready to go back to work." Such introductory statements can then be followed with a similarly concise and straightforward description of the examination procedures, as in "This will be a psychological examination in which I will be asking you questions about various things and having you do some tasks for me, and I'll be telling you more about these tests when we get started."

Examiners should next identify the remaining steps in the evaluation process, as in "After we finish the testing, I'll analyze the results and then prepare a written report of what the tests indicate." This information should be followed with specific statements about the nature and limits of the confidentiality that will apply in the examinee's case, who will receive the examiner's report, and what if any the examiner's role will be after the report is sent. In clinical and health care evaluations, this role often includes a feedback session for discussing the implications of the test findings, as discussed in the final section of this chapter. In administrative evaluations, examiners seldom interact directly with people they have tested following the filing of their report, and they may even be constrained by the referring party from giving examinees any feedback about what the test results indicate.

Once examinees have been given the preceding information and invited to ask any questions they have about the evaluation process, the time has come for them to agree to being evaluated. This agreement should be obtained in writing, using a form that has been developed for this purpose in the examiner's agency or office practice. In the case of minor children or adults who are incapable of acting on their own behalf, the consent form must be signed by a parent or by some other person who has legal responsibility for the examinee.

Examiners should also be aware that informed consent may be waived in certain circumstances. In forensic settings, court-ordered evaluations have customarily not required informed consent to be examined, and defendants pleading insanity are often considered to have given implicit agreement to undergo psychological evaluation. In organizational settings, consent to be examined may be considered implicit among applicants for a position that includes psychological evaluation as a stated requirement. These considerations are elaborated in the *Standards for Educational and Psychological Testing* (AERA et al., 1999) and in discussions by Kitchener (2000), and Koocher and Rey-Casserly (2003). Regulations for waiver of informed consent may vary over time and in different locales, and personality assessors may find it advisable to obtain written agreement from all the people they examine.

CONDUCTING PERSONALITY ASSESSMENTS

Personality assessments should be conducted in a manner that helps people feel comfortable during the evaluation, promotes their cooperation with the testing procedures, and elicits from them data that can be interpreted according to standard guidelines. To foster comfort and cooperation in a testing session, examiners must display a supportive demeanor that minimizes anxiety and encourages openness. To obtain interpretable data, examiners need to communicate clearly and adhere closely to standardized procedures for test administration. Examiners must also decide whether and how to use computerized methods of recording and scoring test responses.

Fostering Comfort and Cooperation

Helping examinees feel comfortable begins with getting their informed consent, which as just described includes reviewing the purposes of the evaluation and describing the procedures that will be followed. Having been given this information, most people feel at least a little less anxious and uncertain about the examination than before, and at least a little more confident that they will be treated with consideration and dignity. After consent has been obtained from the person to be examined, some further discussion of relevant matters can help establish a positive rapport. This further discussion may take the form of an extended clinical interview, particularly if the person being evaluated has not previously been interviewed at length by a mental health professional. Should detailed interview information already be available, the examiner's pretesting interview might be limited to verifying or inquiring about a few items of information, as in "Do you have a family?" "What school do you go to?" or "Am I correct that you've been having these problems for the last six months?"

Examiners whose comments, tone of voice, and nonjudgmental attitude convey interest, respect, and impartiality ordinarily increase examinees' comfort level and the amount of information they feel inclined to provide. Being brusque, impatient, unfriendly, critical, or judgmental can make people angry or anxious and discourage them from being forthcoming. Masling (1998) has similarly noted that openness is facilitated when examinees perceive the testing situation as a mutually respectful interaction intended to obtain helpful information about the kind of person they are, but stifled when they experience being tested as an authoritarian investigation intended to ferret out their defects and shortcomings.

Personal characteristics over which examiners have no control, such as their age, gender, and ethnicity, can also affect an examinee's comfort level and responsiveness. Some people are more relaxed in the company of men than women, and vice versa; some people may prefer confiding in a person close to them in age rather than a much older or younger person; and people of all kinds may be less responsive to an examiner whose ethnicity and sociocultural background differ sharply from theirs. Examiners can do little to alter or disguise objective features of themselves that interfere with the assessment process. If they can recognize this type of interference when it occurs, they may reduce examinees' discomfort or reticence by discussing it with them.

Obtaining Interpretable Data

Personality assessment procedures are largely language-based, and clear communication is essential for obtaining test data that can be interpreted with confidence. Even when test-takers are feeling comfortable and being responsive, misunderstandings can detract from the interpretive value of the obtained data. Clear communication flows from language facility, and there is widespread consensus that examiners and the people they examine should both be speaking either in their native language or in a second language in which they are proficient (AERA et al., 1999, chap. 9). The use of interpreters to circumvent language barriers in the assessment process rarely provides a satisfactory solution to this problem, unless certain requirements are met. In particular, test responses obtained through an interpreter are likely to be dependable only when the interpreter is (a) fully conversant with the idiomatic expressions and cultural referents in both languages, (b) familiar with standard procedures in psychological assessment, and (c) a stranger to the examinee, rather than a friend, relative, or member of the same closely knit subcultural community.

Similar considerations apply for self-report inventories. The written instructions and test items in these inventories must be written in language that the examinee can understand fully. To ensure equivalence of self-report inventories in cross-cultural applications, their translation requires close attention to the idiomatic vagaries of each new language and to culture-specific contents of individual items. Adequate preparation of foreign language versions of an English language inventory usually involves not only translation into the new language, but also back-translation into English to ensure that item content has remained equivalent (see Allen & Walsh, 2000; Butcher, Mosch, Tsai, & Nezami, 2006; McCrae, 2002).

Obtaining data that can be interpreted according to established guidelines also requires adherence to standard procedures for test administration. Interpretive guidelines for an adequately developed personality assessment instrument are derived from determining how groups of people respond to the same version of the instrument administered to them in the same way. Accordingly, any deviation from a standard administration can detract from the interpretability of the obtained data, and only when examiners administer a test as specified in the test manual or in authoritative textbooks can they infer with confidence what a person's test responses indicate. Chapters 6 through 14 of the present book include precise instructions for administering the particular tests being discussed.

Using Computerized Formats

Software programs are available to facilitate data collection and management for most widely used personality assessment instruments. Programs designed for use with self-report inventories typically provide for online administration of test items, automated coding of item responses to produce scale scores, and quantitative manipulation of these scale scores to yield summary scores and indices. For performance-based measures that require inquiry and coding by the examiner, software programs accept manually entered response codes and translate them into the test's quantitative indices. Programs of both kinds typically store the test results in files that can later be accessed or exported, and some programs include computational packages that can generate descriptive statistics for sets of test records held in storage.

The online administration and coding of self-report inventories help examinees avoid mechanical errors in filling out test forms manually, and they eliminate errors that examiners sometimes make in scoring responses (see Allard & Faust, 2000). The utility of performance-based test results depends on accurate coding and data entry by the examiner. Once the data are entered, software programs eliminate examiner error in the calculation of summary scores and indices. The data storage features of many software programs facilitate assessment research, particularly for investigators seeking to combine databases from different sources, and they can also help satisfy requirements in most states and many agencies for keeping assessment information on file for some period of time. For these reasons, the vast majority of assessment psychologists report that they use software for test scoring and feel comfortable doing so (McMinn, Ellens, & Soref, 1999).

Computerized collection of assessment information has potential disadvantages as well. When assessment measures are administered online, first of all, the reliability of the data can be compromised by a lack of equivalence between an automated testing procedure and a noncomputerized administration of the measure on which it is based. The extent of such equivalence is currently an unresolved issue (see Butcher, 2003; Butcher, Perry, & Hahn, 2004; D. K. Snyder, 2000), although some data suggest that computerized versions of self-report personality assessment instruments can achieve fairly good equivalence with booklet forms of these instruments (see Atlis, Hahn, & Butcher, 2006; Finger & Ones, 1999).

As a second potential drawback of automated procedures, they permit personality testing by individuals who are untrained in assessment and would otherwise be unable to collect and score test protocols. The availability of software programs for collecting and scoring personality test thus creates a risk that assessment methods may be misused and examinees may be poorly served. This disadvantage is not an unavoidable by-product of comput-erized assessment procedures, but it represents a possibly harmful abuse of technology by uninformed and irresponsible persons who act beyond the limits of their professional competence. As mentioned in the next section of this chapter, the risk of poor quality assess-ment by untrained persons is amplified when they report computer-based test interpretations verbatim as their test findings.

INTERPRETING PERSONALITY ASSESSMENT DATA

The interpretation of personality assessment data consists of drawing inferences about an individual's current mental and emotional state and about the person's dispositions to think, feel, and act in certain ways. When organized into clear and coherent descriptions of personality functioning, accurate interpretations provide a basis for formulating conclu-sions and recommendations that are responsive to whatever referral questions have been raised. Chapters 6 through 14 of this *Handbook* provide detailed guidelines for interpreting the most widely used personality assessment instruments. This introductory chapter on the personality assessment process addresses three general considerations in interpreting personality assessment data: (1) the basis on which inferences should be drawn, (2) the possible effect of impression management on test findings, and (3) the relevance of cultural and experiential contexts in formulating conclusions and recommendations.

Basis of Inferences

Examiners have several options when they draw inferences from their test data. They can base their conclusions on either empirical or conceptual grounds, on either statistical rules or clinical judgment, and on either nomothetic or idiographic aspects of the data, and they can additionally choose whether and how to rely on computer-generated interpretive statements in formulating their impressions.

Empirical and Conceptual Grounds

Empirical grounds for test interpretation consist of the replicated results of methodolog-ically sound research. Repetitive demonstrations that a test finding correlates with some personality characteristic warrant inferring the presence of that characteristic in a person who shows this test finding. Conceptual grounds for interpretation consist of psychological constructs that provide a logical bridge between test findings and the inferences drawn from them. If subjectively felt distress contributes to a person remaining in and benefiting from psychotherapy (for which there is ample evidence; see Clarkin & Levy, 2004), and if a personality assessment instrument includes a valid index of subjectively felt distress (which many do), then it is reasonable to expect a positive finding on this test index to increase the likelihood of a favorable outcome in psychotherapy.

Both empirical and conceptual grounds for interpretation bring distinct benefits to the personality assessment process. Empirical perspectives are valuable because they provide a psychometric foundation for reasonable certainty in arriving at conclusions. Quantita-tive data concerning the normative distribution, adequate reliability, and valid correlates of test variables allow assessors to interpret them with confidence. Lack of normative expectations to use for comparative purposes limits the certainty with which assessors can draw conclusions from their data, as do questionable reliability and undocumented correlates.

Conceptual perspectives are valuable in the assessment process because they explain why certain findings are associated with certain personality characteristics. In addition to helping assessors understand why their measures work as they do, constructs that link test findings with inferences drawn from them identify which findings are most relevant to answering referral questions. Asked whether a disturbed person has schizophrenia, conceptually informed assessors know that the core feature of schizophrenia is disordered thinking and will focus on variables that measure thought disorder as they interpret and comment on their test data.

Despite their value as grounds for interpretation, both empirical and conceptual perspectives have shortcomings. Empiricism provides the scientific foundations of personality assessment and a basis for certainty in drawing conclusions from test data, but it encompasses only what has already been identified and verified. Used in isolation from conceptualization, empiricism does not bring into the interpretive process ideas not previously conceived or inferences not previously proved. Conceptualization, on the other hand, enriches the interpretive process with explanatory hypotheses that can broaden an examiner's understanding of people being evaluated and suggest facets of their personality style and life experiences that go beyond previously confirmed implications of test data. Used in isolation from empirical support, however, conceptually based interpretations lack the certainty of conclusions that are supported by research findings.

For these reasons, personality assessors can respond to referral questions most fully and confidently when their conclusions are grounded in both empirical data and conceptual formulations. In practice, examiners must sometimes rely on empirically supported but conceptually unclear relationships between test variables and personality characteristics in formulating their conclusions and recommendations. At other times, they must depend on conceptually compelling but not yet empirically tested linkages between test variables and personality characteristics. Both empirically supported relationships that are not fully understood and conceptually compelling relationships that have yet to be empirically tested warrant interpretive inferences, and neither should be neglected. At the same time, examiners should continue scholarly efforts to formulate conceptual explanations of empirically demonstrated relationships and generate empirical support for compelling conceptual linkages.

Statistical Rules and Clinical Judgment

Empirical grounds for personality test interpretation have customarily been operationalized as statistical rules for drawing conclusions from test data. These statistical rules consist of formulas, or algorithms, that provide an objective, actuarial basis for deciding what test findings indicate. When statistical rules are applied to personality assessment data, the formula determines whether an individual has certain personality characteristics or is likely to behave in certain ways. Reliance on statistical rules ensures that examiners who apply them correctly to the same set of data will come to the same conclusion about what these data signify.

As a shortcoming of statistical rules in personality test interpretation, however, their generality is limited by the composition of the database from which they have been derived.

Statistical rules derived from sampling people of a certain age, gender, socioeconomic status, and cultural background may not generalize to persons with other demographic characteristics, and rules developed in one kind of setting may not be valid in other settings. Actuarial interpretations also tend to be limited in scope. A statistical rule may be effective in identifying suicide potential, but it provides little information about the attitudes and concerns that have fostered a person's self-destructive tendencies. For many of the varied types of people seen in assessment practice, and in response to the many complex and multifaceted referral questions that are about them, most statistical rules provide less than fully adequate answers. Discussing these considerations in some detail, Garb (2000, 2003) commented, "Statistical-prediction rules are of limited value because they have typically been based on limited information that has not been demonstrated to be optimal and they have almost never been shown to be powerful" (2000, p. 31). He concluded, "Relatively few statistical prediction rules can be recommended for clinical use" (2003, p. 31).

Basing conclusions on statistical rules can also be problematic when numerical scores generate artificially discrete qualitative descriptions. The manual for the previously mentioned BDI-II (Beck et al., 1996) lists a score of 14 to 19 as indicating "mild depression" and a score of 20 to 28 as indicating "moderate depression." This being the case, two people with almost identical BDI-II scores of 19 and 20 would be categorized differently by the statistical rule, one as being mildly depressed and the other as being moderately depressed. Such an artificially sharp distinction could be eased by further specification of the BDI-II categories, as by designating scores of 17 to 19 the "high mild" range and scores of 20 to 22 the "low moderate" range. The awkwardness of such terminology aside, there are limits to how many data points on a quantitative scale can be assigned separate qualitative designations, and there are corresponding limits to reducing the artificiality of statistical rules by creating categorical descriptions for narrowly defined score ranges.

Clinical judgment as a basis of personality test interpretation consists of the cumulative wisdom that practitioners acquire from their experience. Although created from impressions formed by individual practitioners, this cumulative wisdom comes over time to represent the shared beliefs of large numbers of experienced clinicians. In contrast to the quantitative nature of statistical rules, clinical judgment is a qualitative approach to arriving at conclusions. As a further important difference from reliance on statistical rules, decisions in applying clinical judgment to assessment data are made by the practitioner, not by a formula. Clinical judgments concerning the interpretive significance of personality test data are consequently less uniform than actuarial decisions and less likely to be based on established fact. Whereas the breadth and the relevance of statistical rules are limited by their database, the potential applicability of clinical judgments in personality assessment is limited only by the capacity of examiners to reason logically about possible relationships between the test data and personality characteristics relevant to addressing a referral question.

The relative merits of statistical rules and clinical judgment in personality assessment have been debated at length since Meehl (1954) formulated this distinction in a classic book, *Clinical versus Statistical Prediction*. Influential opinions on the matter can be found in contributions by Garb (1998, 2003), Grove and Meehl (1996), Holt (1958, 1986), Karon (2000), Meehl (1986), and Swets, Dawes, and Monahan (2000). The debate aside, both statistical prediction and clinical judgment have inherent strengths and limitations, as just noted, and there is a closer relationship between them than has often been appreciated by advocates of relying on one or the other as the sole basis for test interpretation. Westen and Weinberger (2004) have reviewed research showing that clinical descriptions can readily be turned into statistical predictions by appropriate psychometric procedures.

As additional evidence of the relationship between statistical and clinical approaches, the development of statistical rules for personality test interpretation typically begins with clinical judgments in forming a pool of test items thought to be associated with certain personality characteristics or behavioral tendencies. Item analysis, cross-validation, and other test construction methods are then used to shape these clinically suggested test items into valid actuarial scales for measuring the characteristics and tendencies to be predicted. Because reliable statistical rules combine clinical wisdom with the sharpening of this wisdom by replicated research findings, they should be expected to produce more accurate results than clinical judgment alone in specifically defined circumstances.

This expectation has been confirmed in two meta-analytic investigations. In the first of these, Grove, Zald, Lebow, Snitz, and Nelson (2000) compared the accuracy of statistical versus clinical prediction methods in 136 studies of human health and behavior. Statistical predictions were on the average approximately 10% more accurate than clinical predictions and substantially more accurate in 33% to 47% of the studies examined, depending on the type of analysis that had been done. Clinical predictions still were often as accurate as statistical predictions, and they were substantially more accurate than statistical predictions in 6% to 16% of the studies. In the other meta-analysis, Ægisdóttir et al. (2006) reported a similar finding of a 13% increase in accuracy of statistical over clinical prediction in 67 studies.

As these data and good sense indicate, then, relying solely on clinical judgment in interpreting personality test findings when adequate actuarial guidelines are available is poor practice. Whereas clinical methods of assessment at their best depend on the impressions and judgment of individual practitioners, statistical methods at their best constitute established fact that has been built on clinical wisdom. Even the best judgment of the most experienced practitioner can at times be clouded by inadvertent bias, insufficient awareness of base rates, and other sources of influence, as elaborated by Garb (1998, 2003) and in Chapter 3 of this *Handbook*. Given a reasonable choice, assessment decisions are more advisedly based on established fact than on clinical judgment.

On the other hand, the nature of people and the circumstances that lead to their being referred for an evaluation are, as already noted, diverse. Because of this diversity, assessment questions regularly arise for which there are no available statistical rules, and patterns of assessment data often resemble but do not closely match the patterns for which empirically demonstrated correlates exist. Moreover, the artificially sharp categorical distinctions sometimes produced by adjacent scores on actuarial scales often call for qualitative explanation, lest they lead to misleading inferences.

In the absence of validated statistical rules for answering a referral question, personality assessors can opt to defer any conclusions or recommendations, pending greater certainty about what the test data show. As a preferable option, assessors in less than completely certain situations can supplement whatever empirical guidelines are available with logical reasoning and cumulative clinical wisdom, thereby allowing them to formulate conclusions and recommendations that are more responsive and more likely to be helpful than not responding at all. Meehl (1957) endorsed this same perspective on clinical practice a half century ago in an article titled, "When Should We Use Our Heads instead of the

Formula?" his answer being that we use our heads when "no formula exists" (p. 269; see also Kleinmuntz, 1990).

In this sense, statistical rules and clinical judgment are complementary components of effective decision making instead of mutually exclusive alternatives. This same view was also recommended half a century ago by Holt (1958), in an article titled "Clinical *and* Statistical Prediction." Wrote Holt, "We should try to find the optimal combination of actuarially controlled methods and sensitive clinical judgment for any particular predictive enterprise" (p. 12).

Nomothetic and Idiographic Emphases

Empirical guidelines and statistical rules constitute a basically nomothetic approach to interpreting assessment information, whereas conceptual guidelines and clinical judgment underlie a basically idiographic approach. As described in Chapter 1 (see pp. 12–13), nomothetic interpretations address ways in which people resemble each other and share various psychological characteristics. These interpretations are accordingly based on comparing an individual's test responses with responses typically obtained from groups of people with certain known characteristics, as in concluding, "This person's test scores show a pattern often seen in people who feel uncomfortable in social situations and are inclined to withdraw from them." Nomothetic interpretations are derived and expressed in primarily quantitative terms and may even specify the precise frequency with which an assessment finding occurs in particular groups of people.

Idiographic interpretations, by contrast, address ways in which people differ from most other kinds of people and show psychological characteristics that diverge from general expectations. These interpretations typically invoke psychological processes to attribute person-specific meaning to assessment data, as in saying, "This person gives many indications of being a passive and dependent individual who is more comfortable being a follower than a leader and would be unlikely to function effectively in an executive position." Deriving and expressing idiographic interpretations is largely a qualitative procedure in which examiners are guided by informed impressions rather than by quantitative empirical comparisons.

As also discussed in Chapter 1, people ordinarily show some personality characteristics that they share with many other people and some in which they differ from most other people. Little can be gained from pondering whether individuals can be described better in terms of how they resemble or how they differ from other people. Nomothetic and idiographic emphases, like empirical and conceptual perspectives and like statistical rules and clinical judgment, complement each other. Balanced attention to formulating both nomothetic and idiographic interpretive statements accordingly helps promote the fullest possible understanding of what people are like.

Computer-Generated Interpretive Statements

In addition to assisting in the collection and scoring of test data, software programs for most published tests generate interpretive statements. Like computerized data collection and scoring, computer-based test interpretation (CBTI) avoids certain kinds of error in the assessment process. By guaranteeing a thorough scan of the test data, CBTI eliminates the possibility of overlooking some items of information in a test protocol. By ensuring that particular patterns of test data always generate the same interpretive statements, CBTI eliminates examiner variability in deriving these statements. CBTI can also facilitate the teaching and learning of personality assessment methods by using computer-generated narratives as an exercise in which students are asked to identify which test scores have keyed particular interpretive statements.

These and other potential benefits of computerizing test interpretations, as well as some drawbacks of doing so, are elaborated by Butcher (2002, 2003), Butcher, Perry, and Hahn (2004), and Lichtenberger (2006). The following four CBTI limitations are particularly important for examiners to keep in mind as they formulate their conclusions and recommendations:

1. Although test software generates interpretive statements by means of quantitative algorithms, these computer programs are not entirely empirically based. Typically, they combine empirically validated correlates of test scores with clinical judgments about the interpretive significance of various patterns of scores, and program algorithms represent beliefs as well as established fact concerning the meaning of these score patterns. Available test programs vary in the extent to which their interpretive statements are research based, and considerable additional research remains to be done to establish a totally empirical basis for computerized interpretations (see Garb, 2000).

2. The previously noted shortcoming of statistical rules in assigning qualitative descriptions to quantitative score ranges characterizes CBTI algorithms as well. Computer programs require fixed cutting points, below which one kind or degree of descriptive statement is keyed and at or above which a different kind or degree of description is keyed. Consequently, a computer narrative may describe two people with just a single point difference on some test variable in different terms (e.g., "This person shows *better than average* capacities for managing stress" versus "this person shows *average* capacities for managing stress").

3. Despite often referring specifically to the person who took the test (as in "he," "she," "this person"), and thereby appearing to be idiographic, computer-generated interpretations do not describe the person who has been examined. Instead, CBTI statements describe test protocols. They report what research findings or clinical wisdom have had to say about people in general who show the kinds of test scores and patterns the computer has found in the protocol being scanned. Computer narratives, therefore, are basically nomothetic, and most of them phrase at least some of their interpretive statements in terms of normative comparisons.

   Because no two people are exactly alike, moreover, and because no one person matches any comparison group perfectly, some computer generated interpretive statements may even describe an individual examinee in ways that other reliable evidence indicates are obviously incorrect. For this reason, most CBTI narratives include a caveat advising examiners (a) that the interpretive statements contained therein describe groups of people, not necessarily the person who took the test; (b) that misleading and erroneous statements might occur as a consequence of psychological characteristics or environmental circumstances unique to the person being examined and not widely shared with any normative reference group; and (c) that other sources of information and the assessor's judgment would be necessary to determine which statements in the interpretive narrative characterize the examinee and which do not.

4. The availability of computer-generated interpretive statements allows persons who know little or nothing about interpreting personality tests to copy CBTI narratives into their assessment reports. Ethical professionals, whatever the level of their psychodiagnostic sophistication, do not use computer narratives in this way. They rely on CBTI printouts only for assistance in ensuring that they have addressed all the relevant data, in resolving differences between narrative statements and information from other sources, and in deciding how to organize their reports and what to emphasize in them. Should examiners be tempted to insert some particularly clear and well-crafted CBTI statements into a report they are writing, integrity requires them to find ways of expressing these statements in their own words, or else to put copied material in quotations and identify its source.

Effects of Impression Management

In drawing conclusions from their test data, personality assessors must be alert to possible effects of impression management, which consists of conscious and deliberate attempts by examinees to paint a misleading picture of themselves. In one form of impression management, often referred to as *malingering, faking bad,* or *overreporting,* people try to appear more disturbed or psychologically dysfunctional than they really are. In an opposite from of impression management, known as *deception, faking good,* or *underreporting,* people try to conceal their difficulties and limitations in order to appear better adjusted and more psychologically capable than they are.

Malingering can range in extent from slight exaggeration of actual problems and concerns to total fabrication of nonexistent serious difficulties. Deception can range from occasionally minimizing one's shortcomings to claiming numerous fictitious capacities and accomplishments. Both malingering and deception stem from a variety of motivations to mislead an examiner, and both usually produce telltale patterns of inconsistency in the assessment data.

Motivations to Mislead

People in clinical settings who overreport personality problems and concerns are usually trying to increase the attention and help they are getting. They may exaggerate or fabricate symptoms of disorder to persuade mental health professionals that they should be taken into psychotherapy, should be seen more frequently if they are already in psychotherapy, should be admitted to an inpatient facility, or should be kept in such a facility if they are already in one. In forensic evaluations, plaintiffs in personal injury cases may overreport psychological incapacity in hopes of increasing the damages they receive, and criminal defendants may malinger psychological disturbance in an effort to reduce the penalties that are imposed on them. In employment situations, people applying for workers' compensation may be motivated to exaggerate their functioning impairments.

Clinical patients may underreport their adjustment difficulties when they want to be discharged from an inpatient facility or convince mental health professionals that they are not in need of psychological treatment. In forensic cases, wanting to make a positive impression can be a powerful inducement to deception among parents seeking custody of their children and prison inmates requesting parole. In personnel evaluations, applicants for positions, candidates for promotion, and people seeking reinstatement after being suspended for mental health reasons may overstate their assets and minimize their limitations.

Patterns of Inconsistency

Malingering usually results in inconsistencies between parts of individual tests, between test data and interview observations, or between test and interview data and case history information. In the first of these three patterns of discrepancy, people who are attempting to look more disturbed than they are respond within the normal range on some portions of a personality test but in a markedly deviant manner on other portions of the same test. In the second pattern, people appear calm and relaxed during an interview, talk sensibly about various matters, and behave in a socially appropriate fashion, but then produce test protocols containing dramatic indications of emotional distress, morbid preoccupations, disordered thinking, and interpersonal animosity. In the third pattern, a person whose test responses and interview behavior both suggest serious psychological disturbance is found to have no history of ever being considered maladjusted, referred for counseling or psychotherapy, or prescribed psychotropic medication. These and other clues to malingering psychological disorder are elaborated by Berry, Wetter, and Baer (2002), McCann (1998), and Rogers (1997).

Efforts to deceive are similarly likely to produce telltale inconsistencies in assessment data. Individuals who are trying to conceal their problems and concerns often give guarded, skimpy, and benign personality test protocols that show few signs of what is known from other sources to be a current history of severe symptom formation or behavioral disturbance. Guardedness and reticence can prevent personal shortcomings and adjustment difficulties from becoming apparent in test protocols, but they also alert examiners that these protocols may not tell the full story of an individual's personality limitations.

With reference to specific personality assessment instruments, the previously mentioned validity scales in self-report inventories are based on inconsistent and unlikely responses that help identify both overreporting and underreporting (see Chapter 5). The performance-based measures presented in Chapters 11 through 14 do not include formal validity scales, as noted, but they can also be sensitive to inconsistencies that suggest malingering or deception (see Elhai, Kinder, & Frueh, 2004; Schretlen, 1997). Weiner (2005) has noted that relatively unstructured measures may even be less susceptible to impression management than relatively structured measures, because they give examinees fewer clues to what their responses might signify. This does not mean that performance-based measures are impervious to malingering and defensiveness, which they are not, but only that efforts to mislead may be more apparent and less likely to go undetected on these measures than on self-report inventories.

Related to the ease or difficulty of faking assessment measures is the extent to which people can be taught to mislead examiners with convincingly good-looking or bad-looking test responses. Research findings indicate that even psychologically naive individuals who are given information about certain psychological disorders or personality characteristics can shape their test responses to make themselves resemble a target group (e.g., people who are depressed) more closely than they could have done without such instruction. Misleading findings are especially likely to occur when people have been coached in how to answer certain questions on self-report inventories without elevating their validity scales (Ben-Porath, 1994; Storm & Graham, 2000; Victor & Abeles, 2004). However, the group findings in these research studies do not indicate whether people who have been given some general instruction or test-specific coaching can successfully mislead experienced examiners in actual practice. The answer to this question awaits further investigation.

As a final note on malingering and deception, both types of impression management differ from instances in which people give self-favorable or self-unfavorable responses without any conscious intent to mislead the examiner. The motivations for these types of response on self-report inventories and their interpretive significance are discussed in Chapter 5.

Relevance of Cultural and Experiential Context

The behavioral implications of personality characteristics identified by test responses are likely to vary with a person's life circumstances, and research findings have shown that cultural expectations can result in similar personality characteristics having either adaptive or maladaptive consequences (see Kazarian & Evans, 1998). Hence, adequate attention to an individual's cultural and experiential context is an essential aspect of translating personality descriptions into useful conclusions and recommendations.

With respect to cultural expectations, a dependent and generally acquiescent person might be at risk for adjustment difficulties in a national, neighborhood, or family culture that values assertiveness and self-reliance, whereas an independent and competitive person, other things being equal, would be likely to feel comfortable and function effectively in a subculture that embraces these values. Conversely, an independently minded and competitive person might feel alienated and adapt poorly in a society that subordinates individual needs and preferences to the wishes and welfare of the group, whereas a dependent and acquiescent person might get along very well in such a society.

Experiential circumstances can lead to personality characteristics having different implications for peace of mind and effective functioning. Suppose a person choosing a career or looking for a job is a contemplative individual who completes tasks carefully and reaches conclusions deliberately. In a career or job that calls for accuracy and thoroughness and rarely involves time pressure, this contemplative person is likely to feel comfortable and perform well, other things being equal. However, in a work situation that requires meeting tight deadlines and making quick decisions on the basis of sketchy information, this same person would be at risk for becoming anxious and performing poorly. In addition to helping people make advisable career choices, the implications of personality characteristics for job satisfaction and success can help identify the sources of difficulty in individuals who are experiencing stress and failing to thrive in their career or work situation.

REPORTING PERSONALITY ASSESSMENT FINDINGS

Sigmund Freud (1904/1953) once wrote, "There are many ways and means of practicing psychotherapy. All that lead to recovery are good" (p. 259). The same can be said for writing personality assessment reports. There are many ways of reporting assessment findings, and suitable reports range widely in style and form. The various clinical, health care, forensic, educational, and organizational settings in which psychologists provide assessments are likely to have different expectations for how reports should be structured and what they should contain, and individual agencies within these settings often have special requirements for the organization of reports. Practitioners complying with expectations and requirements in these settings may imbue their reports with personal preferences as well. These variations in report writing account for a substantial volume of possible formats that prove effective and helpful in the individual case, and there is no single best way to prepare a personality assessment report.

Nevertheless, there are some general areas in which personality assessors can enhance the effectiveness and utility of their reports, whatever the setting in which they are consulting. These include (a) providing adequate identifying data concerning the person who has been examined, (b) giving clear answers to whatever referral questions have been raised, and (c) writing in ways that maximize readability and communication value. In conducting clinical as opposed to administrative evaluations, as differentiated in this *Handbook* (see Chapter 1, pp. 21–22), assessment psychologists can also enhance the benefits of their reports with collaborative feedback sessions, sometimes in the form of a planned therapeutic assessment.

Providing Identifying Data

Personality assessment reports should ordinarily begin with certain identifying data, either in an itemized list or in narrative form. Itemized lists are commonly a required report heading in agency settings and consist of such items as the examinee's name, date of birth, age, marital status, education level, and Social Security or other identification number, together with the date and place of the examination, the identity of the examiner, and the referral question. Individual practitioners writing a report in the form of a narrative letter to a referring person might begin as follows:

> On June 5, 2007, I examined in my office Mr. John Smith, a 27-year-old unmarried Caucasian high school teacher, who consulted you with complaints of anxiety, moodiness, and dissatisfaction with his life. You referred Mr. Smith for evaluation of possible bipolar disorder and recommendations concerning his amenability to psychotherapy.

This illustrative opening conveys who the examinee is, when and where the person was evaluated, and why the person was referred for an assessment. This opening statement might be followed with additional identifying or case history information, as in, "According to his report, he has performed adequately in his teaching position and has not previously sought or received mental health care." Following this initial information, examiners should next indicate either in list or narrative form the procedures they followed, including the tests they administered, whatever case-related documents they reviewed, and the identity of any collateral persons from whom they obtained information. In narrative form, this portion of the identifying data might read as follows:

> For the purposes of my evaluation, I had the opportunity to read the summary of Ms. Jones' personnel file, dated May 5, 2007, which was mailed to me by the human resources manager in her company. In my office, I interviewed Ms. Jones with respect to her personal and work history, and I also spoke briefly with her husband, who accompanied her to the evaluation. I then administered to Ms. Jones a battery of psychological tests that included the following measures: [a list of tests administered then follows]

Answering the Referral Questions

Following the identifying data, the body of a personality assessment report should describe personality characteristics that can be inferred from the test data and relate these characteristics to aspects of the referral questions. In the hypothetical example of Mr. Smith, his report might include indications that his test responses identify a stable and reserved affective style, as opposed to labile and expansive emotionality; that this finding is atypical in bipolar disorder; and that he is therefore unlikely to have such a disorder. In similar fashion, the examiner might report that Mr. Smith appears from his test responses to be a reasonably well-integrated, interpersonally accessible, and psychologically minded individual who accordingly has some good capacities for participating in and benefiting from expressive or interpersonal psychotherapy.

Adequate response to referral questions often requires not only describing and drawing conclusions from an individual's personality characteristics, but also recommending some course of action. A clinical referral might ask specifically, "What type of treatment approach might work best in meeting this patient's needs?" to which an examiner might respond, "This person's acute distress and the limited support systems in his life would appear to call for a crisis-oriented cognitive-behavioral treatment approach at the present time." A family court judge might ask, "Which of these parents is most likely to provide their child a stable and secure home life?" which obliges examiners either to state which parent they think will provide the better home life or to indicate why they cannot make this determination. In personnel work, fitness-for-duty consultations commonly ask examiners to recommend whether and when persons should return to their jobs or professional practices and to suggest modifications in their work situation that might help them function comfortably and effectively.

In structural terms, then, personality assessment reports should generally comprise three sections:

1. An opening section for providing identifying data, which may include background and case history information
2. The main body of the report, which responds to the referral question by presenting test-based descriptions of the examinee's personality characteristics and case-relevant conclusions to which they lead
3. A final section in which assessors complete their response to the referral question by summarizing their conclusions and providing appropriate recommendations

Promoting Readability and Communication Value

Whatever the setting in which reports are prepared and to whomever they are addressed, examiners should strive to write them in ways that promote their readability and communication value. They should avoid jargon, describe people rather than processes, identify personality strengths as well as limitations, and indicate the certainty of the conclusions being drawn.

Avoid Jargon

Personality assessors should write their reports in ordinary, everyday language and avoid using technical jargon. Technical terminology may sometimes be unavoidable, as when a formal diagnosis must be given. Otherwise, however, the language of reports should flow in a clear and uncomplicated manner that is easy for readers to follow and understand.

This recommendation holds even for reports addressed to psychologically sophisticated persons who are familiar with technical terminology. In most venues, reports to knowledgeable colleagues frequently end up being read as well by people with limited psychological sophistication, including examinees, nonpsychiatric physicians, personnel managers, and, in the case of young people, parents and teachers. In addition, reports of personality assessments that were not part of a forensic evaluation may at some future point become relevant to courtroom proceedings, where they may come under the scrutiny of lawyers, judges, and juries. With these considerations in mind, personality assessors may find it beneficial to engage in an imaginary conversation with an intelligent but psychologically unsophisticated person in which they relate their findings, conclusions, and recommendations in everyday language—and then write their report in the same words they have used in this imaginary oral presentation.

Describe People, Not Processes

Personality assessors can enhance the communication value of their reports by writing about the person they have evaluated, not about psychological processes. Personalized statements bring reports to life and give readers a better sense of the individual who has been examined than impersonal statements. Thus stating, "Ms. Brown appears to compare herself unfavorably to other people and consequently to have low self-esteem and limited self-confidence" communicates more clearly and effectively than writing, "Self-esteem is low and self-confidence is limited." When impersonal descriptions of psychological processes combine with jargon, the regrettable result needs no further comment, except to compare "Homophobia is pronounced" with "Mr. Edwards tends to avoid people because he is fearful of being harmed or taken advantage of by others."

Identify Strengths as Well as Limitations

As reviewed in Chapter 1, personality assessment instruments were developed to identity adjustment difficulties and facilitate differential diagnosis of psychopathology. As a consequence, a tradition emerged in which reports of personality assessments focused on cognitive, emotional, coping, and social deficits in people and paid little attention to their adaptive capacities, positive potentials, and admirable qualities. Contemporary clinical psychology has become much more attuned than in the past to the role of personality assets in avoiding and overcoming adjustment difficulties and enriching one's life, and increased attention is being paid to the intrinsic value of promoting positive personality characteristics in people as well as minimizing negative ones (see Duckworth, Steen, & Seligman, 2005; Frisch, 2006; Seligman & Csikszentmihalyi, 2000; Snyder & Lopez, 2007; Tedeschi & Kilmer, 2005).

Accordingly, assessment reports should identify whatever personality strengths are in evidence, even when the person being examined has been referred primarily for differential diagnosis of psychopathology or identification of the origins of aberrant behavior. In a clinical case, a report describing a woman who appears to have an anxiety or affective disorder, but not a cognitive or interpersonal disorder, might include the positive statement, "Ms. Clark gives evidence of being a well-organized person who for the most part can think clearly and logically and exercise good judgment; and she has good capacities to form close and collaborative relationships with other people." A balanced presentation of an individual's personality assets and liabilities can help examiners avoid a subsequent complaint that "the psychologist said only bad things about me." A complaint of this kind, especially when warranted, can lead to an unpleasant cross-examination in the courtroom and even allegations of ethical misconduct on the examiner's part.

Indicate Certainty of Conclusions

Some responses in a personality test battery always point more clearly than others to probable inferences. With this in mind, examiners should sharpen the precision of their reports by referring to the strength of the evidence for the conclusions they are drawing and indicating how certain they are of them. Suppose that a person's test findings contain abundant and compelling evidence of some personality characteristic. In that case, examiners can justifiably phrase their interpretive statement in fairly certain terms that indicate what this person is quite probably like, as in saying, "Mr. Williams gave considerable evidence of long-standing negative self-attitudes, and his characteristically low self-esteem has very probably contributed to his recurrent depressive episodes," or "Ms. Thomas appears to be an impulsive person who is very likely to show limited self-control."

Along with providing an indication of the examiner's level of certainty, these illustrative interpretations embody two other stylistic features that can improve communication in an assessment report. The statement about Mr. Williams explicitly relates the inference to its source by referring to the evidence he gave. This and similar references to what the "tests show" or what the "examination results indicate" inform readers that the examiner's conclusions are factually derived from the test data and are not merely subjective impressions. Such references to the evidential basis of conclusions do not need to accompany every interpretive statement, but they should be used frequently enough to leave no doubt that the conclusions in the report are tied to test evidence.

The statement about Ms. Thomas qualifies a reasonably certain conclusion by referring to how she "appears to be." This qualification reflects that personality assessment instruments are inferential measures that can generate probabilities, but never warrant absolute certainty. Inferences from test data should never be presented as if they were final truth. Instead, even conclusions that are well supported by the test data should be expressed in such qualified terms as what "seems to be," what "may be," or what "is probably" the case. In addition to using qualifiers, examiners should consider phrasing their conclusions in ways that indicate more or less certainty about what they are reporting. Depending on the strength of the data, a conclusion might be stated as "The test findings strongly suggest that . . . ," or "The test findings suggest that . . . ," or "There is some suggestion in the test data that. . . ."

To go one step further, test protocols containing only fragmentary evidence of some personality characteristic call for speculation and reference to possible rather than probable features of a person's nature or behavioral tendencies. The following statements illustrate such tentative conclusions: "This child's test responses raise the possibility that she may be unusually fearful of being left alone"; "Ms. Gilbert occasionally shows a tendency to be inflexible in her approach to solving problems, which might limit the quality of her decision making in an executive position"; "The data provide some basis for speculating that his lack of effort represents a passive-aggressive way of dealing with underlying anger and resentment he feels toward people who have burdened him with excessive demands and unrealistic expectations."

Additional discussion of ways to promote the readability and communication value of personality assessment reports can be found in contributions by Groth-Marnat and Horvath (2006), Harvey (2006), Lichtenberger, Mather, Kaufman, and Kaufman (2004), and Weiner (2006).

Collaborative Feedback and Therapeutic Assessment

In some circumstances, the reporting of personality assessment results may include a final phase of providing face-to-face feedback to the person who has been examined. Examiner feedback is seldom appropriate in administrative evaluations and, as mentioned, may be expressly forbidden in these cases. People being evaluated for clinical or health care purposes may for various reasons be unavailable for a feedback session or may prefer to learn the results of their examination from the primary care professional who referred them for it. When it is appropriate and can be arranged, however, properly presented examiner feedback of personality test results is usually beneficial to people who have been evaluated.

Properly presented feedback is accurate, informative, understandable, and, above all, collaborative. Like their written reports, examiners' oral feedback should present a clear picture of what the test results suggest about the individual's personality assets and liabilities and what these findings imply with respect to the questions or concerns that prompted referral for the evaluation. As for collaboration, the feedback presentation should not be a one-sided conversation in which the examiner provides information and the examinee listens in silence. Instead, to be maximally effective, feedback sessions should be an interactive process in which examinees are asked if they understand and agree with what they are being told. Perplexity on the part of the examinee calls for further explanation, and both agreement and disagreement call for exploration of the reasons behind them.

Exploration of an examinee's agreement or disagreement with inferences from the test data often helps examiners sharpen their conclusions, especially those about which they are less certain. Collaborative feedback presented in this way also helps examinees grasp the implications of the test findings and, having been an active participant in discussing these implications, to take them to heart. Research reported by Finn and Tonsager (1992, 1997) has indicated that persons who receive feedback following personality testing are likely to be much more satisfied with the evaluation process than those for whom there is no feedback. These and other aspects of collaborative feedback are elaborated by Finn (1996), Fischer (2000), and Fischer, Georgievska, and Melczak (2004).

As in writing reports, there is no single best way of conducting a feedback session. Nevertheless, examiners can usually enhance the benefit of collaborative feedback to people who receive it. First, a feedback session, like the testing session that preceded it, should be conducted in a supportive manner that helps recipients feel comfortable and encourages them to discuss the report. Second, to promote perception of the feedback as a supportive and beneficial process, examiners should consider beginning their feedback discussion with the individual's personality strengths, as indicated by the test findings, and then turning to indications of apparent concerns, problems, and functioning limitations. In bringing up liabilities, moreover, it can be helpful to start with those that are most clearly suggested by the test data and then move on to less certain and more speculative inferences. Relatively definite conclusions are usually easier to explain and more likely to be congruent with a person's self-perceptions than relatively speculative conclusions.

Collaborative feedback can also be integrated within a general procedure for therapeutic assessment developed by Finn (1996, 1998; see also Finn & Tonsager, 1992, 1997). In the therapeutic assessment model, examiners precede any testing by discussing with people not only their understanding of why they have been referred for an evaluation, but also what they hope to get out of being assessed. The examination procedures focus not only on obtaining accurate information and making sound recommendations, but also on ensuring that examinees feel respected, understood, and listened to by the assessor. The feedback process, which may be ongoing during the examination as well as in posttesting sessions, is aimed at helping individuals learn new ways of thinking and feeling about themselves and others and fostering their self-exploration of what they have learned and its application to their problems in living.

REFERENCES

Achenbach, T. (1992). *Manual for the Child Behavior Checklist*. Burlington: University of Vermont Department of Psychiatry.

Acklin, M. W. (2002). How to select personality tests for a test battery. In J. N. Butcher (Ed.), *Clinical personality assessment* (2nd ed., pp. 13–23). New York: Oxford University Press.

Ægisdóttir, S., White, M. J., Spengler, P. M., Maugherman, A. S., Anderson, L. A., Cook, R. S., et al. (2006). The meta-analysis of clinical judgment project: Fifty-six years of accumulated research on clinical versus statistical judgment. *Counseling Psychologist, 34*, 341–382.

Allard, G., & Faust, D. (2000). Errors in scoring objective personality tests. *Assessment, 7*, 137–145.

Allen, J., & Walsh, J. A. (2000). A construct-based approach to equivalence: Methodologies for cross-cultural/multicultural personality assessment research. In R. H. Dana (Ed.), *Handbook of cross-cultural and multicultural personality assessment* (pp. 63–86). Mahwah, NJ: Erlbaum.

American Educational Research Association, American Psychological Association, and National Council on Measurement in Education. (1999). *Standards for educational and psychological testing*. Washington, DC: American Educational Research Association.

American Psychiatric Association. (2000). *Diagnostic and statistical manual of mental disorders* (4th ed., text rev.). Washington, DC: Author.

Aspendorf, J. B., Banse, R., & Mucke, D. (2002). Double dissociation between implicit and explicit personality self-concept: The case of shy behavior. *Journal of Personality and Social Psychology, 83*, 380–393.

Atlis, M. M., Hahn, J., & Butcher, J. N. (2006). Computer-based assessment with the MMPI-2. In J. N. Butcher (Ed.), *MMPI-2: A practitioner's guide* (pp. 445–476). Washington, DC: American Psychological Association.

Beck, A. T., Steer, R. A., & Brown, G. K. (1996). *Manual for the Beck Depression Inventory-II*. San Antonio, TX: Psychological Corporation.

Ben-Porath, Y. S. (1994). The ethical dilemma of coached malingering research. *Psychological Assessment, 6*, 14–15.

Berry, D. T. R., Wetter, M. W., & Baer, R. (2002). Assessment of malingering. In J. N. Butcher (Ed.), *Clinical personality assessment* (2nd ed., pp. 269–301). New York: Guilford Press.

Beutler, L. E., Malik, M., Talebi, H., Fleming, J., & Moleiro, C. (2004). Use of psychological tests/instruments for treatment planning. In M. E. Maruish (Ed.), *The use of psychological testing for treatment planning and outcomes assessment* (Vol. 1, pp. 111–146). Mahwah, NJ: Erlbaum.

Bornstein, R. F. (1999). Criterion validity of objective and projective dependency tests: A meta-analytic assessment of behavioral prediction. *Psychological Assessment, 11*, 48–57.

Briere, J. (1995). *Trauma Symptom Inventory (TSI): Professional manual*. Odessa, FL: Psychological Assessment Resources.

Butcher, J. N. (1997). Introduction to the special section on assessment in psychological treatment: A necessary step for effective intervention. *Psychological Assessment, 9*, 331–333.

Butcher, J. N. (2002). How to use computer-based reports. In J. N. Butcher (Ed.), *Clinical personality assessment* (2nd ed., pp. 109–125). New York: Oxford University Press.

Butcher, J. N. (2003). Computerized psychological assessment. In I. B. Weiner (Editor-in-Chief), J. R. Graham & J. A. Naglieri (Vol. Eds.), *Handbook of psychology: Vol. 10. Assessment psychology* (pp. 141–164). Hoboken, NJ: Wiley.

Butcher, J. N., Mosch, S. C., Tsai, J., & Nezami, E. (2006). Cross-cultural applications of the MMPI-2. In J. N. Butcher (Ed.), *MMPI-2: A practitioner's guide* (pp. 505–538). Washington, DC: American Psychological Association.

Butcher, J. N., Perry, J., & Hahn, J. (2004). Computers in clinical assessment: Historical developments, present status, and future challenges. *Journal of Clinical Psychology, 60*, 331–345.

Campbell, D. T., & Fiske, D. W. (1959). Convergent and discriminant validation by the multitrait-multimethod matrix. *Psychological Bulletin, 56*, 81–105.

Clarkin, J. F., & Levy, K. N. (2004). The influence of client variables on psychotherapy. In M. J. Lambert (Ed.), *Bergin and Garfield's handbook of psychotherapy and behavior change* (5th ed., pp. 194–226). Hoboken, NJ: Wiley.

Cull, J. G., & Gill, W. S. (1988). *Suicide Probability Scale: Manual*. Los Angeles: Western Psychological Services.

Duckworth, A. L., Steen, T. A., & Seligman, M. E. P. (2005). Positive psychology in clinical practice. *Annual Review of Clinical Psychology, 1*, 609–651.

Elhai, J. D., Kinder, B. N., & Frueh, B. C. (2004). Projective assessment of malingering. In M. Hersen (Editor-in-Chief), M. J. Hilsenroth & D. L. Segal (Vol. Eds.), *Comprehensive handbook of psychological assessment: Vol. 2. Personality assessment* (pp. 533–561). Hoboken, NJ: Wiley.

Fernandez-Ballesteros, R. (1997). Guidelines for the assessment process (GAP). *European Psychologist, 2*, 352–355.

Finger, M. S., & Ones, D. S. (1999). Psychometric equivalence of the computer and booklet forms of the MMPI: A meta-analysis. *Psychological Assessment, 11*, 58–66.

Finn, S. E. (1996). Assessment feedback integrating MMPI-2 and Rorschach findings. *Journal of Personality Assessment, 67*, 543–557.

Finn, S. E. (1998). Teaching therapeutic assessment in a required graduate course. In L. Handler & M. J. Hilsenroth (Eds.), *Teaching and learning personality assessment* (pp. 359–374). Mahwah, NJ: Erlbaum.

Finn, S. E., & Tonsager, M. E. (1992). Therapeutic effects of providing MMP-2 test feedback to college students awaiting therapy. *Psychological Assessment, 4*, 278–287.

Finn, S. E., & Tonsager, M. E. (1997). Information-gathering and therapeutic models of assessment: Complementary paradigms. *Psychological Assessment, 9*, 374–385.

Fischer, C. T. (2000). Collaborative, individualized assessment. *Journal of Personality Assessment, 74*, 2–14.

Fischer, C. T., Georgievska, E., & Melczak, M. (2004). Collaborative exploration with projective techniques: A life-world approach. In M. Hersen (Editor-in-Chief), M. J. Hilsenroth & D. L. Segal (Vol. Eds.), *Comprehensive handbook of psychological assessment: Vol. 2. Personality assessment* (pp. 586–594). Hoboken, NJ: Wiley.

Freud, S. (1953). On psychotherapy (Standard Ed., Vol. 7, pp. 257–268). London: Hogarth Press. (Original work published 1904)

Frisch, M. B. (2006). *Quality of life therapy: Applying a life satisfaction approach to positive psychology and cognitive therapy*. Hoboken, NJ: Wiley.

Garb, H. N. (1998). *Studying the clinician*. Washington, DC: American Psychological Association.

Garb, H. N. (2000). Computers will become increasingly important for psychological assessment: Not that there's anything wrong with that! *Psychological Assessment, 12*, 31–39.

Garb, H. N. (2003). Clinical judgment and mechanical prediction. In I. B. Weiner (Editor-in-Chief), J. R. Graham & J. A. Naglieri (Vol. Eds.), *Handbook of psychology: Vol. 10. Assessment psychology* (pp. 27–43). Hoboken, NJ: Wiley.

Garner, D. (2004). *The Eating Disorder Inventory-3: Professional manual*. Lutz, FL: Psychological Assessment Resources.

Groth-Marnat, G., & Horvath, L. S. (2006). The psychological report: A review of current controversies. *Journal of Clinical Psychology, 62*, 73–82.

Grove, W. M., & Meehl, P. E. (1996). Comparative efficiency of informal (subjective, impressionistic) and formal (mechanical, algorithmic) prediction procedures: The clinical-statistical controversy. *Psychology, Public Policy, and Law, 2*, 295–323.

Grove, W. M., Zald, D. H., Lebow, B. S., Snitz, B. E., & Nelson, C. (2000). Clinical versus mechanical predication: A meta-analysis. *Psychological Assessment, 12*, 19–30.

Hare, R. D. (1990). *Hare Psychopathy Checklist: Revised manual*. Toronto: Multi-Health Systems.

Harvey, V. S. (2006). Variables affecting the clarity of psychological reports. *Journal of Clinical Psychology, 62*, 5–18.

Holt, R. R. (1958). Clinical and statistical prediction: A reformulation and some new data. *Journal of Abnormal and Social Psychology, 56*, 1–12.

Holt, R. R. (1986). Clinical and statistical prediction: A retrospective and would-be integrative perspective. *Journal of Personality Assessment, 50*, 376–385.

Hurt, S. W., Reznikoff, M., & Clarkin, J. F. (1991). *Psychological assessment, psychiatric diagnosis, and treatment planning*. New York: Brunner/Mazel.

Karon, B. P. (2000). The clinical interpretation of the Thematic Apperception Test, Rorschach, and other clinical data: A reexamination of statistical versus clinical prediction. *Professional Psychology, 31*, 230–233.

Kazarian, S., & Evans, D. R. (Eds.). (1998). *Cultural clinical psychology*. New York: Oxford University Press.

Kitchener, K. S. (2000). *Foundations of ethical practice, research, and teaching in psychology*. Mahwah, NJ: Erlbaum.

Kleinmuntz, B. (1990). Why we still use our heads instead of formulas: Toward an integrative approach. *Psychological Bulletin, 107*, 296–310.

Koocher, G. P., & Rey-Casserly, C. M. (2003). Ethical issues in psychological assessment. In I. B. Weiner (Editor-in-Chief), J. R. Graham & J. A. Naglieri (Vol. Eds.), *Handbook of psychology: Vol. 10. Assessment psychology* (pp. 165–180). Hoboken, NJ: Wiley.

Lambert, M. J., & Hawkins, E. J. (2004). Use of psychological tests for assessing treatment outcomes. In M. E. Maruish (Ed.), *The use of psychological testing for treatment planning and outcomes assessment* (*Vol. 1*, pp. 171–196). Mahwah, NJ: Erlbaum.

Lichtenberger, E. O. (2006). Computer utilization and clinical judgment in psychological assessment reports. *Journal of Clinical Psychology, 62*, 19–32.

Lichtenberger, E. O., Mather, N., Kaufman, N. L., & Kaufman, A. S. (2004). *Essentials of assessment report writing*. Hoboken, NJ: Wiley.

Masling, J. M. (1998). Interpersonal and actuarial dimensions of projective testing. In L. Handler & M. J. Hilsenroth (Eds.), *Teaching and learning personality assessment* (pp. 119–135). Mahwah, NJ: Erlbaum.

Matarazzo, J. D. (1990). Psychological assessment versus psychological testing: Validation from Binet to the school, clinic, and courtroom. *American Psychologist, 45*, 999–1017.

McCann, J. T. (1998). *Malingering and deception in adolescents*. Washington, DC: American Psychological Association.

McClelland, D. C., Koestner, R., & Weinberger, J. (1989). How do self-attributed and explicit motives differ? *Psychological Review, 96*, 690–702.

McCrae, R. R. (2002). NEO PI-R data from 36 cultures. In R. R. McCrae & U. Allik (Eds.), *The Five-Factor Model of personality across cultures* (pp. 105–125). New York: Kluwer Academic/ Plenum Press.

McMinn, M. F., Ellens, B. M., & Soref, E. (1999). Ethical perspectives and practice behaviors involving computer-based test interpretations. *Assessment, 6*, 71–77.

Meehl, P. E. (1954). *Clinical versus statistical prediction.* Minneapolis: University of Minnesota Press.

Meehl, P. E. (1957). When shall we use our heads instead of the formula. *Journal of Counseling Psychology, 4*, 268–273.

Meehl, P. E. (1986). Causes and effect of my disturbing little book. *Journal of Personality Assessment, 50*, 370–375.

Meyer, G. J., Finn, S. E., Eyde, L. D., Kay, G. G., Moreland, K. L., Dies, R. R., et al. (2001). Psychological testing and psychological assessment: A review of evidence and issues. *American Psychologist, 56*, 128–165.

Reynolds, W. M. (2002). *Reynolds Adolescent Depression Scale professional manual* (2nd ed.). Odessa, FL: Psychological Assessment Resources.

Rogers, R. (1997). *Clinical assessment of malingering and deception* (2nd ed.). New York: Guilford Press.

Schretlen, D. J. (1997). Dissimulation on the Rorschach and other projective measures. In R. Rogers (Ed.), *Clinical assessment of malingering and deception* (2nd ed., pp. 208–222). New York: Guilford Press.

Seligman, M. E. P., & Csikszentmihalyi, M. (2000). Positive psychology: An introduction. *American Psychologist, 55*, 5–14.

Selzer, M. L. (1971). The Michigan Alcoholism Screening Test. *American Journal of Psychiatry, 127*, 1653–1658.

Snyder, C. R., & Lopez, S. F. (2007). *Positive psychology: The scientific and practical application of human strengths.* Thousand Oaks, CA: Sage.

Snyder, D. K. (2000). Computer-assisted judgment: Defining strengths and liabilities. *Psychological Assessment, 12*, 52–60.

Spielberger, C. D. (1998). *State-Trait Anger Expression Inventory-2: Research edition.* Odessa, FL: Psychological Assessment Resources.

Storm, J., & Graham, J. R. (2000). Detection of coached malingering on the MMPI-2. *Psychological Assessment, 12*, 158–165.

Swets, J. A., Dawes, R. M., & Monahan, J. (2000). Psychological science can improve diagnostic decisions. *Psychological Science in the Public Interest, 1*, 1–26.

Tedeschi, R. G., & Kilmer, R. P. (2005). Assessing strengths, resilience, and growth to guide clinical interventions. *Professional Psychology, 36*, 230–237.

Victor, T. L., & Abeles, N. (2004). Coaching clients to take psychological and neuropsychological tests: A clash of ethical obligation. *Professional Psychology, 33*, 373–379.

Weiner, I. B. (2004). Monitoring psychotherapy with performance-based measures of personality functioning. *Journal of Personality Assessment, 83*, 322–330.

Weiner, I. B. (2005). Integrative personality assessment with self-report and performance-based measures. In S. Strack (Ed.), *Handbook of personality and psychopathology* (pp. 317–331). Hoboken, NJ: Wiley.

Weiner, I. B. (2006). Writing forensic reports. In I. B. Weiner & A. K. Hess (Eds.), *Handbook of forensic psychology* (pp. 631–651). Hoboken, NJ: Wiley.

Westen, D., & Weinberger, J. (2004). When clinical description becomes statistical prediction. *American Psychologist, 59*, 595–613.

Zaccaro, S. J. (2007). Trait-based perspectives of leadership. *American Psychologist, 62*, 6–16.

Chapter 3

PSYCHOMETRIC FOUNDATIONS OF ASSESSMENT

This chapter provides an overview of the general psychometric information that clinicians must consider when interpreting any assessment test or technique. It is assumed that the reader is familiar with basic descriptive statistics such as measures of central tendency (mean, median, mode), dispersion (standard deviation, variance), and deviations from a normal distribution (kurtosis, skewness). This chapter also describes a multitude of issues that arise when making decisions about clinical patients. The emphasis is on maximizing the accuracy and effectiveness of these decisions, not on the issues per se, which have been described thoroughly by Garb (1998).

All the assessment tests and techniques reviewed in this *Handbook* follow classical test theory (CTT) rather then item response theory (IRT). The assumption in CTT is that the person's actual or obtained score on an assessment test or technique is a function of both a true score and the error associated with measuring it, and that this error is invariant across the entire range of scores. Classical test theory weights items equally regardless of their actual difficulty, so that infrequently endorsed (difficult) items are weighted equally to frequently endorsed (easy) items. To the extent that any of these assumptions cannot be met, which is more often than not, there are potential limitations in CTT.

There are many excellent sources of information on IRT (cf., Embretson & Reise, 2000), and further consideration of it is outside the scope of the present *Handbook*. However, IRT has been proposed as an alternative method in scale construction for addressing problems that arise when CTT assumptions are not met. Because IRT is not sample dependent, it allows generalization of results across samples more directly than CTT. Item response theory also allows for the effectiveness of items to be assessed at all different levels of a scale or at any specific level, if that is desired. The field of personality assessment needs to consider whether moving away from CTT toward IRT, or some other approach, would be beneficial.

The following sections cover basic considerations in assessing reliability, determining validity, and making decisions based on assessment data. For additional discussion of psychometric aspects of psychological testing, readers are referred to the classic book on CTT by Gulliksen (1950) and contemporary texts by Anastasi and Urbina (1997), Kaplan and Saccuzzo (2001), and Urbina (2004).

RELIABILITY

Any variable must be assessed reliably before its validity can be examined, where reliability is defined as the consistency with which a variable is measured. The reliability of an assessment test or technique also sets the upper limits for its validity. Consequently, reliable measurement with any assessment test or technique is mandatory before its validity can even be considered.

Reliability is usually reported as a correlation coefficient, with reliability coefficients of at least .75 as a general standard for whether a variable is being assessed reliably. Three types of reliability are discussed here: (1) test-retest or temporal reliability; (2) internal consistency reliability; and (3) interrater reliability. Two other types of reliability—parallel-form or alternate-form reliability and split-half reliability—are not discussed, because they are not used with any of the assessment tests or techniques reviewed in this *Handbook*. Three related constructs are also examined in this section on reliability: (1) standard error of measurement and cutting scores; (2) stability of test scores; and (3) redundancy of test scores.

In reviewing the reliability of a scale, clinicians need to give some thought to the appropriateness of the measure of reliability that has been used as well as to the magnitude of the correlation coefficient that has been obtained. They can compare the reliability of the scale that is being considered for use with similar scales and their reliability, if they exist. Clinicians should provide the rationale for using a scale whose reliability is significantly lower than similar scales with comparable validity. This rationale could be included in the psychological report to inform readers of the decision that has been made.

Generally speaking, the longer a scale is, the more reliable it is likely to be, and vice versa, because the more items there are in a scale, the more adequately the scale samples the domain being measured. One of the potential shortcomings of brief scales is their limited reliability. Test developers must contend with the challenge of keeping a scale as short as possible while maintaining adequate reliability.

Test-Retest (Temporal) Reliability

Test-retest reliability is assessed by administering an assessment test or technique twice to the same group of participants within some relatively short interval of time, ranging from 1 day to a few weeks. Such brief retest intervals are used when the construct being assessed is expected to vary across time, just as a person's mood is likely to change from time to time. Most of the assessment tests and techniques reviewed in this *Handbook* meet or exceed the criterion of .75 for short-term test-retest reliability when it is used as the measure of reliability. There is, however, a growing trend in the field of assessment to use internal consistency together with or instead of test-retest as the measure of reliability.

Internal Consistency Reliability

A measure of internal consistency for a scale assesses the homogeneity among the items it contains and is basically the average intercorrelation among all the items on the scale. Cronbach's coefficient alpha (1951) is the measure most often used to report internal consistency. Again, the criterion of at least .75 is a general standard for an acceptable level of internal consistency for a scale, and most assessment tests and techniques will meet or exceed this criterion. Because published scales seldom fail to meet this criterion, it is easy for clinicians to overlook the importance of checking the reliability of any assessment tests and techniques that they use.

There is ordinarily a preferred upper limit to the internal consistency of a given scale because as coefficient alpha approaches 1.00, the items become increasingly redundant and provide little, if any, additional information about the underlying construct being assessed. In addition, if the construct is relatively heterogeneous, then the scale must also embody some heterogeneity. In such an instance, a lower level of internal consistency, possibly even as low as .70, might be acceptable. A scale measuring moods that consists entirely of items assessing depression, and does not include items assessing anxiety, anger, and other affective states, might have excellent internal consistency, but still be a poor measure of the more general construct of moods, which the scale was intended to assess.

Interrater Reliability

Intuitively, determining interrater reliability would seem to be simple—just count the number of times two raters agree and calculate the percentage of agreement in their judgments or decisions. This simplicity dissipates quickly when consideration is given to the chance level of agreement expected in these judgments or decisions, how frequently the measured behaviors or symptoms occur, and how many categories are being judged simultaneously. It is much easier to achieve reliable agreement when ratings are only for whether a given behavior or symptom is present than when they are quantified into three or more levels.

There are three methods for measuring the consistency of interrater agreement: (1) the percentage of agreement just mentioned, (2) the interclass correlation coefficient, and (3) the kappa coefficient. These different methods have evolved because two raters can rank order their judgments similarly, and appear to be in perfect agreement, but one can be assigning consistently higher or lower scores than the other, which would mean that there is actually little agreement in their ratings. Interclass correlation coefficients provide a measure of the consistency of the scores assigned, not merely their rank order, either for a single rater or as a measure of the consistency in ratings among several raters. As for the limitation of a percentage of agreement, it is necessary to determine the chance level of agreement to evaluate whether the raters are achieving an increment in consistency beyond what would be expected by chance.

To this end, Cohen (1960) proposed the kappa coefficient, which is generally a better measure for evaluating the agreement between two raters than percentage of agreement, because it provides a correction for the level of agreement expected by chance. If two raters are deciding the presence or absence of a behavior or symptom across a number of individuals, they should agree 50% of the time simply by chance. They would need to improve beyond this level of 50% agreement to demonstrate that they were rating the behavior or symptom reliably. In this example, if two raters agreed 85% of the time, they would demonstrate that their ratings are better than chance using the kappa coefficient. In fact, the kappa coefficient is determined by the formula: (Observed agreement − Chance agreement)/(1 − Chance agreement), so in this instance kappa = (.85 − .50)/(1 − .50) = .70.

Standard Error of Measurement (Confidence Intervals)

In classical test theory, a person's true score on a scale or test is assumed to be composed of two components, the person's actual or obtained score and the error associated with that score. This error is expressed as the standard error of measurement (*SEM*), which is

Table 3.1   **Changes in the standard error of measurement (*SEM*) with changes in the reliability of a scale**

$r = .90$	$SEM = 10 \times \text{SQRT}(1 - .90)$	$=$	10×0.32	$=$	3.20
$r = .80$	$SEM = 10 \times \text{SQRT}(1 - .80)$	$=$	10×0.45	$=$	4.50
$r = .70$	$SEM = 10 \times \text{SQRT}(1 - .70)$	$=$	10×0.55	$=$	5.50
$r = .60$	$SEM = 10 \times \text{SQRT}(1 - .60)$	$=$	10×0.63	$=$	6.30
$r = .50$	$SEM = 10 \times \text{SQRT}(1 - .50)$	$=$	10×0.71	$=$	7.10

Note: The standard deviation was assumed to be 10 in these examples.

the normal variability that would be expected in an individual's score if the scale or test were administered a large number of times. The *SEM* is a direct function of the standard deviation and reliability of the scale ($SEM = SD \times \text{SQRT}[1 - r]$). As the scale becomes less reliable, the *SEM* increases correspondingly. This variability, which is assumed to follow a normal distribution, is expressed in standard deviation units within which the individual's "true" score is expected to fall. If the reliability for most assessment tests or techniques is approximately .80, the *SEM* is about .5 *SD* (see Table 3.1).

If the *SEM* for a scale is 5.0 points, then two-thirds of the time, the individual's true score will be within ±5.0 points of the obtained score. This range of ±1.0 *SEM* is the 68% confidence interval, the range of ±2.0 *SEM* is the 95% confidence interval, and so on. Confidence intervals sometimes are called the error bands for a score.

The *SEM* and confidence intervals become very important when cutting scores are being employed on a scale. When the obtained score on the scale is exactly at the cutting point at least 50% of the time, the individual's true score would be expected to be below the cutting score. If the cutting score for a scale is 25 to indicate the presence of some behavior or symptom, 50% of the time the individual's true score is below 25. If the *SEM* is 3.0, even when the individual has an obtained score of 28 (+1.0 *SEM*), 16% of the time the individual's true score still would be below the cutting score of 25. If the individual has an obtained score of 22 (−1.0 *SEM*), 16% of the time the individual's true score will be above the cutting score. As a general rule of thumb, an individual's obtained score should be at least .5 to 1.0 *SEM* above the cutting score so that there is reasonable probability that the individual's true score would exceed the cutting score. By the same token, it is optimal when an individual's obtained score is at least .5 to 1.0 *SEM* below the cutting score, so there is a reasonable probability that the individual's true score does not exceed the cutting score.

When a cutting score is developed on a scale, the scale is being validated as a dichotomous or categorical variable, that is, whether the person is above or below the cutting score. Consequently, higher scores on the scale above the cutting score have a higher probability that the person's true score is above the cutting score, not that the person has more symptoms or that the symptoms are more severe. Conversely, lower scores below the cutting score have a higher probability that the person's true score is below the cutting score, not that the person has fewer symptoms or the symptoms are less severe. Another way of saying the same thing is that a dichotomous or categorical variable has been validated, not a dimension of quantity or severity of the behavior or symptom.

It is important to realize that artificially dichotomizing any variable that is dimensional will result in a loss of power and is generally not recommended (Cohen, 1983). Taxometric procedures have been developed by Meehl and his colleagues (cf. Waller & Meehl, 1997) as a means of determining whether a variable is dimensional, and hence should not be dichotomized, or categorical.

Stability of Test Patterns or Profile Scores

The stability of test scores is sometimes used as an alternate way of referring to the short-term test-retest (temporal) reliability already discussed, but there is some advantage in reserving this term for descriptions of test-retest correlations over an extended period. As used here, then, stability of test patterns or profile scores refers to similarity or change in test scores across some extended interval and indicates how consistently individuals obtain the same pattern of scores on two administrations of an assessment instrument, one at the beginning and the other at the end of this period of time.

The assessment instruments presented in Chapters 6 through 14 of this *Handbook* are interpreted primarily or in part on the basis of patterns of scores that persons obtain on them. In addition to establishing the reliability of the individual scales used for this purpose, as indicated by either short-term test-retest or internal consistency data, it is important to determine whether there also is stability over time in the pattern of scores on which interpretations are based.

There has only been limited research on this topic, most of which has been restricted to the original Minnesota Multiphasic Personality Inventory (MMPI) and to the Rorschach Inkblot Method (RIM). With respect to the MMPI, Graham, Smith, and Schwartz (1986) reported 42.7%, 44.0%, and 27.7% agreement across an average interval of approximately 3 months for high-point, low point, and two-highest scales, respectively, in 405 psychiatric inpatients. Greene, Davis, and Morse (1993, March) provided similar data on 454 alcoholic inpatients who had taken the MMPI during two different hospitalizations separated by at least 6 months. Approximately 40% of the men and 32% of the women had the same high-point scale on the two successive administrations of the MMPI. However, they had the same two highest scales only 12% and 13% of the time, respectively. Finally, Livingston, Jennings, Colotla, Reynolds, and Shercliffe (2006) reported 45% and 24% agreement for high-point scale and two highest scales on the MMPI-2, respectively, in 94 injured workers evaluated after approximately 2 years (see also Chapter 6).

Two conclusions are readily apparent from these limited data. First, a pattern of test or profile scores on self-report inventories appears to be stable in fewer than 50% of the individuals who have been evaluated. Consequently, clinicians should be very cautious about making any long-term predictions from a single administration of a self-report inventory, because a different pattern of test or profile scores is more likely than not, if the person is reevaluated. Second, more research is needed on the stability of the pattern of test or profile scores for all self-report inventories.

As for the RIM, Exner (1993, chap. 11) reported retest correlations for a sample of 100 adult nonpatients examined after a 3-year interval and a separate sample of 50 adult nonpatients examined after a 1-year interval. Over the 3-year interval, 22 of 32 Rorschach variables examined had retest correlations of .75 or more (with nine at .85 or higher); and over the 1-year interval, 30 of 41 variables examined reached the .75 criterion of adequacy (with 15 at .85 or higher). Most of the examined variables with stability coefficients below

.75 are intended to measure state dimensions of personality (e.g., moods) that are expected to change over time.

Sultan, Andronikof, and Réveillère (2006) reported retest correlations for the Rorschach in a sample of 75 French nonpatient adults who were retested after a 3-month interval. The median correlation was .53, significantly lower than the values reported by Exner (2003). There were a number of factors that appeared to moderate the stability of these coefficients: overall level of engagement in the task, level of state distress, and number of responses.

In Rorschach assessment, then, there is some basis for making long-term predictions related to trait characteristics of individuals. However, such predictions are not warranted on the basis of variables measuring states of the individual, and the stability of scores derived from other performance-based measures has yet to be examined.

Redundancy of Test Scores

Sometimes clinicians confuse the redundancy of self-report inventory scores with their validity. For example, they might administer the MCMI-III, MMPI-2, and Beck Depression Inventory (BDI: Beck, Steer, & Brown, 1996) to the same person and find elevated scores on all the scales assessing depression on these inventories (MCMI-III: Depressive [*2B*], Dysthymic Disorder [*D*], and Major Depression [*CC*]; MMPI-2: Scale 2 [*D*] and Depression [*DEP*]; BDI). The clinician might then be prone to conclude that this individual must really be depressed because of the similar pattern of elevated scores across all of these self-report inventories. In doing so, they would fail to realize that variations of the same questions are asked on all these measures. The individual has been very reliable (consistent) about reporting symptoms of depression, but this does not make the person any more depressed. This redundancy of test scores can be seen by examining the intercorrelations among all these scales, which exceed .70 in most cases.

This issue of redundant test scores should be considered carefully when selecting a battery of assessment instruments for a specific individual. At the same time, avoidance of redundancy in test selection should be distinguished from the confirmatory value of congruent findings that are obtained from different kinds of measures. As discussed in Chapter 2, patterns of convergence and divergence between self-report and performance-based test protocols can provide valuable information about an examinee's psychological condition and frame of mind.

A second type of redundancy in the interrelations among a set of variables derives from heterogeneity in the variables and may be particularly difficult to recognize. If assessors wish to predict school learning problems in adolescents, for example, they need to appreciate that a number of psychosocial variables have a low negative (−.16 to .30) relationship with academic performance, including behavior problems at school, alcohol and drug use, family instability, and poor interpersonal relationships. These variables may mistakenly be construed as being independent, when they actually reflect a complex set of specific variables that assess the same general set of problem variables. This redundancy can be demonstrated by a hierarchical regression analysis that examines incremental validity (covered in the next section) with the addition of each variable. There is almost no increment in the ability to predict academic performance as each of the just mentioned variables is added, even though they might seem to be assessing different behaviors.

VALIDITY

Until an assessment test or technique produces reliable data, there is no reason to proceed to the step of attempting to validate it. Once an assessment test or technique has been determined to be reliable enough to meet the previously indicated psychometric standard, then the issue of its validity becomes paramount. The validity of an assessment test or technique consists of how well or accurately it measures the constructs it is intended to measure.

Unlike the case with reliability coefficients, there is little consensus about the magnitude validity coefficients should attain. Nevertheless, it is important to keep in mind that the reliability coefficient for a score or scale sets the upper limit for its validity coefficient. A validity coefficient for a score or scale cannot exceed the square root of its reliability coefficient. That is, a score or scale with a reliability coefficient of .80 cannot correlate higher than .89 with any other measurement; a score or scale with a reliability coefficient of .70 cannot have any validity coefficient greater than .84; and so on. Validity coefficients between two self-report scales should be larger than validity coefficients between a self-report scale and a behavioral rating, or between a self-report scale and a performance-based scale. The shared method variance between two self-report scales (i.e., the constructs are being measured in the same manner), almost inevitably produces larger correlations than the other two types of comparison.

It cannot be stated too strongly that any assessment test or technique is not valid in the abstract, but is valid for the assessment of a specific construct or set of constructs within a given assessment setting. One of the fundamental issues of validity is how well the results of an assessment test or technique in one set of circumstances generalize to other circumstances. An assessment test or technique may adequately identify a behavior or symptom in one clinical setting, but for a variety of reasons may not work as well in another setting or with different patients. The comparability of the clinical setting and individuals used in the validation process has to be considered carefully when clinicians consider adopting an assessment test or technique they have not previously used in their particular setting.

There are multiple ways of classifying validity as well as a growing trend to consider all forms of validity as construct validity, which refers to how well an assessment test or technique measures a specific construct. Only three types of validity are considered here: convergent, discriminant, and incremental.

Convergent Validity

Convergent validity is a measure of how well an assessment test or technique correlates with other assessment tests or techniques that are measuring *similar* constructs. A new scale designed to measure depression should correlate with extant measures of depression; if not, there is something amiss with one or the other of them. Whether another scale of depression is needed is addressed in discussing incremental validity.

A problem with most self-report inventories is that they assess the general negative emotional distress or misery that is common to all types of psychopathology and consequently demonstrate a substantial level of convergent validity regardless of the specific construct being assessed. This problem is reflected in discussions of whether depression and anxiety are separate diagnostic entities or different manifestations of general negative emotional distress (see Barlow & Campbell, 2000). The inclusion of a diagnosis of mixed anxiety and depression in *DSM-IV-TR* (American Psychiatric Association, 2000) appears to attest to the comorbidity of these disorders.

In self-report assessment of psychopathology, a current issue is whether inventories can assess specific constructs independently of general negative emotional distress or misery. As elaborated in Chapter 6, the Restructured Clinical scales of the MMPI-2 (Tellegen et al., 2003) represent an attempt to remove general negative emotional distress (demoralization) from the clinical scales of the MMPI-2. The interested reader should consult the ongoing debate about the success of this venture (Caldwell, 2006; Nichols, 2006; Tellegen, Ben-Porath, & Sellbom, 2006). It is not clear what mood states like depression, anxiety, and anger would consist of if the general negative emotional distress were removed from them.

Discriminant Validity

Discriminant validity is a measure of whether an assessment test or technique is relatively unrelated to other assessment tests or techniques that assess *dissimilar* constructs. If a scale measuring depression has a significant positive correlation with a scale measuring assertiveness and positive self-regard, there is a rather serious validity problem with one or the other scale. However, a significant and large negative correlation with a scale measuring assertiveness and positive self-regard could be an example of convergent validity because these two constructs should be inversely related.

It is difficult to know how unrelated two scales measuring dissimilar constructs actually should be, because in most cases, it would be unusual for them to be correlated negatively. Validity coefficients for two dissimilar variables should be lower than those for convergent validity for two similar constructs. Campbell and Fiske (1959) advocated multitrait, multimethods for ascertaining the convergent and discriminant validity of a set of constructs simultaneously, so that these validity coefficients can be compared directly.

Incremental Validity

Incremental validity addresses two issues: (1) whether additional information from another assessment test or technique improves or enhances the clinical judgments that are made, and (2) whether any new scale or index contributes additional information beyond extant scales or indices to the prediction of relevant behaviors. There is a rather consistent literature indicating that clinicians' judgments become less accurate when they consider more than three or four variables simultaneously (see Garb, 1998). With multiple variables to evaluate, it can be difficult, sometimes impossible, for clinicians to determine which variables are the most important for a specific judgment and how to weight these variables to maximize accuracy.

Whether a new scale should demonstrate incremental validity over extant scales is less clear. This expectation can be justified to the extent that it limits the proliferation of scales, but it does not take into account the not uncommon differential validity of scales across settings and situational demands. At a minimum, the developer of a new scale or index should report its relationship with conceptually related scales or indices, along with a rationale for why this new scale or index should supplant an existing scale or index if incremental validity is not demonstrated.

Garb (2003) has reviewed the results for the incremental validity of the addition of various assessment tests and techniques to the clinical interview in the evaluation of psychopathology in adults. There was no general pattern to the results that Garb reported, partly because of the paucity of such research. Several specific scales or indices were found to provide incremental validity, including the Borderline scale of the Personality Assessment Inventory (Morey, 1991) in the longitudinal prediction of academic performance and interpersonal problems in college students (Trull, Useda, Conforti, & Doan, 1997) and Rorschach measures of thought disorder. The importance of such demographic variables as the age of onset of the disorder, lifetime history of psychopathology, family history of psychopathology, and social and familial support have not been considered in this research.

CLINICAL DECISION MAKING

The psychometric foundations of personality assessment include several special considerations that clinicians must take into account when they make decisions based on the information they obtain. The most important of these considerations are the impact of prevalence (base rate) data, the distinction between clinical and statistical judgment, the meaning of risk factors and odds ratios, the effects of heterogeneity among patients within diagnostic groups, the implications of diagnostic efficiency statistics, and setting of cutting scores. Each of these considerations is amplified in the sections that follow.

Prevalence (Base Rate) Data

No concept is more important in making decisions in clinical settings than the concept of prevalence (base rate), which is the frequency with which a given behavior or symptom occurs in a given group of individuals or patients. *DSM-IV-TR* (American Psychiatric Association, 2000) is an excellent source for basic information on the frequency of various forms of psychopathology in the general population. According to estimates, the lifetime prevalence of major depressive disorder is 10% to 25% in women and 5% to 12% in men; the lifetime prevalence of alcohol dependence in men is 15%; and the lifetime prevalence of schizophrenia is .5% to 1.5%. These prevalence estimates mean that 20% to 25% of women in the general population will experience an episode of diagnosable depression in their lifetime; nearly 15% of men will be diagnosed as alcoholic; and about 1% of people will experience a schizophrenic episode. Stated in another way, clinicians are likely to see approximately 25 depressed women patients and 15 male alcoholic patients for every schizophrenic patient.

Somewhat surprisingly, there are fewer sources of statistics on the frequency with which various forms of psychopathology are seen in clinical settings than there are concerning their prevalence, probably because these statistics are influenced by the clinical setting. A setting that specializes in the diagnosis and treatment of a specific disorder like borderline personality disorder or posttraumatic stress disorder is quite likely to have a higher prevalence for these disorders than a community clinic that is required to treat all types of patients.

The more specific the information clinicians have about the prevalence of various behaviors and symptoms in their specific setting, the more likely they are to make good decisions. Meehl (1954) long ago recognized the need for local norms, that is, the frequency with which a given behavior or symptom occurs in a specific setting. Most clinical settings are likely to attract particular types of patients. Hence the general prevalence that is presented in *DSM-IV-TR* (American Psychiatric Association, 2000) may be misleading for patients who are seen more or less frequently in any specific setting.

In settings in which the prevalence of some behavior or symptom is either very high (>80%) or very low (<20%), assessors face the formidable task of finding assessment methods that can achieve more than 80% accuracy. In many such circumstances, clinicians can simply use the prevalence of the behavior or symptom to decide whether it is present in an individual, which will make them accurate 80% of the time without any reliance on assessment tests or techniques.

Clinical versus Statistical Judgment

The discussion in Chapter 2 of the basis on which inferences can be drawn from test data distinguished between clinical and statistical judgment as alternative avenues for arriving at conclusions. Because of the importance of this distinction in the clinical decision-making process, and because research findings concerning the interpretive accuracy of these two methods are often ignored, some further attention to clinical versus statistical judgment is appropriate for the present chapter on psychometric foundations of psychological assessment.

To recap these approaches to decision making, statistical judgment is a quantitative approach in which empirical data are mechanically combined to provide actuarial rules for determining what test findings indicate. Clinical judgment, by contrast, is a qualitative approach in which shared beliefs of experienced clinicians are cumulated to determine what test findings signify. Readers are encouraged to consult the several sources referenced in Chapter 2 to gain an in-depth appreciation of these alternative avenues of interpretation and the controversy that has at times swirled around them.

Clinical and statistical judgment have often been pitted against each other—both in the minds of assessment psychologists and in comparative research studies—about which is the better and more accurate way to interpret test data. The empirical findings in this regard are as clear as perhaps any findings pertaining to issues in clinical psychology. As shown in the meta-analyses mentioned in Chapter 2 by Grove, Zald, Lebow, Snitz, and Nelson (2000) of 136 studies of the relative accuracy of clinical and statistical judgment, and by Ægisdóttir et al. (2006) of 67 such studies, statistical judgment is consistently as good as and typically better than clinical judgment in making accurate decisions.

Three other findings in these meta-analyses are important to note. First, the accuracy of both clinical and statistical judgments varied with the type of decision being made, the setting in which data are collected, the type of statistical formula used, and the amount of information available to the clinicians and for inclusion in the formulas. Second, the increase in accuracy of statistical over clinical judgments was modest, with statistical judgments being 13% more accurate on the average than clinical judgments in the Ægisdóttir et al. (2006) study and 10% more accurate in the Grove et al. (2000) study. Third, clinical judgment equaled the accuracy of statistical judgment in many instances and in some cases was even more accurate than a formula. As suggested in Chapter 2, clinical and statistical methods are better seen as complementary than as mutually exclusive approaches to decision making (see pp. 31–34). Relying on both approaches in a balanced manner based on their probable value in a given instance is thus a good way for assessors to enhance the accuracy of the conclusions they draw from their test data.

There are, however, few areas within clinical psychology where available research is ignored more routinely than in appreciating the differential accuracy of clinical and statistical judgment. Some practicing clinicians may place more confidence in their clinical judgment and give less credence to statistical judgment than is warranted by research findings. Psychologists practicing personality assessment may even be unaware of the content and implications of literature concerning the accuracy of clinical and statistical judgments. Studies reviewed by Garb (1998) suggest that clinicians are often uncertain of the variables on which a judgment should be based, or at least of the relative importance of variables pertinent to this judgment, and that they commonly rely in their decision making on variables with little demonstrated relationship to what they are trying to determine. Routine application of available statistical guidelines in making clinical decisions would contribute substantially to improving the overall quality of personality assessments and therapeutic interventions as well.

Moreover, the limitations of statistical judgments noted in Chapter 2, although important to keep in mind, do not necessarily prevent them from serving useful purposes. With respect to generalization, a statistical rule that is less accurate in a different setting or with a demographically different group than it was in its original derivation may still be more accurate in the new circumstances than a clinical impression that is formed without attention to empirical guidelines.

Similarly, the fact that statistical judgments concern a group of individuals rather than any specific, unique individual does not preclude their providing accurate information about a person who has been examined. To the contrary, although reliable information from other sources may indicate that certain statistically based interpretations do not apply in a particular case, a set of carefully developed statistical rules is likely to include many that describe most persons accurately. In those instances in which a statistical rule clearly does not apply, or when no empirical guideline is available, assessment psychologists must rely on informed clinical judgment. They should not, however, allow their clinical impressions to dissuade them from appropriate consideration of research findings, and they should strive always to base their decisions on a well-reasoned integration of statistical and clinical judgments.

Risk Factors and Odds Ratios

Risk factors are behaviors or symptoms that have been identified empirically as related to some outcome. This concept is frequently used in discussions of factors associated with dangerousness to the self (Packman, Marlitt, Bongar, & Pennuto, 2004) or to others (Monahan et al., 2005). Factors that increase the likelihood of people harming themselves include impulsivity, a sense of hopelessness, a history of previous suicidal behavior, and evidence of having a lethal plan. Because each of these factors increases the risk of dangerousness to the self, they are known as *risk factors*. With respect to dangerousness to others, Monahan et al. developed an actuarial model for violence risk assessment that exemplifies the previously noted soundness of statistical judgments when there are sufficient facts to support them.

Odds ratios are one way of expressing the risk of a specific behavior or symptom, provided that clinicians keep in mind relevant prevalence data. Suppose it is known that the odds of developing a schizophrenic disorder are increased by 3.5:1 if a certain condition or risk factor is present. With the previously noted lifetime prevalence of schizophrenia being 0.5% to 1.5% (American Psychiatric Association, 2000), a 3.5 increase in the odds ratio would raise the likelihood of becoming schizophrenic only to 1.75% to 5.25%, which is far from being a probable outcome. Even if the prevalence of schizophrenia were 12.5%, a 3.5 increase in the odds for a particular person would raise the likelihood just to 43.75%, and this person would still have less than a 50% probability of becoming schizophrenic.

Given that the lifetime prevalence for most forms of psychopathology is well below 10%, odds ratios can sometimes be misunderstood by clinicians and by their patients as well. For infrequently occurring disorders, increased odds ratios do not substantially increase their likelihood of being present. The only exceptions, and the only disorders with a lifetime prevalence exceeding 10%, as previously noted, are major depression in women (10% to 25%) and alcohol dependence in men (15%; American Psychiatric Association, 2000).

Heterogeneity in Patients within the Same Diagnostic Group

Experienced clinicians are well aware that there is considerable variability among persons within any diagnostic group. Despite this awareness, clinicians often talk about typical patients by referring to them in such terms as "alcoholics" and "borderlines," as if persons with alcohol dependence or borderline personality disorder are all alike. One of the many exciting aspects of clinical work is the discovery of the uniqueness of each patient within a specific diagnostic group.

This erroneous idea of homogeneity in diagnostic groups may seem to be supported by the fact that group mean profiles or a set of expectations for them can be constructed for the assessment tests and techniques discussed in this *Handbook*. Moreover, these group mean profiles and expectations are different for various diagnostic groups, which could be taken as further evidence of homogeneity within those groups. Data such as these could lead clinicians to assume that all patients within a diagnostic group produce pretty much the same set of scores. To the contrary, only a small portion of patients in a diagnostic group are likely to show the same scores as the group mean profile. Because of this heterogeneity, clinicians should be wary of any study that reports only a mean profile on an assessment test or technique. Frequency distributions of the various scores produced in each diagnostic group provide clinicians with more information on group performance on any measure than that provided by the group mean profile.

The use of polythetic criteria for diagnoses in the *Diagnostic and Statistical Manual* (*DSM-IV-TR*) published by the American Psychiatric Association (2000) contributes to the heterogeneity of groups of patients within specific diagnostic categories. Polythetic diagnostic criteria require only that some of the common features of a condition be present for it to be diagnosed, as in calling for any five or more of nine listed features in diagnosing Major Depressive Episode and five of nine features in diagnosing Borderline Personality Disorder. When disorders are defined by polythetic criteria, it is possible for two patients with the same disorder to share only a few, or even none, of the features of the disorder. As notable exceptions, *DSM* diagnoses of Eating Disorders and Sleep Disorders require the presence of all their listed features, which means that these diagnostic groups are likely to be relatively homogeneous.

Polythetic diagnostic criteria reflect the heterogeneity seen in clinical practice among persons with various disorders, as well as commonly occurring overlaps and lack of firm boundaries between disorders. In this sense, they are quite appropriate to apply, provided that their heterogeneity is kept in mind. As a point of historical interest, successive editions of the *DSM* over the years have defined an increasing number of disorders by polythetic criteria, thereby increasing as well the heterogeneity of these disorders.

Diagnostic Efficiency Statistics

The term *diagnostic efficiency statistics* refers to several ways of describing the accuracy or efficiency of decisions made on the basis of assessment data. A thorough understanding of the implications of these statistics is a basic aspect of any judgment about whether a personality or behavioral characteristic is present in an individual or group of individuals. In particular, diagnostic efficiency statistics demonstrate the impact of prevalence on the accuracy of judgments that are being made and show how important it is for clinicians to be aware of available prevalence data for whatever characteristics are being judged.

As background for defining and illustrating diagnostic efficiency statistics, clinicians should recognize that, in whatever kind of setting they are conducting assessments, they are constantly making judgments, such as deciding in mental health settings whether a person is anxious, depressed, schizophrenic, suicidal, passive-dependent, obsessive-compulsive, or interpersonally aversive. Most such states and dispositions can exist and be measured in degrees (e.g., highly anxious, mildly depressed, somewhat dependent, severely obsessive), but they can also be characterized in a dichotomous fashion as being present or absent, or at least as being more likely to be present than absent, and vice versa.

In similar fashion, the development and validation of an assessment instrument also involves dichotomous distinctions. If an assessment specialist wants to develop a new test for assessing problems with alcohol, an essential requirement is identifying some gold standard against which the new test can be validated. A frequently used standard in developing a test for alcohol problems is a group of people participating in an alcohol treatment program. Scores on the new test in this alcohol treatment group can then be compared with the scores of other persons in the same treatment facility who are not in the alcohol program or of normal individuals in the community. Which of these two possible comparison groups is used can substantially affect the diagnostic efficiency statistics, as illustrated next.

The use of persons being treated in an alcohol program as the gold standard is somewhat problematic because the individuals the test developer really wants to identify are people whose current and ongoing alcohol use is having a negative impact on their work, social, and interpersonal functioning. Such people are difficult to identify in sufficient numbers to validate an assessment test or technique, whereas persons in alcohol treatment programs, who may or may not currently be experiencing these negative impacts, are plentiful and relatively easily accessed. Because convenience samples of treatment program participants are often used as the gold standard in validating alcohol problems assessment measures, practitioners using one of these measures should read the description of its validation samples carefully and decide how comparable it is to people in their particular setting.

Table 3.2 shows a model for reporting the diagnostic efficiency statistics for a hypothetical new assessment test for alcohol problems. The various terms in Table 3.2 are defined next, following which actual examples are used to demonstrate the impact of different

Table 3.2   Defining terms for diagnostic efficiency statistics

		Gold Standard Criterion	
		Present	Absent
New Test — Present		*True positives* **a**	*False positives* **b**
New Test — Absent		*False negatives* **c**	*True negatives* **d**

True positives (sensitivity)	=	$a/(a+c)$
False negatives	=	$c/(a+c)$
True negatives (specificity)	=	$d/(b+d)$
False positives	=	$b/(b+d)$
Overall correct classification	=	$(a+d)/(a+b+c+d)$

Note: **a** = Alcoholic patients identified as alcoholics by the new test; **b** = Normal individuals misidentified by the new test as alcoholics; **c** = Alcoholics misidentified as normal individuals by the new test; **d** = Normal individuals identified as normal individuals by the new test.

prevalence rates on the diagnostic efficiency statistics. Deferring for the moment the method of determining an optimal cutting score on the new assessment test for identifying individuals with alcohol problems, scores above the cutting score are hypothesized as indicating that alcohol problems are present, and scores below the cutting score as indicating that alcohol problems are not present. In this first example, it is assumed that the comparison group for the alcohol treatment group is normal individuals from the community. Once the new test has been given to both groups of individuals, there are four possible outcomes:

1. *True positives,* which consist of alcohol patients who are identified correctly by the new test as having alcohol problems.
2. *False positives,* which consist of normal individuals who are identified incorrectly by the new test as having alcohol problems.
3. *False negatives,* which consist of alcohol patients who are identified incorrectly by the new test as not having alcohol problems.
4. *True negatives,* which consist of normal individuals who are identified correctly by the test as not having alcohol problems.

The true positive rate also is known as the *sensitivity* of the test, and the true negative rate is known as the *specificity* of the test. The *hit rate* or *overall correct classification* rate is the total of true positives plus true negatives divided by the total number of participants in both groups, which gives the percentage of correct classifications. An assessment test or technique with a high rate of true positives or sensitivity would be very good at identifying that alcohol problems are present, other things being equal; whereas an assessment test or technique with a high rate of true negatives or specificity would be very good at identifying that alcohol problems are absent.

Table 3.3   Diagnostic efficiency statistics for prevalence = 50%

| | | Gold Standard Criterion | |
		Alcoholic Patients	Normal Individuals
New Test	Present	*True positives* **85**	*False positives* **20**
	Absent	*False negatives* **15**	*True negatives* **80**
	Total	**100**	**100**

True positives (sensitivity)	=	85/100	=	85.0%
False negatives	=	15/100	=	15.0%
True negatives (specificity)	=	80/100	=	80.0%
False positives	=	20/100	=	20.0%
Overall correct classification	=	165/200	=	82.5%

Table 3.3 illustrates how percentages for the diagnostic efficiency statistics are calculated. In this example, it is assumed that there are 100 participants in each group and that the new test for alcohol problems correctly identifies 85 of the alcoholic patients as having alcohol problems and 80 of the normal individuals as not having alcohol problems. The true positive rate (sensitivity) is accordingly 85.0%, and the true negative rate (specificity) is 80.0%.

Much can be learned by observing the changes that occur in diagnostic efficiency statistics as the prevalence changes. In the present hypothetical example, a prevalence of 50% is created by assigning an equal number of persons to the alcohol patient and normal groups. Designing experiments to have equal sample sizes, and thereby artificially creating a 50% prevalence rate, has the advantage of increasing the power of the statistical techniques. In their focus on the usefulness of a new measure, test developers and practitioners may assume this 50% prevalence and overlook that the prevalence of alcoholism, and all other forms of psychopathology as well, varies widely with the type of setting in which it occurs. Accordingly, several different prevalence rates much lower than 50% need to be considered, because they are likely to affect some aspects of diagnostic efficiency.

To illustrate the potentially limiting effect of prevalence rates on diagnostic efficiency statistics, Table 3.4 shows these statistics for the hypothetical new test for alcohol problems when the prevalence is reduced to 15.0%, which is the previously noted lifetime prevalence for alcohol dependence (American Psychiatric Association, 2000). In this example, it is assumed that the sensitivity and specificity of the new test remain at 85% and 80%, respectively. The hit rate or overall correct classification rate has decreased slightly, from 82.5% to 81.0%.

Figure 3.1 presents the same information as Table 3.4, but uses a different conceptual layout, which many individuals find easier to understand the bases for the various calculations

Table 3.4   Diagnostic efficiency statistics for prevalence = 15%

New Test		Gold Standard Criterion	
		Alcoholic Patients	Normal Individuals
	Present	*True positives* **13**	*False positives* **17**
	Absent	*False negatives* **2**	*True negatives* **68**
	Total	**15**	**85**

True positives (sensitivity)	=	13/15	=	86.7%
False negatives	=	2/15	=	13.3%
True negatives (specificity)	=	68/85	=	80.0%
False positives	=	17/85	=	20.0%
Overall correct classification	=	81/100	=	81.0%

(cf. Gigerenzer, 2002). The results are identical in both Table 3.4 and Figure 3.1, so it does not make any difference which approach the clinician uses for laying out the data.

Assuming in this example that the sensitivity and specificity are unchanged is a typical assumption when an assessment test or technique is used with similar individuals in similar settings. A test validated to assess public speaking problems among college students in a large state university counseling center would be expected to show similar sensitivity and specificity among students in another large state university, and in most other colleges and universities for that matter. However, a test of psychopathy validated in a maximum security penitentiary would be expected to show very different sensitivity and specificity in a university counseling center.

Although sensitivity and specificity remain the same in Table 3.4, the relative number of true positives to false positives in the two groups has changed drastically. In Table 3.3, where the prevalence is 50%, there are 85 true positives and 20 false positives, whereas in Table 3.4, where the prevalence is 15%, there are 13 true positives and 17 false positives.

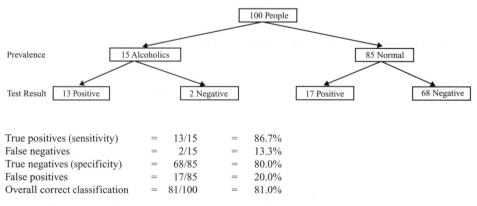

True positives (sensitivity)	=	13/15	=	86.7%
False negatives	=	2/15	=	13.3%
True negatives (specificity)	=	68/85	=	80.0%
False positives	=	17/85	=	20.0%
Overall correct classification	=	81/100	=	81.0%

Figure 3.1   Alternative conceptual layout for diagnostic efficiency statistics.

Table 3.5   Calculating positive and negative predictive power

Positive predictive power	=	True positives/(True positives + False positives)		
Negative predictive power	=	True negatives/(True negatives + False negatives)		
Using data from Table 3.3 where prevalence = **50%**				
Positive predictive power	=	85/(85+20)	=	81.0%
Negative predictive power	=	80/(80+15)	=	84.2%
Using data from Table 3.4 where prevalence = **15%**				
Positive predictive power	=	13/(13+17)	=	43.3%
Negative predictive power	=	68/(68+2)	=	97.1%

With the prevalence decreased from 50% to 15%, an individual hypothesized to have alcohol problems on the basis of the new alcohol test is actually more likely to be a normal individual. That is, the new test is incorrect in more instances than it is correct at a prevalence of 15%, even though the sensitivity and specificity of the test are unchanged and remain quite respectable.

Once an assessment test or technique has been validated, however, assessors should be less interested in sensitivity and specificity than in the ratio of true positives to false positives and true negatives to false negatives. The percentages derived from these ratios are reported respectively as *positive predictive power* and *negative predictive power.* As shown in Table 3.5, positive predictive power is the number of true positive scores divided by the total number of true positive and false positive scores. Using the data from Tables 3.3 and 3.4, it can be seen in Table 3.5 that the positive predictive power for the hypothetical test is 81.0% when the prevalence rate is 50% and 43.3% when the prevalence rate is 15%. Negative predictive power is the number of true negative scores divided by the total number of true negative and false negative scores. The negative predictive power is 84.2% when the prevalence rate is 50% and 97.1% when the prevalence rate is 15%.

The effects of varying the probability of false positive (10%, 20%, 25%) and false negative (10%, 20%, 25%) outcomes in conjunction with the change in the prevalence (2%, 5%, 10%, 20%, 25%, 50%) are summarized in Table 3.6. When the prevalence is 50%, there are significant improvements in the hit rate or overall classification rate over the prevalence even when the false positive and false negative percentages are 25%. However, as the prevalence decreases to 10%, 5%, and 2%, there is limited improvement in the hit rate or overall classification rate over the prevalence and in some cases there appears to be an actual decrease in the accuracy of classification.

These data demonstrate the difficulty of assessing characteristics or predicting behaviors that have a very low or very high prevalence in the setting in which people are being evaluated, particularly in finding an assessment method that is more accurate than simply identifying every person as not having the characteristic (when the prevalence is very low) or identifying every person as having the characteristic (when the prevalence is very high). On this basis, beginning with Meehl (1954), assessment specialists have consistently pointed out that tests work best when the prevalence rates for what is being measured hover around 50%, become increasingly less efficient as prevalence diverges from 50%, and must be used cautiously in situations involving very low or very high prevalence.

As also shown in Table 3.6, clinicians should attend not only to the hit or overall classification rates, which can sometimes be misleading, but also to the positive (*PPP*) and negative (*NPP*) predictive power of whatever measures they use. The NPP is excellent at

Table 3.6   Changes in PPP and NPP as a function of prevalence and percentage of false positives and false negatives

Prevalence	True Positive	False Negative	True Negative	False Positive	N	Hit Rate	PPP	NPP
2	90	10	4,410	490	5,000	90.0	15.5	99.8
2	90	10	3,920	980	5,000	80.2	8.4	99.7
2	90	10	3,675	1,225	5,000	75.3	6.8	99.7
2	80	20	4,410	490	5,000	89.8	14.0	99.5
2	80	20	3,920	980	5,000	80.0	7.5	99.5
2	80	20	3,675	1,225	5,000	75.1	6.1	99.5
2	75	25	4,410	490	5,000	89.7	13.3	99.4
2	75	25	3,920	980	5,000	79.9	7.1	99.4
2	75	25	3,675	1,225	5,000	75.0	5.8	99.3
5	90	10	1,710	190	2,000	90.0	32.1	99.4
5	90	10	1,520	380	2,000	80.5	19.1	99.3
5	90	10	1,425	475	2,000	75.8	15.9	99.3
5	80	20	1,710	190	2,000	89.5	29.6	98.8
5	80	20	1,520	380	2,000	80.0	17.4	98.7
5	80	20	1,425	475	2,000	75.3	14.4	98.6
5	75	25	1,710	190	2,000	89.3	28.3	98.6
5	75	25	1,520	380	2,000	79.8	16.5	98.4
5	75	25	1,425	475	2,000	75.0	13.6	98.3
10	90	10	810	90	1,000	90.0	50.0	98.8
10	90	10	720	180	1,000	81.0	33.3	98.6
10	90	10	675	225	1,000	76.5	28.6	98.5
10	80	20	810	90	1,000	89.0	47.1	97.6
10	80	20	720	180	1,000	80.0	30.8	97.3
10	80	20	675	225	1,000	75.5	26.2	97.1
10	75	25	810	90	1,000	88.5	45.5	97.0
10	75	25	720	180	1,000	79.5	29.4	96.6
10	75	25	675	225	1,000	75.0	25.0	96.4
20	90	10	360	40	500	90.0	69.2	97.3
20	90	10	320	80	500	82.0	52.9	97.0
20	90	10	300	100	500	78.0	47.4	96.8
20	80	20	360	40	500	88.0	66.7	94.7
20	80	20	320	80	500	80.0	50.0	94.1
20	80	20	300	100	500	76.0	44.4	93.8
20	75	25	360	40	500	87.0	65.2	93.5
20	75	25	320	80	500	79.0	48.4	92.8
20	75	25	300	100	500	75.0	42.9	92.3
25	90	10	270	30	400	90.0	75.0	96.4
25	90	10	240	60	400	82.5	60.0	96.0
25	90	10	225	75	400	78.8	54.5	95.7
25	80	20	270	30	400	87.5	72.7	93.1
25	80	20	240	60	400	80.0	57.1	92.3
25	80	20	225	75	400	76.3	51.6	91.8
25	75	25	270	30	400	86.3	71.4	91.5
25	75	25	240	60	400	78.8	55.6	90.6

Table 3.6   (*Continued*)

Prevalence	True Positive	False Negative	True Negative	False Positive	N	Hit Rate	*PPP*	*NPP*
25	75	25	225	75	400	75.0	50.0	90.0
50	90	10	90	10	200	90.0	90.0	90.0
50	90	10	80	20	200	85.0	81.8	88.9
50	90	10	75	25	200	82.5	78.3	88.2
50	80	20	90	10	200	85.0	88.9	81.8
50	80	20	80	20	200	80.0	80.0	80.0
50	80	20	75	25	200	77.5	76.2	78.9
50	75	25	90	10	200	82.5	88.2	78.3
50	75	25	80	20	200	77.5	78.9	76.2
50	75	25	75	25	200	75.0	75.0	75.0

Note: PPP = Positive predictive power; *NPP* = Negative predictive power.

all prevalences, and at its worst is still accurate 75% of the time with a 50% prevalence that yields 25% false negatives and 25% false positives. The *PPP*, by contrast, is less than 50% accurate, that is, inaccurate more often than it is accurate, for all combinations of false positive and false negative values with all prevalence rates less than 20%, with one exception. In other words, any judgment that the behavior or symptom is present (*PPP*) when the prevalence is less than 20% will be inaccurate more often than it is accurate.

The relatively small improvements in the hit rate or overall classification rate over the prevalence as the prevalence decreases to 10%, 5%, and 2%, and the generally very limited positive predictive power (*PPP*), raise the issue of the cost involved in making these judgments in low prevalence situations. It is possible that such small improvements in classification accuracy are not worth the cost in professional time and expense necessary to collect and evaluate assessment data. This is a complex question that will not be pursued in the present discussion. Clinicians must realize, however, that it is imperative to have some reasonable estimate of the prevalence of characteristics and behaviors that are being classified and the percentage of false positive and false negative outcomes that can be tolerated when any scale and its cutting score are used in a new setting. Even a small change in these psychometric features can have an appreciable effect on the accuracy of classification, as is evident in Table 3.6. Assessors should also investigate whether adjustments in cutting scores when scales are used in different settings might enhance the accuracy of classification; this is discussed in the next section.

Finally, with respect to prevalence, Wiggins (1973, p. 252) has pointed out that any test or predictor with a validity coefficient greater than .00 cannot result in a decreased proportion of correct decisions compared with judgments based on prevalence, the reason for this being that prediction from the prevalence rate sets the false positive rate at 0%. Hence, the negative result when the hit rates in Table 3.6 are compared with the prevalence assumes that both have the same percentage of false positive and false negatives, which is not correct. For example, if the prevalence for alcoholic dependence is 15% and false positives plus false negatives equal 25%, the hit rate is 75%, which is a 10% decrease from the prevalence (see last row of first section of Table 3.6). However, any classification made from the prevalence would set the false positive rate at 0% and the false negative rate at 15%, thereby accounting for the 10% decrease from the prevalence to the 75% hit rate.

The relative disadvantages of false positive and false negative outcomes are often more important to consider than the overall classification rate of a measure or scale, particularly in clinical evaluations. Prevalence rates predict all negative outcomes, so that the only errors are false negatives, whereas cutting scores on a measure of symptoms or problem behavior classify accurately some percentage of persons who have the symptom or problem (true positives) and classify inaccurately some percentage of persons who do not (false positives). In most clinical settings, false negatives tend to be more disadvantageous than false positives. Failure to identify a disorder and provide treatment for a distressed person (false negative) is a more serious error than recommending treatment for a well-functioning person who does not need it (false negative), and failing to detect suicidal risk in people who are in fact poised to take their own lives is a more serious error than instituting suicide precautions for people who are in fact unlikely to harm themselves. Although such clinical realities must always be kept in clinicians' minds, they do not alter the primary point of the present discussion, which concerns the effects of prevalence and the percentage of false positives and negatives on the accuracy of classification. Articles by Meehl and Rosen (1955) and Streiner (2003) are recommended for additional reading about these and other matters related to diagnostic efficiency statistics.

Cutting Scores

The final consideration to be discussed about clinical decision making is the derivation of appropriate cutting scores for particular scales in specific settings. The optimal cutting score can be determined fairly easily by plotting the frequency distribution of hits and misses on the same axes, as illustrated in Figure 3.2, because the optimal cutting score is the point

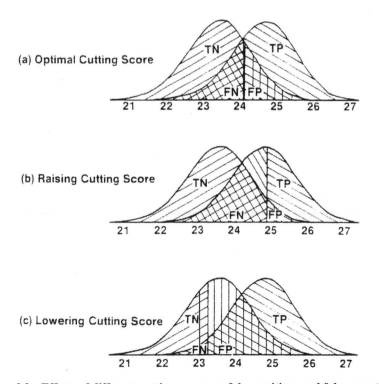

Figure 3.2   Effects of different cutting scores on false positives and false negatives.

at which the two frequency distributions overlap. These examples assume that both groups are of equal size and have equal variances. Rorer and Dawes (1982) provide information on how to select the optimal cutting score when these assumptions are not met. These authors also show how an optimal cutting score can be estimated even when the prevalence in the local setting is not known. As can be seen in Figure 3.2a, the alcoholic persons who fall above this cutting score are true positives, and the normal individuals are false positives. The alcoholic persons who fall below this cutting score are false negatives, and the normal individuals are true negatives. Raising (Figure 3.2b) or lowering (Figure 3.2c) this cutting score changes the percentage of individuals classified in each category. It is thus possible not only to identify an optimal cutting score, but also to investigate the relative effects on false positives and false negatives of altering this cutting score.

Because the hit rate may not be as important as the relationship between the number of false positive and false negative outcomes in most clinical settings, clinicians should consider all these variables in selecting the most appropriate cutting score for a particular scale in a particular setting. A statistical test of the difference between the means of the two distributions provides much less information than the data concerning the prevalence of the behavior and the relative number of false positives and false negatives associated with a cutting score. As few as 100 patients in each group is sufficient to provide reasonable estimates of the prevalence of the behavior and the frequency of false positives and false negatives (Meehl, 1973), and a smaller number of patients can provide approximations of these variables while more data are being collected. This type of information is generally available in most applied settings, although most clinicians do not realize its importance.

Consideration of base rates and optimal cutting scores also applies directly to the *DSM-IV-TR* (American Psychiatric Association, 2000). Finn (1982) showed that the polythetic criteria used to define many diagnoses such as Borderline Personality Disorder, as mentioned previously, can result in a changed prevalence rate and different rates of false positives and false negatives, depending on how many of the criteria are required to make the diagnosis. If the number of required criteria for diagnosing Borderline Personality Disorder were increased above five, the percentage of false positives would decrease; conversely, decreasing the number of required criteria below five would increase the frequency of false positives. This type of information on the changing rate of false positives and false negatives as the number of required criteria is altered does not appear in the *DSM-IV-TR,* and clinicians must look elsewhere for assistance in estimating how such alterations influence the prevalence of specific disorders in a particular setting.

IMPEDIMENTS TO ACCURATE DECISIONS

In any setting in which assessment data are collected, there are likely to be several impediments to making accurate decisions, most of which reflect implicit theories that everyone has about the causes and explanations of behavior. Prime examples of such implicit theories are social roles and stereotypes that people construct in their minds to ease and simplify their everyday interactions. Instead of learning what behaviors to expect from each person with whom they come in contact, people use social roles and stereotypes to make decisions about other individuals more rapidly than would otherwise be possible, and with less information. Being aware of social roles, as in expecting that store clerks will help you find a product you are looking for and will sell it to you, allows you to carry out the daily requirements of life more quickly than having to deduce the expected conduct of each person you encounter. In similar fashion, stereotypes provide generalizations about certain types of people that simplify social interactions with them.

People typically collect information from their everyday experience in ways that support their implicit theories and produce numerous inherent biases. In this process, the apparent accuracy of social roles and stereotypes is commonly buttressed by propensities to note only information that confirms them and to ignore contradictory information. In addition, people tend to interpret ambiguous data that support whatever concepts of social roles or stereotypes they have formed.

It is easy to see how the processes that produce and buttress social roles and stereotypes can cloud the judgment of assessment psychologists and influence their conclusions in untoward ways. The paragraphs that follow describe some specific impediments to accurate decision making and discuss ways of minimizing their impact. Several general texts that explore this issue in depth are recommended for further reading (e.g., Dawes, 1996; Gilovich, Griffin, & Kahneman, 2002).

Vividness (Saliency)

All clinicians encounter persons whose symptoms or clinical presentation are so dramatic or vivid that they are easily recalled. These cases are frequently mentioned to colleagues and students to illustrate various aspects of the assessment and treatment process. The ease of recalling these individuals with vivid or salient characteristics often leads clinicians to overestimate how frequently these characteristics occur among the typical persons they evaluate in their office, agency, or institutional setting.

Accordingly, presentation of vivid case examples to illustrate psychological assessment issues should include information about their prevalence. Including this information helps ensure that those who read or hear about these dramatic cases have an accurate appreciation of the frequency with which they are likely to occur.

Confirmatory Bias

Once clinicians formulate a hypothesis about a person, they should strive to keep an open mind as they examine other data to determine whether they confirm or disconfirm the hypothesis. Confirmatory bias results when the data search attends only to data that support a preliminary judgment and ignore data that contradict it. Looking specifically for redundancy among test scores can exacerbate this problem, as can any preexisting biases a clinician may have concerning the implications of certain assessment findings. Along with confirmatory bias, clinicians may find themselves engaging in hindsight bias, which consists of recalling the data that supported their conclusions and forgetting data that pointed in other directions.

Confirmatory bias can also support illusory correlations, which involve seeing relationships between variables that are actually unrelated. Illusory correlations emerge when clinicians intuit some relationship between two variables and then look for information to confirm this relationship, instead of proceeding in the more appropriate opposite way by inferring relationships only on the basis of data that warrant them.

After clinicians have formulated data-based hypotheses about an individual they have examined, they should then be alert to any information that would disconfirm their hypotheses. This emphasis on looking for disconfirming information is necessary because of the ease with which clinicians can inadvertently interpret ambiguous data as confirming their hypotheses. Clinicians should also write down their conclusions, usually in the form of their reports, prior to receiving any explicit feedback on the accuracy of their judgments. Proceeding in this way prevents assessors who have been mistaken (which all clinicians are at least once in a while) from reshaping what they meant to conclude and thereby continuing to believe that their judgment was accurate, without learning anything from their mistake.

Lack of Feedback on the Accuracy of Interpretations

Feedback on the accuracy of the statements that assessment psychologists make in their reports may not always be available. Ideally, an assessment and the preparation of an assessment report are followed by some discussion with a referring person or agency concerning the extent to which the report provided clear and useful conclusions and was consistent with other known facts about the person who was examined. In addition, as discussed in Chapter 2, examiners may have opportunities for feedback sessions that verify or disprove interpretations they have made.

Often, however, feedback concerning the accuracy of their interpretations may not be available to assessors. They conduct their examination, construct their interpretations, prepare and submit their reports, and move on to the next case. In many agencies, institutions, and organizations—particularly when evaluations have been conducted for administrative rather than clinical purposes—it may be unusual for clinicians to discuss their reports with anyone who can provide useful feedback.

In the absence of feedback, and without being confronted with any contradictory information, clinicians can maintain belief in the accuracy of their judgments. As a more desirable process, discussing assessment results with referring parties and with people they have examined helps clinicians keep abreast of when they are being clear and accurate and when they are not, and by so doing improve the quality of their decision making and report writing.

Lack of Awareness of Relevant Variables

Clinicians are often insufficiently aware of the variables or factors on which they are basing their decisions. When asked to make these factors explicit, they frequently emphasize variables that are unrelated to the behavior or symptom about which they have made a judgment. Even when they are familiar with the factors relevant to a particular judgment, they often do not know very much about the optimal weighting of these factors. Insufficient awareness among clinicians of the factors and their optimal weighting for determining whether a characteristic is present impedes the accuracy of their decision making and accounts for the previously mentioned superiority of statistical to clinical prediction when the necessary empirical data are available.

With this consideration in mind, it cannot be emphasized too strongly that assessment psychologists consulting in clinical settings should be familiar with the empirical literature concerning the specific types of psychopathology that are frequently encountered in their setting. This familiarity with the literature should include knowing which variables are most relevant for identifying each of these types of psychopathology and what if any statistical procedures are available for combining these variables in some weighted fashion. Frequency counts of the presence and absence of variables thought to be relevant for each type of psychopathology can be developed with little difficulty in the clinician's particular setting when such data are not available in the empirical literature.

Task Complexity

Clinicians' cognitive capacity and memory functions can easily be overwhelmed by the sheer amount of data that must be processed in conducting a psychological evaluation. This complexity and the challenge it poses to accurate decision making are likely to increase if examiners do not take extensive notes on an examinee's behavior during the assessment process. Audiotaping or videotaping an assessment procedure is an efficient way to capture all the information provided by people's behavior during testing as well as by their test responses. These tapes can then be consulted as necessary to assist in formulating interpretations and preparing a written report.

Using computerized interpretations of assessment measures that are available is another means of decreasing examiners' reliance on their memory. Computer-based test interpretation is discussed in Chapter 2 of this *Handbook*.

Incomplete Information

The accuracy of decision making can also be impeded when clinicians lack important bits of information. The nature of most settings in which assessment psychologists consult is such that some types of information are routinely not available. Incomplete or missing information in particular can result in clinicians failing to appreciate fully the importance of certain variables and their prevalence. To continue with the example of an alcohol treatment program, clinicians working in such a setting can readily come to the conclusion that no one can recover from alcoholism without participating in a formal treatment program. This belief is instilled by working with the people they encounter in their treatment program, who in fact did not recover without treatment.

What clinicians working in alcohol treatment programs do not acquire, however, and which would disconfirm their belief, is information about individuals with alcohol problems who find ways of recovering on their own without being treated in a formal program. Generally speaking, statements about alcoholism that are generated within an alcohol treatment program cannot be considered valid for all persons who are alcohol dependent, because the subset of persons being sampled comprises only alcoholics who are receiving formal treatment. Incomplete information about any factor that has a substantial bearing on drawing a particular conclusion can contribute to clinicians forming mistaken beliefs and judgments and making inaccurate decisions.

CONCLUDING COMMENTS

Clinicians who conduct psychological evaluations should not feel overwhelmed by the considerable information presented in this chapter or dejected by the many troublesome issues that are raised. The information provides a basic primer in psychometrics and should, for the most part, be familiar to readers who received instruction in statistics and measurement courses prior to beginning their study of personality assessment methods. As for the troublesome issues, which are all too often ignored in many applied settings, they will not go away and must constantly be kept in clinicians' minds as they conduct psychological evaluations. At least one potential solution is provided for each of these issues in the course of the chapter, and there are also four general considerations for examiners to keep in mind that will serve them well in carrying out their clinical decision-making responsibilities.

First, whatever the type of setting in which clinicians are providing diagnostic consultation, they need to be well informed about the prevalence of the psychological characteristics and disorders that are seen in this setting and about the most salient behaviors or symptoms that differentiate among them. Being well informed requires knowing the extant empirical literature and keeping up to date with changes that occur in the field.

Second, attempting to understand and describe the nature of people, their personality assets and limitations, their adjustment problems and disorders, if any, is a complex task that cannot be carried out quickly. Despite the popularity of Dr. Phil, Ann Landers, and Oprah, no clinical assessment can be made in a few minutes of discussion or based on a few sentences describing the problem.

Third, personality assessment is a probabilistic rather than a causal endeavor. No behavior or symptom has just a single cause, and the frequency of its occurrence depends on multiple variables. Once it is truly understood that any statement about an individual is a probabilistic statement, not a fact, both clinicians and the individuals they assess are less likely to be misled.

Finally, clinicians cannot rely on their memory to assimilate and store all the complex information available about the prevalence of and relationships among all of the behaviors or symptoms in all forms of psychopathology. Regular recourse to appropriate books and journals and increased reliance on computers to store and process relevant information are keys to maintaining and enhancing personality assessments.

REFERENCES

Ægisdóttir, S., White, M. J., Spengler, P. M., Maugherman, A. S., Anderson, L. A., Cook, R. S., et al. (2006). The meta-analysis of clinical judgment project: Fifty-six years of accumulated research on clinical versus statistical judgment. *Counseling Psychologist, 34*, 341–382.

American Psychiatric Association. (2000). *Diagnostic and statistical manual of mental disorders* (4th ed., text rev.). Washington, DC: Author.

Anastasi, A., & Urbina, S. (1997). *Psychological testing* (7th ed.). Upper Saddle River, NJ: Prentice-Hall.

Barlow, D. H., & Campbell, L. A. (2000). Mixed anxiety-depression and its implications for models of mood and anxiety disorders. *Comprehensive Psychiatry, 41*, 55–60.

Beck, A. T., Steer, R. A., & Brown, G. K. (1996). *Manual for the Beck Depression Inventory-II*. San Antonio, TX: Psychological Corporation.

Caldwell, A. B. (2006). Maximal measurement or meaningful measurement: The interpretive challenges of the MMPI-2 Restructured Clinical (RC) Scales. *Journal of Personality Assessment, 87*, 193–201.

Campbell, D. T., & Fiske, D. W. (1959). Convergent and discriminant validation by the multitrait-multimethod matrix. *Psychological Bulletin, 56*, 81–105.

Cohen, J. (1960). A coefficient of agreement for nominal scales. *Educational and Psychological Measurement, 20,* 37–46.

Cohen, J. (1983). The cost of dichotomization. *Applied Psychological Measurement, 7,* 249–253.

Cronbach, L. J. (1951). Coefficient alpha and the internal structure of tests. *Psychometrikia, 16,* 297–334.

Dawes, R. (1996). *House of cards: Psychology and psychotherapy built on myth.* New York: Free Press.

Embretson, S. E., & Reise, S. P. (2000). *Item response theory for psychologists.* Mahwah, NJ: Erlbaum.

Exner, J. E., Jr. (2003). *The Rorschach: A comprehensive system: Vol. 1. Basic foundations and principles of interpretation* (4th ed.). Hoboken, NJ: Wiley.

Finn, S. E. (1982). Base rates, utilities, and DSM-III: Shortcomings of fixed-rule systems of psychodiagnosis. *Journal of Abnormal Psychology, 91,* 294–302.

Garb, H. N. (1998). *Studying the clinician: Judgment research and psychological assessment.* Washington, DC: American Psychological Association.

Garb, H. N. (2003). Incremental validity and the assessment of psychopathology in adults. *Psychological Assessment, 15,* 508–520.

Gigerenzer, G. (2002). *Calculated risks: How to know when numbers deceive you.* New York: Simon & Schuster.

Gilovich, T., Griffin, D., & Kahneman, D. (2002). *Heuristics and biases: The psychology of intuitive judgment.* New York: Cambridge University Press.

Graham, J. R., Smith, R. L., & Schwartz, G. F. (1986). Stability of MMPI configurations for psychiatric inpatients. *Journal of Consulting and Clinical Psychology, 54,* 375–380.

Greene, R. L., Davis, L. J., Jr., & Morse, R. P. (1993, March). *Stability of MMPI code types in alcoholic inpatients.* Paper presented at the midwinter meeting of the Society for Personality Assessment, San Francisco.

Grove, W. M., Zald, D. H., Lebow, B. S., Snitz, B. E., & Nelson, C. (2000). Clinical versus mechanical predication: A meta-analysis. *Psychological Assessment, 12,* 19–30.

Gulliksen, H. (1950). *Theory of mental tests.* New York: Wiley.

Kaplan, R. M., & Saccuzzo, D. P. (2001). *Psychological testing: Principles, applications, and issues* (5th ed.). Belmont, CA: Wadsworth/Thompson Learning.

Livingston, R. B., Jennings, E., Colotla, V. A., Reynolds, C. A., & Shercliffe, R. J. (2006). MMPI-2 code-type congruence of injured workers. *Psychological Assessment, 18,* 126–130.

Meehl, P. E. (1954). *Clinical versus statistical judgment.* Minneapolis: University of Minnesota Press.

Meehl, P. E. (1973). Why I do not attend case conferences. In P. E. Meehl (Ed.), *Psychodiagnosis: Selected papers* (pp. 225–302). Minneapolis: University of Minnesota Press.

Meehl, P. E., & Rosen, A. (1955). Antecedent probability and the efficiency of psychometric signs, patterns, or cutting scores. *Psychological Bulletin, 52,* 194–216.

Monahan, J., Steadman, H. J., Robbins, P. C., Appelbaum, P., Banks, S., Grisso, T., et al. (2005). An actuarial model of violence risk assessment for persons with mental disorders. *Psychiatric Services, 56,* 810–815.

Morey, L. C. (1991). *Personality Assessment Inventory: Professional manual.* Odessa, FL: Psychological Assessment Resources.

Nichols, D. S. (2006). The trials of separating bath water from baby: A review and critique of the MMPI–2 Restructured Clinical Scales. *Journal of Personality Assessment, 87,* 121–138.

Packman, W. L., Marlitt, R. E., Bongar, B., & Pennuto, T. O. (2004). A comprehensive and concise assessment of suicide risk. *Behavioral Sciences and the Law, 22,* 667–680.

Rorer, L. G., & Dawes, R. M. (1982). A base-rate bootstrap. *Journal of Consulting and Clinical Psychology, 50,* 419–425.

Streiner, D. L. (2003). Diagnosing tests: Using and misusing diagnostic and screening tests. *Journal of Personality Assessment, 81*, 209–219.

Sultan, S., Andronikof, A., & Réveillère, C. (2006). A Rorschach stability study in a nonpatient adult sample. *Journal of Personality Assessment, 87*, 330–348.

Tellegen, A., Ben-Porath, Y. S., McNulty, J. L., Arbisi, P. A., Graham, J. R., & Kaemmer, B. (2003). *MMPI–2 Restructured Clinical (RC) scales: Development, validation, and interpretation.* Minneapolis: University of Minnesota Press.

Tellegen, A., Ben-Porath, Y. S., & Sellbom, M. (2006). Further evidence on the validity of the MMPI-2 Restructured Clinical (RC) Scales: Addressing questions raised by Rogers, Sewell, Harrison, Jordan, and Nichols. *Journal of Personality Assessment, 87*, 148–171.

Trull, T. J., Useda, J. D., Conforti, K., & Doan, B. (1997). Borderline personality disorder features in nonclinical young adults: Pt. 2. Two-year outcome. *Journal of Abnormal Psychology, 106*, 307–314.

Urbina, S. (2004). *Essentials of psychological testing.* Hoboken, NJ: Wiley.

Waller, N. S., & Meehl, P. E. (1997). *Multivariate taxometric procedures: Distinguishing types from continua.* Thousand Oaks, CA: Sage.

Wiggins, J. S. (1973). *Personality and judgment: Principles of personality assessment.* Reading, MA: Addison-Wesley.

Chapter 4

ETHICAL CONSIDERATIONS IN PERSONALITY ASSESSMENT

A number of standards in the most recent *Ethical Principles and Code of Conduct* of the American Psychological Association (APA, 2002) are relevant to the assessment process. These standards have been abbreviated for the sake of brevity in this chapter. Each of these abbreviated standards is presented in bold font so that the reader can distinguish between the standard and any comments that are made about it. The reader should consult the *Ethical Principles and Code of Conduct* for the complete and exact wording of each standard. These standards are organized following the numbering used for the principles so that the reader can refer directly to them if desired. The number of each standard is indicated parenthetically throughout this chapter to facilitate referencing it. The standard on Test Construction (9.05) is not covered because it is outside the scope of this *Handbook*.

Several of these standards are entirely new in the 2002 *Ethical Principles and Code of Conduct* (APA, 2002): Student Disclosure of Personal Information (7.04); Use of Assessments (9.02b and 9.02c); and Informed Consent in Assessments (9.03). There has been a significant change in Release of Test Data (9.04). In the previous edition of the *Ethical Principles and Code of Conduct* (APA, 1992), examiners were to refrain from releasing raw test results or raw data to persons who were not qualified to use such information. In the 2002 *Ethical Principles and Code of Conduct,* pursuant to an appropriately signed release, examiners provide test data to the person *or other persons identified in the release regardless of their qualifications.* Previously, the test data were only released to another professional, usually a psychologist; now the data can be released to anyone who is identified in the release regardless of their professional training or experience.

The *Rights and Responsibilities of Test Takers: Guidelines and Expectations* by the Working Group of the Joint Committee on Testing Practices (1998) has been relied on extensively in writing this chapter. It provides an excellent overview of the multiple issues that the examiner and the examinee encounter in the assessment process. Every student and clinician would be well advised to review these rights and responsibilities.

All individuals have the right to be treated with courtesy, respect, and impartiality, regardless of their age, disability, ethnicity, gender, religion, sexual orientation, or other personal characteristics. They also should be provided with reasonable access to testing services. Examiners should advise individuals that they are entitled to request reasonable accommodations in test administration that are likely to increase the validity of their test scores if they have a disability recognized under the Americans with Disabilities Act or other relevant legislation. Examiners need to ask the person about any accommodations that may be needed or any physical condition or illness that may interfere with performance rather than simply assuming that they will recognize the need for such accommodations. If documentation is required to support the person's request for accommodation, examiners should inform the person as soon as possible. They also should let the person know that if they do not receive a testing accommodation, they can request information about why the request was denied. Individuals also need to be told to let the examiner know if they have difficulty comprehending the language in which the test is given.

The *Ethical Principles and Code of Conduct* (APA, 2002), like all other sets of ethical principles, provides very general or abstract guidelines for what behavior is or is not expected. The information on how to implement these standards frequently is lacking and thus may be open to various interpretations. Consultation with a colleague is highly recommended any time the examiner is unsure how to proceed in an ethical dilemma.

In most instances, unethical or misuse of assessment tests and techniques is likely to be a function of lack of information or misinformation rather than negligence or malfeasance on the part of the examiner. Thus, one purpose of this chapter is to familiarize the reader with the appropriate ethical considerations for the use of assessments tests and techniques.

STUDENT DISCLOSURE OF PERSONAL INFORMATION (7.04)

Professors do not require students to disclose personal information in course- or program-related activities, either orally or in writing, regarding sexual history, history of abuse and neglect, psychological treatment, and relationships with parents, peers, and spouses or significant others.

This standard becomes particularly important when graduate students taking assessment courses assess themselves or fellow students to gain practice. Although practicing with fellow students may help prepare them to administer and score assessment tests and techniques, students must not be required to reveal personal information. This procedure places students in a multiple relationship (Multiple Relationships [3.05]) with their colleagues, which is to be avoided according to the *Ethical Principles and Code of Conduct* (APA, 2002).

Asking students to role-play specific psychological disorders rather than to provide their own responses is a means of maintaining safeguards on the type of information that is reported. Role-playing eliminates the potential for the inadvertent release of confidential material if students are providing their own responses and negates the need for feedback on their performance. Role-playing of specific disorders also allows students to see how well they can simulate the disorder that is an important consideration in the interpretation of all assessment tests and techniques. There is a fairly extensive history on role-playing of psychological disorders and their impact on assessment tests and techniques, particularly with the MMPI-2 (see Greene, 2000, pp. 120–122).

BASES FOR ASSESSMENTS (9.01)

Examiners base the opinions contained in their reports and evaluative statements on information and techniques sufficient to substantiate their findings only after they have conducted an examination of the individual adequate to support their statements or conclusions.

It goes without saying that the examiner should actually examine the individual directly before rendering an opinion. It is a more complex issue to determine what constitutes an examination *sufficient to substantiate their findings* in a report, and few guidelines exist to help in this determination.

Psychologists are generally reluctant to develop guidelines for what constitutes a personality evaluation or what tests/procedures should be included. Even though guidelines reflect aspirational goals rather than standards, there is unwillingness in the field of assessment to develop such guidelines. Consensus is lacking about such basic issues as should all the items of a self-report inventory be administered and should all the scales on the inventory be scored and profiled. It seems imperative to develop such guidelines so that examiners and students learning assessment tests and techniques have an informed opinion on the ones that have been validated for what purposes as well as the basic issues about their administration, scoring, and interpretation. Such guidelines also would assist examiners in knowing whether they are competent with any assessment test or technique, and whether their evaluation was sufficient to substantiate their conclusions.

USE OF ASSESSMENTS (9.02)

Examiners use assessment tests and techniques whose validity and reliability have been established for use with individuals of the population being assessed. When such validity or reliability has not been established, examiners describe the strengths and limitations of the results and interpretations of assessment tests and techniques.

In keeping with this standard, examiners should know how to select the appropriate assessment tests and techniques for the intended purposes including whether they are appropriate to an individual's language preference and competence. As discussed in Chapter 2, whether an alternative language should be used in the assessment process is a complex issue that involves determining whether the alternative language is relevant to the assessment issues, the examiner's competence in that language, and whether such a procedure is fair for persons from different ethnic groups.

When testing persons with documented disabilities and other special characteristics that require special testing conditions or interpretation of results, examiners should have the necessary skills and knowledge for such testing and interpretation. They also need to ensure that testing conditions (especially if unusual) do not unduly interfere with the assessment process. As mentioned in Chapter 2, testing conditions should normally be similar to those used to standardize the assessment test or technique and provide individuals with a reasonable amount of time to complete the assessment test or technique, unless it has a time limit. The examiner should take reasonable actions to safeguard against fraudulent actions (e.g., cheating) that could place honest persons at a disadvantage. In this vein, it is a good practice to ask routinely what information the person has received or been given, and by whom, about the forthcoming evaluation.

A task force of the American Psychological Association (Moreland, Eyde, Robertson, Primoff, & Most, 1995) identified 12 minimum competencies for all users of assessment tests and techniques (see Table 4.1). In the opinion of the task force, two comprehensive elements are broad enough to serve as major categories for the original 86 competencies that had been rated by a 19-person interdisciplinary panel: (1) knowledge of the assessment

Table 4.1   Twelve minimum competencies for proper use of tests

1. Avoiding errors in scoring and recording

2. Refraining from labeling people with personally derogatory terms like dishonest on the basis of a test score that lacks perfect validity

3. Keeping scoring keys and test materials secure

4. Seeing that every examinee follows directions so that test scores are accurate

5. Using settings for testing that allow for optimum performance by persons (e.g., adequate room)

6. Refraining from coaching or training individuals or groups on test items, which results in misrepresentation of the person's abilities and competencies

7. Willingness to give interpretation and guidance to persons in counseling situations

8. Not making photocopies of copyrighted materials

9. Refraining from using homemade answer sheets that do not align properly with scoring keys

10. Establishing rapport with examinees to obtain accurate scores

11. Refraining from answering questions from persons in greater detail than the test manual permits

12. Not assuming that a norm for one job applies to a different job (and not assuming that norms for one group automatically apply to other groups)

Source: "Assessment of Test User Qualifications: A Research-Based Measurement Procedure," by K. L. Moreland, L. D. Eyde, G. J. Robertson, E. S. Primoff, and R. B. Most, 1995, *American Psychologist, 50,* pp. 14–23. Reprinted with permission.

test or technique and its limitations; and (2) accepting responsibility for competent use of the assessment test or technique.

Clinicians who rely solely on their judgment in using assessment tests and techniques, without attention to empirical findings or in the absence of supportive evidence, fail to appreciate the importance of this standard concerning the bases of assessment. A well-documented fact in clinical psychology is that almost all empirically validated tests and techniques consistently provide more accurate inferences than clinical judgment (see Garb, 1998). As discussed in detail in Chapter 2, both available statistical rules and informed clinical judgment bring strengths and limitations to the assessment process, and integrated reliance on both as bases for test interpretation often broadens the scope and enhances the utility of a personality assessment.

INFORMED CONSENT IN ASSESSMENTS (9.03)

Examiners obtain informed consent for assessments, evaluations, or diagnostic services.

To recap and elaborate the discussion in Chapter 2 of this ethical consideration, informed consent includes a general explanation of the nature and purpose of the assessment, fees, involvement of third parties, if any, and limits of confidentiality. There should be sufficient opportunity for examinees to ask questions and receive answers so that their consent can be informed. Examiners also should describe the general feedback and interpretation that is routinely provided. It is normally the responsibility of the person who administers an assessment test or technique to inform individuals of their rights and responsibilities (see

Table 4.2   The rights of persons

As a person you have the right to:

1. Be informed of your rights and responsibilities;
2. Be treated with courtesy, respect, and impartiality, regardless of your age, disability, ethnicity, gender, national origin, religion, sexual orientation, or other personal characteristics;
3. Be tested with measures that meet professional standards and that are appropriate, given the manner in which the test results will be used;
4. Receive a brief oral or written explanation prior to testing about the purpose(s) for testing, the kind(s) of tests to be used, if the results will be reported to you or to others, and the planned use(s) of the results. If you have a disability, you have the right to inquire and receive information about testing accommodations. If you have difficulty in comprehending the language of the test, you have a right to know in advance of testing whether any accommodations may be available to you;
5. Know in advance of testing when the test will be administered, if and when test results will be available to you, and if there is a fee for testing services that you are expected to pay;
6. Have your test administered and your test results interpreted by appropriately trained individuals who follow professional codes of ethics;
7. Know if a test is optional and learn of the consequences of taking or not taking the test, fully completing the test, or canceling the scores. You may need to ask questions to learn these consequences;
8. Receive a written or oral explanation of your test results within a reasonable amount of time after testing and in commonly understood terms;
9. Have your test results kept confidential to the extent allowed by law; and
10. Present concerns about the testing process or your results and receive information about procedures that will be used to address such concerns.

Source: "Rights and Responsibilities of Persons: Guidelines and Expectations," by the American Psychological Association, retrieved from http://www.apa.org/science/ttrr.html. Reprinted with permission.

Tables 4.2 and 4.3) so that they have an informed basis for consenting to the assessment test or technique.

If requested to do so, examiners may provide the individual with general information about the appropriateness of the assessment test or technique for its intended purpose, to the extent that such information does not involve the release of proprietary information. They also may provide information about how the assessment test or technique will be scored and in what detail. On assessment tests and techniques scored using professional judgment, a general description of the scoring procedures might be provided except when such information is proprietary or would tend to influence performance inappropriately.

Examiners should inform persons about the consequences of not taking an assessment test or technique should they choose not to take it. Once so informed, it is their responsibility to accept such consequences. Examiners should inquire directly about whether examinees have any questions about these consequences rather than assume that they will make these concerns known to their examiner, even though it is the responsibility of the individual to ask such questions.

Table 4.3   The responsibilities of persons

As a test taker you have the responsibility to:

1. Read and/or listen to your rights and responsibilities;
2. Treat others with courtesy and respect during the testing process;
3. Ask questions prior to testing if you are uncertain about why the test is being given, how it will be given, what you will be asked to do, or what will be done with the results;
4. Read or listen to descriptive information in advance of testing and listen carefully to all test instructions. You should inform an examiner in advance of testing if you wish to receive a testing accommodation or if you have a physical condition or illness that may interfere with your performance on the test. If you have difficulty comprehending the language of the test, it is your responsibility to inform an examiner;
5. Know when and where the test will be given, pay for the test if required, appear on time with any required materials, and be ready to be tested;
6. Follow the test instructions you are given and represent yourself honestly during the testing;
7. Be familiar with and accept the consequences of not taking the test, should you choose not to take the test;
8. Inform appropriate person(s), as specified to you by the organization responsible for testing, if you believe that testing conditions affected your results;
9. Ask about the confidentiality of your test results, if this aspect concerns you; and
10. Present concerns about the testing process or results in a timely, respectful way, if you have any.

Source: "Rights and Responsibilities of Persons: Guidelines and Expectations," by the American Psychological Association, retrieved from http://www.apa.org/science/ttrr.html. Reprinted with permission.

Examiners should promptly inform the person if they decide that there is a need to deviate from the assessment tests and techniques and processes to which the person initially agreed and provide an explanation for the change. For example, the examiner may decide, based on the person's performance on one assessment test or technique, that another or different assessment test or technique should be administered subsequently.

RELEASE OF TEST DATA (9.04)

The term *test data* refers to raw and scaled scores, responses to questions or stimuli, and examiners' notes and recordings concerning the person's statements and behavior during an examination. Pursuant to an appropriately signed and dated release, examiners provide test data to the individual *or other persons identified in the release regardless of their qualifications*. Examiners may refrain from releasing test data to protect the person or others from substantial harm or misuse or misrepresentation of the data or the test, recognizing that in many instances release of confidential information under these circumstances is regulated by law.

In the absence of an appropriately signed and dated release, examiners provide test data only as required by law or court order.

Individuals have the right to request and receive information about the specific test data that will or will not be released to them. It also should be explained ahead of time that some *testing materials* are proprietary and protected by copyright law and will not be released. The change in the 2002 *Ethical Principles and Code of Conduct* (APA, 2002) to allow the release of test data to the individual *or other persons identified in the release regardless of their qualifications* has generated significant discussion as to its implications for the field of assessment. A special section of the June 2004 issue of the *Journal of Personality Assessment* was devoted to this topic. The interested reader should consult this journal issue for a more in-depth review of the complex issues that arise in the consideration of releasing test data.

The Committee on Legal Issues of the APA (2006) has provided some general information on strategies that may be available to psychologists for responding to subpoenas or compelled court testimony. This source as well as colleagues should be consulted if the psychologist is placed in this situation.

INTERPRETING ASSESSMENT RESULTS (9.06)

When interpreting assessment results, including automated interpretations, examiners take into account the purpose of the assessment as well as the various test factors and other characteristics of the person being assessed such as linguistic and cultural differences that might affect examiners' judgments or reduce the accuracy of their interpretations. They indicate any significant limitations of their interpretations.

Examiners retain the ultimate responsibility for any interpretations that are made of an assessment technique even when automated or computerized interpretations are used. It cannot be stressed strongly enough that, as mentioned in Chapter 2, most, if not all, automated or computerized interpretations are written about a *group* of individuals who obtained a similar pattern or set of scores, *not about this specific individual.* Consequently, examiners must determine which specific aspects of the automated or computerized interpretation are relevant for this particular individual. They also should provide their rationale for the exclusion of portions that are not included.

ASSESSMENT BY UNQUALIFIED PERSONS (9.07)

Examiners do not promote the use of psychological assessment tests and techniques by unqualified persons, except when such use is conducted for training purposes with appropriate supervision.

Again, it is remarkable that there are no established guidelines as to what qualifies an examiner to administer, score, and interpret assessment tests and techniques. For example, is a single, graduate-level course that surveys all assessment tests and techniques sufficient to qualify the person, or is supervised experience needed? If supervised experience is needed, how long must the person be supervised or for how many administrations, scoring, and interpretations? Are continuing education programs or professional workshops needed to maintain one's qualifications? The development of such guidelines would make it easier both to identify professionals who are unqualified to use a specific assessment test or technique, and for examiners and students learning the assessment test or technique, to know whether they are competent.

The Task Force on Test Users Qualifications (Turner, DeMers, Fox, & Reed, 2001) was established by the American Psychological Association to develop guidelines for the competent and responsible use of psychological tests. These guidelines described two types of test user qualifications: (1) generic psychometric knowledge and skills that are the bases for most of the assessment tests and techniques discussed in this *Handbook,* and (2) more specific qualifications for the use of tests in particular settings or for specific purposes. This second type of qualifications is outside the scope of this *Handbook,* but a good portion of the generic psychometric knowledge and skills described by the task force is covered in Chapter 3. As for the remaining knowledge and skills, they are described in such an abstract or general manner as to be of little use in acquainting psychologists or students with the actual qualifications that are required. The task force document indicates that the knowledge needed for the appropriate selection of tests (figure 2, p. 1102) includes validity evidence of test scores; validity generalization; convergent; divergent [*sic*]; and cross-validation.

A conference on competencies organized by the Association of Psychology Postdoctoral and Internship Centers resulted in a report by Krishnamurthy et al. (2004) that identified eight core competencies related to psychological assessment (see Table 4.4). The report

Table 4.4   Eight core competencies in psychological assessment

1. A background in the basics of psychometric theory.
2. Knowledge of the scientific, theoretical, empirical, and contextual bases of psychological assessment.
3. Knowledge, skill, and techniques to assess the cognitive, affective, behavioral, and personality dimensions of human experience with reference to individuals and systems.
4. The ability to assess outcomes of treatment/intervention.
5. The ability to evaluate critically the multiple roles, contexts, and relationships within which clients and psychologists function, and the reciprocal impact of these roles, contexts, and relationships on assessment activity.
6. The ability to establish, maintain, and understand the collaborative professional relationship that provides a context for all psychological activity including psychological assessment.
7. An understanding of the relationship between assessment and intervention, assessment as an intervention, and intervention planning.
8. Technical assessment skills that include:
   (a) Problem and/or goal identification and case conceptualization
   (b) Understanding and selection of appropriate assessment methods including both test and nontest data (e.g., suitable strategies, tools, measures, time lines, and targets)
   (c) Effective application of the assessment procedures with clients and the various systems in which they function
   (d) Systematic data gathering
   (e) integration of information, inference, and analysis
   (f) Communication of findings and development of recommendations to address problems and goals
   (g) Provision of feedback that is understandable, useful, and responsive to the client, regardless of whether the client is an individual, group, organization, or referral source

Source: "Achieving Competency in Psychological Assessment: Directions for Education and Training," by R. Krishnamurthy et al., (2004), *Journal of Clinical Psychology, 60,* pp. 725–739.

Table 4.5   Four recommendations for training in psychological assessment

1. Academic courses should be relevant to a broad range of assessment models that provide instruction in the core competencies. Course work should include foundational courses on the theoretical and empirical bases of assessment, including psychological theories, psychometrics, and psychopathology, as well as courses relevant to specific assessment methods.

2. Practicum training experiences in psychological assessment should be coherent and consistent with the graduate program's model and philosophy of training and should involve exposure to diverse populations and settings. Practicum supervision in psychological assessment should be provided in individual and small-group modalities, be intensive in nature, and be organized around a supervisory relationship with an experienced mentor.

3. There should be an integration of course work and practicum experiences in learning and applying assessment knowledge and skills.

4. Essential psychological assessment skills should be developed within a framework of coherent and cumulative learning involving progressively increasing complexity, consistent with the program's training model and philosophy.

Source: "Achieving Competency in Psychological Assessment: Directions for Education and Training," by R. Krishnamurthy et al., (2004), *Journal of Clinical Psychology, 60,* pp. 725–739.

included four recommendations for training methods and modalities (see Table 4.5) and identified three central principles to employ in evaluating competency in psychological assessment (see Table 4.6).

The Society for Personality Assessment (2006) has proposed that the *minimal* standards for education in psychological assessment are two or more graduate-level courses. This course work should be composed of didactic and practical experience in the following areas: (a) psychometric theory; (b) theory, administration, and interpretation of cognitive assessment instruments, performance-based measures of psychopathology such as the Rorschach, and self-report inventories such as the MCMI-III, MMPI-2, or PAI-R; (c) appropriate selection of assessment test and techniques to answer specific referral questions; (d) integration of data from multiple sources into a report including feedback to the individual; and (e) the relationship between assessment and treatment. Supervised practicum, internship, and postdoctoral training in psychological assessment also is essential for the development of competence. Such training should occur under the supervision of a licensed professional with expertise in assessment through education and training.

Table 4.6   Three principles for evaluating competency in psychological assessment

1. The evaluation of psychological assessment competency should focus on the comprehensive and integrated set of psychological assessment activities extending from the initial interview and psychological testing and intervention to the evaluation of outcome of psychological service.

2. The content areas evaluated should reflect core competencies and methods of training.

3. The evaluation should be individualized and personally sensitive, and provide adequate, meaningful feedback.

Source: "Achieving Competency in Psychological Assessment: Directions for Education and Training," by R. Krishnamurthy et al., (2004), *Journal of Clinical Psychology, 60,* pp. 725–739.

These competency requirements and standards for education and training in psychological assessment proposed by the Task Force on Test Users Qualifications (Turner et al., 2001), the Association of Psychology Postdoctoral and Internship Centers (Krishnamurthy et al., 2004), and the Society for Personality Assessment (2006) represent the first step in this process. The standards for education proposed by the Society for Personality Assessment have specific content that is not provided by either the Task Force on Test Users Qualifications or the Association of Psychology Postdoctoral and Internship Centers groups. It still remains to be defined explicitly by any group how much supervised training is sufficient. On the one hand, students who administer, score, and interpret one assessment test or technique per month during their practicum, internship, and postdoctoral training probably would not have sufficient experience to be competent simply because the training is so separated in time. On the other hand, students probably do not need to administer, score, and interpret five or more assessment tests or techniques per week to be competent.

Johnson and Campbell (2002) have asked why there are not character and fitness requirements for admission to graduate programs in clinical psychology and licensure as a psychologist, as there are in other professions such as law. Such requirements would limit the impact of unqualified individuals on the general public, which the *Ethical Principles and Code of Conduct* of the APA (2002) is intended to protect. Johnson and Campbell suggest that fitness involves personality adjustment, psychological health, and not using psychoactive substances, and that character involves integrity, prudence, and caring.

OBSOLETE TESTS AND OUTDATED TEST RESULTS (9.08)

Examiners do not base their assessment or intervention decisions or recommendations on data or test results that are outdated for the current purpose.

Exactly what makes a test obsolete is not clear except when a newer version of the test is available. Even in that instance, there may be strong justification for using the previous edition, such as its being better standardized or more appropriate for the specific person being assessed.

Norcross, Koocher, and Garofalo (2006) had 101 assessment experts rate 30 tests and techniques on a continuum from not at all discredited to certainly discredited. Only five tests (Luscher Color; Szondi; Bender Visual Motor Gestalt; Eneagrams; Lowenfeld Mosaic) were rated as being discredited for a specific purpose by 25% or more of these experts. It is not clear what bases these experts used for determining that the assessment test or technique was discredited for a specific purpose. There does not appear to be anything approaching a consensus on what assessment tests or techniques are obsolete or outdated. Instead, such a determination tends to be in the eye of the examiner.

One guideline that could be used in making the determination of whether a specific assessment test or technique is obsolete would be recent reviews or meta-analyses of research findings published in refereed journals. Such reviews or meta-analyses could perform a valuable function for the field of assessment, in general, and individual examiners, in particular, by providing a state of the art summary of the status of the assessment test or technique. Even more compelling would be publication of multiple reviews and meta-analyses, should such ever become available.

TEST SCORING AND INTERPRETATION SERVICES (9.09)

Examiners select scoring and interpretation services (including automated services) on the basis of evidence of the validity of the program and procedures. They retain the responsibility for the appropriate scoring and interpretation of all assessment instruments, whether they score and interpret such tests themselves or use automated or other services.

Examiners tend to assume without verification that commercial scoring services are reliable. Such a belief assumes that the data have been verified, if hand entered for computer scoring, and that optical scanners are 100% accurate, if the data have been scanned. Although commercial test scorers state that their scanners are 100% accurate, no published studies have actually examined their reliability. Errors in scoring self-report inventories are discussed in more depth in Chapter 5.

Examiners who persist in hand-scoring any assessment test or technique, which is neither time- nor cost-effective, should score it twice. Even better is to have another person hand-score the test or technique and resolve any discrepancies by scoring again. Similar precautions need to be taken when plotting any scores or looking them up in reference tables. Because of these and other concerns discussed in Chapter 2, automated scoring of test responses, when programs are available for doing so, have many advantages over hand-scoring. The discussion in Chapter 2 also touched on ethical considerations in drawing on computer-generated interpretive statements in preparing assessment reports. Greene (2005) provides some further specific guidelines for ethical utilization of computer printouts in writing reports.

Greene (2005) recommended beginning to create psychological reports by having assessment tests or techniques interpreted by computer programs when they are available. These computer interpretations would then become one of the basic building blocks of the report. The examiner's task would be to integrate the computer interpretations of the various assessment tests or techniques that were administered along with the clinical history and interview into the final report. This process should be guided by the following four rules.

First, it would be expected that the examiner would modify and adapt the computer interpretation to correct any inaccuracies that might be contained therein. The computer interpretation would *never* be a stand-alone product that is accepted as is, but would be an electronic assistant that quickly provides the basic interpretation of any assessment test or technique. Rather than the examiner looking up the basic interpretation from the standard references on the various tests or techniques and then entering that information into the word processor, the electronic assistant would provide this information.

Second, any modification made of the computer interpretation would require the examiner to point out explicitly the information that contradicts the computer interpretation. That is, examiners cannot use their clinical judgment to override a statement simply because they do not like it or feel in their heart that it cannot be correct. Meehl (1957) reminded us that we are to use our clinical judgment infrequently in this type of task.

Third, computerized interpretations should be used routinely, to promote the examiner's familiarity with and use of them in more complex cases. If computerized interpretations are only used in complex cases, the examiner loses the learning experience of working with computerized interpretations in straightforward cases where potential problems can be seen more easily.

Fourth and finally, it must be remembered that every statement in a computerized interpretation is a hypothesis that must be validated by additional information.

EXPLAINING ASSESSMENT RESULTS (9.10)

Examiners take reasonable steps to ensure that explanations of results are given to the individual or designated representative unless the nature of the relationship precludes provision of an explanation of results, and this fact has been clearly explained in advance to the person being assessed. Recommendations made on the basis of test results should use language that is understandable and not use psychological jargon that is easily misunderstood.

As discussed in Chapter 2, test results should be communicated in an appropriate and sensitive manner, without negative labels or comments likely to inflame or stigmatize the individual. Terms such as the patient *denies* (does not report), the person reports physical *complaints* (symptoms), the person is *paranoid* (very sensitive and aware of the actions of others) should be avoided at all times.

With further respect to other obligatory aspects of explaining test results, examiners who are releasing test scores or reports to examinees or to other persons or institutions should provide understandable explanations about the nature, purposes, and results of the testing and how scores were used. There should be an explanation of what the scores mean, their confidence intervals, and any significant reservations about the accuracy or limitations of their interpretations. Michaels (2006) has described some ethical considerations that arise when writing assessment results and ways to address them. Some of these considerations include (a) how conclusions or included data may have negative consequences or bias how others might see the individual; (b) how the inclusion of some information might breach confidentiality; and (c) how the included data may be of limited reliability or validity.

On request, examiners can provide information about the sources used in interpreting their test results and a description of the comparison group(s). They also can provide information about the options for obtaining a second interpretation of the test results, such as other appropriately trained professionals. It is particularly important to make sure that individuals understand to ask questions if they do not understand their results, or if they believe that the testing conditions affected the results.

Examiners should provide corrected test scores to the person as rapidly as possible should an error occur in the processing or reporting of scores. The length of time is often dictated by individuals responsible for processing or reporting the scores, rather than the individuals responsible for testing, should the two parties be different individuals.

Examiners should inform persons how they can question the results of the testing if they do not believe that the assessment test or technique was administered properly or scored correctly, or other such concerns. Examiners should inform them of the procedures for appealing decisions that they believe are based in whole or in part on erroneous test results. They should inform the person, if that person's test results are canceled or not released for normal use, why that action was taken. The person is entitled to request and receive information on the types of evidence and procedures that have been used to make that determination.

MAINTAINING TEST SECURITY (9.11)

The term *test materials* refers to manuals, instruments, protocols, and test questions or stimuli and does not include *test data* as defined in Release of Test Data (9.04). Examiners make reasonable efforts to maintain the integrity and security of test materials and other assessment tests and techniques consistent with law and contractual obligations, and in a manner that permits adherence to this Ethical Standard.

Examiners should ensure that records of test results, whether in paper or electronic form, are safeguarded and maintained so that only individuals who have a legitimate right to access them can do so. They should provide persons, on request, with information regarding who has a legitimate right to access their test results (when individually identified) and in what form. Examiners should respond appropriately to questions about the reasons such individuals may have access to test results and how they may use the results. They should advise persons that they are entitled to limit access to their results (when individually identified) to those persons or institutions, and for those purposes, revealed to them prior to testing. Exceptions may occur when persons, or their guardians, consent to release the test results to others or when examiners are authorized by law to release test results. The examiner should keep confidential any requests for testing accommodations and the documentation supporting the request.

Examiners generally obtain permission from the copyright holder prior to reprinting test items. Examiners may also consider alternatives to providing test items to persons not qualified in assessment by (a) developing similar items having little or no overlap with content in the original test items and (b) using factors, clusters, or content-categories and their descriptions.

Persons in training who use test materials, or who have access to test data, should be supervised directly by a qualified professional. Academic departments and faculty should maintain the security of all test materials under conditions that prevent access by unauthorized individuals. Access to psychological test materials (e.g., test booklets, protocols, administration manuals, scoring keys) should be granted only to qualified examiners or other professionals who use the material in their teaching, research, or clinical practice. Testing materials should *not* be available to the general public in college or university bookstores. Access to testing materials that are stored in a library should be limited to appropriate personnel and to students in training.

TRAINING STUDENTS IN PERSONALITY ASSESSMENT

A variety of ethical considerations arise in teaching students how to administer, score, interpret, and provide feedback for assessment tests and techniques (see Yalof & Brabender, 2001). The professor can describe the various ethical considerations that arise in learning assessment tests and techniques and involve the students in an interactive process on how they might be addressed. Such a process models how professionals interact with their colleagues to discuss ethical concerns.

Before students administer any kind of psychological test, they should have completed appropriate prerequisite coursework in tests and measurements, statistics, and psychometrics, and they should be thoroughly trained in the proper administration of the specific assessment test or technique being used. It is ill advised and borders at least on unprofessional practice to instruct students to "just read the manual, it will tell you everything that you need to know," as their training in any assessment test or technique. Such an attitude toward assessment by the professor hardly begets an appropriate appreciation of the process in students. Hence, students must be supervised in practice and initial administrations, as well as in scoring of responses, and deriving interpretations for any and all assessment tests and techniques.

Communicating the results of a practice administration or interpretation of any assessment test or technique should be avoided except under the most unusual circumstances. If it becomes necessary to share the results or interpretations of a practice administration, this information should be reported by students only under the supervision of a qualified faculty member or supervisor. Students should be thoroughly trained in appropriate language and procedures for reporting all types and levels of scores.

Rupert, Kozlowski, Hoffman, Daniels, and Piette (1999) noted that two types of problems were reported with some frequency in their survey of adult and child instructors of courses in psychological testing: (1) Volunteers or their parents exert pressure for feedback, and (2) testing reveals a problem that may require intervention. With adult volunteers, such problems generally took the form of severe distress or psychopathology and suicidal risk. One way to negate the need for any type of feedback would be to have students role-play disorders for practice administrations.

Rupert et al. (1999) made the following eight suggestions for practice testing by graduate students:

1. Students should be educated about the ethical issues associated with dual relationships and should be cautioned against testing acquaintances, friends, relatives, and any individual or child of an individual with whom they have an established relationship.

2. A formalized procedure for securing volunteers through university or community contacts should be established to avoid many of the problems associated with the use of personal contacts to secure volunteers.

3. Regardless of the source of volunteers, a screening process (either a brief questionnaire or telephone interview) should be instituted to maximize the possibility that volunteers are appropriate for training purposes.

4. Encourage practice with classmates as a helpful procedure for allowing students to develop skill in administering tests before they do any testing of practice participants. However, care should be taken to avoid placing students in situations where they are required to reveal personal information.

5. When testing is conducted with community individuals solely for training purposes, a no-feedback policy seems justified. This policy must be clearly thought out, however, with consideration given to possible exceptions and procedures for handling emergency situations, and must be communicated in writing to the participants.

6. When clinical patients are tested, a procedure for giving feedback should be incorporated into the content of the testing class.

7. A thorough consent procedure should be instituted with both community volunteers and clinical patients.

8. Special care should be taken to protect the confidentiality of practice participants. Whenever possible, names and identifying data should be removed from test protocols. Policies must be established for either destroying test data or ensuring that it is securely maintained once training purposes have been served.

DIVERSITY ISSUES

In Chapter 2, we discussed briefly the relevance of a person's cultural and experiential context to the implications of whatever personality characteristics are identified by the individual's test responses. In concluding this chapter on ethical considerations in personality assessment, we want to stress the importance of attention to diversity issues. Because of their impact on the assessment process generally and the interpretation of results in particular, diversity issues cannot be emphasized too strongly. These diversity issues include age, disability, ethnicity, gender, religion, and sexual orientation. Most assessment instrument techniques handle age and gender issues in the normative and interpretive process, and these issues are accordingly discussed in reference to specific tests in Chapters 6 through 14. Ethnicity, religion, and sexual orientation are considered here, with some further comments on the issue of English as a second language in the section on ethnicity.

Ethnicity

The typical investigation of the effects of ethnic group membership on performance on an assessment test or technique consists of obtaining a sample of individuals from some specific ethnic group and then comparing their obtained scores against the normative group for the test or technique. If differences occur between the two groups on any scale, the typical conclusion is that the test or technique as a whole or some subset of scales is affected by membership in that ethnic group. These studies rarely determine whether the differences still persist when other potentially confounding factors such as socioeconomic status and educational level are controlled. If ethnic group membership affects the scores on an assessment test or technique when potential confounding factors are controlled, the critical issue becomes whether the differences are of sufficient magnitude to affect clinical interpretation.

Membership within the ethnic group whose performance is being evaluated is rarely specified when this type of research is conducted. Most often, the participants are self-described as black, Hispanic, Asian American, and so on, with little consideration of the heterogeneity that exists within any ethnic group. Okazaki (1998) noted that Asian and Pacific Islander Americans "can trace their roots to 28 countries of origin or ethnic group or to 25 identified Pacific Island cultures" (p. 56), and Allen (1998) stated that there are "510 federally recognized Native entities, including American Indian tribes and Alaska Native Villages" (p. 18). Similar heterogeneity occurs among blacks (Lindsey, 1998) and Hispanics (Cuellar, 1998). A further limiting factor is the relative absence of studies to determine whether different scores between two ethnic groups actually affect the empirical correlates of the scale(s), because even if clinically significant mean score differences are found between groups, the issue remains of whether these differences are real or artifactual.

The use of standardized assessment tests and techniques with different ethnic groups has been questioned for years. While standardized tests and techniques provide an opportunity for comparisons across groups, these tests and techniques often have been cited as deficient when used with different ethnic groups. These deficiencies may lead to both false positive and false negative attributions within these groups (Allen, 1998).

When evaluating assessment tests or techniques with different ethnic groups, it is important to consider whether to take an *emic* or *etic* approach (Dana, 1993). An emic approach attempts to understand the individual as unique within the relativistic context of his or her specific ethnic group and requires little standardization. An etic approach adopts a more universal view by comparing individuals across ethnic groups using standardized measures and has as a major goal the discovery of laws governing the processes under study. Virtually all assessment tests or techniques use an etic approach.

While some contend that emic-based assessments may be more accurate for use within specific ethnic groups, such assessments have considerable developmental costs and may not allow for comparisons across ethnic groups (Malgady & Zayas, 2001). For example, considering the existence of over 500 distinct American Indian tribal groups (Allen, 1998), one can understand the enormity of the task in adopting a totally emic-based assessment approach. To illustrate how these complex issues may be addressed, Hansen (2002) has outlined a process for teaching culturally sensitive psychological assessment and Dana (1993) has devoted an entire book to this topic.

Numerous issues arise when the person being evaluated has English as a second language or is not conversant with English at all. These issues arise at all stages of the assessment process. Does the person understand the description of the assessment process so that consent can be meaningfully provided? Does the person understand the instructions for the various assessment tests or techniques? Are there any norms for the use of the specific test or technique with the person's ethnic group, if ethnicity has an impact on the scoring or interpretation?

The degree of acculturation also arises for the person with English as a second language, regardless of their familiarity with and fluency in English. The use of any idiomatic expressions in the assessment process will be particularly difficult for such individuals. In addition, ambiguity is inherent in the meaning of many statements made in the assessment process and the items on self-report inventories. It is assumed in the assessment process that a statement has a single meaning and both the examiner and individual concur in that meaning. The statement "I am a good mixer" is an excellent example of the multiple interpretations that can be made of the content of a single statement. There are at least 13 meanings of what is being referred to by this item.

The best solution in the assessment of any individual for whom English is a second language occurs when the examiner is fluent in the language. When such an examiner is not available for whatever reason, a professional interpreter who is skilled in the assessment process is invaluable, as noted in Chapter 2. There are few circumstances in which a relative of the person or anyone who has an investment in the outcome of the assessment process should be used as the interpreter.

Religion and Spirituality

Probably the most neglected areas within the field of diversity are religion and spirituality, with little emphasis on teaching or training within assessment or psychology more generally.

This lack of emphasis is surprising given that religion is both a source of support for some individuals and torment for others. Even if examiners recognize the importance of assessing religion and spirituality, they are unlikely to assess it. Also, these two terms usually are used as synonyms despite their different referents. Brawer, Handal, Fabricatore, Roberts, and Wajda-Johnston (2002) and Hage (2006) provide suggestions on how to include training in religion and spirituality in diversity training within psychology programs.

Hathaway, Scott, and Garver (2004) surveyed 1,000 clinical psychologists, who paid the practice assessment fee to the American Psychological Association, about the importance of the person's religion or spirituality in a clinical setting. Although most of them thought it was an important area of functioning, slightly over one-half of the respondents reported asking about religion or spirituality less than 50% of the time during the assessment. Slightly less than 20% reported never asking about the person's religion or spirituality. Over one-half of the respondents indicated that they rarely or never examined the impact a disorder might have on the person's religious or spiritual functioning.

Brawer et al. (2002) reported that religion and spirituality are covered in some manner in most clinical training programs, usually as part of the content of a more general course on diversity. Few programs, however, provide training in this area in a systematic manner. Russell and Yarhouse (2006) found that almost two-thirds of internship programs provided no didactic training with religion or spirituality as a content area. Most internship sites seem to expect the supervisor to handle such issues when they are raised by the person.

Sexual Orientation

Sexual orientation per se is not an ethical issue. The ethical considerations that arise in the assessment of gay, lesbian, and bisexual individuals primarily involve the examiners' familiarity with the multiple social and familial issues these individuals face and their competency for working with them. Examiners may be subtly influenced by the negative view society has of these individuals, which can impact the interpretations of the assessment results. Historically, this bias was apparent in defining homosexuality as a disease that needed to be cured.

There are the beginnings of a movement to provide specific information for assessing and treating gay, lesbian, and bisexual individuals (Eubanks-Carter, Burckell, & Goldfried, 2005). Davison (2001, 2005) has been a vocal advocate for the multiple issues faced by gay, lesbian, and bisexual individuals and the process for dealing with them. His work will help enlighten examiners' awareness of these issues.

CONCLUDING COMMENTS

The overarching issues in the ethical considerations in psychological assessment are consent, competence, and confidentiality. The individual has to be competent, of legal age, and understand thoroughly the various aspects of the assessment process so that informed consent may be given. The examiner must be competent in the administration, scoring, and interpretation of the specific assessment test or technique, and produce an understandable and relevant report within a reasonable time. Finally, all the materials must remain confidential to the full extent of the law and *Ethical Principles and Code of Conduct* (APA, 2002).

Consultation with a colleague always is recommended any time there is an ambiguity in what should or should not be done in a given circumstance. The complexity of the ethical considerations that arise in the assessment process will require such consultation on a regular basis.

REFERENCES

Allen, J. (1998). Personality assessment with American Indians and Alaska Natives: Instrument considerations and service delivery style. *Journal of Personality Assessment, 70*, 17–42.

American Psychological Association. (1992). Ethical principles of examiners and code of conduct. *American Psychologist, 47*, 1597–1611.

American Psychological Association. (2002). Ethical principles of examiners and code of conduct. *American Psychologist, 57*, 1060–1073.

Brawer, P. A., Handal, P. J., Fabricatore, A. N., Roberts, R., & Wajda-Johnston, V. A. (2002). Training and education in religion/spirituality within APA-accredited clinical training programs. *Professional Psychology: Research and Practice, 33*, 203–206.

Committee on Legal Issues of the American Psychological Association. (2006). Strategies for private practitioners coping with subpoenas or compelled testimony for client records of test data. *Professional Psychology: Research and Practice, 37*, 215–222.

Cuellar, I. (1998). Cross-cultural clinical psychological assessment of Hispanic Americans. *Journal of Personality Assessment, 70*, 71–86.

Dana, R. H. (1993). *Multicultural assessment perspectives for professional psychology*. Boston: Allyn & Bacon.

Davison, G. C. (2001). Conceptual and ethical issues in therapy for the psychological problems of gay men, lesbians, and bisexuals. *Journal of Clinical Psychology, 57*, 695–704.

Davison, G. C. (2005). Issues and nonissues in the gay-affirmative treatment of patients who are gay, lesbian, or bisexual. *Clinical Psychology: Science and Practice, 12*, 25–28.

Eubanks-Carter, C., Burckell, L. A., & Goldfried, M. R. (2005). Enhancing therapeutic effectiveness with lesbian, gay, and bisexual clients. *Clinical Psychology: Science and Practice, 12*, 1–18.

Garb, H. N. (1998). *Studying the clinician: Judgment research and psychological assessment*. Washington, DC: American Psychological Association.

Greene, R. L. (2000). *The MMPI-2: An interpretive manual*. Boston: Allyn & Bacon.

Greene, R. L. (2005). Computer scoring and interpretation in psychological report writing. *SPA Exchange, 17*, 6.

Hage, S. M. (2006). A closer look at the role of spirituality in psychology training programs. *Professional Psychology: Research and Practice, 37*, 303–310.

Hansen, N. D. (2002). Teaching cultural sensitivity in psychological assessment: A modular approach used in a distance education program. *Journal of Personality Assessment, 79*, 200–206.

Hathaway, W. L., Scott, S. Y., & Garver, S. A. (2004). Assessing religious/spiritual functioning: A neglected domain in clinical practice? *Professional Psychology: Research and Practice, 35*, 97–104.

Johnson, W. B., & Campbell, C. D. (2002). Character and fitness requirements for professional psychologists: Are there any? *Professional Psychology: Research and Practice, 33*, 46–53.

Krishnamurthy, R., VandeCreek, L., Kaslow, N. J., Tazeau, Y. N., Miville, M. L., Kerns, R., et al. (2004). Achieving competency in psychological assessment: Directions for education and training. *Journal of Clinical Psychology, 60*, 725–739.

Lindsey, M. L. (1998). Culturally competent assessment of African American clients. *Journal of Personality Assessment, 70*, 43–53.

Malgady, R., & Zayas, L. H. (2001). Cultural and linguistic considerations in psychodiagnosis with Hispanics: The need for an empirically informed process model. *Social Work, 46,* 39–49.

Meehl, P. E. (1957). When shall we use our heads instead of the formula? *Journal of Counseling Psychology, 4,* 268–273.

Michaels, M. H. (2006). Ethical considerations in writing psychological assessment reports. *Journal of Clinical Psychology, 62,* 47–58.

Moreland, K. L., Eyde, L. D., Robertson, G. J., Primoff, E. S., & Most, R. B. (1995). Assessment of test user qualifications: A research-based measurement procedure. *American Psychologist, 50,* 14–23.

Norcross, J. C., Koocher, G. P., & Garofalo, A. (2006). Discredited psychological treatments and tests: A Delphi poll. *Professional Psychology: Research and Practice, 37,* 515–522.

Okazaki, S. (1998). Psychological assessment of Asian Americans: Research agenda for cultural competency. *Journal of Personality Assessment, 70,* 54–70.

Rupert, P. A., Kozlowski, N. F., Hoffman, L. A., Daniels, D. D., & Piette, J. M. (1999). Practical and ethical issues in teaching psychological testing. *Professional Psychology: Research and Practice, 30,* 209–214.

Russell, S. R., & Yarhouse, M. A. (2006). Training in religion/spirituality within APA-accredited psychology predoctoral internships. *Professional Psychology: Research and Practice, 37,* 430–436.

Society for Personality Assessment. (2006). Standards for education and training in psychological assessment position of the Society for Personality Assessment. *Journal of Personality Assessment, 87,* 355–357.

Turner, S. M., DeMers, S. T., Fox, H. R., & Reed, G. M. (2001). APA's guidelines for test user qualifications. *American Psychologist, 56,* 1099–1113.

Working Group of the Joint Committee on Testing Practices. (1998, August). *Person rights and responsibilities.* Washington, DC: American Psychological Association. Retrievable at http://www.apa.org/science/ttrr.html.

Yalof, J., & Brabender, V. (2001). Ethical dilemmas in personality assessment courses: Using the classroom for in vivo training. *Journal of Personality Assessment, 77,* 203–213.

Part II

SELF-REPORT INVENTORIES

Chapter 5

OVERVIEW

Several issues are common to all self-report inventories. Instead of repeating the same material in each of the ensuing chapters, these issues are summarized in the present chapter, and the aspects that are specific to each inventory are addressed in Chapters 6 through 10. Because of this focus on issues that are common to all self-report instruments, the organization of this chapter differs somewhat from the preceding and following chapters. This focus also allows for direct comparisons among the instruments that may influence which ones are selected to be part of the test battery for a particular individual. If it is important to compare a person with a normal group of people, any of the self-report inventories discussed in this *Handbook* other than the Millon Multiaxial Clinical Inventory-III (MCMI-III; Millon, Davis, & Millon, 1997) would be appropriate, because the MCMI-III only uses a clinical group for standardization purposes (see section on Standardization Group). Conversely, if an assessor wanted to compare the individual with a clinical group, then the MCMI-III would be appropriate, as would the Personality Assessment Inventory (PAI; Morey, 1991), which is standardized on both clinical and community samples. The sections of this chapter compare and contrast self-report inventories with respect to their nature, item characteristics, methods of scale development, administration and scoring, standardization group, validity assessment, and interpretive process.

NATURE OF SELF-REPORT INVENTORIES

Self-report inventories can be divided into two major categories: Some are *broadband* multidimensional measures that provide global assessments of the type and severity of psychopathology or the dimensions of normal personality; others are *narrowband* unitary measures that assess a single symptom, type of psychopathology, or personality characteristic. The Beck Depression Inventory-II (Beck, Steer, & Brown, 1996) and the Beck Anxiety Inventory (Beck & Steer, 1993) are frequently used measures in this second category, although literally hundreds of such inventories are available (cf. *Buros Mental Measurements Yearbook;* Plake & Impara, 2001; Plake, Impara, & Spies, 2003; Spies & Plake, 2005). Self-report inventories limited to a single symptom or type of psychopathology are not discussed in this *Handbook,* in part because of their sheer number. Of the five self-report inventories in Chapters 6 through 10, four are broadband measures of global psychopathology (the Minnesota Multiphasic Personality Inventory-2 [MMPI-2], Butcher, Dahlstrom, Graham, Tellegen, & Kaemmer, 1989; Butcher et al., 2001; the MMPI-A, Butcher et al., 1992; the MCMI-III, Millon et al., 1997; and the PAI, Morey, 1992), and the fifth is a broadband measure of dimensions of normal personality (NEO PI-R; Costa & McCrae, 1992).

In this chapter, the expression "all self-report inventories" refers only to these five inventories, to avoid repeatedly appending the expression "discussed in this *Handbook.*" A rough idea of the relative frequency with which these self-report inventories are used is reflected in how often they occur in the title of articles listed in *MEDLINE* and *Psy-choInfo* since 1990:[1] MMPI—2,725; MCMI—399; NEO—1,253; and PAI—278. Surveys of the frequency of usage of self-report inventories in clinical practice provide similar results, with the MMPI-2 and MCMI-III being ranked as the top two inventories (Belter & Piotrowski, 2001; Watkins, Campbell, Nieberding, & Hallmark, 1995). The MMPI-2 (86%; 83%), MCMI-III (38%; 40%), MMPI-A (30%;—), and PAI (—; 21%) are the self-report inventories that are most frequently taught in clinical psychology training programs (Childs & Eyde, 2002) and that clinical psychology internship directors most want interns to have learned (Clemence & Handler, 2001), respectively.

To orient readers about what each of these self-report inventories is trying to measure and how they differ from each other, Table 5.1 identifies the major scales on each of them.

ITEM CHARACTERISTICS

Test developers must make numerous decisions about the items on the self-report inventory, including (a) the format for responding to the items, (b) the "true/agree" and "false/disagree" balance in each scale, (c) whether to write the items in the affirmative or in the negative, (d) whether to use items on more than one scale, (e) the breadth and depth of the items on a scale, (f) the inherent ambiguity in the meaning of the item content, (g) potential biases in item content, and (h) how to weight items in scoring responses on a scale. Each of these decisions is reviewed next.

Format for Responding to Items

All self-report inventories provide individuals with explicit statements (items) and a limited number of alternatives from which to select their response. In most of these inventories, individuals are given simple declarative statements about specific behaviors or symptoms and are asked to indicate with dichotomous choices (e.g., true/false or agree/disagree) whether they apply to them. On the MMPI-2, MMPI-A, and MCMI-III, a statement like "I am depressed most of the time" must be marked "true" or "false." The PAI uses a 4-point scale ranging from "false, not at all true," to "slightly true," "mainly true," and finally "very true." The NEO PI-R offers five alternatives: "strongly agree," "agree," "neutral," "disagree," and "strongly disagree."

Providing more response alternatives with each statement allows for greater differentiation in the frequency and intensity of a behavior or symptom within a single item than is available with dichotomous choices. Multiple alternatives also allow for a wider range of total scores on a scale, because each item now comprises four or five possible scores instead of two. If desired for some reason, self-report inventories that offer more than two response alternatives can easily be transformed into dichotomous scores.

---

[1] These searches were made on August 24, 2007, using the inventory names as the search term.

Table 5.1   Scales on self-report inventories assessing psychopathology

MMPI-2	MMPI-A	Scale Name
Validity Scales (8–7)		
VRIN	VRIN	Variable Response Inconsistency
TRIN	TRIN	True Response Inconsistency
F	F	Infrequency
FB		Back Infrequency
Fp		Infrequency Psychopathology
	F1	Infrequency—First Half
	F2	Infrequency—Second Half
L	L	Lie
K	K	Correction
S		Superlative
Clinical Scales (10)		
1	1	Hs: Hypochondriasis
2	2	D: Depression
3	3	Hy: Hysteria
4	4	Pd: Psychopathic Deviant
5	5	Mf: Masculinity-Femininity
6	6	Pa: Paranoia
7	7	Pt: Psychasthenia
8	8	Sc: Schizophrenia
9	9	Ma: Hypomania
0	0	Si: Social Introversion
Content Scales (15)		
ANX	A-anx	Anxiety
FRS		Fears
OBS	A-obs	Obsessions
DEP	A-dep	Depression
HEA	A-hea	Health Concerns
	A-aln	Alienation
BIZ	A-biz	Bizarre Mentation
ANG	A-ang	Anger
CYN	A-cyn	Cynicism
ASP		Antisocial Practices
	A-con	Conduct Problems
TPA		Type A
LSE	A-lse	Low Self-Esteem
	A-las	Low Aspirations
SOD	A-sod	Social Discomfort
FAM	A-fam	Family Problems
WRK		Work Interference
	A-sch	School Problems
TRT	A-trt	Negative Treatment Indicators

(continued)

Table 5.1   *(Continued)*

MMPI-2	MMPI-A	Scale Name
Restructured Clinical Scales (9)		
RCdem	—	Demoralization
RC1som	—	Somatization
RC2lpe	—	Low Positive Emotionality
RC3cyn	—	Cynicism
RC4asb	—	Antisocial Behavior
RC6per	—	Ideas of Persecution
RC7dne	—	Dysfunctional Negative Emotions
RC8abx	—	Aberrant Experiences
RC9hpm	—	Hypomanic Activation
PSY-5 Scales (5)		
AGGR	*AGGR*	Aggression
PSYC	*PSYC*	Psychoticism
DISC	*DISC*	Disconstraint
NEGE	*NEGE*	Negative Emotionality
INTR	*INTR*	Introversion/Low Positive Emotionality
Broad Personality Characteristics (5–2)		
A	*A*	Anxiety
R	*R*	Repression
Es	—	Ego Strength
Do	—	Dominance
Re	—	Social Responsibility
Generalized Emotional Distress (3–0)		
Mt	—	College Maladjustment
PK	—	Posttraumatic Stress Disorder—Keane
MDS	—	Marital Distress
Behavioral Dyscontrol (5–4)		
Ho	—	Hostility
O-H	—	Overcontrolled Hostility
	IMM	Immaturity
MAC-R	*MAC-R*	MacAndrews Alcoholism -Revised
AAS	—	Addiction Admission
	ACK	Alcohol/Drug Problem Acknowledgment
APS	—	Addiction Potential
	PRO	Alcohol/Drug Problem Proneness
Gender Role (2–0)		
GM	—	Gender Role—Masculine
GF	—	Gender Role—Feminine

MCMI-III	Scale Name
Modifying Indices (4)	
V	Validity
X	Disclosure
Y	Desirability
Z	Debasement

Table 5.1   (*Continued*)

MCMI-III	Scale Name

Personality Disorder Scales (11)

1	Schizoid
2A	Avoidant
2B	Depressive
3	Dependent
4	Histrionic
5	Narcissistic
6A	Antisocial
6B	Sadistic (Aggressive)
7	Compulsive
8A	Negativistic (Passive Aggressive)
8B	Masochistic Self-Defeating

Severe Personality Disorder Scales (3)

S	Schizotypal
C	Borderline
P	Paranoid

Clinical Syndrome Scales (10)

A	Anxiety
H	Somatoform
N	Bipolar: Manic
D	Dysthymia
B	Alcohol Dependence
T	Drug Dependence
R	Posttraumatic Stress Disorder

Severe Syndrome Scales (3)

SS	Thought Disorder
CC	Major Depression
PP	Delusional Disorder

PAI	Scale Name

Validity Scales (4)

ICN	Inconsistency
INF	Infrequency
NIM	Negative Impression
PIM	Positive Impression

Clinical Scales (11)

SOM	Somatic Complaints
ANX	Anxiety
ARD	Anxiety-Related Disorders
DEP	Depression
MAN	Mania
PAR	Paranoia
SCZ	Schizophrenia

(*continued*)

Table 5.1   (*Continued*)

PAI	Scale Name
BOR	Borderline Features
ANT	Antisocial Features
ALC	Alcohol Problems
DRG	Drug Problems
Treatment Scales (5)	
AGG	Aggression
SUI	Suicidal Ideation
STR	Stress
NON	Nonsupport
RXR	Treatment Rejection
Interpersonal Scales (2)	
DOM	Dominance
WRM	Warmth

"True/Agree" and "False/Disagree" Balance

Another decision that must be made is the relative balance of "true/agree" and "false/disagree" responses that are scored in the same direction. If all the scored responses are keyed "true/agree" as an indication of some personality characteristic, a person could be endorsing these items because of a bias to be agreeable or yea-saying, not because of the items' content. If all the scored responses for identifying a symptom or behavior are keyed "false/disagree," a person could be negating them because of a bias to be disagreeable or nay-saying.

Slightly over three-fourths (79%) of the scored responses on the 11 clinical personality pattern scales on the MCMI-III are keyed "true." For 8 of these 11 scales, over 90% of the scored responses are keyed "true." Of the 11 PAI clinical scales, almost three-fourths (74%) of the scored responses are keyed "true," with a range from 54% to 92%. On the five domains of the NEO PI-R, slightly over one-half (56%) of the scored responses are keyed "agree" or "strongly agree," and there are virtually no differences across the domains. Roughly one-half of the scored responses on the 10 MMPI-2 (53%) and MMPI-A (53%) clinical scales are keyed "true," with a range from 22% on Scale *3* (*Hy:* Hysteria) to 81% on Scale *7* (*Pt:* Psychasthenia).

The MMPI-2 and MMPI-A both contain a True Response Consistency (*TRIN*) scale that indicates whether a person is responding to items with a "true" or "false" bias. The Pearson Assessments computer scoring for the MMPI-2 and MMPI-A provides the "true" and "false" percentage at the bottom of the profile for the basic validity and clinical scales. None of the other three self-report inventories indicates whether there is a preponderance of "true/agree" or "false/disagree" responses, nor do the computerized scoring programs for these other inventories report the percentage of "true/agree" or "false/disagree" responses. If a paper-and-pencil format is used for the administration of these other self-report inventories, examiners can at least review the answer sheet to get an impression of the tendency to respond either "true/agree" or "false/disagree." When these inventories are administered by computer and the item responses are not printed out, there is no way currently to ascertain the "true/agree" or "false/disagree" percentage.

Items Written in the Affirmative or Negative

Items written in an affirmative manner are easier for test developers to create and easier for test takers to respond to than items written in the negative, which is one reason for the preponderance of affirmative items on self-report inventories. An item like "I am in good health" is straightforward, whether the person wants to say "true/agree" or "false/disagree." An item written in the negative, as in "I do not get angry often," can be challenging to interpret. The meaning of a "true/agree" response to this item is fairly clear, but it is much less clear what saying "false/disagree" actually means. Is the person saying that he or she gets angry often, or gets angry sometimes but not often, or something else entirely? Reading items written in the negative when the person wants to respond "false/disagree" can be a complex task. This complexity is not reflected in the estimated reading level required for each of the self-report inventories being discussed.

Items Used on More Than One Scale

Once an item has been selected for a specific scale, test developers must decide whether that item can be used again on another scale. Creating items is a difficult and time-consuming process, and fewer items are needed if at least some of them can be used on more than one scale. Part of the decision-making process of whether an item should be scored on more than one scale (known as *item overlap*) is a trade-off between the total number of items desired on a self-report inventory and the relative independence of the individual scales. A self-report inventory that can use a single item for several different scales will need a smaller number of total items than a self-report inventory that requires scoring only a single scale. Although items that are used on more than one scale are typically scored in the same direction, this does not have to be the case. A test item can easily be scored as "true/agree" on one scale and "false/disagree" on another scale. The MMPI-2 and MMPI-A are the two self-report inventories in which the same items are most frequently scored in an opposite manner on different scales.

More specifically, the NEO PI-R and PAI do not have any overlapping items; every item on these inventories is scored only on one scale. The MCMI-III, MMPI-2, and MMPI-A include numerous items that are on two, three, and sometimes even more scales. Scales *7 (Pt:* Psychasthenia) and *8 (Sc:* Schizophrenia) on the MMPI-2 and MMPI-A share 17 (35%) items. On the MCMI-III, Scales *6A* (Antisocial) and *6B* (Sadistic [Aggressive]) share 8 (47%) items, and Scales *4* (Histrionic) and *5* (Narcissistic) share 6 items (35%).

The greater the item overlap between two scales, the more statistically correlated they become, no matter how independent the scales were meant to be. Most scales on a self-report inventory have substantial intercorrelations to begin with, because some form of generalized emotional distress is common to most of the scales on self-report inventories that are global measures of psychopathology. The average magnitude of the correlations among the 8 clinical scales on the MMPI-2 and MMPI-A (excluding Scale *5* [*Mf:* Masculinity-Femininity] and Scale *0* [*Si:* Social Introversion]), the 11 clinical personality pattern scales on the MCMI-III, and the 9 clinical scales (excluding Alcohol Problems [*ALC*] and Drug

Problems [*DRG*]) on the PAI is .59, .49, .50, and .50, respectively.[2] Taken together, then, item overlap and generalized emotional distress account for one-fourth (.50 × .50 = 25%) of the variance in these scales. The pervasiveness of this factor of generalized emotional distress is evident in that the average scale intercorrelation on the PAI is virtually identical to the scale intercorrelations on the other three inventories, even though the PAI has no overlapping items.

Breadth and Depth of Items on the Scale

With respect to the breadth and depth of the items selected for a specific scale, a scale measuring a construct like depression has many potential components, including negative cognitive evaluations, dysphoric mood, such physical or vegetative symptoms as fatigue, sleep difficulties, and changes in appetite, social or interpersonal withdrawal and isolation, and suicidal ideation. A decision must be made concerning how many items, if any, should be assigned to each of these components of depression. A minimum of approximately 10 dichotomous items is generally necessary for a scale to provide a reliable estimate of what is being measured. If the decision is made to assign items equally to each of these five components of depression, the total scale will need approximately 50 items. If a test developer is willing to sacrifice the breadth of the scale, then fewer items can be used, but at the price of potentially missing those patients who have components of depression that are not reliably assessed, if at all.

No self-report inventory could contain an adequate number of items to assess every component of all forms of psychopathology without being so long that no one would be willing to complete it. Consequently, test developers are faced with the dilemma of how many forms of psychopathology they can assess and how thorough the assessment can be. Accordingly, the MMPI-2, MMPI-A, and PAI focus primarily on Axis I disorders in the *DSM-IV-TR*, with less emphasis on Axis II, whereas the MCMI-III has just the opposite focus. The NEO PI-R focuses primarily on different dimensions of normal personality with little or no direct attention to psychopathology.

Inherent Ambiguity in the Meaning of Item Content

An assumption is made, whether explicitly or implicitly, that every item on a self-report inventory has a single meaning that is understood by both the person taking the test and the clinician administering it. As mentioned in Chapter 1, the fault with this assumption can readily be illustrated with items like "I am a good mixer." It takes little effort to identify numerous perspectives from which this item can be endorsed, such as the mixing done by a bartender, chef, painter, chemist, pharmacist, sound recorder, light technician, boxer, or socialite. Even though individuals can report accurately that they are a good mixer, examiners have no way of knowing what specific kind of "mixing" is being reported. The tenuousness of assuming a single meaning of items led Hathaway and McKinley (1940) to adopt an empirical method of selecting items for the original MMPI, which is described later

---

[2]These correlations are taken from the *Manuals* for these self-report inventories: MMPI-2 (p. 128); MMPI-A (p. C-3); MCMI-III (p. 65); and PAI (p. 134).

in this chapter. Over the past two decades, the trend in developing self-report inventories has been toward deriving scales rationally rather than empirically, because paying close attention to item content can make scales more sensitive to ambiguity than relying solely on an empirical derivation.

This difficulty of knowing exactly what items mean is also illustrated by the ambiguity introduced by adverbs. When a person says "true/agree" or "false/disagree" to an item like "I have headaches often," just how often does the person have headaches? One person may say "true/agree" because of headaches that occur once a week, whereas another person who has a headache every few days may say "false/disagree." The actual frequency of these persons' headaches could be just the opposite of what their evaluations suggest. One solution to this problem is to omit frequency adverbs for items, but doing so would be at the cost of not getting any estimate of the frequency of the behavior or whether it is problematic for the person. Most of the time, an adverb has to be included in an item for the person to respond to it in any meaningful way. The item "I have headaches" clamors for specification, and a response to it would have almost no informational value.

Potential Biases in Item Content

Several potential biases in item content must be dealt with in selecting the items for a self-report inventory, including biases related to age, gender, ethnicity, education, socioeconomic level, and marital status. After an initial pool of items has been created, most test developers have a panel of judges review them for obvious biases as well as ambiguity in wording and content. They must decide whether potential problems of bias should be dealt with at the item level, at the scale level, or in the standardization of raw scores. At the item level, test developers can select only items that demonstrate minimal effects of bias in the initial validation stage. At the scale level, test developers do not attend to biases in any single item, but instead balance the total items on a scale so that any effects of item bias are canceled out or negated. Thus, one item slightly biased toward men can be balanced by selecting another item that is slightly biased for women. In the standardization of raw scores for the scales on a self-report inventory, gender bias can be avoided by developing separate norms for males and females. This particular solution doubles the number of persons that must be included in the standardization sample for a dichotomous variable (male/female), would triple it for a trichotomous variable (upper class/middle class/lower class), and so on. For this reason, multiple standardization samples as a correction for bias are typically used for only a few mainly dichotomous variables, with gender being most common.

The self-report inventories presented in Chapters 6 through 10 differ in how they handle potential gender bias in their items. The MCMI-III, MMPI-2, MMPI-A, and NEO PI-R use separate norms for men and women; this eliminates differences in response rates by gender to individual items when raw scores are converted to T scores. Only the PAI uses unigender norms. In selecting the final set of items for the PAI, items that had significant correlations with gender were deleted, but some gender differences still remain. In general, mean differences between men and women on the primary PAI scales average 4 T points, which is approximately the standard error of measurement.

Both of these methods for handling item bias are confounded by the fact that some biases may reflect the underlying characteristics of whatever psychopathology is being assessed.

It is well known that symptoms of depression are reported more frequently by women than men, and symptoms of alcohol and drug use are reported more often by men than women (*DSM-IV-TR:* American Psychiatric Association, 2000). In a similar vein, there are ethnic differences in reporting psychological symptoms, age differences in physical energy and activity level, and so on. Attempting to remove these types of biases could result in a scale that does not reflect accurately the conditions, symptoms, or behaviors that the scale is designed to measure.

Weighting Items

After all the items have been selected for a scale, test developers must decide how many points to assign each item when it is answered in the scored direction. On most self-report inventories, examiners merely add the number of items answered in the scored direction, which means that each item has a weight of 1. Multiple weighting of individual items produces some of the same advantages and disadvantages of more response alternatives. Giving some items on a scale a weight of 2 or 3 increases the range of total scores on the scale and can decrease the total number of items required on the self-report inventory. Multiple item weights also allow core or prototypical items to be given more emphasis and thereby contribute additional variance to the scale.

As a disadvantage, hand scoring of a self-report inventory that weights the items is more cumbersome and more likely to lead to errors than scoring unweighted items. When a single template is used for scoring such a scale with multiple item weights, examiners must be especially cognizant of how many points to assign each item when it is endorsed in the scored direction. Only the MCMI-III uses weighting, by assigning 2 points to items on the personality disorder scales that are considered prototypical for that disorder.

A few specific scales on several self-report inventories do use statistical weights (logistic or discriminant functions) for individual items or component scales. The Common Alcohol Logistic scale (Malinchoc, Offord, Colligan, & Morse, 1994) on the MMPI-2 uses logistic weights to compute a total score, and Rogers's (Rogers, Sewell, & Morey, 1992) discriminative function on the PAI weights all the PAI scales to identify individuals who may be trying to simulate schizophrenia, major depression, or anxiety. On the NEO PI-R, calculating the factor scores (*N, E, O, A, C*) by hand is too complex and time consuming to be time- or cost-efficient. The domain scores on the NEO PI-R are more easily scored by hand than the factor scores and provide a close approximation of them. Generally speaking, the complexity of attempting to score or combine statistically weighted scales makes computer scoring almost mandatory.

Despite the inherent difficulty and complexity of developing quality items and organizing them into the many kinds of scales that are discussed here, practitioners and researchers remain undaunted and continue to churn out new self-report inventories at a furious pace. Contemporary editions of *Buros' Mental Measurements Yearbook* list 296 new or revised self-report inventories in the 14th edition (Plake & Impara, 2001), 207 in the 15th edition (Plake et al., 2003), and 198 in the 16th edition (Spies & Plake, 2005). Every 2 years in the present century, then, approximately 200 or more new or revised inventories have been introduced.

ADMINISTRATION AND SCORING

Before administering any self-report inventory for the first time, even experienced clinicians should read the *Manual* and review standard interpretive texts for the inventory. Numerous considerations in using self-report inventories can be overlooked if these materials are not reviewed regularly. Some of these considerations are fairly straightforward and uncomplicated, such as noting the age range for which a self-report inventory is appropriate to administer and using the correct gender profile when there are male/female forms. Other examples include being sure to code on the MCMI-III whether the person is an inpatient or an outpatient, and if an inpatient, the length of hospitalization, because these variables are used in adjusting the base rate scores on this measure (see Chapter 8). The sections that follow address several additional considerations that bring some complexity to administering and scoring self-report inventories, including reading level, method for administering items, standardization of raw scores, and errors in scoring.

Reading Level

Reading level is a crucial factor in determining whether a person can complete a self-report inventory, and inadequate reading ability is a major cause of inconsistent patterns of item endorsement (to be discussed later). It is important to realize that the estimates of the required grade reading level for a specific self-report inventory are typically conservative (i.e., low), because they are based on assessments of the readability of individual items or groups of items. These estimates are not based on the previously mentioned difficulty of understanding what is meant by saying either "true/agree" or "false/disagree" to a specific item.

   This issue of the reading level required to complete self-report inventories becomes a particular concern when it is realized that most freshman-level college texts are written at the ninth-grade level and most newspapers at the sixth-grade level. This means that although more people are receiving more years of education than in the past, the ability to read the items on self-report inventories remains a potential problem. It is also possible for examinees with limited formal education to take these self-report inventories if their reading comprehension is adequate. If assessors suspect that a person's reading level may be deficient, they should ascertain the person's reading level by administering a brief reading test or, as an alternative, ask the person whether reading is difficult and administration with a CD or cassette tape might be easier. Reading level is especially important to consider among ethnic minorities who speak English fluently but may be unable to read it. Persons who cannot read may be reluctant to acknowledge this limitation, and individuals have been known to respond to all the items on a self-report inventory even though they were unable to read them.

   Clinicians are strongly recommended not to read the items on a self-report inventory to an individual, particularly inventories that assess psychopathology (MCMI-III, MMPI-2, MMPI-A, PAI). In addition to requiring an inordinate amount of the clinician's time, reading the items changes the assessment process and makes it no longer comparable to a standard administration of the self-report inventory. Few explicit guidelines exist regarding how much assistance examiners can provide for individuals who have marginal reading skills. It seems reasonable to give standard dictionary definitions of terms if people ask for them, or to allow them to consult a dictionary. Most self-report inventories can be presented by CD or cassette tape, which as just noted can be very helpful to individuals who have limited reading skills but adequate language comprehension (see Table 5.2). If for some reason it seems absolutely necessary to read the items, the examinee should be instructed to record the responses in a private manner, to maintain confidentiality during the examination. In such a situation, consideration should be given to whether a structured clinical interview might be more appropriate than a self-report inventory.

In the case of the NEO PI-R, which is assessing normal personality dimensions, Costa and McCrae (1992) allow for some modification of standard procedures of administration, when necessary. These modifications include reading the test items aloud and marking the person's responses on the answer sheet even though CD and cassette tape versions are available (see Table 5.2). The NEO PI-R also allows the measure to be completed at home, as long as the examiner ensures that all the test materials are returned. Completing self-report inventories at home raises some additional issues that are discussed in the next section.

Method for Administering Items

Self-report inventories customarily provide examinees with a test booklet and an answer sheet on which to indicate their responses to the items. Most self-report inventories can also be administered by computer, and, as noted in discussing reading level, the items can be presented by a CD or cassette tape for people who have difficulty reading them. All these self-report inventories have Spanish versions, and most are available in additional languages as well.

After determining that a person is capable of completing the self-report inventory, the clinician should ensure that the individual is seated comfortably and has a sharpened pencil with an eraser. Using a pencil with an eraser makes it easy for individuals to change any response, should they so wish. Because few problems are likely to occur in the administration of self-report inventories, they can usually be given to small groups of individuals, provided there is sufficient room to respect each person's privacy.

The individual should read the instructions for the self-report inventory, the clinician should answer any questions the person has about them, and then the person taking the test should proceed at his or her own pace to complete it. On occasion, examinees may question the appropriateness of the content of some items. Persons who raise such objections can usually be reassured by being told that their answers will remain confidential and that how they respond to groups of items, rather than to any individual item, is what is important. Should this reassurance be insufficient, examinees may be allowed to omit an objectionable item. The number of such omissions must be kept at a minimum because the validity of the inventory becomes an issue if too many items are omitted, as elaborated later on.

The clinician should be available throughout the test session to respond to any questions that may arise, especially about definitions of unfamiliar words. Even when people are not asking any questions, the examiner should unobtrusively check on their progress in completing the test, especially if they appear confused, to make sure that they are correctly entering answers on the answer sheet. Although it is preferable to have people complete a self-report inventory in a single session, it is not mandatory. If a second session is necessary,

Table 5.2   Comparison of self-report inventories on demographic variables

	MCMI-III	MMPI-2	PAI	PAI	MMPI-A	NEO PI-R
Setting	Clinical	Clinical	Clinical	Clinical	Clinical	Normal
Age Range	Adults	Adults	Adults	Adults	Adolescents	Adults Adolescents
Normative Group	Clinical	Normal	Normal	Clinical	Normal	Normal
Number	600	2,600	1,000	1,265	1,620	1,000
Age	36.7*	41.0	44.2	—	15.6	45.0*
Gender						
Men (%)	41.0	43.8	48.0	61.4	49.7	50.0
Women (%)	59.0	56.2	52.0	38.6	50.3	50.0
Education						
Mean (years)	13.1*	14.7	13.7	—	10.1	14.7
Less than 12 years	17.0	5.0	11.3	19.2	—	—
12 years	30.2	24.6	31.4	31.5	—	—
13–15 years	31.6	25.0	25.4	28.9	—	—
16 years	11.5	26.9	19.3	11.3	—	—
More than 16 years	8.3	18.5	12.6	9.2	—	—
Ethnicity						
White	86.3	81.4	85.1	78.8	76.2	85.1
Hispanic	2.8	—	—	—	2.1	—
Black	8.7	12.1	11.7	12.6	12.3	11.6
Asian	0.3	0.7	—	—	2.8	—
Native American	1.0	3.0	—	—	2.9	—
Other	0.8	—	3.2	8.6	3.6	3.3
Standard Scores	Base Rate Scores	Uniform T Scores	T Scores	T Scores	Uniform T Scores	T Scores
Mean/Median	60	50	50	50	50	50
Standard Deviation	~15	10	10	10	10	10
Elevated	≥60	≥65	≥70	≥70	≥65	≥56
Administer to	18+	18+	18+	18+	13–17	12+
Number of Items	175	567	344	344	478	240
Item Responses						
Format	True/ False	True/ False	True/ False	True/ False	True/ False	Agree/ Disagree
Number	2	2	4	4	2	5
Reading Level	8th	6th	4th	4th	5th–7th	4th
Time to Complete (min)	25–30	60–90	40–50	40–50	90–120	30–40
Administration Format						
Paper/pencil	Yes	Yes	Yes	Yes	Yes	Yes
Computer	Yes	Yes	Yes	Yes	Yes	Yes
Cassette Tape	No	Yes	Yes	Yes	Yes	Yes
CD	Yes	Yes	Yes	Yes	Yes	Yes
Languages						
Spanish	Yes	Yes	Yes	Yes	Yes	Yes
Additional	No	Yes	Yes	Yes	Yes	Yes
Sign	No	Yes	No	No	No	No

*These values were estimated from the ranges of data provided in the *Manual* (Millon, Davis, & Millon, 1997).

every effort should be made to have the inventory completed within a few days, to minimize the possibility of any significant changes in the individual's current status during the testing period. Because the length of an inventory may appear formidable if it must be completed in a single session, persons being tested are frequently relieved to know that they can take some breaks during the session or even be allowed to complete it over a few days' time. Being sensitive to a person's needing to complete an inventory over a period of days and allowing the person to do so should increase the likelihood of obtaining a valid administration.

Standardization of Raw Scores

Most self-report inventories convert raw scores on the inventory to some form of standard score, although the standard score that is used varies widely. Knowing the individual's standard score on a specific scale is important for two reasons. First, it shows how the individual scored on the scale compared with the group on whom the inventory was standardized. Knowing that an individual has a raw score of 26 on some scale means virtually nothing, but knowing that the person scored at the 50th percentile on this scale tells the clinician that the person's score on this scale is at the mean of the standardization group. Second, standard scores enable clinicians to compare an individual's scores on the various scales with one another. Knowing that an individual has a raw score of 26 on one scale and 39 on another scale means very little; knowing that the individual has a score at the 50th percentile on one scale and the 90th percentile on the other, however, allows assessors to determine the relative deviation from average and the interpretive importance of these two scales for this specific individual.

Table 5.3 lists the various standard scores that are used on self-report inventories and how they are related to each other. All these standard scores, except the uniform T scores used with the MMPI-2 and MMPI-A and the base rate scores used with the MCMI-III, are *linear* standard scores, because they are linear transformations of the raw scores that maintain the underlying distributions of the raw scores. The linear and uniform T scores have a mean of 50 and a standard deviation of 10. Thus, a T score of 70 is two standard deviations above the mean of 50 and is at the 97.5 percentile, meaning that only 2.5% of the standardization sample had a higher score. The percentile equivalents of other T scores are provided in Table 5.3.

Inherent in the use of linear standard scores is the assumption that these scores have similar distributions from one scale to the next; the standard score has the same probability of occurrence on each scale. However, this assumption is valid only if the scales involved have similar distributions. If the underlying raw score distributions for each scale are not similar, which is typically the case, then a standard score will not be equivalent across the scales. These differences in the probability of occurrence of the linear standard score across scales tend to be relatively minor, and in most cases are less than the standard error of measurement.

Assessors should realize that small differences in linear standard scores between two scales are not statistically reliable and even less likely to be clinically meaningful. A good rule of thumb for inferring a reliable and meaningful difference is to require the difference between two scales to exceed the standard error of measurement (the random error that is associated with any score). Standard errors of measurement are used to create confidence intervals around the scores that an individual obtains on a given scale. If the standard error

Table 5.3   Comparison of standard scores and standard errors of measurement

		WAIS-III	MCMI-III	NEO PI-R PAI	MMPI-2 MMPI-A
Percentiles	Z Scores	IQ Scores	Base Rate	Linear T Scores	Uniform T Scores
99	3.00	145	—	80	80
97.5	2.00	130	—	70	70
93	—	—	85	65	65
90	—	—	—	—	—
84	1.00	115	—	60	60
75	—	—	—	—	—
70	—	—	75	—	—
60	—	—	—	—	—
55	—	—	—	—	50
50	0.00	100	60	50	—
40	—	—	—	—	—
30	—	—	—	—	—
25	—	—	—	—	—
16	−1.00	85	—	40	40
10	—	—	—	—	—
2.5	−2.00	70	—	30	30
1	−3.00	—	—	—	—

of measurement for a scale is 4 points, then two-thirds of the time, an individual's true score on the scale will be within plus or minus 4 points of the obtained score.

Linear transformations of raw scores into standard scores also assume that the underlying forms of psychopathology or scale content are equally prevalent, which is not the case. Referring once more to the *DSM-IV-TR* (American Psychiatric Association, 2000) for examples, widely varying prevalences characterize Major Depressive Disorder (men, 5% to 12%; women, 10% to 25%); Schizophrenia (1.0%); Antisocial Personality Disorder (men, 3%; women, 1%); and Borderline Personality Disorder (men, 0.5%; women, 2.0%). The MCMI-III is the only self-report inventory being discussed that uses base rate scores derived from the prevalence of forms of psychopathology, instead of some form of T, as a standard score. The base rates for the MCMI-III scale scores were created to tie the probability of elevating a specific scale to the prevalence of being assessed by the scale. The development and use of base rate scores with the MCMI-III is elaborated in Chapter 8.

The methodology for the derivation of uniform T scores that are used with the MMPI-2 and MMPI-A is fairly complex and is described in detail by Tellegen and Ben-Porath (1992). Suffice it to say that uniform T scores create uniform percentiles across the MMPI-2 and MMPI-A scales, so that two scales with the same uniform T score have the same probability of occurrence. Uniform T scores adjust for the different probabilities across scales that occur with linear transformations, but they do not adjust for the differences in the underlying prevalence of disorders, nor do they materially change the shapes of the underlying distributions involved.

When clinicians are interpreting self-report inventories, they need to know the percentile or relative likelihood of a scale score being at a given level, as well as the degree of elevation that would denote clinical significance. Because T scores are used on the MMPI-2, MMPI-A, PAI, and NEO PI-R, comparison among them is relatively straightforward. Comparing the MCMI-III with any of the other self-report inventories is complicated by the use of base rate rather than T standard scores.

The MMPI-2 and MMPI-A use a T score of 65 or more to denote clinical significance, and the PAI uses a T score of 70 or more. A base rate score of 75 on the MCMI-III indicates the presence of a personality disorder trait or clinical syndrome, and a base rate score of 85 indicates the presence of a personality disorder or prominence of a clinical syndrome. Roughly speaking, a T score of 65 on the MMPI-2, MMPI-A, PAI, and NEO PI-R and a base rate score of 85 on the MCMI-III are at the 92nd percentile (see Table 5.3).

Errors in Scoring

Little attention has been paid to the problem of scoring errors in self-report inventories, perhaps because the accuracy of scoring has been almost taken for granted. At first blush, it seems nonsensical to inquire about the accuracy of scoring a scale when all that is required is for examiners to count the number of responses that a person has made in the deviant or scored direction, a skill that is well learned by the 2nd or 3rd grade. However, to elaborate some surprising research on this matter that was mentioned in Chapter 2, Allard and Faust (2000) found that 20 (13.3%) out of 150 administrations of the Beck Depression Inventory, 56 (28.7%) of 300 administrations of the State-Trait Anxiety Inventory, and 22 (14.7%) of 150 administrations of the MMPI had scoring errors of some kind. The frequency of scoring errors on these three self-report inventories ranged from 2% to 51% across three different clinical settings (Veterans Affairs inpatient, Veterans Affairs outpatient, and private inpatient).

The Test User Qualification Group established by the American Psychological Association (Moreland, Eyde, Robertson, Primoff, & Most, 1995) stated that avoiding errors in scoring and recording—the first of 12 minimum test user's competencies—may not be met by all clinicians. It may well be that many clinicians comfortably assume that their scoring is accurate, without verifying whether this is the case, and assume that the scoring errors found in research studies are made by clinicians less careful than they. It is essential for clinicians to verify their scoring of self-report inventories, because the ensuing steps in providing a psychodiagnostic consultation can be no better than the data that are generated at this stage in the assessment process.

When self-report inventories are scored by hand, errors almost always lower the raw scores, because deviant responses are the ones being summed, and one or two items can easily be missed. If the data are entered into a computer for scoring without verification, errors of data entry can either raise or lower the raw scores, because erroneous entries can produce either "deviant/scored" or "nondeviant/nonscored" responses to items. An advantage of computer administration of self-report inventories, as noted in Chapter 2, is that computer scoring eliminates this source of error. However, errors in computer scoring and profiling of score results are not unheard of, which means that assessors cannot assume that using a computer to administer and score a self-report inventory will eliminate all potential sources of error.

Even though computer scoring of self-report inventories may not be perfect, and without losing sight of the potential drawbacks of computerized administration mentioned in

Chapter 2 (see p. 29), there is good reason to recommend automated scoring, whether responses are entered by the person being examined or entered manually by the examiner. Hand scoring is neither efficient nor cost-effective given the time it takes to score all the scales on an inventory, and the propensity to errors. Moreover, examiners who hand-score a self-report inventory may be tempted not to score all the numerous possible scales and sub-scales and thereby sacrifice information that would have been valuable for the interpretive process.

It is estimated that from one-half to two-thirds of MMPI-2s are still hand scored. The Variable Response Inconsistency (*VRIN*) and True Response Inconsistency (*TRIN*) scales on the MMPI-2 and MMPI-A are the scales most likely to be omitted from hand scoring, because of the complex process necessary to determine them. Of further note, Iverson and Barton (1999) found in reviewing 55 hand-scored MMPI-2 protocols that 15 (27%) of them had scoring errors on *VRIN*. Working with a missing or an erroneous *VRIN* score deprives examiners of valuable information concerning whether a person has endorsed items consistently. Similarly on the PAI, the Inconsistency (*ICN*) scale is likely to be omitted from hand scoring because of its complexity. Hand-scoring errors commonly occur on the MCMI-III when raw scores are converted into base rate scores and scale scores are adjusted according to these base rates, again because of the complexity of the process (Millon et al., 1997).

STANDARDIZATION (NORMATIVE) GROUP

The raw scores on the scales for most self-report inventories are standardized on groups of normal individuals, which are accordingly termed a *standardization* or *normative* group. Table 5.2 provides the basic demographic variables of the standardization group for the five self-report inventories discussed in Chapters 6 through 10. The standardization groups for these inventories are all large and almost equally divided between men and women. As noted in introducing this chapter, all the inventories being discussed except for the MCMI-III used normal individuals as the standardization group. The MCMI-III used only clinical patients as its standardization group, and the PAI was standardized on both normal and clinical patient groups.

The persons in the standardization groups for the four adult self-report inventories average around 40 years of age and 13 to 14 years of education (see Table 5.2). Over three-fourths of the standardization groups are Caucasian, with non-Caucasian groups represented roughly in accord with their prevalence in the United States Census. The presence of minority group members in the standardization samples does not by itself address whether these groups differ systematically in their responses to the inventory. Possible effects of race, culture, and ethnicity on these inventories are discussed in the specific chapters devoted to them.

In other respects as well, there is considerable similarity among the standardization groups for the four adult self-report inventories. This similarity occurs because census parameters were used as general guidelines in selecting individuals for the normative samples. Only the MMPI-2 deviates substantially from these census parameters, in that its standardization group includes more individuals at the higher levels of education and fewer individuals at the lower levels of education than the other inventories.

METHOD OF SCALE DEVELOPMENT

There are three basic methods of selecting the items for use in a self-report inventory: empirical (criterion) keying, rational (theoretical) selection, and factorial selection. The MMPI-2 and MMPI-A were developed by empirical methods, and the MCMI-III, PAI, and NEO PI-R were developed with rational methods, although the NEO PI-R is based on a factor-analytic method of identifying dimensions of personality. Each of these methods for selecting items in scale construction is examined next, along with considerations in the naming of the scales on which they are scored.

Constructing Scales

In empirical keying, a criterion group and a comparison group are tested, and items that differentiate between them become the items on a scale for measuring whether people resemble the criterion group. These items are selected from an initial item pool that test developers accumulate using a variety of sources. Because the items comprising a scale are going to be selected empirically, little attention is paid to the adequacy or comprehensiveness with which items in the pool sample any specific set of symptoms or behaviors.

The construction of the MMPI-2 clinical scales exemplifies this empirical methodology. In developing Scale *1* (*Hs:* Hypochondriasis) on the original MMPI, Hathaway and McKinley (1940) contrasted the responses of a criterion group of hypochondriacal patients with a comparison group of normal individuals on all the items in the MMPI item pool. Items that differentiated these two groups became the set of items on Scale *1* (*Hs:* Hypochondriasis). This method of empirically selecting items results in heterogeneous sets of items, some of which may not have any apparent relationship with the criterion group. Individuals who endorse the items on Scale *1* (*Hs:* Hypochondriasis) in the scored direction are responding to the items in the same way as members of the criterion group. However, it cannot be said that these individuals are necessarily hypochondriacal, because they may share common characteristics with hypochondriacal patients other than core features of hypochrondriasis. Additional research is always required to determine the meaning or correlates of an empirically keyed scale. Among the well-established correlates of Scale *1* (*Hs:* Hypochondriasis), persons with elevated scores (T > 64) will spend more time in rehabilitation, will use more pain medication, and are more likely to be in litigation than persons who do not elevate on this scale (Greene, 2000).

In rational or theoretical selection of items for a scale, test developers start with an explicit definition of the scale and then select or create items to fit that definition. If a depression scale is being developed rationally, a test developer would begin by formulating an explicit definition of the construct of depression that includes all the behaviors and symptoms expected to characterize persons with depression. Items would then be written to fit this construct and its expected behavioral and symptomatic manifestations. This initial group of items would be reviewed by a panel of judges for ambiguity in meaning, consistency with, and representativeness of the construct of depression. Once items were corrected as much as possible for ambiguities and judged to be consistent with and representative of the construct of depression, the test developer would begin the validation process by administering them to a group of depressed individuals and various comparison groups. Items that did not differentiate the depressed group from the comparison groups would either be deleted or rewritten and revalidated. This refining process would continue until the test developer was satisfied that the set of items adequately measured the construct of depression.

It should be readily apparent that any differences in the presence or absence of specific behaviors or symptoms in the initial definition of depression can result in rationally derived depression scales containing very different items. The test developer must decide whether dangerousness to self is a component of depression, and if so, how much emphasis should be placed on it in the total set of items. One scale measuring depression may not include any dangerousness-to-self items, possibly because the test developer also has a rationally derived suicide scale. Another scale measuring depression may have a number of dangerousness-to-self items because the test developer believes that they tap a core aspect of depression. This issue can be illustrated by comparing two rationally derived scales of depression on the MMPI-2, Content Depression (*DEP*) and Wiggins's Depression (*DEP*). Both scales consist of 33 items, yet they have only 16 items in common and correlate .88.

In factorial selection of items for a personality assessment scale, test developers start with a large pool of items, usually involving personality descriptors or trait adjectives, and then use multivariate procedures to identify common groupings among them. Factor-analytic studies of personality descriptors and trait adjectives served as the basis for the five-factor models of personality that are currently prominent in personality theory and research. The NEO PI-R exemplifies such a five-factor model, but it is classified as a rationally developed inventory because its items were selected to fit this model.

Naming of Scales

Each of the three methods of scale construction has a typical way of naming its scales. An empirically derived scale is customarily named for the criterion group that was used to develop it; a rationally derived scale is named for the construct that served as the basis for its development and guided the writing of its items; and a factorially derived scale is named for the core factor common to the items on it.

Scales with the same or similar names derived by these different methods often vary substantially in their intercorrelations and number of shared items. To draw an example from the original MMPI, it includes—in addition to the empirically developed Scale 2 (*D:* Depression)—the Wiggins content scale of Depression (*DEP*), which was developed rationally, and the TSC Cluster scale of Depression (*D*), which was developed by cluster analysis, a variation of factor analysis. Table 5.4 shows the number of items on each of these three depression scales and their intercorrelations. There are a total of 95 different items on these three scales, 75 of which are unique to just one of them. Only six items appear on all three scales. The correlations show that the Wiggins content scale of Depression (*DEP*) and the TSC Cluster scale of Depression (*D*) are virtually identical ($r = .90$), even though they share only 14 (42.4%) items. Scale 2 (*D:* Depression) shares about one-quarter of its variance ($.52 \times .52 = .27$) with these other two depression scales. Hence these three depression scales with the same name are undoubtedly sampling different aspects of depression.

Table 5.5 shows the intercorrelations for depression scales on the MCMI-III, MMPI-2, and PAI. All these correlations are in the range .63 to .70. Hence these depression scales appear to measure some common components of depression, but still over one-half

Table 5.4   Item overlap and intercorrelations among MMPI scales with the same name

	Wiggins's Content Depression (*DEP*) 33 items [rational]	TSC-Cluster Depression (*D*) 28 items [factorial]
Item Overlap		
Scale 2 (*D*: Depression) [empirical] 60 items	8	9
Content Depression (*DEP*) [rational] 33 items	—	14
Intercorrelations		
Scale 2 (*D*: Depression) [empirical] 60 items	.52	.55
Content Depression (*DEP*) [rational] 33 items	—	.90

($.70 \times .70 = 49\%$) of the variance of each scale is accounted for by components that are unique to that scale.

As these examples make clear, assessors cannot take the scale names from two inventories literally and expect them to be measuring the same construct. Experience over time with frequent use of a specific self-report inventory is usually necessary to grasp these nuances and appreciate how they affect the interpretative process. This process becomes particularly challenging when clinicians are faced with integrating results from two or more self-report inventories they have administered into a coherent report.

VALIDITY ASSESSMENT

Assessment of the validity of a specific administration of a self-report inventory is usually limited to inventories that are standardized against clinical samples. Self-report inventories designed for use with normal individuals, such as the NEO PI-R, typically have no or few

Table 5.5   Intercorrelations across self-report inventories for depression scales

MCMI-III Dysthymia (*D*)	
MMPI-2 Scale 2 (*D*: Depression)	.68
MCMI-III Major Depression (*CC*)	
MMPI-2 Scale 2 (*D*: Depression)	.71
Personality Assessment Inventory Depression (*DEP*)	
MMPI-2 Scale 2 (*D*: Depression)	.66

Note: These correlations are reported in the *Manuals* for these inventories: MCMI-III, pp. 105, 107; and PAI, p. 184.

validity scales. The deemphasis on validity assessment in these latter inventories reflects an assumption that there is no reason to expect individuals to distort their responses on them and therefore no reason to assess it. This assumption is probably warranted, mainly because the item content of the NEO PI-R and similarly standardized inventories tends to be fairly innocuous, particularly when compared with the item content on inventories intended for examining clinical samples. Self-report inventories that are designed for evaluating aspects of psychological disorder, including the MCMI-III, MMPI-A, MMPI-2, and PAI, assume that some type of distortion is often likely to occur and include various scales for detecting it.

Several sequential steps need to be carried out in ascertaining the validity of a specific administration of a self-report inventory that is being used to assess the presence and severity of psychopathology or adjustment difficulties in a person being examined. The issues involved in this process, which are common to all self-report inventories, are discussed in general terms in this chapter and with specific reference to individual inventories in Chapters 6 through 10. Following a note concerning the concept of validity in self-report assessment, this chapter addresses sequential considerations related to (a) providing a collaborative and therapeutic assessment; (b) noting the number of items that must be answered to allow for scoring of scales, or alternatively, the number of items that can be omitted without disallowing scoring; (c) determining the consistency with which the items have been endorsed; and (d) determining the accuracy with which the items have been endorsed. An overview of these steps appears in Figure 5.1.

The Concept of Validity in Self-Report Assessment

The concept of validity has traditionally meant the degree to which a test actually measures what it purports to measure (see Chapter 3). A graduate school aptitude test is valid to the extent that it identifies students who will succeed in graduate school. The validity of the

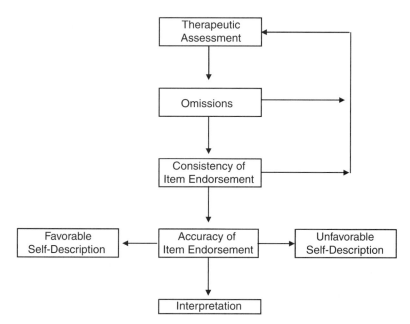

Figure 5.1   Flow chart for assessing validity.

test would be indicated by the relationship between scores on the test and some index of success in graduate school, such as grade-point average or completion of a graduate degree. Similarly with the MCMI-III, MMPI-2, and PAI, the overall relationship of the test to some external criterion (e.g., its accuracy in predicting variables like psychiatric diagnosis and length of hospitalization) would be an index of its validity.

The concept of validity in the administration of a self-report inventory has a second, somewhat different meaning. It describes the test-taking attitudes of an individual, that is, whether the individual has endorsed the test items consistently and accurately or has instead endorsed them in some distorted manner. If a person has provided a consistent and accurate self-description when responding to the items on a self-report inventory, the administration of the inventory is considered to be valid. Hence it is possible for a person to give a valid set of responses on one occasion, an invalid set at another time, and a valid set on a third testing. In this second context, then, validity refers to how individuals have gone about deciding which items to endorse—whether consistently and accurately—and not to the validity of the inventory as reflected in the accuracy of predictions based on it.

Clinicians need to be aware of these alternate meanings of validity in psychodiagnostic assessment. They should also recognize that the consistency of item endorsement within a single administration of a self-report inventory would be described more appropriately by the term *reliability* than by referring to it as validity. Moreover, people can endorse inventory items in a consistently distorted pattern that makes them appear more or less disturbed than they actually are. In other words, a consistent set of responses may be inaccurate and hence not valid at all. Using the term *validity* in referring to the dependability of a test administration has a long history, however, and attempts to convince several generations of clinicians to use more appropriate terms have little likelihood of success.

Collaborative and Therapeutic Assessment

The first consideration in administering a self-report inventory is ensuring that the individual is invested in the process. Spending a few extra minutes answering any questions the person may have about why the inventory is being administered and how the results will be used typically pays excellent dividends. Fischer (1994) has described individualizing psychological assessment so that the individual and the clinician collaborate to obtain the desired information. Finn (1996a) has described how to make the assessment process with the MMPI-2 therapeutic for the individual in ways that apply to any test administration. These aspects of conducting collaborative and therapeutic assessments are elaborated in Chapter 2, but some additional information concerning the work of Fischer and Finn is relevant to the present discussion.

The major thesis of Fischer's and Finn's texts is that clinicians should determine in advance what an individual who is to be tested wants to learn from the assessment process and should then make sure that the person receives it. Finn (1996a, 1996b) provides specific examples of how people might be given feedback about troublesome behaviors and symptoms that clinicians just learning this process will find instructive. An individual who is reporting an unusual significant amount of generalized emotional distress might be told, "You reported a great deal of distress, and it is possible that you may have downplayed some of your strengths to make sure that I heard how much you are hurting." An individual who is concerned about relationship difficulties might be told the following:

You are not sure how safe it is to get close to others. You start worrying about whether you might get hurt if something goes wrong and you will not be able to cope with all of the feelings associated with such a loss. At times, these feelings become so strong that you start thinking that you might be overwhelmed by them. Consequently, it is quite easy and natural for you to start having second thoughts, once someone starts to express an interest in getting close to you.

Examiners who follow the procedures suggested by Fischer and Finn should find that they help reduce the frequency of validity issues. Individuals who genuinely want to learn something from completing a self-report inventory and are active participants or collaborators in the process have little reason for trying to take the test in some inappropriate or misleading manner.

Item Omissions

Although the instructions for all self-report inventories encourage individuals to respond to all items, people often cannot or will not respond to one or more items. Omissions also include items in which people have given more than one response alternative, as in marking both "true" "false," or have placed a mark that does not fit within any of the spaces for a response on the answer sheet. Individuals sometimes write comments on the answer sheet about items they are omitting, and these comments should be read carefully. There are several reasons people may decide not to respond to certain items on a self-report inventory: (a) they may not be able to respond to a specific item because they are not familiar with or have no experience with the item content; (b) they may believe that neither a "true" or "false" response is appropriate, because the item is true for them some of the time and false at other times; (c) in personnel settings, job applicants may believe, quite appropriately, that such item content as religious beliefs or sexual practices is not relevant to the position they are seeking; and (d) in forensic settings, parents being evaluated as part of a child custody dispute may think that an item needs explanation or qualification beyond what they can give with a true/false or agree/disagree response.

All self-report inventories have a minimum number of items that must be answered to make the resulting scores reliable. For some self-report inventories, the number of items that can be omitted has been determined on the basis of research studies, whereas in others the excessive number of item omissions or the minimum number of required responses is simply stated. In either case, examiners need to be aware of the criterion for excessive item omissions on an inventory they are using and before ending the test check a person's sheet carefully to make sure that the individual has not exceeded this limit. Most individuals omit only a small number of items, and these omissions are usually dispersed throughout the inventory, which means that they may not be spotted with only a cursory glance at the answer sheet. In perusing the answer sheet carefully, the clinician should mark any item that has been omitted and encourage the examinee to go back and reconsider whether the item can be answered.

One of the few disadvantages of computer administration of self-report inventories is that the omitted items cannot be determined until the inventory is scored, by which time the examinee may no longer be available to look at them again. If suppression of item level responses is chosen when the inventory is computer scored, the clinician must rely on the computer profiling and interpretation of the inventory to include a listing of the omitted items. Every self-report inventory indicates the number of omitted items, but the ease of accessing this information varies from one inventory to another. Examiners using a self-report inventory that has been computer administered and computer scored with suppression of printing of item level data should note whether omitted items are listed in a manner that makes them easy to review.

In standard scoring procedures, as mentioned, omitted items are considered to be answered in the nondeviant direction, because only items answered in the deviant direction are counted. Hence item omissions have the potential effect of lowering the elevation of scales on which they are scored, inasmuch as the individual, if answering them, might have given a deviant response. Most scales on self-report inventories comprise 20 to 25 items and have a standard deviation of approximately 3 items. Thus examinees have to omit only three items on a given scale that they would have endorsed in the deviant direction to lower the total score by one standard deviation ($\sim$10 T points). Because scale scores can be lowered quickly and substantially by omission of just a few items for persons who have omitted numerous items, it is important to identify the specific scales on which these omissions have occurred. Clinicians also need to review the content of omitted items to determine if there is any common theme to them. Individuals should be queried in particular about omission of any items related to dangerousness to self or dangerousness to others, and their explanation of these omissions should be recorded.

Despite the importance of checking to see if people have omitted any items and identifying the scales on which these items are scored, this step is frequently overlooked in scoring self-report inventories, mainly because items are omitted rather infrequently. The usual dispersion of omitted items throughout an inventory that can make them difficult to detect also fosters the impression that items are omitted infrequently. Moreover, of the inventories being discussed, only the MMPI-A and the MMPI-2 indicate the number of omitted items on their profile sheet. The computerized scoring of the MMPI-A and MMPI-2 by Pearson Assessments also identifies the specific scales on which the omitted items are scored.

Implementation of Flowchart in Figure 5.1

No specific scales are provided in Figure 5.1 for deciding whether an excessive number of items have been omitted or whether items have been endorsed inconsistently or inaccurately. The figure shows only the generic process described in this chapter for assessing the validity of a self-report inventory. Because self-report inventories differ in the specific scales they use for making these decisions about the validity of an assessment, the main inventory-specific scales for this purpose are discussed in Chapters 6 through 10. Percentiles are provided in Chapters 6 through 10 for each of these inventory-specific scales to assist in making assessment validity decisions, but no particular percentile for any scale is suggested as indicating whether the number of items omitted is excessive or whether the items have been endorsed inconsistently or inaccurately. Instead, the text presents the range of percentiles for each scale and allows examiners to choose how stringent a criterion to use in making their decisions. Cutting scores in the range of the 93rd percentile (1.5 standard deviations above the mean) to the 99th percentile (2.0 standard deviations above the mean) are typically appropriate in most settings.

There are several reasons absolute criteria cannot be provided for specific scales in implementing the flowchart in Figure 5.1. First, any interpretive statement generated from a self-report inventory is a hypothesis that must be considered along with other available data. With respect to validity assessment, a conclusion that a person has endorsed the items on a test inconsistently must be evaluated in the context of the person's intellectual level, reading ability, reasons for being evaluated, motivation for possibly endorsing the items inconsistently, and the total number of items endorsed inconsistently.

Second, the relative costs of false positive (identifying a valid profile as invalid) or false negative (identifying an invalid profile as valid) decisions must be weighed in each setting to determine the optimal cutting score for a validity scale. Consider the far-reaching consequences of hypothesizing that an individual has endorsed the items inaccurately when the person is being evaluated for a disability and the amount of compensation will depend on the extent and severity of the disability. The clinician in this instance might use a relatively stringent criterion (slightly higher percentile) when there are substantial external data to document the existence of a disability, to be sure that the appropriate decision is made. A less stringent criterion (slightly lower percentile) might be appropriate when the circumstances supporting the disability are not fully trustworthy and the amount and severity of the distress being reported are not commensurate with the clinical history.

Third, individuals do not experience the same type and severity of psychological distress in response to the same traumatic event, nor can they be expected to report their distress in the same manner. Not all persons who experience a traumatic event are traumatized by it, and those who are traumatized are not all affected in the same manner and to the same degree. For all these reasons, absolute criteria are not viable in making assessment validity decisions, and clinicians making these decisions must take into account all the available data that may be relevant to making them wisely.

Consistency of Item Endorsement

After any omitted items have been identified, the number of omitted items determined not to be excessive, and the thematic content of these omitted items reviewed, the next step in assessing the validity of an administration of a self-report inventory is to verify the consistency of item endorsement (see Figure 5.1). Consistency of item endorsement verifies that the individual has endorsed the items in a reliable manner for this specific administration of the self-report inventory. It is necessary to ensure that an individual has endorsed the items consistently before proceeding to evaluate the accuracy with which the person has endorsed the items.

Another way of understanding the difference between the consistency and accuracy of item endorsement may clarify why they are distinct steps in assessing the validity of a self-report inventory administration. Think of the consistency of item endorsement as being independent of or irrelevant to item content, whereas the accuracy of item endorsement is dependent on or relevant to item content. In other words, measures of the consistency of item endorsement assess whether people have provided a reliable pattern of responding to the items throughout the test, regardless of their content, whereas measures of the accuracy of item endorsement assess whether people have attempted to distort their responses to particular items in some specific manner.

There are two general classes of reasons for providing an inconsistent pattern of item endorsement: (1) lack of necessary skills, including reading disability, limited intellectual ability, inadequate language comprehension, and disorders that impair attention and concentration; and (2) unwillingness to comply with the assessment process. Approximately three-fourths of the instances of inconsistent item endorsement on the MMPI-2 are caused by lack of the necessary skills (Greene, 2000). In most of these instances, the cause of the inconsistent item endorsement can be determined and addressed in an appropriate manner, and the self-report inventory can then be successfully readministered.

If reading comprehension skills are causing inconsistent item endorsement, the self-report inventory can be presented by a CD or cassette tape, as mentioned earlier. Table 5.3 indicates which self-report inventories have CD or cassette tape versions available. If a neurological or psychiatric condition is causing inconsistent item endorsement, the self-report inventory can be readministered once the person's attention and concentration difficulties have been alleviated. If noncompliance is the cause of the inconsistent item endorsement, this issue should be addressed directly. Noncompliance during an assessment can generalize to similar negative attitudes during subsequent therapeutic interventions, and it can have a negative influence on decisions that are made about a person who is being evaluated for forensic or personnel selection purposes. In instances of noncompliance, examiners should review their administrative process to make sure that they have not contributed to the problem by failing to provide a sufficiently comfortable and therapeutic testing atmosphere. More often than not, noncompliance reflects test-taking attitudes for which examinees bear responsibility, and examiners should consider advising noncompliant persons to complete the inventory again, in a more appropriate manner, for their own good and to provide an interpretable test record.

It is important to recognize that psychopathology by itself does not cause people to endorse self-report items inconsistently. Patients can be floridly psychotic and still endorse the items in a consistent manner, as long as they are lucid enough to follow the instructions for completing the inventory and understand how to fill out the answer sheet or respond to the items on the computer. Inconsistent item endorsement appears more frequently on some diagnostic groups than others, particularly among those in which, as in Antisocial Personality Disorder, noncompliance is a relatively common characteristic.

There are three general methods for evaluating the consistency of item endorsement in self-report inventories. The first method involves repeating a certain number of items verbatim within the inventory and then evaluating the number of times an individual provides different responses to these items. The Test-Retest Index (TR Index; Dahlstrom, Welsh, & Dahlstrom, 1972) on the original MMPI, which consisted of 16 items repeated verbatim, is the only instance of this method in the self-report inventories being discussed. This method for assessing consistency of item endorsement provides an easy way of demonstrating their inconsistency to individuals who have been inconsistent in their responses. Being shown only two or three pairs of identical items to which they have given different answers is usually sufficient for them to see the nature of the problem. This first method of paired identical items is not used in any current self-report inventory, because individuals taking the original MMPI were often bothered by the repeated items and expressed their dislike to examiners.

The second method involves using sets of items with similar, but not identical, content to evaluate the consistency of item endorsement. This second method is used frequently in self-report inventories, as illustrated by the Carelessness scale (*CLS;* Greene, 1978) on the original MMPI, the Variable Response Consistency scale (*VRIN*) and True Response Consistency scale (*TRIN*) on the MMPI-2 (Butcher et al., 1989) and MMPI-A (Butcher et al., 1992), and the Inconsistency scale (*ICN*) on the PAI (Morey, 1991). People are less likely to be aware of and concerned about the recurrence of similar items than they are about items repeated verbatim. A disadvantage of this second method is that not even the most careful selection of pairs of items can eliminate circumstances in which individuals can honestly respond to the items in what appears to be an inconsistent manner. For example, consider the pair of items, "I almost never dream" and "I dream frequently." Most people will endorse one of these items true and the other item false, and that is in fact the manner in which this pair of items is typically endorsed (see Greene, 1980, p. 55). Yet individuals could endorse both of them as false because they dream some of the time.

The third method of evaluating consistency of item endorsement uses a set of items with implausible content. When a person endorses too many of these items, the items are deemed to be endorsed inconsistently. An item like "I frequently travel to Jupiter and Pluto to visit friends" is clearly implausible and unlikely to be endorsed by anyone who has read it. Some individuals will consider items of this kind demeaning to them and to the assessment process, so they need to be used judiciously. Both the MCMI-III Validity Index (*V*) and the PAI Infrequency scale (*INF*) use this third method of implausible items to assess consistency of item endorsement.

Most normal individuals are more inconsistent in endorsing the items on a self-report inventory than might be expected. On the original MMPI, a typical normal individual would endorse four (25%) of the 16 pairs of repeated items in an inconsistent manner (Greene, 1980). Normal individuals typically endorse about five pairs of items on the Variable Response Inconsistency scale (*VRIN*) on the MMPI-2 (Table 6.1), about three pairs of items on the Variable Response Inconsistency scale (*VRIN*) on the MMPI-A (Table 7.1), and four pairs of items on the Inconsistency scale (*ICN*) on the PAI in an inconsistent manner (Table 9.1).

Clinicians need to be aware of the pattern of scores that results on each self-report inventory when the items have been endorsed in a random manner, which is the most extreme form of inconsistent item endorsement. A way of simulating inconsistent responses involves generating item responses based on repeated patterns of item endorsements, such as TF/TF/TF TTF/TTF/FFT, FFT/FFT/FFT, and so on. Huba (1986) has developed a statistical test to assess whether a person switches between true and false responses more or less often than would be expected by chance. The test requires computer scoring of the inventory and implements a search for all specific sequences of stereotyped responses. Somewhat surprisingly, his test has not been implemented in any self-report inventory.

Clinicians also should be familiar with the profile produced on each self-report inventory when all the items are endorsed as true or false. Although such profiles are not technically inconsistent, they still indicate that the person is responding to the items irrespective of their content. Most persons who are responding to the items in this manner do not respond to all the items as either true or false. Instead they alternate randomly with a few items answered in the other direction throughout their string of responses. An example of random, "all-true," and "all-false" responses is provided for each self-report inventory in its respective chapter.

The advent of computer-administered self-report inventories makes it possible to examine a person's reaction time in responding to each item. Very rapid reaction times suggest that an individual has not taken the time to read the items carefully and probably point to inconsistent item endorsement. Research that evaluates such a hypothesis and provides guidelines for interpreting reaction times has yet to be undertaken. Future research could also measure changes in reaction times across blocks of items to determine if these indicate variations in a person's motivation. Research to test other response styles also is feasible. Individuals who have very slow reaction times may be trying to distort their responses to the items in some manner because they want to provide the desired response to each item. Holden and Kroner (1992) and Brunetti, Schlottmann, Scott, and Hollrah (1998) provide an introduction to these issues as they relate to the MMPI-2.

Accuracy of Item Endorsement

After item omissions and consistency of item endorsement have been checked and deemed to be acceptable or good enough to proceed, the next step in assessing the validity of an administration of a self-report inventory is verifying the accuracy of item endorsement (see Figure 5.1). Verification of the accuracy of item endorsement indicates whether individuals have attempted to describe themselves in either self-unfavorable or self-favorable terms with respect to their personal qualities, adjustment difficulties, and the presence and severity of psychopathology. The discussion in Chapter 2 of impression management addresses instances in which examinees consciously and deliberately seek to give a misleading picture of themselves as being either more psychologically dysfunctional than they really are (referred to as malingering, faking bad, or overreporting) or as being adjusted and more psychologically capable than they really are (known as deception, faking good, or underreporting; see pp. 36–38). These types of impression management do not include instances in which people give self-favorable or self-unfavorable responses without any conscious intent to mislead the examiner.

Motivations for giving self-unfavorable and self-favorable descriptions can range from being fully conscious to being entirely outside a person's awareness. The present discussion of verifying accuracy expands on Chapter 2 by considering both deliberate and unintended (at least not consciously) item distortions. Self-report test data can reveal only that items have been endorsed inaccurately; whether an individual's motivation for inaccurate item endorsement has been explicit (conscious) or implicit (unconscious) must be determined from a clinical interview and a review of the reasons for this person's evaluation.

Assessing accuracy of item endorsement is undertaken with several considerations in mind. First, it is assumed that self-unfavorable and self-favorable descriptions are a unitary dimension with self-unfavorable and self-favorable description at opposite ends (Figure 5.2). This means that accurate patterns of item endorsement shade gradually into self-unfavorable or self-favorable descriptions as one moves toward either end of this dimension; there is no exact point at which an individual's performance changes suddenly from one to the other type of distortion. Instead, a probability statement can be made concerning the likelihood of an individual's response reflecting either a self-unfavorable or self-favorable description.

Second, it is assumed that individuals who are endorsing items inaccurately are giving self-unfavorable descriptions of psychopathology in a generic sense rather than trying to simulate any specific mental disorder or a set of symptoms. It is difficult for individuals to simulate a specific mental disorder accurately on any self-report inventory. As noted in Chapter 2, people who have been coached in how to answer certain questions on self-report inventories may mislead examiners, but there is as yet no consistent research evidence

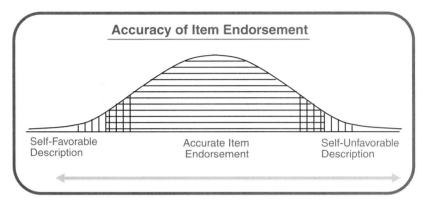

Figure 5.2   The dimension of accuracy of item endorsement.

that coached examinees can produce a valid self-report protocol entirely compatible with a specific disorder they do not have. Interested readers are encouraged to take any of the self-report inventories being discussed with a specific mental disorder in mind, and see how well the scales designed to assess accuracy of item endorsement detect it.

Third, a self-unfavorable or self-favorable description of psychopathology cannot be evidence that individuals do or do not have actual psychopathology, because people who actually have some specific mental disorder can distort how they report their psychopathology. The scales for assessing accuracy indicate only whether people have provided an accurate self-description and have no bearing on their level of adjustment.

Finally, the scales used to assess consistency of item endorsement are not appropriate for assessing the accuracy of item endorsement, and the scales used to assess accuracy of item endorsement are not appropriate for assessing the consistency of item endorsement. Consistency and accuracy assessment are independent sequential steps in determining the validity of a self-report inventory administration, using appropriate scales at each step. Scales for assessing the accuracy of item endorsement are presented next, first for self-unfavorable descriptions and then for favorable self-descriptions.

Self-Unfavorable Description Scales

Whether an individual is making a self-unfavorable description is typically addressed in two ways: with infrequency scales that consist of items that are endorsed infrequently by either normal individuals or psychiatric patients, and response distortion scales that evaluate the extent to which individuals are making an overly negative evaluation of themselves. All the self-report inventories intended for conducting clinical evaluations use one or both of these methods to assess whether people are describing themselves unfavorably. Both infrequency scales (MMPI-2: Infrequency [F], Back Infrequency [F_B], and Infrequency Psychopathology [$F(p)$]; MMPI-A: Infrequency [F]) and response distortion scales (Gough, 1950; Dissimulation Index [$F - K$]) are used on the MMPI-2 and MMPI-A to assess whether an individual is making a self-unfavorable description. The Debasement Index (Z) on the MCMI-III and the Negative Impression Management (*NIM*) on the PAI are response distortion scales for assessing a self-unfavorable description. The Disclosure Index (X) on the MCMI-III is a general dimensional measure relating self-unfavorable to self-favorable descriptions, with very high scores reflecting that the person has been unusually frank and self-revealing in acknowledging problems. Both the MCMI-III (Validity Index [V]) and PAI (Infrequency scale [INF]) use infrequency scales to assess consistency of item endorsement rather than accuracy of item endorsement, as previously noted.

Infrequency scales developed within normal samples, such as the MMPI-2 and MMPI-A infrequency scales (MMPI-2: Infrequency [F], Back Infrequency [F_B]; MMPI-A: Infrequency [F, F_1, F_2]), do not work as well in identifying whether individuals are making self-unfavorable descriptions as infrequency scales developed within clinical samples, such as the MMPI-2 Infrequency Psychopathology scale ($F[p]$) or the MMPI-A Infrequency Psychopathology scale (Fp - A). Infrequency scales developed within normal samples can be elevated by inconsistent item endorsement, inaccurate item endorsement, or severe psychopathology. Consistency scales can be examined in conjunction with infrequency scales to rule out this particular possibility, but examiners still must determine whether inaccurate item endorsement or an accurate report of severe psychopathology is producing the scale elevations. By contrast, infrequency scales developed within clinical samples are elevated solely by inaccurate item endorsement and not by psychopathology, which makes it easy to differentiate between them and argues for using these infrequency scales rather than those developed within normal samples.

If it is determined that an individual has given an extremely unfavorable self-description, the interpretive process stops. The examiner needs instead to talk with the person about the reasons for the inaccurate item endorsement. If this interview seems productive, the inventory can be readministered, although this procedure rarely results in an accurate self-description. Once people are motivated, whether consciously or unconsciously, to describe themselves unfavorably, it is very difficult to get them to endorse the items accurately during the current evaluation. There are no available data concerning whether a self-unfavorable description is likely to persist across different self-report inventories or in a subsequent evaluation at a different point of time or in a different setting.

Although self-report test profiles cannot be interpreted when people provide an extremely unfavorable description of themselves, it can be ascertained whether there are empirical correlates of such profiles, following Marks, Seeman, and Haller's (1974) description of a $K+$ profile on the original MMPI. In studies by Greene (1988) and Hale, Zimostrad, Duckworth, and Nicholas (1986, March), persons with self-unfavorable profiles who entered psychotherapy were very likely to terminate treatment within the first few sessions and frequently did not return after the initial session. This tendency of unusually self-critical patients to terminate treatment quickly is just the opposite of what might be anticipated, given that such patients are commonly described as "crying for help" and would be expected to remain in treatment longer than most other patients. Except for additional investigation by Greene and Clopton (2004), the research on the relationship of self-unfavorable description of psychopathology to treatment outcome has been scanty. Additional studies are needed to confirm the early findings and identify other possible correlates showing an extremely unfavorable self-description.

Self-Favorable Description Scales

The only typical method of assessing the prominence of self-favorable descriptions in personality inventories consists of response distortion scales. All the self-report inventories used for clinical evaluations include one or more response distortion scales designed specifically to assess whether individuals are making overly positive evaluations of themselves.

The response distortion method for assessing whether individuals are describing themselves in favorable ways takes into account two possibilities suggested by Paulhu's (1984, 1986) model of social desirability. In some instances, positive self-descriptions can reflect an unconscious motivation to see oneself in favorable terms, in which case they involve self-deception as well as deception of the examiner. The other possibility, positive self-descriptions, can arise as a consciously motivated strategy for making a deceptively good impression on the examiner. A pattern of self-favorable responses stemming from an impression management strategy corresponds to what Block (1965) identified as the "Alpha" factor, whereas self-favorable responses involving self-deception correspond to Wiggins's (1964) "Gamma" factor.

On the MMPI-2 and MMPI-A, the L scale is a measure of positive impression management, and the K scale is a measure of self-deception. Additionally on the MMPI-2, the S (Superlative) scale provides a measure of self-deception. The Desirability (Y) Index on the MCMI-III is a positive impression management scale. The Disclosure Index (X) on the MCMI-III is a dimensional index of the ratio of self-unfavorable to self-favorable descriptions, with very low scores reflecting that a person has been reluctant to acknowledge any type of problem. The nature of the Positive Impression Management (PIM) on the PAI is identified by its name.

Generalization of Validity Scales across Inventories

With respect to the generalization of validity scales across inventories, there is surprisingly little commonality in the accuracy of item endorsement across any two of the self-report measures being used. It is not unheard for individuals to describe themselves favorably on one inventory and unfavorably on another inventory taken at the same time. Table 5.6 shows the intercorrelations for scales measuring unfavorable and favorable self-descriptions on several self-report measures. The correlations for the unfavorable self-description scales range from .54 to .69. The moderate magnitude of these correlations (.54 to .69) indicates

Table 5.6   Self-description scales

Unfavorable Self-Description Scales	
MMPI-2 F (Infrequency) Scale	
MCMI-III Debasement (X)	.69
PAI Infrequency (INF)	.11
PAI Negative Impression Management (NIM)	.54
Favorable Self-Description Scales	
MMPI-2 L (Lie) Scale	
MCMI-III Desirability (Y)	.39
PAI Positive Impression Management (PIM)	.41

Note: These correlations are reported in the *Manuals* except for the MCMI-III.
Source: "A Comparison of the MCMI-III Personality Disorder and Modifier Indices with the MMPI-2 Clinical Scales," by M. R. Schoenberg, D. Dorr, C. D. Morgan, and M. Burke, 2004, *Journal of Personality Assessment, 82,* p. 276; PAI (p. 184).

the uncertainty of trying to generalize accuracy of item endorsement across self-report inventories. The correlations for these favorable self-description scales approximate .40, and the correlations among positive impression management scales generally tend to be lower than the correlations among negative impression management scales (Greene, 2000). Hence it would be even more uncertain to generalize across inventories with respect to positive than to negative impression management scales.

Assessors are also advised to avoid generalizing from an individual's scores on the validity scales of one self-report inventory to how the person is likely to respond to a clinical interview or a different self-report inventory that has no validity scales. Although it may be tempting to assume that people who have responded accurately to one self-report inventory would respond in similarly accurate fashion in a clinical interview or when completing other self-report inventories without validity scales or performance-based measures, there is little research support for such an assumption. Instead, the finding that self-descriptions can vary across two self-report inventories given at the same time cautions against generalizing assessment validity from any one self-report inventory to other measures in a test battery.

THE PROCESS OF INTERPRETATION

For those self-report inventories with validity scales, interpretation begins after it has been determined that the person being examined has endorsed the items in a valid manner. As emphasized throughout this *Handbook,* the interpretive process generates hypotheses, not facts, and the likely implications of self-report inventory data for an individual's personality characteristics remain to be verified by convergence of information from multiple sources.

The first step in the interpretation of a self-report inventory consists of determining which, if any, of its scales are elevated to a statistically and clinically significant level. This determination can be made separately for each individual scale and also for groups of scales, which means that a decision must be made for a particular protocol whether it is more important to examine scales scores separately or with a configural approach focused on combinations of scales. A configural approach is exemplified by the codetypes on the MMPI-2 and MMPI-A based on the two highest clinical scales with a T score above 64.

The second step in interpretation involves recognizing how global or specific the various scales are for the characteristic they assess. The more global a scale is, the more it is limited to supporting only general hypotheses, but the more reliably it supports these hypotheses. The more specific a scale is, the more precise the hypotheses it supports, but the less reliable these hypotheses are likely to be. A total scale for depression is relatively global and can support a relatively general and reliable hypothesis concerning whether a person is depressed, whereas subscales for cognitive, vegetative, interpersonal, and psychomotor manifestations of depression can provide relatively precise hypotheses for these specific symptoms, but do not do so as reliably as the total depression scale suggests whether the person is depressed.

The third step in the interpretive process for most self-report inventories is a review of certain individual items (sometimes called "critical" or "stop" items) that usually warrant further investigation when they are endorsed. An item on the order of "I see objects or things that other people do not see" could be considered a critical item, because a person endorsing it may be experiencing visual hallucinations. By exploring why critical items like this one have been endorsed, examiners are likely to unearth many possibilities, not all of which are pathological. Thus people who report seeing objects or things that other people do not see may not be hallucinatory at all, but merely have very keen vision or are more attuned and sensitive than most people to what is going on around them.

Computer Interpretation Recommended

Once self-report inventory responses have been computer scored, most programs for this purpose can be instructed to generate a computer based test interpretation (CBTI). This CBTI then becomes one of the basic building blocks of the assessment psychologist's evaluation report. In preparing the final report, the clinician's task is to integrate the computer interpretation of the self-report inventories that were administered with interview and performance-based test data and with the examinee's clinical history. The use of CBTI in the assessment process was discussed in Chapter 2, and three considerations with respect to self-report inventories merit further mention in concluding the present chapter.

First, clinicians must take responsibility for modifying and adapting computer interpretations to correct any inaccuracies they might contain. CBTIs are never a stand-alone product to be accepted as they are; instead, they must be regarded only as an electronic assistant that quickly provides the basic interpretation for a self-report inventory. This electronic assistant spares examiners from having to look up basic interpretations in standard references on the various self-report inventories and then having to enter that information into the word processor. The electronic assistant is tireless and provides this information in the same manner for every case.

Second, any modifications that examiners make of the computer interpretation should be based on specific information that contradicts what the computer has generated. Clinicians must avoid any temptation to override an automated interpretive statement simply because they dislike it or because they have formed an impression—without any concrete evidence they can identify—that it cannot be correct.

Third, the routine use of computerized interpretations is recommended to familiarize examiners with their use and help them apply CBTI in complex cases. If drawing on computerized interpretations for assistance is reserved for complicated and difficult cases only, clinicians miss learning how to work with computerized interpretations in relatively straightforward cases in which potential problems are more likely to be apparent. Finally, assessors should keep in mind that computerized interpretations, like all inferences based on personality test responses, are hypotheses that must be validated by additional information.

REFERENCES

Allard, G., & Faust, D. (2000). Errors in scoring objective personality tests. *Assessment, 7*, 119–129.

American Psychiatric Association. (2000). *Diagnostic and statistical manual of mental disorders* (4th ed., text rev.). Washington, DC: Author.

Beck, A. T., & Steer, R. A. (1993). *Manual for the Beck Anxiety Inventory*. San Antonio, TX: Psychological Corporation.

Beck, A. T., Steer, R. A., & Brown, G. K. (1996). *Manual for the Beck Depression Inventory-II*. San Antonio, TX: Psychological Corporation.

Belter, R. W., & Piotrowski, C. (2001). Current status of doctoral-level training in psychological testing. *Journal of Clinical Psychology, 57*, 717–726.

Block, J. (1965). *The challenge of response sets: Unconfounding meaning, acquiescence, and social desirability in the MMPI.* New York: Appleton-Century-Crofts.

Brunetti, D. G., Schlottmann, R. S., Scott, A. B., & Hollrah, J. L. (1998). Instructed faking and MMPI-2 response latencies: The potential for assessing response validity. *Journal of Clinical Psychology, 54*, 143–153.

Butcher, J. N., Dahlstrom, W. G., Graham, J. R., Tellegen, A., & Kaemmer, B. (1989). *MMPI-2: Manual for administration and scoring.* Minneapolis: University of Minnesota Press.

Butcher, J. N., Graham, J. R., Ben-Porath, Y. S., Tellegen, A., Dahlstrom, W. G., & Kaemmer, B. (2001). *MMPI-2: Manual for administration and scoring* (Rev. ed.). Minneapolis: University of Minnesota Press.

Butcher, J. N., Williams, C. L., Graham, J. R., Archer, R. P., Tellegen, A., Ben-Porath, Y. S., et al. (1992). *MMPI-A (Minnesota Multiphasic Personality Inventory—Adolescent): Manual for administration, scoring, and interpretation.* Minneapolis: University of Minnesota Press.

Childs, R. A., & Eyde, L. D. (2002). Assessment training in clinical psychology doctoral programs: What should we teach? What do we teach? *Journal of Personality Assessment, 78*, 130–144.

Clemence, A. J., & Handler, L. (2001). Psychological assessment on internship: A survey of training directors and their expectations of students. *Journal of Personality Assessment, 76*, 18–45.

Costa, P. T., & McCrae, R. R. (1992). *NEO PI-R professional manual.* Odessa, FL: Psychological Assessment Resources.

Dahlstrom, W. G., Welsh, G. S., & Dahlstrom, L. E. (1972). *An MMPI handbook: Vol. I. Clinical interpretation* (Rev. ed.). Minneapolis: University of Minnesota Press.

Finn, S. E. (1996a). *A manual for using the MMPI-2 as a therapeutic intervention.* Minneapolis: University of Minnesota Press.

Finn, S. E. (1996b). Assessment feedback integrating MMPI-2 and Rorschach findings. *Journal of Personality Assessment, 67*, 543–557.

Fischer, C. T. (1994). *Individualizing psychological assessment.* Hillsdale, NJ: Erlbaum.

Gough, H. G. (1950). The *F* minus *K* dissimulation index for the MMPI. *Journal of Consulting Psychology, 14*, 408–413.

Greene, R. L. (1978). An empirically derived MMPI carelessness scale. *Journal of Clinical Psychology, 34*, 407–410.

Greene, R. L. (1980). *The MMPI: An interpretive manual.* New York: Grune & Stratton.

Greene, R. L. (1988). Assessment of malingering and defensiveness by objective personality measures. In R. Rogers (Ed.), *Clinical assessment of malingering and deception* (pp. 123–158). New York: Guilford Press.

Greene, R. L. (2000). *The MMPI-2: An interpretive manual* (2nd ed.). Boston: Allyn & Bacon.

Greene, R. L., & Clopton, J. R. (2004). MMPI-2. In M. Maruish (Ed.), *The use of psychological testing for treatment planning and outcomes assessment: Vol. 3: Instruments for adults* (3rd ed., pp. 449–477). Mahwah, NJ: Erlbaum.

Hale, G., Zimostrad, S., Duckworth, J., & Nicholas, D. (1986, March). *The abusive personality: MMPI profiles of male batterers.* Paper presented at the 21st Annual Symposium on Recent Developments in the Use of the MMPI, Clearwater, FL.

Hathaway, S. R., & McKinley, J. C. (1940). A multiphasic personality schedule (Minnesota): Pt. I. Construction of the schedule. *Journal of Psychology, 10*, 249–254.

Holden, R. R., & Kroner, D. G. (1992). Relative efficacy of differential response latencies for detecting faking on a self-report measure of psychopathology. *Psychological Assessment, 4*, 170–173.

Huba, G. J. (1986). The use of the runs test for assessing response validity in computer scored inventories. *Educational and Psychological Measurement, 46*, 929–932.

Iverson, G. I., & Barton, E. (1999). Interscorer reliability of the MMPI-2: Should *TRIN* and *VRIN* be computer scored? *Journal of Clinical Psychology*, *55*, 65–69.

Malinchoc, M., Offord, K. P., Colligan, R. C., & Morse, R. M. (1994). The Common Alcohol Logistic—Revised Scale (CAL-R): A revised alcoholism scale for the MMPI and MMPI-2. *Journal of Clinical Psychology*, *50*, 436–445.

Marks, P. A., Seeman, W., & Haller, D. L. (1974). *The actuarial use of the MMPI with adolescents and adults*. Baltimore: Williams & Wilkins.

Millon, T., Davis, R., & Millon, C. (1997). *Millon Clinical Multiaxial Inventory-III: Manual* (2nd ed.) Minneapolis, MN: National Computer Systems.

Moreland, K. L., Eyde, L. D., Robertson, G. J., Primoff, E. S., & Most, R. B. (1995). Assessment of test user qualifications: A research-based measurement procedure. *American Psychologist*, *50*, 14–23.

Morey, L. C. (1991). *Personality Assessment Inventory: Professional manual*. Odessa, FL: Psychological Assessment Resources.

Paulhus, D. L. (1984). Two-component models of socially desirable responding. *Journal of Personality and Social Psychology*, *46*, 598–609.

Paulhus, D. L. (1986). Self-deception and impression management in test responses. In A. Angleitner & J. S. Wiggins (Eds.), *Personality assessment via questionnaires: Current issues in theory and measurement* (pp. 143–165). Berlin: Springer-Verlag.

Plake, B. S., & Impara, J. C. (2001). *The fourteenth mental measurements yearbook*. Lincoln, NB: Buros Institute of Mental Measurements.

Plake, B. S., Impara, J. C., & Spies, R. A. (2003). *The fifteenth mental measurements yearbook*. Lincoln, NB: Buros Institute of Mental Measurements.

Rogers, R., Sewell, K. W., & Morey, L. C. (1992). Detection of feigned mental disorders on the Personality Assessment Inventory: A discriminant analysis. *Journal of Personality Assessment*, *67*, 629–640.

Schoenberg, M. R., Dorr, D., Morgan, C. D., & Burke, M. (2004). A comparison of the MCMI-III personality disorder and modifier indices with the MMPI-2 clinical scales. *Journal of Personality Assessment*, *82*, 273–280.

Spies, R. A., & Plake, B. S. (2005). *The sixteenth mental measurements yearbook*. Lincoln, NB: Buros Institute of Mental Measurements.

Tellegen, A., & Ben-Porath, Y. S. (1992). The new uniform T scores for the MMPI-2: Rationale, derivation, and appraisal. *Psychological Assessment*, *4*, 145–155.

Watkins, C. E., Jr., Campbell, V. L., Nieberding, R., & Hallmark, R. (1995). Contemporary practice of psychological assessment by clinical psychologists. *Professional Psychology: Research and Practice*, *26*, 54–60.

Wiggins, J. S. (1964). Convergences among stylistic response measures from objective personality tests. *Educational and Psychological Measurement*, *24*, 551–562.

Chapter 6

MINNESOTA MULTIPHASIC PERSONALITY INVENTORY-2

The Minnesota Multiphasic Personality Inventory-2 (MMPI-2: Butcher, Dahlstrom, Graham, Tellegen, & Kaemmer, 1989; Butcher et al., 2001) is a broadband measure of the major dimensions of psychopathology found in Axis I disorders and some Axis II disorders of the *DSM-IV-TR* (American Psychiatric Association, 2000). The MMPI-2 consists of 9 validity and 10 clinical scales in the basic profile, along with 15 content scales, 9 restructured clinical scales, and 20 supplementary scales (see Table 6.1).

There also are subscales for most of the clinical and content scales with easily over 120 scales that can be scored and interpreted on the MMPI-2. Table 6.2 provides general information on the MMPI-2.

HISTORY

Hathaway and McKinley (1940) sought to develop a multifaceted or multiphasic personality inventory, now known as the Minnesota Multiphasic Personality Inventory (MMPI), that would surmount the shortcomings of the previous personality inventories. These shortcomings included (a) relying on how the researcher thought individuals should respond to the content of items rather than validating how they actually responded to the items; (b) using only face-valid items whose purpose or intent was easily understood; and (c) failing to assess whether individuals were trying to distort their responses to the items in some manner. Instead of using independent sets of tests, each with a specific purpose, Hathaway and McKinley included in a single inventory a wide sampling of behavior of significance to psychologists. They wanted to create a large pool of items from which various scales could be constructed, in the hope of evolving a greater variety of valid personality descriptions than was currently available.

MMPI (Original Version)

To this end, Hathaway and McKinley (1940) assembled more than 1,000 items from psychiatric textbooks, other personality inventories, and clinical experience. The items were written as declarative statements in the first-person singular, and most were phrased in the affirmative. Using a subset of 504 items, Hathaway and McKinley constructed a series of quantitative scales that could be used to assess various categories of psychopathology. The items had to be answered differently by the criterion group (e.g., hypochondriacal

Table 6.1   Minnesota Multiphasic Personality Inventory-2 (MMPI-2) scales

Validity Scales

?	Cannot Say
VRIN	Variable Response Consistency
TRIN	True Response Consistency
F	Infrequency
F_B	Back Infrequency
Fp	Infrequency Psychopathology
L	Lie
K	Correction
S	Superlative

Clinical Scales

1 (Hs)	Hypochondriasis
2 (D)	Depression
3 (Hy)	Hysteria
4 (Pd)	Psychopathic Deviate
5 (Mf)	Masculinity-Femininity
6 (Pa)	Paranoia
7 (Pt)	Psychasthenia
8 (Sc)	Schizophrenia
9 (Ma)	Hypomania
0 (Si)	Social Introversion

Restructured Clinical Scales

RCd	Demoralization
RC1som	Somatization
RC2lpe	Low Positive Emotionality
RC3cyn	Cynicism
RC4asb	Antisocial Behavior
RC6per	Persecutory Ideas
RC7dne	Dysfunctional Negative Emotions
RC8abx	Aberrant Experiences
RC9hpm	Hypomanic Activation

Content Scales

ANX	Anxiety
FRS	Fears
OBS	Obsessions
DEP	Depression
HEA	Health Concerns
BIZ	Bizarre Mentation
ANG	Anger
CYN	Cynicism
ASP	Antisocial Practices
TPA	Type A
LSE	Low Self-Esteem
SOD	Social Discomfort
FAM	Family Problems
WRK	Work Interference
TRT	Negative Treatment Indicators

Table 6.1   *(Continued)*

PSY-5 Scales	
AGGR	Aggression
PSYC	Psychoticism
DISC	Disconstraint
NEGE	Negative Emotionality
INTR	Introversion/Low Positive Emotionality
Supplementary Scales	
Broad Personality Characteristics	
A	Anxiety
R	Repression
Es	Ego Strength
Do	Dominance
Re	Social Responsibility
Generalized Emotional Distress	
Mt	College Maladjustment
PK	PTSD—Keane
MDS	Marital Distress
Behavioral Dyscontrol	
Ho	Hostility
O-H	Overcontrolled Hostility
MAC-R	MacAndrew Alcoholism-Revised
AAS	Addiction Admission
APS	Addiction Potential
Gender Role	
GF	Gender Role–Feminine
GM	Gender Role–Masculine

patients) as compared with normal groups. Since their approach was strictly empirical and no theoretical rationale was posited as the basis for accepting or rejecting items on a specific scale, it is not always possible to discern why a particular item distinguishes the criterion group from the normal group. Rather, items were selected solely because the criterion group answered them differently than other groups. For each of the criterion groups and the normative group, the frequency of "True" and "False" responses was calculated for each item. An item was tentatively selected for a scale if the difference in frequency of response between the criterion group and the normative group was at least twice the standard error of the proportions of true/false responses of the two groups being compared. Having selected items according to this procedure, Hathaway and McKinley then eliminated some of them for various reasons. First, the frequency of the criterion group's response was required to be greater than 10% for nearly all items; those items that yielded infrequent deviant response rates from the criterion group were excluded even if they were highly significant statistically because they represented so few criterion cases. Additionally, items whose responses appeared to reflect biases on variables such as marital status or socioeconomic

Table 6.2 Minnesota Multiphasic Personality Inventory-2 (MMPI-2)

Authors:	Butcher, Dahlstrom, Graham, Tellegen, and Kaemmer
Published:	1989
Edition:	2nd
Publisher:	Pearson Assessments
Website:	www.PearsonAssessments.com
Age Range:	18+
Reading Level:	6th–8th grade
Administration Formats:	paper/pencil, computer, CD, cassette
Additional Languages:	Spanish, Hmong, and French for Canada
Number of Items:	567
Response Format:	True/False
Administration Time:	60–90 minutes
Primary Scales:	9 Validity, 10 Clinical, 15 Content
Additional Scales:	5 PSY-5, 9 Restructured Clinical, 20 Supplementary
Hand Scoring:	Templates
General Texts:	Friedman et al. (2001); Graham (2006); Greene (2000); Nichols (2001)
Computer Interpretation:	Caldwell Report (Caldwell); Pearson Assessments (Butcher); Psychological Assessment Resources (Greene)

status were excluded. Evaluation of several methods of weighting individual items showed no advantage over using unweighted items. Therefore, each item simply received a weight of "one" in deriving a total score. In other words, a person's score on any MMPI scale is equal to the total number of items that the individual answers in the same manner as the criterion group.

The empirical approach to item selection used by Hathaway and McKinley, in fact, freed them of any concerns about how any individual interprets specific items because it assumes that the individual's self-report is just that and makes no a priori assumptions about the relationships between the individual's self-report and the individual's behavior. Items are selected for inclusion in a specific scale only because the criterion group answered the items differently than the normative group irrespective of whether the item content is actually an accurate description of the criterion group. Any relationship between individuals' responses on a given scale and their behavior must be demonstrated empirically.

MMPI-2 (Restandardized Version)

The MMPI-2 (Butcher et al., 1989, 2001) represents the restandardization of the MMPI that was needed to provide current norms for the inventory, develop a nationally representative and larger normative sample, provide appropriate representation of ethnic minorities, and update item content where needed. Continuity between the MMPI and the MMPI-2 was maintained because new criterion groups and item derivation procedures were *not* used on the standard validity and clinical scales. Thus, the items on the validity and clinical scales of the MMPI are essentially unchanged on the MMPI-2 except for the elimination of 13 items based on item content and the rewording of 68 items.

In the development of the MMPI-2, the Restandardization Committee (Butcher et al., 1989) started with the 550 items on the original MMPI; that is, they first deleted the 16 repeated items. They reworded 141 of these 550 items to eliminate outdated and sexist language and to make these items more easily understood. Rewording these items did not change the correlations of the items with the total scale score in most cases (Ben-Porath & Butcher, 1989). Many of these items were omitted on the original MMPI because individuals did not understand them. Greene (1991, p. 57) provides examples of these items such as playing drop the handkerchief. The Restandardization Committee then added 154 provisional items that resulted in the 704 items on Form AX, which was used to collect the normative data for the MMPI-2.

When finalizing the items to be included on the MMPI-2, the Restandardization Committee deleted 77 items from the original MMPI in addition to the 13 items deleted from the standard validity and clinical scales and the 16 repeated items. Consequently, most special and research scales that have been developed on the MMPI are still capable of being scored unless the scale has an emphasis on religious content or the items are drawn predominantly from the last 150 items on the original MMPI.

The Restandardization Committee included 68 of the 141 items that had been rewritten, and they incorporated 107 of the provisional items to assess major content areas that were not covered in the original MMPI item pool. The rationale for including and dropping items from Form AX that resulted in the 567 items on the MMPI-2 has not been made explicit.

The MMPI-2 was standardized on a sample of 2,600 individuals who resided in seven different states (California, Minnesota, North Carolina, Ohio, Pennsylvania, Virginia, and Washington) to reflect national census parameters on age, marital status, ethnicity, education, and occupational status. The normative sample for the MMPI-2 varies significantly from the original normative sample for the MMPI in several areas: years of education, representation of ethnic minorities, and occupational status. The individuals in the normative sample for the MMPI-2 also are more representative of the United States as a whole because national census parameters were used in their collection. However, they still varied from the census parameters on years of education and occupational status. The potential impact of this higher level of education and occupation in the MMPI-2 normative sample on codetype and scale interpretation has been a focus of concern (Caldwell, 1997c; Helmes & Reddon, 1993). However, Schinka and LaLone (1997) compared a census-matched subsample created within the MMPI-2 restandardization sample and found only one difference that exceeded 3 T score points between these two samples on the standard validity and clinical scales, content scales, and supplementary scales.

The extant literature that has examined the empirical correlates of MMPI-2 scales and codetypes has been consistent with the correlates reported for their MMPI counterparts (Archer, Griffin, & Aiduk, 1995; Graham, Ben-Porath, & McNulty, 1999). It appears safe to assume that the correlates of well-defined MMPI-2 codetypes (the two highest clinical scales composing the codetype should be at least five T points higher than the next highest clinical scale) and the individual validity and clinical scales will be very similar to those for the MMPI. The data are less clear for MMPI-2 codetypes that are not well-defined, although it still will be safe to interpret the individual validity and clinical scales in these codetypes using MMPI correlates given the minimal change at the scale level.

New sets of scales have been developed with the MMPI-2 item pool: content scales (Butcher, Graham, Williams, & Ben-Porath, 1990); content component scales (Ben-Porath

& Sherwood, 1993); personality psychopathology five scales (PSY-5: Harkness, McNulty, Ben-Porath, & Graham, 2002); and restructured clinical scales (Tellegen et al., 2003).

Several major reviews of the MMPI-2 (Butcher, Graham, & Ben-Porath, 1995; Butcher & Rouse, 1996; Caldwell, 1997c; Greene, Gwin, & Staal, 1997; Helmes & Reddon, 1993) provide summaries from a variety of perspectives on this venerable instrument. These reviews provide the interested reader with an excellent starting point for looking at the current status of the MMPI-2. Butcher et al. (1995) and Greene et al. (1997) also outline the general steps that researchers need to follow and issues that need to be addressed in conducting research with the MMPI-2. It is to be hoped that researchers will heed the advice dispensed in these reviews to enhance the quality of the data that are being collected.

Unlike the MMPI which was used with all ages, *the MMPI-2 is to be used only with adults 18 years of age and older.* Adolescents are to be tested with the MMPI-A (Butcher et al., 1992), which is designed specifically for them (see Chapter 7).

ADMINISTRATION

The first requirement in the administration of the MMPI-2 is ensuring that the individual is invested in the process. It will pay excellent dividends to spend a few extra minutes answering any questions the individual may have about why the MMPI-2 is being administered and how the results will be used. The clinician should work diligently to make the assessment process a collaborative activity with the individual to obtain the desired information. This issue of therapeutic assessment (Finn, 1996; Fischer, 1994) was covered in more depth in Chapter 2 (pp. 43–44).

Reading level is a crucial factor in determining whether a person can complete the MMPI-2; inadequate reading ability is a major cause of inconsistent patterns of item endorsement to be discussed later. Butcher et al. (1989) suggest that most clients who have had at least *8* years of formal education can take the MMPI-2 with little or no difficulty because the items are written on an eighth-grade level or less. A number of authors (Dahlstrom, Archer, Hopkins, Jackson, & Dahlstrom, 1994; Paolo, Ryan, & Smith, 1992; Schinka & Borum, 1993) have studied the readability of MMPI-2 and MMPI-A items. There was general concurrence that the average readability of the MMPI-2 and MMPI-A is in the range of *fifth to sixth* grade. The scales requiring the highest reading levels were 9 (*Ma:* Hypomania), the three content scales of Antisocial Practices (*ASP*), Cynicism (*CYN*), and Type A (*TPA*), several of the Harris and Lingoes (1955) subscales: Hy_2 (Need for Affection), Pa_3 (Naivete), Sc_5 (Lack of Ego Mastery, Defective Inhibition), Ma_1 (Amorality), Ma_2 (Psychomotor Acceleration), Ma_3 (Imperturbability), and Ma_4 (Ego Inflation). On most of these scales, at least 25% of their items required more than an eighth-grade reading level. These estimates of the required grade level are conservative because they are based on assessing the readability of individual MMPI-2 items or groups of items. They are *not* based on the difficulty of understanding what is meant by saying either "true" or "false" to a specific item. The reader can assess this problem directly by trying to understand exactly what is meant by saying "false" to an MMPI-2 item that is worded in the negative. What do individuals actually mean when they say "false" to an item such as "I do not always have pain in my back"? Schinka and Borum did suggest that individuals be asked to read MMPI-2 items 114, 226, and 445 if they have completed less than a 10th grade education to determine whether their reading skills are adequate. Dahlstrom et al. (1994) also noted that the instructions for the MMPI-2 actually were more difficult than the items on the test so clinicians should be sure the individual fully understands them.

SCORING

Scoring the MMPI-2 is relatively straightforward either by hand or computer. If the MMPI-2 is administered by computer, the computer automatically scores it. If the individual's responses to the items have been placed on an answer sheet, these responses can be entered into the computer by the clinician for scoring or they can be hand-scored. If the clinician enters the item responses into the computer for scoring, they should be double entered so that any data entry errors can be identified.

The first step in hand-scoring is to examine the answer sheet carefully and indicate omitted items and double-marked items by drawing a line with brightly colored ink through both the "true" and "false" responses to these items. Also, cleaning up the answer sheet helps facilitate scoring. Responses that were changed need to be erased completely if possible, or clearly marked with an "X" so that the clinician is aware that this response has not been endorsed by the client.

There is one scale that must always be scored without a template. The Cannot Say (?) scale score is the total number of items not marked and double marked. All the other scales are scored by placing a plastic template over the answer sheet with a small box drawn at the scored (deviant) response—either "true" or "false"—for each item on the scale. The total number of such items marked equals the client's raw score for that scale; this score is recorded in the proper space on the answer sheet. One scale—Scale 5 (Mf: Masculinity-Femininity)—is scored differently for men and women, and unusually high or low scores on this scale might indicate that the wrong template was used. Among women, a raw score less than 30 is unusual, and such raw scores should at least arouse a suspicion that the wrong template was used in scoring the scale. All scoring templates are made of plastic and must be kept away from heat.

Plotting the profile is the next step in the scoring process. In essence, the clinician transfers all the raw scores from the answer sheet to the appropriate column of the profile sheet (see Figure 6.1). Some precautions must be taken and data calculations performed. First, separate profile sheets are used for men and women as with the scoring templates for Scale 5; an unusually high or low score plotted for Scale 5 should alert the clinician to the possibility that the wrong profile sheet was selected. Second, each column on the profile sheet is used to represent the raw scores for a specific scale. Each dash represents a raw score of 1 with the larger dashes marking increments of 5. Thus, the clinician notes the individual's raw score on the scale being plotted and makes a point or dot at the appropriate dash. Once the clinician has plotted the individual's scores on the eight validity scales, a solid line is drawn to connect them. The raw score on the Cannot Say (?) scale is merely recorded in the proper space in the lower left-hand corner of the profile sheet.

A similar procedure is followed to plot the 10 clinical scales except that five of the clinical scales (1 [Hs: Hypochondriasis], 4 [Pd: Psychopathic Deviate], 7 [Pt: Psychasthenia], 8 [Sc: Schizophrenia], and 9 [Ma: Hypomania]) are K-corrected; that is, a fraction of K is added to the raw score before the individual's score is plotted. For these five scales that

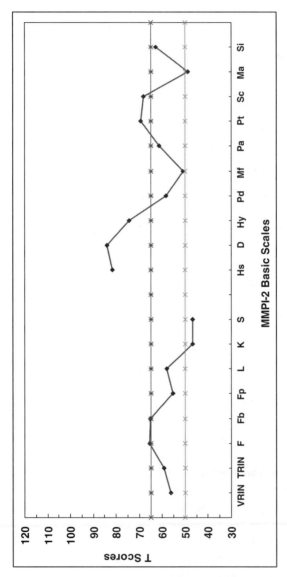

Figure 6.1 MMPI-2 profile for basic validity and clinical scales for a *1-2/2-1* codetype. Reproduced by permission of the University of Minnesota Press.

are *K*-corrected, the clinician plots the raw score on the scale with *K* added. Once the clinician has plotted the individual's scores on the 10 clinical scales, another solid line is drawn to connect them. The clinician should note that the validity and clinical scales are *not* connected, because the determination of the validity of the MMPI-2 is independent of or precedes the evaluation of the clinical scales. A similar process is followed for scoring the restructured clinical scales, content scales, and supplementary scales.

The left and right columns of the profile for basic scales provide the T score equivalents for the raw scores on each scale (see Figure 6.1). The profile form for the basic scales provides a direct means of converting the raw scores on the standard validity and clinical scores into the appropriate T scores. The development and the use of T scores were described in Chapter 5.

Hand scoring of the MMPI-2 is to be discouraged for several reasons. First, hand scoring is extremely time consuming, and clinicians will be tempted not to score all the possible MMPI-2 scales to save time. Currently, 129 scales and indexes are scored on the Pearson Assessments Extended Score Report for the MMPI-2. If it takes only 10 seconds to score each scale or index, the clinician will spend over 20 minutes simply scoring the MMPI-2. Second, hand scoring is prone to error even when clinicians are very careful. Third, hand scoring of the two inconsistency scales on the MMPI-2 (Variable Response Inconsistency [*VRIN*] and True Response Inconsistency [*TRIN*]) requires that the clinician copy 138 of the individual's responses onto an additional answer sheet before scoring these two scales; this provides another opportunity to introduce errors. In fact, hand scoring the *VRIN* and *TRIN* scales several times is sufficient to convince most clinicians to use computer scoring of the MMPI-2. The extra time required to hand-score the *VRIN* and *TRIN* scales may tempt clinicians to omit scoring these two scales, which are vital in assessing the consistency of item endorsement on the MMPI-2 described in the next section.

ASSESSING VALIDITY

Figure 6.2 provides a flowchart for assessing the validity of this administration of the MMPI-2, and the criteria for using this flowchart are provided in Table 6.3. The criteria provided in Table 6.3 are continuous, yet ultimately the decisions that must be made in implementing the flowchart in Figure 6.2 are dichotomous. General guidelines are provided for translating these continuous data into dichotomous decisions on the MMPI-2, but these guidelines need to be considered within the constraints of this specific individual and the circumstances for the evaluation.

Item Omissions

The Cannot Say (*?*) Scale consists of the total number of items that the individual fails to answer or answers both "true" and "false." The raw score on the Cannot Say (*?*) scale is located at the bottom left-hand corner of the profile form and can be easily overlooked, particularly if the clinician is not the person who actually scored the MMPI-2. The omitted item(s) should be reviewed to see if there is any theme to them. The individual should be queried carefully about any omitted items among the dangerousness-to-self items (150,

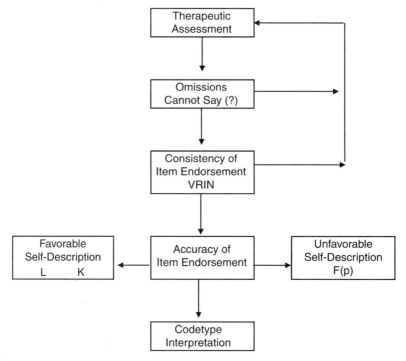

Figure 6.2   Flowchart for assessing MMPI-2 validity.

303, 506, 520, 524, 530) and dangerousness-to-others items (150, 540, 542, 548), and the explanation documented.

Changes in the MMPI-2 codetype (two highest clinical scales) are likely when 10 or more items are omitted, particularly if these omissions are in the first 370 items, even though profile elevation may be reduced only slightly. If most of the omitted items occur after item 370, the three basic validity (*L, F,* and *K*) and 10 clinical scales can be scored. However, the additional validity scales (*VRIN, TRIN, FB, F(p),* and *S*) and the content scales should not be scored without determining the actual number of items omitted on each of these scales.

As the number of omitted items approaches 30, the MMPI-2 profile essentially becomes uninterpretable. If the individual omits more than 10 or 15 items, the clinician can ask the individual to review the omitted items and respond to them based on whether each is *mostly true* or *mostly false*. If the individual still omits more than 10 items, the clinician can question the individual about the reasons for not responding to them.

Few items are generally omitted on the MMPI-2 with nearly 70% of normal and clinical samples and 50% of personnel samples omitting no items (Table 6.3). Omitting more than 10 items is approximately the 98th percentile for the MMPI-2 normative sample (Butcher et al., 1989) and clinical (Caldwell, 1997a) and personnel-screening (Caldwell, 1997b) samples. Few items are omitted on the MMPI-2, and the setting in which the MMPI-2 is administered does not appreciably affect how many items are omitted. It might be expected that individuals in a personnel setting would be more likely to omit items, but omissions actually are somewhat less frequent in this setting.

Table 6.3   Criteria for assessing MMPI-2 validity by type of setting

Setting	Percentile										
	1	2	7	16	30	50	70	84	93	98	99
Item Omissions (Cannot Say [?])											
Normal[a]	—	—	—	—	—	—	0	1	3	10	16
Clinical[b]	—	—	—	—	—	—	0	2	5	12	18
Personnel[c]	—	—	—	—	—	0	1	3	5	11	12
Consistency of Item Endorsement (Variable Response Inconsistency Scale [VRIN])											
Normal[a]	—	0	1	2	3	4	6	7	9	11	12
Clinical[b]	—	0	1	2	3	5	6	8	9	11	12
Personnel[c]	—	—	—	0	1	2	3	4	6	8	10
Accuracy of Item Endorsement											
Self-Unfavorable (Infrequency Psychopathology Scale [$F_{(p)}$])											
Normal[a]	—	—	—	—	—	0	1	2	3	4	5
Clinical[b]	—	—	—	—	0	1	2	3	4	7	8
Personnel[c]	—	—	—	—	0	—	1	2	3	4	5
Self-Favorable (Impression Management (Lie Scale [L])											
Normal[a]	—	0	1	2	3	4	5	6	9	10	
Clinical[b]	0	1	2	3	4	5	7	8	10	11	
Personnel[c]	0	1	2	4	5	7	9	11	12	13	
Self-Favorable Self-Deception (Correction Scale [K])											
Normal[a]	5	8	10	12	15	17	19	22	24	25	
Clinical[b]	5	7	9	12	15	19	21	23	25	26	
Personnel[c]	10	13	16	18	21	23	24	25	26	27	

[a]Butcher et al. (1989).
[b]Caldwell (1997a).
[c]Caldwell (1997b).

Consistency of Item Endorsement

Consistency of item endorsement on the MMPI-2 is assessed by the Variable Response Inconsistency (VRIN) and True Response Inconsistency (TRIN) scales. The Variable Response Inconsistency (VRIN) scale consists of 67 pairs of items that have similar or opposite item content. These pairs are scored if the individual provides inconsistent responses. The VRIN scale actually consists of 49 pairs of unique items, since two separate response patterns are scored for 18 of these 67 item pairs as with items 6 and 90. The True Response Inconsistency (TRIN) scale consists of 23 pairs of items. The TRIN scale is similar to the VRIN scale except that the scored response on the TRIN scale is either "true" or "false" to both items in each pair. The TRIN scale has 14 pairs of items to which the inconsistent response is "true" and 9 item pairs to which the inconsistent response is "false." Scoring the TRIN scale is somewhat complicated. One point is added to the individual's score for each of the 14 item pairs that are scored if endorsed "true," whereas one point is subtracted for each of the 9 item pairs that are scored if endorsed "false." Then 9 points are added to this score. (Nine points are added to prevent obtaining a negative score on the TRIN scale.

If an individual endorsed none of the 14 "true" item pairs and all 9 of the "false" item pairs, a score of –9 would be obtained. Adding 9 points avoids this problem.) The *TRIN* scale is intended to identify individuals who are endorsing the items inconsistently by essentially responding to most of the items as "true" or "false."

Scores on the *VRIN* scale are similar in normal, clinical, and personnel-screening samples (see Table 6.3), which substantiates the point that psychopathology per se does not produce inconsistent item endorsement. Raw scores greater than 9 are above the 93th percentile in both normal and clinical samples. Also, a fair amount of inconsistency (4 to 5 inconsistent pairs of items) is found in both the clinical and normal samples. Again, a specific score on *VRIN* has not been selected to indicate that the items were endorsed inconsistently. Raw scores in the range of 10 to 13 have been suggested as a cutting score by the authors of MMPI-2 interpretive manuals (Butcher et al., 1989 [>13]; Greene, 2000 [>10 to 12]). The clinician will have to decide which cutting score is most appropriate given the specific individual and the setting in which the MMPI-2 is administered.

Figure 6.3 shows the profiles for random, all true, and all false responses on the MMPI-2. The validity scales easily identify all three profiles as being invalid with several scales at T scores of 120 or 30. However, the clinical scales for the random profile look very interpretable if the validity scales are not evaluated.

Accuracy of Item Endorsement

Self-Unfavorable Descriptions

Self-unfavorable descriptions of psychopathology on the MMPI-2 can be assessed by infrequency scales [*F, FB,* and $F(p)$], the *F - K* Dissimulation index (Gough, 1950), the Gough Dissimulation scale (*Ds:* Gough, 1954) scale, and critical item sets (Koss & Butcher, 1973; Lachar & Wrobel, 1974). Only the Infrequency-Psychopathology [$F(p)$] scale (Arbisi & Ben-Porath, 1995) will be described here because it is the best single scale to identify self-unfavorable descriptions. The $F(p)$ scale consists of 27 items that no more than 20% of a sample of 706 men who were psychiatric patients, a second sample of 423 men and women who also were psychiatric patients, and the MMPI-2 normative sample endorsed in the deviant direction. This scale is similar to the standard *F* scale except that the items were endorsed infrequently by a sample of psychiatric patients, hence the name *infrequency-psychopathology*. The scale generally taps a wide variety of heterogeneous content areas reflecting severe psychotic symptoms, unusual habits, highly amoral attitudes, and identity confusion that essentially are endorsed by no one.

Table 6.3 shows that endorsing more than three to four items on the $F(p)$ scale is unusual and at or above the 93rd percentile in normal, clinical, and personnel-screening samples. The $F(p)$ scale contains four items related to familial relations and four items from the *L* scale that can lead to false positive scores. Although these four *L* scale items are infrequently endorsed by psychiatric patients, the *L* scale assesses *self-favorable* descriptions rather than self-unfavorable descriptions. A person, who has endorsed a large number of the *L* scale items and actually is making a self-favorable description, could produce a significant elevation on the $F(p)$ scale because of the four items they have in common. Similarly, a person could endorse the four family items because of extremely poor familial relations

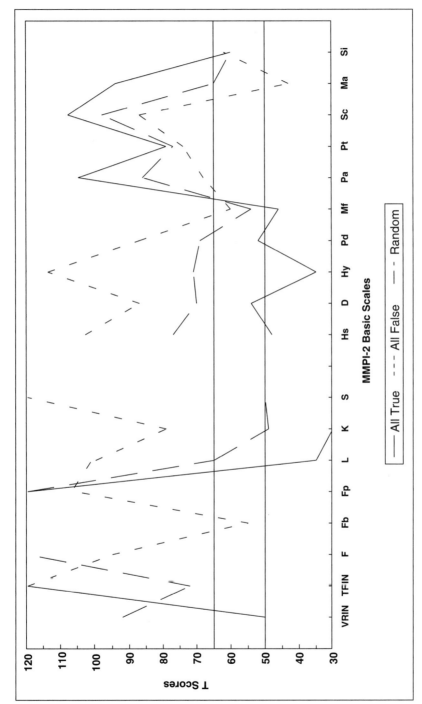

Figure 6.3 MMPI-2 profile for validity and clinical scales for random, all true, and all false responses. Reproduced by permission of the University of Minnesota Press.

that would elevate the $F(p)$ scale. Because these two extraneous factors can produce false positive elevations on the $F(p)$ scale, the clinician needs to examine the specific items endorsed when raw scores are in the range of 3 to 6.

Once it has been determined that the individual has made an extremely self-unfavorable description of psychopathology, the clinician will need to ascertain the reasons for the inaccurate item endorsement by a clinical interview. It remains to be determined whether it is possible to readminister the MMPI-2 to an individual who has made an extremely self-unfavorable description of psychopathology and obtain an accurate pattern of item endorsement. In any event, the clinician must remember that neither the MMPI-2 codetype nor the individual scales can be interpreted, when it has been determined that the individual has made an extremely unfavorable self-description as suggested by a very elevated score on the $F(p)$ scale.

Self-Favorable Descriptions

Self-favorable descriptions of psychopathology are organized within Paulhus's (1984, 1986) model of social desirability responding that distinguishes between self-deception and impression management: *self-deception* refers to a motivated unawareness of one of two conflicting cognitions, whereas *impression management* can be conceptualized as a strategic motive to present oneself in a positive manner. In self-deception, individuals are thought to believe their positive self-evaluation is an accurate description of themselves; whereas in impression management, individuals consciously dissemble to create a favorable impression in others. The L (Lie) scale on the MMPI-2 is a measure of impression management; whereas the K (Correction) and S (Superlative) scales are measures of self-deception.

The L (Lie) scale includes 15 items that were selected on a rational basis to identify persons who are deliberately trying to avoid answering the MMPI frankly and honestly (Dahlstrom, Welsh, & Dahlstrom, 1972). The scale assesses attitudes and practices that are culturally laudable but actually found only in the most conscientious persons. The content areas within the L scale include denial of minor, personal dishonesties and denial of aggression, bad thoughts, and weakness of character.

The K (Correction) scale consists of 30 items that were selected empirically to assist in identifying persons who displayed significant psychopathology yet had profiles within the normal range. Butcher and Han (1995) developed the Superlative (S) scale to assess persons who present themselves in a superlative manner that is encountered frequently in individuals who are being screened in personnel settings. The items for the S scale were selected by contrasting the MMPI-2 item responses of 274 pilot applicants with the 1,138 men in the MMPI-2 normative group. This analysis produced a set of 50 items with a difference in response frequency of at least 25% between the two groups. Butcher and Han suggested that the 41 items on the S scale that do not overlap with the K scale appear to operate as a "virtue-claiming or problem-denying scale." Item content on the S scale reflects general comfort with others who have good intentions, lack of any negative feelings toward others, and avoidance of any type of risk-taking behaviors. Butcher and Han conducted a component analysis of the S scale and identified five factors: Beliefs in Human Goodness; Serenity; Contentment with Life; Patience and Denial of Irritability and Anger; and Denial of Moral Flaws. There is no item overlap among the subscales of the S scale and all 50 items are assigned to one of the five factors.

Table 6.3 shows that endorsing more than 6 to 8 of the items on the L scale is at or above the 93rd percentile in normal and clinical samples, while 11 items is at the 93rd percentile in personnel-screening samples. It would be expected for persons in a personnel-screening setting to show more impression management than normal persons or individuals in a clinical setting. Scores on the K scale also tend to be similar in normal and clinical settings with raw scores of 22 to 23 at the 93rd percentile and only slightly higher at 25 in a personnel-screening setting. Self-deception, which is being measured by the K scale, is thought to be a manifestation of a cognitive variable that would not be expected to vary as greatly by the type of setting.

The person can be described as using impression management to create a favorable self-description when the L (Lie) scale is elevated (T > 59) and the L (Lie) scale is at least 5 T points higher than the K (Correction) and S (Superlative) scales. The person can be described as using self-deception to create a favorable self-description when the K (Correction) and S (Superlative) scales are elevated (T > 59) at least 5 T points higher than the L (Lie) scale. When all three of these scales (L [Lie], K [Correction], and S [Superlative]) are elevated in the same range (T > 55), the person can be described as making a generic self-favorable description.

When a client's responses have been identified as being endorsed inaccurately because of an extremely self-favorable description of psychopathology, the MMPI-2 profile is no longer interpretable. The clinician will have little reason to try to interpret such a profile because extremely self-favorable descriptions result in no clinical scales being elevated over a T score of 65 and frequently no clinical scales are above a T score of 60. The clinician should describe the individual's style of self-favorable description of psychopathology (impression management, self-deception, or a combination of both), determine the potential causes for this self-favorable description, and assess the implications for treatment and intervention. If the clinician can appreciate that the MMPI-2 profile produced by an extremely self-favorable description of psychopathology is not interpretable because no clinical scales are elevated, it may become more apparent that the MMPI-2 profile produced by an extremely self-unfavorable description of psychopathology is equally uninterpretable because most or all clinical scales are elevated.

Individuals who provide extremely self-favorable descriptions of psychopathology see their problems as less troubling to themselves and, hence, are less motivated to change. Their problems also may be more chronic and, consequently, more difficult to treat, if they remain in treatment. None of these potential causes of an extremely self-favorable description of psychopathology is a good prognostic sign for any type of psychological intervention.

INTERPRETATION

Codetypes

Once it has been determined that the individual has omitted few, if any, items, and endorsed the items consistently and accurately, the MMPI-2 can be interpreted. Interpretation of the MMPI-2 begins with and is based on codetypes; that is, the two highest clinical scales elevated to a T score of 65 or higher, or the single clinical scale (spike codetype) when only one scale reaches a T score of 65. This interpretation then is supplemented by the examination of specific scales, such as the clinical, content, and supplementary scales, as well as individual critical items. Fowler, Butcher, and Williams (2000), Friedman, Lewak, Nichols, and Webb (2001), Graham (2006), Greene (2000), and Nichols (2001) provide examples of the general interpretive strategy for the MMPI-2.

Commonly Occurring MMPI-2 Codetypes

The following pages provide the interpretation of 21 commonly occurring two-point MMPI-2 codetypes that have been extracted from the MMPI-2 Adult Interpretive System (Greene & Brown, 2006).[1] Figure 6.1 illustrates the basic profile for the MMPI-2 validity and clinical scales for a *1-2/2-1* codetype. A codetype description is written about a *group* of individuals who have elevated these two specific scales, not about the specific individual who has produced the codetype. Each statement within the codetype description must be considered a hypothesis to be verified with the clinical interview and history of this specific individual. Approximately 10% to 20% of these statements (hypotheses) will not be accurate simply because of the multiplicity of relations that can exist among the set of over 120 individual scales and 567 items on the MMPI-2. For example, the interpretive text for a *2-7/7-2* codetype (see pp. 159–161) contains 12, 14, 10, and 8 sentences in the Moods, Cognitions, Interpersonal Relations, and Other Problem Areas sections, respectively. The total number of actual behaviors or symptoms being reported is actually two or three times larger once it is realized that most sentences contain two or more pieces of separate information. It is expected that a minimum of from four to eight of these statements will need some kind of modification.

The clinician must expect to be making some type of modification to every codetype description on the MMPI-2. This entire process has been made much more straightforward in the MMPI-2 AIS (Greene & Brown, 2006) because every statement is referenced either to a scale(s) and/or item(s). When a scale name is in **bold** font, the individual is expected to have a low score (T < 50) on that scale. In the description of Interpersonal Relations for a *1-2/2-1* codetype (p. 151), the *Pd₁* and *FAM* scales are in bold font because these two scales assess problems and conflicts in family relations that this group of individuals does not report. When an item is listed in **bold** font, the item is endorsed in the **false** direction. Numerous examples can be seen in the Other Problem Areas for a *1-2/2-1* codetype (p. 151).

The clinician should modify any statement for which there are explicit data to support the change. If the codetype description indicates that the individual has endorsed an item as being "true" and it actually was endorsed "false," the clinician has explicit data to change, modify, or delete that item. Similarly, if the interpretive text indicates that a scale is or is not elevated, the individual's actual T score on the scale will support or negate that statement explicitly. The clinician, however, should not change any statement simply because it does not seem to fit this individual or the clinician does not think it is appropriate. It is vital

---

[1]Reproduced by special permission of the Publisher, Psychological Assessment Resources, Inc., 16204 North Florida Avenue, Lutz, Florida 33549, from the MMPI-2 Adult Interpretive System, Version 3, by Roger L. Greene, PhD, Robert C. Brown Jr., PhD, and PAR Staff. Copyright 1992, 1995, 2000, 2005 by PAR, Inc. Further reproduction is prohibited without permission of Psychological Assessment Resources, Inc.

to remember Meehl's (1957) admonition of how infrequently we are to use our clinical judgment when we have empirical data available to us.

The clinician's task of modifying the computer interpretation is much more difficult when no specific information is provided as to the source of each statement, which is characteristic of most computer interpretive systems. Nevertheless, the clinician still must edit each statement based on this individual's T scores on all the MMPI-2 scales and responses to all the items. The fact that this information is not provided explicitly does not absolve the clinician of the responsibility to modify the computer interpretation as needed.

1-2/2-1[2]

Moods   She reports that she is experiencing a mild to moderate level of emotional distress (*A, NEGE, RCd[dem]*) characterized by tension, anxiety (*7[Pt], ANX*), and dysphoria (*2[D], DEP*). She feels unable to get going and get things done in her life (*INTR, RC2[lpe], DEP1, TRT1,* 38T). It is rather unusual for her to report that she is depressed despite how she may appear to others; she is more likely to report being tired, having sleep difficulties, and having physical symptoms (*1[Hs], 2[D]*). She is more sensitive (285T) and feels more intensely than most people (271T). Her feelings are easily hurt (**63F,** 127T), and she is inclined to take things hard (331T). She is often irritable and grouchy (116T, 430T), and it makes her angry to have people hurry her (461T).

Cognitions   She reports that she has problems with attention, concentration (31T, 299T, 325T), and memory (**165F,** 565T). She is greatly bothered by forgetting where she puts things (472T). She often gets confused and forgets what she wants to say (475T). She tends to think in a concrete manner and to focus on her physical ailments (*1[Hs]*).

She believes her judgment is not as good as it was in the past (**43F**).

She thinks that most people will use unfair means and lie to get ahead (*CYN, RC3[cyn],* 58T, 81T, 110T, 374T).

Interpersonal Relations   She reports that she is introverted (*0[Si], SOD1*) and finds it hard to talk when she meets new people (167T). She is shy and reserved around other people (*SOD2*). She is likely not to speak to people until they speak to her (265T). Whenever possible, she avoids being in a crowd (367T). Her relations with her family are good (***Pd₁, FAM***). The only place she feels relaxed is in her own home (558T).

Other Problem Areas   She reports a number of gastrointestinal (*HEA1*) and neurological symptoms (*Sc₆, HEA2*), headaches (40T, **176F,** 536T), and pain in a number of areas of her body (**47F, 57F, 224F**). Her physical health is not as good as that of most of her friends (**45F**) and she worries about her health (**33F**). During the past few years she has not been well most of the time (**141F**). She has difficulty going to sleep because ideas or thoughts are bothering her (**140F**), her sleep is fitful and disturbed (39T), and she does not wake up fresh and rested most mornings (**3F**). She is easily awakened by noise (5T). She tires quickly (**152F**) and feels weak and tired a good deal of the time (175T, **330F,** 464T). She does not have enough energy for her work (**561F**), and she is not as able to work as she once was (**10F**). Her history and background should be reviewed to determine whether a

---

[2]The gender used for the interpretive text for each codetype reflects whether it is more common in men or women.

medical or neurological evaluation is warranted. Careful inquiry about suicidal ideation is recommended because of her masked depressive symptoms (*DEP4,* 150T, 303T, 506T, 520T, 524T, 530T).

Treatment   Her prognosis is poor for any form of traditional psychotherapy because of her difficulty in understanding that her problems might have a psychological component (*1*[*Hs*], *2*[*D*]). Conservative medical treatment is recommended because her physical ailments usually are difficult to document (*1*[*Hs*], *2*[*D*]). Short-term interventions focused on providing symptomatic relief from her physical ailments may be beneficial and can provide the foundation for more traditional psychotherapy (*1*[*Hs*], *2*[*D*]). Although cognitive-behavioral therapy for depression may be warranted (*2*[*D*], *DEP*), treatment should be focused initially on her presenting symptoms rather than depression per se because she is not likely to describe herself as being depressed (*1*[*Hs*], *2*[*D*]).

Two specific issues must be kept in mind when establishing and maintaining the therapeutic alliance: She has difficulty starting to do things (233T), and she seldom asks people for advice (**398F**).

Possible Diagnoses
Axis I
   R/O Somatoform Disorders
      307.80 Pain Disorder Associated with Psychological Factors
      300.81 Somatization Disorder
      300.81 Undifferentiated Somatization Disorder
      300.81 Somatoform Disorder NOS
   R/O Mood Disorders
      296.xx Major Depressive Disorder
      300.4   Dysthymic Disorder
      311   Depressive Disorder NOS
   R/O Anxiety Disorders
      300.23 Social Phobia
Axis II
   R/O Personality Disorders
      301.6   Dependent Personality Disorder
      301.82 Avoidant Personality Disorder

1-3/3-1

Moods   She reports that she is experiencing very mild emotional distress (*A, NEGE, RCd*[*dem*]) characterized by tension and anxiety (*7*[*Pt*], *ANX*). She frequently worries about something (196T). She also experiences a very mild level of dysphoria (*2*[*D*], *DEP*). Her daily life is full of things that keep her interested (9T). Something exciting will almost always make her feel better when she is feeling low (244T).

Cognitions   She reports that she cannot keep her mind on one thing (299T) and that she forgets where she leaves things (533T). It takes a great deal of effort for her to remember what people tell her these days (565T). She is self-confident (**73F**). She has strong opinions that she expresses directly to other people (437T, 452T). She likes to let people know where she stands on things (365T), and she finds it necessary to stand up for what she thinks is right (120T) or if people do something that makes her angry (481T). She tends to think in a concrete manner and to focus on her physical ailments (*1*[*Hs*]).

She believes that most people are honest and can be trusted (*3*[*Hy*], **CYN**, **RC3**[*cyn*]). She does not analyze the motives for her own or others' behavior (*3*[*Hy*]).

Interpersonal Relations   She reports a balance between extroverted and introverted behaviors (*0*[*Si*], **SOD**). She is very sociable and makes friends quickly (49T, 280T, 360T). She likes making decisions and assigning jobs to others (521T) and believes, if given the chance, she would make a good leader of people (350T). She seems to make friends about as quickly as others do (280T). She is very conventional and conforming to social standards (*3*[*Hy*]). Her relations with her family are good (**Pd₁**, **FAM**, **MDS**).

Other Problem Areas   She reports a wide variety of physical (*1*[*Hs*], *HEA*, *Hy₄*, *RC1*[*som*]) and neurological symptoms (*Sc6*, *HEA2*), headaches (**176F**), and pain in a number of areas of her body (**57F**, **224F**). Her physical health is not as good as that of most of her friends (**45F**), and she worries about her health (**33F**). She tires quickly (**152F**) and feels tired a good deal of the time (464T). She has difficulty going to sleep because she is bothered by ideas or thoughts (**140F**), her sleep is fitful and disturbed (39T), and she does not wake up fresh and rested most mornings (**3F**). She is less able to work now than she was in the past (**10F**). Her history and background should be reviewed to determine whether a medical or neurological evaluation is warranted. She is unlikely to get into behavioral problems (**ASP**, **ASP2**) or to have been in trouble with the law (266T).

Treatment   Her prognosis is generally poor because she has little motivation for any type of psychological intervention (*A*, *NEGE*, *RCd*[*dem*]). She prefers to focus on her physical symptoms instead of on any form of psychological process (*1*[*Hs*], *3*[*Hy*]). Conservative medical treatment is recommended because her physical ailments are difficult to document (*1*[*Hs*], *3*[*Hy*]). Short-term interventions focused on providing symptomatic relief from her physical ailments may be beneficial and can provide the foundation for more traditional psychotherapy (*1*[*Hs*], *3*[*Hy*]).

Only one specific issue must be kept in mind when establishing and maintaining the therapeutic alliance: She seldom asks people for advice (**398F**). She is not naturally introspective, which will complicate the implementation of any therapeutic intervention (*3*[*Hy*]).

Possible Diagnoses
Axis I
   R/O Somatoform Disorders
      300.7   Hypochondriasis
      307.80 Pain Disorder Associated with Psychological Factors
      300.81 Somatization Disorder
      300.81 Somatoform Disorder NOS
      300.81 Undifferentiated Somatoform Disorder
   R/O Adjustment Disorders
      309.0   Adjustment Disorder with Depressed Mood

R/O Mood Disorders
    300.4   Dysthymic Disorder
    311   Depressive Disorder NOS
Axis II
    R/O Personality Disorders
    301.50 Histrionic Personality Disorder
    301.6 Dependent Personality Disorder

2-3/3-2

Moods   She reports that she is experiencing a mild to moderate level of emotional distress (*A, NEGE, RCd[dem]*) characterized by dysphoria (*2[D], DEP*), worrying (*7[Pt], ANX*), and anhedonia (*INTR, RC2[lpe], DEP1, TRT1*). Most of the time she feels blue (65T, **95F, 388F**), and her daily life is not full of things that keep her interested (**9F**). She frequently worries about something or someone (196T, 301T, 305T, 415T). She is easily hurt by criticism or scolding (127T) and has difficulty expressing her feelings, describing herself as feeling bottled up (*2[D], 3[Hy]*). She has had long periods of time when she could not take care of things because she could not get going (38T). She is overcontrolled and fearful of losing control (*2[D], 3[Hy]*). She is likely to experience increases in depression, fatigue, and physical symptoms in response to stress (*3[Hy]*). It makes her angry when people hurry her (461T), and she lets them know how she feels about it (481T); otherwise she is unlikely to express her anger overtly (***AGGR, ANG, ANG1***).

Cognitions   She reports that she has problems with attention, concentration (31T, 299T, 325T), and memory (**165F**, 533T, 565T). She has strong opinions that she expresses directly to other people (437T, 452T). She likes to let people know where she stands on things (365T), and she finds it necessary to stand up for what she thinks is right (120T) or if people do something that makes her angry (481T). She has low self-esteem, lacks self-confidence (73T, **239F**), and doubts her own abilities (*LSE1*). She feels inadequate, helpless, and insecure (*LSE*). She certainly thinks she is useless at times (130T).

   She sometimes thinks that she is about to go to pieces (469T). At times, her mind seems to work more slowly than usual (341T). Her judgment is not as good as it was in the past (**43F**).

   She does not analyze the motives for her own or others' behavior (*3[Hy], **CYN, RC3[cyn]***). She is not happy with herself the way she is (377T) and wishes she could be as happy as others seem to be (56T).

Interpersonal Relations   She reports that she is somewhat introverted (*0[Si], SOD, SOD1*) and does not like loud parties or social events (**86F**). She feels socially alienated (*Pd$_4$, Sc$_1$, Si$_2$*) and presents herself as helpless, immature, and dependent (*LSE*). She reports good relations with her family (***Pd$_1$, FAM***).

Other Problem Areas   She reports that she has a wide variety of physical symptoms (*1[Hs], HEA, H$_4$, RC1[som]*) including gastrointestinal symptoms (*HEA1*), neurological symptoms (*Sc$_6$, HEA2*), headaches (**176F**), and generalized pain (**224F**). Her physical health is not as good as that of most of her friends (**45F**) and she worries about her health

(**33F**). During the past few years she has not been well most of the time (**141F**). She has difficulty going to sleep because thoughts or ideas are bothering her (**140F**), her sleep is fitful and disturbed (39T), and she does not wake up fresh and rested most mornings (**3F**). She is easily awakened by noise (5T). She tires quickly (**152F**) and feels tired, weak, and without energy much of the time (175T, **330F,** 464T). She does not have enough energy to do her work (**561F**), and she is not as able to work as she once was (**10F**). Her history and background should be reviewed to determine whether a medical or neurological evaluation is warranted. She is a very conventional individual who is unlikely to have behavioral problems (**ASP**). She is not likely to abuse substances (**AAS**). There is some possibility of suicidal ideation that needs to be evaluated carefully (*DEP4,* 150T, 303T, 506T, 520T, 524T, 530T).

Treatment   Her prognosis is generally poor because she sees little chance for significant change in her life (*2[D], 3[Hy]*). Short-term, behavioral therapy that focuses on her reasons for entering treatment may be beneficial and may allow for the development of a therapeutic alliance that would be necessary for long-term therapy (*2[D], 3[Hy]*). She will prefer to discuss her physical symptoms rather than focus on her psychological processes (*1[Hs]*).

She is not naturally introspective, and that will complicate the therapeutic process (*3[Hy]*). Two specific issues must be kept in mind when establishing and maintaining the therapeutic alliance: She has difficulty starting to do things (233T), and she seldom asks people for advice (**398F**).

Possible Diagnoses
Axis I
   R/O Mood Disorders
      296.xx Major Depressive Disorder
      300.4 Dysthymic Disorder
      311   Depressive Disorder NOS
   R/O Somatoform Disorders
      300.81 Somatoform Disorder NOS
   R/O Adjustment Disorders
      309.0 Adjustment Disorder with Depressed Mood
Axis II
   R/O Personality Disorders
      301.50 Histrionic Personality Disorder
      301.6 Dependent Personality Disorder
      301.83 Borderline Personality Disorder

2-4/4-2

Moods   She reports that she is experiencing a mild to moderate level of emotional distress (*A, NEGE, RCd[dem]*) characterized by dysphoria (*2[D], DEP,* 65T, **95F, 388F**), resentment (*6[Pa]*), agitation (*7[Pt], ANX*), and anhedonia (*INTR, RC2[lpe], DEP1, TRT1*). Her daily life has few things that keep her interested (**9F**). She frequently worries about something or someone (196T, 301T, 305T, 415T). These moods often arise in response to some external problem or difficulty (*4[Pd]*). While she may express guilt and remorse and may promise to change her behavior, her expressions typically are not sincere (4[Pd]). She is more sensitive (285T) and feels more intensely than most people (271T). Her feelings are easily hurt (**63F,** 127T), and she is inclined to take things hard (331T). She is grouchy, irritable, and stubborn (ANG2, 116T, 430T, 486T). It makes her angry when people hurry her (461T), and she has become so angry that she feels as though she will explode (542T).

Cognitions   She reports that her memory is all right (165T). Her judgment is not as good as it was in the past (**43F**). She certainly is lacking in self-confidence and believes that she is not as good as other people (LSE1, 73T, **239F,** 411T, 485T). She certainly thinks she is useless at times (130T). She has sometimes thought that difficulties were piling up so high that she could not overcome them (339T). She is apt to take disappointments so keenly that she cannot put them out of her mind (408T).

She sometimes thinks that she is about to go to pieces (469T).

She doubts the motives of other people and believes that they are interested only in their own welfare (CYN, RC3[cyn], 81T, 110T). She knows who is responsible for most of her troubles (113T). She has made lots of bad mistakes in her life (518T), regrets many things that she has done (82T), and thinks that she has not lived the right kind of life (52T). She is not happy with herself the way she is (377T) and wishes that she could be as happy as others seem to be (56T).

Interpersonal Relations   She reports that she is introverted (0[Si], SOD1). Her interpersonal relations tend to be generally problematic and conflicted (4[Pd], FAM, MDS), and she is alienated from herself (Pd5, Si3) and others (Pd4, Sc1, Si3). Her home life is not as pleasant as that of most people she knows (**125F**). She quarrels with members of her family (FAM1, **83F**) and feels alienated from them (FAM2).

Other Problem Areas   She reports that she worries about her health (**33F**). Her sleep is bothered by her thoughts and ideas (**140F**), and she does not wake up fresh and rested most mornings (**3F**). She tires quickly (**152F**) and feels tired a good deal of the time (464T). She does not feel weak all over much of the time (**175F**). She reported a number of behavioral problems when she was in school (ASP2). She is likely to abuse alcohol or drugs (AAS, 264T, 487T, 489T, 511T), so a careful review should be made of the consequences of her alcohol and drug use. She may have suicidal ideation (DEP4, 150T, 303T, 506T, 520T, 524T, 530T) that needs to be monitored carefully because of her potential to abuse alcohol or drugs.

Treatment   Her prognosis is generally poor for traditional individual psychotherapy (4[Pd]) unless a mood disorder is the primary diagnosis (2[D], DEP). In that instance, cognitive-behavioral psychotherapy focused on her depressive cognitions will be beneficial (2[D], DEP). Evaluation for antidepressant medication may be indicated in cases of more severe depression (2[D], DEP). Group therapy with individuals with similar behaviors may be effective when a mood disorder is not the primary diagnosis (4[Pd]). The consequences of her use of alcohol and drugs cannot be overlooked when determining what interventions need to be made (2[D], 4[Pd]).

Several specific issues must be kept in mind when establishing and maintaining the therapeutic alliance: She has difficulty starting to do things (233T); she gives up quickly when things go wrong (364T) or because she thinks too little of her ability (326T); she is hard to get to know (479T); and she is very stubborn (486T).

Possible Diagnoses
Axis I
R/O Adjustment Disorder
309.0   Adjustment Disorder with Depressed Mood
309.3   Adjustment Disorder with Disturbance of Conduct
R/O Mood Disorders
296.xx Major Depressive Disorder
296.5x Bipolar I Disorder, Most Recent Episode Depressed
296.89 Bipolar II Disorder, Most Recent Episode Depressed
300.4   Dysthymic Disorder
R/O Anxiety Disorders
300.23 Social Phobia
R/O Substance-Related Disorders
291.8   Alcohol-Induced Mood Disorder
305.00 Alcohol Abuse
305.40 Sedative, Hypnotic, or Anxiolytic Abuse
Axis II
R/O Personality Disorders
301.7   Antisocial Personality Disorder
301.81 Narcissistic Personality Disorder
301.82 Avoidant Personality Disorder
301.83 Borderline Personality Disorder

2-6/6-2

Moods   She reports that she is experiencing a moderate level of emotional distress (*A, NEGE, RCd[dem]*) that is characterized by brooding (*D₅*, 215T), dysphoria (*DEP2*, 65T, **95F, 388F**), anger (*ANG*), and anhedonia (*INTR, RC2[lpe], DEP1, TRT1*, 38T). She frequently worries about something or someone (196T, 301T, 305T, 415T). She believes she is more nervous than most others (**223F**). She is more sensitive (285T) and feels more intensely than most people (271T). Her feelings are easily hurt (**63F**, 127T), and she is inclined to take things hard (331T). She easily becomes impatient with people (302T). She is often irritable and grouchy (116T, 430T) and generally feels angry with both herself and others (*6[Pa], ANG*). It makes her angry when people hurry her (461T), and she gets angry with herself for giving in to others so much (519T). She has become so angry that she does not know what comes over her (513T) and she feels as though she will explode (542T).

Cognitions   She reports that she has problems with attention, concentration (31T, 299T, 325T), and memory (**165F**, 533T, 565T). Her judgment is not as good as it was in the past (**43F**). She certainly is lacking in self-confidence, believes that she is not as good as other people (*LSE*, 73T, **239F**, 411T, 485T), and thinks she is useless at times (130T). She has a hard time making decisions (482T, 509T), and she lets other people take charge and make decisions (503T, **521F**). She has sometimes thought that difficulties were piling up so high that she could not overcome them (339T). She thinks that she is about to go to pieces (469T) and to lose her mind (170T). She is sensitive to any form of criticism, assumes others are against her, and anticipates being rejected (6[Pa], Pa₁). She is apt to take disappointments so keenly that she cannot put them out of her mind (408T). She is sure that she is being talked about (259T), someone has it in for her (99T), and strangers are looking at her critically (251T). She is sure that she gets a raw deal from life (17T) and that she has often been punished without cause (145T). In everything she does lately, she thinks she is being tested (549T). She believes that it is safer to trust nobody (241T). She has often been misunderstood when she was trying to be helpful (396T, 403T). She is not happy with herself the way she is (377T) and wishes that she could be as happy as others seem to be (56T).

[*She reports a number of symptoms that may reflect a psychotic process or a long-term, characterological condition. Her presenting problems, background, and history should be reviewed with this possibility in mind.*]

Interpersonal Relations   She reports that she is introverted (0[Si], SOD1) and wishes she was not so shy (185T). She finds it hard to talk when she meets new people (167T) or is in a group of people (243T), and she is likely not to speak to people until they speak to her (265T). Whenever possible, she avoids being in a crowd (367T). She spends most of her spare time by herself (480T). She feels lonely even when she is with people (277T). She reports mild conflict with members of her family (Pd₁, FAM, MDS). She is alienated from herself (Pd₅, Si₃) and others (Pd₄, Sc₁, Si₃).

Other Problem Areas   She reports a number of specific gastrointestinal (HEA1) and neurological symptoms (Sc₆, HEA2), and she is generally concerned about her health (HEA3). She worries about her health (**33F**), and she is not in as good physical health as most of her friends (**45F**). She has difficulty going to sleep because thoughts or ideas are bothering her (**140F**), her sleep is fitful and disturbed (39T), and she does not wake up fresh and rested most mornings (**3F**). She feels tired a good deal of the time (464T). She is not as able to work as she once was (**10F**). Her history and background should be reviewed to determine whether a medical or neurological evaluation is warranted. A theme of hopelessness pervades her thoughts (454T, 554T); hence, suicidal ideation should be evaluated carefully (DEP4, 150T, 303T, 506T, 520T, 524T, 530T).

Treatment   Her prognosis is guarded because her anger and brooding resentment make it difficult to develop a therapeutic alliance (2[D], 6[Pa]). Short-term, behavioral interventions that focus on her reasons for entering treatment will be most beneficial (2[D], 6[Pa]). Cognitive-behavioral therapy that focuses on her dysphoric mood (2[D], DEP) and anger (6[Pa], ANG) also may be appropriate. Evaluation for antidepressant medication may be indicated in cases of more severe depression (2[D], DEP).

Several specific issues must be kept in mind when establishing and maintaining the therapeutic alliance: No one seems to understand her (22T); she has difficulty starting to do things (233T); she believes it is safer to trust nobody (241T); she is so touchy on some subjects that she cannot talk about them (274T); it makes her nervous when people ask her personal questions (375T); she is hard to get to know (479T); and she is bothered greatly by the thought of making changes in her life (497T).

Possible Diagnoses

Axis I

R/O Schizophrenia and Other Psychotic Disorders

295.40 Schizophreniform Disorder

295.70 Schizoaffective Disorder, Depressive Type

297.1   Delusional Disorder

R/O Mood Disorders

296.xx Major Depressive Disorder

296.5x Bipolar I Disorder, Most Recent Episode Depressed

296.89 Bipolar II Disorder, Most Recent Episode Depressed

300.4   Dysthymic Disorder

R/O Anxiety Disorders

300.23 Social Phobia

Axis II

R/O Personality Disorders

301.0   Paranoid Personality Disorder

301.22 Schizotypal Personality Disorder

301.82 Avoidant Personality Disorder

301.83 Borderline Personality Disorder

2-7/7-2

Moods   She reports that she is experiencing a moderate level of emotional distress (*A, NEGE, RCd*[*dem*]) characterized by dysphoric mood (*2*[*D*], *DEP,* 65T, **95F, 388F**), guilt, and anxiety (*7*[*Pt*], *ANX*). She views herself as being irritable and grouchy (*ANG2,* 116T, 430T), although others are more aware of her dysphoric mood (*2*[*D*], *DEP*). She experiences little pleasure from life (*INTR, RC2*[*lpe*], *DEP1, TRT1*) and may be anhedonic. She has had long periods when she could not take care of things because she could not get going (38T). She is a chronic worrier (196T) who broods and ruminates about herself and her problems (*7*[*Pt*], *ANX, OBS,* 301T, 305T, 415T). She is likely to overreact to minor stress with agitation, guilt, and self-punishment (*7*[*Pt*]). She is more sensitive (285T) and feels more intensely than most people (271T). Her feelings are easily hurt (**63F**, 127T), and she is inclined to take things hard (331T). She easily becomes impatient with people (302T). It makes her angry when people hurry her (461T), and she gets angry with herself for giving in to others so much (519T). She has become so angry that she feels as though she will explode (542T). She is unlikely to express anger overtly or to be aggressive toward others (*ANG1, AGGR*).

Cognitions   She reports that she has problems with attention, concentration (31T, 299T, 325T), and memory (**165F**, 308T, 533T, 565T). She often gets confused and forgets what she wants to say (475T). She certainly is lacking in self-confidence and believes that she is not as good as other people (*LSE,* 73T, **239F**, 411T, 485T). She certainly thinks she is useless at times (130T). She has a hard time making decisions (482T, 509T), and she feels helpless when she has to make important decisions (491T). She usually has to stop and think before she acts even in small matters (309T). She has several times given up doing a thing because she thought too little of her ability (326T). She is obsessed with her perceived personal deficiencies (*7*[*Pt*], *ANX, OBS*). She believes that her judgment is not as good as it once was (**43F**). She has difficulty starting to do things (233T) and she gives up quickly when things go wrong (364T). Her inertia and lack of drive reflect her depressive cognitions and negative expectations (*2[D]*, *DEP*). She is pessimistic and hopeless about the possibility of making any substantial changes in her circumstances (*2[D]*, *DEP*). She feels guilty when her high standards and expectations are not met (*7[Pt]*). She is not happy with herself the way she is (377T), and she wishes she could be as happy as others seem to be (56T).

Interpersonal Relations   She reports that she is shy and introverted (*0[Si]*, *SOD1*). She is easily embarrassed (289T), wishes she was not so shy (185T), and frequently has to fight against showing that she is bashful (165T). She finds it hard to talk when she meets new people (167T) and has trouble thinking of the right things to talk about when in a group of people (243T). She will avoid people if given the opportunity (*Si₂*). She is likely not to speak to people until they speak to her (265T). Even when she is with people, she feels lonely much of the time (277T). She is passive and dependent in her relationships and is unlikely to be assertive (*LSE2*). She sometimes finds it hard to stick up for her rights because she is so reserved (446T). She reports mild conflict with members of her family (*Pd₁*, *FAM*, *MDS*). She is alienated from herself (*Pd₅*, *Si₃*) and others (*Pd₄*, *Sc₁*, *Si₃*).

Other Problem Areas   She reports that she has several gastrointestinal (*HEA1*) and neurological symptoms (*Sc₆*, *HEA2*). She worries about her health (*HEA3*), and her health is not as good as that of most of her friends (**45F**). She has difficulty going to sleep because thoughts or ideas are bothering her (**140F**), her sleep is fitful and disturbed (39T), and she does not wake up fresh and rested most mornings (**3F**). She tires quickly (**152F**) and feels tired and without energy a good deal of the time (**330F,** 464T). She does not have enough energy to do her work (**561F**). Her history and background should be reviewed to determine whether a medical or neurological evaluation is warranted. Suicidal thoughts (*DEP4*, 150T, 303T, 506T, 520T, 524T, 530T) and suicide attempts are fairly likely and should be evaluated carefully. Sleep medications should be prescribed cautiously, if at all, because of the potential for suicide.

Treatment   Her prognosis is generally quite good because she sees herself as being responsible for her difficulties and is willing to examine her behavior, even at great length (*2[D]*, *7[Pt]*). Cognitive-behavioral psychotherapy focusing on her depressive cognitions will be very beneficial to her (*2[D]*, *7[Pt]*). Evaluation for antidepressant medication may be indicated in cases of more severe depression (*2[D]*, *DEP*).

   A number of specific issues must be kept in mind when establishing and maintaining the therapeutic alliance: She has difficulty starting to do things (233T); she gives up quickly when things go wrong (364T) or get difficult (554T), or because she thinks too little of her ability (326T); she shrinks from facing a crisis or difficulty (368T); she is passive and nonassertive (369T, 446T, 514T); it makes her nervous when people ask her personal questions (375T); she is hard to get to know (479T); she is bothered greatly by the thought of making changes in her life (497T); and it is hard for her to accept compliments (562T).

Possible Diagnoses

Axis I

R/O Mood Disorders

    296.xx Major Depressive Disorder

    296.5x Bipolar I Disorder, Most Recent Episode Depressed

    296.89 Bipolar II Disorder, Most Recent Episode Depressed

    300.4   Dysthymic Disorder

    311   Depressive Disorder NOS

R/O Adjustment Disorders

    309.0   Adjustment Disorder with Depressed Mood

    309.28 Adjustment Disorder with Mixed Anxiety and Depressed Mood

R/O Anxiety Disorders

    300.02 Generalized Anxiety Disorder

    300.23 Social Phobia

    300.3   Obsessive-Compulsive Disorder

R/O Substance-Related Disorders

    291.8   Alcohol-Induced Anxiety Disorder

    291.8   Alcohol-Induced Mood Disorder

    305.00 Alcohol Abuse

    305.40 Sedative, Hypnotic, and Anxiolytic Abuse

    305.50 Opioid Abuse

Axis II

R/O Personality Disorders

    301.4   Obsessive-Compulsive Personality Disorder

    301.6   Dependent Personality Disorder

    301.82 Avoidant Personality Disorder

2-8/8-2

Moods   She reports that she is experiencing moderate to severe emotional distress (*A, NEGE, RCd*[*dem*]) that is characterized by dysphoria (*2*[*D*], *DEP2,* 65T, **95F, 388F**), anxiety (*7*[*Pt*], *ANX*), and anhedonia (*INTR, RC2*[*lpe*], *DEP1, TRT1*). Her daily life has few things that keep her interested (**9F**). She is depressed, agitated, anxious, and guilty (*2*[*D*], *8*[*Sc*]). She does not seem to care what happens to her (92T), and she has lost her desire to work out her problems (539T). She frequently worries about something or someone (196T, 301T, 305T, 415T). She is more sensitive (285T) and feels more intensely than most people (271T). Her feelings are easily hurt (**63F,** 127T), and she is inclined to take things hard (331T). She easily becomes impatient with people (136T, 302T), and she is irritable and grouchy (*ANG,* 116T, 430T). It makes her angry when people give her advice (378T) or hurry her (461T). She also gets angry with herself for giving in to others so much (519T). She has become so angry that she does not know what comes over her (513T) and she feels as though she will explode (542T).

Cognitions   She reports that she has problems with attention, concentration (31T, 299T, 325T), and memory (**165F,** 308T, 475T, 533T, 565T). Her judgment is not as good as it was in the past (**43F**). She certainly is lacking in self-confidence and believes that she is not as good as other people (*LSE,* 73T, **239F,** 411T, 485T). She has a hard time making decisions (482T, 509T) and she feels helpless when she has to make important decisions (491T). Her plans have frequently seemed so full of difficulties that she had to give them up (394T). She generally feels worthless and inadequate (*LSE*) and avoids facing a crisis or difficulty (368T). She has difficulty starting to do things (233T), and she has little hope of success if she does get started (**318F**). She gives up quickly when things go wrong (364T). Several times a week she thinks something dreadful is about to happen (463T). She has strange and peculiar thoughts (316T) and she thinks and dreams of things that are too bad to talk about (16T, 221T). She also daydreams frequently and would rather daydream than do anything else (48T, **184F**). She thinks that there is something wrong with her mind (170T, 180T) and that she is about to go to pieces (469T). She often thinks things are not real (311T). She thinks that most people will use unfair means and stretch the truth to get ahead (*CYN, RC3*[*cyn*], 58T, 81T, 110T, 374T). She thinks that strangers are looking at her critically (251T) and believes that it is safer to trust nobody (241T). She has often been misunderstood when she was trying to be helpful (396T, 403T). She knows she is a burden to others (526T).

[*She reports a number of symptoms that may reflect a psychotic process or a long-term, characterological condition. Her presenting problems, background, and history should be reviewed with this possibility in mind.*]

Interpersonal Relations   She reports that she is very introverted (*0*[*Si*], *SOD1*) and withdraws from and keeps others at a distance (*8*[*Sc*], *Si₂*). She dislikes having people around her (281T) and spends most of her spare time by herself (480T). She feels lonely even when she is with people (277T). She is likely not to speak to people until they speak to her (265T). She finds it hard to talk when she meets new people (167T) or is in a group of people (243T). She does not seem to make friends as quickly as others do (**280F**). Her withdrawal and isolation only exacerbate her symptoms (*8*[*Sc*]). Her family is critical of her (*Pd₁, FAM1*) and she feels alienated from them (*FAM2*). She is alienated from herself (*Pd₅, Si₃*) and others (*Pd₄, Sc₁, Si₃*).

Other Problem Areas   She reports several neurological (*Sc₆, HEA2*) and gastrointestinal symptoms (*HEA1*). She has difficulty going to sleep because thoughts or ideas are bothering her (**140F**), her sleep is fitful and disturbed (39T), and she does not wake up fresh and rested most mornings (**3F**). She tires quickly (**152F**) and feels tired, weak, and without energy a good deal of the time (175T, **330F,** 464T). She does not have enough energy to do her work (**561F**). Her history and background should be reviewed carefully to determine whether a medical or neurological evaluation is needed. She is worried about sex (166T). Suicidal ideation is very likely (*DEP4,* 150T, 303T, 506T, 520T, 524T, 530T) and suicide potential should be evaluated carefully and monitored regularly. She also is hopeless, which increases the risk of suicidal behavior (**75F,** 454T, 516T, 539T).

Treatment   Her prognosis is generally poor because her problems are chronic (*2*[*D*], *8*[*Sc*]). Hospitalization may be required to stabilize her condition (*2*[*D*], *8*[*Sc*]). Psychopharmacological interventions may be necessary to deal with her concerns that she may be losing her mind, to help her sleep, and to elevate her mood (*2*[*D*], *8*[*Sc*]). The probability of meaningful long-term change is low (*2*[*D*], *8*[*Sc*]). Short-term, behavioral interventions that focus on her reasons for entering treatment will be most beneficial once she has been stabilized (2[D], 8[Sc]).

Several specific issues must be kept in mind when establishing and maintaining the therapeutic alliance: No one seems to understand her (22T); she does not seem to care what happens to her (92T); she has difficulty starting to do things (233T); she believes it is safer to trust nobody (241T); she is so touchy on some subjects that she cannot talk about them (274T); she gives up quickly when things go wrong (364T) or get difficult (554T), or because she thinks too little of her ability (326T); she shrinks from facing a crisis or difficulty (368T); she is very passive and nonassertive (369T, 421T, 446T, 514T); it makes her nervous when people ask her personal questions (375T); she feels unable to tell anyone all about herself (391T); she seldom asks people for advice (**398F**); the future seems hopeless to her (454T); she is hard to get to know (479T); she is very stubborn (486T); she is bothered greatly by the thought of making changes in her life (497T) and is not sure that she can make these changes (500T); she hates going to doctors even when she is sick (499T); she has had a tragic loss in her life that she will never get over (512T); she believes her life is empty and meaningless (516T); and it is hard for her to accept compliments (562T).

Possible Diagnoses
Axis I
R/O Mood Disorders
    296.xx Major Depressive Disorder
    296.5x Bipolar I Disorder, Most Recent Episode Depressed
    296.89 Bipolar II Disorder, Most Recent Episode Depressed
R/O Schizophrenia and Other Psychotic Disorders
    295.30 Schizophrenia, Paranoid Type
    295.40 Schizophreniform Disorder
    295.70 Schizoaffective Disorder, Depressive Type
R/O Anxiety Disorders
    300.23 Social Phobia
Axis II
R/O Personality Disorders
    301.22 Schizotypal Personality Disorder
    301.82 Avoidant Personality Disorder
    301.83 Borderline Personality Disorder

2-0/0-2

Moods   He reports that he is experiencing mild emotional distress (*A, NEGE, RCd*[*dem*]) characterized by chronic brooding (215T), dysphoria (2[D], *DEP2*), and anhedonia (*INTR, RC2*[*lpe*], *DEP1, TRT1*). He has had long periods when he could not take care of things because he could not get going (38T). He frequently worries about something or someone (196T, 301T, 305T, 415T). He is more sensitive (285T) and feels more intensely than most people (271T). His feelings are easily hurt (**63F,** 127T), and he is inclined to take things hard (331T). He is often irritable and grouchy (*ANG2,* 116T, 430T), and he easily becomes impatient with people (136T, 302T). It makes him angry when people give him advice (378T) or hurry him (461T). He also gets angry with himself for giving in to others so much (519T). He has become so angry that he feels as if he will explode (542T). Despite these angry feelings, he is very unlikely to be overtly aggressive (*ANG1, AGGR*).

Cognitions　He reports that he has problems with attention and concentration (31T, 325T). He certainly is lacking in self-confidence and believes that he is not as good as other people (*LSE,* 73T, **239F,** 411T, 485T). He finds it hard to be assertive because he is so reserved (*LSE2*). At times he thinks he is useless (130T). He shrinks from facing a crisis or difficulty (368T) and is easily downed in an argument (70T). He has a hard time making decisions (482T, 509T) and having to make important decisions makes him nervous (491T). He has often lost out on things because he could not make up his mind quickly enough (135T). He is apt to feel disappointments so keenly that he cannot put them out of his mind (408T). He gives up quickly when things go wrong (364T), when others criticize him, or when he thinks that he is unable to do something (326T). He is apt to pass up something he wants to do when others feel that it is not worth doing (369T). He thinks that most people will use unfair means and stretch the truth to get ahead (*CYN, RC3[cyn]*, 58T, 81T, 110T, 374T) and it is safer to trust nobody (241T). He has often been misunderstood when he was trying to be helpful (396T, 403T). He is not happy with himself the way he is (377T) and wishes he could be as happy as others seem to be (56T).

Interpersonal Relations　He reports that he is very socially introverted (*0[Si], SOD1*). He is easily embarrassed (289T), unusually self-conscious (**335F**), wishes he were not so shy (185T), and frequently has to fight against showing that he is bashful (161T). He avoids interactions with others (*Si2*), and he spends most of his spare time by himself (480T). Whenever possible, he avoids being in a crowd (367T) and he does not enjoy the excitement of a crowd (**359F**). At parties, he is more likely to sit by himself or with just one other person than to join in with the crowd (337T). He finds it hard to make talk when he meets new people (167T) or when in a group of people (243T), and he is likely not to speak to people until they speak to him (265T). He does not seem to make friends as quickly as others seem to do (**280F**). He sees himself as socially inept and awkward (*LSE1*); others are more likely to describe him as shy and reserved (*SOD2*). He feels lonely even when he is with people (277T). He sometimes finds it hard to stand up for his rights because he is so reserved (446T). He is alienated from himself (*Pd5, Si3*) and others (*Pd4, Sc1, Si3*).

Other Problem Areas　He reports general concerns about his physical health, but few specific symptoms (*HEA3*). He is unlikely to abuse substances (*AAS*) or to get into trouble because of his behavior (*Pd2, ASP2*, 266T).

Treatment　His prognosis is only fair because he is accustomed to his characterological problems, and he is reluctant to think of making changes in his life (*2[D], 0[Si]*). Social skills and assertiveness training are frequently beneficial (*0[Si]*). He responds well to structured treatment approaches that prescribe what he is to do (*2[D], 0[Si]*). Cognitive-behavioral approaches that focus on his depressive cognitions also will be beneficial (*2[D], DEP*). Group psychotherapy will be helpful in providing a social perspective for his problems and in dealing directly with his avoidant behaviors (*0[Si]*).

　　A number of specific issues must be kept in mind when establishing and maintaining the therapeutic alliance: He has difficulty starting to do things (233T); it is safer to trust nobody (241T); he gives up quickly when things go wrong (364T) or get difficult (554T), or because he thinks too little of his ability (326T); he shrinks from facing a crisis or difficulty (368T); he is passive and nonassertive (369T, 446T, 514T); it makes him nervous when people ask him personal questions (375T); he feels unable to tell anyone all about himself (391T); he seldom asks people for advice (**398F**); he is hard to get to know (479T); he is very stubborn (486T); he is bothered greatly by the thought of making changes in his life (497T); he hates going to doctors even when he is sick (499T); and it is hard for him to accept compliments (562T).

Possible Diagnoses
Axis I
R/O Adjustment Disorders
309.0   Adjustment Disorder with Depressed Mood
R/O Mood Disorders
300.4   Dysthymic Disorder
311   Depressive Disorder NOS
R/O Anxiety Disorders
300.23 Social Phobia
Axis II
R/O Personality Disorders
301.6   Dependent Personality Disorder
301.82 Avoidant Personality Disorder

Spike 3

Moods   She reports that she is not experiencing any type of emotional distress (*A, NEGE, RCd*[*dem*]). She is happy most of the time (**65F,** 95T, 388T) and finds her daily life interesting and pleasurable (9T). She sees herself as bright, cheerful, and optimistic (*3*[*Hy*]). She uses repression and denial to maintain her cheerful outlook on life (*3*[*Hy*]). She is very unlikely to display anger or be aggressive toward other people (*Hy$_5$, ANG, AGGR*). She is usually calm and not easily upset (405T).

Cognitions   She reports that her attention, concentration (**31F, 299F, 325F**), and memory seem to be all right (165T, **565F**). She has strong opinions that she expresses directly to other people (437T, 452T). She likes to let people know where she stands on things (365T) and she finds it necessary to stand up for what she thinks is right (120T) or if people do something that makes her angry (481T). She believes that she thinks clearly and logically, but others perceive her to be flighty and unfocused (*3*[*Hy*]); she has a histrionic cognitive style. She can make up her mind easily (**482F, 491F**), and she believes that her judgment is better than it has ever been (43T). She is self-confident (**73F**). She does not analyze the motives for her own or others' behavior (*3*[*Hy*]). She believes that others can be trusted and that they have her best interests at heart (*3*[*Hy*], *Pa$_3$, CYN, RC3*[*cyn*]).

Interpersonal Relations   She reports that she interacts easily with others and likes to be in social situations (*0*[*Si*]). She is very sociable and makes friends quickly (49T, 280T, 360T). She enjoys social gatherings and parties (353T, 370T) and the excitement of a crowd (359T, **367F**). She likes making decisions and assigning jobs to others (521T) and believes, if given the chance, she would make a good leader of people (350T). She has good relations with her family (*Pd₁*, *FAM*).

Other Problem Areas   She reports almost no physical symptoms (*1[Hs]*, *HEA*, *RC1[som]*). She is in just as good physical health as most of her friends (45T) and she seldom worries about her health (33T). She sleeps very well and wakes up fresh and rested most mornings (3T, **39F,** 140T, **304F**). She does not tire quickly (152T) and is not tired, weak, or without energy a good deal of the time (**175F,** 330T, **464F**). She usually has enough energy to do her work (561T). She is unlikely to abuse substances (*AAS*) or to have behavioral problems (*ASP, ASP2*).

Treatment   Her prognosis is guarded for any type of intervention because she is experiencing little emotional distress (*A, NEGE, RCd[dem]*). Short-term, behavioral interventions that focus on her reasons for entering treatment will be most beneficial (*3[Hy]*).

Only two specific issues that must be kept in mind when establishing and maintaining the therapeutic alliance: She is happy most of the time (95T) and she sees little that needs to be changed (**377F,** 534T).

Possible Diagnoses
Axis I
  R/O Depressive Disorders
      311   Depressive Disorder NOS
  R/O Adjustment Disorders
      309.3 Adjustment Disorder with Disturbance of Conduct
      309.4 Adjustment Disorder with Mixed Disturbance of Emotions and Conduct
  R/O Dissociative Disorders
      300.15 Dissociative Disorder NOS
Axis II
  R/O Personality Disorders
      301.50 Histrionic Personality Disorder
      301.81 Narcissistic Personality Disorder

3-6/6-3

Moods   She reports that she is experiencing a mild to moderate level of emotional distress (*A, NEGE, RCd[dem]*) characterized by dysphoria (*2[D]*, *DEP2*) and tension (*7[Pt]*, *ANX*). She frequently worries about something or someone (196T, 301T, 305T). She is fearful and generally apprehensive about what is happening around her (*FRS1*). She is more sensitive (285T) and feels more intensely than most people (271T). Her feelings are easily hurt (**63F**), and she is inclined to take things hard (331T). She feels unable to get going and to get things done in her life (38T) and may be anhedonic (*INTR, RC2[lpe], DEP1, TRT1*). It makes her angry when people hurry her (461T), and she lets them know how she feels about it (481T). She has become so angry that she feels as though she will explode (542T). Others may see her as an angry, hostile individual who strongly denies these readily apparent feelings (*3[Hy], 6[Pa]*). She usually expresses her anger in indirect, passive ways (*3[Hy], 6[Pa]*).

Cognitions   She reports that her memory seems to be all right (165T). She has strong opinions that she expresses directly to other people (437T, 452T). She likes to let people know where she stands on things (365T), and she finds it necessary to stand up for what she thinks is right (120T) or if people do something that makes her angry (481T). She makes decisions easily (**482F**), yet she believes that her difficulties are piling up so high that she cannot overcome them (339T). She sometimes thinks that she is about to go to pieces (469T). She does not analyze the motives for her own or others' behavior (*3[Hy]*, *Pa₃, CYN, RC3[cyn]*). She is sure that she is being talked about (259T) and that she has enemies who really wish to harm her (**314F**). She knows who is responsible for most of her problems (113T). Her hardest battles are with herself (89T).

Interpersonal Relations   Although she reports that she is slightly introverted (*0[Si]*), she is very sociable and makes friends quickly (49T, 280T, 360T). She likes making decisions and assigning jobs to others (521T) and believes, if given the chance, she would make a good leader of people (350T). She has good relations with her family (*Pd₁, FAM*), but she is alienated from herself (*Pd₅*) and others (*Pd₄, Sc₁*). She believes that her home life is as pleasant as that of most people she knows (125T).

Other Problem Areas   She reports a number of gastrointestinal (*HEA1*) and neurological (*Sc₆, HEA2*) symptoms as well as general concern about her health (*1[Hs], HEA3*). She has difficulty going to sleep because she is excited (304T) or thoughts or ideas are bothering her (**140F**), her sleep is fitful and disturbed (39T), she is easily awakened by noise (5T), and she does not wake up fresh and rested most mornings (**3F**). She feels tired a good deal of the time (464T). Her history and background should be reviewed to determine whether a medical or neurological evaluation is warranted. She is unlikely to have been in trouble because of her behavior (*ASP, ASP2*) or to abuse substances (*AAS*).

Treatment   Her prognosis is generally guarded to poor because of the characterological nature of her problems (*3[Hy], 6[Pa]*). Her tendency not to analyze the motives for her own or others' behavior complicates most interventions (*3[Hy], Pa₃, CYN, RC3[cyn]*). Short-term, behavioral interventions that focus on her reasons for entering treatment will be most beneficial (*3[Hy], 6[Pa]*).

No specific issues must be kept in mind when establishing and maintaining the therapeutic alliance.

Possible Diagnoses
Axis I
R/O Mood Disorders
    296.xx Major Depressive Disorder
    300.4   Dysthymic Disorder
    311   Depressive Disorder NOS
R/O Somatoform Disorders
    300.81 Somatoform Disorder NOS
R/O Adjustment Disorders
    309.3   Adjustment Disorder with Disturbance of Conduct

Axis II

R/O Personality Disorders

301.0 Paranoid Personality Disorder

301.50 Histrionic Personality Disorder

301.81 Narcissistic Personality Disorder

301.83 Borderline Personality Disorder

Spike 4

Moods He reports minimal emotional distress (***A, NEGE, RC***[***dem***]) and is very comfortable with himself and his behavior. Life is not a strain for him (**273F**), and he is happy most of the time (**65F**, 95T, 388T). His daily life is full of things that keep him interested (9T). He believes that he is no more nervous than most others (223T). He is less sensitive (**285F**) and feels less intensely than most people do (**271F**). Criticism or scolding does not hurt him terribly (**127F**), and he is not inclined to take things hard (**331F**). Something exciting will always pull him out of it when he is feeling low (244T).

Cognitions He reports that his attention, concentration (**31F, 299F, 325F**), and memory seem to be all right (165T, **472F, 533F, 565F**). He has strong opinions that he expresses directly to other people (437T, 452T). He likes to let people know where he stands on things (365T), and he finds it necessary to stand up for what he thinks is right (120T) or if people do something that makes him angry (481T). At times, he thinks that he can make up his mind with unusually great ease (206T). He believes his judgment is better than it ever was (43T). He believes that he thinks clearly and rationally and has good insight into his own behavior (*4*[*Pd*]). He usually has an easy time deciding what to do (**482F**). His confidence and assurance in his abilities may be a façade for underlying feelings of insecurity, inadequacy, and dependency (*4*[*Pd*]).

Interpersonal Relations He reports that he is extroverted (*0*[*Si*]) and comfortable in social situations (*Pd₃*, **SOD**). He is very sociable and makes friends quickly (49T, 280T, 360T). He likes making decisions and assigning jobs to others (521T) and believes, if given the chance, he would make a good leader of people (350T). He enjoys social gatherings and parties (353T, 370T) and the excitement of a crowd (359T, **367F**). He makes a good first impression on others, but this impression does not last long (*4*[*Pd*]). His interpersonal relations are often shallow and superficial (*4*[*Pd*]). His relations typically are not reciprocal and are marked by distrust, a lack of empathy, and irresponsibility (*4*[*Pd*]). His family is critical of him and he is alienated from them (*FAM2*). He reports very mild alienation from others (*Pd₄*). He believes his home life is as pleasant as that of most people he knows (125T). When things get really bad, he knows that he can count on his family for help (383T).

Other Problem Areas He reports that he is in good physical health (*1*[*Hs*], **HEA**, *Hy₄*, **RC1**[***som***]). He has few or no pains (57T, 224T) and very few headaches (176T). During the past few years he has been well most of the time (141T), and he is in just as good physical health as most of his friends (45T). He sleeps very well and wakes up fresh and rested most mornings (3T, **39F**, 140T, **304F**). He does not tire quickly (152T) and is not tired, weak, and without energy a good deal of the time (**175F**, 330T, **464F**). He usually has enough energy to do his work (561T) and is about as able to work as he ever was (10T). He is likely to abuse alcohol or drugs (*AAS*, 264T, 487T, 489T, 511T), so a careful review should be made of the consequences of his alcohol and drug use. He is very likely to have engaged in antisocial behaviors during his school years (*ASP2*) and to continue to engage in reckless behaviors that may or may not be explicitly illegal (*4[Pd]*). He has been in trouble with the law (**266F**). He has done dangerous things for the thrill of it (**100F**).

Treatment   His prognosis is guarded unless treatment begins early in the life of the individual (*4[Pd]*). He is experiencing little personal distress (*A, NEGE, RCd[dem]*), and he expects others to change to meet his expectations (*4[Pd]*). Short-term, behavior interventions focused on his reasons for entering treatment will be most effective (*4[Pd]*).

No specific issues must be kept in mind when establishing and maintaining the therapeutic alliance other than that despite his sincere-sounding intentions, he is not inclined to undertake any serious examination of his own behavior (*4[Pd]*).

Possible Diagnoses
Axis I
    R/O Adjustment Disorders
        309.3   Adjustment Disorder with Disturbance of Conduct
    R/O Substance-Related Disorders
        305.00 Alcohol Abuse
        305.60 Cocaine Abuse
        305.70 Amphetamine Abuse
Axis II
    R/O Personality Disorders
        301.7   Antisocial Personality Disorder
        301.81 Narcissistic Personality Disorder

4-7/7-4

Moods   He reports that he is experiencing a mild to moderate level of emotional distress (*A, NEGE, RCd[dem]*) characterized by anxiety and agitation (*7[Pt]*, *ANX*). He is unmotivated and feels unable to do much to help himself at this time and may be anhedonic (*INTR, RC2[lpe], DEP1*, TRT1). He frequently worries about something or someone (196T, 301T, 305T, 415T). He is more sensitive (285T) and feels more intensely than most people (271T). His feelings are easily hurt (**63F,** 127T), and he is inclined to take things hard (331T). He is grouchy and irritable (*ANG*) and easily becomes impatient with people (302T). It makes him angry when people hurry him (461T), and he gets angry with himself for giving in to others so much (519T). He has become so angry that he feels as if he will explode (542T).

Cognitions   He reports that he has problems with attention and concentration (31T, 299T, 325T), but his memory seems to be all right (165T). He has a hard time making decisions (482T, 509T). He certainly is lacking in self-confidence and believes that he is not as good as other people (*LSE,* 73T, **239F,** 411T, 485T). He exhibits a cyclical pattern of acting-out followed by excessive concern, regret, and remorse over his behavior (*4[Pd], 7[Pt]*). However, his remorse does not inhibit the repetition of this behavior and further episodes of acting-out (*4[Pd], 7[Pt]*). He does many things that he later regrets (82T). He believes that he has not lived the right kind of life (52T), has made lots of bad mistakes in his life (518T), is not happy with himself the way he is (377T), and wishes he could be as happy as others seem to be (56T). He is apt to take disappointments so keenly that he cannot put them out of his mind (408T). He does not analyze the motives for his own or others' behavior (*Pa3, CYN, RC3[cyn]*).

Interpersonal Relations   He reports that he is slightly introverted (*0[Si]*), but he is very sociable and makes friends quickly (49T, 280T, 360T). He enjoys social gatherings and parties (353T, 370T) and the excitement of a crowd (359T, **367F**). His familial and interpersonal relations are marked by conflict and are often disrupted by episodic acting-out (*4[Pd], Pd₁, Pd₂, FAM, MDS*). When things get really bad, he knows that he can count on his family for help (383T). He is not particularly sensitive or responsive to the needs of others, except after something has happened (*4[Pd]*). He is alienated from himself (*Pd₅, Si₃*) and others (*Pd₄, Sc₁, Si₃, FAM2*).

Other Problem Areas   He reports a few general concerns about his health (*HEA3*). He has few or no pains (57T, 224T) and very few headaches (176T). He is in just as good physical health as most of his friends (45T). Most nights he does not go to sleep without thoughts or ideas bothering him (**140F**), and he does not wake up fresh and rested most mornings (**3F**). He usually has enough energy to do his job (561T), and he is about as able to work as he ever was (10T). He is likely to abuse alcohol or drugs (*AAS,* 264T, 487T, 489T, 511T) so a careful review should be made of the consequences of his alcohol and drug use. He reported a number of behavior problems when he was in school (*ASP2*), and he is likely to have been in trouble with the law (**266F**).

Treatment   His prognosis is generally poor for short-term psychotherapy and guarded for long-term, intensive psychotherapy because of the characterological nature of his problems (*4[Pd], 7[Pt]*). His remorse and guilt over acting-out may give the impression of more insight and motivation to change than are actually present (*4[Pd], 7[Pt]*). Once his remorse and guilt have dissipated, his motivation will disappear quickly (*4[Pd], 7[Pt]*). Helping him to recognize his cyclic patterns and then to understand their dynamics is a primary goal in treatment (*4[Pd], 7[Pt]*).

Several specific issues must be kept in mind when establishing and maintaining the therapeutic alliance: He has difficulty starting to do things (233T); he gives up quickly when things go wrong (364T) or because he thinks too little of his ability (326T); he has done some bad things in the past that he will never tell anyone about (373T); he works out things for himself rather than ask for advice (**398F,** 440T); and he is very stubborn (486T).

Possible Diagnoses
Axis I
   R/O Anxiety Disorders
      300.00 Anxiety Disorder NOS
      300.02 Generalized Anxiety Disorder
      300.23 Social Phobia
   R/O Adjustment Disorders
      309.24 Adjustment Disorder with Anxiety
      309.3   Adjustment Disorder with Disturbance of Conduct

R/O Substance-Related Disorders
    291.8   Alcohol-Induced Anxiety Disorder
    305.00 Alcohol Abuse
    305.40 Sedative, Hypnotic, or Anxiolytic Abuse

Axis II
R/O Personality Disorders
    301.81 Narcissistic Personality Disorder
    301.82 Avoidant Personality Disorder
    301.83 Borderline Personality Disorder

4-8/8-4

Moods   He reports that he is experiencing a moderate to severe level of emotional distress (*A, NEGE, RCd[dem]*) characterized by dysphoric mood (*2[D], DEP2*), agitation (*7[Pt], 9[Ma]*), and anhedonia (*INTR, RC2[lpe], DEP1, TRT1*). He frequently finds himself worrying about something (196T), finds it difficult to get things done in his life, and has little hope of being successful if he could get motivated at something (*INTR, RC2[lpe], DEP1, TRT1*). He is more sensitive (285T) and feels more intensely than most people (271T). His feelings are easily hurt (**63F**, 127T), and he is inclined to take things hard (331T). He easily becomes impatient with people (302T). He often feels resentful, angry (*6[Pa], ANG*), irritable, and grouchy (116T, 430T). He has difficulty controlling or expressing his anger appropriately (*8[Sc], DISC*). In response to stress, he is likely to either withdraw completely (*8[Sc]*) or to act out his angry impulses (*6[Pa], ANG, DISC*). It makes him angry when people give him advice (378T) or hurry him (461T), and he lets them know how he feels about it (481T). He also gets angry with himself for giving in to others so much (519T). He has become so angry that he does not know what comes over him (513T) and he feels as if he will explode (542T). At times, he has a strong urge to do something harmful or shocking (85T).

Cognitions   He reports that he has problems with attention and concentration (31T, 299T, 325T). He has strong opinions that he expresses directly to other people (437T, 452T). He likes to let people know where he stands on things (365T), and he finds it necessary to stand up for what he thinks is right (120T) or if people do something that makes him angry (481T). He certainly is lacking in self-confidence and believes that he is not as good as other people (*LSE, LSE1*, 73T, **239F**, 411T, 485T). He exhibits poor judgment and is often unpredictable and impulsive (*4[Pd], 8[Sc]*). His judgment is not as good as it once was (**43F**). He feels insecure, isolated, rejected, and unwanted (*8[Sc]*). He is threatened by a world that he views as hostile and dangerous (*8[Sc]*). He has had very peculiar and strange experiences (32T) and thoughts (316T). He thinks and dreams of things that are too bad to talk about (16T, 221T). He is very sensitive to the motives of others and hypervigilant (*6[Pa]*). He has often thought that strangers were looking at him critically (251T). He thinks that most people will use unfair means and stretch the truth to get ahead (*CYN, RC3[cyn]*, 58T, 81T, 110T, 374T). He often wonders what hidden reason another person may have for being nice to him (124T). He believes that it is safer to trust nobody (241T). He has not lived the right kind of life (52T), made lots of bad mistakes in his life (518T), and done many things that he later regrets (82T). He has often been misunderstood when he was trying to be helpful (396T, 403T), and his way of doing things is apt to be misunderstood by others (225T).

[*He reports a number of symptoms that may reflect a psychotic process or a long-term, characterological condition. His presenting problems, background, and history should be reviewed with this possibility in mind.*]

Interpersonal Relations He reports that he is introverted (*0[Si]*) and has difficulty with close, emotional relationships (*8[Sc]*). He lacks basic social skills (*4[Pd], 8[Sc]*) and tends to be socially withdrawn and isolated (*0[Si]*), yet he enjoys social gatherings and parties (353T, 370T) and the excitement of a crowd (359T, **367F**). He sees himself as being very sociable and making friends quickly (49T, 280T, 360T), although he is emotionally distant, feels lonely, and knows that no one understands him and his problems (*8[Sc]*). His tendency to feel rejected by others often leads to hostility and conflict that only exacerbate his feelings of being alienated from others (*4[Pd], 8[Sc]*). He sees his family as extremely uncaring and critical and his home life as very unpleasant (*Pd$_1$, FAM*). Once in a while, he feels hate toward members of his family whom he usually loves (256T). He has very little to do with his relatives now (550T). The things that some of his family have done have frightened him (292T). Some of his family members have habits that bother and annoy him very much (205T). He is alienated from himself (*Pd$_5$, Si$_3$*) and others (*Pd$_4$, Sc$_1$, Si$_3$, FAM2*).

Other Problem Areas He reports a few gastrointestinal symptoms (*HEA1*) and a number of neurological symptoms (*Sc$_6$, HEA2*). He does not wake up fresh and rested most mornings (**3F**). He does not feel weak all over much of the time (**175F**). At times, he is all full of energy (330T). His physical and neurological symptoms warrant careful review and possible referral for a medical or neurological evaluation. He is likely to abuse substances (*AAS,* 264T, 487T, 489T, 511T) that exacerbate all his problems. His problems frequently involve inappropriate sexual behavior (*4[Pd], 8[Sc]*, **34F**). He had a number of behavioral problems while in school (*ASP2*) and has been in trouble with the law (**266F**). If he commits a crime, it is likely to be poorly planned and executed and may involve bizarre or violent behavior (*4[Pd], 8[Sc]*). He is likely to have a history of suicidal behavior, so suicide ideation should be evaluated carefully (*DEP4,* 150T, 303T, 506T, 520T, 524T, 530T). His isolation (*8[Sc], 0[Si]*) and proneness to act out impulsively toward himself or others (*8[Sc], MAC-R, DISC*) increase the risk of suicide.

Treatment His prognosis is generally very poor because of the characterological nature of his problems (*4[Pd], 8[Sc]*). Psychopharmacological interventions, other than possibly antidepressants, also are unlikely to be very effective because of the characterological problems involved (*4[Pd], 8[Sc]*). Interventions focused on specific behavioral objectives may be useful (*4[Pd], 8[Sc]*). Any form of insight-oriented therapy is contraindicated (*4[Pd], 8[Sc]*). Social skills and assertiveness training in a group setting may be very beneficial (*8[Sc], 0[Si]*).

His difficulties in forming an emotional relationship and his reluctance to self-disclose make the establishment of a therapeutic alliance problematic at best (*4[Pd], 8[Sc]*). A number of specific issues must be kept in mind when establishing and maintaining the therapeutic alliance: No one seems to understand him (22T); he has difficulty starting to do things (233T); it is safer to trust nobody (241T); he is so touchy on some subjects that he cannot talk about them (274T); he gives up quickly when things go wrong (364T) or because he thinks too little of his ability (326T); he shrinks from facing a crisis or difficulty

(368T); he has done some bad things in the past that he will never tell anyone about (373T); he is hard to get to know (479T); and he is very stubborn (486T).

Possible Diagnoses
Axis I
R/O Schizophrenia and Other Psychotic Disorders
    295.40 Schizophreniform Disorder
    295.30 Schizophrenia, Paranoid Type
    295.70 Schizoaffective Disorder, Depressive Type
R/O Mood Disorders
    296.xx Major Depressive Disorder
    296.5x Bipolar I Disorder, Most Recent Episode Depressed
    296.89 Bipolar II Disorder, Most Recent Episode Depressed
R/O Anxiety Disorders
    300.23 Social Phobia
R/O Paraphilias
    302.9 Paraphilia NOS
R/O Impulse-Control Disorders Not Elsewhere Classified
    312.34 Intermittent Explosive Disorder
R/O Substance-Related Disorders
    305.00 Alcohol Abuse
Axis II
R/O Personality Disorders
    301.0 Paranoid Personality Disorder
    301.22 Schizotypal Personality Disorder
    301.7 Antisocial Personality Disorder
    301.81 Narcissistic Personality Disorder
    301.82 Avoidant Personality Disorder
    301.83 Borderline Personality Disorder

4-9/9-4

Moods   He reports that he is experiencing minimal emotional distress or concern (*A, NEGE, RCd[dem]*) about his behavior or present circumstances. In fact, he is happy most of the time (**65F**, 95T). He dislikes being bored and inactive and will stir up excitement if he gets bored (*9[Ma]*, 169T). Once a week or oftener, he becomes very excited (242T). Something exciting will almost always pull him out of it when he is feeling low (244T). He frequently has intense feelings of anger and hostility that result in episodic outbursts of anger (*9[Ma], ANG, AGGR, DISC, RC9[hpm]*). He is likely to exhibit increased anger and hostility in response to stress (*4[Pd], 9[Ma]*). He is oppositional when he is not overtly angry (*4[Pd], 9[Ma]*). It makes him angry when people hurry him (461T), and he lets them know how he feels about it (481T).

Cognitions   He reports that his attention, concentration (**31F, 299F, 325F**), and memory (165T, **565F**) seem to be all right. He has strong opinions that he expresses directly to other people (437T, 452T). He likes to let people know where he stands on things (365T) and he finds it necessary to stand up for what he thinks is right (120T) or if people do something that makes him angry (481T). He exhibits poor judgment, often acts without considering the consequences of his actions, and has difficulty learning from experience (*4[Pd]*, *9[Ma]*). He is unwilling to accept responsibility for his own behavior, and he exhibits a persistent tendency to get into trouble (*4[Pd]*, *9[Ma]*). He thinks that most people will use unfair means and stretch the truth to get ahead (*CYN, RC3[cyn]*, 58T, 81T, 110T, 374T). He has made a lot of bad mistakes in his life (518T).

Interpersonal Relations   He reports that he is extroverted and mixes easily with others (***0[Si]***, ***SOD***). He is very sociable and makes friends quickly (49T, 280T, 360T). He likes making decisions and assigning jobs to others (521T) and believes, if given the chance, he would make a good leader of people (350T). He enjoys social gatherings and parties (353T, 370T) and the excitement of a crowd (359T, **367F**). He is socially facile (**167F, 243F**), and he makes a good first impression (*4[Pd]*, ***0[Si]***). More long-term contact will reveal that his interpersonal relations are superficial and marked by impulsivity, distrust, a lack of empathy, and egocentricity (*4[Pd]*, *9[Ma]*). He has numerous, long-standing problems with his family and persons in positions of authority (*4[Pd]*, *Pd₁*, *Pd₂*, *FAM, MDS*). Some of his family have habits that bother and annoy him very much (205T). He is alienated from himself (*Pd₅*, *Si₃*) and others (*Pd₄*, *Sc₁*, *Si₃*).

Other Problem Areas   He reports that he is in good physical health (***1[Hs]***, ***HEA, Hy₄, RC1[som]***). He has few or no pains (224T) and very few headaches (176T). He is in just as good physical health as most of his friends (45T). Sometimes he becomes so excited that he finds it hard to get to sleep (304T), but his sleep is not fitful or disturbed (**39F**). He does not tire quickly (152T) and is not tired, weak, and without energy a good deal of the time (**175F**, 330T, **464F**). He usually has enough energy to do his work (561T) and is about as able to work as he ever was (10T). He is impulsive, risk-taking (*4[Pd]*, *9[Ma]*, *MAC-R, DISC*) and is likely to abuse substances (*AAS*, 264T, 487T, 489T, 511T) so a careful review should be made of the consequences of his alcohol and drug use. He has done dangerous things for the thrill of it (**100F**). He has a history of legal and school problems and acting-out, even if he is not in legal trouble at the present time (*4[Pd]*, *9[Ma]*, *ASP, ASP2*, **266F**).

Treatment   His prognosis is guarded unless treatment begins early in his life because this characterological process tends to result in fixed behavior patterns that are difficult to change (*4[Pd]*, *9[Ma]*). He is experiencing minimal emotional distress that might serve as motivation to change his behavior (*A, NEGE, RCd[dem]*). Behavioral or short-term interventions that focus on the specific behaviors that led him to treatment will be most effective (*4[Pd]*, *9[Ma]*). Group therapies with similar individuals frequently are helpful in confronting his characterological pattern of relating to others (*4[Pd]*, *9[Ma]*).

Only one specific issue must be kept in mind when establishing and maintaining the therapeutic alliance: He is very stubborn (486T).

Possible Diagnoses
Axis I
   R/O Adjustment Disorders
      309.3   Adjustment Disorder with Disturbance of Conduct
   R/O Mood Disorders
      296.40 Bipolar I Disorder, Most Recent Episode Hypomanic
      296.89 Bipolar II Disorder, Most Recent Episode Hypomanic
      301.13 Cyclothymic Disorder

R/O Substance-Related Disorders

    291.8   Alcohol-Induced Mood Disorder

    305.00 Alcohol Abuse

    305.60 Cocaine Abuse

    305.70 Amphetamine Abuse

Axis II

R/O Personality Disorders

    301.7   Antisocial Personality Disorder

    301.81 Narcissistic Personality Disorder

Spike 6

Moods He reports that he is not experiencing any emotional distress (**A, NEGE, RCd[*dem*]**). He is happy most of the time (**65F,** 95T, 388T), and his daily life is full of things that keep him interested (9T). He believes he is no more nervous than most others (223T).

Cognitions He reports that his attention, concentration (**31F, 299F, 325F**), and memory seem to be all right (165T, **308F, 565F**). He has strong opinions that he expresses directly to other people (437T, 452T). He likes to let people know where he stands on things (365T), and he finds it necessary to stand up for what he thinks is right (120T) or if people do something that makes him angry (481T). His judgment is better than it ever was (43T). He is self-confident (**73F**). He is very vigilant of what goes on around him (6[*Pa*]). He does not analyze the motives for his own or others' behavior and believes that they can be trusted (**CYN, RC3[*cyn*],** *Pa₃*).

    [*He reports a number of symptoms that may reflect a psychotic process or a long-term, characterological condition. His presenting problems, background, and history should be reviewed with this possibility in mind.*]

Interpersonal Relations He reports that he is extroverted (*0*[*Si*]). He is very sociable and makes friends quickly (49T, 280T, 360T). He enjoys social gatherings and parties (353T, 370T) and the excitement of a crowd (359T, **367F**). He likes making decisions and assigning jobs to others (521T) and believes, if given the chance, he would make a good leader of people (350T). He appears to be comfortable around others, which actually reflects his aloofness from and lack of genuine involvement with others (6[*Pa*]). Others see him as being defensive and guarded (6[*Pa*]). He reports that his relations with his family are good (***Pd₁, FAM, MDS***). He is somewhat alienated from others (*Pd₄*).

Other Problem Areas He reports very few physical symptoms (*1*[*Hs*], *Hy₄*, **HEA, RC1[*som*]**), and he is in good physical health (45T, 141T). He has few or no pains (57T, 224T) and very few headaches (176T). He sleeps very well and wakes up fresh and rested most mornings (3T, **39F,** 140T). He does not tire quickly (152T) and is not tired, weak, and without energy a good deal of the time (**175F,** 330T, **464F**). He usually has enough energy to do his work (561T) and is about as able to work as he ever was (10T). He is not likely to abuse substances (***AAS***).

Treatment His prognosis is guarded because of his lack of emotional distress and consequent reluctance to consider that he might have any psychological problems (**A, NEGE,**

RCd[*dem*]). Behavioral or cognitive-behavioral interventions that do not require insight are most likely to be successful with him (*6*[*Pa*]).

A number of specific issues must be kept in mind when establishing and maintaining the therapeutic alliance: He is happy most of the time (95T); he sees little that needs to be changed (**377F,** 534T); and he works out things for himself rather than asking for advice (**398F,** 440T). Forging a therapeutic alliance is difficult because of his propensity to distance himself emotionally from others (*6*[*Pa*]). The discrepancy between how he perceives himself and how others perceive him and his behavior also complicates establishing a therapeutic alliance with him (*6*[*Pa*]).

Possible Diagnoses
Axis I
   R/O Adjustment Disorders
      309.3   Adjustment Disorder with Disturbance of Conduct
   R/O Schizophrenia and Other Psychotic Disorders
      297.1   Delusional Disorder
      296.9   Psychotic Disorder NOS
Axis II
   R/O Personality Disorders
      301.0   Paranoid Personality Disorder
      301.81 Narcissistic Personality Disorder
      301.9   Personality Disorder NOS

6-8/8-6

Moods   He reports that he is experiencing severe emotional distress (*A, NEGE, RCd*[*dem*]) characterized by dysphoric mood (*2*[*D*], *DEP2*), agitation (*9*[*Ma*]), worrying (*7*[*Pt*], *ANX*), and anhedonia (*INTR, RC2*[*lpe*], *DEP1, TRT1*). His affect is likely to be blunted or inappropriate (*6*[*Pa*], *8*[*Sc*]). He sees little opportunity for improving his circumstances further dampening his mood (*6*[*Pa*], *8*[*Sc*]). He is very fearful (*FRS*), easily frightened, and generally apprehensive (*FRS1*). Several times a week, he feels as if something dreadful is about to happen (463T). He frequently worries about something or someone (196T, 301T, 305T, 415T). He is more sensitive (285T) and feels more intensely than most people (271T). His feelings are easily hurt (**63F,** 127T), and he is inclined to take things hard (331T). He easily becomes impatient with people (136T, 302T) and often has serious disagreements with people who are close to him (382T). He is often irritable and grouchy (*ANG2*, 116T, 430T). He gets angry with people who give him advice (378T) or hurry him (461T), and he lets them know how he feels about it (481T). He also gets angry with himself for giving in to others so much (519T). He has become so angry that he does not know what comes over him (513T) and he feels as if he will explode (542T). At times, he has a strong urge to do something harmful or shocking (85T). At times, he feels like smashing things (37T). At times, he has fits of laughing and crying that he cannot control (23T).

Cognitions   He reports that he has problems with attention, concentration (31T, 299T, 325T), and memory (**165F,** 308T, 533T, 565T). He has strong opinions that he expresses directly to other people (437T, 452T). He likes to let people know where he stands on things (365T), and he finds it necessary to stand up for what he thinks is right (120T) or if people do something that makes him angry (481T). He certainly is lacking in self-confidence, believes that he is not as good as other people (73T, **239F,** 411T, 485T), and feels inferior and insecure (*LSE*). He has a hard time making decisions (482T, 509T) and he feels helpless when he has to make some important decisions (491T). Sometimes some unimportant thought will run through his mind and bother him for days (328T). His plans have frequently seemed so full of difficulties that he has had to give them up (394T).

He has very strange and peculiar experiences (32T) and thoughts (316T). He thinks and dreams of things that are too bad to talk about (16T, 221T, 448T). He daydreams frequently and he would rather daydream than do anything else (48T, 184T). He thinks that there is something wrong with his mind (170T, 180T) and that he is about to go to pieces (469T). He has had blank spells in which his activities were interrupted and he did not know what was going on around him (229T) and periods in which he carried on activities without knowing later what he had been doing (168T). Everything is going on too fast around him (525T). He sometimes seems to hear his thoughts being spoken out loud (551T). Bad words, often terrible words, come into his mind, and he cannot get rid of them (327T). He often feels as if things are not real (311T). He has often thought that strangers were looking at him critically (251T) and he is bothered by people on the street or in stores watching him (424T). He is sure he is being talked about (259T); he believes he is being plotted against (138T), people say vulgar and insulting things about him (333T), and someone has it in for him (99T). He has enemies who wish to harm him (**314F**). If people had not had it in for him, he would have been much more successful (42T). Much of the time, he thinks he has done something wrong or evil (94T) and believes he is a condemned person (234T). He is sure he gets a raw deal from life (17T) and that he is often being punished without cause (145T). In everything he does lately, he thinks that he is being tested (549T).

He thinks that most people will use unfair means and stretch the truth to get ahead (*CYN, RC3*[cyn], 58T, 81T, 110T, 374T). He often wonders what hidden reason another person may have for doing something nice for him (124T). He believes that it is safer to trust nobody (241T). He has often been misunderstood when he was trying to be helpful (396T, 403T). He does many things that he later regrets (82T). He knows he is a burden to others (526T).

[*He reports symptoms that may reflect a psychotic process or a long-term, character-ological condition. His presenting problems, background, and history should be reviewed with this possibility in mind.*]

Interpersonal Relations He reports that he is extremely introverted (*0*[*Si*], *SOD1*) and very uncomfortable around others (*SOD*). His behavior is likely to be unpredictable and inappropriate also making others uneasy around him (*6*[*Pa*], *8*[*Sc*]). He is suspicious and distrustful of others, and he avoids serious emotional relationships (*6*[*Pa*], *8*[*Sc*]). He generally feels apathetic, socially isolated and withdrawn, and he believes that no one understands him (*6*[*Pa*], *8*[*Sc*]). He feels lonely most of the time even when he is with people (277T). He has poor relations with his family (*Pd₁, FAM, MDS*) and is alienated from himself (*Pd₅, Si₃*) and others (*Pd₄, Sc₁, Si₃*). Once in a while he feels hate toward members of his family whom he usually loves (256T).

Other Problem Areas He reports a number of specific gastrointestinal (*HEA1*) and neuro-logical symptoms (*Sc₆, HEA2*) as well as a wide variety of more general physical symptoms (*1*[*Hs*], *HEA, Hy₄, RC1*[*som*]). His head seems to hurt all over much of the time, and he has frequent headaches (40T, 101T, **176F,** 536T). He has difficulty going to sleep because he is excited (304T) or thoughts or ideas are bothering him (**140F**), his sleep is fitful and disturbed (39T), and he does not wake up fresh and rested most mornings (**3F**). He tires quickly (**152F**) and feels weak and tired a good deal of the time (175T, 464T). He does not have enough energy to do his work (**561F**). His history and background should be reviewed to determine whether a medical or neurological evaluation is warranted. He is very likely to abuse substances (*AAS,* 264T, 487T, 489T, 511T). He is worried about sex (166T). He is likely to have suicidal ideation (*DEP4,* 150T, 303T, 505T, 506T, 520T, 524T, 530T, 546T) and he feels hopeless (306T, 454T, 516T), which increases his risk of suicide.

Treatment　His prognosis is generally poor because his problems are chronic and severe (*6[Pa]*, *8[Sc]*). His ability to work may not be severely impaired as long as the job does not involve any appreciable amount of contact with people (*6[Pa]*, *8[Sc]*). Some type of psychopharmacological intervention may be necessary to stabilize his thought processes and mood and to help him sleep (*6[Pa]*, *8[Sc]*). Short-term, behavioral interventions are warranted rather than any form of insight-oriented psychotherapy (*6[Pa]*, *8[Sc]*).

Many specific issues must be kept in mind when establishing and maintaining the therapeutic alliance: No one seems to understand him (22T); he has difficulty starting to do things (233T); it is safer to trust nobody (241T); he is so touchy on some subjects that he cannot talk about them (274T); he gives up quickly when things go wrong (364T) or get difficult (554T), or because he thinks too little of his ability (326T); he shrinks from facing a crisis or difficulty (368T); he is very passive and nonassertive (369T, 421T, 446T, 514T); he has done some bad things in the past that he will never tell anyone about (373T); it makes him nervous when people ask him personal questions (375T); he feels unable to tell anyone all about himself (391T); the future seems hopeless to him (454T); he is hard to get to know (479T); he is very stubborn (486T); he is bothered greatly by the thought of making changes in his life (497T) and is not sure that he can make these changes (500T); he hates going to doctors even when he is sick (499T); he has had a tragic loss in his life that he will never get over (512T); his life is empty and meaningless (516T); and it is hard for him to accept compliments (562T).

Possible Diagnoses
Axis I
　R/O Schizophrenia and Other Psychotic Disorders
　　295.10 Schizophrenia, Disorganized Type
　　295.30 Schizophrenia, Paranoid Type
　　295.40 Schizophreniform Disorder
　　295.70 Schizoaffective Disorder, Depressive Type
　R/O Substance-Related Disorders
　　291.8　Alcohol-Induced Anxiety Disorder
　　291.8　Alcohol-Induced Mood Disorder
　　305.00 Alcohol Abuse
　　305.40 Sedative, Hypnotic, or Anxiolytic Abuse
　R/O Anxiety Disorders
　　300.02 Generalized Anxiety Disorder
　　300.23 Social Phobia
　　300.3　Obsessive-Compulsive Disorder

R/O Mood Disorders
    296.xx Major Depressive Disorder
    296.5x Bipolar I Disorder, Most Recent Episode Depressed
    296.89 Bipolar II Disorder, Most Recent Episode Depressed
R/O Other Cognitive Disorders
    294.9   Cognitive Disorder NOS

Axis II

R/O Personality Disorders
    301.22 Schizotypal Personality Disorder
    301.82 Avoidant Personality Disorder
    301.83 Borderline Personality Disorder

6-9/9-6

Moods   He reports that he is experiencing a mild to moderate level of emotional distress (*A, NEGE, RCd[dem]*) characterized by agitation, tension, and excitement (*9[Ma]*). His daily life is full of things that keep him interested (9T). Something exciting will almost always pull him out of it when he is feeling low (244T). When he gets bored, he likes to stir up excitement (169T). Once a week or oftener, he becomes very excited (242T). Sometimes without any reason or even when things are going wrong he feels excitedly happy or unusually cheerful (226T, 267T). He has very few fears compared to his friends (261T). He also reports mild dysphoric mood (*DEP2*), yet he is happy most of the time (**65F,** 95T). He feels more intensely than most people do (271T). He has difficulty expressing his feelings appropriately and may vacillate between overcontrolling and undercontrolling his emotions (*6[Pa], 9[Ma]*). It makes him angry when people hurry him (461T), and he lets them know how he feels about it (481T). He has become so angry that he feels as if he will explode (542T). Others will perceive him as being irritable, grouchy, and angry (*9[Ma], RC9[hpm], ANG, AGGR*).

Cognitions   He reports that his attention, concentration (**31F**), and memory seem to be all right (165T). He has strong opinions that he expresses directly to other people (437T, 452T). He likes to let people know where he stands on things (365T) and he finds it necessary to stand up for what he thinks is right (120T) or if people do something that makes him angry (481T). He has had very strange and peculiar experiences (32T). He often exercises poor judgment, although he thinks that his judgment is better than it ever was (*6[Pa], 9[Ma]*, 43T). At times, he cannot seem to stop talking (529T). At times, he can make up his mind with unusually great ease (206T). He is sure he is being talked about (259T) and being punished without cause (145T). He is grandiose and egocentric (*6[Pa], 9[Ma]*, 61T). He thinks that most people will use unfair means and stretch the truth to get ahead (*CYN, RC3[cyn]*, 58T, 81T, 110T, 374T). He has often been misunderstood when he was trying to be helpful (396T, 403T).

   [*He reports a number of symptoms that may reflect a psychotic process or a long-term, characterological condition. His presenting problems, background, and history should be reviewed with this possibility in mind.*]

Interpersonal Relations   He reports that he is extroverted (*0[Si]*) and comfortable in social situations (*SOD*). He is very sociable and makes friends quickly (49T, 280T, 360T). He likes making decisions and assigning jobs to others (521T) and believes, if given the chance, he would make a good leader of people (350T). He enjoys social gatherings and parties (353T, 370T) and the excitement of a crowd (359T, **367F**). His relations with his family (Pd_1, *FAM, MDS*) and others (Pd_2) tend to be strained at best. He is alienated from himself (Pd_5, Si_3) and others (Pd_4, Sc_1, Si_3).

Other Problem Areas   He reports a number of gastrointestinal (*HEA1*) and neurological symptoms (Sc_6, *HEA2*), but states that he is in just as good physical health as most of his friends (45T) with few or no pains (224T). Sometimes he becomes so excited he finds it hard to get to sleep (304T). He wakes up fresh and rested most mornings (3T). He does not tire quickly (152T) and is not tired, weak, and without energy a good deal of the time (**175F**, 330T, **464F**). He has enough energy to do his work (561T) and is about as able to work as he ever was (10T). His history and background should be reviewed to determine whether a medical or neurological evaluation is warranted. He is prone to abuse substances (*AAS*, 264T, 487T, 489T, 511T). He reported a number of behavioral problems when he was in school (*ASP2*) and he has been in trouble with the law (**266F**). He is a risk taker and sensation-seeker (*MAC-R*, **100F**).

Treatment   His prognosis is generally poor because of his limited concerns about his own behavior (6[*Pa*], 9[*Ma*]). Psychopharmacological interventions are frequently warranted because of the agitation and excitement (6[*Pa*], 9[*Ma*]). Short-term, behavioral interventions that focus on his reasons for entering treatment will be most effective (6[*Pa*], 9[*Ma*]).

There are specific issues that must be kept in mind when establishing and maintaining the therapeutic alliance: He has done some bad things in the past that he will never tell anyone about (373T); he works out things for himself rather than to ask for advice (**398F**, 440T); and he is very stubborn (486T).

Possible Diagnoses
Axis I
>   R/O Mood Disorders
>>   296.40 Bipolar I Disorder, Most Recent Episode Hypomanic
>>   296.89 Bipolar II Disorder, Most Recent Episode Hypomanic
>>   301.13 Cyclothymic Disorder
>   R/O Schizophrenia and Other Psychotic Disorders
>>   295.70 Schizoaffective Disorder, Bipolar Type
>   R/O Substance-Related Disorders
>>   291.8 Alcohol-Induced Mood Disorder
>>   305.00 Alcohol Abuse
>>   305.60 Cocaine Abuse
>>   305.70 Amphetamine Abuse

Axis II
>   R/O Personality Disorders
>>   301.22 Schizotypal Personality Disorder
>>   301.7 Antisocial Personality Disorder
>>   301.81 Narcissistic Personality Disorder
>>   301.83 Borderline Personality Disorder

7-8/8-7

Moods   He reports that he is experiencing a moderate to severe level of emotional distress (*A, NEGE, RCd*[*dem*]) characterized by dysphoric mood (*DEP2,* 65T), brooding, and agitation (*2*[*D*], *DEP,* *7*[*Pt*], *ANX*). He frequently worries about something or someone (196T, 301T, 305T, 320T, 415T). He is chronically stressed, and he becomes more agitated or withdrawn as his level of stress increases (*7*[*Pt*], *8*[*Sc*]). He is generally apprehensive and fearful of his environment (*FRS, FRS1*). Several times a week, he feels as if something dreadful is about to happen (463T). He obtains little pleasure from life and is likely to be anhedonic (*INTR, RC2*[*lpe*], *DEP1, TRT1*). He is more sensitive (285T) and feels more intensely than most people (271T). His feelings are easily hurt (**63F,** 127T) and he is inclined to take things hard (331T). He easily becomes impatient with people (136T, 302T). He is often irritable and grouchy (*ANG1,* 116T, 430T). It makes him angry when people give him advice (378T) or hurry him (461T). He also gets angry with himself for giving in to others so much (519T). He has become so angry that he does not know what comes over him (513T), and he feels as if he will explode (542T). At times, he has a strong urge to do something shocking or harmful (85T).

Cognitions   He reports that he has problems with attention, concentration (31T, 299T, 325T), and memory (**165F,** 308T, 475T, 533T, 565T). He certainly is lacking in self-confidence and believes that he is not as good as other people (*LSE,* 73T, **239F,** 411T, 485T). He has a hard time making decisions (482T, 509T), and he feels helpless when he has to make some important decisions (491T). He has often lost out on things because he could not make up his mind quickly enough (135T). His plans have frequently seemed so full of difficulties that he had to give them up (394T).

Sometimes an unimportant thought will run through his mind and bother him for days (328T). He has strange and peculiar thoughts (316T) and thinks and dreams of things that are too bad to talk about (16T, 221T). He daydreams frequently and prefers to daydream rather than do anything else (48T, **184F**). He often engages in sexual fantasies and his sexual adjustment is likely to be poor (*7*[*Pt*], *8*[*Sc*]). He often thinks that things are not real (311T), there is something wrong with his mind (170T, 180T), and that he is about to go to pieces (469T). Much of the time he feels as if he has done something wrong or evil (94T). He has had periods in which he carried on activities without knowing later what he had been doing (168T, 229T).

He thinks that most people will use unfair means and stretch the truth to get ahead (*CYN, RC3*[*cyn*], 58T, 81T, 110T, 374T). He often wonders what hidden reason another person may have for being nice to him (124T). He believes it is safer to trust nobody (241T). He has often felt that strangers were looking at him critically (251T). He has often been misunderstood when he was trying to be helpful (396T, 403T) and his way of doing things is apt to be misunderstood by others (225T). He does many things that he later regrets (82T).

[*He reports symptoms that may reflect a psychotic process or a long-term, character-ological condition. His presenting problems, background, and history should be reviewed with this possibility in mind.*]

Interpersonal Relations   He reports that he is extremely introverted (*0*[*Si*], *SOD1*) and socially uncomfortable (*SOD*) and has poor social skills and judgment (*7*[*Pt*], *8*[*Sc*]). When in a group of people, he has trouble thinking of the right things to talk about (243T). He is easily embarrassed (289T) and wishes he were not so shy (185T). He has difficulty forming close, personal relationships (7[Pt], 8[Sc]). Even when he is with people he feels lonely much of the time (277T). His relations with his family tend to be very poor (Pd₁, FAM, MDS). He is very alienated from himself (Pd₅, Si₃) and others (Pd₄, Sc₁, Si₃, FAM2).

Other Problem Areas   He reports a number of physical symptoms (1[Hs], HEA, Hy₄, RC1[som]), general concern about his health (HEA3), gastrointestinal symptoms (HEA1), and neurological symptoms (Sc₆, HEA2). He has difficulty going to sleep because he is excited (304T), or thoughts or ideas are bothering him (**140F**), his sleep is fitful and disturbed (39T), and he does not wake up fresh and rested most mornings (**3F**). He tires quickly (**152F**) and feels weak and tired a good deal of the time (175T, 464T). He does not have enough energy to do his work (**561F**) and he is not as able to work as he once was (**10F**). His history should be reviewed to determine whether a medical or neurological evaluation is warranted. He is worried about and bothered by thoughts about sex (166T, 268T). He is likely to abuse substances (AAS, 264T, 487T, 489T, 511T). He is likely to have suicidal ideation that should be monitored carefully (DEP4, 150T, 303T, 506T, 520T, 524T, 530T). He is hopeless which increases the risk of suicide (505T, 554T).

Treatment   His prognosis is generally poor given the characterological nature of his problems and his diminished motivation to work (7[Pt], 8[Sc]). Establishing a therapeutic relationship is challenging because of the serious character pathology that is present (7[Pt], 8[Sc]). Psychopharmacological intervention may be necessary to decrease his level of agitation and to help him sleep (7[Pt], 8[Sc]). Cognitive-behavioral interventions focused on his depressive and anxious cognitive processes will be beneficial (2[D], DEP, 7[Pt], ANX).

Many specific issues must be kept in mind when establishing and maintaining the therapeutic alliance: No one seems to understand him (22T); he has difficulty starting to do things (233T); it is safer to trust nobody (241T); he is so touchy on some subjects that he cannot talk about them (274T); he gives up quickly when things go wrong (364T) or get difficult (554T), or because he thinks too little of his ability (326T); he shrinks from facing a crisis or difficulty (368T); he is very passive and nonassertive (369T, 421T, 446T, 514T); he has done some bad things in the past that he will never tell anyone about (373T); it makes him nervous when people ask him personal questions (375T); he feels unable to tell anyone all about himself (391T); he is hard to get to know (479T); he is very stubborn (486T); he is bothered greatly by the thought of making changes in his life (497T); he hates going to doctors even when he is sick (499T); and it is hard for him to accept compliments (562T).

Possible Diagnoses
Axis I
   R/O Anxiety Disorders
      300.02 Generalized Anxiety Disorder
      300.23 Social Phobia
      300.3   Obsessive-Compulsive Disorder

R/O Mood Disorders
  296.xx Major Depressive Disorder
  296.5x Bipolar I Disorder, Most Recent Episode Depressed
  296.89 Bipolar II Disorder, Most Recent Episode Depressed
R/O Schizophrenia and Other Psychotic Disorders
  295.30 Schizophrenia, Paranoid
  295.10 Schizophrenia, Disorganized Type
  295.40 Schizophreniform Disorder
  295.70 Schizoaffective Disorder, Depressive Type
R/O Substance-Related Disorders
  291.8   Alcohol-Induced Anxiety Disorder
  291.8   Alcohol-Induced Mood Disorder
  305.00 Alcohol Abuse
  305.40 Sedative, Hypnotic, or Anxiolytic Abuse

Axis II
R/O Personality Disorders
  301.22 Schizotypal Personality Disorder
  301.82 Avoidant Personality Disorder
  301.83 Borderline Personality Disorder

8-9/9-8

Moods   He reports that he is experiencing moderate to severe emotional distress (*A, NEGE, RCd*[*dem*]) characterized by agitation and excitement (*8*[*Sc*], *9*[*Ma*]). He is often first seen in an acute state of hyperactivity, excitement, confusion, and disorientation (*8*[*Sc*], *9*[*Ma*]). When he gets bored, he likes to stir up some excitement (169T). Sometimes without any reason or even when things are going wrong, he feels excitedly happy (226T). He has periods in which he feels unusually cheerful without any special reason (267T). Something exciting will almost always pull him out of it when he is feeling low (244T). He easily becomes impatient with people (302T) and often has serious disagreements with people who are close to him (382T). He is often angry, irritable, and grouchy (*ANG, AGGR, RC9*[*hpm*], 116T, 430T). It makes him angry when people give him advice (378T) or hurry him (461T), and he lets them know how he feels about it (481T). He also gets angry with himself for giving in to others so much (519T). He has become so angry that he does not know what comes over him (513T), and he feels as if he will explode (542T). At times he has a strong urge to do something shocking or harmful (85T).

Cognitions   He reports that he has problems with attention and concentration (31T, 299T, 325T), but his memory seems to be all right (165T). He has strong opinions that he expresses directly to other people (437T, 452T). He likes to let people know where he stands on things (365T), and he finds it necessary to stand up for what he thinks is right (120T) or if people do something that makes him angry (481T).

He thinks and dreams of things that are too bad to talk about (16T, 221T) and he has strange and peculiar experiences (32T) and thoughts (316T). He has had periods in which he carried on activities without knowing later what he had been doing (168T, 229T). At times, he cannot seem to stop talking (529T). In response to stress, he is likely to become more disorganized and agitated or to engage in more daydreaming and fantasy (*8*[*Sc*], *9*[*Ma*]).

He thinks that most people will use unfair means and stretch the truth to get ahead (*CYN*, *RC3*[cyn], 58T, 81T, 104T, 110T, 374T). Most people make friends because friends are likely to be useful to them (254T). He often wonders what hidden reason another person may have for doing something nice for him (124T). He believes that it is safer to trust nobody (241T). He has often been misunderstood when he was trying to be helpful (396T, 403T), and his way of doing things is apt to be misunderstood by others (225T). He likes to keep people guessing what he is going to do next (393T).

[*He reports symptoms that may reflect a psychotic process or a very long-term, characterological condition. His presenting problems, background, and history should be reviewed with this possibility in mind.*]

Interpersonal Relations   He reports a balance between extroverted and introverted behaviors (*0*[*Si*]) and he is comfortable in social situations (*SOD*). He is very sociable and makes friends quickly (49T, 280T, 360T). He enjoys social gatherings and parties (86T, 353T, 370T) and the excitement of a crowd (359T, **367F**). He likes to be with a crowd that play jokes on one another (231T). He likes making decisions and assigning jobs to others (521T) and believes, if given the chance, he would make a good leader of people (350T). His behavior may be unpredictable, and he may act out unexpectedly (*8*[*Sc*], *9*[*Ma*]). He is fearful of relating to others; consequently, close relationships are usually lacking (*8*[*Sc*], *9*[*Ma*]). His relations with his family (*Pd$_1$*, *FAM*, *MDS*) and others (*Pd$_2$*) are marked by conflict. Once in a while, he feels hate toward members of his family whom he usually loves (256T). He is alienated from himself (*Pd$_5$*, *Si$_3$*) and others (*Pd$_4$*, *Sc$_1$*, *Si$_3$*, *FAM2*).

Other Problem Areas   He reports a number of general physical symptoms (*1*[*Hs*], *HEA*, *Hy$_4$*, *RC1*[som]), gastrointestinal symptoms (*HEA1*), and neurological symptoms (*Sc$_6$*, *HEA2*). Sometimes he becomes so excited that he finds it hard to get to sleep (304T). His history should be reviewed to determine whether a medical or neurological evaluation is warranted. He is very likely to abuse substances so a careful review should be made of the consequences of his alcohol and drug use (*AAS*, 264T, 487T, 489T, 511T). He is a risk taker and sensation seeker (*MAC-R*) who is likely to have legal and behavioral problems (*ASP*). He reported a number of behavioral problems when he was in school (*ASP2*).

Treatment   His prognosis is generally poor because of the serious characterological nature of his problems (*8*[*Sc*], *9*[*Ma*]). Psychopharmacological intervention may be helpful in reducing his agitation (*8*[*Sc*], *9*[*Ma*]). The difficulties he experiences in focusing on specific issues and his fear of relating to others often preclude good therapeutic contact and outcome (*8*[*Sc*], *9*[*Ma*]). Short-term, behavioral interventions that focus on his reasons for entering treatment will be most effective (*8*[*Sc*], *9*[*Ma*]).

Some specific issues must be kept in mind when establishing and maintaining the therapeutic alliance: He has difficulty starting to do things (233T); it is safer to trust nobody (241T); he is so touchy on some subjects that he cannot talk about them (274T); he has done some bad things in the past that he will never tell anyone about (373T); he works out things for himself rather than ask for advice (**398F,** 440T); he is hard to get to know (479T); and he is very stubborn (486T).

Possible Diagnoses
Axis I
  R/O Mood Disorders
    296.40 Bipolar I Disorder, Most Recent Episode Hypomanic
    296.89 Bipolar II Disorder, Most Recent Episode Hypomanic
    301.13 Cyclothymic Disorder
  R/O Substance-Related Disorders
    291.8   Alcohol-Induced Mood Disorder
    305.00 Alcohol Abuse
    305.60 Cocaine Abuse
    305.70 Amphetamine Abuse
  R/O Schizophrenia and Other Psychotic Disorders
    295.70 Schizoaffective Disorder, Bipolar Type
Axis II
  R/O Personality Disorders
    301.22 Schizotypal Personality Disorder
    301.81 Narcissistic Personality Disorder
    301.83 Borderline Personality Disorder

Spike 9

Moods   He reports that he is not experiencing any emotional distress (*A, NEGE, RCd*[*dem*]). He is happy most of the time (**65F,** 95T, 388T). His daily life is full of things that keep him interested (9T). Once a week or oftener, he becomes very excited (242T). He has periods in which he feels unusually cheerful without any special reason (226T, 267T). When he gets bored, he likes to stir up some excitement (169T). Something exciting will almost always pull him out of it when he is feeling low (244T). He has very few fears compared with his friends (261T).

Cognitions   He reports that his attention, concentration (**31F, 299F, 325F**), and memory seem to be all right (165T, **475F, 565F**). He has strong opinions that he expresses directly to other people (437T, 452T). He likes to let people know where he stands on things (365T) and he finds it necessary to stand up for what he thinks is right (120T) or if people do something that makes him angry (481T).

His judgment is better than it ever was (43T). At times, he thinks that he can make up his mind with unusually great ease (206T). He is entirely self-confident (**73F,** 239T).

He thinks that most people will use unfair means and stretch the truth to get ahead (58T, 81T, 110T).

Interpersonal Relations   He reports that he is very extroverted (*0*[*Si*]) and very comfortable in social situations (*SOD*). He is very sociable and makes friends quickly (49T, 280T, 360T). He enjoys social gatherings and parties (353T, 370T) and the excitement of a crowd (359T, **367F**). He likes making decisions and assigning jobs to others (521T) and believes, if given the chance, he would make a good leader of people (350T). It is not hard for him to ask for help from his friends even though he knows he cannot return the favor (200T).

Other Problem Areas   He reports that he is in good physical health (*1[Hs]*, ***Hy₄***, ***HEA***, ***RC1[som]***, 45T, 141T). He has few or no pains (47T, 57T, 224T) and very few headaches (176T). He sleeps very well and wakes up fresh and rested most mornings (3T, **39F**, 140T, **304F**). He does not tire quickly (152T) and is not tired, weak, and without energy a good deal of the time (**175F**, 330T, **464F**). He usually has enough energy to do his work (561T) and is about as able to work as he ever was (10T). He is a risk taker and sensation seeker (*MAC-R*).

Treatment   His prognosis is poor because he is experiencing little emotional distress limiting his motivation for any intervention (***A, NEGE, RCd[dem]***). Short-term, behavioral interventions that focus on his reasons for entering treatment may be effective (*9[Ma]*).

Some specific issues must be kept in mind when establishing and maintaining the therapeutic alliance: He may have unrealistic ideas of his self-importance (61T, 239T); he is happy most of the time (95T); he sees little that needs to be changed (**377F**, 534T); he works out things for himself rather than ask for advice (**398F**, 440T); and he is very stubborn (486T).

Possible Diagnoses
Axis I
   R/O Adjustment Disorders
      309.3   Adjustment Disorder with Disturbance of Conduct
   R/O Mood Disorders
      296.40 Bipolar I Disorder, Most Recent Episode Hypomanic
      296.89 Bipolar II Disorder, Most Recent Episode Hypomanic
      301.13 Cyclothymic Disorder
Axis II
   R/O Personality Disorders
      301.81 Narcissistic Personality Disorder
      301.9   Personality Disorder NOS

Individual Scales

The interpretive text for each MMPI-2 codetype provides the broad overview of how the *group* of individuals within the codetype scored on the various scales. The task for the clinician at this juncture is to review all the individual scales (clinical, restructured clinical, content, and supplementary) and critical items for this specific individual to determine how the interpretive text needs to be modified. Greene and Brown (2006) provide several examples of this process. Once the interpretive text for the MMPI-2 has been rendered internally consistent, the clinician then must integrate the clinical history and background into the interpretation.

The individual scales on the MMPI-2 can be organized within two large categories that reflect how the scales were developed: empirically and rationally. The 10 clinical scales were developed empirically, as described earlier; and the 15 content scales (Butcher et al., 1989), 9 restructured clinical scales (Tellegen et al., 2003), and 5 personality psychopathology scales (PSY-5: Harkness et al., 2002) were developed rationally. These two approaches are conceptually opposed to one another, as described in Chapter 5 (pp. 116–117), and provide two different methods for interpreting the MMPI-2. When the individual endorses the items accurately, these two approaches provide a similar interpretation of the MMPI-2 profile and the clinician's task is relatively straightforward. When the individual for any reason is motivated to provide either a self-unfavorable or self-favorable description, these two approaches will provide more or less divergent interpretations. In these instances, the clinician's task becomes more daunting because the clinician must determine which set of interpretations is more appropriate.

Clinical and Content Scales

Tables 6.4 and 6.5 provide general interpretive text for the clinical and content scales, respectively, when they are elevated above a T score of 64 or below a T score of 45. Figure 6.1 illustrated the profile for the basic validity and clinical scales for a *1-2/2-1* codetype, and Figure 6.4 illustrates the profile for the content scales for the same codetype. The major emphasis in the interpretation of the MMPI-2 is on elevated scales, yet important information frequently is found in scales that are not elevated. Individuals in a clinical setting who do not elevate Scales *2 (D:* Depression) and *7 (Pt:* Psychasthenia) are reporting that they are not experiencing any distress about the behavior or symptoms that led them to the clinical setting or about being evaluated.

Factor Scales

Factor-analytic studies of the MMPI-2 clinical scales have consistently identified two factors that are variously labeled and interpreted. The first factor is generally acknowledged to be a measure of generalized emotional distress and negative affect, and Welsh (1956) developed his Anxiety *(A)* scale to measure this factor. There are 10 to 20 other scales in the MMPI-2 that measure this factor of generalized emotional distress and negative affect, all of which have high positive correlations with the *A* scale: Scales *7 (Pt:* Psychasthenia, .95) and *8 (Sc:* Schizophrenia, 90); the Content Scales of Work Interference *(WRK:* .94), Depression *(DEP:* .92), Anxiety *(ANX:* .90), Obsessions *(OBS:* .89), and Low Self-Esteem *(LSE:* .87); and the supplementary scales of Posttraumatic Stress Disorder—Keane *(PK:* .93), College Maladjustment *(Mt:* .93), and Marital Distress Scale *(MDS:* .79). Several MMPI-2 scales also have high negative correlations with the *A* scale, and as such are simply inverted measures of generalized distress and negative affect: Ego Strength *(Es:* −.83) and *K* (Correction: −.79). All these scales can be characterized as generalized measures of emotional distress and negative affect with little or no specificity despite the name of the scales, and there are little empirical data to support any distinctions among them. These scales also illustrate how scale names can be misleading. Although each of these scales has a different name, they are measuring a single construct—generalized emotional distress and negative affect.

The second factor identified in these factor-analytic studies of the MMPI-2 clinical scales is a measure of control and inhibition, and Welsh (1956) developed his Repression *(R)* scale to measure this factor. The major content area of the *R* scale is the denial, suppression, constriction, and inhibition of all kinds of interests either positive or negative; these individuals like to keep their behavior within very narrow limits. There are 5 to 10 other scales in the MMPI-2 that measure this factor of control and inhibition, but the pattern of correlations with the *R* scale is much more variable and smaller than found with the *A* scale: Scale *9 (Ma:* Hypomania, −.45), Antisocial Practices *(ASP:* −.36), MacAndrew

Table 6.4   Interpretation of the MMPI-2 clinical scales

Scale	Potential Issues
1 (Hs) > 64	Individuals focus on vague physical ailments. They are reluctant to consider that they might have psychological problems. They are pessimistic about being helped. They are argumentative with staff. Conservative interventions should be used whenever possible.
1 (Hs) < 45	No specific interpretations can be made.
2 (D) > 64	Individuals are reporting generalized distress and are likely to be depressed. Their depressive mood should be readily apparent. It is important to determine whether internal or external factors are producing the negative mood state and to plan treatment accordingly.
2 (D) < 45	Individuals are not reporting any type of emotional distress either as a result of their presence in treatment or the behaviors/symptoms that led them to consider treatment. The possibility of acting out in an impulsive manner should be evaluated. There is little internal motivation for any type of treatment or intervention.
3 (Hy) > 64	Individuals are naive, suggestible, and lack insight into their own and others' behavior. They deny any type of psychological problem. Under stress, specific physical ailments will be seen. They look for simplistic, concrete solutions to their problems. Treatment should focus on short-term goals because of limited motivation. They may initially be enthusiastic about treatment, then later resist treatment or fail to cooperate.
3 (Hy) < 45	Individuals are caustic, sarcastic, and socially isolated. They have few defenses for coping with any problems that they encounter. Well-structured, behavioral interventions should be used whenever possible.
4 (Pd) > 64	Individuals are in conflict either with family members or persons in positions of authority. They may make a good initial impression, but more long-term contact will reveal that they are egocentric and have little concern for others. Any treatment should focus on short-term goals with emphasis on behavior change rather than on their verbalized intent to change, no matter how sincere they may sound. Low scores on Scales *2 (D*: Depression) and *7 (Pt*: Psychasthenia) make elevations on Scale *4* particularly pathognomonic.
4 (Pd) < 45	Individuals are rigid, conventional, and have little psychological insight into themselves or others. Explicit, behavioral directives to change will be most productive if there is sufficient motivation to follow them.
5 (Mf) > 64	Individuals do not identify with their traditional gender role and are concerned about sexual issues. Men frequently worry and their feelings are easily hurt. Women are confident and satisfied with themselves.
5 (Mf) < 40	Individuals identify with their traditional gender role. Men are confident and self-assured. Women are trusting of and depend on others and lack self-confidence. Their feelings are easily hurt and they cry easily.
6 (Pa) > 64	Individuals are suspicious, hostile, and overly sensitive, which is readily apparent to everyone. Any treatment is problematic because of the difficulty in developing a therapeutic relationship based on trust. Any intervention must be instituted slowly.

Table 6.4   (*Continued*)

Scale	Potential Issues
6 (Pa) < 45	Individuals have narrow interests and they tend to be insensitive to and unaware of the motives of others. Explicit, behavioral directives to change will be most productive if there is sufficient motivation to follow them.
7 (Pt) > 64	Individuals are worried, tense, and indecisive, which is readily apparent to everyone. Ineffective ruminative and obsessive behaviors will be seen. It may be necessary to lower their level of anxiety before implementing treatment of other symptoms.
7 (Pt) < 45	Individuals are secure and comfortable with themselves, which augurs poorly for any type of intervention in a clinical setting.
8 (Sc) > 64	Individuals feel alienated and remote from the environment and others. At higher elevations ($T > 79$), difficulties in logic and judgment may become evident. Interventions should be directive and supportive. Psychotropic medications may be needed.
8 (Sc) < 45	Individuals are conventional, concrete, and unimaginative. Any intervention should be behavioral, directive, and focused on short-term goals.
9 (Ma) > 64	Individuals are overactive, impulsive, emotionally labile, and euphoric with occasional outbursts of anger. They may need to be evaluated for a manic mood disorder. Short-term behavioral goals should be pursued.
9 (Ma) < 45	Individuals have a low energy and activity level. They may be manifesting significant signs of psychomotor retardation that should be evaluated carefully.
0 (Si) > 64	Individuals are introverted, shy, and socially insecure. They withdraw from and avoid significant others, which exacerbates their distress. Interventions need to address specifically their tendency to withdraw and avoid others.
0 (Si) < 45	Individuals are extroverted, gregarious, and socially poised. They may have difficulty in forming intimate relationships with others at very low scores ($T < 35$). They are unlikely to have a thought disorder. The probability of acting out is increased. Group therapies are particularly useful with these individuals.

Alcoholism-Revised (*MAC-R:* −.52), Social Responsibility (*Re:* .38), and the PSY-5 scales of Aggression (*AGGR:* −.53) and Disconstraint (*DISC:* −.46). The specific correlates of the second factor will be a function of the scale that is used to define it, but this group of MMPI-2 scales is characterized by significant dyscontrol or dysinhibition associated with acting-out or externalization of psychopathology.

Conjoint interpretations of the first two factors of the MMPI-2 (generalized emotional distress and control/inhibition) provide a succinct approach for how individuals are coping with the behaviors and symptoms that led them to treatment (see Greene, 2000, table 6.5, p. 225). The *A* scale provides a quick estimate of how much generalized emotional distress the individual is experiencing, and the *R* scale indicates whether the individual is trying to inhibit or control the expression of this distress. It is particularly noteworthy in a clinical setting when the *A* scale is *not* elevated (T < 50) because it signifies that the individual is

Table 6.5   Interpretation of the MMPI-2 content scales

Scale	Potential Issues
ANX (Anxiety) > 64	Individuals report general symptoms of anxiety, nervousness, worry, and sleep and concentration difficulties. Depending on the level of anxiety, psychotropic medications or other anxiety-reducing techniques may be needed before implementing other interventions.
FRS (Fears) > 64	Individuals report generalized fearfulness (*FRS1*) as well as many specific fears (*FRS2*). These specific fears respond well to systematic desensitization if they are not part of a larger set of fear and anxiety symptoms.
OBS (Obsessions) > 64	Individuals have great difficulty making decisions, ruminate and worry excessively, and have intrusive thoughts. They are good candidates for most insight-oriented therapies.
DEP (Depression) > 64	Individuals have difficulty getting going and getting things done in their life (*DEP1*). They have a depressive mood and thoughts (*DEP2*) and a negative self-concept (*DEP3*). Suicide potential should be evaluated (*DEP4*). Their depression has an angry component that involves blaming others, particularly when *DEP* is higher (+15 T points) than Scale *2* (*D*: Depression).
HEA (Health Concerns) > 64	Individuals report gastrointestinal symptoms (*HEA1*) and symptoms associated with neurological functioning (*HEA2*), as well as general concerns about their health (*HEA3*). Their physical symptoms may be another manifestation of their emotional distress. They need to be reassured that their symptoms are being taken seriously.
BIZ (Bizarre Mentation) > 64	Individuals report overtly psychotic symptoms such as paranoid ideation and hallucinations and various peculiar and strange experiences (*BIZ2*). Psychotropic (*BIZ1*) medications may be indicated, as well as hospitalization.
ANG (Anger) > 64	Individuals report explosive tendencies such as hitting and smashing things (*ANG1*), as well as being irritable, grouchy, and impatient (*ANG2*). Assertiveness training and/or anger-control techniques should be implemented as part of treatment.
CYN (Cynicism) > 64	Individuals believe others are only interested in their own welfare (*CYN1*) and are suspicious of others' motives (*CYN2*). Establishing a trusting relationship is a difficult process, but imperative if any progress is to be made in therapy.
ASP (Antisocial Practices) > 64	Individuals have attitudes similar to individuals who break the law (*ASP1*), even if they do not actually engage in antisocial behavior. They report stealing things and other problem behaviors and antisocial practices *during their school years* (*ASP2*). It is important to determine whether these behaviors are still being displayed. Group interventions with similar individuals will be most productive.
TPA (Type A) > 64	Individuals frequently become impatient, grouchy, irritable, and annoyed (*TPA1*). They are hard-driving, fast-moving, and competitive individuals (*TPA2*). The possibility of a manic mood disorder should be considered.
LSE (Low Self-Esteem) > 64	Individuals have very low opinions of themselves (*LSE1*), and they are uncomfortable if people say nice things about them. They give in easily to others (*LSE2*). Interventions need to be supportive and allow ample time for change.

Table 6.5   (*Continued*)

Scale	Potential Issues
SOD Social (Discomfort) > 64	Individuals are very uneasy around others and are happier by themselves (*SOD1*). They see themselves as shy and uncomfortable in social situations (*SOD2*). They need to be supported and encouraged to participate in treatment until they are comfortable interacting with others.
FAM (Family Problems) > 64	Individuals report considerable familial discord (*FAM1*). Their families are reported to lack love, support, and companionship. They feel alienated from and unattached to their family (*FAM2*). Involvement of the family system in treatment may be important unless the individual needs to be emancipated from them.
WRK (Work Interference) > 64	Individuals report that they are not as able to work as they once were, and that they work under a great deal of tension. They are tired, lack energy, and are sick of what they have to do. It is important to determine specifically whether the reported symptoms and behaviors actually interfere with their work because *WRK* is primarily a measure of generalized emotional distress. *Work-related problems actually can be ascertained more directly by asking the individual.*
TRT (Negative Treatment Indicators) > 64	Individuals are unmotivated and feel unable to help themselves (*TRT1*). They dislike going to doctors and they believe that they should not discuss their personal problems with others (*TRT2*). They prefer to take drugs or medicine because talking about problems does not help them. Individuals with depressive mood disorders will elevate *TRT* because it is primarily a measure of generalized emotional distress, so clinicians need to be cautious about interpreting *TRT* in a characterological manner.

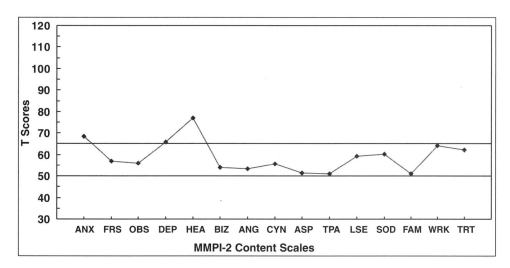

Figure 6.4   MMPI-2 profile for content scales for a *1-2/2-1* codetype.

not experiencing any distress about the behaviors and symptoms that led (usually) someone else to refer them to treatment. Similarly low scores ($T < 45$) on the R scale suggest that the individual has no coping skills or abilities to control or inhibit the overt expression of his distress. When either of these two scales is elevated significantly and the other scale is unusually low, clinicians should give serious consideration to the hypothesis that the individual has provided a self-unfavorable ($A > 75$; $R < 45$) or self-favorable ($A < 45$; $R > 60$) description of her psychopathology. It is particularly pathognomonic when both the A and R scales are low ($T < 50$), a pattern that is seen in chronic, ego-syntonic psychopathology.

Restructured Clinical Scales

Tellegen et al. (2003) developed the Restructured Clinical (RC) Scales in an attempt to remove first-factor variance (generalized emotional distress) from each of the extant clinical scales. They developed a new marker for this first-factor variance, *RCd* (Demoralization), which was used to remove the generalized emotional distress from each clinical scale, and then they identified the salient area of content. Although their attempt to remove generalized emotional distress was only marginally successful at best (see Caldwell, 2006), they identified a single area of salient content within each clinical scale (see Table 6.6). After identifying this content area, they added items from the entire item pool to each scale. Nearly one-half of the items from each RC scale are not found on the parent clinical scale, so the RC scales actually are a single content area from the entire MMPI-2 item pool that has direct relevance to each clinical scale. The RC scales are redundant to a number of extant MMPI-2 scales so little new information is provided (see Table 6.7). The RC scales are helpful in identifying whether this single content area is causing the elevation on the parent clinical scale. There is one important change in the relationship between the RC scales and the parent clinical scales; *RC3cyn* (Cynicism) has been inverted with respect to Scale *3* (*Hy:* Hysteria).

The entire October 2006 issue of the *Journal of Personality Assessment* is devoted to the RC scales. This issue should be reviewed by any clinician who is using the RC scales.

Table 6.6   Correlations with Demoralization (*RCdem*) for clinical and restructured clinical scales in clinical patients

Restructured Clinical Scale		Demoralization		Clinical Scale
RC1som	Somatic Complaints	.69	.72	*1* (*Hs*: Hypochondriasis)
RC2lpe	Low Positive Emotionality	.74	.80	*2* (*D*: Depression)
RC3cyn	Cynicism	.53	.48	*3* (*Hy*: Hysteria)
RC4asb	Antisocial Behavior	.46	.75	*4* (*Pd*: Psychopathic Deviate)
RC6per	Ideas of Persecution	.56	.67	*6* (*Pa*: Paranoia)
RC7dne	Dysfunctional Negative Emotions	.83	.93	*7* (*Pt*: Psychasthenia)
RC8abx	Aberrant Experiences	.62	.88	*8* (*Sc*: Schizophrenia)
RC9hpm	Hypomanic Activation	.38	.41	*9* (*Ma*: Hypomania)

Source: Caldwell (1997a).

Table 6.7   Correlations between restructured clinical scales and extant MMPI-2 scales

Restructured Clinical Scale		Correlation	Similar Scale
Rcdem	Demoralization	.94	Welsh Anxiety (A)
RC1som	Somatic Complaints	.96	Health Concerns (HEA)
RC2lpe	Low Positive Emotionality	.88	Introversion/Low Positive Emotionality (INTR)
RC3cyn	Cynicism	.93	Cynicism (CYN)
RC4asb	Antisocial Behavior	.82	Addiction Admission (AAS)
RC6per	Ideas of Persecution	.88	Persecutory Ideas (Pa₁)
RC7dne	Dysfunctional Negative Emotions	.90	Negative Emotionality (NEGE)
RC8abx	Aberrant Experiences	.92	Bizarre Mentation (BIZ)
RC9hpm	Hypomania	.67	Aggression (AGGR)

Source: Caldwell (1997a).

Supplementary Scales

A total of 20 supplementary scales are scored routinely on the MMPI-2. Only eight of these scales will be covered here: three alcohol and drug scales and the personality psychopathology five (PSY-5) scales. The other supplementary scales, which are used less frequently, are described in the standard references to the MMPI-2 (Fowler et al., 2000; Friedman et al., 2001; Graham, 2006; Greene, 2000; Nichols, 2001).

The alcohol and drug scales on the MMPI-2 can be easily subdivided into rationally derived or direct measures (Addiction Admission [*AAS*]) and empirically derived or indirect measures (MacAndrew Alcoholism-Revised [*MAC-R*] and Addiction Potential [*APS*]). These different methodologies yielded very different item groupings on these three scales that can be seen in the low positive intercorrelations among them: *MAC- R* with *AAS* .48 and *APS* .29; and *AAS* with *APS* .34. Consequently, the manifestations of alcohol and drug abuse in specific individuals will differ depending on which scale is elevated.

The *MAC-R* scale (MacAndrew, 1965) is best conceptualized as a general personality dimension. Individuals who produced elevated scores (raw scores > 24 to 26) on the *MAC-R* scale are described as being impulsive, risk-taking, and sensation-seeking; and they frequently have a propensity to abuse alcohol and stimulating drugs. They are uninhibited, sociable individuals who appear to use repression and religion in an attempt to control their rebellious, delinquent impulses. They also are described as having a high energy level, having shallow interpersonal relationships, and being generally psychologically maladjusted. Low scorers (raw scores < 18 to 20) are described as being risk-avoiding, introverted, and depressive; and if they abuse substances, they abuse sedative-hypnotics and alcohol. Once the MAC-R scale is understood as a general personality dimension of risk-taking versus risk-avoiding, the fact that mean scores vary drastically by codetype makes sense. In men, the mean raw score on the *MAC-R* scale in a *4-9/9-4* (risk-taking) codetype is 26.5 and in a *2-0/0-2* (risk-avoiding) codetype is 17.1 (see Greene, 2000, appendix D), a difference of over two standard deviations.

A number of issues must be kept in mind when interpreting the *MAC-R* scale: Men score about two raw-score points higher than women across most samples, which indicates that different cutting scores are necessary by gender; there is not a single, optimal cutting score, with raw scores anywhere from 24 to 29 being used in different studies; clinicians need to be very cautious in using the *MAC-R* scale in nonwhite ethnic groups, if it is used at all. Classification accuracy decreases when clinicians are trying to discriminate between substance abusers and nonsubstance abusing, psychiatric patients, which is a frequent differential diagnosis; and classification accuracy may be unacceptably low in medical samples.

The Addiction Potential Scale (*APS:* Weed, Butcher, McKenna, & Ben-Porath, 1992) consists of 39 items that differentiated among groups of male and female substance abuse patients, normal individuals, and psychiatric patients. Individuals with elevated (T > 64) scores on the *APS* scale are generally distressed and upset as well as angry and resentful. They also are concerned about what others think of them, a concern that is not evident in individuals who elevate the *MAC-R* scale. The *APS* scale appears to be more accurate at discriminating between substance-abuse patients and psychiatric patients than the *MAC-R* scale. The *APS* scale also tends to be less gender biased than the *MAC-R* scale and to be less codetype sensitive. In men, the mean T score on *APS* in a *4-9/9-4* codetype is 56.2 and in a *2-0/0-2* codetype, it is 49.0 (see Greene, 2000, appendix D), a difference slightly over one-half of a standard deviation.

The Addiction Admission Scale (*AAS:* Weed et al., 1992) consists of 13 items directly related to the use of alcohol and drugs. Clinicians should review the clinical history and background of any individual who elevates the AAS scale (T > 59) because of the explicit nature of the items and the fact that three or more of these items have been endorsed in the deviant direction to produce this elevation. The *AAS* scale typically performs better at identifying individuals who are abusing substances than less direct measures such as the *APS* and *MAC-R* scales, even though the items are face valid allowing individuals not to report the substance abuse if they so desire. Weed, Butcher, and Ben-Porath (1995) have provided a thorough review of all MMPI-2 measures of substance abuse.

The specific MMPI-2 items related to alcohol and drug use (264, 489, 511, 544) warrant further inquiry any time they are endorsed in the deviant direction. Most of these items are phrased in the past tense so the clinician cannot assume without inquiry whether the alcohol and drug use is a current or past event.

Harkness and McNulty (1994) created a five-factor model within the MMPI-2 item pool called the Personality Psychopathology Five scales (PSY-5) to aid in the description of normal personality and to complement the diagnosis of personality disorders. Using replicated rational selection, Harkness and McNulty identified five factors within 60 descriptors of normal and abnormal human behavior: Aggressiveness (*AGGR*), Psychoticism (*PSYC*), Disconstraint (*DISC*), Negative Emotionality/Neuroticism (*NEGE*), and Introversion/Low Positive Emotionality (*INTR;* Harkness et al., 2002). The *AGGR* scale assesses offensive aggression and possibly the enjoyment of dominating, frightening, and controlling others, and the lack of regard for social rules and conventions. The *PSYC* scale assesses the cognitive ability of the individual to model the external, objective world in an accurate manner. Persons who are low on the *PSYC* construct can realize that their model is not working and accommodate or revise the model to fit their environment. Although the *PSYC* scale has its largest correlations with Scales *F, 8 (Sc)*, and Bizarre Mentation (*BIZ*), it appears to be measuring a generalized emotional distress factor, much like the *NEGE* scale. The *DISC* scale assesses a dimension from rule following versus rule breaking and criminality. The *DISC* scale is not correlated to most of the other MMPI-2 scales and, thus, would appear to have the potential to contribute additional information when interpreting the

MMPI-2. The largest correlations of the *DISC* scale are with Scales *9* (*Ma:* Hypomania), the MacAndrew Alcoholism-Revised (*MAC-R*), and Antisocial Practices (*ASP*). The *NEGE* scale assesses a broad affective disposition to experience negative emotions focusing on anxiety and nervousness. The *NEGE* scale is another of the numerous markers for the first factor of generalized emotional distress and negative affect on the MMPI-2. The *INTR* construct assesses a broad disposition to experience negative affects and to avoid social experiences. Although the *INTR* scale generally has its largest correlations with MMPI-2 markers for the first factor, the *INTR* scale is a measure of anhedonia that is suggestive of serious psychopathology. Such an interpretation of the *INTR* scale is particularly likely when the *NEGE* scale is *not* elevated significantly.

Critical Items

A variety of critical item sets (Koss & Butcher, 1973; Lachar & Wrobel, 1974) can be reviewed in every MMPI-2 profile. The interpretation of individual items reflects the ultimate level of specificity in describing the content of a specific MMPI-2 profile. This increased specificity, however, is at the price of lowered reliability and the potential for idiographic interpretation of the content. This problem can be illustrated by interviewing individuals about their reasons for endorsing any critical items. They will provide reasons that range the gamut from inane to profound for endorsing the same item.

Comparison Groups

Any MMPI-2 profile can be compared with numerous different groups, and the interpretation that is made will vary as a function of which comparison group is used. In the standard MMPI-2 profile, the client is being compared with all men or women in the MMPI-2 normative group (Butcher et al., 1989, 2001). The client also can be compared with all psychiatric patients (Caldwell, 1997a), personnel-screening applicants (Caldwell, 1997b; Cord, Sajwaj, Tolliver, & Ford, 1997), child-custody litigants (Bathurst, Gottfried, & Gottfried, 1997), prison inmates (Megargee, Mercer, & Carbonell, 1999), personal-injury plaintiffs (Lees-Haley, 1997), and pain patients (Caldwell, 1998).

Table 6.8 illustrates how the individual's T score on the *F* (Infrequency) and *K* (Correction) validity scales and Scales *2* (*D:* Depression) and *8* (*Sc:* Schizophrenia) will have

Table 6.8   Effects of setting on several MMPI-2 validity and clinical scales

Setting/Author(s)	Mean T Score			
	F	*K*	*2(D)*	*8(Sc)*
Civilian personnel screening (Caldwell, 1997b)	46.8	60.9	46.9	49.8
Nuclear power plant personnel screening (Cord et al., 1997)	44.2	56.9	—	—
Child-custody litigants (Bathurst et al., 1997)	44.7	56.7	46.6	46.9
Normal individuals (Butcher et al., 1989)	50.0	50.0	50.0	50.0
Pain patients (Caldwell, 1997c)	56.8	53.1	66.2	61.4
Prison inmates (Megargee et al., 1999)	56.0	49.0	55.5	56.5
Personal-injury plaintiffs (Lees-Haley, 1997)	62.0	50.0	70.0	65.0
Psychiatric patients (Caldwell, 1997a)	59.7	51.3	63.1	61.9

different interpretations depending on which sample is being used as a comparison group. An individual with a T score of 60 on the *F* scale is 15 points higher than the mean of the child-custody litigants (Bathurst et al., 1997) and personnel-screening applicants (Caldwell, 1997b; Cord et al., 1997), and slightly lower than the mean of the psychiatric patients (Caldwell, 1997a) and personal-injury plaintiffs (Lees-Haley, 1997). In the former group, a T score of 60 is relatively unusual, whereas in the latter two groups, it is common. Similar differences by comparison group can be found on the *K* (Correction) scale and Scales *2* (*D:* Depression) and *8* (*Sc:* Schizophrenia).

Another group with which the MMPI-2 can be compared in the interpretive process is some subgrouping of the entire group that has been considered previously. The most common subgrouping of the MMPI-2 is based on codetype analysis. Although the frequency with which a specific codetype occurs will vary drastically by the type of setting (e.g., clinical versus medical), the prototypic MMPI-2 profile for individual codetypes appears to be relatively invariant across settings. For example, *1-3/3-1* codetypes comprise nearly 31.9% of all codetypes in a pain setting (Keller & Butcher, 1991) and less than 14.8% in a clinical setting (Caldwell, 1997a).

Table 6.9 provides the mean scores on the *F* (Infrequency) and *K* (Correction) validity scales and Scales *2* (*D:* Depression) and *8* (*Sc:* Schizophrenia) for 20 different MMPI-2 codetypes. The mean T score on the *F* scale varies from 46.6 in Spike *3* codetypes to 96.9 in *6-8/8-6* codetypes, and the *K* scale varies from 36.1 in *6-8/8-6* codetypes to 60.0 in

Table 6.9   Effects of MMPI-2 codetype on several MMPI-2 validity and clinical scales

Codetype	Mean T Score			
	F	*K*	*2(D)*	*8(Sc)*
1-2/2-1	65.3	46.7	84.1	66.0
1-3/3-1	57.3	55.1	70.7	65.0
2-3/3-2	63.4	50.2	86.0	70.0
2-4/4-2	66.3	46.3	80.0	66.8
2-6/6-2	74.4	43.0	85.5	72.9
2-7/7-2	67.8	45.9	86.8	72.9
2-8/8-2	86.6	40.6	90.5	90.4
2-0/0-2	63.1	40.1	77.9	60.2
Spike *3*	46.6	60.0	53.0	50.9
3-6/6-3	64.6	50.4	71.1	69.2
Spike *4*	50.6	59.5	51.2	53.2
4-7/7-4	64.6	49.2	67.6	66.9
4-8/8-4	82.2	45.3	67.9	82.9
4-9/9-4	62.8	47.9	52.3	61.7
Spike *6*	50.0	53.5	50.6	50.6
6-8/8-6	96.9	36.1	77.7	95.0
6-9/9-6	66.7	43.9	51.7	63.6
7-8/8-7	84.4	41.5	77.8	91.2
8-9/9-8	76.2	41.4	56.5	79.0
Spike *9*	49.0	51.3	44.9	50.9

Spike *3* codetypes. A client with a T score of 60 on the *F* scale is almost 15 points higher than the mean for Spike *3* codetypes, and nearly 40 points lower than the mean for *6-8/8-6* codetypes. A T score of 60 is unusual in both of these codetypes; in the former it is higher than expected and in the latter it is much lower than expected. Similar variations can be seen in the T scores for Scales *2* (*D:* Depression) and *8* (*Sc:* Schizophrenia).

A codetype analysis can be further refined by considering additional clinical scales to create three- and four-point codetypes. A number of two-point codetypes have frequent three-point variants that should be considered in the interpretation of the MMPI-2, such as variants of *2-4/4-2* (*2-4/4-2-(3)*, *2-4/4-2-(7)*, *2-4/4-2-(8)*) and *2-7/7-2* (*2-7/7-2-(1)*, *2-7/7-2-(3)*, *2-7/7-2-(8)*, *2-7/7-2-(0)*) codetypes. Again, the interpretation of a client's score on a given scale will change as the prototypic score changes in the three-point codetypes within a particular group.

The final "group" with which the MMPI-2 can be compared in the interpretive process is the individual, or idiographic, interpretation. In this comparison, the relative elevations of the scales become important because they indicate which content domains are more or less important for this particular individual. An individual who has T scores of 75 and 60 on the content scales of Depression (*DEP*) and Anxiety (*ANX*), respectively, is saying that symptoms of depression are more of a problem than symptoms of anxiety. The MMPI-2 content (Butcher et al., 1990) and content component (Ben-Porath & Sherwood, 1993) scales are an excellent means of developing such an idiographic interpretation of an individual's MMPI-2 profile, because the various content domains can be juxtaposed so that the clinician can compare them directly.

APPLICATIONS

As a self-report inventory, the MMPI-2 is easily administered in a wide variety of settings and for a variety of purposes. Although the MMPI was developed originally in a clinical setting with a primary focus on establishing a diagnosis for the person (Hathaway & McKinley, 1940), its uses quickly broadened to include more general descriptions of the behavior and symptoms of most forms of psychopathology (cf. Dahlstrom et al., 1972). This use was followed by extensions into the screening of applicants in personnel selection settings and a multitude of uses in forensic settings.

Somewhat different issues must be considered in the administration of the MMPI-2 in personnel selection and forensic settings compared with the more usual clinical setting. First, not only is the administration not going to be therapeutic, the MMPI-2 results have the potential to cause a fairly negative impact on the individual. The individual may not be selected in a personnel-screening setting or be less likely to be considered for custody of children because of the acknowledgment of significant psychopathology.

Second, the assessment of validity is particularly important because different forensic settings can have a significant impact on the data that are obtained from an individual. Items particularly sensitive to this impact are likely to be those items about which an individual is not sure or ambivalent in responding. In civil forensic settings such as personal injury, workers' compensation, and insurance disability claims, this impact is likely to be in the opposite direction from that in parenting examinations or personnel selection. Portraying oneself as being more impaired in cases for civil damages is likely to benefit an individual's claim; portraying oneself as being less impaired and more psychologically healthy is likely to benefit an individual's chances of being selected, or at least not screened out, in a personnel-screening setting. Consequently, it behooves the forensic psychologist to know what types of MMPI-2 scores and profiles are to be expected in every forensic setting.

There also are different expectations of whether to report problematic behaviors and symptoms in criminal cases. Individuals who are being evaluated for competency to stand trial or for the introduction of mitigating circumstances during the sentencing phase after a conviction for murder versus probation or parole should have different expectations of the problematic behaviors and symptoms of psychopathology that are, or are not, to be reported. Individuals in the former forensic contexts would be expected to report any and all problematic behaviors or symptoms that might be in any way relevant to their circumstances, while individuals in the latter would not be expected to report any problematic behaviors or symptoms.

Third, in a forensic setting it must be kept in mind that the MMPI-2 is being used to address a specific psycholegal issue rather than as a general screen for psychopathology. Thus, the interpretations provided of the MMPI-2 must be relevant to this psycholegal issue. For example, the mere presence of psychopathology as indicated by elevation of several clinical scales on the MMPI-2 may not be directly relevant to the psycholegal issue of quality of parenting skills in a child-custody examination or the ability to understand legal proceedings in a competency hearing.

Finally, whether it is the prosecution (plaintiff) or the defense (defendant) that has retained the forensic psychologist also may impact the problematic behaviors and symptoms reported by an individual, but there are minimal empirical data on this point. Hasemann (1997) provided data on workers' compensation claimants who were evaluated by forensic psychologists for both the defense and the plaintiff. The claimant reported more symptoms and distress to the forensic psychologist retained by the defense attorney. Consequently, some of the differences in examinations performed by forensic psychologists on the same individual may reflect that he actually describes problematic behaviors and symptoms differently depending on whether he believes that the forensic psychologist is likely to be sensitive or insensitive to his self-report. The underlying heuristic of an individual is likely to be that the opposing forensic psychologist will require more proof to be able or willing to perceive and report an individual as being impaired. These results suggest that being examined by the plaintiff's expert and then by the defense's expert over the same psycholegal issue should be considered as different forensic contexts rather than as the same one.

PSYCHOMETRIC FOUNDATIONS

Demographic Variables

Age

Specific norms are not provided by age on the MMPI-2, even though it is well known that there are substantial effects of age below the age of 20. These age effects are reflected in the development of separate sets of adolescent norms for the original MMPI (Marks & Briggs, 1972), and the restandardization of a different form of the MMPI for adolescents

(MMPI-A: Butcher et al., 1992). Colligan and his colleagues (Colligan, Osborne, Swenson, & Offord, 1983, 1989) found substantial effects of age on MMPI performance in their contemporary normative sample with differences of 10 or more T points between 18- and 19-year-olds and 70-year-olds on Scales *L* (Lie) and *9* (*Ma:* Hypomania). Several MMPI-2 scales demonstrate differences of nearly 5 T points between 20-year-olds and 60-year-olds (Butcher et al., 1989, 2001; Caldwell, 1997b, 1997c; Greene & Schinka, 1995) with scores on Scales *L* (Lie: women only), *1* (*Hs:* Hypochondriasis), and *3* (*Hy:* Hysteria) increasing and Scales *4* (*Pd:* Psychopathic Deviate) and *9* (*Ma:* Hypomania) decreasing with age. Given that these age comparisons involve different cohorts, it is not possible to know whether these effects actually reflect the influence of age or simply differences between the cohorts. Butcher et al. (1991) found few effects of age in older (>60) men and they saw no reason for age-related norms in these men.

Gender

Gender does not create any general issues in MMPI-2 interpretation because separate norms (profile forms) are used for men and women. Any gender differences in how individuals responded to the items on each scale are removed when the raw scores are converted to T scores. Consequently, men and women with a T score of 70 on Scale *2* (*D:* Depression) are one standard deviation above the mean, although women have endorsed more items (30) than men (28). When the MMPI-2 is computer scored by Pearson Assessment, unigender norms also are provided for each scale. Even a cursory perusal of these unigender norms will show that men and women have very similar scores on all MMPI-2 scales except for those three scales specifically related to gender (Scale *5* [*Mf:* Masculinity-Femininity]; Gender-Role Feminine [*GF*]; Gender-Role Masculine [*GM*]).

Education

The potential effects of education have not been investigated in any systematic manner either on the MMPI or the MMPI-2, although such research is needed. When the men and women in the MMPI-2 normative group with less than a high school education were contrasted with men and women with postgraduate education (Dahlstrom & Tellegen, 1993, pp. 58–59), the differences on the following scales exceeded 5 T points: *L* (Lie: women only), *F* (Infrequency), *K* (Correction), *5* (*Mf:* Masculinity-Femininity), and *0* (*Si:* Social Introversion). Men and women with less than a high school education had a higher score in all these comparisons except for Scales *K* (Correction) and *5* (*Mf:* Masculinity-Femininity). When psychiatric patients with 8 years or less of education were contrasted with patients with 16 or more years of education (Caldwell, 1997b), the differences ranged from 4 to 8 T points on all the scales except *3* (*Hy:* Hysteria). The individuals with less education had higher scores in all these comparisons except for Scales *K* (Correction) and *5* (*Mf:* Masculinity-Femininity).

Occupation

There do not appear to be any systematic effects for occupation or income within the MMPI-2 normative group (Dahlstrom & Tellegen, 1993; Long, Graham, & Timbrook, 1994). There have been no studies of the effects of these two factors in psychiatric patients.

Ethnicity

The effects of ethnicity on MMPI performance have been reviewed by Dahlstrom, Lachar, and Dahlstrom (1986) and Greene (1987), and they concluded that there is not any consistent pattern of scale differences between any two ethnic groups. A similar conclusion has been offered in several other reviews of the effect of ethnicity on MMPI-2 performance (Greene, 1991, 2000; Hall, Bansal, & Lopez, 1999).

Multivariate regressions of age, education, gender, ethnicity, and occupation on the standard validity and clinical scales in the MMPI-2 normative group (Dahlstrom & Tellegen, 1993) and psychiatric patients (Caldwell, 1997 [age, education, and gender only]; Schinka, LaLone, & Greene, 1998) have shown that the percentage of variance accounted for by these factors does not exceed 10%. Such small percentages of variance are unlikely to impact the interpretation of most MMPI-2 profiles. The one exception is Scale 5 (*Mf:* Masculinity-Femininity) in which slightly over 50% of the variance is accounted for by gender.

In summary, demographic variables appear to have minimal impact on the MMPI-2 profile in most individuals. It may be important to monitor the validity of the MMPI-2 profile more closely in persons with limited education and lower occupations. A major reason that demographic effects are seen in these persons may simply reflect that the reading level of the MMPI-2 is approximately the eighth grade (Butcher et al., 1989, 2001; Greene, 2000).

Reliability

The *MMPI-2 Manual* (Butcher et al., 1989, 2001, Appendix E) reports the reliability data for 82 men and 111 women who were retested after an average of 8.58 days. The test-retest correlations ranged from .54 to .93 across the 10 clinical scales and averaged .74. The standard error of measurement is about 5 T points for the clinical scales, that is, the individual's true score on the clinical scales will be within ±5 T points two-thirds of the time.

The test-retest correlations for the 15 content scales range from .77 to .91 and averaged .85. The standard error of measurement is about 4 T points for the content scales, that is, the individual's true score on the content scales will be within ±4 points two-thirds of the time.

Codetype Stability

There is little empirical data indicating how consistently clients will obtain the same codetype on two successive administrations of the MMPI or the MMPI-2. The research on the stability of the MMPI historically focused either on the reliability of individual scales as discussed, which leaves unanswered whether clients' codetypes have remained unchanged. There would be at least some cause for concern if a client obtained a *4-9/9-4* codetype on one occasion and on a second administration of the MMPI-2 a few months later in another setting obtained a *2-7/7-2* codetype.

Graham, Smith, and Schwartz (1986) have provided the only empirical data on the stability of MMPI codetypes for a large sample ($N = 405$) of psychiatric inpatients. They reported 42.7%, 44.0%, and 27.7% agreement across an average interval of approximately 3 months for high-point, low-point, and two-point codetypes, respectively. If the patients were classified into the categories of neurotic, psychotic, and characterological, 58.1% remained in the same category when retested.

Greene, Davis, and Morse (1993, August) reported the stability of the MMPI in 454 alcoholic inpatients who had been retested after an interval of approximately 6 months. Approximately 40% of the men and 32% of the women had the same single high-point scale on the two successive administrations of the MMPI. However, they had the same two-point codetype only 12% and 13% of the time, respectively. Almost 30% of these men and women had two totally different high-point scales when they took the MMPI on their second admission.

These data on codetype stability, or more accurately the lack thereof, suggest several important conclusions. First, clinicians should be cautious about making long-term predictions from a single administration of the MMPI-2. Rather an MMPI-2 profile should be interpreted as reflecting the individual's current status. Second, it is not clear whether the shifts that do occur in codetypes across time reflect meaningful changes in the clients' behaviors, psychometric instability of the MMPI-2, or some combination of both factors.

CONCLUDING COMMENTS

The MMPI-2 (Butcher et al., 1989, 2001) is the oldest and the most widely used of the self-report inventories. The numerous validity scales have served it well in assessing the many forms of response distortion that are encountered in the various settings in which the MMPI-2 is administered. The MMPI-2 is the prototype of an empirically derived test in which the correlates of individual scales and codetypes are determined through research. There is an extensive research base on most of the major issues in the assessment of psychopathology reflecting its long history of use.

REFERENCES

American Psychiatric Association. (2000). *Diagnostic and statistical manual of mental disorders* (4th ed., text rev.). Washington, DC: Author.

Arbisi, P. A., & Ben-Porath, Y. S. (1995). An MMPI-2 infrequent response scale for use with psychopathological populations: The Infrequency Psychopathology scale: $F(p)$. *Psychological Assessment, 7*, 424–431.

Archer, R. P., Griffin, R., & Aiduk, R. (1995). MMPI-2 clinical correlates for ten common codes. *Journal of Personality Assessment, 65*, 391–407.

Bathurst, K., Gottfried, A. W., & Gottfried, A. E. (1997). Normative data for the MMPI-2 in child custody litigation. *Psychological Assessment, 9*, 205–211.

Ben-Porath, Y. S., & Butcher, J. N. (1989). Psychometric stability of rewritten MMPI items. *Journal of Personality Assessment, 53*, 645–653.

Ben-Porath, Y. S., & Sherwood, N. E. (1993). *The MMPI-2 content component scales: Development, psychometric characteristics, and clinical application.* Minneapolis: University of Minnesota Press.

Butcher, J. N., Aldwin, C. M., Levenson, M. R., Ben-Porath, Y. S., Spiro, A., & Bosse, R. (1991). Personality and aging: A study of the MMPI-2 among older men. *Psychology and Aging, 6*, 361–370.

Butcher, J. N., Dahlstrom, W. G., Graham, J. R., Tellegen, A. M., & Kaemmer, B. (1989). *MMPI-2: Manual for administration and scoring*. Minneapolis: University of Minnesota Press.

Butcher, J. N., Graham, J. R., & Ben-Porath, Y. S. (1995). Methodological problems and issues in MMPI, MMPI-2, and MMPI-A research. *Psychological Assessment, 7*, 320–329.

Butcher, J. N., Graham, J. R., Ben-Porath, Y. S., Tellegen, A. M., Dahlstrom, W. G., & Kaemmer, B. (2001). *MMPI-2: Manual for administration and scoring* (Rev. ed.). Minneapolis: University of Minnesota Press.

Butcher, J. N., Graham, J. R., Williams, C. L., & Ben-Porath, Y. S. (1990). *Development and use of the MMPI-2 content scales*. Minneapolis: University of Minnesota Press.

Butcher, J. N., & Han, K. (1995). Development of an MMPI-2 scale to assess the presentation of self in a superlative manner: The *S* scale. In J. N. Butcher & C. D. Spielberger (Eds.), *Advances in personality assessment* (*Vol. 10*, pp. 25–50). Hillsdale, NJ: Erlbaum.

Butcher, J. N., & Rouse, S. V. (1996). Personality: Individual differences and clinical assessment. *Annual Review of Psychology, 47*, 87–111.

Butcher, J. N., Williams, C. L., Graham, J. R., Archer, R. P., Tellegen, A., Ben-Porath, Y. S., et al. (1992). *MMPI-A (Minnesota Multiphasic Personality Inventory—Adolescent): Manual for administration, scoring, and interpretation*. Minneapolis: University of Minnesota Press.

Caldwell, A. B. (1997a). [MMPI-2 data research file for clinical patients]. Unpublished raw data.

Caldwell, A. B. (1997b). [MMPI-2 data research file for personnel applicants]. Unpublished raw data.

Caldwell, A. B. (1997c). Whither goest our redoubtable mentor the MMPI/MMPI-2? *Journal of Personality Assessment, 68*, 47–66.

Caldwell, A. B. (1998). [MMPI-2 data research file for pain patients]. Unpublished raw data.

Caldwell, A. B. (2006). Maximal measurement or meaningful measurement: The interpretive challenges of the MMPI-2 Restructured Clinical (RC) scales. *Journal of Personality Assessment, 87*, 193–201.

Colligan, R. C., Osborne, D., Swenson, W. M., & Offord, K. P. (1983). *The MMPI: A contemporary normative study*. New York: Praeger.

Colligan, R. C., Osborne, D., Swenson, W. M., & Offord, K. P. (1989). *The MMPI: A contemporary normative study* (2nd ed.). Odessa, FL: Psychological Assessment Resources.

Cord, E. L. J., Sajwaj, T. E., Tolliver, D. K., & Ford, T. W. (1997, June). *Normative update on MMPI-2 data for a large federal power utility*. Paper presented at the 32nd annual Symposium on Recent Developments in the use of the MMPI-2 and MMPI-A, Minneapolis, MN.

Dahlstrom, W. G., Archer, R. P., Hopkins, D. G., Jackson, E., & Dahlstrom, L. E. (1994). *Assessing the readability of the Minnesota Multiphasic Inventory Instruments: The MMPI, MMPI-2, MMPI-A*. Minneapolis: University of Minnesota Press.

Dahlstrom, W. G., Lachar, D., & Dahlstrom, L. E. (1986). *MMPI patterns of American minorities*. Minneapolis: University of Minnesota Press.

Dahlstrom, W. G., & Tellegen, A. (1993). *Socioeconomic status and the MMPI-2: The relation of MMPI-2 patterns to levels of education and occupation*. Minneapolis: University of Minnesota Press.

Dahlstrom, W. G., Welsh, G. S., & Dahlstrom, L. E. (1972). *An MMPI handbook: Vol. I. Clinical interpretation* (Rev. ed.). Minneapolis: University of Minnesota Press.

Finn, S. (1996). *Using the MMPI-2 as a therapeutic intervention*. Minneapolis: University of Minnesota Press.

Fischer, C. T. (1994). *Individualizing psychological assessment*. Hillsdale, NJ: Erlbaum.

Fowler, R. A., Butcher, J. N., & Williams, C. L. (2000). *Essentials of MMPI-2 and MMPI-A interpretation* (2nd ed.). Minneapolis: University of Minnesota Press.

Friedman, A. F., Lewak, R., Nichols, D. S., & Webb, J. T. (2001). *Psychological assessment with the MMPI-2* (2nd ed.). Hillsdale, NJ: Erlbaum.

Gough, H. G. (1950). The *F* minus *K* dissimulation index for the MMPI. *Journal of Consulting Psychology, 14*, 408–413.

Gough, H. G. (1954). Some common misconceptions about neuroticism. *Journal of Consulting Psychology, 18*, 287–292.

Graham, J. R. (2006). *MMPI-2: Assessing personality and psychopathology* (4th ed.). New York: Oxford University Press.

Graham, J. R., Ben-Porath, Y. S., & McNulty, J. L. (1999). *MMPI-2 correlates for outpatient community mental health settings.* Minneapolis: University of Minnesota Press.

Graham, J. R., Smith, R. L., & Schwartz, G. F. (1986). Stability of MMPI configurations for psychiatric inpatients. *Journal of Consulting and Clinical Psychology, 54*, 375–380.

Greene, R. L. (1987). Ethnicity and MMPI performance: A review. *Journal of Consulting and Clinical Psychology, 55*, 497–512.

Greene, R. L. (1991). *The MMPI-2/MMPI: An interpretive manual.* Boston: Allyn & Bacon.

Greene, R. L. (2000). *The MMPI-2: An interpretive manual.* Boston: Allyn & Bacon.

Greene, R. L., & Brown, R. C. (2006). *MMPI-2 adult interpretive system* (3rd ed.). Lutz, FL: Psychological Assessment Resources.

Greene, R. L., Davis, L. J., Jr., & Morse, R. M. (1993, August). *Stability of MMPI codetypes in alcoholic inpatients.* Paper presented at the annual meeting of the American Psychological Association, San Francisco.

Greene, R. L., Gwin, R., & Staal, M. (1997). Current status of MMPI-2 research: A methodological overview. *Journal of Personality Assessment, 68*, 20–36.

Greene, R. L., & Schinka, J. A. (1995). [MMPI-2 data research file for psychiatric inpatients and outpatients]. Unpublished raw data.

Hall, G. C. N., Bansal, A., & Lopez, I. R. (1999). Ethnicity and psychopathology: A meta-analytic review of 31 years of comparative MMPI/MMPI-2 research. *Psychological Assessment, 11*, 186–197.

Harkness, A. R., & McNulty, J. L. (1994). The Personality Psychopathology Five (PSY-5): Issue from the pages of a diagnostic manual instead of a dictionary. In S. Strack & M. Lorr (Eds.), *Differentiating normal and abnormal personality* (pp. 291–315). New York: Springer.

Harkness, A. R., McNulty, J. L., Ben-Porath, Y. S., & Graham, J. R. (2002). *MMPI-2 Personality Psychopathology Five (PSY-5) scales: Gaining an overview for case conceptualization and treatment planning.* Minneapolis: University of Minnesota Press.

Harris, R. E., & Lingoes, J. C. (1955). *Subscales for the MMPI: An aid to profile interpretation.* Unpublished manuscript, University of California.

Hasemann, D. M. (1997). *Practices and findings of mental health professionals conducting workers' compensation evaluations.* Unpublished doctoral dissertation, University of Kentucky.

Hathaway, S. R., & McKinley, J. C. (1940). A multiphasic personality schedule (Minnesota): Pt. I. Construction of the schedule. *Journal of Psychology, 10*, 249–254.

Helmes, E., & Reddon, J. R. (1993). A perspective on developments in assessing psychopathology: A critical review of the MMPI and MMPI-2. *Psychological Bulletin, 113*, 453–471.

Keller, L. S., & Butcher, J. N. (1991). *Assessment of chronic pain patients with the MMPI-2.* Minneapolis: University of Minnesota Press.

Koss, M. P., & Butcher, J. N. (1973). A comparison of psychiatric patients' self-report with other sources of clinical information. *Journal of Research in Personality, 7*, 225–236.

Lachar, D., & Wrobel, T. A. (1974). Validating clinicians' hunches: Construction of a new MMPI critical item set. *Journal of Consulting and Clinical Psychology, 47*, 277–284.

Lees-Haley, P. R. (1997). MMPI-2 base rates for 492 personal injury plaintiffs: Implications and challenges for forensic assessment. *Journal of Clinical Psychology, 53*, 745–755.

Long, K. A., Graham, J. R., & Timbrook, R. E. (1994). Socioeconomic status and MMPI-2 interpretation. *Measurement and Evaluation in Counseling and Development, 27*, 158–177.

MacAndrew, C. (1965). The differentiation of male alcoholic outpatients from nonalcoholic psychiatric outpatients by means of the MMPI. *Quarterly Journal of Studies on Alcohol, 26*, 238–246.

Marks, P. A., & Briggs, P. F. (1972). Adolescent norm tables for the MMPI. In W. G. Dahlstrom, G. S. Welsh, & L. E. Dahlstrom (Eds.), *An MMPI handbook: Vol. 1. Clinical interpretation* (Rev. ed., pp. 388–399). Minneapolis: University of Minnesota Press.

Meehl, P. E. (1957). When should we use our heads instead of the formula? *Journal of Counseling Psychology, 4*, 268–273.

Megargee, E. I., Mercer, S. J., & Carbonell, J. L. (1999). MMPI-2 with male and female state and federal prison inmates. *Psychological Assessment, 11*, 177–185.

Nichols, D. S. (2001). *Essentials of MMPI-2 assessment.* New York: Wiley.

Paolo, A. M., Ryan, J. J., & Smith, A. J. (1992). Reading difficulty of MMPI-2 subscales. *Journal of Clinical Psychology, 47*, 529–532.

Paulhus, D. L. (1984). Two-component models of socially desirable responding. *Journal of Personality and Social Psychology, 46*, 598–609.

Paulhus, D. L. (1986). Self-deception and impression management in test responses. In A. Angleitner & J. S. Wiggins (Eds.), *Personality assessment via questionnaires: Current issues in theory and measurement* (pp. 143–165). Berlin, Germany: Springer-Verlag.

Schinka, J. A., & Borum, R. (1993). Readability of adult psychopathology inventories. *Psychological Assessment, 5*, 384–386.

Schinka, J. A., & LaLone, L. (1997). MMPI-2 norms: Comparisons with a census-matched subsample. *Psychological Assessment, 9*, 307–311.

Schinka, J. A., LaLone, L., & Greene, R. L. (1998). Effects of psychopathology and demographic characteristics on MMPI-2 scale scores. *Journal of Personality Assessment, 70*, 197–211.

Tellegen, A., Ben-Porath, Y. S., McNulty, J. L., Arbisi, P. A., Graham, J. R., & Kaemmer, B. (2003). *The MMPI-2 Restructured Clinical Scales: Development, validation, and interpretation.* Minneapolis: University of Minnesota Press.

Weed, N. C., Butcher, J. N., & Ben-Porath, Y. S. (1995). MMPI-2 measures of substance abuse. In J. N. Butcher & C. D. Spielberger (Eds.), *Advances in personality assessment* (*Vol 10*, pp. 121–145). Hillsdale, NJ: Erlbaum.

Weed, N. C., Butcher, J. N., McKenna, T., & Ben-Porath, Y. S. (1992). New measures for assessing alcohol and drug abuse with the MMPI-2: The APS and AAS. *Journal of Personality Assessment, 58*, 389–404.

Welsh, G. S. (1956). Factor dimensions A and R. In G. S. Welsh & W. G. Dahlstrom (Eds.), *Basic readings on the MMPI in psychology and medicine* (pp. 264–281). Minneapolis: University of Minnesota Press.

Chapter 7

MINNESOTA MULTIPHASIC PERSONALITY INVENTORY— ADOLESCENT

The Minnesota Multiphasic Personality Inventory—Adolescent (MMPI-A: Butcher et al., 1992) is a downward extension of the MMPI-2 (see Chapter 6) for adolescents between the ages of 14 and 18. Like the MMPI-2, the MMPI-A is a broadband measure of the major dimensions of psychopathology found in Axis I disorders and some Axis II disorders of the *DSM-IV-TR* (American Psychiatric Association, 2000). The MMPI-A consists of 8 validity and 10 clinical scales in the basic profile, along with 15 content scales, and 11 supplementary scales (see Table 7.1). There also are subscales for the clinical scales and content scales with more than 100 scales that can be scored and interpreted on the MMPI-A. Table 7.2 provides general information on the MMPI-A.

HISTORY

The original standardization sample of the MMPI consisted of white Minnesota adults, primarily between the ages of 16 and 55 (Hathaway & McKinley, 1940). Hathaway and Monachesi (1963), in an extensive study of the MMPI performance of adolescents, administered the MMPI to 3,971 ninth graders (mean age about 15) in the Minneapolis public school system during the 1947 to 1948 school year. Two and four years later, they determined how many of these students had records with the local juvenile division of the police department or probation office. During the spring of 1954, these researchers tested 11,329 additional ninth graders who represented a sample of the entire state of Minnesota. Three years later, they determined how many of these students had records by examining local community police and court files.

In 1957, when most of this second set of ninth graders were now twelfth graders (mean age about 18), Hathaway and Monachesi readministered the MMPI to 3,976 students. Hathaway and Monachesi obviously have a wealth of data, only part of which is relevant to the issue of how adolescents differ from adults in terms of their MMPI performance. (The reader who is interested in the use of the original MMPI to predict delinquency in adolescents, which was the main thrust of Hathaway and Monachesi's research project, should consult their book.)

Relevant to the current topic of MMPI norms, Hathaway and Monachesi found that ninth graders had mean scores with *K*-corrections on Scales *4* (*Pd:* Psychopathic Deviate), *8* (*Sc:* Schizophrenia), and *9* (*Ma:* Hypomania), which were approximately 10 T points

Table 7.1   MMPI-A scales

Validity Scales

?	Cannot Say
VRIN	Variable Response Consistency
TRIN	True Response Consistency
F_1	Infrequency (First Half)
F_2	Infrequency (Second Half)
F	Infrequency
L	Lie
K	Correction

Clinical Scales

1 (Hs)	Hypochondriasis
2 (D)	Depression
3 (Hy)	Hysteria
4 (Pd)	Psychopathic Deviate
5 (Mf)	Masculinity-Femininity
6 (Pa)	Paranoia
7 (Pt)	Psychasthenia
8 (Sc)	Schizophrenia
9 (Ma)	Hypomania
0 (Si)	Social Introversion

Content Scales

A-anx	Anxiety
A-obs	Obsessions
A-dep	Depression
A-hea	Health Concerns
A-aln	Alienation
A-biz	Bizarre Mentation
A-ang	Anger
A-cyn	Cynicism
A-con	Conduct Problems
A-lse	Low Self-Esteem
A-las	Low Aspirations
A-sod	Social Discomfort
A-fam	Family Problems
A-sch	School Problems
A-trt	Negative Treatment Indicators

Supplementary Scales

MAC-R	MacAndrew Alcoholism—Revised
ACK	Alcohol/Drug Acknowledgment
PRO	Alcohol/Drug Problems Proneness
IMM	Immaturity
A	Anxiety
R	Repression

PSY-5 Scales

AGGR	Aggression
PSYC	Psychoticism
DISC	Disconstraint
NEGE	Negative Emotionality
INTR	Introversion/Low Positive Emotionality

Table 7.2   Minnesota Multiphasic Personality Inventory-A (MMPI-A)

Authors:	Butcher, Williams, Graham, Archer, Tellegen, Ben-Porath, & Kaemmer
Published:	1992
Edition:	1st
Publisher:	Pearson Assessments
Website:	www.PearsonAssessments.com
Age range:	14–18
Reading level:	6th grade
Administration formats:	Paper/pencil, computer, CD, cassette
Additional languages:	Spanish
Number of items:	478
Response format:	True/False
Administration time:	45–60 minutes
Primary scales:	8 Validity, 10 Clinical, 15 Content
Additional scales:	11 Supplementary
Hand scoring:	Templates
General texts:	Archer (2005), Archer & Krishnamurthy (2002), Fowler et al. (2000)
Computer interpretation:	Caldwell Report (Caldwell); Pearson Assessments (Butcher); Psychological Assessment Resources (Archer)

higher than the original Minnesota normative sample of adults. On the rest of the validity and clinical scales, the ninth graders scored similarly to the adult sample. Thus, these adolescents were more likely to have elevations on Scales *4* (*Pd:* Psychopathic Deviate), *8* (*Sc:* Schizophrenia), and *9* (*Ma:* Hypomania), if adult MMPI norms were used. They also were less likely to have profiles in which all clinical scales were below a T score of 70 than were the normal adults.

Hathaway and Monachesi did not directly address whether these MMPI scale elevations in normal adolescents reflected some form of psychological distress and maladjustment that was characteristic of the turmoil of adolescence or whether these elevations reflected mere differences in the frequency of item endorsement that may not have psychopathological implications. Hathaway and Monachesi seemed to favor the former interpretation because they did not advocate special adolescent norms with the MMPI. Instead, they suggested that both the standard adult-normed profile and an adolescent-normed profile should be plotted so that the clinician can understand the contrast between adolescents and adults. The clinician, however, when provided with the potentially divergent and contradictory information from two profiles on the same adolescent, needs to know which source of information is more accurate, and Hathaway and Monachesi (1963) did not answer this question.

The students who were retested with the MMPI in the 12th grade provided some interesting information on profile stability. Test-retest reliability coefficients were highest for the *K* (Correction) scale—.52 for males and .56 for females—and Scale *0* (*Si:* Social Introversion)—.54 for males and .61 for females. By contrast, Scales *4* (*Pd:* Psychopathic Deviate)—.36 for males and .38 for females—and *6* (*Pa:* Paranoia)—.32 for males and .36 for females—had the lowest reliability coefficients.

As might be expected, profile stability as defined by the single high-point scale was highest when that scale was a T score of 70 or higher. More than half of the adolescents, both male and female, with a T score of 70 or higher on Scale *4* (*Pd:* Psychopathic Deviate) on initial testing, had Scale *4* (*Pd:* Psychopathic Deviate) as one of the two highest scales when retested. This relationship, however, did not hold for all scales. Scale *5* (*Mf:* Masculinity-Femininity), for example, was likely to shift from a high-point scale to one of the three lowest clinical scales across this 3-year interval.

Marks, Seeman, and Haller (1974) described how the adolescent norms for the MMPI were derived, primarily crediting Peter F. Briggs. Briggs selected 100 boys and 100 girls aged 14, 15, and 16 years, and 80 boys and 40 girls aged 17 years from the students studied by Hathaway and Monachesi (1963). To obtain a larger and more nationally representative sample, Marks et al. collected 1,046 additional MMPI profiles in 1964 and 1965 from both rural and urban, public and private school students residing in Alabama, California, Kansas, Missouri, North Carolina, and Ohio. All these students were presumed to be white and at the time of testing were neither institutionalized nor being treated for emotional disturbance (Marks et al., 1974). By combining these two groups of students, the adolescent norms for the MMPI validity and clinical scales for boys and girls in four age groups (14 and below, 15, 16, and 17 and 18) were constructed (see appendix H, tables 6 to 9, Dahlstrom, Welsh, & Dahlstrom, 1972). Although Marks et al. (1974) advocated that emotional disturbance in adolescents needs to be evaluated against adolescent norms, they concurred with Hathaway and Monachesi (1963) that adolescent scores on the MMPI also should be compared with adult norms. Thus, Marks et al. recommended that both an adult- and an adolescent-normed profile should be constructed for adolescents.

Several issues arise when the MMPI is used with adolescents. The first issue is whether adult norms, adolescent norms, or both sets of norms should be used with adolescents. As noted, Hathaway and Monachesi (1963) and Marks et al. (1974) recommended that adult- and adolescent-normed profiles should be constructed for adolescents. However, Archer (1984, 1987) advocated that adolescent norms should be used exclusively with adolescents, and he presented a cogent rationale for their use that clinicians should read. Williams (1986) also indicated that adolescent norms were the most appropriate for adolescents, but she suggested that both profiles should be plotted for adolescents.

A final issue is whether the adolescent or the adult correlates provide a more accurate interpretation once adolescent norms serve as the base to derive a codetype. Using adolescent and adult norms, Lachar, Klinge, and Grisell (1976) obtained valid profiles on 100 adolescents, most of whom were hospitalized. Interpretations of the two profiles for each adolescent were generated using Lachar's (1974) automated interpretive system for adults. Clinicians then were asked to rate these interpretations for accuracy. The interpretations of profiles generated from adolescent norms, compared with interpretations of profiles generated from adult norms, were rated more accurate 61 times, as accurate 13 times, and less accurate 26 times. Only 10% of the adolescent norm interpretations were judged to be inaccurate, and 20% of the adult norm interpretations were judged to be inaccurate. Wimbish (1984) reported similar findings in a sample of inpatient adolescent substance abusers.

Hence, it appears that even when an interpretive system (Lachar's) based on adults is used, profiles based on adolescent norms provide a more accurate description of adolescents than do profiles based on adult norms. It remains to be seen, however, whether other adult interpretive systems and individual clinicians will demonstrate the same improvement in accuracy with the use of adolescent norms.

Once the decision had been made to use adolescent norms for the MMPI, the clinician had three different sets of norms from which to choose. Marks et al.'s (1974) norms, described previously, have served as the standard for adolescent MMPIs since they were first published. Gottesman, Hanson, Kroeker, and Briggs (1987) developed their norms by using the MMPI responses of 12,953 15-year-olds and 3,492 18-year-olds, who composed the entire sample of adolescents studied by Hathaway and Monachesi (1963). Colligan and Offord (1989) developed their norms by collecting a sample of adolescents in the Mayo Clinic catchment area. This issue of which set of norms to use with the MMPI has been resolved with the development of the MMPI-A (Butcher et al., 1992) and the decision of the University of Minnesota Press to discontinue publishing the original MMPI in the fall of 1997.

The MMPI-A (Butcher et al., 1992) represents the restandardization of the MMPI to create a version that is specifically adapted for adolescents. Restandardization of the MMPI was needed to provide item content that was appropriate for adolescents, develop scales to assess symptoms and behaviors more common to adolescents, and create current norms for the inventory. Continuity between the MMPI and the MMPI-A was maintained as much as possible, although it was recognized that some changes would be necessary to adapt the MMPI for adolescents. Thus, the items on the validity and clinical scales of the MMPI are basically unchanged on the MMPI-A except for the F (Infrequency) scale and Scale 5 ($Mf:$ Masculinity-Femininity), which lost 27 and 16 items, respectively. The MMPI-A still retains 12 of the 27 items that were dropped from the F scale.

In the development of the MMPI-A, the Restandardization Committee (Butcher et al., 1992) started with the 550 items on the original MMPI (they first deleted the 16 repeated items). They reworded 82 of these 550 items to eliminate outdated and sexist language and to make these items more easily understood. Williams, Ben-Porath, and Hevern (1994) determined that the psychometric properties of 20 of these reworded items were the same or better than the original items. They also included 58 items from Form AX that was used to collect the normative data for the MMPI-2. The Restandardization Committee then added 96 provisional items "to assess problems, behaviors, and attitudes of adolescents in areas related to identity formation, negative peer-group influence, school and teachers, relationships with parents and families, and sexuality" (Butcher et al., 1992, p. 5). Thus, Form TX had a total of 704 items and was used to collect the normative data for the MMPI-A.

When finalizing the items to be included on the MMPI-A, the Restandardization Committee deleted 121 items from the original MMPI in addition to the 54 items deleted from the standard validity and clinical scales and the 16 repeated items. The rationale for including and dropping items from Form TX that resulted in the 478 items on the MMPI-A has not been made explicit to date.

The MMPI-A was standardized on a sample of 1,620 adolescents who resided in eight different states (California, Minnesota, New York, North Carolina, Ohio, Pennsylvania, Virginia, and Washington). These adolescents "were derived from samples of generally limited representativeness in terms of ethnicity, geographical region, and rural-urban residence" (Butcher et al., 1992, p. 10). Similar to the MMPI-2, the MMPI-A normative sample is predominantly white and the adolescents' parents tended to be well educated and to be in professional and managerial occupations.

The MMPI-A is intended to be used with adolescents in the age range of 14 to 18 years. The Restandardization Committee thought that the validity of the data for 13-year-olds was too questionable to warrant inclusion in the normative sample. Bright, mature 12- and 13-year-olds might be able to take the MMPI-A appropriately, but research is needed to document this position. The Restandardization Committee also suggested that the MMPI-A be used for 18-year-olds who are in high school and the MMPI-2 be used for those who are in college and living an independent lifestyle. Shaevel and Archer (1996) have suggested that a conservative approach would be to plot both the MMPI-A profile and the MMPI-2 profile for 18-year-olds when the clinician cannot decide which form of the test is more appropriate. The data on age effects on the MMPI-2 (see Chapter 6, pp. 198–199) would suggest that all 18-year-olds should be given the MMPI-A, but research is needed to answer this question definitively.

ADMINISTRATION

Special efforts must be made to provide adequate instructions and monitoring for all adolescents, because of their age and developmental stage (cf. Archer, 2005, pp. 50–61), and are extremely important for younger adolescents (<15). The adolescent must be able to understand why the MMPI-A is being administered and how the results will be used in order to assent to the assessment process. The clinician should work diligently to make the assessment process a collaborative activity with the adolescent to obtain the desired information. This issue of therapeutic assessment was covered in more depth in Chapter 2 (pp. 43–44).

Completing the 478 items may seem like a nearly impossible task for younger adolescents and any adolescent with language or attention deficits. Before they start, these adolescents need to be aware that there will be frequent breaks any time they become necessary. A number of shorter sessions that are planned beforehand are more likely to produce valid results than relying on these adolescents to recognize when breaks are necessary. Pena, Megargee, and Brody (1996) reported by splitting the MMPI-A administration into two sessions 94% of their sample of delinquent boys produced a valid profile.

Supervision and monitoring of adolescents taking the MMPI-A is important in a group setting. Some adolescents may respond out loud to the MMPI-A items and provoke responses from others that, if not dealt with quickly, have the potential to not only disrupt the session, but render the entire assessment process questionable. The initial instructions should make it explicit that they are to raise their hand if they have a question and the proctor will come to them. Under no circumstances are they to ask out loud about any of the items. The proctors also need to know what types of assistance are allowed and never indicate what the response to any item should be. Butcher et al. (1992, p. 29) suggest that it usually is sufficient to say, "Just answer as you think best."

Although the proctors need to monitor actively the adolescents' performance in a group setting, the proctors should not linger near any of the adolescents to prevent them from thinking that their specific responses are of interest. Any type of conversation among the proctors also should be minimized so that the adolescents do not get the impression that their responses are being discussed. The proctors need to make sure that adolescents' responses on the answer sheet correspond to their place in the test booklet as nonobtrusively as possible.

Reading level is a crucial factor in determining whether the adolescent can complete the MMPI-A, and if possible, reading level should be checked before the MMPI-A is administered rather than relying on the inconsistency scales to identify these problems. The adolescent should have at least a sixth-grade reading level to take the MMPI-A (Butcher et al., 1992). Krakauer, Archer, and Gordon (1993) have developed the *Items–Easy* and *Items–Difficult* scales for the MMPI-A to identify adolescents who are having reading difficulties. The clinician must check measures of consistency (Baer, Ballenger, Berry, & Wetter, 1997) and accuracy of item endorsement carefully with adolescents because of the higher probability that they will be noncooperative or noncompliant with the assessment process, in addition to the potential problems of reading comprehension.

SCORING

Scoring the MMPI-A is identical to scoring the MMPI-2 (see pp. 141–143), with one major exception, and will not be repeated here. The primary major difference in scoring the MMPI-A compared with the MMPI-2 is that the five clinical scales (*1* [*Hs:* Hypochondriasis], *4* [*Pd:* Psychopathic Deviate], *7* [*Pt:* Psychasthenia], *8* [*Sc:* Schizophrenia], and *9* [*Ma:* Hypomania]), that are *K*-corrected on the MMPI-2, are *not K*-corrected on the MMPI-A. Consequently, a similar procedure is followed to score and plot all the validity, clinical, content, and supplementary scales on the MMPI-A.

ASSESSING VALIDITY

Figure 7.1 provides the flowchart for assessing the validity of this specific administration of the MMPI-A, and the criteria for using this flowchart are provided in Table 7.3. The clinician is reminded that the criteria provided in Table 7.3 are continuous, yet ultimately the decisions that must be made in implementation of the flowchart in Figure 7.1 are dichotomous. General guidelines are provided for translating these continuous data into dichotomous decisions on the MMPI-A, but these guidelines need to be considered within the constraints of this specific adolescent and the circumstances for the evaluation.

Item Omissions

The Cannot Say scale (*?*) consists of the total number of items that the adolescent fails to answer or answers both "true" and "false." The raw score on the Cannot Say scale (*?*) is located at the bottom left-hand corner of the profile form and can be easily overlooked, particularly if the clinician is not the person who actually scored the MMPI-A. These omitted item(s) should be reviewed to see if there is any theme to them. The individual should be queried carefully about any omitted items among the dangerousness-to-self items (177, 283) and dangerousness-to-others items (445, 453, 458, 465), and the explanation documented.

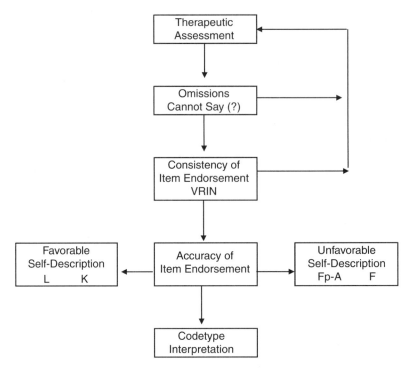

Figure 7.1   Flowchart for assessing validity of the MMPI-A.

Butcher et al. (1992) and Archer (2005) state that if 30 or more items are omitted and they are evenly distributed throughout the MMPI-A, it should not be scored. Clinicians may want to ask the adolescent to attempt to answer any omitted items if there are more than 10 omitted items, after determining that reading difficulties are not the cause of the omissions. If most of the omitted items occur after item 350, the basic validity (F_1, L, and K) and the 10 clinical scales can be scored.

Archer (2005, p. 83) reported the items most frequently omitted by the MMPI-A normative sample: 203 (2.9%); 199 (1.5%); 93 (1.2%); and 16 (1.0%). All the other items on the MMPI-A were omitted by less than 1% of the normative group. These very low rates of item omissions suggest that the restandardization process was successful at rendering the items appropriate for adolescents.

Few items are generally omitted on the MMPI-A with nearly 70% of normal adolescents and 50% of clinical samples omitting no items (Table 7.3). Omitting 10 items is around the 98th percentile for the MMPI-A normative sample (Butcher et al., 1992) and the 93rd percentile in a clinical sample (Archer, Handel, & Mason, 2006). The setting in which the MMPI-A is administered does not appreciably affect the number of items that are omitted.

Consistency of Item Endorsement

The clinician should carefully note the time that the adolescent started and completed the MMPI-A. Unusually short administration times, such as less than 40 minutes to complete all 478 items, will alert the clinician to potential problems in consistency of item endorsement.

Table 7.3   Criteria for assessing MMPI-A validity by type of setting

Setting					Percentile						
	1	2	7	16	30	50	70	84	93	98	99
Item Omissions (Cannot Say [?])											
Normal[a]	—	—	—	—	—	—	0	1	3	7	11
Clinical[b]	—	—	—	—	—	0	1	4	9	27	83
Consistency of Item Endorsement (Variable Response Inconsistency Scale [VRIN])											
Normal[a]	—	—	0	1	2	3	5	7	9	12	13
Clinical[b]	—	0	1	2	3	4	6	9	12	15	17
Accuracy of Item Endorsement											
Self-Unfavorable (Infrequency Psychopathology Scale [Fp-A])											
Normal[a]	—	—	—	0	1	2	5	9	13	16	17
Clinical[b]	—	—	0	1	2	4	7	12	17	21	22
Accuracy of Item Endorsement											
Self-Unfavorable (Infrequency Scale [F])											
Normal[a]	—	—	0	1	2	5	11	17	23	28	30
Clinical[b]	0	1	3	4	6	10	16	24	30	34	40
Self-Favorable Impression Management (Lie Scale [L])											
Normal[a]	—	—	—	0	1	2	3	4	6	8	9
Clinical[b]	—	0	1	2	3	4	6	7	9	11	12
Self-Deception (Correction Scale [K])											
Normal[a]	2	3	5	7	9	11	14	16	19	22	23
Clinical[b]	4	5	7	9	11	14	16	19	22	25	27

[a]Butcher et al. (1992).
[b]Archer et al. (2006).

This information is easily overlooked, however, unless the clinician routinely notes the administration time.

Consistency of item endorsement on the MMPI-A is assessed by the Variable Response Inconsistency (*VRIN*) and True Response Inconsistency (*TRIN*) scales in an identical manner as on the MMPI-2 and the Infrequency scales F_1 and F_2. The Variable Response Inconsistency (*VRIN*) scale consists of 50 pairs of items that have similar or opposite item content. These pairs of items are scored if the adolescent is inconsistent in his or her responses. The *VRIN* scale actually consists of 42 pairs of unique items, since two separate response patterns are scored for 8 of these 50 item pairs as with items 6 and 86.

The True Response Inconsistency (*TRIN*) scale consists of 24 pairs of items. The *TRIN* scale is very similar to the *VRIN* scale except that the scored response on the *TRIN* scale is either "true" or "false" to both items in each pair. The TRIN scale has 15 pairs of items to which the inconsistent response is "true" and 9 item pairs to which the inconsistent response is "false." Scoring the *TRIN* scale is somewhat complicated. One point is added to the client's score for each of the 15 item pairs that are scored if endorsed "true," whereas one point is subtracted for each of the 9 item pairs that are scored if endorsed "false." Then

9 points are added to this score. (Nine points are added to the score so that it is not possible to obtain a negative score on the *TRIN* scale. If a client endorsed none of the 15 "true" item pairs and all 9 of the "false" item pairs, a score of –9 would be obtained. Adding 9 points avoids this problem.) The *TRIN* scale is intended to identify adolescents who are endorsing the items inconsistently by essentially responding to most of the items as "true" or "false."

The *F* (Infrequency) scale on the MMPI-A has been divided into two 33-item subscales. The items on the F_1 scale are found in the first half of the test and the items on the F_2 scale are found in the second half of the test. Butcher et al. (1992) suggested that the *T scores* on the F_1 and F_2 scales can be compared to assess whether the adolescent has endorsed more or less of these infrequently endorsed items on the second half of the test. An adolescent who has an elevated T score on the F_2 scale compared with the F_1 scale may have lost interest in the assessment process and began to respond randomly to the items somewhere in the latter half of the MMPI-A. However, Archer, Handel, Lynch, and Elkins (2002) found that the difference between the T scores on the F_1 and F_2 scales was ineffective at identifying profiles with varying levels of random responding. Consequently, clinicians should be cautious about putting too much emphasis on interpreting the relationship between the T scores on the F_1 and F_2 scales as a possible indicator of inconsistent item endorsement in the latter half of the MMPI-A until additional research validates its use. Archer et al. also noted that none of the measures of consistency of item endorsement was very effective when partial (<50%) random responding occurred in the last half of the test. Pinsoneault (2005) reported similar difficulties in the identification of partially random MMPI-A profiles. He did suggest a number of subscales of VRIN (Variable Response Inconsistency) and algorithms based on the relationships among the family of *F* (Infrequency) scales to identify these partially random profiles.

Scores on the *VRIN* scale are very similar in normal and clinical samples (see Table 7.3), which substantiates the point that psychopathology per se does not produce inconsistent item endorsement. Also, a fair amount of inconsistency (3 to 4 inconsistent pairs of items) is found in both the clinical and normal samples. Again, a specific score on *VRIN* has not been selected to indicate that the items were endorsed inconsistently. Raw scores in the range of 12 to 15 have been suggested as a cutting score by the authors of MMPI-A interpretive manuals (Archer, 2005 [girls >12; boys - >14]; Butcher et al., 1992 [girls >11; boys > 13]). The clinician will have to decide which cutting score is most appropriate given the specific adolescent and the setting in which the MMPI-A is administered.

Figure 7.2 shows the profiles for random, "all-true," and "all-false" responses on the MMPI-A. The validity scales easily identify the "all-true," and "all-false" profiles as being invalid with several scales at T scores greater than 100 or below 40. Scales *1* (*Hs:* Hypochondriasis), *2* (*D:* Depression), and *3* (*Hy:* Hysteria) when compared with Scales *6* (*Pa:* Paranoia), *7* (*Pt:* Psychasthenia), *8* (*Sc:* Schizophrenia), and *9* (*Ma:* Hypomania) also are elevated in very divergent manners in these two profiles. The validity scales do not identify a random profile very well with T scores around 80 on *VRIN* (Variable Response Inconsistency) and the family of *F* (Infrequency) scales. Validity scores in this T score range can be seen in adolescents who are accurately reporting relatively severe psychopathology. The clinical scales for the random profile also look interpretable and do not assist the clinician in the identification of a random profile. In short, it is very difficult to identify a randomly generated MMPI-A profile, which underscores the importance of both obtaining the cooperation of adolescents before taking the MMPI-A and monitoring their

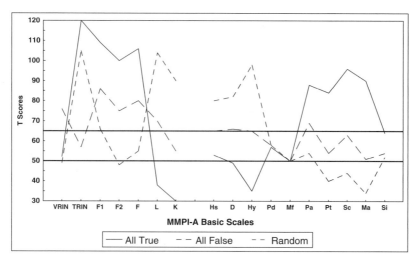

Figure 7.2   Random, all true, and all false MMPI-A profiles.

performance during the test. Figure 7.2 can be compared with Figure 6.3, which provides similar data on the MMPI-2, to note some of the differences between the MMPI-A and MMPI-2.

Accuracy of Item Endorsement

Self-Unfavorable Descriptions

Self-unfavorable descriptions of psychopathology on the MMPI-A can be assessed by infrequency scales [F, F_1, F_2, and Fp - A] and the F - K Dissimulation index (Gough, 1950). Only the F (Infrequency) and Infrequency-Psychopathology (Fp - A) scale (McGrath et al., 2000) will be described here because they are the two best scales to identify self-unfavorable descriptions. The Fp - A scale consists of 40 items that no more than 20% of a sample of 475 inpatient adolescents, a second sample of 356 inpatients adolescents from the same facility, 140 high school students faking the MMPI-A (Stein, Graham, & Williams, 1995), and the MMPI-A normative sample endorsed in the deviant direction. Nearly three-quarters (31) of the items on the Fp - A scale also are found on the F scale. Given the redundancy between these two scales, the incremental validity for the Fp - A scale is relatively small. McGrath et al.'s data also suggested that the MMPI-A F scale may be a better indicator of a self-unfavorable description than the MMPI-2 F scale.

Table 7.3 shows that endorsing a number of the F and Fp - A items is typical in both normal and clinical samples. The adolescent must endorse 13 to 17 of the Fp - A items (32% to 42%) and 23 to 30 of the F items (35% to 45%) to reach the 93rd percentile in both samples. Adolescents are much more likely to endorse these infrequency items on the MMPI-A than adults endorse the infrequency items on the MMPI-2 (see Table 6.3).

Self-Favorable Description

Self-favorable descriptions of psychopathology will be organized within Paulhus's (1984, 1986) model of social desirability responding that distinguishes between self-deception and impression management: *self-deception* refers to a motivated unawareness of one of two conflicting cognitions, whereas *impression management* can be conceptualized as a strategic simulation, a motive, or a skill. In self-deception, individuals are thought to believe their positive self-evaluation is an accurate description of themselves, whereas in impression management, individuals consciously dissemble to create a favorable impression in others. The L (Lie) scale on the MMPI-A is a measure of impression management, whereas the K (Correction) scale is a measure of self-deception.

The L (Lie) scale includes 15 items that were selected on a rational basis to identify persons who are deliberately trying to avoid answering the MMPI frankly and honestly (Dahlstrom et al., 1972). The scale assesses attitudes and practices that are culturally laudable but actually found only in the most conscientious persons. The content areas within the L scale include denial of minor, personal dishonesties and denial of aggression, bad thoughts, and weakness of character. The K (Correction) scale consists of 30 items that were empirically selected to assist in identifying persons who displayed significant psychopathology yet had profiles within the normal range.

Table 7.3 shows that endorsing more than 6 to 9 of the items on the L (Lie) scale and 19 to 22 items on the K (Correction) scale is at or above the 93rd percentile in normal and clinical samples. These ranges on the MMPI-A L (Lie) and K (Correction) scales are similar to the ranges found on the MMPI-2 (see Table 6.3). The similarity in the scores on these self-favorable scales between the MMPI-A and MMPI-2 is in sharp contrast to the differences that were found on the self-unfavorable scales.

The person can be described as using impression management to create a favorable self-description when the L (Lie) scale is elevated (T > 59) and the L (Lie) scale is at least 5 T points higher than the K (Correction) scale. The person can be described as using self-deception to create a favorable self-description when the K (Correction) is elevated (T > 59) and at least 5 T points higher than the L (Lie) scale. When both of these scales (L [Lie], K [Correction]) are elevated in the same range (T > 55), the person can be described as making a generic self-favorable description.

When an adolescent's responses have been identified as being endorsed inaccurately because of an extremely self-favorable description of psychopathology, the MMPI-A profile is no longer interpretable. The clinician will have little reason to try to interpret such a profile, however, because extremely self-favorable descriptions result in no clinical scales being elevated over a T score of 60. The clinician should describe the adolescent's style of self-favorable description of psychopathology (impression management, self-deception, or a combination of both), determine the potential causes for this self-favorable description, and assess the implications for treatment and intervention.

Adolescents who provide extremely self-favorable descriptions of psychopathology see their problems as less troubling to themselves and, hence, are less motivated to change. Their problems also may be more chronic in nature, and consequently, they may be more difficult to treat if they remain in treatment. None of these potential causes of an extremely self-favorable description of psychopathology is a good prognostic sign for any type of psychological intervention.

INTERPRETATION

The clinician whose primary focus has been on the MMPI-2 must be particularly careful when interpreting the MMPI-A for the first time because of the numerous subtle and not

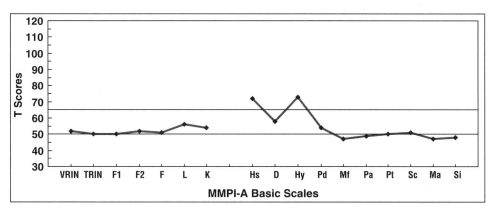

Figure 7.3   MMPI-A basic validity and clinical scales for a *1-3/3-1* codetype.

so subtle differences between the two tests. The interpretive guidelines for the MMPI-2 simply *cannot* be applied directly to the MMPI-A. A prime example of this difference in interpretive strategy on the MMPI-A is the use of *marginally* elevated T score values between 60 and 64 in addition to the more usual *clinically* elevated T scores of 65 and higher (see Figure 7.3). The T scores in this marginally elevated range are indicated by the shaded area on the MMPI-A profile sheets. Probably the major difference between the MMPI-A and the MMPI-2 is that the MMPI-A is being interpreted for an adolescent who is still growing and maturing rather than for an adult. Generally, MMPI-A profiles will be characterized by less chronicity and severity of psychopathology than the same MMPI-2 profile simply because of the relative youth of adolescents. Any inferences drawn from the MMPI-A must reflect that adolescents are in a state of developmental transition to adulthood.

Codetypes

Once it has been determined that the adolescent has omitted few, if any, items, and endorsed the items consistently and accurately, the MMPI-A can be interpreted. Interpretation of the MMPI-A begins with, and is based on codetypes; that is, the two highest clinical scales elevated to a T score of 65 or higher, or the single clinical scale (spike codetype) when only one scale reaches a T score of 65. In contrast to the MMPI-2, marginally elevated T scores in the range of 60 to 64 on the MMPI-A are considered to be in a transition range between normal and elevated profiles. (This range is indicated by the gray or shaded background on the profile form for the basic validity and clinical scales). Scores in this marginally elevated range are expected to reflect some, but not all, of the behaviors reflected in elevated scores. The interpretation of the MMPI-A codetype then is supplemented by the examination of specific scales, such as the clinical, content, and supplementary scales, as well as individual critical items. Archer (2005), Archer and Krishnamurthy (2002), and Fowler, Butcher, and Williams (2000) have provided examples of the general interpretive strategy for the MMPI-A.

The following pages provide the interpretation of 15 commonly occurring two-point MMPI-A codetypes, which have been adapted from the MMPI-2 Adult Interpretive System

(Greene & Brown, 2006) based on the work of Marks et al. (1974) and Archer (2005). The 60 new items on the MMPI-A that are not found on the MMPI-2 were not available to be included in these descriptions so the clinician will need to add these items to the description where appropriate. Most of these 60 items are found on the MMPI-A content and supplementary scales that have been included in these codetype descriptions. Figure 7.3 illustrates the basic profile for the MMPI-A validity and clinical scales for a *1-3/3-1* codetype. A codetype description is written about a *group* of adolescents who have elevated these two specific scales, not about this specific adolescent who has produced the codetype. Each statement within the codetype description must be considered a hypothesis to be verified with the clinical interview and history of this specific adolescent.

The clinician must expect to be making some modification to every codetype description on the MMPI-A. This entire process has been made much more straightforward in these descriptions because every statement is referenced either to a scale(s) and/or item(s). When a scale name is in **bold** font, the individual is expected to have a low score (T < 50) on that scale. In the description of Interpersonal Relations for a *1-3/3-1* codetype (p. 219), the *Pd₁* and *A-fam* scales are in bold font because these two scales assess problems and conflicts in family relations that this group of adolescents does *not* report. When an item is listed in **bold** font, the item is endorsed in the **false** direction. Numerous examples can be seen in the Other Problem Areas for a *1-3/3-1* codetype (p. 219).

The clinician should modify any statement for which there are explicit data to support the change. If the codetype description indicates that the adolescent has endorsed an item as being "true" and it actually was endorsed "false," the clinician has explicit data to change/modify/delete that item. Similarly, if the interpretive text indicates that a scale is/is not elevated, the adolescent's actual T score on the scale will support/negate that statement explicitly. The clinician, however, should *not* change any statement simply because it does not seem to fit this individual or the clinician does not think it is appropriate. It is vital to remember Meehl's (1957) admonition of how infrequently we are to use our clinical judgment when we have empirical data available to us.

1-3/3-1[1]

Moods   She reports that she is experiencing very mild emotional distress (*A, NEGE*) characterized by tension and anxiety (*7[Pt]*, *A-anx*). She frequently worries about something (185T). She also experiences a very mild level of dysphoria (*2[D]*, *A-dep*). Her daily life is full of things that keep her interested (9T). Something exciting will almost always make her feel better when she is feeling low (228T).

Cognitions   She reports that she cannot keep her mind on one thing (279T). She is self-confident (**70F**). She likes to let people know where she stands on things (341T), and she finds it necessary to stand up for what she thinks is right (115T). She tends to think in a concrete manner and to focus on her physical ailments (*1[Hs]*).

She believes that most people are honest and can be trusted (*3[Hy]*, *A-cyn*). She does not analyze the motives for her own or others' behavior (*3[Hy]*).

---

[1]The gender used for the interpretive text for each codetype reflects whether it is more common in boys or girls.

Interpersonal Relations   She reports a balance between extroverted and introverted behaviors (*0[Si]*, *A-sod*). She is very sociable and makes friends quickly (46T, 262T, 336T). She believes, if given the chance, she would make a good leader of people (329T). She seems to make friends about as quickly as others do (262T). She is very conventional and conforming to social standards (*3[Hy]*). Her relations with her family are good (*Pd₁*, *A-fam*).

Other Problem Areas   She reports a variety of physical (*1[Hs]*, *A-hea*, *Hy₄*) and neurological symptoms (*Sc₆*, *A-hea2*), headaches (**168F**), and pain in a number of areas of her body (**54F, 210F**). Her physical health is not as good as that of most of her friends (**42F**), and she worries about her health (**4F**). She tires quickly (**146F**). She has difficulty going to sleep because she is bothered by ideas or thoughts (**134F**), her sleep is fitful and disturbed (36T), and she does not wake up fresh and rested most mornings (**3F**). She is less able to work now than she was in the past (**10F**). Her history and background should be reviewed to determine whether a medical or neurological evaluation is warranted. She is unlikely to have behavioral problems (*A-con*, *A-con2*), have been in trouble with the law (249T), or use alcohol or drugs (*ACK, PRO*).

Treatment   She often is referred for treatment because of problems or concerns in academic settings (*1[Hs]*, *3[Hy]*) that reflect attention-seeking behavior or somatic symptoms. She is able to talk at least superficially about her psychological problems and is not evasive in treatment (*1[Hs]*, *3[Hy]*). Conservative medical treatment is recommended because her physical ailments are difficult to document (*1[Hs]*, *3[Hy]*). Short-term interventions that are focused on providing symptomatic relief from her physical ailments may be beneficial and can provide the foundation for more traditional psychotherapy (*1[Hs]*, *3[Hy]*).

   She is not naturally introspective, which will complicate the implementation of any therapeutic intervention (*3[Hy]*).

2-3/3-2

Moods   She reports that she is experiencing a mild to moderate level of emotional distress (*A, NEGE*) characterized by dysphoria (*2[D]*, *A-dep*), worrying (*7[Pt]*, *A-anx*), and anhedonia (*INTR, A-dep1, A-trt1*). Most of the time she feels blue (62T, **91F, 360F**), and her daily life is not full of things that keep her interested (**9F**). She frequently worries about something or someone (185T, 281T, 285T, 383T). She is easily hurt by criticism or scolding (121T) and has difficulty expressing her feelings, describing herself as feeling bottled up (*2[D]*, *3[Hy]*). She has had long periods of time when she could not take care of things because she could not get going (35T). She is overcontrolled and fearful of losing control (*2[D]*, *3[Hy]*). She is likely to experience increases in depression, fatigue, and physical symptoms in response to stress (*3[Hy]*). She is unlikely to express her anger overtly (*AGGR, A-ang*).

Cognitions   She reports that she has problems with attention, concentration (28T, 279T, 305T), and memory (**158F**). She likes to let people know where she stands on things (341T), and she finds it necessary to stand up for what she thinks is right (115T). She has low self-esteem, lacks self-confidence (70T, **223F**), and doubts her own abilities (*A-lse*).

She feels inadequate, helpless, and insecure (*A-lse*). She certainly thinks she is useless at times (124T).

She sometimes thinks that she is about to go to pieces (404T). At times, her mind seems to work more slowly than usual (320T). Her judgment is not as good as it was in the past (**40F**).

She does not analyze the motives for her own or others' behavior (*3[Hy]*, **A-cyn**). She wishes she could be as happy as others seem to be (53T).

Interpersonal Relations   She reports that she is somewhat introverted (*0[Si]*, *A-sod*, *A-sod1*) and does not like loud parties or social events (**82F**). Her activities are usually engaged in alone (*2[D]*, *3[Hy]*). She feels socially alienated (*Pd₄*, *Sc₁*, *Si₂*) and presents herself as helpless, immature, and dependent (*A-lse*). She reports good relations with her family (**Pd₁, A-fam**).

Other Problem Areas   She reports a wide variety of physical symptoms (*1[Hs]*, *A-hea*, *Hy₄*) including neurological symptoms (*Sc₆*, *A-hea2*), headaches (**168F**), and generalized pain (**210F**). Her physical health is not as good as that of most of her friends (**42F**) and she worries about her health (**4F**). During the past few years, she has not been well most of the time (**135F**). She has difficulty going to sleep because thoughts or ideas are bothering her (**134F**), her sleep is fitful and disturbed (36T), and she does not wake up fresh and rested most mornings (**3F**). She is easily awakened by noise (5T). She tires quickly (**146F**) and feels tired, weak, and without energy a good deal of the time (167T, **289F**). She is not as able to work as she once was (**10F**). Her history and background should be reviewed to determine whether a medical or neurological evaluation is warranted. She is a very conventional individual who is unlikely to have behavioral problems (**A-con**). She is not likely to abuse substances (*ACK, PRO*).

Treatment   Her prognosis is generally poor because she sees little chance for significant change in her life (*2[D]*, *3[Hy]*). She is referred for treatment because of poor relationships with peers; at school, she is liked by few students and outside school, she has few friends of any kind (*2[D]*, *3[Hy]*). Short-term, behavioral therapy that focuses on her reasons for entering treatment may be beneficial and may allow for the development of a therapeutic alliance that would be necessary for long-term therapy (*2[D]*, *3[Hy]*). She will prefer to discuss her physical symptoms rather than focus on her psychological processes (*1[Hs]*).

She is not naturally introspective, which will complicate the therapeutic process (*3[Hy]*).

2-4/4-2

Moods   He reports that he is experiencing a mild to moderate level of emotional distress (*A, NEGE*) characterized by dysphoria (*2[D]*, *A-dep2*, 62T, **91F, 360F**), resentment (*6[Pa]*), agitation (*7[Pt]*, *A-anx*), and anhedonia (*INTR, A-dep1, A-trt1*). His daily life has few things that keep him interested (**9F**). He frequently worries about something or someone (185T, 281T, 285T, 383T). These moods often arise in response to some external problem or difficulty (*4[Pd]*). While he may express guilt and remorse and may promise to change his behavior, his expressions typically are not sincere (*4[Pd]*). He is more sensitive (266T) and feels more intensely than most people (253T). His feelings are easily hurt (**60F**, 121T), and he is inclined to take things hard (311T). He is grouchy, irritable, and stubborn (*A-ang2,* 111T, 388T, 416T).

Cognitions   He reports that his memory seems to be all right (158T). His judgment is not as good as it was in the past (**40F**). He certainly is lacking in self-confidence and believes that he is not as good as other people (*A-lse1,* 70T, **223F,** 379T). He certainly thinks he is useless at times (124T). He has sometimes thought that difficulties were piling up so high that he could not overcome them (318T). He is apt to take disappointments so keenly that he cannot put them out of his mind (377T).

He sometimes thinks that he is about to go to pieces (404T).

He doubts the motives of other people and believes that they are interested only in their own welfare (*A-cyn,* 77T, 107T). He knows who is responsible for most of his troubles (109T). He regrets many things that he has done (78T) and thinks that he has not lived the right kind of life (49T).

Interpersonal Relations   He reports that he is introverted (*0[Si], A-sod1*). His interpersonal relations tend to be generally problematic and conflicted (*4[Pd], A-fam*), and he is alienated from himself (*Pd5, Si3*) and others (*Pd4, Sc1, Si3*). His home life is not as pleasant as that of most people he knows (**119F**). He quarrels with members of his family (*A-fam1,* **79F**) and feels alienated from them (*A-fam2*). He has no one in his family with whom to discuss his personal problems (*2[D], 4[Pd]*).

Other Problem Areas   He reports that he worries about his health (**4F**). His sleep is bothered by his thoughts and ideas (**134F**), and he does not wake up fresh and rested most mornings (**3F**). He tires quickly (**146F**). He does not feel weak all over much of the time (**167F**). He reported a number of conduct problems (*A-con2*). He is likely to abuse alcohol or drugs with the exception of narcotics (*ACK, PRO,* 247T); a careful review should be made of the consequences of his alcohol and drug use.

Treatment   His prognosis is generally poor for traditional methods of individual psychotherapy (*4[Pd]*) unless a mood disorder is the primary diagnosis (*2[D], A-dep*). In that instance, cognitive-behavioral psychotherapy focused on his depressive cognitions will be beneficial (*2[D], A-dep*). Evaluation for antidepressant medication may be indicated in cases of more severe depression (*2[D], A-dep*). He frequently is referred for treatment because he has difficulty concentrating (*2[D], 4[Pd]*). Group therapy with individuals with similar behaviors may be effective when a mood disorder is not the primary diagnosis (*4[Pd]*). The consequences of his use of alcohol and drugs cannot be overlooked when determining the interventions that need to be made (*2[D], 4[Pd]*).

Several specific issues must be kept in mind when establishing and maintaining the therapeutic alliance: He has difficulty starting to do things (218T); he gives up quickly when things go wrong (340T) or because he thinks too little of his ability (306T); he is hard to get to know (408T); and he is very stubborn (416T).

2-7/7-2

Moods   He reports that he is experiencing a moderate level of emotional distress (*A, NEGE*) characterized by dysphoric mood (*2[D], A-dep2,* 62T, **91F, 360F**), guilt, and anxiety (*7[Pt],*

A-anx). He views himself as being irritable and grouchy (*A-ang2*, 111T, 388T), although others are more aware of his dysphoric mood (*2[D]*, *A-dep2*). He experiences little pleasure from life (*INTR, A-dep1, A-trt1*) and may be anhedonic. He has had long periods when he could not take care of things because he could not get going (35T). He is a chronic worrier (185T) who broods and ruminates about himself and his problems (*7[Pt]*, *A-anx, A-obs*, 281T, 285T, 383T). He is likely to overreact to minor stress with agitation, guilt, and self-punishment (*7[Pt]*). He is more sensitive (266T) and feels more intensely than most people (253T). His feelings are easily hurt (**60F,** 121T) and he is inclined to take things hard (311T). He easily becomes impatient with people (282T). He is unlikely to express anger overtly or to be aggressive toward others (*AGGR*).

Cognitions   He reports that he has problems with attention, concentration (28T, 279T, 305T), and memory (**165F,** 288T). He certainly is lacking in self-confidence and believes that he is not as good as other people (*A-lse1,* 70T, **223F,** 379T). He certainly thinks he is useless at times (130T). He usually has to stop and think before he acts even in small matters (310T). He has several times given up doing a thing because he thought too little of his ability (306T). He is obsessed with his perceived personal deficiencies (*7[Pt]*, *A-obs*). He believes that his judgment is not as good as it once was (**40F**). He has difficulty starting to do things (218T), and he gives up quickly when things go wrong (340T). His inertia and lack of drive reflect his depressive cognitions and negative expectations (*2[D]*, *A-dep*). He is pessimistic and hopeless about making any substantial changes in his circumstances (*2[D]*, *A-dep*). He feels guilty when his high standards and expectations are not met (*7[Pt]*). He wishes he could be as happy as others seem to be (53T).

Interpersonal Relations   He reports that he is shy and introverted (*0[Si]*, *A-sod1*). He is easily embarrassed (270T), wishes he was not so shy (178T), and frequently has to fight against showing that he is bashful (158T). He finds it hard to talk when he meets new people (160T) and he has trouble thinking of the right things to talk about when in a group of people (227T). He will avoid people if given the opportunity (*Si_2*). He is likely not to speak to people until they speak to him (248T). Even when he is with people, he feels lonely much of the time (259T). He is passive and dependent in his relationships and is unlikely to be assertive (*A-lse2*). He reports mild conflict with members of his family (*Pd_1*, *A-fam1*). He is alienated from himself (*Pd_5, Si_3*) and others (*Pd_4, Sc_1, Si_3*).

Other Problem Areas   He reports that he has a number of gastrointestinal (*A-hea1*) and neurological symptoms (*Sc_6*, *A-hea2*). He worries about his health (**4F**), and his health is not as good as that of most of his friends (**42F**). He has difficulty going to sleep because thoughts or ideas are bothering him (**134F**), his sleep is fitful and disturbed (36T), and he does not wake up fresh and rested most mornings (**3F**). He tires quickly (**146F**) and feels tired and without energy a good deal of the time (**289F**). His history and background should be reviewed to determine whether a medical or neurological evaluation is warranted. Suicidal thoughts are quite common and should be monitored carefully (*2[D]*, *7[Pt]*).

Treatment   His prognosis is generally quite good because he sees himself as being responsible for his difficulties and is willing to examine his behavior, even at great length (*2[D]*, *7[Pt]*). Cognitive-behavioral psychotherapy focusing on his depressive cognitions will be very beneficial to him (*2[D]*, *7[Pt]*). Evaluation for antidepressant medication may be indicated in cases of more severe depression (*2[D]*, *A-dep*). The primary reasons for his referral for treatment are tearfulness, restlessness, nervousness, anxiety, and worry, as well as excessive fantasy and daydreaming.

A number of specific issues must be kept in mind when establishing and maintaining the therapeutic alliance: He shrinks from facing a crisis or difficulty (27T); he has difficulty starting to do things (218T); he is passive and nonassertive (280T); he gives up quickly when things go wrong (340T) or because he thinks too little of his ability (306T); he is hard to get to know (408T); and he is bothered greatly by the thought of making changes in his life (444T).

2-0/0-2

Moods   She reports that she is experiencing mild emotional distress (*A*, *NEGE*) characterized by chronic brooding (203T), dysphoria (*2[D]*, *A-dep2*), and anhedonia (*INTR, A-dep1, A-trt1*). She has had long periods when she could not take care of things because she could not get going (35T). She frequently worries about something or someone (185T, 281T, 285T, 383T). She is more sensitive (266T) and feels more intensely than most people (253T). Her feelings are easily hurt (**60F,** 121T) and she is inclined to take things hard (311T). She is often irritable and grouchy (*A-ang2*, 116T, 388T), and she easily becomes impatient with people (130T, 282T). Despite these angry feelings, she is very unlikely to be overtly aggressive (***A-ang1, AGGR***).

Cognitions   She reports that she has problems with attention and concentration (28T, 305T). She certainly is lacking in self-confidence and believes that she is not as good as other people (*A-lse1*, 70T, **223F,** 379T). She finds it hard to be assertive because she is so reserved (*A-lse2*). At times, she thinks she is useless (124T). She shrinks from facing a crisis or difficulty (27T) and is easily downed in an argument (67T). She has often lost out on things because she could not make up her mind quickly enough (129T). She is apt to feel disappointments so keenly that she cannot put them out of her mind (377T). She gives up quickly when things go wrong (340T), when others criticize her, or when she thinks that she is unable to do something (306T). She is apt to pass up something she wants to do when others feel that it is not worth doing (280T). She thinks that most people will use unfair means and stretch the truth to get ahead (*A-cyn*, 55T, 77T, 107T) and it is safer to trust nobody (225T). She has often been misunderstood when she was trying to be helpful (403T). She wishes she could be as happy as others seem to be (56T).

Interpersonal Relations   She reports that she is very socially introverted (*0[Si]*, *A-sod1*). She is easily embarrassed (270T), wishes she was not so shy (178T), and frequently has to fight against showing that she is bashful (154T). She avoids interactions with others (*Si₂*), and she spends most of her spare time by herself (410T). Whenever possible, she avoids being in a crowd (304T), and she does not enjoy the excitement of a crowd (**335F**). At parties she is more likely to sit by herself or with just one other person than to join in with the crowd (316T). She finds it hard to talk when she meets new people (160T) or is in a group of people (227T), and she is likely not to speak to people until they speak to her (248T). She does not seem to make friends as quickly as others seem to do (**262F**). She sees herself as socially inept and awkward (*A-lse1*); others are more likely to describe her as shy and reserved (*A-sod2*). She feels lonely even when she is with people (259T). She is alienated from herself (*Pd5, Si3*) and others (*Pd4, Sc1, Si3*).

Other Problem Areas   She reports general concerns about her physical health, but few specific symptoms (*A-hea3*). There is an increased frequency of eating disorders, including bulimia and anorexia (*2[D], 0[Si]*) so eating behavior should be reviewed carefully. She is unlikely to abuse substances (***ACK, PROS***) or to get into trouble because of her behavior (***Pd2, A-con***, 249T).

Treatment   Her prognosis is only fair because she is very accustomed to her character-ological problems and she is reluctant to think of making changes in her life (*2[D], 0[Si]*). She often is referred for treatment because she is nervous and anxious, listless, apathetic, shy, and fearful (*2[D], 0[Si]*). She is essentially friendless at school (*2[D], 0[Si]*). Social skills and assertiveness training will frequently be beneficial (*0[Si]*). She responds well to structured treatment approaches that prescribe what she is to do (*2[D], 0[Si]*). Cognitive-behavioral approaches that focus on her depressive cognitions also will be beneficial (*2[D], A-dep*). Group psychotherapy will be helpful in providing a social perspective for her problems and in dealing directly with her avoidant behaviors (*0[Si]*).

   Several specific issues must be kept in mind when establishing and maintaining the therapeutic alliance: She shrinks from facing a crisis or difficulty (27T); she has difficulty starting to do things (218T); she believes it is safer to trust nobody (225T); she is passive and nonassertive (280T); she gives up quickly when things go wrong (340T) or because she thinks too little of her ability (306T); and she feels unable to tell anyone all about herself (369T).

4-6/6-4

Moods   He reports that he is experiencing mild to moderate emotional distress (*A, NEGE*) that is characterized by brooding (*6[Pa], D5*), dysphoric mood (*2[D], A-dep2*), and anhe-donia (*INTR, A-dep1, A-trt1*). He broods and worries constantly over what is happening to him (*6[Pa]*, 285T). He is more sensitive (266T) and feels more intensely than most people (253T). His feelings are easily hurt (**60F,** 121T), and he is inclined to take things hard (311T). He is generally stubborn, argumentative, and angry (*6[Pa]*). He is usually able to control the expression of his anger, but he does exhibit episodic angry outbursts, particularly in response to stress (*A-ang1, AGGR, DISC*).

Cognitions   He reports that his attention, concentration (**28F, 305F**), and memory seem to be all right (165T). He remembers very well, and for a long time, anything that people say or do to him (*6[Pa]*). He likes to let people know where he stands on things (341T), and he finds it necessary to stand up for what he thinks is right (115T). He has very peculiar and strange experiences (29T). At times, his thoughts have raced ahead faster than he could speak them (116T). He has sometimes thought that difficulties were piling up so high he could not overcome them (318T). He is very sensitive to and resentful of any demands being placed on him (*6[Pa]*). He is sure that he is being talked about (286T). He knows who is responsible for most of his troubles (109T). He has not lived the right kind of life (49T) and wishes that he could be as happy as others seem to be (53T). His way of doing things is apt to be misunderstood by others (211T).

[*He reports symptoms that may reflect a psychotic process or a long-term, character-ological condition. His presenting problems, background, and history should be reviewed with this possibility in mind.*]

Interpersonal Relations   He reports a balance between extroverted and introverted be-haviors (*0[Si]*) and that he is comfortable in social situations (*A-sod*). He is very sociable and makes friends quickly (46T, 262T, 336T). He believes, if given the chance, he would make a good leader of people (329T). He enjoys social gatherings and parties (331T, 292T) and the excitement of a crowd (335T, **304F**). However, he is likely to have a long history of poor interpersonal relations (*4[Pd]*, *6[Pa]*) often characterized by resentment, anger, and suspiciousness (*6[Pa]*). He sees his family as extremely uncaring and critical and his home life as very unpleasant (*Pd, Pd$_1$, A-fam*). He is constantly in trouble with his parents because of his misbehavior (*4[Pd]*, *6[Pa]*). He is alienated and detached from himself (*Pd$_5$*) and others (*Pd$_4$, Sc$_1$, A-fam2*).

Other Problem Areas   He reports only a few general concerns about his physical health (*1[Hs]*, *Hy$_4$*, *A-hea3*). He has few or no pains (54T, 210T) and very few headaches (168T). He is in just as good physical health as most of his friends (42T). His sleep is not fitful and disturbed (**36F**), but he does not wake up fresh and rested most mornings (**3F**). He does not tire quickly (146T) and is not tired, weak, or without energy a good deal of the time (**167F,** 289T). He is about as able to work as he ever was (10T). He is likely to abuse alcohol or drugs (*ACK PRO*, 247T) so a careful review should be made of the consequences of his alcohol and drug use. He reported a number of conduct problems (*A-con2*) and that he has been in trouble with the law (**249F**). He has done dangerous things for the thrill of it (**96F**).

Treatment   His prognosis is generally quite poor due to his lack of awareness of his role in his problems, which are chronic and characterological (*4[Pd]*, *6[Pa]*). He is frequently referred for treatment by the legal system because he is defiant, disobedient, tense, restless, and negativistic (*4[Pd]*, *6[Pa]*). He will be very demanding and will engage in frequent testing of the therapist (*4[Pd]*, *6[Pa]*). He typically makes excessive demands on others for attention and sympathy but is resentful of even mild demands that may be placed on him (*4[Pd]*, *6[Pa]*). Short-term, behavioral interventions that are presented in a direct and explicit manner will be most effective (*4[Pd]*, *6[Pa]*).

   The therapeutic alliance must be developed slowly and cautiously because of his distrust of others (*6[Pa]*).

4-7/7-4

Moods   He reports that he is experiencing a mild to moderate level of emotional distress (*A, NEGE*) characterized by anxiety and agitation (*7[Pt]*, *A-anx*). He is unmotivated and feels unable to do much to help himself at this time and may be anhedonic (*INTR, A-dep1, A-trt1*). He frequently worries about something or someone (185T, 281T, 285T, 383T). He is more sensitive (266T) and feels more intensely than most people (253T). His feelings are easily hurt (**60F,** 121T) and he is inclined to take things hard (311T). He is grouchy and irritable (*A-ang2*) and easily becomes impatient with people (282T).

Cognitions   He reports that he has problems with attention and concentration (28T, 279T, 305T), but his memory seems to be all right (165T). He certainly is lacking in self-confidence and believes that he is not as good as other people (*A-lse,* 70T, **223F**, 379T). He exhibits a cyclical pattern of acting-out followed by excessive concern, regret, and remorse over his behavior (*4[Pd]*, *7[Pt]*). His remorse, however, does not inhibit the repetition of this behavior and further episodes of acting-out (*4[Pd]*, *7[Pt]*). He does many things that he later regrets (78T). He believes that he has not lived the right kind of life (49T) and wishes he could be as happy as others seem to be (53T). He is apt to take disappointments so keenly that he cannot put them out of his mind (377T). He does not analyze the motives for his own or others' behavior (*Pa₃*, **A-cyn**).

Interpersonal Relations   He reports that he is slightly introverted (*0[Si]*), but he is very sociable and makes friends quickly (46T, 262T, 336T). He enjoys social gatherings and parties (331T, 292T) and the excitement of a crowd (335T, **304F**). His familial and interpersonal relations are marked by conflict and are often disrupted by episodic acting-out (*4[Pd]*, *Pd₁*, *Pd₂*, A-fam). He is not particularly sensitive or responsive to the needs of others, except after something has happened (*4[Pd]*). He is alienated from himself (*Pd₅*, *Si₃*) and others (*Pd₄*, *Sc₁*, *Si₃*, A-fam2).

Other Problem Areas   He reports a few general concerns about his health (*A-hea3*). He has few or no pains (54T, 210T) and very few headaches (168T). He is in just as good physical health as most of his friends (42T). Most nights his thoughts or ideas bother his sleep (**134F**), and he does not wake up fresh and rested most mornings (**3F**). He is about as able to work as he ever was (10T). He is likely to abuse alcohol or drugs (*ACK, PRO,* 247T) so a careful review should be made of the consequences of his alcohol and drug use. He reported a number of conduct problems (*A-con2*), and he is likely to have been in trouble with the law (**249F**).

Treatment   His prognosis is generally poor for short-term psychotherapy and guarded for long-term, intensive psychotherapy because of the characterological nature of his problems (*4[Pd]*, *7[Pt]*). He sees his main problems as picking the right kind of friends and his parents not liking his friends (*4[Pd]*, *7[Pt]*). His remorse and guilt over acting-out may give the impression of more insight and motivation to change than are actually present (*4[Pd]*, *7[Pt]*). Once his remorse and guilt have dissipated, his motivation will disappear quickly (*4[Pd]*, *7[Pt]*). Helping him to recognize his cyclic patterns and then to understand their dynamics is a primary goal in treatment (*4[Pd]*, *7[Pt]*).

Some specific issues must be kept in mind when establishing and maintaining the therapeutic alliance: He has difficulty starting to do things (218T); he gives up quickly when things go wrong (340T) or because he thinks too little of his ability (306T); and he is very stubborn (416T).

4-8/8-4

Moods   He reports that he is experiencing a moderate to severe level of emotional distress (*A, NEGE*) characterized by dysphoric mood (*2[D]*, *A-dep2*), agitation (*7[Pt]*, *9[Ma]*), and anhedonia (*INTR, A-dep1, A-trt1*). He frequently finds himself worrying about something (185T), finds it very difficult to get things done in his life, and has little hope of being successful even if he could get motivated at something (*INTR, A-dep1, A-trt1*). He is more sensitive (266T) and feels more intensely than most people (253T). His feelings are easily hurt (**60F,** 121T), and he is inclined to take things hard (311T). He easily becomes impatient with people (282T). He often feels resentful, angry (*6[Pa], A-ang*), irritable, and grouchy (111T, 388T). He has difficulty controlling or expressing his anger appropriately (*8[Sc]*, *DISC*). In response to stress, he is likely to either withdraw completely (*8[Sc]*) or to act out his angry impulses (*6[Pa], A-ang, DISC*). At times, he has a strong urge to do something harmful or shocking (81T).

Cognitions   He reports that he has problems with attention and concentration (28T, 279T, 305T). He likes to let people know where he stands on things (341T) and he finds it necessary to stand up for what he thinks is right (115T). He certainly is lacking in self-confidence and believes that he is not as good as other people (*A-lse,* 70T, **223F,** 379T). He exhibits poor judgment and is often unpredictable and impulsive (*4[Pd], 8[Sc]*). His judgment is not as good as it once was (**40F**). He feels insecure, isolated, rejected, and unwanted (*8[Sc]*). He is threatened by a world that he views as hostile and dangerous (*8[Sc]*). He has had peculiar and strange experiences (29T) and thoughts (296T). He thinks and dreams of things that are too bad to talk about (15T, 208T). He is very sensitive to the motives of others and hypervigilant (*6[Pa]*). He has often thought that strangers were looking at him critically (235T). He thinks that most people will use unfair means and stretch the truth to get ahead (*A-cyn,* 55T, 77T, 107T). He often wonders what hidden reason another person may have for being nice to him (118T). He believes that it is safer to trust nobody (225T). He has not lived the right kind of life (49T) and has done many things that he later regrets (78T). He has often been misunderstood when he was trying to be helpful (373T), and his way of doing things is apt to be misunderstood by others (211T).

[*He reports symptoms that may reflect a psychotic process or a long-term, character-ological condition. His presenting problems, background, and history should be reviewed with this possibility in mind.*]

Interpersonal Relations   He reports that he is introverted (*0[Si]*) and has difficulty with close, emotional relationships (*8[Sc]*). He lacks basic social skills (*4[Pd], 8[Sc]*) and tends to be socially withdrawn and isolated (*0[Si]*), yet he enjoys social gatherings and parties (331T, 292T) and the excitement of a crowd (335T, **304F**). He sees himself as being sociable and making friends quickly (46T, 262T, 336T), although he is emotionally distant, feels lonely, and knows that no one understands him and his problems (*8[Sc]*). His tendency to feel rejected by others often leads to hostility and conflict that only exacerbate his feelings of being alienated from others (*4[Pd], 8[Sc]*). He sees his family as extremely uncaring and critical and his home life as very unpleasant (*Pd₁, A-fam*). He is constantly in trouble with his family because of his misbehavior (*4[Pd], 8[Sc]*). Once in a while, he feels hate toward members of his family whom he usually loves (240T). The things that some of his family have done have frightened him (302T). Some of his family have habits that bother and annoy him very much (194T). He is alienated from himself (*Pd₅, Si₃*) and others (*Pd₄, Sc₁, Si₃, A-fam2*).

Other Problem Areas   He reports a few gastrointestinal symptoms (*A-hea1*) and a number of neurological symptoms (*Sc₆, A-hea2*). He does not wake up fresh and rested most mornings (**3F**). He does not feel weak all over much of the time (**167F**). At times he is all full of energy (289T). His physical and neurological symptoms warrant careful review and possible referral for a medical or neurological evaluation. He may abuse substances (*ACK, PRO,* 247T), which will exacerbate all his problems, so a careful review should be made of the consequences of his use of substances. His problems frequently involve inappropriate sexual behavior (*4[Pd]*, *8[Sc]*, **31F**). He reported a number of conduct problems (*A-con2*) and has been in trouble with the law (**249F**). If he commits a crime, it is likely to be poorly planned and executed and may involve bizarre or violent behavior (*4[Pd]*, *8[Sc]*).

Treatment   His prognosis is generally very poor because of the characterological nature of his problems (*4[Pd]*, *8[Sc]*). Psychopharmacological interventions, other than possibly antidepressants, also are unlikely to be very effective because of the characterological problems involved (*4[Pd]*, *8[Sc]*). He frequently is referred because of immaturity coupled with extreme narcissism (*4[Pd]*, *8[Sc]*). He has very poor academic achievement and poor grades (*4[Pd]*, *8[Sc]*). Interventions focused on specific behavioral objectives may be useful (*4[Pd]*, *8[Sc]*). Any form of insight-oriented therapy is contraindicated (*4[Pd]*, *8[Sc]*). Social skill and/or assertiveness training in a group setting may be beneficial (*8[Sc]*, *0[Si]*).

His difficulties in forming an emotional relationship and his reluctance to self-disclose make the establishment of a therapeutic alliance problematic at best (*4[Pd]*, *8[Sc]*). Some specific issues that must be kept in mind when establishing and maintaining the therapeutic alliance: No one seems to understand him (20T); he shrinks from facing a crisis or difficulty (27T); he has difficulty starting to do things (218T); it is safer to trust nobody (225T); he is so touchy on some subjects that he cannot talk about them (256T); he gives up quickly when things go wrong (340T) or because he thinks too little of his ability (306T); and he is very stubborn (416T).

4-9/9-4

Moods   He reports that he is experiencing minimal emotional distress or concern (*A, NEGE*) about his behavior or present circumstances. In fact, he is happy most of the time (**62F,** 91T). He dislikes being bored and inactive and will stir up excitement if he gets bored (*9[Ma]*, 162T). Once a week or oftener, he becomes very excited (226T). Something exciting will almost always pull him out of it when he is feeling low (228T). He frequently has intense feelings of anger and hostility that result in episodic outbursts of anger (*9[Ma]*, *A-ang, AGGR, DISC*). He is likely to exhibit increased anger and hostility in response to stress (*4[Pd]*, *9[Ma]*). He is oppositional when he is not overtly angry (*4[Pd]*, *9[Ma]*).

Cognitions   He reports that his attention, concentration (**28F, 278F, 305F**), and memory (165T) seem to be all right. He likes to let people know where he stands on things (341T), and he finds it necessary to stand up for what he thinks is right (115T). He exhibits very poor judgment, often acts without considering the consequences of his actions, and has difficulty learning from experience (*4[Pd]*, *9[Ma]*). He is unwilling to accept responsibility for his own behavior and he exhibits a persistent tendency to get into trouble (*4[Pd]*, *9[Ma]*). He thinks that most people will use unfair means and stretch the truth to get ahead (*A-cyn,* 55T, 77T, 107T).

Interpersonal Relations   He reports that he is extroverted and mixes easily with others (*0[Si]*, *A-sod*). He is very sociable and makes friends quickly (46T, 262T, 336T). He believes, if given the chance, he would make a good leader of people (329T). He enjoys social gatherings and parties (331T, 292T) and the excitement of a crowd (335T, **304F**). He is socially facile (**160F, 227F**), and he makes a good first impression (*4[Pd]*, *0[Si]*). More long-term contact will reveal that his interpersonal relations are superficial and marked by impulsivity, distrust, a lack of empathy, and egocentricity (*4[Pd]*, *9[Ma]*). He has numerous, long-standing problems with his family and persons in positions of authority (*4[Pd]*, *Pd₁*, *Pd₂*, *A-fam*). Some of his family have habits that bother and annoy him very much (194T). He is alienated from himself (*Pd₅*, *Si₃*) and others (*Pd₄*, *Sc₁*, *Si₃*).

Other Problem Areas   He reports that he is in good physical health (*1[Hs]*, *A-hea*, *Hy₄*). He has few or no pains (210T) and very few headaches (168T). He is in just as good physical health as most of his friends (42T). Sometimes he becomes so excited that he finds it hard to get to sleep (284T), but his sleep is not fitful or disturbed (**36F**). He does not tire quickly (146T) and is not tired, weak, and without energy a good deal of the time (**167F**, 289T). He is about as able to work as he ever was (10T). He is impulsive, risk-taking (*4[Pd]*, *9[Ma]*, *MAC-R*, *DISC*), and is very likely to abuse substances (*ACK*, *PRO*, 247T) so a careful review should be made of the consequences of his alcohol and drug use. He has done dangerous things for the thrill of it (**96F**). He has a history of legal and school problems and acting-out, even if he is not in legal trouble at the present time (*4[Pd]*, *9[Ma]*, *A-con2*, **249F**). He does not like school because of lack of interest in and dislike of the subjects being taught (*4[Pd]*, *9[Ma]*).

Treatment   His prognosis is guarded because this characterological process tends to result in fixed behavior patterns that are difficult to change (*4[Pd]*, *9[Ma]*). He often is referred for treatment because he is defiant, disobedient, impulsive, provocative, mischievous, and truant from school (*4[Pd]*, *9[Ma]*). He is experiencing minimal emotional distress that might serve as motivation to change his behavior (*A, NEGE*). Behavioral or short-term interventions that focus on the specific behaviors that led him to treatment will be most effective (*4[Pd]*, *9[Ma]*). Group therapies with similar adolescents frequently are helpful in confronting his characterological pattern of relating to others (*4[Pd]*, *9[Ma]*).

Only one specific issue must be kept in mind when establishing and maintaining the therapeutic alliance: He is very stubborn (416T).

4-0/0-4

Moods   He reports that he is experiencing a mild level of emotional distress (*A, NEGE*) characterized by dysphoric mood (*2[D]*, *A-dep2*) and anhedonia (*INTR, A-dep1, A-trt1*). He is more sensitive (266T) and feels more intensely than most people (253T). His feelings are easily hurt (**60F**, 121T), and he is inclined to take things hard (311T). He easily becomes impatient with people (130T, 282T). He is often irritable and grouchy (111T, 388T).

Cognitions   He reports that his attention, concentration (**279F, 305F**), and memory seem to be all right (165T). He certainly is lacking in self-confidence and believes that he is not as good as other people (*A-lse*, 70T, **223F**, 379T). He thinks that most people will use unfair means and stretch the truth to get ahead (*A-cyn*, 55T, 77T, 107T). He often wonders what hidden reason a person may have for doing something nice for him (118T). He has often thought that strangers were looking at him critically (235T). He believes that it is safer to trust nobody (225T). He believes that he has not lived the right kind of life (49T) and has done many things that he later regrets (78T). He has often been misunderstood when he was trying to be helpful (373T) and others are apt to misunderstand his way of doing things (211T). He wishes that he could be as happy as others seem to be (53T).

Interpersonal Relations   He reports that he is a shy, retiring individual (*0[Si]*) who actively avoids social interactions (*A-sod, Si₂*). Whenever possible, he avoids being in a crowd (**335F,** 304T). He is easily embarrassed (269T) and has to fight against showing that he is bashful (154T). He is likely not to speak to people unless they speak to him (248T). He does not like to meet strangers (**336F**) and finds it hard to talk when he meets new people (160T) or is in a group of people (227T). He does not seem to make friends as quickly as others do (**262F**). He is troubled by how slow he is in making friends and tends to have only a few rather close friends (*4[Pd], 0[Si]*). His relations with his family are unpleasant, with little love or companionship (*4[Pd], Pd₁, A-fam*). He is alienated from himself (*Pd₅, Si₃*) and others (*Pd₄, Sc₁, Si₃*).

Other Problem Areas   He reports that he is in good physical health (*1[Hs], A-hea, Hy₄*). His sleep is not fitful and disturbed (**36F**), but he does not wake up fresh and rested most mornings (**3F**). He does not feel weak all over much of the time (**167F**). He is about as able to work as he ever was (10T). He is likely to abuse substances (*ACK, PRO,* 247T), so a careful review should be made of the consequences of his alcohol and drug use. He reported a number of conduct problems (*A-con2*) and he has been in trouble with the law (**249F**).

Treatment   His prognosis is guarded because of the characterological nature of his problems (*4[Pd], 0[Si]*). Group interventions focused on social skills or assertiveness training frequently will be beneficial (*0[Si], A-sod*). It will be important for the therapist to provide him support in initial group sessions because of his shyness (*0[Si], A-sod2*). He has little motivation for any long-term intervention (*A, NEGE*).

Many specific issues must be kept in mind when establishing and maintaining the therapeutic alliance: No one seems to understand him (20T); he shrinks from facing a crisis or difficulty (27T); he has difficulty starting to do things (218T); he believes it is safer to trust nobody (225T); he is so touchy on some subjects that he cannot talk about them (256T); he is passive and nonassertive (280T); he gives up quickly when things go wrong (340T) or because he thinks too little of his ability (306T); and he is very stubborn (416T). Developing a therapeutic alliance must proceed slowly because of his sensitivity and shy, retiring style (*0[Si]*). He questions the motives of others and is distrustful of people in general (*4[Pd], 0[Si]*), which makes the whole therapeutic process more difficult.

6-8/8-6

Moods   She reports that she is experiencing severe emotional distress (*A, NEGE*) characterized by dysphoric mood (*2[D], A-dep2*), agitation (*9[Ma]*), worrying (*7[Pt], A-anx*), and anhedonia (*INTR, A-dep1, A-trt1*). Her affect is likely to be blunted or inappropriate (*6[Pa], 8[Sc]*). She sees little opportunity of improving her circumstances, further dampening her mood (6[*Pa*], 8[*Sc*]). She is very fearful, easily frightened, and generally apprehensive (8[*Sc*]). Several times a week she feels as if something dreadful is about to happen (402T). She frequently worries about something or someone (185T, 281T, 285T, 383T). She is more sensitive (266T) and feels more intensely than most people (253T). Her feelings are easily hurt (**60F,** 121T), and she is inclined to take things hard (311T). She easily becomes impatient with people (130T, 282T). She is often irritable and grouchy (*A-ang,* 111T, 388T) and has a violent temper (6[*Pa*], 8[*Sc*]). She gets angry when people hurry her (401T). At times, she has a strong urge to do something harmful or shocking (81T), and she feels like smashing things (34T). At times she has fits of laughing and crying that she cannot control (21T).

Cognitions   She reports that she has problems with attention, concentration (28T, 279T, 305T), and memory (**158F,** 288T). She likes to let people know where she stands on things (341T) and she finds it necessary to stand up for what she thinks is right (115T). She certainly is lacking in self-confidence, believes that she is not as good as other people (70T, **223F,** 379T), and feels inferior and insecure (*A-lse*). Sometimes some unimportant thought will run through her mind and bother her for days (308T). Her plans have frequently seemed so full of difficulties that she has had to give them up (370T).

   She has had very strange and peculiar experiences (29T) and thoughts (296T). She thinks and dreams of things that are too bad to talk about (15T, 208T). She prefers to daydream rather than do anything else (45T). She thinks that there is something wrong with her mind (163T, 173T) and that she is about to go to pieces (404T). She has had blank spells in which her activities were interrupted and she did not know what was going on around her (214T) and periods in which she carried on activities without knowing later what she had been doing (161T). Bad words, often terrible words, come into her mind and she cannot get rid of them (307T). She often feels as if things are not real (329T). She has often thought that strangers were looking at her critically (235T). She is sure that she is being talked about (286T), she is being plotted against (132T), people say vulgar and insulting things about her (314T), and someone has it in for her (95T). She has enemies who wish to harm her (**294F**). If people had not had it in for her, she would have been much more successful (39T). Much of the time, she thinks she has done something wrong or evil (90T) and believes she is a condemned person (219T). She is sure she gets a raw deal from life (16T) and that she is often being punished without cause (137T).

   She thinks that most people will use unfair means and stretch the truth to get ahead (*A-cyn,* 55T, 77T, 107T). She often wonders what hidden reason another person may have for doing something nice for her (118T). She believes that it is safer to trust nobody (225T). She has often been misunderstood when she was trying to be helpful (373T). She does many things that she later regrets (78T).

   [*She reports symptoms that may reflect a psychotic process or a long-term, character-ological condition. Her presenting problems, background, and history should be reviewed with this possibility in mind.*]

Interpersonal Relations   She reports that she is extremely introverted (0[*Si*]) and very uncomfortable around others (*A-sod*). Her behavior is likely to be unpredictable and in-appropriate, also making others uneasy around her (6[*Pa*], 8[*Sc*]). She is suspicious and distrustful of others, and she avoids serious emotional relationships (6[*Pa*], 8[*Sc*]). She generally feels apathetic, socially isolated, and withdrawn, and she believes that no one understands her (6[*Pa*], 8[*Sc*]). She feels lonely most of the time even when she is with people (259T). She is liked by few students and has few friends of any kind; any friends that she might have are older (6[*Pa*], 8[*Sc*]). She has poor relations with her family (*Pd₁*, *A-fam*) and is alienated from herself (*Pd₅*, *Si₃*) and others (*Pd₄*, *Sc₁*, *Si₃*). Once in a while she feels hate toward members of her family whom she usually loves (240T).

Other Problem Areas   She reports a number of specific gastrointestinal (*A-hea1*) and neurological symptoms (*Sc₆*, *A-hea2*) as well as a wide variety of more general physical symptoms (*1*[*Hs*], *A-hea*, *Hy₄*). Her head seems to hurt all over much of the time, and she has frequent headaches (37T, 97T, **168F**). She has difficulty going to sleep because she is excited (284T) or thoughts or ideas are bothering her (**134F**), her sleep is fitful and disturbed (36T), and she does not wake up fresh and rested most mornings (**3F**). She tires quickly (**146F**) and feels weak and tired a good deal of the time (167T). Her history and background should be reviewed to determine whether a medical or neurological evaluation is warranted. She is likely to abuse substances (*ACK, PRO,* 247T), so a careful review should be made of the consequences of her alcohol and drug use. She is worried about sex (159T).

Treatment   Her prognosis is generally poor because her problems are chronic and severe (6[*Pa*], 8[*Sc*]). She is usually referred because of her bizarre behavior or excessive fantasies (6[*Pa*], 8[*Sc*]). Her ability to work may not be severely impaired as long as the job does not involve any appreciable amount of contact with people (6[*Pa*], 8[*Sc*]). Some type of psychopharmacological intervention may be necessary to stabilize her thought processes and mood and to help her sleep (6[*Pa*], 8[*Sc*]). Short-term, behavioral interventions are warranted rather than any form of insight-oriented psychotherapy (6[*Pa*], 8[*Sc*]).

A number of specific issues must be kept in mind when establishing and maintaining the therapeutic alliance: No one seems to understand her (20T); she shrinks from facing a crisis or difficulty (27T); she has difficulty starting to do things (218T); she believes it is safer to trust nobody (225T); she is so touchy on some subjects that she cannot talk about them (256T); she is very passive and nonassertive (280T, 385T); she gives up quickly when things go wrong (340T) or because she thinks too little of her ability (306T); she feels unable to tell anyone all about herself (369T); the future seem hopeless to her (399T); she is hard to get to know (408T); she is very stubborn (416T); she is bothered greatly by the thought of making changes in her life (444T) and is not sure that she can make these changes (426T); and she hates going to doctors even when she is sick (434T).

6-9/9-6

Moods   He reports that he is experiencing a mild to moderate level of emotional distress (*A, NEGE*) characterized by agitation, tension, and excitement (9[*Ma*]). His daily life is full of things that keep him interested (9T). Something exciting will almost always pull him out of it when he is feeling low (228T). When he gets bored, he likes to stir up excitement (162T). Once a week or oftener, he becomes very excited (226T). Sometimes without any reason or even when things are going wrong he feels excitedly happy or unusually cheerful (212T, 298T). He has very few fears compared with his friends (244T). He also reports mild dysphoric mood (*A-dep2*), yet he is happy most of the time (**62F**, 91T). He feels more intensely than most people do (253T). He has difficulty expressing his feelings appropriately and may vacillate between overcontrolling and undercontrolling his emotions (6[Pa], 9[Ma]). It makes him angry when people hurry him (401T). Others will perceive him as being irritable, grouchy, and angry (9[Ma], A-ang, AGGR).

Cognitions   He reports that his attention, concentration (**28F**), and memory seem to be all right (158T). He likes to let people know where he stands on things (341T), and he finds it necessary to stand up for what he thinks is right (115T). He has had very strange and peculiar experiences (29T). He often exercises poor judgment, although he thinks that his judgment is better than it ever was (6[Pa], 9[Ma], 40T). At times, he can make up his mind with unusually great ease (195T). He is sure he is being talked about (286T) and being punished without cause (137T). He is grandiose and egocentric (6[Pa], 9[Ma], 58T). He thinks that most people will use unfair means and stretch the truth to get ahead (A-cyn, 55T, 77T, 107T). He has often been misunderstood when he was trying to be helpful (373T).

[*He reports symptoms that may reflect a psychotic process or a long-term, characterological condition. His presenting problems, background, and history should be reviewed with this possibility in mind.*]

Interpersonal Relations   He reports that he is extroverted (*0[Si]*) and comfortable in social situations (*A-sod*). He is very sociable and makes friends quickly (46T, 262T, 336T). He believes, if given the chance, he would make a good leader of people (329T). He enjoys social gatherings, parties (292T, 331T), and the excitement of a crowd (335T, **304F**). His relations with his family (*Pd_1, A-fam*) and others (*Pd_2*) tend to be strained at best. He is alienated from himself (*Pd_5, Si_3*) and others (*Pd_4, Sc_1, Si_3*).

Other Problem Areas   He reports gastrointestinal (*A-hea1*) and neurological symptoms (*Sc_6, A-hea2*), but states that he is in just as good physical health as most of his friends (42T), with few or no pains (210T). Sometimes he becomes so excited, he finds it hard to get to sleep (284T). He wakes up fresh and rested most mornings (3T). He does not tire quickly (146T) and is not tired, weak, and without energy a good deal of the time (**167F**, 289T). He is about as able to work as he ever was (10T). His history and background should be reviewed to determine whether a medical or neurological evaluation is warranted. He is prone to abuse substances (*ACK, PRO*, 247T), so a careful review should be made of the consequences of his alcohol and drug use. He reported a number of conduct problems (*A-con2*) and he has been in trouble with the law (**249F**). He is a risk-taker and sensation-seeker (*MAC-R*, **96F**).

Treatment   His prognosis is generally poor because of his limited concerns about his own behavior (6[Pa], 9[Ma]). Psychopharmacological interventions are frequently warranted because of the agitation and excitement (6[Pa], 9[Ma]). Short-term, behavioral interventions that focus on his reasons for entering treatment will be most effective (6[Pa], 9[Ma]).

7-8/8-7

Moods   She reports that she is experiencing a moderate to severe level of emotional distress (*A, NEGE*) characterized by dysphoric mood (*A-dep2*, 62T), brooding, and agitation (2[D], *A-dep*, 7[Pt], *A-anx*). She frequently worries about something or someone (185T, 281T,

285T, 300T, 383T). She is chronically stressed, and she becomes more agitated or withdrawn as her level of stress increases (*7[Pt]*, *8[Sc]*). She is generally apprehensive and fearful of her environment (*8[Sc]*). Several times a week she feels as if something dreadful is about to happen (402T). She obtains little pleasure from life and is likely to be anhedonic (*INTR, A-dep1, A-trt1*). She is more sensitive (266T) and feels more intensely than most people (253T). Her feelings are easily hurt (**60F,** 121T), and she is inclined to take things hard (311T). She easily becomes impatient with people (130T, 282T). She is often irritable and grouchy (*A-ang1*, 111T, 388T). It makes her angry when people hurry her (401T). At times, she has a strong urge to do something shocking or harmful (81T).

Cognitions   She reports that she has problems with attention, concentration (28T, 279T, 305T), and memory (**158F,** 288T). She certainly is lacking in self-confidence and believes that she is not as good as other people (*A-lse,* 70T, **223F,** 379T). She has often lost out on things because she could not make up her mind quickly enough (129T). Her plans have frequently seemed so full of difficulties that she had to give them up (370T).

Sometimes some unimportant thought will run through her mind and bother her for days (308T). She has had strange and peculiar thoughts (296T) and thinks and dreams of things that are too bad to talk about (15T, 208T). She prefers to daydream rather than do anything else (45T). She often engages in sexual fantasies and her sexual adjustment is likely to be poor (*7[Pt]*, *8[Sc]*). She often thinks that things are not real (291T), there is something wrong with her mind (163T, 173T), and she is about to go to pieces (404T). Much of the time she feels as if she has done something wrong or evil (90T). She has had periods in which she carried on activities without knowing later what she had been doing (161T, 214T). Her thinking may be quite deviant and she may have experienced either auditory or visual hallucinations (*7[Pt]*, *8[Sc]*).

She thinks that most people will use unfair means and stretch the truth to get ahead (*A-cyn,* 55T, 77T, 107T). She often wonders what hidden reason another person may have for being nice to her (118T). She believes it is safer to trust nobody (225T). She has often felt that strangers were looking at her critically (235T). She has often been misunderstood when she was trying to be helpful (373T) and her way of doing things is apt to be misunderstood by others (211T). She does many things that she later regrets (78T).

[*She reports symptoms that may reflect a psychotic process or a long-term, characterological condition. Her presenting problems, background, and history should be reviewed with this possibility in mind.*]

Interpersonal Relations   She reports that she is extremely introverted (*0[Si]*) and socially uncomfortable (*A-sod*) and has poor social skills and judgment (*7[Pt]*, *8[Sc]*). When in a group of people she has trouble thinking of the right things to talk about (227T). She is easily embarrassed (270T) and wishes she was not so shy (178T). She has difficulty forming close, personal relationships (*7[Pt]*, *8[Sc]*). Even when she is with people, she feels lonely much of the time (259T). Her relations with her family tend to be poor (*Pd1, A-fam*). She is very alienated from herself (*Pd5, Si3*) and others (*Pd4, Sc1, Si3*).

Other Problem Areas   She reports a number of physical symptoms (*1[Hs], A-hea, Hy4*), general concern about her health (*A-hea3*), gastrointestinal symptoms (*A-hea1*), and neurological symptoms (*Sc6, A-hea2*). She has difficulty going to sleep because she is excited

(284T) or thoughts or ideas are bothering her (**134F**), her sleep is fitful and disturbed (36T), and she does not wake up fresh and rested most mornings (**3F**). She tires quickly (**146F**) and feels weak and tired a good deal of the time (167T). She is not as able to work as she once was (**10F**). Her history should be reviewed to determine whether a medical or neurological evaluation is warranted. She is worried about and bothered by thoughts about sex (159T, 251T). She is likely to abuse substances (*AAS, PRO*, 247T), so a careful review should be made of the consequences of her alcohol and drug use.

Treatment   Her prognosis is generally poor given the characterological nature of her problems and her diminished motivation to work (*7[Pt]*, *8[Sc]*). Establishing a therapeutic relationship is challenging because of the serious character pathology that is present (*7[Pt]*, *8[Sc]*). Psychopharmacological intervention may be necessary to decrease her level of agitation and to help her sleep (*7[Pt]*, *8[Sc]*). Cognitive-behavioral interventions focused on her depressive and anxious cognitive processes will be beneficial (*2[D]*, *A-dep*, *7[Pt]*, *A-anx*).

Numerous specific issues must be kept in mind when establishing and maintaining the therapeutic alliance: No one seems to understand her (20T); she shrinks from facing a crisis or difficulty (27T); she has difficulty starting to do things (218T); she believes it is safer to trust nobody (225T); she is so touchy on some subjects that she cannot talk about them (256T); she is passive and nonassertive (280T, 385T); she gives up quickly when things go wrong (340T) or because she thinks too little of her ability (306T); she feels unable to tell anyone all about herself (369T); she is hard to get to know (408T); she is very stubborn (416T); she hates going to doctors even when she is sick (434T); and she is bothered greatly by the thought of making changes in her life (444T).

7-0/0-7

Moods   He reports that he is experiencing a moderate level of emotional distress (*A, NEGE*) characterized by dysphoric mood (*2[D]*, *A-dep2*), worrying (*7[Pt]*, *A-anx*), and guilt (*7[Pt]*). He gets little pleasure from life and may be anhedonic (*INTR, A-dep1, A-trt1*). He frequently worries about something or someone (185T, 281T, 285T, 383T). He is more sensitive (266T) and feels more intensely than most people (253T). His feelings are easily hurt (**60F**, 121T), and he is inclined to take things hard (311T). He easily becomes impatient with people (130T, 282T). He is often irritable and grouchy (*A-ang1*, 111T, 388T).

Cognitions   He reports that he has problems with attention and concentration (28T, 279T, 305T), but his memory seems to be all right (158T). He certainly is lacking in self-confidence and believes that he is not as good as other people (*A-lse*, 70T, **223F**, 379T). He has often lost out on things because he could not make up his mind quickly enough (129T). He usually has to stop and think before he acts even in small matters (310T). He lets other people take charge (430T). He shrinks from facing a crisis or difficulty (27T). He is easily downed in an argument (67T). He is apt to pass up something he wants to do because others think it is not worth doing (280T). He takes disappointments so keenly that he cannot put them out of his mind (377T).

He thinks that most people will use unfair means and stretch the truth to get ahead (*A-cyn*, 55T, 77T, 107T). He has often thought that strangers were looking at him critically

(235T). He has often been misunderstood when he was trying to be helpful (373T). He does many things that he later regrets (78T).

Interpersonal Relations   He reports that he is introverted (*0[Si]*) and uncomfortable in social situations (*A-sod*). He is shy (178T), bashful (154T), and easily embarrassed (270T). At parties, he is more likely to sit by himself or with one other person than to join in with the crowd (316T). Whenever possible, he avoids being in a crowd (304T, **335F**). Even when he is with people, he feels lonely much of the time (259T). He finds it hard to talk when he meets new people (160T) or in a group of people (227T). He is not likely to speak to people until they speak to him (248T). He does not seem to make friends as quickly as others do (**262F**). He spends most of his spare time by himself (410T). He reports conflicted relations with his family (*Pd₁, A-fam*). He is alienated from himself (*Pd₅, Si₃*) and others (*Pd₄, Sc₁, Si₃*).

Other Problem Areas   He reports a few physical symptoms (*A-hea, Hy₄*) and general concern about his health (*A-hea3*), but states that he is in just as good physical health as most of his friends (42T). His sleep is not fitful or disturbed (**36F**), but he does not wake up fresh and rested most mornings (**3F**). He tires quickly (**146F**) and feels tired a good deal of the time (167T). He is about as able to work as he ever was (10T). He is not likely to abuse substances (***ACK, PRO***). His social isolation and fear of social interaction (*7[Pt]*, *0[Si]*) decrease the possibility of conduct problems (***A-con***).

Treatment   His prognosis is good for long-term therapy because he is experiencing a significant degree of emotional distress (*A, NEGE*), and he is willing to think about his problems (*7[Pt], A-obs*). He usually is referred for his shyness and extreme sensitivity (*7[Pt], 0[Si]*). He is generally a serious person who is given to anticipating problems and difficulties (*7[Pt], 0[Si]*). Social-skill training or assertiveness training may be beneficial (*0[Si]*).

Some specific issues must be kept in mind when establishing and maintaining the therapeutic alliance: He shrinks from facing a crisis or difficulty (27T); he has difficulty starting to do things (218T); he is so touchy on some subjects that he cannot talk about them (256T); he is passive and nonassertive (280T, 385T); he gives up quickly when things go wrong (340T) or because he thinks too little of his ability (306T); he feels unable to tell anyone all about himself (369T); he is hard to get to know (408T); he is very stubborn (416T); and he is bothered greatly by the thought of making changes in his life (444T).

8-9/9-8

Moods   He reports that he is experiencing moderate to severe emotional distress (*A, NEGE*) characterized by agitation and excitement (*8[Sc], 9[Ma]*). He is often first seen in an acute state of hyperactivity, excitement, confusion, and disorientation (*8[Sc], 9[Ma]*). When he gets bored, he likes to stir up some excitement (162T). Sometimes without any reason or even when things are going wrong, he feels excitedly happy (212T). He has periods in which he feels unusually cheerful without any special reason (298T). Something exciting will almost always pull him out of it when he is feeling low (228T). He easily becomes impatient with people (282T). He is often angry, irritable, and grouchy (*A-ang,*

AGGR, 111T, 388T). At times, he has a strong urge to do something shocking or harmful (81T).

Cognitions   He reports that he has problems with attention and concentration (28T, 279T, 305T), but his memory seems to be all right (158T). He likes to let people know where he stands on things (341T), and he finds it necessary to stand up for what he thinks is right (115T).

He thinks and dreams of things that are too bad to talk about (15T, 208T) and he has strange and peculiar experiences (29T) and thoughts (296T). He has had periods in which he carried on activities without knowing later what he had been doing (161T, 214T). In response to stress, he is likely to become more disorganized and agitated or to engage in more daydreaming and fantasy (*8[Sc], 9[Ma]*).

He thinks that most people will use unfair means and stretch the truth to get ahead (*A-cyn,* 55T, 77T, 100T, 107T). Most people make friends because friends are likely to be useful to them (238T). He often wonders what hidden reason another person may have for doing something nice for him (118T). He believes that it is safer to trust nobody (225T). He has often been misunderstood when he was trying to be helpful (373T), and his way of doing things is apt to be misunderstood by others (211T).

[*He reports symptoms that may reflect a psychotic process or a long-term, characterological condition. His presenting problems, background, and history should be reviewed with this possibility in mind.*]

Interpersonal Relations   He reports a balance between extroverted and introverted behaviors (*0[Si]*) and he is comfortable in social situations (*A-sod*). He is sociable and makes friends quickly (46T, 262T, 336T). He enjoys social gatherings and parties (82T, 292T, 331T) and the excitement of a crowd (**304F,** 335T). He likes to be with people who play jokes on one another (217T). He believes, if given the chance, he would make a good leader of people (329T). His behavior may be unpredictable, and he may act out unexpectedly (*8[Sc], 9[Ma]*). He is fearful of relating to others; consequently, intimate relationships are usually lacking (*8[Sc], 9[Ma]*). His relations with his family (*Pd₁, A-fam*) and others (*Pd₂*) are marked by conflict. Once in a while, he feels hate toward members of his family whom he usually loves (240T). He is alienated from himself (*Pd₅, Si₃*) and others (*Pd₄, Sc₁, Si₃*).

Other Problem Areas   He reports a number of general physical symptoms (*1[Hs], A-hea, Hy₄*), gastrointestinal symptoms (*A-hea1*), and neurological symptoms (*Sc₆, A-hea2*). Sometimes he becomes so excited that he finds it hard to get to sleep (282T). His history should be reviewed to determine whether a medical or neurological evaluation is warranted. He is likely to abuse substances, so a careful review should be made of the consequences of his alcohol and drug use (*ACK, PRO,* 247T). He is a risk-taker and sensation seeker (*MAC-R*) who is likely to have legal and conduct problems (*A-con2*).

Treatment   His prognosis is generally poor because of the serious characterological nature of his problems (*8[Sc], 9[Ma]*). Psychopharmacological intervention may be helpful in reducing his agitation (*8[Sc], 9[Ma]*). The difficulties he experiences in focusing on specific issues and his fear of relating to others often preclude good therapeutic contact and outcome (*8[Sc], 9[Ma]*). He has little capacity for forming close interpersonal relationships, yet he is rarely referred for poor peer or sibling relationships (*8[Sc]*, *9[Ma]*). Short-term, behavioral interventions that focus on his reasons for entering treatment will be most effective (*8[Sc]*, *9[Ma]*).

The following specific issues must be kept in mind when establishing and maintaining the therapeutic alliance: He has difficulty starting to do things (218T); it is safer to trust nobody (225T); he is so touchy on some subjects that he cannot talk about them (256T); he is hard to get to know (408T); and he is very stubborn (416T).

Individual Scales   The interpretive text for every MMPI-A codetype provides the broad overview of how the *group* of adolescents within the codetype scored on the various scales. The task for the clinician at this juncture is to review all the individual scales (clinical, content, and supplementary) and critical items for this specific adolescent to determine how the interpretive text needs to be modified. Once the interpretive text for the MMPI-A has been rendered internally consistent, the clinician then must integrate the clinical history and background into the interpretation.

The individual scales on the MMPI-A can be organized within two large categories that reflect how the scales were developed: empirically or rationally. The 10 clinical scales for the MMPI-2 and MMPI-A were developed empirically and the 15 content scales (Williams, Butcher, Ben-Porath, & Graham, 1992), and PSY-5 scales (McNulty, Harkness, Ben-Porath, & Williams, 1997) were developed rationally. These two approaches are conceptually opposed to one another as described in Chapter 5 (pp. 116–117) and provide two methods for interpreting the MMPI-A. When the adolescent endorses the items accurately, these two approaches provide a similar interpretation of the MMPI-A profile, and the clinician's task is relatively straightforward. When the adolescent for any reason is motivated to provide either a self-unfavorable or self-favorable description, the approaches will provide divergent interpretations, and the clinician's task becomes more daunting because it is necessary to determine the basis for these divergent interpretations.

Clinical and Content Scales

Tables 7.4 and 7.5 provide general interpretive text for the clinical and content scales, respectively, when they are elevated above a T score of 64 or below a T score of 45. Figure 7.3 illustrated the profile for the basic validity and clinical scales, and Figure 7.4 illustrates the profile for the content scales for the same *1-3/3-1* codetype. The major emphasis in the interpretation of the MMPI-A is on elevated scales, yet very important information frequently is found in scales that are not elevated. For example, adolescents in a clinical setting who do not elevate Scales *2* (*D:* Depression) and *7* (*Pt:* Psychasthenia) are reporting that they are not experiencing any distress about the behavior or symptoms that led them to the clinical setting or about being evaluated.

A total of 15 new content scales have been developed for the MMPI-A (Williams et al., 1992): Anxiety, Obsessiveness, Depression, Health Concerns, Alienation, Bizarre Mentation, Anger, Cynicism, Conduct Problems, Low Self-Esteem, Low Aspirations, Social Discomfort, Family Problems, School Problems, and Negative Treatment Indicators (see Table 7.1 and Figure 7.4). These scales were developed in a similar manner to the MMPI-2 content (Butcher, Graham, Williams, & Ben-Porath, 1990) scales. The stages in the development of the MMPI-A content scales are outlined in Butcher et al. (1992, p. 61)

Table 7.4   Interpretation of the MMPI-A clinical scales

Scale	Potential Issues
1 (Hs) > 64	Adolescents have a preoccupation with vague physical ailments. They are pessimistic about being helped. They are unlikely to be doing well in school, reporting increasing problems, primarily academic.
1 (Hs) < 45	No specific interpretations can be made.
2 (D) > 64	Adolescents are reporting generalized distress and likely to be depressed. Their depressive mood should be readily apparent. It is important to determine whether internal or external factors are producing the negative mood state and to plan treatment accordingly.
2 (D) < 45	Adolescents are not reporting any type of emotional distress either as a result of their presence in treatment or the behaviors/symptoms that led them to consider treatment. The possibility of acting out in an impulsive manner should be evaluated. There is little internal motivation for any type of treatment or intervention.
3 (Hy) > 64	Adolescents are dependent, suggestible, and lack insight into their own and others' behavior. They deny any type of psychological problems. Under stress, specific physical ailments will be seen. They look for simplistic, concrete solutions to their problems. Treatment should focus on short-term goals because there is limited motivation. They initially may be enthusiastic about treatment, then later resist treatment or fail to cooperate.
3 (Hy) < 45	Adolescents are caustic, sarcastic, and socially isolated. They have few defenses for coping with any problems that they encounter. Well-structured, behavioral interventions should be used whenever possible.
4 (Pd) > 64	Adolescents are in conflict either with family members or with persons in positions of authority. They are likely to abuse alcohol or drugs. They may make a good initial impression, but more long-term contact will reveal that they are egocentric and have little concern for others. Any treatment should focus on short-term goals with emphasis on behavior change rather than their verbalized intent to change, no matter how sincere they may sound. Low scores on Scales *2 (D:* Depression) and *7 (Pt:* Psychasthenia) make elevations on Scale *4* particularly pathognomonic.
4 (Pd) < 45	Adolescents are rigid, conventional, and have little psychological insight into themselves or others. Explicit, behavioral directives to change will be most productive if there is sufficient motivation to follow them.
5 (Mf) > 64	Adolescents do not identify with their traditional gender role and are concerned about sexual issues. Boys frequently worry and their feelings are easily hurt. Girls are confident and satisfied with themselves.
5 (Mf) < 40	Adolescents identify with their traditional gender role. Men are confident and self-assured. Women are trusting of and depend on others and lack self-confidence. Their feelings are easily hurt and they cry easily.
6 (Pa) > 64	Adolescents are suspicious, hostile, and overly sensitive, which is readily apparent to everyone. Any treatment is problematic because of the difficulty in developing a therapeutic relationship based on trust. Any intervention must be instituted slowly.

(continued)

Table 7.4 (*Continued*)

Scale	Potential Issues
6 (*Pa*) < 45	Adolescents have narrow interests, and they tend to be insensitive to and unaware of the motives of others. Explicit, behavioral directives to change will be most productive if there is sufficient motivation to follow them.
7 (*Pt*) > 64	Adolescents are worried, tense, and indecisive, which is readily apparent to everyone. Ineffective ruminative, and obsessive behaviors will be seen. It may be necessary to lower their level of anxiety before implementing treatment of other symptoms.
7 (*Pt*) < 45	Adolescents are secure and comfortable with themselves, which augurs poorly for any type of intervention in a clinical setting.
8 (*Sc*) > 64	Adolescents feel alienated and remote from the environment and others. At higher elevations (>79), difficulties in logic and judgment may become evident. Interventions should be directive and supportive. Psychotropic medications may be needed.
8 (*Sc*) < 45	Adolescents are conventional, concrete, and unimaginative. Any intervention should be behavioral, directive, and focused on short-term goals.
9 (*Ma*) > 64	Adolescents are overactive, impulsive, emotionally labile, and euphoric with occasional outbursts of anger. Short-term behavioral goals should be pursued.
9 (*Ma*) < 45	Adolescents have low energy and activity levels. They may be manifesting significant signs of psychomotor retardation that should be evaluated carefully.
0 (*Si*) > 64	Adolescents are introverted, shy, and socially insecure. They withdraw from and avoid significant others who exacerbate their distress. Interventions need to address specifically their tendency to withdraw and avoid others.
0 (*Si*) < 45	Adolescents are extroverted, gregarious, and socially poised. They may have difficulty in forming intimate relationships with others at very low scores (T < 35). They are unlikely to have a thought disorder. The probability of acting out is increased. Group therapies are particularly useful with these adolescents.

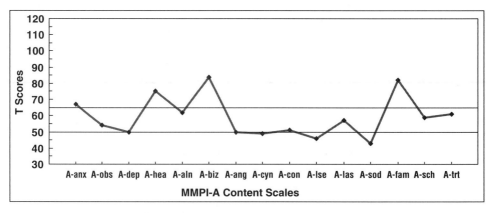

Figure 7.4   **MMPI-A content scales for a *1-3/3-1* codetype.**

Table 7.5   Interpretation of the MMPI-A content scales

Scale	Potential Issues
A-anx (Anxiety) > 64	Adolescents report general symptoms of anxiety, nervousness, worries, and sleep and concentration difficulties. Depending on the level of anxiety, psychotropic medications or other anxiety-reducing techniques may be needed before implementing other interventions.
A-obs (Obsessiveness) > 64	Adolescents have great difficulty making decisions, ruminate and worry excessively, and have intrusive thoughts. They are good candidates for most insight-oriented therapies.
A-dep (Depression) > 64	Adolescents have difficulty getting going and getting things done in their lives (*A-dep1*). They have a dysphoric mood (*A-dep2*) and thoughts and a negative self-concept (*A-dep3*). Their depression has an angry component that involves blaming others, particularly when *A-dep* is higher (+15 T points) than Scale *2* (*D*: Depression).
A-hea (Health Concerns) > 64	Adolescents report gastrointestinal symptoms (*A-hea1*) and symptoms associated with neurological functioning (*A-hea2*), as well as general concerns about their health (*A-hea3*). Their physical symptoms may be another manifestation of their emotional distress. They need to be reassured that their symptoms are being taken seriously.
A-aln (Alienation)	Adolescents report considerable social distance from others. They do not believe that they are liked by others and they do not get along well with others. They believe that others are out to get them and are unkind to them.
A-biz (Bizarre Mentation) > 64	Adolescents report overtly psychotic symptoms such as paranoid ideation and hallucinations (*A-biz1*) and various peculiar and strange experiences (*A-biz2*). Psychotropic medications may be indicated, as well as hospitalization.
A-ang (Anger) > 64	Adolescents report a number of explosive tendencies such as hitting and smashing things (*A-ang1*), as well as being irritable, grouchy, and impatient (*A-ang2*). Assertiveness training and anger-control techniques should be implemented as part of treatment.
A-cyn (Cynicism) > 64	Adolescents expect others are only interested in their own welfare (*A-cyn1*) and are suspicious of others' motives (*A-cyn2*). Establishing a trusting relationship is a difficult process, but imperative, if any progress is to be made in therapy.
A-con (Conduct Problems) > 64	Adolescents have attitudes similar to adolescents who break the law (*A-con1*), even if they do not have conduct problems. They report stealing things and other problematic conduct (*A-con2*). Group interventions with similar adolescents will be most productive.

(continued)

Table 7.5   *(Continued)*

Scale	Potential Issues
A-lse (Low Self-Esteem) > 64	Adolescents have very low opinions of themselves (*A-lse1*), and they are uncomfortable if people say nice things about them (*A-lse2*). They give in easily to others. Interventions need to be very supportive and allow ample time for change.
A-las (Low Aspirations) > 64	Adolescents are not interested in being successful. They report difficulty starting things and quickly give up when things go wrong. They let other people solve problems, and they avoid facing difficulties. They believe that others block their success; others say they are lazy.
A-sod (Social Discomfort) > 64	Adolescents are very uneasy around others and are happier by themselves (*A-sod1*). They see themselves as shy and uncomfortable in social situations (*A-sod2*). They need to be supported and encouraged to participate in treatment until they are comfortable interacting with others.
A-fam (Family Problems) > 64	Adolescents report considerable familial discord (*A-fam1*). Their families are reported to lack love, support, and companionship. They feel alienated from and unattached to their family (*A-fam2*). Involvement of the family system in treatment may be important unless the adolescent needs to be emancipated from them.
A-sch (School Problems) > 64	Adolescents have numerous school problems such as poor grades, suspensions, truancy, negative attitudes toward teachers, and a dislike of school. They do not participate in school activities.
A-trt (Negative Treatment Indicators) > 64	Adolescents are unmotivated and feel unable to help themselves (*A-trt1*). They dislike going to doctors and they believe that they should not discuss their personal problems with others (*A-trt2*). They prefer to take drugs or medicine because talking about problems does not help them. Adolescents with depressive mood disorders will elevate *TRT* because it is primarily a measure of general distress, so clinicians need to be cautious about interpreting *TRT* in a characterological manner.

and explained more fully in Williams et al. (1992). Sherwood, Ben-Porath, and Williams (1997) developed component scales for the MMPI-A content scales again similar to the MMPI-2 content component scales (Ben-Porath & Sherwood, 1993). Arita and Baer (1998) examined the convergent and discriminant validity of the content scales of Anxiety, Depression, Health Concerns, Alienation, Anger, Conduct Problems, and Social Discomfort in adolescent inpatients. Neither the Anxiety nor the Depression scale discriminated among the various other measures and appear to be more general measures of nonspecific distress. The other content scales that they studied demonstrated reasonable convergent and discriminant validity.

Supplementary Scales

There are many supplementary scales to assist the clinician in interpreting the MMPI-A codetype. Three of these supplementary scales will be familiar to the clinician who has used the MMPI-2 and will have generally similar interpretations: MacAndrew Alcoholism-Revised (*MAC-R*) scale and Welsh's Anxiety (*A*) and Repression (*R*) scales. These scales have had a few minor changes made in them at the item level. Three new scales are represented in the supplementary scales on the MMPI-A: Alcohol/Drug Problem Acknowledgment (*ACK:* Weed, Butcher, & Williams, 1994); Alcohol/Drug Proneness (*PRO:* Weed et al., 1994); and Immaturity (*IMM:* Archer, Pancoast, & Gordon, 1994). The Alcohol/Drug Problem Acknowledgment (ACK) and Alcohol/Drug Proneness (PRO) scales were developed in the same manner as the Addiction Admission (*AAS*) and Addiction Potential (*APS*) scales on the MMPI-2, respectively. McNulty et al. (1997) developed scales to measure the Personality Psychopathology Five (PSY-5) in adolescents from the MMPI-A items; and Bolinskey, Arnau, Archer, and Handel (2004) developed facet subscales for these PSY-5 scales.

MMPI-A Structural Summary

The MMPI-A Structural Summary (Archer & Krishnamurthy, 1994) has been created to provide a conceptual framework for the eight factors that have been identified in the MMPI-A item pool (Archer, Belevich, & Elkins, 1994; Archer & Krishnamurthy, 1997): general maladjustment; immaturity; disinhibition/excitatory potential; social discomfort; health concerns; naivete; familial alienation; and psychoticism. These factors are listed in relative order of the amount of variance for which they accounted. Krishnamurthy and Archer (1999) showed that simply counting the number of scales within each factor—and if a majority of them are elevated to a T score of 65 or higher to consider a factor as being elevated—produced similar results as computing the average T score for all scales within the factor.

The MMPI-A Structural Summary organizes all the MMPI-A scales and subscales within each of these factors based on their degree of correlation with each factor. Archer, Krishnamurthy, and Jacobson (1994) and Archer (1997) describe the MMPI-A Structural Summary in more detail and also provide examples of its use with clinical cases.

Critical Items

Archer and Jacobson (1993) investigated the frequency with which the Koss and Butcher (1973) critical items were endorsed by adolescents in the MMPI-A normative group and clinical samples. Both groups of adolescents endorsed these critical items more often than adults. However, the adolescents in clinical settings did not endorse these items more often than the normal adolescents, which should serve as a caution to clinicians who might be tempted to interpret these critical items in adolescents.

Forbey and Ben-Porath (1998) developed a critical item set specifically for adolescents based on the MMPI-A items. They used a multiple-step process that involved comparing endorsement rates of the individual items among normal and various clinical samples and review of potential critical items by judges experienced with adolescents and the MMPI-A. This process resulted in 82 items that Forbey and Ben-Porath rationally placed in 15 content groupings: Aggression; Anxiety; Cognitive Problems; Conduct Problems; Depressed/Suicidal Ideation; Eating Problems; Family Problems; Hallucinatory Experiences; Paranoid Ideation; School Problems; Self Denigration; Sexual Concerns; Somatic Complaints; Substance Use/Abuse; and Unusual Thinking. There have been no published studies on these MMPI-A critical items, but they appear to be much more suitable for adolescents than the MMPI-2 critical item sets that were designed for adults.

Summary

Archer (2005), Archer and Krishnamurthy (2002), Fowler et al. (2000), and Williams et al. (1992) have provided interpretive guidelines for the individual validity, clinical, content, and supplementary scales of the MMPI-A. These references are required reading for any clinician who is interpreting the MMPI-A. Archer (1997) and Butcher, Graham, and Ben-Porath (1995) have provided general guidelines for research with the MMPI-A that should be consulted by anyone who is interested in working in this area.

APPLICATIONS

The applications of the MMPI-A have been generally limited to the identification of psychopathology within a clinical setting and delinquent behaviors in criminal justice settings. The former application was the primary purpose of the original MMPI and also is the primary application of the MMPI-A. Consequently, this application has been the focus of the entire chapter and will not be pursued further here.

The identification of delinquent behavior was the focus of Hathaway and Monachesi's (1963) longitudinal investigations. They found that elevations on Scales *4* (*Pd:* Psychopathic Deviate), *8* (*Sc:* Schizophrenia), and *9* (*Ma:* Hypomania) as "excitatory" scales increased the risk of delinquent behavior, while elevations on Scales *2* (*D:* Depression), *5* (*Mf:* Masculinity-Femininity), and *0* (*Si:* Social Introversion) as "inhibitory" decreased the risk of delinquent behavior. The effects of these excitatory and inhibitory scales were relatively small, however, with approximately a 7% increase or decrease from the base rate for delinquent behavior of 35%, respectively. Several subsequent studies (e.g., Huesmann, Lefkowitz, & Eron, 1978; Pena et al., 1996; Rempel, 1958) supported these general findings of the effects of the excitatory and inhibitory scales on delinquent behaviors.

More recent studies of using the MMPI-A to identify delinquent behavior have found somewhat divergent results. Cashel, Rogers, Sewell, and Holliman (1998) reported the external correlates of the MMPI-A clinical scales. Scales *4* (*Pd:* Psychopathic Deviate), *7* (*Pt:* Psychasthenia), and *8* (*Sc:* Schizophrenia) were related significantly to most of the correlates, while Scales *5* (*Mf:* Masculinity-Femininity) and *0* (*Si:* Social Introversion) were related to none of them. The correlates of Scales *2* (*D:* Depression) and *9* (*Ma:* Hypomania) were as expected, depressive and excitatory variables, respectively. However, Scale *3* (*Hy:* Hysteria) was related to cruelty toward others and suicidal ideation, neither of which would be expected from either the adult or adolescent research. They also reported that White delinquents tended to have higher scores on the clinical scales than African American or Mexican American delinquents. That is, there was no tendency for the MMPI-A to overpathologize African American or Mexican American delinquents.

Morton, Farris, and Brenowitz (2002) compared a large sample of male delinquents with the MMPI-A normative group. Lower scores on Scale 5 (*Mf:* Masculinity-Femininity) characterized the delinquent boys and was the most effective Scale to differentiate the two groups. Elevations on Scales 4 (*Pd:* Psychopathic Deviate) and 6 (*Pa:* Paranoia) also were common in the delinquent boys.

Thus, it appears that elevations on Scales 4 (*Pd:* Psychopathic Deviate), 8 (*Sc:* Schizophrenia), and 9 (*Ma:* Hypomania) as excitatory scales must be considered in evaluating adolescents for increased risk for delinquent behaviors. In addition, elevations on Scales *F* (Infrequency), 3 (*Hy:* Hysteria), and 6 (*Pa:* Paranoia) and lower scores on Scale 5 (*Mf:* Masculinity-Femininity) must be considered as potential risk factors.

PSYCHOMETRIC FOUNDATIONS

Demographic Variables

Age

There were substantial differences in performance between adolescents and adults on the original MMPI that resulted in the development of the MMPI-A specifically for adolescents. Within the limited age range of the MMPI-A (14 to 18), there is little reason to expect much difference as the function of age. Younger adolescents (< 15) would be expected to have more trouble reading the MMPI-A items because of their developmental level in reading skills.

Gender

Gender does not create any general issues in MMPI-A interpretation because separate norms (profile forms) are used for boys and girls. Any gender differences in how adolescents responded to the items on each scale are removed when the raw scores are converted to T scores.

Education

The limited levels of education represented in ages 14 to 18 also limit any potential effect of education on the MMPI-A.

Ethnicity

Only very limited research has looked specifically at the effects of ethnicity on either the original MMPI or the MMPI-A in adolescents. This limited research in adolescents is somewhat surprising given the vast number of studies of ethnicity with the MMPI and MMPI-2 in adults. The effects of ethnicity on the MMPI and MMPI-2 in adults were summarized in Chapter 6 (see p. 200) and should be perused to provide a context for looking at this issue in adolescents.

The MMPI-A has been examined in three studies with normal Hispanic adolescents (Gumbiner, 1998; Mendoza-Newman, 1999; Negy, Leal-Puente, Trainor, & Carlson, 1997), all of which found minimal differences when compared with the MMPI-A normative group. Negy et al. (1997) found that MMPI-A profiles did vary as a function of acculturation and socioeconomic status (SES). Gumbiner (1998) found that boys scored higher than girls on several scales and she concluded that the scale elevations might be related to SES. Mendoza-Newman (1999) examined the relationship between acculturation and SES on Scales *L* (Lie) and *5* (*Mf:* Masculinity-Femininity) and found no relationship between acculturation or SES as individual variables. However, there was a significant negative correlation between the combination of acculturation and SES and Scale *L* (Lie), but not for Scale *5* (*Mf:* Masculinity-Femininity). All three studies suggest that normal Hispanic adolescents score very similarly to the MMPI-A normative group and underscore the importance of considering the importance of acculturation and SES in looking at the effects of ethnicity when any differences are found.

Gomez, Johnson, Davis, and Velasquez (2000) found no differences on any of the MMPI-A scales between small samples of African American and Mexican American first-time offenders. They did find that the African American offenders produced more within-normal-limit profiles (50% versus 25%).

Multivariate regressions of age, gender, and ethnicity on the MMPI-A scales (Schinka, Elkins, & Archer, 1998) have shown that the total percentage of variance accounted for by these factors did not exceed 10% for any of the MMPI-A scales. The largest percentage of variance (9.50%) was found on the Bizarre Mentation (*BIZ*) scale. Such small percentages of variance are unlikely to impact the interpretation of most MMPI-A profiles. Ethnicity (White versus nonwhite) accounted for 7.73% of the variance in the *F* (Infrequency) scale and typically was in the range of 1% to 3% on most of the MMPI-A scales. Gender only accounted for 0.79% of the variance on Scale *5* (*Mf:* Masculinity-Femininity) on the MMPI-A, in contrast to the MMPI-2 in which slightly over 50% of the variance was accounted for by gender.

It appears that demographic variables will have minimal impact on the MMPI-A profile in most individuals. It is important to monitor the validity of the MMPI-A profile more closely in younger adolescents because of the potential limitations on their reading level because of their level of education.

Reliability

The *MMPI-A Manual* (Butcher et al., 1992, Appendix E) reports the reliability data for 45 boys and 109 girls who were retested 1 week later. The test-retest correlations ranged from .65 to .84 across the 10 clinical scales and averaged .74. The test-retest correlations ranged from .62 to .82 across the 15 content scales and averaged .73. The standard error of measurement is 4 to 6 T points for the clinical and content scales; that is, the individual's true score on the clinical and content scales will be within ±4 to 6 T points two-thirds of the time.

Codetype Stability

There are no data on the stability of MMPI-A codetypes. It would be assumed that MMPI-A codetypes, at best, would be no more stable than MMPI-2 codetypes (see pp. 200–201), and probably would be less stable than MMPI-2 codetypes. Consequently, any interpretation should describe the adolescent's *current* status rather than be used for any long-term predictions.

REFERENCES

American Psychiatric Association. (2000). *Diagnostic and statistical manual of mental disorders* (4th ed., text rev.). Washington, DC: Author.

Archer, R. P. (1984). Use of the MMPI with adolescents: A review of salient issues. *Clinical Psychology Review, 4*, 241–251.

Archer, R. P. (1987). *Using the MMPI with adolescents*. Hillsdale, NJ: Erlbaum.

Archer, R. P. (1997). Future directions for the MMPI-A: Research and clinical issues. *Journal of Personality Assessment, 68*, 95–109.

Archer, R. P. (2005). *MMPI-A: Assessing adolescent psychopathology* (3rd ed.). Mahwah, NJ: Erlbaum.

Archer, R. P., Belevich, J. K. S., & Elkins, D. E. (1994). Item-level and scale-level factor structures of the MMPI-A. *Journal of Personality Assessment, 62*, 332–345.

Archer, R. P., Handel, R. W., Lynch, K. D., & Elkins, D. E. (2002). MMPI-A validity scale uses and limitations in detecting varying levels of random responding. *Journal of Personality Assessment, 78*, 417–431.

Archer, R. P., Handel, R. W., & Mason, J. A. (2006). [MMPI-A data from a community outpatient setting]. Unpublished raw data.

Archer, R. P., & Jacobson, J. M. (1993). Are critical items "critical" for the MMPI-A? *Journal of Personality Assessment, 61*, 547–556.

Archer, R. P., & Krishnamurthy, R. (1994). A structural summary approach for the MMPI-A: Development and empirical correlates. *Journal of Personality Assessment, 63*, 554–573.

Archer, R. P., & Krishnamurthy, R. (1997). MMPI-A scale-level factor structure: Replication in a clinical sample. *Assessment, 4*, 337–349.

Archer, R. P., & Krishnamurthy, R. (2002). *Essentials of MMPI-A assessment*. Hoboken, NJ: Wiley.

Archer, R. P., Krishnamurthy, R., & Jacobson, J. M. (1994). *MMPI-A casebook*. Odessa, FL: Psychological Assessment Resources.

Archer, R. P., Pancoast, D. L., & Gordon, R. A. (1994). The development of the MMPI-A Immaturity scale: Findings for normal and clinical samples. *Journal of Personality Assessment, 62*, 145–156.

Arita, A. A., & Baer, R. A. (1998). Validity of selected MMPI-A Content scales. *Psychological Assessment, 10*, 59–63.

Baer, R. A., Ballenger, J., Berry, D. T. R., & Wetter, M. W. (1997). Detection of random responding on the MMPI-A. *Journal of Personality Assessment, 68*, 139–151.

Ben-Porath, Y. S., & Sherwood, N. E. (1993). *The MMPI-2 Content Component scales: Development, psychometric characteristics, and clinical application*. Minneapolis: University of Minnesota Press.

Bolinskey, P. K., Arnau, R. C., Archer, R. P., & Handel, R. W. (2004). A replication of the MMPI-A PSY-5 scales and development of facet subscales. *Assessment, 11*, 40–48.

Butcher, J. N., Graham, J. R., & Ben-Porath, Y. S. (1995). Methodological problems and issues in MMPI, MMPI-2, and MMPI-A research. *Psychological Assessment, 7*, 320–329.

Butcher, J. N., Graham, J. R., Williams, C. L., & Ben-Porath, Y. S. (1990). *Development and use of the MMPI-2 Content scales*. Minneapolis: University of Minnesota Press.

Butcher, J. N., Williams, C. L., Graham, J. R., Archer, R. P., Tellegen, A., Ben-Porath, Y. S., et al. (1992). *Minnesota Multiphasic Personality Inventory—Adolescent (MMPI-A): Manual for administration, scoring, and interpretation*. Minneapolis: University of Minnesota Press.

Cashel, M. L., Rogers, R., Sewell, K. W., & Holliman, N. B. (1998). Preliminary validation of the MMPI-A for a male delinquent sample: An investigation of clinical correlates and discriminant validity. *Journal of Personality Assessment, 71*, 49–69.

Colligan, R. C., & Offord, K. P. (1989). The aging MMPI: Contemporary norms for contemporary teenagers. *Mayo Clinic Proceedings, 64*, 3–27.

Dahlstrom, W. G., Welsh, G. S., & Dahlstrom, L. E. (1972). *An MMPI handbook: Vol. I. Clinical interpretation (Rev. ed.).* Minneapolis: University of Minnesota Press.

Forbey, J. D., & Ben-Porath, Y. S. (1998). *A critical item set for the MMPI-A.* Minneapolis: University of Minnesota Press.

Fowler, R. A., Butcher, J. N., & Williams, C. L. (2000). *Essentials of MMPI-2 and MMPI-A interpretation* (2nd ed.). Minneapolis: University of Minnesota Press.

Gomez, F. C., Johnson, R., Davis, Q., & Velasquez, R. J. (2000). MMPI-A performance of African and Mexican American adolescent first-time offenders. *Psychological Reports, 87,* 309–314.

Gottesman, I. I., Hanson, D. R., Kroeker, T. A., & Briggs, P. F. (1987). New MMPI normative data and power-transformed T-score tables for the Hathaway-Monachesi Minnesota cohort of 14,019 15-year-olds and 3,674 18-year-olds. In R. P. Archer (Ed.), *Using the MMPI with adolescents* (pp. 241–297). Hillsdale, NJ: Erlbaum.

Gough, H. G. (1950). The *F* minus *K* dissimulation index for the MMPI. *Journal of Consulting Psychology, 14,* 408–413.

Greene, R. L., & Brown, R. C. (2006). *MMPI-2 adult interpretive system* (3rd ed.). Lutz, FL: Psychological Assessment Resources.

Gumbiner, J. (1998). MMPI-A profiles of Hispanic adolescents. *Psychological Reports, 82,* 659–672.

Hathaway, S. R., & McKinley, J. C. (1940). A multiphasic personality schedule (Minnesota): Pt. I. Construction of the schedule. *Journal of Psychology, 10,* 249–254.

Hathaway, S. R., & Monachesi, E. D. (1963). *Adolescent personality and behavior: MMPI patterns of normal, delinquent, dropout, and other outcomes.* Minneapolis: University of Minnesota Press.

Huesmann, L. R., Lefkowitz, M. M., & Eron, L. D. (1978). Sum of MMPI scales *F, 4,* and *9* as a measure of aggression. *Journal of Consulting and Clinical Psychology, 46,* 1071–1078.

Koss, M. P., & Butcher, J. N. (1973). A comparison of psychiatric patients' self-report with other sources of clinical information. *Journal of Research in Personality, 7,* 225–236.

Krakauer, S. Y., Archer, R. P., & Gordon, R. A. (1993). The development of Items-easy (*Ie*) and Items-difficult (*Id*) scales for the MMPI-A. *Journal of Personality Assessment, 60,* 561–571.

Krishnamurthy, R., & Archer, R. P. (1999). A comparison of two interpretive approaches for the MMPI-A structural summary. *Journal of Personality Assessment, 73,* 245–259.

Lachar, D. (1974). *The MMPI: Clinical assessment and automated interpretation.* Los Angeles: Western Psychological Services.

Lachar, D., Klinge, V., & Grisell, J. L. (1976). Relative accuracy of automated MMPI narratives generated from adult norm and adolescent norm profiles. *Journal of Consulting and Clinical Psychology, 44,* 20–24.

Marks, P. A., Seeman, W., & Haller, D. L. (1974). *The actuarial use of the MMPI with adolescents and adults.* Baltimore: Williams & Wilkins.

McGrath, R. E., Pogge, D. L., Stein, L. A. R., Graham, J. R., Zaccario, M., & Piacentini, T. (2000). Development of an Infrequency-Psychopathology scale for the MMPI-A: The *Fp - A* scale. *Journal of Personality Assessment, 74,* 282–295.

McNulty, J. L., Harkness, A. R., Ben-Porath, Y. S., & Williams, C. L. (1997). Assessing the Personality Psychopathology Five (PSY-5) in adolescents: New MMPI-A scales. *Psychological Assessment, 9,* 250–257.

Meehl, P. E. (1957). When should we use our heads instead of the formula? *Journal of Counseling Psychology, 4,* 268–273.

Mendoza-Newman, M. C. (1999). *Level of acculturation, socioeconomic status, and the MMPI-A performance of a non-clinical Hispanic adolescent sample.* Unpublished doctoral dissertation, Pacific Graduate School of Psychology, Palo Alto, CA.

Morton, T. L., Farris, K. L., & Brenowitz, L. H. (2002). MMPI-A scores and high points of male juvenile delinquents: Scales, *4, 5,* and, *6,* as markers of juvenile delinquency. *Psychological Assessment, 14,* 311–319.

Negy, C., Leal-Puente, L., Trainor, D. J., & Carlson, R. (1997). Mexican American adolescents' performance on the MMPI-A. *Journal of Personality Assessment*, *69*, 205–214.

Paulhus, D. L. (1984). Two-component models of socially desirable responding. *Journal of Personality and Social Psychology*, *46*, 598–609.

Paulhus, D. L. (1986). Self-deception and impression management in test responsesy. In A. Angleitner & J. S. Wiggins (Eds.), *Personality assessment via questionnaires: Current issues in theory and measurement* (pp. 143–165). Berlin, Germany: Springer-Verlag.

Pena, L. M., Megargee, E. I., & Brody, P. (1996). MMPI-A patterns of male juvenile delinquents. *Psychological Assessment*, *8*, 388–397.

Pinsoneault, T. B. (2005). Detecting random, partially random, and nonrandom MMPI-A protocols. *Psychological Assessment*, *17*, 476–480.

Rempel, P. P. (1958). The use of multivariate statistical analysis of MMPI scores in the classification of delinquent and nondelinquent high school boys. *Journal of Consulting Psychology*, *22*, 17–23.

Schinka, J. A., Elkins, D. E., & Archer, R. P. (1998). Effects of psychopathology and demographic characteristics on MMPI-A scale scores. *Journal of Personality Assessment*, *71*, 295–305.

Shaevel, B., & Archer, R. P. (1996). Effects of MMPI-2 and MMPI-A norms on T-score elevations for 18-year-olds. *Journal of Personality Assessment*, *67*, 72–78.

Sherwood, N. E., Ben-Porath, Y. S., & Williams, C. L. (1997). *The MMPI-A Content Component scales: Development, psychometric characteristics, and clinical applications*. Minneapolis: University of Minnesota Press.

Stein, L. A. R., Graham, J. R., & Williams, C. L. (1995). Detecting fake-bad MMPI-A profiles. *Journal of Personality Assessment*, *65*, 415–427.

Weed, N. C., Butcher, J. N., & Williams, C. L. (1994). Development of MMPI-A Alcohol/Drug Problem scales. *Journal of Studies on Alcohol*, *55*, 296–302.

Williams, C. L. (1986). MMPI profiles for adolescents: Interpretive strategies and treatment considerations. *Journal of Child and Adolescent Psychotherapy*, *3*, 179–193.

Williams, C. L., Ben-Porath, Y. S., & Hevern, V. W. (1994). Item level improvements for use with the MMPI with adolescents. *Journal of Personality Assessment*, *63*, 284–293.

Williams, C. L., Butcher, J. N., Ben-Porath, Y. S., & Graham, J. R. (1992). *MMPI-A Content scales: Assessing psychopathology in adolescents*. Minneapolis: University of Minnesota Press.

Wimbish, L. G. (1984). *The importance of appropriate norms for the computerized interpretations of adolescent MMPI profiles*. Unpublished doctoral dissertation, Ohio State University, Columbus.

Chapter 8 ———————————————————

MILLON CLINICAL MULTIAXIAL INVENTORY-III

The Millon Clinical Multiaxial Inventory-III (MCMI-III: Millon, Davis, & Millon, 1994, 1997) is a broadband measure of the major dimensions of psychopathology found in Axis II disorders and some Axis I disorders of the *DSM-IV-TR* (American Psychiatric Association, 2000). The MCMI-III consists of 4 validity (modifier) scales, 11 personality style scales, 3 severe personality style scales, 7 clinical syndrome scales, and 3 severe clinical syndrome scales (see Table 8.1). Table 8.2 provides the general information on the MCMI-III. In contrast to the MMPI-2 (Butcher, Dahlstrom, Graham, Tellegen, & Kaemmer, 1989) that has 120+ additional scales, the MCMI-III does not have any subscales for these basic sets of scales or separate content scales so there are only 28 total scales on the MCMI-III. Consequently, learning to interpret the MCMI-III is more straightforward than the MMPI-2. Recently Grossman and del Rio (2005) described the development of 35 facet scales for the 14 personality style scales that represent the first such attempt to create subscales for any of the versions of the MCMI. These facet scales are very new so there is little research on them or clinical information on their use. They are described briefly later in this chapter.

HISTORY

Millon (1983; Millon & Davis, 1996) conceptualized an evolutionary framework for personality in which the interface of three polarities (pleasure-pain; active-passive; self-other) determines an individual's specific personality style as an adaptation to the environment. The pleasure-pain polarity involves either seeking pleasure as a way of enhancing life or avoiding pain as a way of constricting life. The active-passive polarity involves either working to change unfavorable aspects of the environment or accepting unfavorable aspects that cannot be changed.

Table 8.3 presents the functional processes and structural domains for each of the 14 personality disorder styles in the MCMI-III. Millon et al. (1997) believe that each cell of this matrix contains the diagnostic attribute or criterion that best captures the personality style within that specific functional process or structural domain. Reading down each column provides an overview of how each personality style differs on each functional process or structural domain. Reading across each row provides an overview of how each personality style can be described.

Millon's conceptual system for personality disorders does not map directly onto the *DSM-IV-TR* (American Psychiatric Association, 2000) Axis II personality disorders. The latter is an atheoretical categorical system that describes the behaviors and symptoms needed

Table 8.1   Millon Clinical Multiaxial Inventory-III (MCMI-III)

Modifying Indices (Validity Scales)

V	Validity Index
X	Disclosure Index
Y	Desirability Index
Z	Debasement Index

Personality Styles

1	Schizoid
2A	Avoidant
2B	Depressive
3	Dependent
4	Histrionic
5	Narcissistic
6A	Antisocial
6B	Sadistic (Aggressive)
7	Compulsive
8A	Negativistic (Passive-Aggressive)
8B	Masochistic

Severe Personality Styles

S	Schizotypal
C	Borderline
P	Paranoid

Clinical Syndromes

A	Anxiety Disorder
H	Somatoform Disorder
N	Bipolar Disorder: Manic
D	Dysthymic Disorder
B	Alcohol Dependence
T	Drug Dependence
R	Posttraumatic Stress Disorder

Severe Clinical Syndromes

SS	Thought Disorder
CC	Major Depression
PP	Delusional Disorder

to make a specific personality disorder diagnosis. Millon also includes personality disorders such as Sadistic (Aggressive) and Depressive on the MCMI-III that are not included in the *DSM-IV-TR*.

MCMI (First Edition)

The original MCMI (Millon, 1977) had five major distinguishing features when compared with the MMPI (Hathaway & McKinley, 1951), which was the primary self-report inventory in use at the time. First, the MCMI was developed following Millon's comprehensive

Table 8.2   Millon Multiaxial Clinical Inventory-III (MCMI-III)

Authors:	Millon, Davis, Millon
Published:	1994
Edition:	3rd
Publisher:	Pearson Assessments
Website:	www.PearsonAssessments.com/tests/MCMI_3
Age range:	18+
Reading level:	8th grade
Administration formats:	Paper/pencil, computer, CD, cassette
Languages:	Spanish
Number of items:	175
Response format:	True/False
Administration time:	25–30 minutes
Primary scales:	4 Validity, 11 Personality Styles, 3 Severe Personality Styles, 7 Clinical Syndromes, 3 Severe Clinical Syndromes
Additional scales:	35 (42) Facet
Hand scoring:	Templates
General texts:	Choca (2004), Craig (2005), Jankowski (2002), Millon et al. (1997), Retzlaff (1995), Strack (2002)
Computer interpretation:	Pearson Assessments (Millon); Psychological Assessment Resources (Craig)

clinical theory described earlier, in contrast to the atheoretical or empirical development of the original MMPI (see Chapter 6). Second, the MCMI contained specific scales to assess personality disorders, the more enduring personality characteristics of patients, which would be incorporated into Axis II of the forthcoming diagnostic system at the time, that is, *DSM-III* (American Psychiatric Association, 1980). Third, the comparison group consisted of a representative sample of psychiatric patients instead of normal individuals, which would facilitate differential diagnosis among patients. Fourth, scores on the scales were transformed into actuarial base rates. These base rates reflected the actual frequency with which various forms of psychopathology occurred rather than traditional standard scores, which measure how far the person deviates from the mean of normal individuals. Finally, the MCMI was designed to use as few items as possible to achieve these goals. At 175 items, the MCMI was and remains the shortest self-report inventory that is a broadband measure of the major dimensions of psychopathology.

The original MCMI had four items that evaluated whether the person had read the items. These four items will become the Validity (*V*) scale on the ensuing editions of the MCMI that assess the consistency of item endorsement.

The original MCMI did not have explicit validity scales to assess the accuracy of item endorsement. Instead a weight factor was developed based on the variation of the person's score from the midpoint of the total raw score for the eight basic personality scales. When this total raw score was below 110, the person was thought to be too cautious in reporting problematic behaviors and symptoms of psychopathology so their scores would need to be adjusted upward. Conversely, when the total raw score was above 130, the person was thought to be too open or self-revealing so their scores would need to be adjusted downward.

Table 8.3   Expression of personality disorders across the functional and structural domains of personality

	Disorder	Functional Processes			
		Expressive Arts	Interpersonal Conduct	Cognitive Style	Regulatory Mechanisms
1	**Schizoid**	Impassive	Unengaged	Impoverished	Intellectualization
2A	**Avoidant**	Fretful	Aversive	Distracted	Fantasy
2B	**Depressive**	Disconsolate	Defenseless	Pessimistic	Asceticism
3	**Dependent**	Incompetent	Submissive	Naïve	Introjection
4	**Histrionic**	Dramatic	Attention-Seeking	Flighty	Dissociation
5	**Narcissistic**	Haughty	Exploitive	Expansive	Rationalization
6A	**Antisocial**	Impulsive	Irresponsible	Deviant	Acting Out
6B	**Sadistic**	Precipitate	Abrasive	Dogmatic	Isolation
7	**Compulsive**	Disciplined	Respectful	Constricted	Reaction Formation
8A	**Negativistic**	Resentful	Contrary	Skeptical	Displacement
8B	**Masochistic**	Abstinent	Deferential	Diffident	Exaggeration
S	**Schizotypal**	Eccentric	Secretive	Autistic	Undoing
C	**Borderline**	Spasmodic	Paradoxical	Capricious	Regression
P	**Paranoid**	Defensive	Provocative	Suspicious	Projection

	Disorder	Structural Attributes			
		Self-Image	Object Representation	Morphologic Organization	Mood/ Temperament
1	**Schizoid**	Complacent	Meager	Undifferentiated	Apathetic
2A	**Avoidant**	Alienated	Vexations	Fragile	Anguished
2B	**Depressive**	Worthless	Forsaken	Depleted	Melancholic
3	**Dependent**	Inept	Immature	Inchoate	Pacific
4	**Histrionic**	Gregarious	Shallow	Disjointed	Fickle
5	**Narcissistic**	Admirable	Contrived	Spurious	Insouciant
6A	**Antisocial**	Autonomous	Debased	Unruly	Callous
6B	**Sadistic**	Combative	Pernicious	Eruptive	Hostile
7	**Compulsive**	Conscientious	Concealed	Compartmentalized	Solemn
8A	**Negativistic**	Discontented	Vacillating	Divergent	Irritable
8B	**Masochistic**	Undeserving	Discredited	Inverted	Dysphoric
S	**Schizotypal**	Estranged	Chaotic	Fragmented	Distraught or Insensitive
C	**Borderline**	Uncertain	Incompatible	Split	Labile
P	**Paranoid**	Inviolable	Unalterable	Inelastic	Irascible

Note: Self-Other are reversed in Compulsive and Negativistic.
Source: MCMI-III Manual, second edition (p. 27), by T. Millon, R. Davis, and C. Millon, 1997, Minneapolis, MN: National Computer Systems. Reprinted with permission from table 2.2.

This weight factor will become an explicit validity (modifier) scale (Disclosure [X]) on the ensuing forms of the MCMI.

MCMI-II (Second Edition)

The second edition of the MCMI (MCMI-II: Millon, 1987) appeared in 1987 to enhance several features of the original MCMI. Two new personality disorder scales (Aggressive/Sadistic and Self-Defeating [Masochistic]) and three validity (modifier) scales (Disclosure [X], Desirability [Y], and Debasement [Z]) scales were added to the profile form. Forty-five new items (45/175 = 25.7%) were added to replace 45 extant items that did not add sufficient discriminating power to their scales. Modifications also were made in the MCMI-II items to bring the scales into closer coordination with *DSM-III-R* (American Psychiatric Association, 1987). An item-weighting procedure was added wherein items with greater prototypicality for a given scale were given higher weights of 2 or 3. If an item was endorsed in the nonscored direction, it was assigned a weight of 0. If an item was endorsed in the scored direction, it was assigned a weight of 1, 2, or 3 depending on how prototypical the item was for that scale with the most prototypical items assigned a weight of 3.

The replacement of one-quarter of the items from the original MCMI limits the generalizability of its results to the MCMI-II. Even though the scales still have the same name, the actual items composing a scale may have changed substantially. The introduction of the increased weighting of prototypical items on each MCMI-II scale also alters the relationship among the items within the scale and with other scales.

MCMI-III (Third Edition)

The third edition of the MCMI (Millon et al., 1994, 1997) appeared in 1994 with four major changes. First, 95 (95/175 = 54.3%) new items were introduced to parallel the substantive nature of the then forthcoming *DSM-IV* criteria (American Psychiatric Association, 1994). Second, two new scales were added: one personality style (Depressive) and one clinical syndrome scale (Posttraumatic Stress Disorder). Third, a small set of items was added to strengthen the Noteworthy responses in the areas of child abuse, anorexia, and bulimia. Finally, the weighting of items was reduced to only two levels with the more prototypical items for a specific scale adding two points to the raw score.

The generalizability of the research results from the MCMI-II to the MCMI-III need to be made cautiously because over one-half of the items were changed. The emphasis in these new items also tended to be on *DSM-IV* criteria. It appears that the emphasis in the MCMI-III is toward the *DSM-IV* criteria for personality disorders; whereas the emphasis in the MCMI-II was toward Millon's theory.

ADMINISTRATION

The first issue in the administration of the MCMI-III is ensuring that the individual is invested in the process. Taking a few extra minutes to answer any questions the individual may have about why the MCMI-III is being administered and how the results will be used will pay excellent dividends. This issue may be even more important with the MCMI-III than with other self-report inventories because of the relatively limited number of items on each scale and the extensive item overlap that quickly compounds the effect of the individual distorting responses to even a few items. The clinician should work diligently to make the assessment process a collaborative activity with the individual to obtain the desired information. This issue of therapeutic assessment (Finn, 1996; Fischer, 1994) was covered in more depth in Chapter 2 (pp. 43–44).

Reading level is a crucial factor in determining whether a person can complete the MCMI-III; inadequate reading ability is a major cause of inconsistent patterns of item endorsement. Millon et al. (1997) suggest that most clients who have had at least *8* years of formal education can take the MCMI-III with little or no difficulty because the items are written on an eighth-grade level or less. If there is some concern about the person's reading level, he or she can be asked to read a few items out loud to obtain a quick estimate of whether reading is a problem. In those individuals for whom reading is difficult, the MCMI-III can be presented by CD or audiocassette tape.

SCORING

Scoring the MCMI-III by hand is a complex process that commonly results in scoring errors (Millon et al., 1997, p. 112). If computer scoring is not available, each MCMI-III should be hand scored and profiled independently by two different individuals and their scores verified to catch such errors. If the MCMI-III is administered by computer, the computer automatically scores it. If the individual's responses to the items have been placed on an answer sheet, these responses can be entered into the computer by the clinician for scoring or they can be hand scored. If the clinician enters the item responses into the computer for scoring, they should be double entered to identify any data entry errors.

The first step in hand scoring is to examine the answer sheet carefully and indicate omitted items and double-marked items by drawing a line through both the "true" and "false" responses to these latter items in brightly colored ink. Also, cleaning up the answer sheet is helpful and facilitates scoring. Responses that were changed need to be erased completely if possible, or clearly marked with an "X" so that the clinician is aware that this response has not been endorsed by the client.

The next step is to determine whether any of the three Validity (*V*) scale items (65, 110, 157) have been endorsed as being "True." If two or more of these items have been endorsed as being "True," scoring is unwarranted and should stop; it is probably unwarranted even if only one of them has been endorsed as "True."

The number of omitted items, which is the total number of items not marked and double marked, is scored without a template. There is no standard place on the profile form on which the number of omitted items is reported so the clinician should make it explicit if, and how many, items have been omitted when it does occur. All the other scales except for Scale *X* (Disclosure) are scored by placing a plastic template over the answer sheet with a small box drawn at the scored (deviant) response—either "true" or "false"—for each item on the scale. The responses on the MCMI-III are weighted either "1" or "2," with the responses weighted "2" being prototypic for that scale. The sum of these *weighted* responses equals the client's raw score for that scale; this raw score is recorded in the proper space on the hand-scoring worksheet. All scoring templates are made of plastic and must be kept away from heat.

The raw score on Scale X (Disclosure) is the sum of the raw scores for the 11 personality style scales (Scales *1* through *8B*) except that Scale *5* is weighted by two-thirds because it is longer than the other scales. If the total score is a fraction of some number, it is rounded to the nearest whole number. The raw score on Scale X is then entered in the proper space on the hand-scoring worksheet.

Once the client's raw score for each scale has been determined, then the base rate (BR) score must be looked up in the appropriate table in the *MCMI-III Manual* (Millon et al., 1997) based on the client's gender (men: Appendix C-1; women: Appendix C-2). The BR scores are entered in the proper space on the hand-scoring worksheet; these scores are *not* the final BR scores that ultimately will be entered on the bottom of the hand-scoring profile. The Validity Scale (*V*) is *not* transformed into a BR score; rather it is interpreted as a raw score.

Four potential adjustments can be made in these BR scores before they are plotted: Disclosure; Anxiety/Depression; Inpatient; and Denial/Complaint. Each of these adjustments is based on the assumption that the factor in question (excessive or minimal disclosure; presence of an anxiety or depression diagnosis; inpatient status; and excessive denial) requires a general raising or lowering of the BR scores. The Disclosure Adjustment raises or lowers all the BR scores on all 11 personality style scales (Scales *1* through *8B*). If Scale X (Disclosure) is low (<61) then all scales are increased, whereas if the Scale X is high (>123) then all scores are decreased. The exact amount of increase or decrease in BR score must be looked up in Appendix D. No Disclosure Adjustment is made when the Disclosure scale is in the range of 61 to 123.

The Anxiety/Depression Adjustment is used to lower the BR scores of five scales (*2A* [Avoidant]; *2B* [Depressive]; *8B* [Masochistic]; *S* [Schizotypal]; and *C* [Borderline]) if the individual is in the midst of an acute emotional state. This adjustment is made if the individual's score on Scale *A* (Anxiety) or *D* (Dysthymia) is equal to or greater than a BR score of 75, which is the cutting score that indicates the presence of one or the other of these syndromes. When either Scale *A* or *D* is elevated in this range, the A/D value is computed by subtracting 75 from the BR score for that Scale. When both Scales are elevated in this range, the A/D value is computed by adding the BR scores for these two scales and subtracting 150. The specific table that is used within Appendix D in making the BR adjustment for this A/D value depends on whether the person is an inpatient or an outpatient, and the length of hospitalization.

The Inpatient Adjustment is determined by the person's treatment setting and the duration of the Axis I disorder. The BR score for three severe clinical syndrome scales (*SS* [Thought Disorder]; *CC* [Major Depression]; *PP* [Delusional Disorder]) is adjusted when the person is an inpatient. The exact amount of the adjustment depends on the duration of the Axis I disorder.

If any of these four adjustments in the BR score for a scale result in a BR less than 0 or greater than 115, then the BR is changed to 0 or 115. There should not be any BR scores less than 0 or greater than 115. If the increase of the BR for any scale, because of one of these four adjustments, results in a BR greater than 115, such as 119 or 124, it is lowered to a BR score of 115. Similarly, if the decrease of the BR for any scale results in a BR less than 0, such as −5 or −9, it is increased to a BR score of 0.

Plotting the profile is the next step in the scoring process. In essence, the clinician transfers all the final BR scores from the hand-scoring worksheet to the appropriate column of the profile sheet (see Figure 8.1). Each column on the profile sheet is used to represent the final BR scores for a specific scale. Each dash represents a raw score of 1 with the larger dashes marking increments of 5. Thus, the clinician notes the individual's final BR score on the scale being plotted and makes a point or dot at the appropriate dash. A similar procedure is followed for the other sets of scales on the profile sheet: personality style scales; severe personality style scales; clinical syndrome scales; and severe clinical syndrome scales.

Raw scores on the MCMI-III are transformed into base rate (BR) scores rather than standard scores such as the T scores used on the original MMPI. Millon et al. (1997) believed that there are two problems with the standard scores used by other self-report inventories, which compare the individual to some reference group. First, if the distribution of the raw scores for each scale is not the same, which is almost always the case, the T scores do not have the same meaning from one scale to the next. (The use of uniform T scores on the MMPI-2 addressed this issue by making the percentiles of the raw scores equivalent across all the scales before converting them to T scores.) Second, the prevalence rate of most clinical disorders rarely matches the normal distribution that underlines standard scores in which 2.0% of the sample will score two standard deviations above the mean. For a disorder such as Alcohol Dependence, which has a lifetime prevalence of about 8% in adults (*DSM-IV*: American Psychiatric Association, 1994), using a cutting score of two standard deviations above the mean would miss approximately 6% of these adults.

These problems of standard scores are avoided by using criterion referencing that underlies the BR scores used on the MCMI-III. The initial base rate transformations for each of the MCMI-III scales were anchored at three BR scores. A BR score of 0 was assigned to a raw score of 0, a BR score of 60 was assigned to the median value on the scale, and a BR score of 115 was assigned to the maximum raw score. Next BR scores of 75 and 85 were defined for each scale. For the 14 personality style scales (Scales *1* [Schizoid] through *P* [Paranoid]), a BR of 75 indicated the *presence of a trait*, and a BR of 85 indicated the *presence of a disorder*. For the remaining scales (Scales *A* [Anxiety] through *PP* [Delusional Disorder]), a BR of 75 indicated the *presence of a syndrome*, and a BR of 85 indicated the *prominence of a syndrome*. A BR score of 85 was fixed at the point on the raw score distribution that matched the prevalence rate of the disorder or prominence of the syndrome being measured by that scale. A BR score of 75 was assigned to the raw score that matched the sum of the presence of a trait and disorder or the sum of the presence and prominence of the syndrome being measured by that scale. Once these five BR scores were defined, the intermediate BR scores were assigned by linear interpolation.

The BR scores for the three validity scales (Scales *X* [Disclosure]; *Y* [Desirability]; and *Z* [Debasement]) were assigned somewhat differently. A BR score of 85 was set to indicate the highest 10% of the patient sample and BR scores of 75 to 84 indicated the next 15%. BR scores below 35 were defined as the lowest 15% of the patient sample. A person who has a BR score of at or above 85 on Scale *X* would be in the highest 10% of individuals in the patient sample that was used to create the norms for the MCMI-III. A person who has a BR score below 35 on Scale *X* would be in the lowest 15% of individuals in the patient sample.

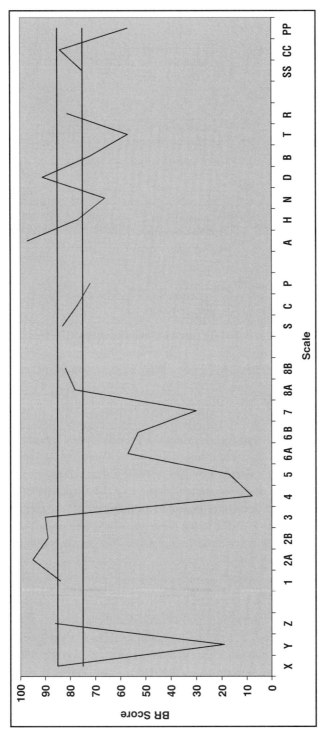

Figure 8.1 MCMI-III profile 2a30: avoidant—dependent.

259

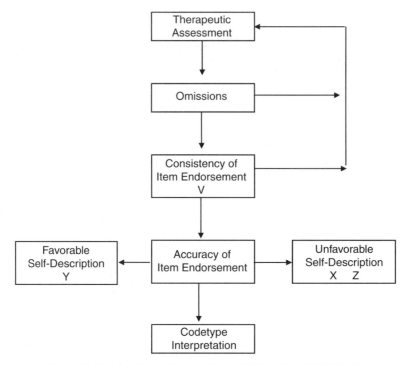

Figure 8.2   Flowchart for assessing validity of the MCMI-III.

ASSESSING VALIDITY

Figure 8.2 provides the flowchart for assessing the validity of this specific administration of the MCMI-III and the criteria for using this flowchart are provided in Table 8.4. The clinician is reminded that the criteria provided in Table 8.4 are continuous, yet ultimately the decisions that must be made in implementation of the flowchart in Figure 8.2 are dichotomous. General guidelines will be provided for translating these continuous data into dichotomous decisions on the MCMI-III, but these guidelines need to be considered within the constraints of a specific client and the circumstances for the evaluation.

Item Omissions

Item omissions consist of the total number of items that the individual fails to answer, or answers both "true" and "false." These omitted item(s) should be reviewed to see if there is any theme to them. The individual also should be queried carefully about any omitted items among the Noteworthy Responses to Self-Destructive Potential (24, 44, 112, 128, 142, 150, 151, 154, 171), and the explanation documented.

Mandell (1997) examined the effects of randomly omitting 11 items from the MCMI-II in a sample of clinical patients, who originally had omitted no items. Omitting 11 items lowered the base rate score, originally above a cutting score of 75, below this cutting

Table 8.4   Criteria for assessing MCMI-III validity by type of setting

	Percentile										
	1	2	7	16	30	50	70	84	93	98	99
Item Omissions											
Clinical[a]	—	—	—	—	—	—	0	1	4	13	20
Consistency of Item Endorsement (Validity [V])											
Clinical[a]	—	—	—	—	—	—	—	—	—	0	1
Correctional[b]	—	—	—	—	—	—	—	—	—	0	1	2
Accuracy of Item Endorsement											
Self-Unfavorable (Disclosure Index [Scale X])											
Clinical[a]	52	56	68	82	97	118	140	158	169	—	—
Clinical[c]	—	—	—	60	—	—	122	146	—	—	—
Correctional[b]	41	45	53	60	68	81	98	117	137	161	172
Self-Unfavorable (Debasement Index [Scale Z])											
Clinical[a]	—	—	1	4	8	14	20	24	27	30	31
Correctional[b]	—	—	—	0	1	3	7	12	18	24	26
Clinical[c]	—	—	—	1	—	—	18	24	—	—	—
Accuracy of Item Endorsement											
Self-Favorable (Desirability Index [Scale Y])											
Clinical[a]	1	2	4	6	9	12	14	16	18	19	20
Correctional[b]	—	5	9	11	14	16	17	18	19	20	21
Clinical[c]	—	—	—	6	—	—	15	18	—	—	—

[a]Haddy et al. (2005).
[b]Retzlaff et al. (2002).
[c]Millon et al. (1997).

score in more than 25% of these patients for six scales: 7 (Compulsive); *P* (Paranoid); *H* (Somatoform); *N* (Bipolar: Manic); *PP* (Delusional Disorder); and *Y* (Desirability). Such a reduction in the base rate score would have resulted in raising different interpretive and diagnostic hypotheses. At a cutting score of 85, six additional scales (*4* [Histrionic], *S* [Schizotypal], *C* [Borderline], *D* [Dysthymia], *CC* [Major Depression], and *X* [Disclosure]) fell below this cutting score more than 25% of the time. She concluded that Scales 7 (Compulsive) and *N* (Bipolar: Manic) were particularly sensitive to the omission of items. She did not suggest an actual number of items that could be omitted and the MCMI-II still interpreted safely. She did suggest that this number is less than the 12 items reported by Millon (1987).

Item omissions are particularly troublesome on the MCMI-III because of the extensive item overlap that characterizes the scales with 120 (68.6%) items scored on more than one scale, although items are only assigned a 2-point weight on a single scale. Nine items (7, 22, 41, 83, 141, 142, 148, 151, 166) are scored on six or more scales and item 148 actually is scored on 11 different scales.

Millon et al. (1997) stated that 12 omitted items is excessive, and they encourage the clinician to have the individual try to answer these items. Haddy, Strack, and Choca (2005) are the only researchers who have provided data on the frequency with which items are omitted on the MCMI-III (see Table 8.4). Few items are omitted on the MCMI-III with 70% of clinical patients omitting no items. Omitting 12 items is approximately the 98th percentile in this sample, which would support the contention of Millon et al. that 12 omitted items is excessive.

Consistency of Item Endorsement

Consistency of item endorsement on the MCMI-III is assessed by the Validity (V) scale, which consists of three implausible items that empirically are not endorsed by anyone. The total score on the V scale is the number of these three items that are endorsed in the deviant ("true") direction. The V scale is the only MCMI-III scale that is scored as a raw score, that is, it is not transformed into a base rate score. Scores on the V scale (see Table 8.4) are very similar in clinical (Haddy et al., 2005) and correctional inmate samples (Retzlaff, Stoner, & Kleinsasser, 2002) with raw scores of one at or above the 98th percentile. Endorsing even one of the items on the V scale should raise serious concerns about the consistency of item endorsement and whether interpretation should proceed at all past this point.

Figure 8.3 shows the profiles for random, "all-true," and "all-false" responses on the MCMI-III. These profiles were constructed making only the Scale X (Disclosure) and Anxiety/Depression adjustments to the BR scores. The validity (modifier) scales of X (Disclosure) and Z (Debasement), the three severe personality scales and all of the clinical syndrome scales easily identify "all-true," and "all-false" profiles with all of these scales being at BR scores of 90+ or 20, respectively. However, all the validity (modifier), personality style, and clinical syndrome scales for the random profile look very interpretable if the Validity (V) scale is not evaluated. Charter and Lopez (2002) demonstrated that 12.4% of random profiles will produce a raw score of zero and 37.7% a raw score of one on the V scale. Their data would suggest that raw scores of even one on the V scale should be considered to be inconsistent.

Accuracy of Item Endorsement

Self-Unfavorable Descriptions

Self-unfavorable descriptions of psychopathology on the MCMI-III can be assessed by Scales X (Disclosure Index) and Z (Debasement Index). Scale X is the sum of the raw scores for the 11 personality style scales (Scales 1 through $8B$) except that Scale 5 is weighted by two-thirds because it is longer than the other scales. Scale X is basically a measure of how much the person deviates from the mean number of items endorsed by all patients. Higher scores indicate that the person has endorsed more items than the typical patient, which may reflect a self-unfavorable description or the presence of more severe psychopathology. The raw score on Scale X is converted to a base rate (BR) score by looking it up in the appropriate table in the *MCMI-III Manual* (Millon et al., 1997) based on the client's gender (men: Appendix C-1; women: Appendix C-2). When the *raw* score on

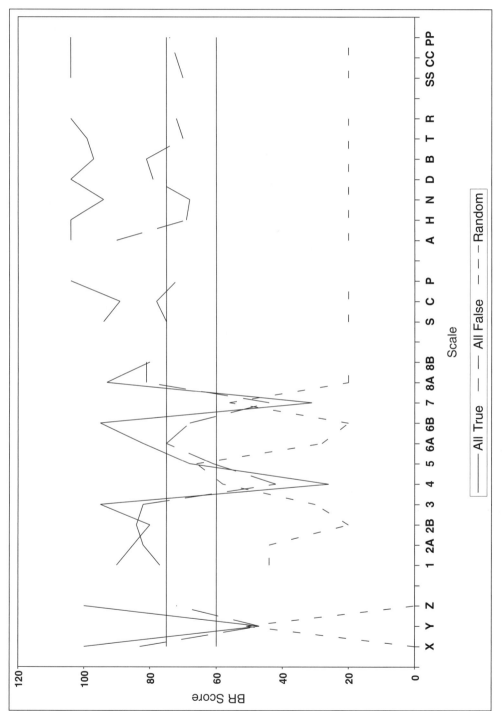

Figure 8.3 MCMI-III profile for random, all true, and all false responses.

Scale X is above 178, the profile should be considered as invalid because of the extremely self-unfavorable description.

Scale Z (Debasement) assesses whether individuals are being more self-deprecating or devaluing of themselves by reporting a larger number of symptoms and deviant behaviors than would be expected based on an objective review of their clinical status. There are no unique items on Scale Z and no prototypical items; its items are all scored on at least one other scale. High scores on Scale Z may reflect a plea for help from a patient who is experiencing overwhelming psychological distress. In such cases, this extreme level of distress should be readily apparent in the clinical interview. If such an extreme level of distress is not apparent, the clinician should entertain the hypothesis that the person is self-deprecating.

Table 8.4 shows that raw scores above 160 (BR score of 91) on Scale X (Disclosure Index) are at the 93rd percentile in clinical samples (Haddy et al., 2005) and the 98th percentile in correctional inmate samples (Retzlaff et al., 2002). Raw scores above 24 (BR score of 83) on Scale Z (Debasement Index) are at the 93rd percentile in clinical samples (Haddy et al., 2005) and the 99th percentile in correctional inmate samples (Retzlaff et al., 2002). Clinical patients appear to be slightly more likely to make a self-unfavorable description than correctional inmates.

Once it has been determined that the individual has made an extremely self-unfavorable description of psychopathology, the clinician will need to ascertain the reasons for the inaccurate item endorsement by a clinical interview. It remains to be determined whether it is possible to readminister the MCMI-III to an individual who has made an extremely self-unfavorable description of psychopathology and obtain an accurate pattern of item endorsement. In any event, the clinician must remember that none of the MCMI-III scales can be interpreted when it has been determined that the individual has made an extremely unfavorable self-description as suggested by very elevated raw and BR scores on Scales X (Disclosure Index) and Z (Debasement Index).

Self-Favorable Description

Self-favorable descriptions of psychopathology on the MCMI-III are assessed by Scale Y (Desirability Index). Scale Y assesses the person's tendency to appear socially attractive and emotionally well composed. There are no unique items on Scale Y and no prototypical items; its items are all scored on at least one other scale. BR scores equal to or greater than 75 indicate a tendency to describe oneself in favorable terms. As Scale Y goes higher than 75, it is more likely that the person is trying very diligently not to report any type of psychopathology or interpersonal difficulties. Millon et al. (1997) do not attempt to determine whether this favorable self-description assessed by Scale Y reflects impression management or self-deception (Paulhus, 1984).

Table 8.4 shows that raw scores above 18 (BR score of 84) on Scale Y (Desirability Index) are at the 98th percentile in clinical samples (Haddy et al., 2005) and the 84th percentile in correctional inmate samples (Retzlaff et al., 2002) and the total MCMI-III normative group (Millon et al., 1997). Raw scores on Scale Y appear to be less variable across settings than Scales X (Disclosure Index) and Z (Debasement Index), which assess self-unfavorable descriptions.

When a client's responses have been identified as being endorsed inaccurately because of an extremely self-favorable description of psychopathology, the MCMI-III profile is no longer interpretable. The clinician will have little reason to try to interpret such a profile, because extremely self-favorable descriptions result in no individual scales being elevated over a BR score of 60 and frequently most scales are near a BR score of 0. The clinician should determine the potential causes for this self-favorable description, and assess the implications for treatment and intervention. An MCMI-III profile produced by an extremely self-favorable description of psychopathology is not interpretable because no scales are elevated, which is the antithesis of the MCMI-III profile produced by an extremely self-unfavorable description of psychopathology.

Individuals who provide extremely self-favorable descriptions of psychopathology see their problems as less troubling to themselves and, hence, are less motivated to change. Their problems also may be more chronic in nature and, consequently, they may be more difficult to treat if they remain in treatment. None of these potential causes of an extremely self-favorable description of psychopathology is a good prognostic sign for any type of psychological intervention.

INTERPRETATION

Once it has been determined that the individual has omitted few, if any, items, and endorsed the items consistently and accurately, the MCMI-III can be interpreted. Millon et al. (1997) suggest that the MCMI-III can either be interpreted by individual scales or configurally, by looking at combinations of individual scales. In the former approach, the clinician simply determines which individual scales are at or exceed the BR cutting scores of 75 and 85. BR scores at or above 75 indicate the presence of clinically significant traits for Axis II disorders and the presence of a syndrome for Axis I disorders. BR scores at or above 85 indicate that the psychopathology is pervasive enough to be called a personality disorder for Axis II disorders, and the prominence of a syndrome for Axis I disorders. The interpretation of these individual scales can then be supplemented by the examination of prototypic items for each scale (Millon et al., 1997). In the latter approach, combinations of the two or three highest scales are considered as a whole, that is, configurally, because the interpretation of one scale can be changed drastically by an elevation on two other scales. The next section provides illustrations of configural interpretation of MCMI-III profiles. Choca (2004), Craig (2005), Jankowski (2002), Millon et al. (1997), Retzlaff (1995), and Strack (2002) provide examples of the general interpretive strategy for the MCMI-III.

Millon et al. (1997, pp. 27–48) provide the prototypic description for each of the personality disorders being assessed by each personality style scale based on the functional and structural organization. The functional processes are divided into expressive acts, interpersonal conduct, cognitive style, and regulatory mechanisms. The structural attributes are divided into self-image, object representations, morphological organization, and mood/temperament. They also include the specific MCMI-III items that map onto each of the *DSM-IV* criteria for that personality disorder. These items illustrate how the MCMI-III maps more onto the *DSM-IV* criteria than Millon's theory of personality disorders.

Millon et al. (1997, pp. 80–88) also provide the median profile of various diagnostic groups on the MCMI-II that illustrate the general configuration of all the scales for each group. To the extent that the MCMI-III corresponds to the MCMI-II, these median profiles provide the clinician with a general idea of what pattern of scores on the various scales would be expected.

Commonly Occurring MCMI-III Configurations

Choca (2004) recommends interpreting configurally only the three highest elevations among the original eight personality style scales (*1* [Schizoid]; *2A* [Avoidant]; *3* [Dependent]; *4* [Histrionic]; *5* [Narcissistic]; *6A* [Antisocial]; *7* [Compulsive]; and *8A* [Negativistic]). This approach does not use Millon's three new personality style scales that were added to the MCMI-II and MCMI-III (*2B* [Depressive]; *6B* [Aggressive/Sadistic]; and *8B* [Self-Defeating]). Using all possible combinations of the three highest scales among the eight original personality style scales would result in a total of 336 potential configural interpretations. Choca (2004) has reduced this number to 80 configural interpretations that represent the most commonly occurring configurations. Some configurations rarely occur in any setting such as configurations involving Scales 1 (Schizoid) and 4 (Histrionic). Retzlaff, Ofman, Hyer, and Matheson (1994) found that 20 configurations of two scales accounted for 80% of the MCMI-II profiles that were encountered in VA patients.

There are 14 two-point codetypes that occurred frequently in Haddy et al.'s (2005) sample of clinical inpatients and outpatients (see Table 8.5). These 14 codetypes accounted for 72.2% of these patients. Interpretations are available for 8 of these codetypes in Choca

Table 8.5   Frequency of MCMI-III two-point codetypes[a]

Ranked by Codetype			Ranked by Frequency		
Two-Point			Two-Point		
Codetype	N	%	Codetype	N	%
1-2A/2A-1	160	13.7	*1-2A/2A-1*	160	13.7
1-2B/2B-1	67	5.7	2A-2B/2B-2A	96	8.2
1-3/3-1	49	4.2	1-6A/6A-1	95	8.1
1-6A/6A-1	95	8.1	2A-3/3-2A	87	7.5
1-8B/8B-1	33	2.8	1-2B/2B-1	67	5.7
2A-2B/2B-2A	96	8.2	2A-6A/6A-2A	62	5.3
2A-3/3-2A	87	7.5	1-3/3-1	49	4.2
2A-6A/6A-2A	62	5.3	7-8A/8A-7	45	3.9
2A-8B/8B-2A	26	2.2	3-6A/6A-3	42	3.6
3-6A/6A-3	42	3.6	5-6A/6A-5	40	3.4
3-8B/8B-3	15	1.3	1-8B/8B-1	33	2.8
5-6A/6A-5	40	3.4	2A-8B/8B-2A	26	2.2
6A-6B/6B-6A	26	2.2	6A-6B/6B-6A	26	2.2
7-8A/8A-7	45	3.9	3-8B/8B-3	15	1.3
All Others	324	27.8	All Others	324	27.8
Total	1167	100.0	Total	843	100.0

Note: All scales were equal to or greater than a BR score of 75.
[a]Haddy et al. (2005).

(2004) and are provided later in this chapter. The last paragraph of each interpretation focuses on the issues encountered in establishing the therapeutic alliance and potential problems that may be encountered in the treatment process. Choca (2004) has provided the interpretation of all 80 commonly occurring MCMI-III configural combinations of the eight basic personality style scales.

These interpretations are based on the *group* of individuals who have endorsed these two personality style scales. The clinician must adapt this interpretation to reflect the specific elevations of all the other MCMI-III scales for this individual as well as the clinical history and interview behavior. The prototypic items that have been endorsed are particularly helpful in adapting the group interpretation for this individual.

Schizoid (1)—Avoidant (2A)[1]

High scores on the Schizoid (*1*) and Avoidant (*2A*) scales of the MCMI-III characterize people who keep a significant emotional distance from others. Such individuals are most comfortable when they are alone and are referred to as the "remote schizoids" (Millon & Davis, 1996). They tend to like jobs or hobbies that involve objects and that have minimal human contact. In extreme cases, these individuals may be single, and their history may show signs of an inability or unwillingness to establish a meaningful relationship outside of the nuclear family. Otherwise, these individuals restrict the number of relationships that they form and tend to have superficial friendships when they do exist.

For these individuals, the inclination to be loners seems to be the result of two different dynamics. First, they appear to be uninterested in interpersonal relations. They are not too adept at understanding and enjoying the subtleties and nuances of interpersonal emotions and communications, a situation that might then have led to their being apathetic about relationships. They typically do not have strong emotions and live fairly bland affective lives. A second dynamic in their lives is that they seem to be sensitive and afraid of being rejected by others. As a result, social situations are a source of significant tension; they feel nervous about and do not look forward to this type of activity. They would like to be accepted and appreciated and realize that they have to take part in social events to obtain that kind of satisfaction. Relating to others, however, is so uncomfortable that they avoid social situations in spite of the positive effects that they could have.

On the positive side, schizoid-avoidant individuals are self-sufficient individuals who do not depend on others for the fulfillment of their own needs. They often lead lives that are fairly free of overemotionality and in which psychological issues tend not to interfere with their behavior. On the other hand, others may perceive them as isolated loners who lead somewhat empty and unproductive lives.

Individuals with this personality style may have difficulty establishing therapeutic alliances. The discomfort that they experience in interpersonal relationships will probably make the sessions unenjoyable. In addition, a therapist also would have to be concerned about such clients feeling rejected any time he or she makes an uncomplimentary interpretation. When the treatment plan involves giving negative feedback or is intended to confront objectionable aspects of the personality or behavior, the client will experience the

[1]From *Interpretive Guide to the Millon Clinical Multiaxial Inventory,* by J. P. Choca, 2004, Washington, DC: American Psychological Association. Reprinted with permission.

therapeutic context as threatening or stressful. To maintain the alliance but still contribute to the client's growth, the therapist must achieve a careful balance between uncritical support and threatening therapeutic work. The therapist also must be ready to allow the emotional distance that such clients may need and to tolerate their inability to talk about their lives and feelings nondefensively. These individuals will feel most enhanced with a therapist who treats them with admiration and respect.

Schizoid (1)—Dependent (3)

Labeled "ineffectual dependent" by Millon (Millon & Davis, 1996), the schizoid-dependent personality style emphasizes introversive aspects accompanied by dependent traits. These individuals lack interest in other people. They do not seem happy when things come out well, nor are they too upset by unfortunate events. They are not interested in interpersonal situations. They are quiet and often stay by themselves, typically taking the role of passive observer, seldom taking sides or verbalizing a strong opinion. Rarely the center of attention, these individuals typically fade into the background. They have few friends; when relationships do exist, they tend to be superficial. They are socially indifferent and have little apparent need to communicate or to obtain support from others.

With the emotional indifference, such clients tend to feel less important or capable than other people. Similar individuals are easily led by others and are submissive and dependent. They are uncomfortable with highly competitive situations, are humble, and try to be as congenial as possible to the people around them. These individuals are probably detached and uninvolved. Cooperative and agreeable individuals, they may be perceived as easygoing and emotionally stable. However, they may be criticized as being somewhat dull, quiet, indifferent, dependent, or apathetic.

A therapist attempting to work with these clients may have difficulty establishing the therapeutic alliance. The therapist will have to be tolerant of these clients' distant way of relating. A somewhat unexciting course of treatment also can be expected. A supportive relationship will be one in which the therapist takes a protective and parental attitude, reassuring clients that problems can be worked out and that help will be available.

Schizoid (1)—Antisocial (6A)

Competitive and introversive traits characterize this "nomadic antisocial" (Millon & Davis, 1996) personality profile of the MCMI-III. Such individuals see their environment as if it were a tournament, with one person pitted against the other. To be able to function in such a situation, they feel that they have to fend for themselves. Such individuals are self-sufficient and do not depend on others to fulfill their needs. They may be somewhat mistrustful and suspicious. They see themselves as being assertive, energetic, self-reliant, strong, and realistic. To make it in the rat race, they believe they must adopt a tough stance. Their assertiveness is justified by pointing to the hostile and exploitative behavior of others.

Individuals with this type of personality may be contemptuous of the weak; they may appear cold, callous, or insensitive to the feelings of others and may tend to be argumentative and contentious. When matters go their way, they may be gracious, cheerful, and friendly. More characteristically, however, their behavior is guarded, reserved, and aggressive. When crossed, pushed, or embarrassed, they may respond impulsively and become angry, vengeful, and vindictive.

In addition these individuals keep an emotional distance from others. These individuals restrict the number of relationships they form and tend to have superficial friendships when they exist and alliances that are more like acquaintanceships than strong friendships.

In the light of this personality style, the establishment of a therapeutic alliance may be somewhat difficult. Clients are not inclined to see psychotherapy as valuable unless it offers a tangible material benefit, such as a way out of a jam. The fact that they are likely to be threatened by or uninterested in emotional closeness also may impede the forming of a relationship. One approach to establishing an alliance in spite of this difficulty may be to accept, at least temporarily, the same competitive outlook that the clients favor. The therapist then may be in the position to help them explore the behaviors and attitudes that get in the way of their being a "winner."

Avoidant (2)—Dependent (3)

Individuals with the avoidant-dependent profile, referred to as "phobic avoidants" by Millon (Millon & Davis, 1996), usually do not have any close friends, so they tend to remain detached and isolated. They view themselves as weak, inadequate, unresourceful, and unattractive. Strongly wishing to be liked and accepted by others, they nevertheless have a great fear of rejection. They often are guarded and experience social situations negatively. They seem apprehensive, shy, or nervous in social situations. These clients usually avoid relating to others, which forces them to give up the support and affection that the relationship might have brought. Thus, life is experienced as a conflict between taking a risk and accepting the discomfort of forming a relationship or retreating to the unfulfilling safety of their isolation. Although these individuals usually are sensitive, compassionate, and emotionally responsive, they also are nervous, awkward, mistrustful, and isolated.

Avoidant (2A)—Antisocial (6A)

According to the MCMI-III, avoidant-antisocial individuals are hypersensitive to the possibility of rejection and look at the environment as a competitive place. Similar individuals feel that to function in this world, they have to fend for themselves. Somewhat distrusting and suspicious, they also see themselves as assertive, energetic, self-reliant, strong, and realistic. They imagine that they have to be tough to make it in the rat race. Justifying their assertiveness by pointing to others' hostile and exploitative behaviors, they may be contemptuous of the weak and may not care whether they are liked, claiming that "good guys come in last."

Individuals with this type of personality are concerned that others will take advantage of their friendship if they are not careful. This fear causes them to be uncomfortable in social situations because they feel that they constantly have to be on guard. As a result, they tend to be nervous and uncomfortable. To avoid the discomfort that is commonly attached to interpersonal contact, they shy away from social situations. These individuals typically like to have friends, but the discomfort associated with the social risk often leads them to forfeit the support that could have been derived from others rather than to take the chance of being mistreated. Such individuals typically are isolated and may function best in situations in which they do not have to interact with many other people.

Individuals obtaining similar MCMI-III scores usually are impulsive. They typically are perceived as being somewhat aggressive and intimidating and perhaps as cold, callous, or insensitive to the feelings of others. They may be argumentative and contentious, even abusive, cruel, or malicious. When matters go their way, they may act in a gracious, cheerful, and friendly manner. More characteristically, however, their behavior is guarded, reserved, and resentful.

In the light of this personality style, such clients can be expected to have some difficulties in establishing a therapeutic alliance. They must overcome a certain amount of discomfort in the relationship and an inability to develop enough trust to truly confide in the therapist. Even after the relationship has been established, the therapist will need to be careful not to offer interpretations that can be experienced as a rejection. To the extent that treatment involves giving negative feedback or confronting objectionable aspects of their personalities or behaviors, these clients will experience the therapeutic context as threatening or conflictual. To maintain the therapeutic alliance while contributing to the client's growth, the therapist must strike a balance between uncritical support and threatening therapeutic work.

Dependent (3)—Antisocial (6A)

The dependent-antisocial profile defines a cooperative personality style with competitive overtones. The life assumption of individuals with this profile is that they are not capable of taking care of themselves and must find someone dependable who will support and protect them. They tend to feel inadequate or insecure and see themselves as being less effective or able than everyone else. They tend to form strong attachments to people who will be the decision makers and take responsibility for their welfare. Concerned with the possibility of losing friends, they may hide their true emotions when the feelings are aggressive or objectionable. These are humble, congenial individuals.

Such individuals perceive the environment as a competitive place. As a result, they are somewhat mistrustful and suspicious of others. Typically, their behavior is guarded and reserved, but they hope that with the help of the people they have risked depending on, they can be strong, realistic, and determined in the rat race of life. Although they do not feel tough or secure by themselves, they look to others to provide protection from a cruel and insensitive world in which people are interested only in personal gain.

In the light of the personality style just described, such clients are likely to be guarded and distant at first, but they nonetheless will be able to form an alliance with any therapist willing to play a benevolent parental role. If guidance is given in an affectionate and understanding manner, the client will experience it as supportive. If part of the treatment plan is to move clients toward more independence or increase their ability to compete in an effective or aggressive manner, clients may feel vulnerable and threatened and may respond with maladaptive behaviors.

Narcissistic (5)—Antisocial (6A)

High scores on the Narcissistic and Antisocial scales suggest a personality style characterized by confident and competitive elements. The main assumption these individuals hold about themselves is that they are special and superior to most other people. Such individuals may tend to exaggerate their abilities and positive attributes, emphasize their past achievements, and depreciate those who refuse to accept their inflated self-image. This narcissism typically is manifested in an air of conviction and self-assurance. When extreme, some individuals are perceived as being conceited and arrogant.

A good person is someone who appears intelligent, outgoing, competent, sophisticated, and so on. Beneath this surface, however, there is a need for approval and a striving to be conspicuous, to evoke affection, and to attract attention from others. These individuals may be impressive at first because they easily express their thoughts and enjoy a natural capacity to draw attention to themselves. They may be capricious, however, and intolerant of frustration. They become bored easily and may move from one enterprise to another.

Another factor in the feelings of superiority may be related to the individuals' tendency to view the environment as a competitive place. They feel that they have to fend for themselves to function. As a result, they are somewhat mistrustful and suspicious. Assertive, energetic, self-reliant, strong, and realistic are adjectives they use to describe themselves. They feel that they have to be tough to survive in a tough world. For them, compassion and warmth are weak emotions that will place them in an inferior position. The competitive outlook fits well with the feelings of superiority as long as they are in situations in which they have a good chance of "winning."

Clients with this personality style may require a therapeutic context in which they feel admired or at least respected. They need to be the center of attention. If confrontation is used in therapy, the therapist must use tact to avoid injuring these clients' narcissism more than they can tolerate. Another problem could arise if clients interpret the confrontation as being part of a competitive relationship and fight it rather than accepting it as useful feedback. On the other hand, there also is a danger that a therapist would be so supportive of the clients' narcissism that he or she gives no negative feedback and does not facilitate growth. Therefore, it is important to find ways to help clients accept their fallibilities and work on their problems without feeling unrecognized or humiliated.

Compulsive (7)—Negativistic (8A)

The compulsive-negativistic personality style may be described as resentful and disciplined. The compulsive-negativistic style results from holding two assumptions about the world that are difficult to integrate. These individuals first assume that they need to rely on others because they are not able to do well without their support. The second premise is that they should strive toward perfection on their own. These two assumptions about life typically bring about one of two different behavior patterns.

In the passive-aggressive substyle, the person handles conflict by being compliant on the surface but not fully supporting the efforts of others along the way. By contrast, the moody variant involves a vacillation between feeling lucky and being able to get more out of life than expected and feeling cheated or mistreated. The behavior changes accordingly. At times these individuals treat others in an agreeable and friendly manner, but they also may be irritable or hostile. Still at other times, these individuals may experience guilt and appear eagerly cooperative and remorseful. An energetic and productive mood, together with high goals, may characterize them on some occasions, but in other instances these individuals are inclined to lower their goals and become less productive.

Such individuals place a premium on avoiding mistakes. They tend to be orderly and plan for the future. They prepare in a conscientious manner and try to do the work on schedule. They strive to be efficient, dependable, industrious, and persistent. They often relate in an overly respectful and ingratiating manner, but they may be somewhat rigid, perfectionistic, and demanding. They have significant problems making decisions by themselves.

Compulsive-negativistic individuals can be moody and irritable. Projection is an important defense, but the direction of the blame tends to change from the self to others. Mostly, these individuals tend to be resentful and conflicted. They typically are difficult to handle and present some problems wherever they go.

Given this personality style, it may be useful to try not to control these clients in ways that are not necessary. Because these clients are bound to resent any control that is placed on them, this tactic can prevent the therapeutic relationship from becoming overly conflictual. They also may benefit from learning how they normally operate and tend to project negative feelings onto others.

Interpretation of Individual Scales

The interpretive text for configurations of MCMI-III scales provides the general description of the *group* of individuals with elevations on these various combinations of scales. The task for the clinician at this juncture is to review all the other individual scales (other personality style scales, severe personality style scales, clinical syndrome scales, and severe clinical syndrome scales) and critical (noteworthy) items for this specific individual to determine how the interpretive text needs to be modified. Once the interpretive text for the MCMI-III has been rendered internally consistent, the clinician then must integrate the clinical history and background into the interpretation.

The individual scales on the MCMI-III are organized within four categories; personality styles; severe personality styles, clinical syndromes, and severe clinical syndromes. Each of these sets of scales will be discussed briefly and general interpretive text for each scale is provided in Table 8.6.

Personality Style Scales

The 11 personality style scales are intended to identify pervasive characteristics of the person's functioning that perpetuate and aggravate their psychological functioning. Eight of these scales correspond to the *DSM-IV* diagnosis with the same name. The other three scales (Scales *2B* [Depressive], *6B* [Sadistic/Aggressive]; *8B* [Masochistic/Self-Defeating]) were not included in *DSM-IV*, but are included in the MCMI-III because they reflect a significant personality style in Millon's theory.

Severe Personality Style Scales

The three severe personality style scales (Scales *S* [Schizotypal]; *C* [Borderline]; *P* [Paranoid]) assess more pathological personality characteristics than the 11 personality style scales. These scales may underlie one or more of the personality style scales.

Clinical Syndrome Scales

The seven clinical syndrome scales identify the major forms of psychopathology found on Axis I of *DSM-IV* (American Psychological Association, 1994). These clinical syndrome scales can be understood as distortions of the person's basic personality pattern that is identified by the preceding two sets of scales. The clinical syndrome scales also are assumed to reflect more transient states, while the former two sets of scales reflect more enduring characteristics of the person.

Severe Clinical Syndrome Scales

The three severe clinical syndrome scales (*SS* [Thought Disorder]; *CC* [Major Depression]; and *PP* [Delusional Disorder]) assess the most serious forms of Axis I psychopathology.

Table 8.6   Interpretation of individual MCMI-III scales

Scale (BR > 74)	Potential Issues
Personality Styles	
1 (Schizoid)	Individuals prefer to do things by themselves and do not show their feelings. They have little desire for close relations and have few close friends other than their family. They experience little pleasure or pain from life.
2A (Avoidant)	Individuals desire, but are fearful of, personal relations because of the possibility of ridicule and rejection from others. They are vigilant and always on guard to avoid rejection. They are very self-conscious and tense in social situations.
2B (Depressive)	Individuals are pervasively sad and guilty and blame themselves when anything goes wrong. They worry constantly and perceive themselves as worthless. They have given up hope that pleasure can be ever happen again.
3 (Dependent)	Individuals are agreeable and submissive, and try to please others even when they dislike them. They fear others' anger or rejection if they disagree with them. They allow others to make their decisions for them and others can change their mind easily. They are frightened of being alone without someone on whom they can depend.
4 (Histrionic)	Individuals show their feelings quickly and easily. They are sociable, outgoing, like to flirt, and are looking to make new friends. They constantly are in search of signs of acceptance and approval from others.
5 (Narcissistic)	Individuals think that they are special and superior individuals who deserve special attention from other people who envy their abilities. They do not blame anyone who takes advantage of others who let them do it. Members of their family believe that they are selfish and only think of themselves.
6A (Antisocial)	Individuals had behavioral problems in school and have been in trouble with the law. They do what they want without worrying about what others might think, and punishment never stops them from doing something they want to do. They are good at making up excuses when they get into trouble. They are irresponsible and impulsive.
6B (Sadistic) [Aggressive]	Individuals often criticize others who annoy them and are rough and mean to keep people in line. They often say cruel things just to make others unhappy. They get personal pleasure and satisfaction in ways that humiliate others. They believe that it is important to place strict controls on others.
7 (Compulsive)	Individuals believe it is important to follow the rules and have a routine for doing things. Others see them as serious, reserved, proper, and moral individuals. Their compulsiveness and perfectionism derive from a conflict between anger toward others and the fear of social disapproval. Their work is well planned and organized and they keep close track of their money.
8A (Negativistic) [Passive-Aggressive]	Individuals are often cross and grouchy and likely to feel angry about and resist what others want them to do. Other people often blame them for things that they did not do. They experience endless conflicts because of their ambivalence about defiance of and deference to others. They have bad luck in life and believe that most successful people are either lucky or dishonest.

(continued)

Table 8.6   (*Continued*)

Scale (BR > 74)	Potential Issues
8B (Masochistic) [Self-Defeating]	Individuals are often mistreated by their friends and they seem to create situations in which they get hurt or feel rejected. They believe that they do not deserve the good things that happen to them. They get confused and upset when people are kind to them and believe that they deserve to be shamed and humiliated.

Severe Personality Styles

S (Schizotypal)	Individuals keep having strange thoughts that they cannot get rid of and, when alone, often feel the presence of someone who cannot be seen. People think that they talk and think about strange or different things. They are concerned that people they do not know might harm them, and they do not understand why some people smile at them.
C (Borderline)	Individuals frequently feel like there is nothing inside them, like they are empty or hollow. Their moods and feelings toward others change from day to day and often swing from loving them to hating them. They may do something desperate to keep a person they love from abandoning them.
P (Paranoid)	Individuals never forgive an insult or forget an embarrassment that someone has caused them. They always are watching out for people who want to cheat them and try to see who can and cannot be trusted. People do not give them enough recognition for what they have done. They take great care to keep their life a private matter so that no one can take advantage of them.

Clinical Syndromes

A (Anxiety)	Individuals are very jumpy, feel tense, and sweat a great deal. Certain thoughts and events from their past come back again and again in their mind. They repeat certain behaviors to reduce their anxiety and to keep bad things from happening.
H (Somatoform)	Individuals feel weak and tired a great deal of the time and worn out for no special reason. They have problems sleeping. They have lost the ability to feel sensations in parts of their body and have difficulty in keeping their balance when walking.
N (Bipolar: Manic)	Individuals feel excited and cheerful at many times for no special reason. People say that they become too interested and excited about too many different things, and talk too much and fast. They have had periods when they have been so cheerful and used up so much energy that they fell into a low mood.
D (Dysthymia)	Individuals feel like a failure and guilty because they cannot do things right anymore. They are quite blue, discouraged, and sad, and cannot snap out of it. They have lost interest in most things that they used to find pleasurable.
B (Alcohol Dependence)	Individuals have an alcohol problem and a great deal of trouble trying to control their impulse to drink to excess. Drinking alcohol helps them when they are feeling down.
T (Drug Dependence)	Individuals have taken drugs in the past that have gotten them into trouble and caused them to miss work and to get into arguments with their family. There have been times when they could not get through the day without street drugs.

Table 8.6   (*Continued*)

Scale (BR > 74)	Potential Issues
R (Posttraumatic Stress Disorder)	Individuals have a very upsetting experience from their past that keeps coming back to haunt their thoughts and causes nightmares. They feel terrified and have flashbacks of some traumatic experience that happened to them in the past.
Severe Clinical Syndromes	
SS (Thought Disorder)	Individuals have to think things over and over again for no special reason and these thoughts will not go away. Lately, they have gone all to pieces. They feel like they are losing touch with the real world. They often hear things so well that it bothers them.
CC (Major Depression)	Individuals feel terribly depressed and sad for no reason that they can figure out. They have completely lost their appetite and have trouble sleeping most nights. They have given serious thoughts to doing away with themselves.
PP (Delusional Disorder)	Individuals believe that people have been spying on them for years and trying to make them think that they are crazy. They believe that they are being plotted against. Someone has been trying to control their minds.

They bear the same relationship to the clinical syndrome scales that the severe personality style scales bear to the personality style scales.

Facet Scales

Grossman and del Rio (2005) described the development of 35 facet scales for the 14 personality style scales. The first step involved the identification of the most salient domains within each scale. For example, the most salient domains for Scale *1* (Schizoid) are impassive expressive acts, unengaged interpersonal behavior, and apathetic mood. The second step involved identifying items on each of the 14 scales that would assess its salient domains. Each of these sets of items was then subjected to an alpha method factor analysis with promax rotation. The resulting scales that had a coefficient alpha greater than .50 were retained. Rational and statistical methods then were employed to finalize the items on each facet scale. For example, the facet scales for Scale *1* (Schizoid) are Apathetic Mood/Temperament, Unengaged Interpersonal Conduct, and Impassive Expressive Behavior. Although Grossman and del Rio identified only two facet scales for eight of the personality style scales, the MCMI-III Profile Report provides three facet scales for each of the 14 personality style scales.

The facet scales are intended to be used to further refine and understand what subsets of items are causing the elevation in the parent scale. Two individuals could have very similar BR scores on one of the personality style scales and very different scores on the facet scales. The actual items found on each facet scale have not been provided, so implementation of them awaits their incorporation into the MCMI-III on a formal basis. The fact that the eight additional facet scales on the MCMI-III Profile Report would be assumed to have a coefficient alpha less than .50, the criterion used by Grossman and del Rio for identifying a facet scale, suggests that these facet scales should be used very cautiously.

Critical Items (Noteworthy Responses)

Critical items on the MCMI-III are identified as Noteworthy Responses (Millon et al., 1997, Appendix E). These Noteworthy Responses are divided into six categories: (1) Health Preoccupations; (2) Interpersonal Alienation; (3) Emotional Dyscontrol; (4) Self-Destructive Potential; (5) Childhood Abuse; and (6) Eating Disorders. The deviant response to all these items is "True." These items are intended to alert the clinician to specific items that warrant close review. All the items except one within Health Preoccupations are found on Scale *H* (Somatoform). The Eating Disorder items are not scored on any extant MCMI-III scale and must be reviewed directly. Items 154 and 171 reflect suicide attempts and suicidal ideation that need to be reviewed any time they are endorsed or omitted.

APPLICATIONS

As a self-report inventory, the MCMI-III is used routinely in clinical settings as well as correctional and substance abuse settings. However, the MCMI-III is not to be used "with normal populations or for purposes other than establishing a diagnostic screening and clinical assessment. . . . To administer the MCMI-III to a wider range of problems or class of subjects, such as those found in business or industry, or to identify neurologic lesions, or to use it for the assessment of general personality traits among college students is to apply the instrument to settings and samples for which it is neither intended nor appropriate" (Millon et al., 1997, p. 6). Choca (2004) has suggested that there is nothing wrong with giving the MCMI-III to normal individuals or other samples on which the MCMI-III was not standardized, as long as the clinician keeps in mind the standardization group to which the person is being compared.

The MCMI-III also is used in forensic settings, and several authors have provided guidelines for its use (McCann, 2002; Schutte, 2001). There has been substantial debate whether the MCMI-III meets the federal standards for evidence in the legal settings with advocates pro (Craig, 2006; Dyer, 2005) and con (Lally, 2003; Rogers, Salekin, & Sewell, 1999). Review of these issues is beyond the scope of this text. The forensic psychologist does need to be well informed about all these issues before using the MCMI-III.

Somewhat different issues must be considered in the administration of the MCMI-III in forensic settings compared with the more usual clinical setting. These issues were reviewed in Chapter 6 on the MMPI-2 (pp. 197–198) and will not be reiterated here. These issues need to be considered carefully because the validity (modifier) scales on the MCMI-III appear to be relatively insensitive to response distortions (Morgan, Schoenberg, Dorr, & Burke, 2002; Schoenberg, Dorr, & Morgan, 2003), although Schoenberg, Dorr, and Morgan (2006) developed a discriminant function that looked promising in identifying college students who were simulating psychopathology.

Millon et al. (1997) have stated that in child-custody settings when "custody battles reach the point of requiring psychological evaluation, they constitute such a degree of interpersonal difficulty that the evaluation becomes a clinical matter" (p. 144). McCann, Flens, and Campagna (2001) have reported normative data for 259 child-custody examinees. The mean MCMI-III profile for these examinees was an elevation on Scale *Y* (Social Desirability) and subclinical elevations on Scales *4* (Histrionic), *5* (Narcissistic), and *7*

(Compulsive). Lampel (1999) reported elevations on the same four MCMI-III scales in 50 divorcing couples. Halon (2001) has questioned whether elevations on these four scales in child-custody samples reflect personality difficulties or normal personality characteristics.

PSYCHOMETRIC FOUNDATIONS

Demographic Variables

Age

There are minimal effects of age on any of the MCMI-III scales (Haddy et al., 2005). There is a slight tendency for raw scores to decrease slightly past the age of 50 except on Scales *4* (Histrionic), *5* (Narcissistic), and *7* (Compulsive). Raw scores increased slightly in individuals over 50 on these three scales. Dean and Choca (2001) reported similar results when male psychiatric patients were classified as younger (18 to 40) or older (60+). The older patients had lower scores on all MCMI-III scales except Scales *4* (Histrionic), *5* (Narcissistic), and *7* (Compulsive).

Gender

Gender does not create any general issues in MCMI-III interpretation because separate base rate (BR) scores are used for men and women. Any gender differences in how individuals responded to the items on each scale are removed when the raw scores are converted to BR scores. Lindsay, Sankis, and Widiger (2000) reported that women were more likely to endorse the items on Scale *4* (Histrionic).

Education

There is no research that has looked at the effects of education on MCMI-III scales.

Ethnicity

About 15% of the development and cross-validation for the MCMI-III were nonwhite. Millon et al. (1997) reported that some differences were found for the demographic variables (unspecified), but these differences appear to reflect known differences in prevalence of the disorder. Some ethnic differences were noted on the MCMI-I and MCMI-II, but no published research has looked at the effects of ethnicity on the MCMI-III. There have been several dissertations that examined ethnic differences on the MCMI-III. This absence of such research on the MCMI-III is remarkable because it is so common with the MMPI/MMPI-2. Until such research is published on the MCMI-III, the MCMI-III should be used cautiously with nonwhite individuals.

Reliability

The *MCMI-III Manual* (Millon et al., 1997, Table 3.3, p. 58) reports the reliability data for 87 individuals who were retested after an average of 5 to 14 days. The test-retest correlations ranged from .82 to .96 across the scales with a median of .91, which is very stable. Measures of the internal consistency of each scale (Cronbach's Alpha) also were quite good with only

Table 8.7   Standard error of measurement for MCMI-III scales in male psychiatric patients[a]

Scale	Raw Scores M	SD	SEM	Alpha*	SEM in BR Units at Base Rate 60	75	85
Personality Styles							
1 (Schizoid)	9.83	5.52	4.47	.81	3.35	2.23	5.14
2A (Avoidant)	8.94	6.64	5.91	.89	3.56	1.35	3.72
2B (Depressive)	9.58	6.77	6.02	.89	3.32	1.66	4.98
3 (Dependent)	8.55	5.86	4.98	.85	4.01	2.81	5.02
4 (Histrionic)	11.80	5.47	4.43	.81	NA	NA	NA
5 (Narcissistic)	13.06	4.75	3.18	.67	6.28	5.34	4.71
6A (Antisocial)	10.78	6.02	4.64	.77	3.45	2.59	2.16
6B (Sadistic)	9.67	6.06	4.79	.79	1.04	1.46	5.43
7 (Compulsive)	14.12	5.34	3.52	.66	3.69	NA	NA
8A (Negativistic)	10.39	6.51	5.41	.83	4.07	1.48	4.44
8B (Masochistic)	7.32	5.69	4.95	.87	1.62	1.01	5.86
Severe Personality Styles							
S (Schizotypal)	8.01	6.65	5.66	.85	1.77	1.77	4.60
C (Borderline)	10.02	6.67	5.67	.85	2.64	3.17	3.53
P (Paranoid)	8.96	6.55	5.50	.84	1.64	4.00	5.45
Clinical Syndromes							
A (Anxiety)	8.25	5.71	4.91	.86	5.09	2.65	2.65
H (Somatoform)	7.23	4.76	4.09	.86	1.95	7.33	7.33
N (Bipolar: Manic)	6.99	4.39	3.12	.71	2.57	4.81	6.41
D (Dysthymia)	9.55	6.03	5.31	.88	3.39	1.32	5.65
B (Alcohol Dependence)	8.93	6.00	4.92	.82	3.86	2.03	3.46
T (Drug Dependence)	8.86	6.29	5.22	.83	1.92	5.56	NA
R (PTSD)	8.92	6.47	5.76	.89	1.74	3.47	NA
Severe Clinical Syndromes							
SS (Thought Disorder)	8.77	6.15	5.35	.87	1.50	4.68	NA
CC (Major Depression)	9.54	6.61	5.95	.90	1.34	4.20	5.04
PP (Delusional Disorder)	3.79	3.83	3.03	.79	2.64	5.61	7.26
Validity Scales (Modifier Scales)							
X (Disclosure)	119.85	34.43	NA	NA	—	—	—
Y (Desirability)	11.92	4.74	4.07	.86	6.14	4.91	NA
Z (Debasement)	14.46	8.84	8.40	.95	1.55	1.79	NA

*$N = 1,924$.
[a] Haddy et al. (2005).

six scales (*5* [Histrionic]—.67; *6A* [Antisocial]—.77; 6B [Sadistic/Aggressive]—.79; *7* [Compulsive]—.66; *N* [Bipolar: Manic]—.71; *PP* [Delusional Disorder]—.79) below .80.

The standard error of measurement for all MCMI-III scales is provided in Table 8.7 at BR scores of 60, 75, and 85 for male psychiatric patients (Haddy et al., 2005). (There were not a sufficient number of women in this sample to compute standard errors of measurement for them. The standard errors of measurement for raw scores in men and women were generally similar suggesting that the standard errors of measurement for men could be used in women, too.) The standard error of measurement was calculated in raw score units for each scale and then converted in BR scores at these three points. For example, the standard error of measurement for Scale *1* (Schizoid) is 3.35, 2.23, and 5.14 at BR scores of 60, 75, and 85, respectively. These values change because the distribution is not uniform around these numbers. When the SEM is about 3 BR points for one of these scales, the individual's true score will be within ±3 BR points two-thirds of the time.

The standard error of measurement for BR scores around 75 tends to be small, which means that BR scores above that cutting score are very likely to remain elevated despite any error of measurement. On the other hand, the standard error of measurement for BR scores around 85 tends to be about twice as large as at 75, which means that BR scores above cutting scores of 85 are more likely to change.

The maximum BR score on Scales 4 (Histrionic) and 7 (Compulsive) in men is 84 and 83, respectively. Thus, it is not possible for a man to have a BR score above 85 on this scale and the standard error of measurement could not be calculated. The maximum BR on these same two scales in women is 92 and 91, respectively.

CONCLUDING COMMENTS

The MCMI-III is the self-report inventory most widely used to assess personality disorders. The MCMI-III should be considered any time the presence of a personality disorder is expected in an individual; it is a frequently overlooked set of diagnoses given the more dramatic symptoms in most Axis I disorders. Computer scoring is almost mandatory for the MCMI-III given its complexity and time-consuming nature. Clinicians must understand the derivation and use of BR scores for the accurate interpretation of the scale scores.

REFERENCES

American Psychiatric Association. (1980). *Diagnostic and statistical manual of mental disorders* (3rd ed.). Washington, DC: Author.

American Psychiatric Association. (1987). *Diagnostic and statistical manual of mental disorders* (3rd ed., rev.). Washington, DC: Author.

American Psychiatric Association. (1994). *Diagnostic and statistical manual of mental disorders* (4th ed.). Washington, DC: Author.

American Psychiatric Association. (2000). *Diagnostic and statistical manual of mental disorders* (4th ed., text rev.). Washington, DC: Author.

Butcher, J. N., Dahlstrom, W. G., Graham, J. R., Tellegen, A. M., & Kaemmer, B. (1989). *MMPI-2: Manual for administration and scoring.* Minneapolis: University of Minnesota Press.

Charter, R. A., & Lopez, M. N. (2002). MCMI-III: The inability of the validity conditions to detect random responders. *Journal of Clinical Psychology, 58,* 1615–1617.

Choca, J. P. (2004). *Interpretive guide to the Millon Clinical Multiaxial Inventory* (3rd ed.). Washington, DC: American Psychological Association.

Craig, R. J. (Ed.). (2005). *New directions in interpreting the MCMI-III: Essays on current issues.* Hoboken, NJ: Wiley.

Craig, R. J. (2006). The MCMI-III. In R. P. Archer (Ed.), *Forensic uses of clinical assessment instruments* (pp. 121–145). Mahwah, NJ: Erlbaum.

Dean, K. J., & Choca, J. (2001, August). *Psychological changes of emotionally disturbed men with age.* Paper presented at the annual meeting of the American Psychological Association, San Francisco.

Dyer, F. J. (2005). Forensic applications of the MCMI-III in light of recent controversies. In R. J. Craig (Ed.), *New directions in interpreting the MCMI-III* (pp. 201–226). Hoboken, NJ: Wiley.

Finn, S. (1996). *Using the MMPI-2 as a therapeutic intervention.* Minneapolis: University of Minnesota Press.

Fischer, C. T. (1994). *Individualizing psychological assessment.* Hillsdale, NJ: Erlbaum.

Grossman, S. D., & del Rio, C. (2005). The MCMI-III facet subscales. In R. J. Craig (Ed.), *New directions in interpreting the MCMI-III* (pp. 3–31). Hoboken, NJ: Wiley.

Haddy, C., Strack, S., & Choca, J. P. (2005). Linking personality disorders and clinical syndromes on the MCMI-III. *Journal of Personality Assessment, 84,* 193–204.

Halon, R. L. (2001). The MCMI-III: The normal quartet in child custody cases. *American Journal of Forensic Psychology, 19,* 57–75.

Hathaway, S. R., & McKinley, J. C. (1951). *MMPI manual.* New York: Psychological Corporation.

Jankowski, D. (2002). *A beginner's guide to the MCMI-III.* Washington, DC: American Psychological Association.

Lally, S. J. (2003). What tests are acceptable for use in forensic evaluations?: A survey of experts. *Professional Psychology: Research and Practice, 34,* 491–498.

Lampel, A. K. (1999). Use of the MCMI-III in evaluating child custody litigants. *American Journal of Forensic Psychology, 17,* 19–31.

Lindsay, K. A., Sankis, L. M., & Widiger, T. A. (2000). Sex and gender bias in self-report personality disorder inventories. *Journal of Personality Disorders, 14,* 218–232.

Mandell, D. (1997). *An investigation of the effects of item omissions on the Millon Clinical Multiaxial Inventory-II (MCMI-II).* Unpublished doctoral dissertation, Fairleigh Dickinson University, Teaneck, NJ.

McCann, J. T. (2002). Guidelines for the forensic applications of the MCMI-III. *Journal of Forensic Psychology Practice, 2,* 55–70.

McCann, J. T., Flens, J. T., & Campagna, V. (2001). The MCMI-III in child custody evaluations: A normative study. *Journal of Forensic Psychology Practice, 1,* 27–44.

Millon, T. (1977). *MCMI manual.* Minneapolis, MN: Interpretive Scoring Systems.

Millon, T. (1983). *Modern psychopathology: A biosocial approach to maladaptive learning and functioning.* Prospect Heights, IL: Waveland Press.

Millon, T. (1987). *Manual for the MCMI-II* (2nd ed.). Minneapolis, MN: National Computer Systems.

Millon, T., & Davis, R. D. (1996). *Disorders of personality: DSM-IV and beyond* (Rev. ed.). New York: Wiley.

Millon, T., Davis, R., & Millon, C. (1994). *MCMI-III manual.* Minneapolis, MN: National Computer Systems.

Millon, T., Davis, R., & Millon, C. (1997). *MCMI-III manual* (2nd ed.). Minneapolis, MN: National Computer Systems.

Morgan, C. D., Schoenberg, M. R., Dorr, D., & Burke, M. J. (2002). Overreport on the MCMI-III: Concurrent validation with the MMPI-2 using a psychiatric inpatient sample. *Journal of Personality Assessment, 78*, 288–300.

Paulhus, D. L. (1984). Two-component models of socially desirable responding. *Journal of Personality and Social Psychology, 46*, 598–609.

Retzlaff, P. D. (1995). *Tactical psychotherapy of the personality disorders: An MCMI-III-based approach*. Needham Heights, MA: Allyn & Bacon.

Retzlaff, P. D., Ofman, P., Hyer, L., & Matheson, S. (1994). MCMI-II high-point codes: Severe personality disorder and clinical syndrome extensions. *Journal of Clinical Psychology, 30*, 228–234.

Retzlaff, P. D., Stoner, J., & Kleinsasser, D. (2002). The use of the MCMI-III in the screening and triage of offenders. *International Journal of Offender Therapy and Comparative Criminology, 46*, 319–332.

Rogers, R., Salekin, R. T., & Sewell, K. W. (1999). Validation of the MCMI for Axis II disorders: Does it meet the Daubert standard? *Law and Human Behavior, 23*, 425–443.

Schoenberg, M. R., Dorr, D., & Morgan, C. D. (2003). The ability of the MCMI-III to detect malingering. *Psychological Assessment, 15*, 198–204.

Schoenberg, M. R., Dorr, D., & Morgan, C. D. (2006). Development of discriminant functions to detect dissimulation for the MCMI-III. *Journal of Forensic Psychiatry and Psychology, 17*, 405–416.

Schutte, J. W. (2001). Using the MCMI-III in forensic evaluations. *American Journal of Forensic Psychology, 19*, 5–20.

Strack, S. (2002). *Essentials of Millon inventories assessment*. Hoboken, NJ: Wiley.

Chapter 9 ———————————————————

PERSONALITY ASSESSMENT INVENTORY

The Personality Assessment Inventory (PAI: Morey, 1991) is a broadband measure of the major dimensions of psychopathology found in Axis I disorders and some Axis II disorders of the *DSM-IV-TR* (American Psychiatric Association, 2000). The PAI consists of 4 validity, 11 clinical, 5 treatment consideration, and 2 interpersonal scales (see Table 9.1). There also are three or four subscales for 9 of the 11 clinical scales and for one treatment consideration scale. Finally, a PAI Structural Summary provides the tables for scoring and profiles for plotting supplemental indices. Table 9.2 provides the general information on the PAI.

HISTORY

The PAI (Morey, 1991) was developed following a sequential, construct-validation strategy. The underlying construct for most of the clinical syndrome scales based on the extant research is multidimensional, and so the scale to measure each clinical syndrome was to be composed of several subscales. Once these component subscales were identified, items were written so that the content was directly relevant for each one. Each item in the original item pool of over 2,200 items then was rated by four individuals for its appropriateness for the specific subscale. Then four experts were asked to assign times to the appropriate scale, and items that did not reach 75% agreement either were dropped or rewritten. These items then were reviewed by a bias-review panel as to whether they could be perceived as being offensive on the basis of gender, race, religion, or ethnic-group membership. Any item that was perceived as being offensive or could inappropriately identify a normal behavior as psychopathology was deleted.

Expert judges, who were nationally recognized within the content area of each scale, then were used to sort the remaining items to ensure that each item was related to its actual construct for each scale on the PAI. The overall agreement was 94.3% among these judges for the 776 items that were retained for the alpha version of the PAI.

Groups of college students then completed the alpha-version of the PAI in one of three conditions: (1) standard, in which students were asked to respond frankly and honestly; (2) positive-impression management, in which the students were asked to respond as if they were trying to impress a potential employer; and (3) malingering, in which the students were asked to simulate the responses of a person with a mental disorder. Items for the beta

Table 9.1   Personality Assessment Inventory (PAI) scales

Validity Scales

ICN	Inconsistency
INF	Infrequency
NIM	Negative Impression Management
PIM	Positive Impression Management

Clinical Scales

SOM	Somatic Complaints
SOM-C	Conversion
SOM-S	Somatization
SOM-H	Health Concerns
ANX	Anxiety
ANX-C	Cognitive
ANX-A	Affective
ANX-P	Physiological
ARD	Anxiety-Related Disorders
ARD-O	Obsessive-Compulsive
ARD-P	Phobias
ARD-T	Traumatic Stress
DEP	Depression
DEP-C	Cognitive
DEP-A	Affective
DEP-P	Physiological
MAN	Mania
MAN-A	Activity Level
MAN-G	Grandiosity
MAN-I	Irritability
PAR	Paranoia
PAR-R	Resentment
PAR-H	Hypervigilance
PAR-P	Persecution
SCZ	Schizophrenia
SCZ-P	Psychotic Experience
SCZ-S	Social Detachment
SCZ-T	Thought Disorder
BOR	Borderline Features
BOR-A	Affective Instability
BOR-I	Identity Problems
BOR-N	Negative Relationships
BOR-S	Self-Harm
ANT	Antisocial Features
ANT-A	Antisocial Behaviors
ANT-E	Egocentricity
ANT-S	Stimulus-Seeking
ALC	Alcohol Problems
DRG	Drug Problems

Table 9.1 (*Continued*)

Treatment Consideration Scales

AGG	Aggression
AGG-A	Aggressive Attitude
AGG-V	Verbal Aggression
AGG-P	Physical Aggression
SUI	Suicidal Ideation
STR	Stress
NON	Nonsupport
RXR	Treatment Rejection

Interpersonal Scales

DOM	Dominance
WRM	Warmth

version of the PAI were selected on six bases: (1) reasonable variability across the construct, essentially an item-difficulty parameter; (2) a positive, corrected part-whole correlation of the item with the total score of the other items on the scale; (3) the corrected part-whole correlation was higher than the correlation with measures of social desirability and positive and negative impression management; (4) a higher correlation with their own scale than other scales; (5) less face valid or "transparent" measures of the construct embodied in the

Table 9.2 Personality Assessment Inventory (PAI)

Authors:	Morey
Published:	1991
Edition:	1st
Publisher:	Psychological Assessment Resources
Website:	www.parinc.com
Age range:	18+
Reading level:	4th grade
Administration formats:	paper/pencil, computer, CD, cassette
Additional languages:	Arabic, French Canadian, Korean, Norwegian, Serbian, Slovene and Swedish
Number of items:	344
Response format:	False/Not at all True, Slightly True, Mainly True, Very True
Administration time:	40–50 minutes
Primary scales:	4 Validity, 11 Clinical, 5 Treatment Considerations, 2 Interpersonal
Additional scales:	Subscales for 9 clinical scales and 1 Treatment Consideration scale
Hand scoring:	Self-scoring answer sheet
General texts:	Morey (2003), Morey (2007a)
Computer interpretation:	Psychological Assessment Resources (Clinical: Morey; Corrections: Morey & Edens)

scale; and (6) absence of gender differences. Using these criteria, a total of 597 items were retained for the beta-version of the PAI.

The beta-version of the PAI was administered to three groups of individuals: (1) community adults; (2) clinical patients; and (3) college students with either positive impression or malingering instructions. Similar item characteristics were assessed for the beta version of the PAI as were assessed with the alpha version. The final 344 items on the PAI represented the best balance of all these item characteristics, including the requirement that no item could be scored on more than one scale—there are no overlapping items on the PAI.

Normative data for the PAI were collected from three groups: (1) 1,462 community-dwelling adults from which a subsample of 1,000 were selected who were census-matched; (2) 1,265 clinical patients from 69 clinical sites; and (3) 1,051 college students. The norms for the PAI are based on 1,000 individuals from the census-matched sample. The skyline profile on the standard profile form demarcates two standard deviations above the mean in the clinical sample allowing the clinician to compare the individual simultaneously with both the census-matched and clinical samples (see Figure 9.1).

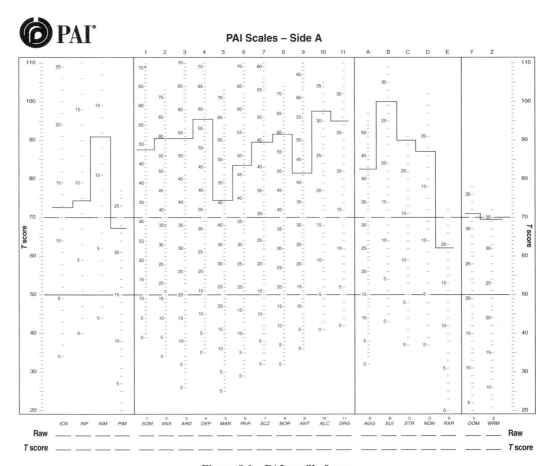

Figure 9.1   PAI profile form.

Short Form of the PAI

The first 160 items of the PAI can be used to provide a reasonable estimate of 20 of the 22 clinical scales for all scales but Inconsistency (*ICN*) and Stress (*STR*). These estimates are possible because the items with the largest item-scale correlations were located at the beginning of the test when the final version of the PAI was developed. Table 11.1 in the *Personality Assessment Inventory Professional Manual* (Morey, 1991, p. 142) provides the descriptive characteristics for these 160 items. The short form only should be used in the most unusual circumstances, and the estimated scores must be considered as generating only the most tentative interpretive hypotheses. Frazier, Naugle, and Haggerty (2006) found that agreement between the short- and full-form of the PAI was affected adversely when the validity scales were elevated. They also noted that individuals with lower levels of ability were more likely to leave items missing and produce invalid protocols. These individuals are the very ones for whom the short form was designed. The hope was that it would provide information about the presence of psychopathology that otherwise might not be available from a self-report inventory.

PAI-A (Adolescent)

As a result of interest by professionals in using the PAI with adolescents in clinical settings, work was begun in 1999 on piloting an adolescent version of the inventory (Morey, 2007b). The intent of this work was to explore the applicability of an adolescent version that would closely parallel the adult version of the PAI. It would retain the structure and, as much as possible, the items of the adult version rather than be an entirely new version targeted specifically at an adolescent population. The development of the PAI-A involved an adaptation of the items of the adult PAI so that the content was meaningful when applied to adolescents. The approach taken was a conservative one—the question was not whether the item was optimized to capture the experience of an adolescent, but rather whether the item would retain its original meaning when read by the adolescent. This conservative approach was merited in that the items on the adult PAI had been selected on the basis of numerous criteria, and the rewording or replacement of items could have significant and unanticipated effects on the final properties of the adolescent version and its interpretability as parallel to the adult version. Thus, these revisions included rewordings of relatively few items and involved close equivalents of the original wording.

The next stage in development involved collecting a diverse and representative sample of adolescent patients, and determining the psychometric comparability of items on the adolescent and adult versions. A relatively small number of items were identified that appeared to have different characteristics in adolescent patients than in adult patients, and the decision was made to explore the impact of elimination of these items. On the basis of these analyses, items were removed in an effort to eliminate the most problematic items and yield an item distribution pattern that would closely parallel the adult instrument. On the basis of this strategy, the final PAI-A included 264 items. The PAI-A was then standardized using a census-matched normative sample of 707 adolescents aged 12 to 18, as well as a diverse clinical sample of 1,160 patients in the same age range. The average internal consistency for the 22 clinical scales was .79 in the community sample and .80 in the clinical sample, while the average test-retest reliability for these scales was .78 over an interval of approximately 18 days.

ADMINISTRATION

The first issue in the administration of the PAI is ensuring that the individual is invested in the process. Taking a few extra minutes to answer any questions the individual may have about why the PAI is being administered and how the results will be used will pay excellent dividends. The clinician should work diligently to make the assessment process a collaborative activity with the individual to obtain the desired information. This issue of therapeutic assessment (Finn, 1996; Fischer, 1994) was covered in depth in Chapter 2 (pp. 43–44).

Reading level is a crucial factor in determining whether a person can complete the PAI; inadequate reading ability (to be discussed) is a major cause of inconsistent patterns of item endorsement. Morey (1991) suggests that most individuals who can read at the fourth-grade level can take the PAI with little or no difficulty because the items are written on an fourth-grade level or less. The PAI has the easiest reading level of any of the self-report inventories reviewed in this *Handbook*. As such, one reason for selecting the PAI is the larger number of clients who can complete it successfully compared with the MMPI-2 (Butcher, Dahlstrom, Graham, Tellegen, & Kaemmer, 1989) and the MCMI-III (Millon, Davis, & Millon, 1997), both of which are written at the eighth-grade level.

SCORING

Scoring the PAI is relatively straightforward either by hand or computer. A different answer sheet is used for hand scoring (Form HS Answer Sheet) and optical scanning (Form SS Answer Sheet), so the proper answer sheet must be selected for the method of scoring. If the PAI is administered by computer, the computer automatically scores it. If the individual's responses to the items have been placed on an answer sheet, these responses can be entered into the computer by the clinician for scoring or they can be hand scored. If the clinician enters the item responses into the computer for scoring, they should be double entered so that any data entry errors can be identified.

The first step in hand scoring is to examine the answer sheet carefully and indicate omitted items and double-marked items by drawing a line through all four responses to these items with brightly colored ink. Also, cleaning up the answer sheet is helpful and facilitates scoring. Responses that were changed need to be erased completely if possible, or clearly marked with an "X" so that the clinician is aware that this response has not been endorsed by the client.

The PAI (Morey, 1991) and the NEO PI-R (Costa & McCrae, 1992) are the only self-report inventories reviewed in this *Handbook* that do not use "true/false" items. Both of these inventories have the same publisher (Psychological Assessment Resources), which may account for not using "true/false" items. The PAI uses a four-point Likert scale ranging from "false, not at all true," "slightly true," "mainly true," to "very true." These potential response options always are presented in this same order on the answer sheet. When "very true" is the scored direction for a specific item, the response options are scored as 0, 1, 2, or 3 ("very true"). When "false, not at all true" is the scored direction, the preceding four response options are scored as 3 ("false, not at all true"), 2, 1, or 0. Thus, the total raw score on an eight-item scale, which is the characteristic number of items on each subscale of the clinical scales, can range from 0 to 24. It is imperative that the clinician realize that *the total score is the sum of the response options for each scale,* not the total number of items endorsed on the scale, which is the method for scoring the MCMI-III, MMPI-2, and MMPI-A.

The PAI is easier to score than other self-report inventories because no templates are required. The answer sheet, on which the person records his or her responses, is self-scoring. The items on each scale are designated by ruled and shaded boxes that are identified by scale abbreviations. The total raw score for each scale or subscale is entered in the corresponding box with the same abbreviation on Side B of the profile form. The subscales for the various scales on the PAI are plotted on Side B of the profile form. The total scores, which are the sum of the scores on the subscales, for all scales are entered on Side A of the profile form.

Although this process of hand scoring may sound somewhat complex, it is straightforward and can be carried out in 10 to 15 minutes. It is advisable to have another person double-check all the scoring and transferring of numbers to catch any scoring or transcription errors before the interpretive process begins.

ASSESSING VALIDITY

Figure 9.2 provides the flowchart for assessing the validity of this specific administration of the PAI and the criteria for using this flowchart are provided in Table 9.3. The clinician is reminded that the criteria provided in Table 9.3 are continuous, yet ultimately the decisions that must be made in implementation of the flowchart in Figure 9.2 are dichotomous. General guidelines will be provided for translating these continuous data into dichotomous decisions on the PAI, but these guidelines need to be considered within the constraints of this specific client and the circumstances for the evaluation.

Item Omissions

Morey (1991) recommends that more than 95% of the items should be endorsed if the PAI is to be interpreted; that is, no more than 17 ($.05 \times 344$) items should be omitted. Table 9.3 shows that omitting 17 items is somewhere between the 93rd and 98th percentile in both normal and clinical samples. Morey also recommends that more than 80% of the items should be endorsed for any individual scale to be interpreted. The subscales of the clinical scales all have six to eight items, so the omission of two items from one of these subscales ($6/8 = 75\%$) would mean that subscale should not be interpreted, although the entire scale could be interpreted if more than 80% of its items were endorsed.

Consistency of Item Endorsement

Consistency of item endorsement on the PAI is assessed by the Inconsistency Scale (*ICN*) and Infrequency Scale (*INF*). The Inconsistency Scale (*ICN*) scale consists of 10 pairs of

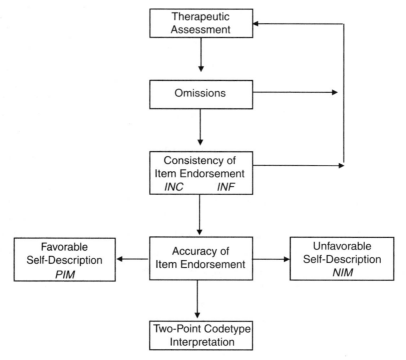

Figure 9.2   Flowchart for assessing validity of the PAI.

items that have similar item content. Scoring of the Inconsistency Scale (*ICN*) is slightly more complicated than scoring the Variable Response Inconsistency Scale (*VRIN*) on the MMPI-A or MMPI-2, because the PAI has four response alternatives ("false, not at all true," "slightly true," "mainly true," and "very true") rather than simply "true" or "false." The item scores for these 10 pairs of items are entered into a box labeled *Raw Score Calculation for ICN* on Side B of the profile sheet and then the *absolute* differences between the scores on these 10 items are summed. The scoring direction is reversed for two pairs of the items (13-190 and 53-270) on the Inconsistency Scale (*ICN*), which further complicates this process. The sum of the absolute differences on these 10 pairs of items becomes the total raw score on the *ICN*. The complexity of hand scoring the *ICN* on the PAI, and the Variable Response Inconsistency Scale (*VRIN*) and True Response Consistency Scale (*TRIN*) on the MMPI-A and MMPI-2, and the ease with which errors can be made, is another strong argument for computer scoring of all self-report inventories.

The Infrequency Scale (*INF*) consists of eight items that were both expected and empirically known *not* to be answered by almost all individuals regardless of their clinical status. Four of these items were expected to be endorsed as "false, not at all true," and the other four as "very true." There is no theme to the content of these eight items.

Scores on the Inconsistency Scale (*ICN*) and Infrequency Scale (*INF*) correlated .39 in the normal sample and .16 in the clinical sample on the PAI. That is, these two scales are very different measures of inconsistency of item endorsement and the clinician occasionally will encounter profiles in which one of these two scales is elevated and the other is not.

Table 9.3   Criteria for assessing PAI validity by type of setting.

					Percentile						
	1	2	7	16	30	50	70	84	93	98	99
Item Omissions											
Normal[a]	—	—	—	—	0	1	3	6	14	24	27
Clinical[b]	—	—	—	—	0	1	2	5	10	19	23
Consistency of Item Endorsement (Inconsistency Scale [ICN])											
Normal[a]	—	0	1	2	3	4	6	8	11	14	15
Clinical[b]	0	1	2	3	4	6	7	9	11	13	14
Consistency of Item Endorsement (Infrequency Scale ([INF])											
Normal[a]	—	—	—	—	0	2	3	4	6	10	11
Clinical[b]	—	—	—	0	1	—	2	5	7	9	9
Accuracy of Item Endorsement											
Self-Unfavorable (Negative Impression Scale [NIM])											
Normal[a]	—	—	—	—	—	0	1	3	5	10	13
Clinical[b]	—	—	—	1	2	3	5	8	11	16	18
Self-Favorable (Positive Impression Scale ([PIM])											
Normal[a]	4	5	8	10	13	15	17	19	21	23	24
Clinical[b]	1	2	4	6	9	12	15	17	19	22	23

Note: The raw scores on all of these scales except for the number of items omitted are sums of the item scores on that scale, they are *not* the number of items endorsed on that scale.
[a]Morey et al. (1991).
[b]Morey et al. (1991).

Because of the very small number of items on the Infrequency Scale (*INF*), the clinician quickly can interview the individual about the few items that have been endorsed in those instances where these two scales do not agree.

Clark, Gironda, and Young (2003) examined the ability of the Inconsistency Scale (*ICN*) and the Infrequency Scale (*INF*) to identify clinical profiles in which increasingly more random responses in blocks of 50 items were introduced beginning from the end of the test. Neither *ICN* nor *INF* was very effective at identifying these random responses until at least 200 random items were introduced. The combined index of *INC* greater than a T score of 72 and *INF* greater than a T score of 74 was the most effective at identifying these random profiles. Five of the 8 *INF* items are in the first 200 items so there are only 3 items that can detect random responding at the end of the test. Similarly, only 3 items in the 10 pairs of items on the *ICN* scale occur after item 200, so again there are few items to detect such random responding. These data underscore the importance of therapeutic assessment to enhance the person's compliance.

Morey and Hopwood (2004) examined the effectiveness of using the differences between the T scores of the short form and full form of two PAI scales (Alcohol Problems [*ALC*]; Suicidal Ideation [*SUI*]) to identify random responses at the end of the test. They found that the discrepancies between these two scores had reasonable sensitivity for identifying random responses at the end of the test. They recommended that the clinician consider discrepancies between the short- and full-form scores on both *ALC* and *SUI* of more than 5 T points as a reliable indicator of inconsistent responding at the end of the test in the absence of elevations on the Inconsistency (*INC*) and Infrequency (*INF*) scales.

The normal and clinical samples have similar scores on the Inconsistency Scale (*ICN;* see Table 9.3); that is, psychopathology is not the cause of inconsistency similar to the findings on the Variable Response Inconsistency (*VRIN*) scale on the MMPI-2 (see Table 6.3, p. 145). A total raw score of six (T score of 52) on the Infrequency Scale (*INF*) is near the 93rd percentile in both normal and clinical samples. The clinician must remember that the total raw score for PAI scales is the *sum of the responses for the scored items,* not the total number of these items endorsed as on the MCMI-III, MMPI-A, and MMPI-2. Morey (1991) indicates that T scores above 75 on the *INF* scale and above 72 on the *ICN* scale should be considered to be invalid because of inconsistent item endorsement.

Figure 9.3 shows the profiles for endorsing all the items on the PAI randomly, "false, not at all true," or "very true." These latter two response patterns would be recognized easily on the answer sheet, but they provide the general parameters within which the PAI scales would be expected to vary based on responding "true" or "false" to all the items. The "very true" profile is easily identified by the validity scales. The simultaneous elevation of virtually all the other scales also would arouse serious concerns about its validity. The validity scales for the random and "false, not at all true" profiles are very elevated and raise serious doubts about their validity, but the other scales look interpretable if the validity scales are not evaluated.

Accuracy of Item Endorsement

Self-Unfavorable Descriptions

Self-unfavorable descriptions of psychopathology on the PAI can be assessed by the Negative Impression Management (*NIM*) scale. The *NIM* scale consists of items that were endorsed infrequently either by normal or clinical samples. As such, the items represent very infrequent or bizarre symptoms. Table 9.3 shows that a total raw score of 10 or above (T score 81) on the *NIM* scale is very unusual and at or above the 93rd percentile in normal and clinical samples. Morey (1991) states that T scores of 92 or higher (total raw score of 13 or higher) on the *NIM* scale should be considered to be invalid because of an extreme self-unfavorable description. Subsequent research has shown that the *NIM* scale is fairly effective at identifying individuals trying to simulate the more severe forms of psychopathology, but its effectiveness is more limited with the less severe forms of psychopathology. This finding would be expected because the less severe forms of psychopathology are much harder to identify.

The Malingering Index (MAL: Morey, 1996a), Rogers' Discriminant Function (*RDF:* Rogers, Sewell, Morey, & Ustad, 1996), and a regression equation comparing *NIM* predicted and obtained clinical scale scores (Hopwood, Morey, Rogers, & Sewell, 2007) have been developed subsequently to assess self-unfavorable descriptions. The *MAL* is composed of eight configural features that are more likely to be found in persons simulating mental disorders than in clinical patients. These configural features can be found in Morey (1996a) or the PAI Structural Summary (Morey, 1996b). The *RDF* was developed through discriminant analysis between naive (undergraduate students) and sophisticated (graduate students)

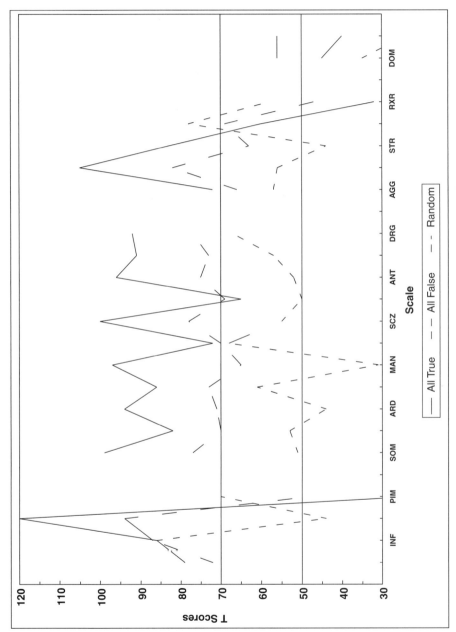

Figure 9.3   PAI profile for endorsing all items random, all false, or all true.

simulators of psychopathology and three clinical groups (generalized anxiety disorder, major depression, and schizophrenia). The *RDF* involves 20 different scales from the PAI and is based on the rationale that individuals simulating psychopathology cannot produce the pattern of scales found in clinical patients. The actual discriminant function can be found in Rogers et al. (1996, p. 640). The Hopwood et al. (2007) regression equation is based on the idea that individuals simulating specific forms of psychopathology cannot produce the pattern of clinical scale scores found in patients with that diagnosis. Their preliminary work with this regression equation looks promising. These *NIM* predicted scores are built into the PAI scoring and interpretation software as an overlay to the observed profile (Morey, 1999).

No meta-analyses have been published on the validity scales and indices to assess self-unfavorable presentations on the PAI. Research has shown that the *NIM* scale was more accurate than the *RDF* in identifying criminal defendants (Kucharski, Toomey, Fila, & Duncan, 2007), the *RDF* was more accurate than the *NIM* scale in identifying prison inmates (Edens, Poythress, & Watkins-Clay, 2007) and students simulating psychopathology (Bagby, Nicholson, Bacchiochi, Ryder, & Bury, 2002), and these two measures were essentially equivalent (Baity, Siefert, Chambers, & Blais, 2007). There was one commonality among the results of these various studies. It was easier for any measure to identify accurately naive individuals who were trying to simulate severe psychopathology than actual clinical patients. The entire February 2007 issue of the *Journal of Personality Assessment* was devoted to the PAI and five of these articles addressed unfavorable self-descriptions that should be reviewed.

Once it has been determined that the individual has made an extremely self-unfavorable description of psychopathology, the clinician will need to ascertain the reasons for the inaccurate item endorsement by a clinical interview. It remains to be determined whether it is possible to readminister the PAI to an individual who has made an extremely self-unfavorable description of psychopathology and obtain an accurate pattern of item endorsement. In any event, the clinician must remember that neither the PAI profile nor the individual scales can be interpreted when it has been determined that the individual has made an extremely unfavorable self-description as suggested by a very elevated score on the *NIM* scale.

Self-Favorable Descriptions

Self-favorable descriptions of psychopathology on the PAI can be assessed by the Positive Impression Management (*PIM*) scale. The *PIM* scale consists of items that were endorsed infrequently either by normal or clinical samples; however, these items were endorsed more frequently by normal individuals than by clinical patients. As such, the items represent a very favorable self-description and not reporting minor faults. Table 9.3 shows that a total raw score of 19 or above (T score of 59) on the *PIM* scale is very unusual and at or above the 93rd percentile in normal and clinical samples. Morey (1991) states that T scores of 68 or higher (total raw score of 23 or higher) on the *PIM* scale should be considered to be invalid because of an extreme self-favorable description.

The Defensiveness Index (*DEF*: Morey, 1996a) and Cashel's Discriminant Function (*CDF*: Cashel, Rogers, & Sewell, 1995) have been developed subsequently to assess self-favorable descriptions. The *DEF*, similar to the *MAL*, is composed of eight configural features that are more likely to be found in persons simulating a positive impression than in clinical patients or normal individuals. These configural features can be found in Morey (1996a) or the PAI Structural Summary (Morey, 1996b). The *CDF* was developed through discriminant analysis between male undergraduate students and male criminals who took the PAI under standard conditions and then were asked to portray themselves in the best possible manner that would still be believable. The *CDF* involves five different scales from the PAI. Because the *CDF* is specific to Cashel et al.'s samples, Morey (1996a) has provided means and standard deviations for the *CDF* based on the PAI normative sample.

No meta-analyses have been published, and very few individual studies, on the validity scales and indices to assess self-favorable presentations on the PAI. Peebles and Moore (1998) found that a total raw score of 18 on *PIM* was optimal for distinguishing between college students taking the PAI validity scale items under standard and "fake good" instructions. Baity et al. (2007) found similar results in psychiatric patients who were given the same instructions as in Peebles and Moore (1998). Only the *PIM* scale differentiated between these two sets of instructions with the optimal cutoff score at a T score of 57 (a total raw score of 18). It appears that a lower cutoff score on *PIM* may be more appropriate than the T score of 68 (a total raw score of 23) suggested by Morey (1991).

When a client's responses have been identified as being endorsed inaccurately because of an extremely self-favorable description of psychopathology, the PAI profile is no longer interpretable. The clinician will have little reason to try to interpret such a profile, however, because extremely self-favorable descriptions result in no clinical scales being elevated at or above a T score of 70 and frequently no clinical scales are above a T score of 60. The clinician should determine the potential causes for this self-favorable description and assess the implications for treatment and intervention. If the clinician can appreciate that the PAI profile produced by an extremely self-favorable description of psychopathology is not interpretable because no clinical scales are elevated, the parallel situation that the PAI profile produced by an extremely self-unfavorable description of psychopathology is equally uninterpretable because most or all clinical scales are elevated may become more apparent.

Individuals who provide extremely self-favorable descriptions of psychopathology see their problems as less troubling to themselves and, hence, are less motivated to change. Their problems also may be more chronic in nature, and consequently, they may be more difficult to treat if they remain in treatment. None of these potential causes of an extremely self-favorable description of psychopathology is a good prognostic sign for any type of psychological intervention.

INTERPRETATION

Once it has been determined that the individual has omitted few, if any, items, and endorsed the items consistently and accurately, the PAI can be interpreted. Interpretation of the PAI can begin either with the individual scales or the two highest of the 11 clinical scales elevated to a T score of 70 or higher (two-point codetypes). In determining these two-point codetypes, either scale can be higher; the only requirement is that they be the two highest clinical scales at or above a T score of 70. Morey (1996a, chap. 3) has provided interpretations of all 55 two-point codetypes that can occur with the 11 clinical scales on the PAI. In the following section, interpretations have been provided for those two-point codetypes that occurred at least 1.0% of the time in a large sample of clinical patients.

Two-Point Codetypes[1]

SOM-ANX/ANX-SOM (Somatic Complaints/Anxiety)

This pattern suggests a person who is reporting marked distress, with particular concerns about physical functioning. Such individuals see their lives as severely disrupted by a variety of physical problems, some of which may be stress-related. These problems render them tense, unhappy, and probably impaired in their ability both to concentrate on and to perform important life tasks. The somatic concerns may have led to friction in close relationships, and other people often perceive these individuals as complaining and demanding. Secondary elevations on Anxiety-Related Disorders *(ARD)* and Depression *(DEP)* are often observed with this codetype, and the level of Stress *(STR)* can be informative in ascertaining the degree of life disruption associated with the somatic concerns. This is a relatively common profile configuration, observed in 1.1% of clinical patients. Common diagnostic correlates include Somatoform Disorders, Posttraumatic Stress Disorder, Adjustment Disorders, and Major Depression. Interestingly, this codetype also is observed disproportionately in Schizophrenia, perhaps reflecting the onset of somatic delusions.

SOM-DEP/DEP-SOM (Somatic Complaints/Depression)

This configuration of the clinical scales suggests a person who is reporting significant distress, with particular concerns about physical functioning. Such people see their lives as severely disrupted by a variety of physical problems. These problems have left them unhappy with little energy or enthusiasm for concentrating on important life tasks and little hope for improvement in the future. Performance in important social roles has probably suffered as a result, and lack of success in these roles will serve as an additional source of stress. Secondary elevations on Anxiety *(ANX)* are frequent, and Suicidal Ideation *(SUI)* is often elevated; this pattern suggests that some probe of suicidal ideation is merited when the *SOM-DEP/DEP-SOM* codetype is observed. This is a relatively common profile, observed in 2.8% of clinical patients. Common diagnostic correlates include Somatoform Disorders, Organic Mental Disorders, and Major Depression.

SOM-ALC/ALC-SOM (Somatic Complaints/Alcohol Problems)

This configuration of the clinical scales suggests a person with a history of drinking problems who is experiencing a number of physiological difficulties that may be partially related to the drinking. These somatic problems might involve withdrawal symptoms, or they might be medical complications of alcohol abuse, for example, problems associated with the central nervous system sequelae of alcoholism. The combination of alcohol use and physical symptomatology is probably causing severe disruptions in relationships and work, and these difficulties are most likely serving as additional sources of stress; secondary

---

[1]Reproduced by special permission of the Publisher, Psychological Assessment Resources, Inc., 16204 North Florida Avenue, Lutz, Florida 33549, from *An Interpretive Guide to the Personality Assessment Inventory (PAI),* chapter 3, by Leslie C. Morey, PhD. Copyright 1996. Further reproduction is prohibited without permission of PAR.

elevations on Stress (*STR*) are often observed with this codetype. Seen in 1.3% of clinical patients, the most common diagnostic correlates include Alcohol Dependence and Organic Mental Disorders.

ANX-ARD/ARD-ANX (Anxiety/Anxiety-Related Disorders)

This clinical scale configuration suggests a person with marked anxiety and tension. Such people may be particularly uneasy and ruminative about their personal relationships, some of which are probably not going well. These relationships may be an important source of current distress, and such people tend to respond to their circumstances by becoming socially withdrawn or passively dependent. The disruptions in their lives often leave them questioning their goals and priorities, and tense and fearful about what the future may hold. Secondary elevations on Depression (*DEP*) and Suicidal Ideation (*SUI*) are often observed with this codetype and are prominent as the distress becomes more debilitating. This is a fairly common profile, observed in 1.9% of clinical patients. Common diagnostic correlates include various types of Anxiety Disorders as well as Major Depression.

ANX-DEP/DEP-ANX (Anxiety/Depression)

This configuration of the clinical scales suggests a person with significant unhappiness, moodiness, and tension. Although such people are quite distressed and acutely aware of their need for help, their low energy level, passivity, and withdrawal may make them difficult to engage in treatment. Typically self-esteem is quite low, and they view themselves as ineffectual and powerless to change their life direction. Often accompanied by elevations on Stress (*STR*), life disruptions can leave such people uncertain about goals and priorities, and tense and pessimistic about what the future may hold. They are likely to have difficulties in concentrating and making decisions, and the combination of hopelessness, agitation, confusion, and stress may place such people at increased risk for self-harm; secondary elevations on Suicidal Ideation (*SUI*) are often observed with this codetype. This pattern is observed in 1.3% of clinical patients, and it is associated with diagnoses of Dysthymic Disorder, Major Depressive Disorder, and Borderline Personality Disorder.

ANX-ALC/ALC-ANX (Anxiety/Alcohol Problems)

This configuration of the clinical scales suggests a person with a history of drinking problems who is experiencing prominent anxiety. The anxiety and alcohol use may be related in a number of different ways. For example, alcohol use may be serving a functional role of tension reduction. The person is also likely to be anxious and guilty about the impairment in social role performance that has resulted from drinking. The alcohol use is probably causing severe disruptions in a relationships and work, with these difficulties serving as additional sources of distress and, perhaps, further aggravating the drinking problems. Secondary elevations on Stress (*STR*) are often observed with this codetype, further supporting the possibility that alcohol is serving a stress-reduction function. This profile pattern, observed in 1.0% of clinical patients, is associated with diagnoses of Alcohol Dependence, Major Depressive Disorder, and Dysthymic Disorder.

ANX-DRG/DRG-ANX (Anxiety/Drug Problems)

This clinical scale configuration suggests a person with a history of substance-abuse problems who is experiencing prominent anxiety. This anxiety and the substance use may be related in a number of different ways. For example, the drug use may be serving a functional role of tension reduction, or the impairments associated with the drug use may be heightening subjective distress. Such people tend to be anxious and guilty about these impairments in social-role performance, including relationships and work. Such difficulties serve as additional sources of stress and, perhaps, further aggravate the tendency to abuse drugs. Secondary elevations on Depression (*DEP*) and Suicidal Ideation (*SUI*) are often observed with this codetype. Also, it is not uncommon to see Treatment Rejection (*RXR*) in a range that suggests limited motivation for treatment, perhaps associated with a reliance on drugs to solve the individual's problems. This profile configuration, observed in 1.0% of clinical patients, is actually relatively uncommon in substance-abusing samples, but it is seen with some frequency in individuals who have psychotic symptoms.

ARD-DEP/DEP-ARD (Anxiety-Related Disorders/Depression)

This configuration of the clinical scales suggests a person with significant tension, unhappiness, and pessimism. Although such people are quite distressed and acutely aware of their need for help, their low energy level, tension, and withdrawal may make them difficult to engage in treatment. Various stressors, both past and present, have adversely affected self-esteem, and they tend to view themselves as ineffectual and powerless to change their life direction. The life disruptions have left them feeling uncertain about goals and priorities, and tense and pessimistic about what the future may hold. They are likely to have difficulties in concentration and making decisions, and the combination of hopelessness, anxiety, and stress places a person at increased risk for self-harm. Secondary elevations on Anxiety (*ANX*) and Suicidal Ideation (*SUI*) are often observed with this codetype. This is a relatively common profile, observed in 2.5% of clinical patients. Common diagnostic correlates include Posttraumatic Stress and other Anxiety Disorders, Major Depression and Dysthymic Disorder, Borderline Personality Disorder, and Schizoaffective Disorder.

ARD-BOR/BOR-ARD (Anxiety-Related Disorders/Borderline Features)

This pattern suggests a person who is uncomfortable, impulsive, angry and resentful. People with this type of profile often are presenting in a state of crisis and marked distress. Such crises often are associated with difficulties or rejection (perceived or actual) in interpersonal relationships. They often feel betrayed or abandoned by others who are close to them. This may be part of a more general pattern of anxious ambivalence in close relationships, marked by bitterness and resentment, on the one hand, and by dependency and anxiety about possible rejection on the other. Various stressors, both past and present, may have both contributed to and maintained this pattern of interpersonal turmoil; Anxiety-Related Disorder-Traumatic Stress (*ARD-T*) and Stress (*STR*) may yield information about the relative importance of recent, as opposed to more distant, stressors. Regardless of the temporal progression, the disruptions in their lives leave such people uncertain about goals and priorities, and tense and cynical about future prospects. Secondary elevations on Depression (*DEP*) and Suicidal Ideation (*SUI*) are often observed with this codetype, which is obtained in 1.6% of clinical patients. Common diagnostic correlates include Borderline Personality Disorder, Major Depression, and Dysthymic Disorder.

DEP-SCZ/SCZ-DEP (Depression/Schizophrenia)

This configuration of the clinical scales suggests a person with significant problems in thinking and concentration problems, accompanied by prominent distress and dysphoria. Such people are likely to be quite withdrawn and isolated, feeling estranged from the people around them. These current difficulties have probably placed a strain on the few close interpersonal relationships that the person does have. Such people see little hope that their circumstances will improve to any significant degree, and this hopelessness and pessimism, combined with the likelihood of impaired judgment, may place them at increased risk for self-harm; secondary elevations on Suicidal Ideation (SUI) are often observed with this codetype. This configuration is reasonably common in clinical settings and was observed in 2.4% of patients in the clinical standardization sample. Common diagnostic correlates include Schizoaffective Disorder, Posttraumatic Stress or other severe Anxiety Disorders, Borderline Personality Disorder, Major Depression, and Schizophrenia.

DEP-BOR/BOR-DEP (Depression/Borderline Features)

This pattern suggests a person who is unhappy emotionally labile, and probably quite angry at some level. Clients with such profiles are typically presenting in a state of crisis with marked distress and depression. The current distress may be associated with difficulties or rejection, perceived or actual, in interpersonal relationships. Individuals with such profiles often feel betrayed or abandoned by those close to them that compounds their feelings of helplessness and hopelessness. For the person, this may be part of a more general pattern of anxious ambivalence in close relationships, marked by bitterness and resentment on the one hand, and by dependency and anxiety about possible rejection on the other. The underlying anger can cause such people to lash out impulsively at those closest to them. However, the anger seems as much self-directed as it is directed at others. Life disruptions leave these individuals quite uncertain and ambivalent about goals and priorities, and tense and pessimistic about what the future may hold. The combination of hopelessness, resentment, and impulsivity may place such people at increased risk for self-harm, and Suicidal Ideation (SUI) and Stress (STR) are typically elevated with this codetype. This is a relatively common profile, observed in 2.5% of clinical patients. Common diagnostic correlates include Borderline Personality Disorder, Major Depression, and Adjustment Disorders.

DEP-ALC/ALC-DEP (Depression/Alcohol Problems)

This configuration of the clinical scales suggests a person with a history of drinking problems who is quite unhappy and pessimistic. For such individuals, alcohol problems probably have led to severe impairment in the ability to maintain their social-role expectations, and this behavior has most likely alienated many of the people who were once central in their lives. Such setbacks have probably led to significant guilt and rumination about their life circumstances, and the urge to drink may be at the center of many of these ruminations. The depression and the alcohol use may be related in a number of different ways. For example, the depression could be driving the alcohol use, or it could be a consequence of the social disruption associated with alcohol use. Regardless of whether the depression is primary or secondary, the person may well be desperate for help, but cynical about the prospects for change or improvement. Secondary elevations on Suicidal

Ideation (*SUI*) are often observed with this codetype and, when present, heighten concerns about the possibility of self-harm, given the potential for disinhibition associated with alcohol use. Observed in 1.7% of clinical patients, this configuration is commonly associated with diagnoses of Alcohol Dependence, Major Depressive Disorder, and Posttraumatic Stress Disorder.

DEP-DRG/DRG-DEP (Depression/Drug Problems)

This configuration of the clinical scales suggests a person with a history of substance-abuse problems who is quite unhappy and pessimistic. The drug use has probably led to severe impairment in the ability to maintain social-role expectations concerning relationships and employment, and the drug-related behaviors have likely alienated many of the people who were once close to the person. The configuration indicates significant guilt and distress about current life circumstances. The depression and drug use may be related in a number of different ways. For example, the depression could be driving the use of drugs, or it could be a consequence of the disruption associated with substance abuse. Regardless of whether the depression is primary or secondary, it has probably left the person quite pessimistic about the prospects for change or improvement. Secondary elevations on Suicidal Ideation (*SUI*) are often observed with this codetype, and this should be monitored closely given the potential for disinhibition associated with drug misuse. This configuration is found in 1.0% of clinical patients, and is commonly associated with diagnoses of Borderline Personality Disorder, Major Depressive Disorder, and disorders involving drug abuse and/or dependence.

PAR-SCZ/SCZ-PAR (Paranoia/Schizophrenia)

This configuration of the clinical scales suggests a person with significant problems in thinking and concentration, accompanied by prominent hostility resentment, and suspiciousness. Sensitivity in social interactions probably serves as a formidable obstacle to the development of close relationships, and, thus, they are likely to be cautious, withdrawn, and isolated, feeling both estranged from and mistreated by the people around them. Their judgment is probably fairly poor, and they are likely to be chronically tense and apprehensive about what the future may hold. If such a person presents for treatment, establishing a therapeutic relationship may be challenging because such people tend to become quite anxious and threatened by the offer of a close interpersonal relationship. Secondary elevations on Negative Impression Management (*NIM*) are often observed with this codetype, raising the possibility that symptom exaggeration may be driving up the scores on Paranoia (*PAR*) and Schizophrenia (*SCZ*). This is a relatively common profile in inpatient settings, observed in 2.4% of patients in the clinical standardization sample. Common diagnostic correlates include Schizophrenia, Schizoaffective Disorder, Antisocial Personality Disorder, and drug dependence.

SCZ-ALC/ALC-SCZ (Schizophrenia/Alcohol Problems)

This configuration of the clinical scales suggests a person with a history of drinking problems who is confused and socially isolated. A general discomfort in social interactions probably serves as a formidable obstacle to the development of close relationships, and, thus, such people are likely to be withdrawn and isolated and to feel estranged from the people around them. Alcohol may be playing a functional role in helping them distance themselves from such relationships or in reducing the anxiety and threat posed by such relationships.

Their judgment is probably fairly poor, and they are generally both apprehensive about what the future may hold and cynical about the prospects for change. Secondary elevations on Negative Impression Management (*NIM*) are often observed with this codetype, raising the possibility that symptom exaggeration may be contributing to the Schizophrenia (*SCZ*) elevation. This codetype is seen in 1.0% of clinical patients. Alcohol dependence is the most common diagnostic correlate of this pattern.

BOR-ALC (Borderline Features/Alcohol Problems)

This configuration of the clinical scales suggests a person with a history of drinking problems who is impulsive and affectively labile. Drinking may be part of a more general pattern of self-destructive behavior. Interpersonal relationships are likely to be volatile and to be characterized by marked conflict. Even those close relationships that have been maintained will have suffered some strain from their impulsive, unpredictable, and probably hostile style of interaction. These relationships likely will have deteriorated even further as a consequence of the drinking. Such people are likely to be particularly disinhibited under the influence of alcohol, and they may display remarkably poor judgment and demonstrate other acting-out behaviors while intoxicated, perhaps blaming the alcohol for their own unacceptable behavior. Secondary elevations on Stress (*STR*) and low scores on Treatment Rejection (*RXR*) are often observed with this codetype and, when present, suggest a desperate recognition of the need for help. This is a relatively common profile, observed in 1.3% of clinical patients. Common diagnostic correlates include Alcohol Dependence, and Antisocial Personality Disorder as well as Borderline Personality Disorder.

BOR-DRG/DRG-BOR (Borderline Features/Drug Problems)

This configuration of the clinical scales suggests a person with a history of substance-abuse problems who is impulsive and affectively labile. The drug use may be part of a more general pattern of self-destructive behavior, and it probably exacerbates an already erratic approach to life. Interpersonal relationships are likely to be volatile and to be characterized by marked conflict. Even those close relationships that have been maintained will have suffered some strain from the unpredictable and hostile style of interaction. These relationships likely will have deteriorated even further as a consequence of the drug abuse. Such people are likely to be particularly disinhibited under the influence of drugs, and they will tend to display particularly poor judgment and to demonstrate other acting-out behaviors while intoxicated. Secondary elevations on Aggression (*AGG*) are often observed with this codetype. This profile, observed in 1.1% of clinical patients, is most commonly associated with drug abuse and/or dependence diagnoses and Borderline Personality Disorder.

ANT-DRG/DRG-ANT (Antisocial Features/Drug Problems)

This configuration of the clinical scales suggests a person with a history of acting-out behavior, most notably in the area of substance abuse, but probably involving other behaviors as well. Impulsivity and drug use have likely led to severe impairment in their ability to maintain stable employment. Their recklessness has probably alienated most of their family and friends. Generally impulsive and thrill-seeking, the use of drugs is likely to further impair their already suspect judgment. Interpersonal relationships are likely to be superficial, volatile, and short-lived. Even those relationships that have been maintained will have suffered some strain from their egocentricity and from the consequences of their drug use. Secondary elevations on Aggression (*AGG*) are often observed with this codetype and, when present, suggest one possible result of the disinhibition associated with drug use. This is a relatively common profile, observed in 2.1% of clinical patients. This pattern is common in groups with drug dependence diagnoses, Borderline Personality Disorder, or both.

ALC-DRG/DRG-ALC (Alcohol Problems/Drug Problems)

This pattern on the clinical scales suggests a person with a history of polysubstance abuse, including alcohol as well as other drugs. When disinhibited by the substance use, other acting-out behaviors may become apparent as well. The substance abuse is probably causing severe disruptions in social relationships and work performance, with these difficulties serving as additional sources of stress and, perhaps, further aggravating the tendency to drink and use drugs. Secondary elevations on Stress (*STR*) are often observed with this codetype. This profile pattern is quite common, observed in 9.0% of clinical patients, and it characterizes roughly one-fourth of the individuals in alcohol or drug treatment. Other common diagnostic correlates include Antisocial Personality Disorder and Bipolar Disorder.

Individual Scales

Table 9.4 provides general interpretive text for the clinical, treatment consideration, and interpersonal scales when they are elevated to a T score of 70 or higher. For scales with subscales, the general interpretive text has been written on the assumption that the three or four subscales contributed approximately equally to the parent scale. When this assumption is not accurate, the interpretation of the parent scale must be modified by emphasizing the subscale(s) that is/are elevated. For example, on the Anxiety (*ANX*) and Depression (*DEP*) scales, the individual can emphasize any combination of the cognitive, affective, and physiological components of either or both scales and have a very different clinical presentation. Morey (1996a, chap. 2) provides examples of the interpretation of all the patterns of the subscales that are found for each scale, and should be consulted any time an unusual configuration is encountered for the first time.

Supplemental Indices

Morey (1996a) developed three configural indices for the PAI: Suicide Potential Index (*SPI*); Violence Potential Index (*VPI*); and Treatment Process Index (*TPI*). These indices consist of 20, 20, and 12 configural rules, respectively. These indices are computed directly on the PAI Supplemental Indexes-Side C scoring form (see Figure 9.4).

Morey (1991) identified 27 critical items on the PAI distributed across seven content areas (see Table 9.5). These critical items were selected on the basis of two criteria: importance of the content as an indicator of a crisis situation, and a low frequency of endorsement in normal samples. Morey (2007a) revised these 27 critical items by deleting four items with overlapping item content and adding four items in two additional content areas (True Response Set and Idiosyncratic Context). All 27 of the original critical items (Morey, 1991) were keyed "true," but four of the new items added to the critical items are keyed "false." Any deviant (scored) response on any of these 27 items is atypical and individuals should be questioned about any of these items and their explanations documented. Because there are only 27 critical items, few of which are endorsed by even most clinical patients, checking each endorsed item is not very time consuming. As can be seen in Table 9.5, 21

Table 9.4   Interpretation of the PAI clinical and facet scales

Scale Subscale	Interpretation
SOM (Somatic Complaints)	
High (T > 69)	Individuals report unusual sensory or motor dysfunctions. They believe that their health problems are complex and difficult to treat successfully. They report frequent headaches, back problems, pain, and other general problems with their health. Their daily functioning has been impaired by numerous and various physical ailments, accompanied by general lethargy and malaise. They view their health problems as complex, and most of their efforts are focused on the amelioration of these problems. They believe that their health is not as good as that of other people, and they are accustomed to being in the patient role.
SOM-C (Conversion)	
High (T > 69)	Individuals report unusual sensory or motor dysfunctions. They believe that their health problems are complex and difficult to treat successfully. Alcoholics who are beginning to show neurological consequences of their drinking frequently elevate this scale as well as individuals with brain dysfunction.
SOM-S (Somatization)	
High (T > 69)	Individuals report frequent headaches, back problems, pain, and other general problems with their health. Their daily functioning has been impaired by numerous and various physical ailments, accompanied by general lethargy and malaise. They tend to be dissatisfied with their general health and treatment and voice these concerns to anyone who will listen.
SOM-H (Health Concerns)	
High (T > 69)	Individuals view their health problems as very complex, and most of their efforts are focused on the amelioration of these problems. They believe that their health is not as good as that of other people, and they are accustomed to being in the patient role.
ANX (Anxiety)	
High (T > 69)	Individuals worry, ruminate, and are overly concerned about events over which they have no control. Their anxiety is extensive enough to interfere with their memory and concentration. They report feelings of tension, anxiety, and apprehension. They have great difficulty in relaxing and tend to be easily fatigued because of their constant apprehensiveness and high level of perceived stress. They report the physical manifestations of anxiety: racing heart, sweaty palms, rapid breathing, and dizziness.
ANX-C (Cognitive)	
High (T > 69)	Individuals worry, ruminate, and are overly concerned about events over which they have no control. Their anxiety is extensive enough to interfere with their memory and concentration.
ANX-A (Affective)	
High (T > 69)	Individuals report feelings of tension, anxiety, and apprehension. They have great difficulty in relaxing and tend to be easily fatigued because of their constant apprehensiveness and high level of perceived stress.

(continued)

Table 9.4 *(Continued)*

Scale Subscale	Interpretation
ANX-P (Physiological)	
High (T > 69)	Individuals report the physical manifestations of anxiety: racing heart, sweaty palms, rapid breathing, and dizziness. They may not describe the symptoms as being anxious in nature although to others the symptoms are obvious.
ARD (Anxiety-Related Disorders)	
High (T > 69)	Individuals are ruminative, detail oriented, and concerned about order and details in their lives. Their ruminations may make it difficult for them to make decisions and to grasp the larger overview of circumstances. They report specific fears of heights, closed spaces, and agoraphobia. They report nightmares, sudden anxiety reactions, and feelings of being irreversibly harmed by some traumatic event.
ARD-O (Obsessive-Compulsive)	
High (T > 69)	Individuals are ruminative, detail oriented, and very concerned about order and details in their lives. Their ruminations may make it difficult for them to make decisions and to grasp the larger overview of circumstances.
ARD-P (Phobias)	
High (T > 69)	Individuals report specific fears of heights, closed spaces, and agoraphobia. They will go out of their way to avoid these phobic objects.
ARD-T (Traumatic Stress)	
High (T > 69)	Individuals report nightmares, sudden anxiety reactions, and feelings of being irreversibly harmed by some traumatic event.
DEP (Depression)	
High (T > 69)	Individuals perceive themselves as being inadequate and helpless in dealing with life's stresses. They attribute any negative outcome to their inadequacies and any positive outcome to luck. They feel distressed, blue, and sad. They have lost a sense of pleasure in events and activities they used to enjoy. They report vegetative signs of depression: sleep and appetite problems; decreased motivation, energy, and libido; and motoric slowing.
DEP-C (Cognitive)	
High (T > 69)	Individuals perceive themselves as being inadequate and helpless in dealing with life's stresses. They attribute any negative outcome to their inadequacies and any positive outcome to luck.
DEP-A (Affective)	
High (T > 69)	Individuals feel distressed, blue, and sad. They have lost a sense of pleasure in events and activities they used to enjoy.
DEP-P (Physiological)	
High (T > 69)	Individuals report vegetative signs of depression: sleep and appetite problems; decreased motivation, energy, libido, and motoric slowing.

Table 9.4   (*Continued*)

Scale Subscale	Interpretation

MAN (Mania)

High (T > 69)   Individuals tend to be involved in a wide variety of activities in a somewhat disorganized manner and to experience accelerated thought processes. They believe that they are good at almost anything and may even be grandiose. They tend to be quite volatile in the face of frustrations and their mood can change abruptly.

MAN-A (Activity Level)

High (T > 69)   Individuals tend to be involved in a wide variety of activities in a somewhat disorganized manner and to experience accelerated thought processes. This high energy level is very perceptible to others.

MAN-G (Grandiosity)

High (T > 69)   Individuals believe that they are good at almost anything. The likelihood of grandiosity that should be considered may range from belief of having exceptionally high levels of common skills to border on the delusion of special and unique talents.

MAN-I (Irritability)

High (T > 69)   Individuals tend to be volatile in the face of frustrations and their mood can change abruptly. They blame others who do not cooperate or agree with them.

PAR (Paranoia)

High (T > 69)   Individuals spend a great deal of time monitoring their environment for any evidence that others are not trustworthy and may be trying to harm or discredit them in some way. They are quick to believe that they are being treated unfairly and that there is a concerted effort among others to undermine their best interests. They are sensitive and easily slighted and respond by holding grudges against others.

PAR-H (Hypervigilance)

High (T > 69)   Individuals spend a great deal of time monitoring their environment for any evidence that others are not trustworthy and may be trying to harm or discredit them in some way. Others view them as hypersensitive and easily insulted.

PAR-P (Persecution)

High (T > 69)   Individuals are quick to believe that they are being treated unfairly and that there is a concerted effort among others to undermine their best interests.

PAR-R (Resentment)

High (T > 69)   Individuals are very sensitive and easily slighted and respond by holding grudges against others. They attribute their misfortunes to the neglect of others and the success of others as being the result of luck or favoritism.

(continued)

Table 9.4   *(Continued)*

Scale Subscale	Interpretation

SCZ (Schizophrenia)

High (T > 69)   Individuals report the positive symptoms of schizophrenia such as delusions and hallucinations, as well as bizarre thought content. They neither desire nor enjoy close relationships. Social isolation and detachment may serve to avoid the discomfort of interpersonal relations. They have a loosening of associations and difficulties in self-expression and communication. There is a strong likelihood of confusion and perplexity.

SCZ-P (Psychotic Experiences)

High (T > 69)   Individuals experience unusual sensory or perceptual events and/or the unusual ideas that may involve delusional beliefs. They report the positive symptoms of schizophrenia such as delusions and hallucinations, as well as bizarre thought content.

SCZ-S (Social Detachment)

High (T > 69)   Individuals neither desire nor enjoy close relationships. Social isolation and detachment may serve to avoid the discomfort of interpersonal relations.

SCZ-T (Thought Disorder)

High (T > 69)   Individuals have a loosening of associations and difficulties in self-expression and communication. There is a strong likelihood of confusion and perplexity.

BOR (Borderline Features)

High (T > 69)   Individuals are highly responsive emotionally, manifesting rapid and extreme mood swings. Their affective instability involves a propensity to become rapidly anxious, angry, depressed, or irritable. They have a profound need for others to help them define who they are, and they fear abandonment. They repeatedly become involved in relationships that are very intense and chaotic. When their expectations are not met in relationships, they feel betrayed and exploited. They have a tendency to act impulsively without considering the consequences of their actions.

BOR-A (Affective Instability)

High (T > 69)   Individuals are highly responsive emotionally, manifesting rapid and extreme mood swings. Their affective instability involves a propensity to become rapidly anxious, angry, depressed, or irritable.

BOR-I (Identity Problems)

High (T > 69)   Individuals have a profound need for others to help them define who they are and they fear abandonment. They have difficulty in developing and maintaining a sense of purpose.

BOR-N (Negative Relationships)

High (T > 69)   Individuals repeatedly become involved in relationships that are very intense and chaotic. When their expectations are not met in relationships, they feel betrayed and exploited.

Table 9.4 *(Continued)*

Scale Subscale	Interpretation

BOR-S (Self-Harm)

High (T > 69)   Individuals have a tendency to act impulsively without considering the consequences of their actions. Their impulsive behavior has interfered with their occupational and social success.

ANT (Antisocial Features)

High (T > 69)   Individuals have a history of difficulties with persons in positions of authority and have trouble following social conventions. They have a callous attitude toward and lack empathy for other people. They feel little responsibility for the welfare of others and have little loyalty to their acquaintances. They have a willingness to take risks and a desire for novelty. Their behavior is potentially dangerous to themselves and others around them.

ANT-A (Antisocial Behaviors)

High (T > 69)   Individuals have a history of difficulties with persons in positions of authority and have trouble following social conventions.

ANT-E (Egocentricity)

High (T > 69)   Individuals have a callous attitude toward and lack empathy for other people. They have little regard for others or the opinions of the society around them. They feel little responsibility for the welfare of others and have little loyalty to their acquaintances.

ANT-S (Stimulus Seeking)

High (T > 69)   Individuals have a willingness to take risks and a desire for novelty. Their behavior is potentially dangerous to themselves and others around them. They are easily bored by routine and convention.

ALC (Alcohol Problems)

High (T > 69)   Individuals are likely to meet the criteria for alcohol abuse, and alcohol is having a negative impact on their lives. Alcohol-related problems are likely including troubled interpersonal relations, social and occupational difficulties, and possibly health complications.

DRG (Drug Problems)

High (T > 69)   Individuals are likely to meet the criteria for drug abuse and drugs are having a negative impact on their lives. Drug-related problems are likely to be manifested in difficulties in interpersonal relations and in social and occupational difficulties.

From *An Interpretive Guide to the PAI,* chap. 2, by L. C. Morey, 1996a, Odessa, FL: Psychological Assessment Resources. Adapted with permission.

of these 27 critical items come from eight scales: Schizophrenia—Psychotic Experiences (*SCZ-P*); Suicidal Ideation (*SUI*); Aggression-Physical (*AGG-P*); Alcohol Problems (*ALC*); Drug Problems (*DRG*); Negative Impression Management (*NIM*); Antisocial Features-Egocentricity (*ANT-E*); and Anxiety-Related Disorders-Traumatic Stress (*ARD-T*). There is a clear duty to protect the individual if items 100 and 340 on Suicide Intentions (*SUI*) are endorsed.

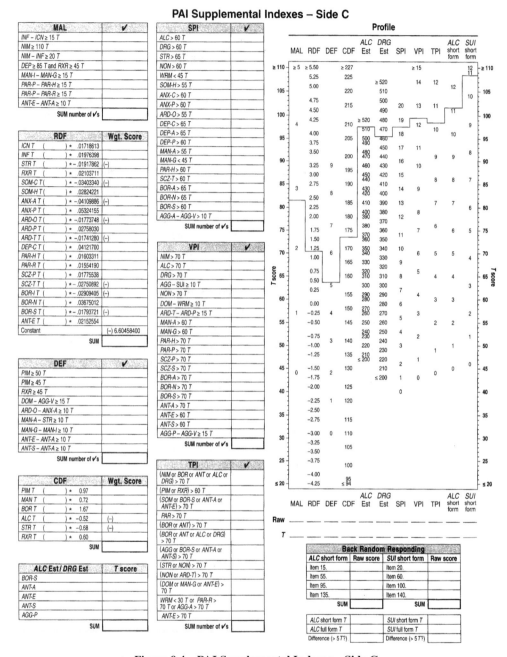

Figure 9.4   PAI Supplemental Indexes—Side C.

Comparison Groups

There are two different groups with which any PAI profile can be compared, and the interpretation that is made will vary as a function of which comparison group is used. In the standard PAI profile (see Figure 9.1), the client is being compared with the census-matched community adults in the PAI normative group (Morey, 1991). The skyline profile that is

Table 9.5   PAI critical items

Item No.	Scale	Sample Statement
Delusions and Hallucinations		
90	*SCZ-P*	Sometimes it seems that my thoughts are broadcast so that others can hear them.
130	*SCZ-P*	
170	*SCZ-P*	
100	*SUI*	
309	*PAR-P*	
183	*BOR-S*	
Potential for Self-Harm		
206	*DEP-A*	
340	*SUI*	
Potential for Aggression		
21	*AGG-P*	.
61	*AGG-P*	
181	*AGG-P*	
Substance Abuse, Current and Historical		
23	*DRG*	
55	*ALC*	
222	*DRG*	
334	*ALC*	My drinking has never gotten me into trouble. (**False**)
Traumatic Stressors		
34	*ARD-T*	I keep reliving something horrible that happened to me.
114	*ARD-T*	
274	*ARD-T*	
Potential Malingering		
49	*NIM*	
129	*NIM*	
249	*NIM*	
Unreliability		
71	*ANT-E*	
311	*ANT-E*	
True Response Set		
75	*DEP-P*	(**False**)
142	*DRG*	(**False**)
Idiosyncratic Context		
80	*INF*	(**False**)
280	*INF*	

Source: An Interpretive Guide to the PAI, table 3-11 (p. 77), by L. C. Morey, 2007a, Odessa, FL: Psychological Assessment Resources. Reprinted with permission.

shown on this form also allows the clinician to compare the individual's scores on each scale with the clinical sample.

APPLICATIONS

As a self-report inventory, the PAI is easily administered in a wide variety of settings and for a variety of purposes. Although the PAI was developed as a broadband measure of psychopathology in clinical settings, its use has gradually been extended to forensic and criminal settings, neuropsychological settings, and medical settings. One of the primary reasons for its rising popularity in these settings is that it is shorter and easier to read than the other self-report inventories.

Somewhat different issues must be considered in the administration of the PAI in personnel selection and forensic settings compared with the more usual clinical setting. These general issues were covered in Chapter 6 with the MMPI-2 (pp. 197–198) and will not be repeated here, but they should be consulted by anyone who is using the PAI in personnel selection or forensic settings for the first time.

One of the considerations in the use of any assessment test or technique in forensic settings is whether it will meet the legal standards for admissibility. These considerations were raised in Chapter 8 with the MCMI-III (pp. 276–277) because various authors have opined that the MCMI-III does or does not meet these legal standards. Morey, Warner, and Hopwood (2007) have described how the PAI meets the legal standards for admissibility. In a survey of forensic psychologists, Lally (2003) reported that the PAI was rated as being acceptable for the evaluation of mental status at the time of the offense, risk for violence, risk for sexual violence, competency to stand trial, and malingering.

The PAI is increasingly being used in correctional settings because it is shorter and easier to read than other self-report inventories. Edens, Cruise, and Buffington-Vollum (2001) have provided a general overview of the issues involved in using the PAI in forensic and correctional settings. Edens and Ruiz (2006) reported that elevated scores on the Positive Impression Management (*PIM* > T56) scale in conjunction with elevated scores on the Antisocial Features (*ANT* > T59) scale predicted institutional misconduct among male inmates. Caperton, Edens, and Johnson (2004) found that elevated scores on the Antisocial Features (*ANT* > T69) scale identified sex offenders who were more likely to be management risks while in prison. Finally, Kucharski, Duncan, Egan, and Falkenback (2006) found that three levels of psychopathy as measured by the PCL-R were not related to scores on Negative Impression Management (*NIM*) scale, the Malingering Index (*MAL*), or Rogers' discriminant function (*RDF*), and that the criminal defendants with higher levels of psychopathy were not more likely to malinger as measured by the PAI scales.

Finally, the PAI is being used in neuropsychological settings to evaluate whether the effects of brain injury have produced any psychological sequelae. Demakis et al. (2007) found that 34.7% of their sample of 95 individuals who had suffered a traumatic brain injury did not elevate any clinical scale on the PAI above a T score of 69. This number of unelevated profiles in individuals with brain injury is commonly found (cf. Warriner, Rourke, Velikonja, & Metham, 2003). The most common two-point codetypes were: *SCZ/BDL*—(Schizophrenia/Borderline Features)—18.9%; *DEP/SCZ*—(Depression/Schizophrenia)—12.6%; and *SOM/ANX*—(Somatic Complaints/Anxiety)—10.5%.

PSYCHOMETRIC FOUNDATIONS

Demographic Variables

Age

Morey (1996a) reported age has minimal impact on the PAI scale scores. Individuals who were 18 to 29 years of age elevated the Paranoia (*PAR*) scale 5 T points, the Borderline Features (*BOR*) scale 6 T points, the Antisocial Features (*ANT*) scale 7 T points, the Aggression (*AGG*) scale 5 T points, and the Stress (*STR*) scale 4 T points higher than other age groups. The primary subscale impacted by this elevation in score was Paranoia-Persecution (*PAR-P*), Borderline Features-Identity Problems (*BOR-I*), Antisocial Features-Stimulus Seeking (*ANT-S*), and Aggression-Verbal Aggression (*AGG-V*). There are no subscales for Stress (*STR*). Individuals who were 60+ years of age lower these same five scales 4 T points. The primary subscale lowered by this elevation was Paranoia-Resentment (*PAR-R*), Borderline Features-Identity Problems (*BOR-I*), Antisocial Features-Antisocial Behavior (*ANT-A*), and Aggression-Physical Aggression (*AGG-P*).

Gender

Gender does not create any general issues in PAI interpretation because the items were selected to eliminate gender bias. Men elevated the Antisocial Features (*ANT*) scale by 3 T points more than women (Morey, 1996a). This elevation primarily impacted the Antisocial Features-Antisocial Behavior (*ANT-A*) subscale.

Education

The potential effects of education have not been investigated in any systematic manner on the PAI, although such research clearly is needed.

Ethnicity

The effects of ethnicity on PAI performance also have not been investigated in any systematic manner. Morey (1996a) reported that nonwhite individuals elevated the Paranoid (*PAR*) scale 6 T points compared with White individuals. This elevation primarily impacted the Paranoid-Hypervigilance (*PAR-H*) subscale.

Reliability

The *PAI Professional Manual* (Morey, 1991, Appendix E) reported the reliability data for 75 community-dwelling adults who were retested after an average of 24 days and 80 undergraduate students who were retested at 28 days. The test-retest correlations ranged from .85 to .94 in the adult sample and ranged from .66 to .90 in the student sample across the 11 clinical scales. The standard error of measurement ranges from 2.8 to 4.6 T points for these 11 clinical scales, that is, the individual's "true" score on the clinical scales will be within ±3 to 5 T points two-thirds of the time.

Codetype Stability

There are limited empirical data that indicate how consistently individuals will obtain the same two highest clinical scales on two successive administrations of the PAI. Codetype stability was examined in all 155 individuals who were part of the examination of retest reliability just described. When only the single highest scale was examined across the two administrations, 57.4% had the same high-point scale. When this analysis was limited only to those individuals with significant elevations (20/155), 76.9% had the same high-point scale. These data should only be considered to be an estimate of the actual codetype stability of the PAI. Because only a single high-point scale was considered, there has to be a lower rate of stability when the two highest scales are required to be the same. On the other hand, clinical samples would produce higher elevations on the PAI clinical scales than these normal individuals and the preceding data suggest that concordance rates would be higher for more elevated profiles.

CONCLUDING COMMENTS

The PAI (Morey, 1991) is the newest of the self-report inventories reviewed in this *Handbook*. The PAI is gradually gaining a wide base of usage because it is shorter than all other self-report inventories except the MCMI-III and it has the lowest reading level of any of them. There has been a substantial increase in research with the PAI in each ensuing year that continues to validate its use in a number of different settings.

REFERENCES

American Psychiatric Association. (2000). *Diagnostic and statistical manual of mental disorders* (4th ed., text rev.). Washington, DC: Author.

Bagby, R. M., Nicholson, R. A., Bacchiochi, J. R., Ryder, A. G., & Bury, A. S. (2002). The predictive capacity of the MMPI-2 and PAI validity scales and indexes to detect coached and uncoached feigning. *Journal of Personality Assessment, 78*, 69–86.

Baity, M. R., Siefert, C. J., Chambers, A., & Blais, M. A. (2007). Deceptiveness with the PAI: A study of naïve faking with psychiatric inpatients. *Journal of Personality Assessment, 88*, 16–24.

Butcher, J. N., Dahlstrom, W. G., Graham, J. R., Tellegen, A. M., & Kaemmer, B. (1989). *MMPI-2: Manual for administration and scoring*. Minneapolis: University of Minnesota Press.

Caperton, J. D., Edens, J. F., & Johnson, J. K. (2004). Predicting sex offender institutional adjustment and treatment compliance using the PAI. *Psychological Assessment, 16*, 187–191.

Cashel, M. L., Rogers, R., & Sewell, K. (1995). The PAI and the detection of defensiveness. *Assessment, 2*, 333–342.

Clark, M. E., Gironda, R. J., & Young, R. W. (2003). Detection of back random responding: Effectiveness of MMPI-2 and PAI validity indices. *Psychological Assessment, 15*, 223–234.

Costa, P. T., Jr., & McCrae, R. R. (1992). *Revised NEO Personality Inventory (NEO PI-R) and NEO Five-Factor Inventory (NEO-FFI) professional manual*. Odessa, FL: Psychological Assessment Resources.

Demakis, G. J., Hammond, F., Knotts, A., Cooper, D. B., Clement, P., Kennedy, J., et al. (2007). The PAI in individuals with traumatic brain injury. *Archives of Clinical Neuropsychology, 22*, 123–130.

Edens, J. F., Cruise, K. R., & Buffington-Vollum, J. K. (2001). Forensic and correctional applications of the PAI. *Behavioral Sciences and the Law, 19*, 519–543.

Edens, J. F., Poythress, N. G., & Watkins-Clay, M. M. (2007). Detection of malingering in psychiatric unit and general population prison inmates: A comparison of the PAI, SIMS, and SIRS. *Journal of Personality Assessment, 88*, 33–42.

Edens, J. F., & Ruiz, M. A. (2006). On the validity of validity scales: The importance of defensive responding in the prediction of institutional misconduct. *Psychological Assessment, 18*, 220–224.

Finn, S. (1996). *Using the MMPI-2 as a therapeutic intervention.* Minneapolis: University of Minnesota Press.

Fischer, C. T. (1994). *Individualizing psychological assessment.* Hillsdale, NJ: Erlbaum.

Frazier, T. W., Naugle, R. I., & Haggerty, K. A. (2006). Psychometric adequacy and comparability of the short and full forms of the PAI. *Psychological Assessment, 18*, 324–333.

Hopwood, C. J., Morey, L. C., Rogers, R., & Sewell, K. (2007). Malingering on the PAI: Identification of specific feigned disorders. *Journal of Personality Assessment, 88*, 43–48.

Kucharski, L. T., Duncan, S., Egan, S. S., & Falkenbach, D. M. (2006). Psychopathy and malingering of psychiatric disorder in criminal defendants. *Behavioral Sciences and the Law, 24*, 633–644.

Kucharski, L. T., Toomey, J. P., Fila, K., & Duncan, S. (2007). Detection of malingering of psychiatric disorder with the PAI: An investigation of criminal defendants. *Journal of Personality Assessment, 88*, 25–32.

Lally, S. J. (2003). What tests are acceptable for use in forensic evaluations? A survey of experts. *Professional Psychology: Research and Practice, 34*, 491–498.

Millon, T., Davis, R., & Millon, C. (1997). *MCMI-III manual* (2nd ed.). Minneapolis, MN: National Computer Systems.

Morey, L. C. (1991). *Personality Assessment Inventory professional manual.* Odessa, FL: Psychological Assessment Resources.

Morey, L. C. (1996a). *An interpretive guide to the PAI.* Odessa, FL: Psychological Assessment Resources.

Morey, L. C. (1996b). *PAI structural summary.* Odessa, FL: Psychological Assessment Resources.

Morey, L. C. (1999). *PAI interpretive explorer module manual.* Odessa, FL: Psychological Assessment Resources.

Morey, L. C. (2003). *Essentials of PAI assessment.* Hoboken, NJ: Wiley.

Morey, L. C. (2007a). *An interpretive guide to the PAI.* Odessa, FL: Psychological Assessment Resources.

Morey, L. C. (2007b). *Personality Assessment Inventory—Adolescent professional manual.* Odessa, FL: Psychological Assessment Resources.

Morey, L. C., & Hopwood, C. J. (2004). Efficiency of a strategy for detecting back random responding on the PAI. *Psychological Assessment, 16*, 197–200.

Morey, L. C., Warner, M. B., & Hopwood, C. J. (2007). Personality Assessment Inventory: Issues in legal and forensic settings. In A. M. Goldstein (Ed.), *Forensic psychology: Emerging topics and expanding roles* (pp. 97–126). Hoboken, NJ: Wiley.

Peebles, J., & Moore, R. J. (1998). Detecting socially desirable responding with the PAI: The Positive Impression Management scale and the Defensiveness Index. *Journal of Clinical Psychology, 54*, 621–628.

Rogers, R., Sewell, K. W., Morey, L. C., & Ustad, K. L. (1996). Detection of feigned mental disorders on the Personality Assessment Inventory: A discriminant analysis. *Journal of Personality Assessment, 67*, 629–640.

Warriner, E. M., Rourke, B. P., Velikonja, D., & Metham, L. (2003). Subtypes of emotional and behavioral sequelae in patients with traumatic brain injury. *Journal of Clinical and Experimental Neuropsychology, 25*, 904–917.

Chapter 10 ———————————————————————

REVISED NEO PERSONALITY INVENTORY

The NEO Personality Inventory (NEO PI; Costa & McCrae, 1985) and the Revised NEO Personality Inventory (NEO PI-R; Costa & McCrae, 1992) measure five broad domains or dimensions of personality in normal adults. Three of these domain scales, measuring Neuroticism (*N*), Extraversion (*E*), and Openness to Experience (*O*), have been researched for years and serve as the basis of the name for the original Inventory (NEO). The NEO PI also includes two additional domains, Agreeableness (*A*) and Conscientiousness (*C*). These five domains allow for a comprehensive description of personality in normal adults. The NEO PI-R consists of five global domains and six facets for each domain (see Table 10.1).

Table 10.2 provides the general information on the NEO PI-R.

HISTORY

A long line of research on five-factor models of personality serve as the basis for the NEO PI-R, most of which is beyond the scope of this *Handbook* (cf. Wiggins, 1996). The rather common finding in the 1980s of five factors in personality research, served as the major impetus for a multitude of studies based on a lexical analysis of words, personality traits, interpersonal theory, or ratings of schoolchildren's behavior. Despite critiques that five-factor models were atheoretical, they have persisted and gained widespread acceptance in the field of personality research. A significant impetus for this widespread acceptance of five-factor models is the prolific work of Costa and McCrae and their publication of the NEO PI (Costa & McCrae, 1985) and NEO PI-R (Costa & McCrae, 1992). A bibliography (Costa & McCrae, 2003) available on the website for Psychological Assessment Resources (www.parinc.com), the publisher of the NEO PI-R, is nearly 60 pages.

Both the NEO PI (Costa & McCrae, 1985) and the NEO PI-R (Costa & McCrae, 1992) have two forms: Form R (Rater) and Form S (Self). Form R is to be completed by a knowledgeable other who is well acquainted with the person and Form S is to be completed by the person being evaluated. Virtually all the research on the NEO PI and NEO PI-R has been conducted with Form S and it is the main form that will be discussed here. More frequent use of Form R in conjunction with Form S seems well warranted because of the important perspective it can provide on the person being evaluated. At a minimum, the reader needs to be aware of the existence of Form R so as to consider the possibility of its use.

Table 10.1 Revised NEO Personality Inventory (NEO PI-R) domain and facet scales

Domain	Facets	
N (Neuroticism)	*N1*	Anxiety
	N2	Angry Hostility
	N3	Depression
	N4	Self-Consciousness
	N5	Impulsiveness
	N6	Vulnerability
E (Extraversion)	*E1*	Warmth
	E2	Gregariousness
	E3	Assertiveness
	E4	Activity
	E5	Excitement-Seeking
	E6	Positive Emotions
O (Openness)	*O1*	Fantasy
	O2	Aesthetics
	O3	Feelings
	O4	Actions
	O5	Ideas
	O6	Values
A (Agreeableness)	*A1*	Trust
	A2	Straightforwardness
	A3	Altruism
	A4	Compliance
	A5	Modesty
	A6	Tender-Mindedness
C (Conscientiousness)	*C1*	Competence
	C2	Order
	C3	Dutifulness
	C4	Achievement Striving
	C5	Self-Discipline
	C6	Deliberation

NEO PI (First Edition)

The NEO PI (Costa & McCrae, 1985) consisted of five domains: Neuroticism (*N*); Extraversion (*E*); Openness (*O*); Agreeableness (*A*); and Conscientiousness (*C*). The name of the inventory—NEO—was formed from the initial letter of the first three names in a concession to an early version of the inventory that contained only those three domains. These five domains measure the broad dimensions of personality in normal adults. The first three domains (Neuroticism [*N*]; Extraversion [*E*], Openness [*O*]) also had six facets or subscales for each domain.

Table 10.2   Revised NEO Personality Inventory (NEO PI-R)

Authors:	Costa & McRae
Published:	1992
Edition:	Revised
Publisher:	Psychological Assessment Resources
Website:	www.parinc.com
Age range:	18+
Reading level:	6th grade
Administration formats:	Paper/pencil, computer, CD, cassette
Languages:	9 published and 25 validated translations
Number of items:	240
Response format:	5-point Likert scale
Administration time:	20–30 minutes
Primary scales:	5 Domains and 30 Facets
Additional scales:	None
Hand scoring:	2-part carbonless Answer Sheet (self-scoring)
General texts:	None
Computer interpretation:	Psychological Assessment Resources (Costa & McRae)

NEO PI-R (Revised Edition)

The NEO PI-R (Costa & McCrae, 1992) consists of the same five domains as in the NEO PI. There are only two minor differences between the NEO PI-R and the NEO PI. First, the facet scales for Agreeableness (*A*) and Conscientiousness (*C*) were added; they had not been available on the NEO PI. Second, 10 (4.2%) items were replaced to allow for more accurate measurement of several facets.

Although the NEO PI-R is the focus of this chapter, two other forms of the NEO need to be mentioned: NEO Five-Factor Inventory (NEO-FFI; Costa & McCrae, 1992); and NEO PI-3 (McCrae, Costa, & Martin, 2005). Each of these other forms of the NEO PI-R is described in turn. This description can be very brief for both of them because they retain the essential features of the NEO PI-R.

NEO Five-Factor Inventory

The NEO-FFI (Costa & McCrae, 1992) is essentially an authorized short form of the NEO PI-R. It consists of 60 items from the NEO PI-R that are used only to score the five domains: Neuroticism (*N*), Extraversion (*E*); Openness (*O*); Agreeableness (*A*); and Conscientiousness (*C*). It does not contain the items for assessing the facets within each domain. The NEO-FFI is designed for use in circumstances in which time is too limited to present the entire NEO PI-R or only scores on the five domains are required. All the information provided on the domains for the NEO PI-R will apply to the NEO-FFI so it does not need to be discussed explicitly.

NEO PI-3

McCrae et al. (2002) identified 30 items on the NEO PI-R (Costa & McCrae, 1992) that were not endorsed by at least 2% of nearly 2,000 adolescents. A number of these

30 items contained words that adolescents, and even some adults, might not understand. An additional 18 items were identified that had item-total scores on the facet scales less than .30. Alternative items were developed for these 48 items and McCrae et al. (2005) found acceptable replacements for 37 of them. The original version of the other 11 items was retained on the NEO PI-3. The items on the NEO PI-3 are easier to read than those on the NEO PI-R and the NEO PI-3 can be used for adolescents 12 years of age and older. Further research currently is being conducted to determine whether the NEO PI-3 can be considered as a replacement for the NEO PI-R at all ages.

The entire December 2000 issue of the journal *Assessment* was devoted to the NEO PI-R. Anyone who is using the NEO PI-R should review this issue to get a better idea of the broad extent and wide nature of its usage.

ADMINISTRATION

The first issue in the administration of the NEO PI-R is ensuring that the individual is invested in the process. Taking a few extra minutes to answer any questions the individual has about why the NEO PI-R is being administered and how the results will be used will pay excellent dividends. The examiner should work diligently to make the assessment process a collaborative activity with the individual to obtain the desired information. This issue of therapeutic assessment (Finn, 1996; Fischer, 1994) was covered in more depth in Chapter 2 (pp. 43–44). The transparent nature of the items on the NEO PI-R and the lack of extensive means for assessing the validity of item endorsement (see later section in this chapter) make the task of getting the individual appropriately engaged in completing the NEO PI-R all the more important.

Reading level is not a crucial factor in determining whether a person can complete the NEO PI-R. First, the reading level of the NEO PI-R is the sixth grade. Second, the examiner may read the items to individuals whose reading abilities are limited and record the responses (Costa & McCrae, 1992, p. 5). The NEO PI-R is the only self-report inventory discussed in this *Handbook* that allows the examiner to read the items to the individuals. All other self-report inventories explicitly discourage or forbid this procedure (see Chapter 5).

SCORING

Scoring the NEO PI-R is relatively straightforward either by hand or computer. If the NEO PI-R is administered by computer, the computer automatically scores it. If the individual's responses to the items have been placed on an answer sheet, these responses can be entered into the computer by the clinician for scoring or they can be hand scored. If the clinician enters the item responses into the computer for scoring, they should be double entered so that any data entry errors can be identified.

One of the advantages of computer scoring is that the factor score for each domain is computed directly. The factor scores can be calculated for the domains using the formulas presented in the *Manual* (Costa & McCrae, 1992, p. 8), and it is recommended that researchers use the factor scores. "In most cases, the domain scale scores are a good approximation to factor scores, and it is probably not worth the effort to apply these formulas by hand to individual cases" (Costa & McCrae, 1992, p. 7).

The NEO PI-R (Costa & McCrae, 1992) and the Personality Assessment Inventory (PAI: Morey, 1991) are the only self-report inventories reviewed in this *Handbook* that do not use "true/false" items. Both of these inventories have the same publisher (Psychological Assessment Resources), and that may account for not using "true/false" items. The NEO PI-R uses a five-point Likert scale ranging from *SD* (Strongly Disagree), *D* (Disagree), *N* (Neutral), *A* (Agree), to *SA* (Strongly Agree). These potential response options always are presented in this same order on the answer sheet. When *SD* (Strongly Disagree) is the scored direction for a specific item, the response options are scored as 4, 3, 2, 1, or 0. When *SA* (Strongly Agree) is the scored direction, the preceding five response options are scored as 0, 1, 2, 3, or 4. Thus, the total raw score on each eight-item facet scale can range from 0 to 32. The total score on a domain, each of which consists of six facet scales, can range from 0 to 192, but the norm tables for adults are truncated at 25 and 172 (Costa & McCrae, 1992, Appendix C, p. 79).

The first step in hand scoring is to examine the answer sheet carefully and indicate omitted items and double-marked items by drawing a line through all five responses to these items with brightly colored ink. Also, cleaning up the answer sheet is helpful and facilitates scoring. Responses that were changed need to be erased completely if possible, or clearly marked with an "X" so that the clinician is aware that this response has not been endorsed by the client.

The answer sheet for the NEO PI-R is self-scoring, that is, no templates or overlays are required for scoring. Instead the top page of the answer sheet is removed and each row of items corresponds to one of the facets for each of the domains. The facets are in numerical order within each domain and the domains are in the order: Neuroticism (*N*); Extraversion (*E*); Openness (*O*); Agreeableness (*A*); and Conscientiousness (*C*). The raw score for each facet is the sum of the circled numbers on its row. The sum of the marked scores for the first row is facet *N1*, the sum of the second row is facet *E1*, and so on. Once the six facet scores have been calculated for each domain, they are summed to create the raw score for each domain. Thus, the sum of facets *N1, N2, N3, N4, N5,* and *N6* becomes the raw score for domain *N*. These raw scores for each domain are entered into the corresponding box at the bottom of the answer sheet.

Plotting the profile is the next step in the scoring process. There are two profile forms that can be used with Form S: adults (21 years of age and older) and college (17 to 20). Profiles are plotted separately for men and women with each of these forms and are on opposite sides of the same page. The college-age profile form is used for all individuals aged 17 to 20 no matter whether they are in college. To remove the ambiguity, it would be more accurate to say that the "young adult" form should be used for all individuals between the ages of 17 and 20 and not call it a "college" profile form.

Once the correct profile form has been selected for the person's age and gender, all the raw scores from the answer sheet are transferred to the appropriate column of the profile sheet (see Figure 10.1). The first five columns on the profile sheet are the five domains (*N, E, O, A,* and *C*) and then the six facets for each domain are presented in order. The raw score on each domain and facet is indicated by either circling the number or marking it with an "x." Once the individual's scores on the five domains have been plotted, a solid line is drawn to connect them. A similar procedure is followed for each of the six facets.

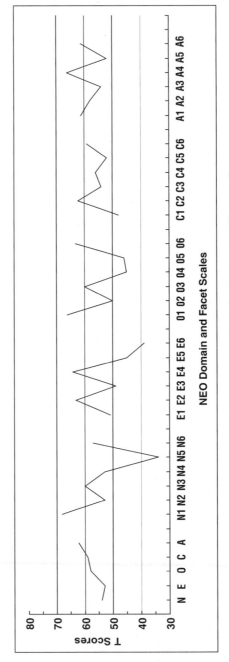

Figure 10.1 NEO PI-R profile form for Domain and Facet scales.

The scores for the domains are not connected to the facet scores, and the sets of facets are plotted separately; that is, there will be seven separate lines or profiles on the form.

ASSESSING VALIDITY

One of the few areas of contention with the NEO PI-R is whether validity scales are necessary at all. The focus of this contention revolves around three issues: (1) whether responses to the NEO PI-R can be distorted and thus should be assessed; (2) the prevalence of such distortions within various groups of individuals; and (3) whether the use of validity scales to remove questionable profiles actually improves correlates with external criteria. Each of these issues is examined in turn.

A variety of studies have demonstrated that the NEO PI-R, like all self-report instruments, can be distorted by students in simulation designs either in a positive (Ballenger, Caldwell-Andrews, & Baer, 2001; Griffin, Hesketh, & Grayson, 2004) or negative direction (Berry et al., 2001).

It seems natural enough that distortions of responses occur less frequently in normal adults, where the NEO PI-R is used most often, because there is little motivation for doing so. The frequency of such distortions of responses also should decrease when the NEO PI-R is filled out anonymously, which typically happens in research. Again, finding that validity scales are not useful in normal adults and research settings would seem to reflect the nature of the participants and settings rather than the usefulness of the validity scales.

However, in clinical and personnel screening settings, it seems probable that individuals may distort their responses in some manner and the preceding research demonstrates that scores on the NEO PI-R can be distorted. In both clinical and personnel selection settings, the examiner is concerned with assessing potential distortions to the domain and facet scales in this specific individual, because it will affect the interpretation of the scores. Thus, the finding that validity scales may be more useful in clinical and personnel selection settings would seem to reflect the nature of the setting.

Several studies found that using the validity scales to remove NEO PI-R profiles with excessive distorted responses did not increase the relationship with external correlates (Piedmont, McCrae, Riemann, & Angleitner, 2000; Yang, Bagby, & Ryder, 2000). These findings typically occur when large groups of participants are assessed and the relative prevalence of such invalid profiles is relatively low.

Several studies also have found that using the validity scales to remove NEO PI-R profiles with excessive distorted responses increased the relationship with external correlates (Caldwell-Andrews, Baer, & Berry, 2000; Young & Schinka, 2001). These findings typically occurred in clinical samples that would be more prone to distort their responses and in most cases were instructed to do so.

Another way of framing this contention is whether response distortion is substance, a characteristic of the individual such as some form of psychopathology, or personality trait or style, an effortful alteration of responses that may be conscious or reflect lack of insight. In true diplomatic fashion, Morey et al. (2002) concluded that both substantive and stylistic variance may be involved in determining responses to the NEO PI-R in clinical patients.

These two sources of substantive and stylistic variance were highly correlated (.71), which may be the reason for the conflicting findings in various samples.

Costa and McCrae (1992), the authors of the NEO PI-R, have another perspective on the issue of protocol validity. They acknowledge that there are potential problems with response distortions, but they are not convinced that validity scales are an appropriate solution. They do offer minimal checks on protocol validity by simply asking persons if they have answered questions honestly and completely, and checking for patterns of grossly random responding. However, they feel that the first effort should be to get the full cooperation of the individual by establishing rapport, explaining reasons for the assessment, and providing feedback on the assessment where appropriate. This point is the idea of therapeutic assessment that has been stressed repeated thoroughly this *Handbook* (see pp. 43–44).

Where it is still questionable whether valid data can be obtained, Costa and McCrae (1992) recommend the use of ratings from knowledgeable others (e.g., spouses, relatives, significant others) on a parallel version of the NEO PI-R, Form R. Evidence on the validity and clinical utility of Form R assessments is provided in Bagby et al. (1998), Costa and McCrae (1992), and Fiedler, Oltmanns, and Turkheimer (2004). The NEO PI-R is the only self-report inventory reviewed in this *Handbook* that has a parallel form that can be used for ratings by knowledgeable others. Their perspective on the person using Form R can make an important contribution to understanding him or her, regardless of the validity of self-reports, and its more widespread use in clinical settings is encouraged.

Because it appears that responses to the NEO PI-R can be distorted, particularly in clinical and personnel selection settings, the same format will be used to assess validity on the NEO PI-R as has been used with the other self-report inventories discussed in this *Handbook*. The NEO PI-R has three simple Validity Checks that need to be reviewed routinely. Beyond these three simple Validity Checks, there is only a limited amount of data on the research scales developed by Schinka, Kinder, and Kremer (1997) to assess validity of the NEO PI-R.

Figure 10.2 provides the flowchart for assessing the validity of this specific administration of the NEO PI-R, and the criteria for using this flowchart are provided in Table 10.3. The reader is reminded that the criteria provided in Table 10.3 are continuous, yet ultimately the decisions that must be made in implementation of the flowchart in Figure 10.2 are dichotomous. General guidelines will be provided for translating these continuous data into dichotomous decisions on the NEO PI-R, but these guidelines need to be considered within the constraints of this specific individual and the circumstances for the evaluation.

Item Omissions

Before the individual leaves the evaluation, the answer sheet should be scanned to see if any item(s) has(have) been omitted, and if so, the individual should be asked to complete them. The individual may use the *N* (Neutral) response option if he or she is unsure how to respond to a specific item. If the individual is no longer available to complete any omitted items, the NEO PI-R should *not* be scored if more than 40 (16.7%) items have been omitted. If fewer than 41 items have been omitted, the omitted items should be scored as if the *N*

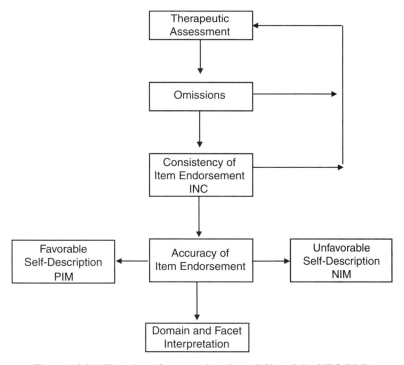

Figure 10.2   Flowchart for assessing the validity of the NEO PI-R.

(Neutral) response was selected. Individual facet scores should *not* be scored if three or more items have been omitted.

Item B, one of the three validity checks on the NEO PI-R at the bottom of the answer sheet, asks whether all the items have been endorsed. An answer of "No" to Item B should be queried by the examiner to determine why the individual cannot respond to the item(s). The individual can be reminded to use the *N* (Neutral) response option if he or she is unsure of how to respond to a specific item.

There are no published frequency data on item omissions on the NEO PI-R. It does seem like omitting 40 responses would have a significant impact on the resulting profile and should be discouraged, if at all possible to do so. Scoring the *N* (Neutral) response option for omitted items seems questionable because it assumes that the item has no relevancy for the individual, and as such, is not considered to be either substance or style.

Consistency of Item Endorsement

There is no extant scale to assess consistency of item endorsement on the NEO PI-R. Validity Check C asks the individual whether responses to the items have been marked in the correct spaces. A response of "No" to Validity Check C for whatever reason normally invalidates formal scoring of the NEO PI-R.

Costa and McCrae (1992) suggest that long strings of the same response option can be used to indicate random responding: 6 consecutive *SD* (Strongly Disagree) responses; 9 consecutive *D* (Disagree) responses, 10 consecutive *N* (Neutral) responses; 14 consecutive *A* (Agree) responses; or 9 consecutive *SA* (Strongly Agree) responses. Any one of these

Table 10.3   Criteria for assessing NEO PI-R validity by type of setting

	Percentile										
Setting	1	2	7	16	30	50	70	84	93	98	99
Item Omissions											
No data are available.											
Consistency of Item Endorsement											
Adults[a]	0	1	2	3	4	5	7	9	10	13	14
Accuracy of Item Endorsement											
Self-Unfavorable Description (Negative Impression Management [*NIM*])											
Adults[a]	0	1	3	5	6	8	10	12	13	16	18
College[b]	1	3	5	7	8	10	12	13	15	17	18
Personnel[b]		0	2	3	4	6	8	9	10	11	12
Personnel[b]		0	2	3	4	6	8	9	11	14	22
Accuracy of Item Endorsement											
Self-Favorable Description (Positive Impression Management [*PIM*])											
Adults[a]	9	10	13	16	18	20	22	24	26	29	30
College[b]		8	12	13	16	17	20	22	25	27	29
Personnel[b]	14	19	21	23	24	26	28	30	31	34	36
Personnel[b]	15	18	21	23	25	28	30	32	34	36	39

[a]Schinka et al. (1997).
[b]Caldwell-Andrews (2001).

long strings of the same response invalidates the NEO PI-R and it should not be scored or interpreted.

Schinka et al. (1997) developed an inconsistency scale (*INC*) for the NEO PI-R that consists of 10 pairs of items (11-71; 39-159; 53-113; 59-199; 72-132; 85-215; 102-162; 110-170; 188-218; 191-221) with the highest relationship. The absolute difference in the scored response for each pair of items is computed and then summed across all 10 pairs of items to get the raw score on the *INC* scale. Five of these pairs were related positively and five pairs were related negatively. High scores on the *INC* scale reflect the number of inconsistent responses to these 10 pairs of items. The *INC* scale accurately identified NEO PI-R protocols generated at random (Schinka et al., 1997).

Scores on the *INC* scale are very low in normal individuals (see Table 10.3) with nearly 90% of them scoring less than a raw score of 10 (Schinka et al., 1997). It would seem that raw scores of 10 or higher on the *INC* scale should be reviewed carefully to examine whether the person had the necessary skills to read the items or answered the items randomly. There are no published data on the frequency of raw scores on the *INC* scale in clinical or personnel-screening samples or what raw score in any sample would render the NEO PI-R uninterpretable because of inconsistent item endorsement.

Accuracy of Item Endorsement

There are no standard scales on the NEO PI-R to assess accuracy of item endorsement. Validity Check A asks the individual whether the items have been answered honestly and accurately. Costa and McCrae (1992) reported that 99% of volunteer participants endorsed Validity Check A as *A* (Agree) or *SA* (Strongly Agree). A *SD* (Strongly Disagree) or *D* (Disagree) response to Validity Check A for whatever reason normally invalidates formal scoring of the NEO PI-R.

Costa and McCrae (1992) suggest that the sum of the *A* (Agree) and *SA* (Strongly Agree) responses can be used to assess whether the individual has an acquiescence or naysaying bias. If the individual has 150 or more of these *A* and *SA* responses, the NEO PI-R should be interpreted with caution, if at all, because of a potential acquiescence bias. If the individual has 50 or fewer of these *A* and *SA* responses, the NEO PI-R should be interpreted with caution, if at all, because of a potential nay-saying bias.

Self-Unfavorable Descriptions

Schinka et al. (1997) developed the Negative Impression Management (*NIM*) scale to assess self-unfavorable descriptions on the NEO PI-R. The initial item pool for the *NIM* scale consisted of 50 potential items with extremely low mean scores (low frequency of endorsement). The final 10 items (Strongly Disagree [*SD*]: 15, 48, 57, 62, 73, 104, 129, 135; Strongly Agree [*SA*]: 31, 161) for the *NIM* scale were selected rationally by the authors. When *SD* (Strongly Disagree) is the scored direction for these eight items, the response options are scored as 4 (*SD*), 3, 2, 1, or 0 (*SA*). When *SA* (Strongly Agree) is the scored direction, the five response options are scored as 0 (*SD*), 1, 2, 3, or 4 (*SA*). The sum of the scores on these 10 items becomes the raw score on the *NIM* scale. There are from one to three items from each domain on the *NIM* scale. Several studies have demonstrated that the *NIM* scale identifies college students and clinical patients who were instructed to make a self-unfavorable description by simulating psychopathology (Berry et al., 2001; Caldwell-Andrews et al., 2000; Young & Schinka, 2001).

Table 10.3 shows that a raw score more than 11 to 15 on the *NIM* scale is very unusual and at or above the 93rd percentile in normal adult, college student, and personnel-screening samples. There is surprisingly little variation among these three samples on the *NIM* scale. It would be assumed that all these groups have little motivation to distort their responses in a self-unfavorable manner, and hence, their scores are similar.

Self-Favorable Descriptions

Schinka et al. (1997) developed the Positive Impression Management (*PIM*) scale to assess self-favorable descriptions on the NEO PI-R. The initial item pool for the *PIM* scale consisted of 22 potential items with extremely high mean scores (high frequency of endorsement). The final 10 items (Strongly Disagree [*SD*]: 30, 42, 113, 146, 162, 196; Strongly Agree [*SA*]: 37, 93, 139, 153) for the *PIM* scale were selected rationally by the authors. When *SD* (Strongly Disagree) is the scored direction for these six items, the response options are scored as 4 (*SD*), 3, 2, 1, or 0 (*SA*). When *SA* (Strongly Agree) is the scored direction, the five response options are scored as 0 (*SD*), 1, 2, 3, or 4 (*SA*). The sum of the scores on these 10 items becomes the raw score on the *PIM* scale. There are two items from each domain on the *PIM* scale. Many studies have investigated the effectiveness of the *PIM* scale because it is more relevant to the settings in which the NEO PI-R is administered such as personnel selection. These studies demonstrate that college students (Caldwell-Andrews et al., 2000), personnel-screening applicants (Griffin et al., 2004; Pauls & Crost, 2005), and psychotherapy outpatients (Ballenger et al., 2001) could simulate being healthy and well adjusted on the NEO PI-R, and the *PIM* scale was reasonably successful at identifying them. The differentiation of normal college students from other groups simulating being healthy and well adjusted was more difficult because of the similarity of these two conditions. Pauls and Crost (2005) found that job applicants could distort their responses in a positive direction, and more importantly, distort their responses to domains that were relevant for the position for which they were applying.

Table 10.3 shows that a raw score more than 25 to 34 on the *PIM* scale is very unusual and at or above the 93rd percentile in normal adult, college student, and personnel-screening samples. There is more variability in performance on the *PIM* scale among these samples than was found on the *NIM* scale. Normal adults and college students, who would be assumed to be psychologically healthy, have similar scores on the *PIM* scale and lower than the scores of police applicants. College students simulating the performance of police applicants have almost identical scores to the actual police applicants (Caldwell-Andrews, 2001).

High scores on either the *NIM* or *PIM* scale on the NEO PI-R are presumptive, rather than definitive, evidence of inaccurate responses. This point is clearest with the *PIM* scale where a very high score could reflect accurately that the person is very psychologically healthy rather than that the person is being screened for some personnel position. As with all other assessment tests and techniques, scores on scales or profiles are used to create hypotheses about the person that must be corroborated by other data. In the example of a high *PIM* score in a personnel screening setting, if it is an accurate self-description, it should be apparent in an interview with the person or even a cursory overview of the social background that the person is psychologically healthy.

INTERPRETATION

Once it has been determined that the individual has omitted few, if any, items, and endorsed the items consistently and accurately, the NEO PI-R can be interpreted. Interpretation of the NEO PI-R begins with, and sometimes ends with, the scores on the five domains, although the facet scores should be interpreted if they have been administered and scored. (The NEO-FFI only can be interpreted at the domain level because no items from the facet scales have been administered.) All scales on the NEO PI-R and NEO-FFI are construed as dimensions, and as such, both high and low scores are interpretable. Scores below a T score of 45 are considered low, T scores of 45 to 55 are average, and T scores above 56 are high.

Table 10.4 provides a brief summary of the interpretation of high and low scores on all the domain and facet scales. Figure 10.3 is a copy of the standard feedback form that is available from the publisher. This feedback form provides a brief description of high, average, and low scores on each domain in the order of Neuroticism (*N*), Extraversion (*E*), and Openness to Experience (*O*), Agreeableness (*A*) and Conscientiousness (*C*).

Table 10.4   Interpretation of the NEO PI-R and NEO-FFI domain and NEO PI-R facet scales

Domain	Facet	Interpretation
N (Neuroticism)	High (T > 55)	Individuals often feel tense, jittery, anxious, and easily frightened. They are easily embarrassed, self-conscious, and feel inferior around other people. They feel sad, blue, and depressed, and sometimes experience a deep sense of guilt and sinfulness. Individuals often get angry and mad, and they are known as being hot blooded and quick tempered. They sometimes do things on impulse that they later regret and often give in to their impulses. They feel helpless, unstable emotionally, and sometimes feel like they are going to pieces.
	Low (T < 45)	Individuals do not worry and rarely feel fearful or anxious. They are even tempered and it takes a lot to get them mad. They rarely feel lonely, sad, or depressed. They are comfortable around other people. They rarely overindulge and seldom give in to their impulses, cravings, or temptation. They can handle themselves pretty well in a crisis or emergency.
N1 (Anxiety)	High (T > 55)	Individuals often feel tense, jittery, anxious, and easily frightened. They often worry about things that might go wrong. They have frightening thoughts and are apprehensive about the future.
	Low (T < 45)	Individuals do not worry and rarely feel fearful or anxious. They are seldom apprehensive about the future and have fewer fears than most people. They do not have frightening thoughts.
N2 (Angry Hostility)	High (T > 55)	Individuals often get angry and mad, and they are known as being hot blooded and quick tempered. They often get disgusted with other people and at times have felt bitter and resentful. Even minor annoyances can be frustrating to them.
	Low (T < 45)	Individuals are even tempered and it takes a lot to get them mad. Minor annoyances are not frustrating to them and they seldom get angry at the way people treat them. They seldom get disgusted with people or feel bitter and resentful.
N3 (Depression)	High (T > 55)	Individuals feel sad, blue, and depressed, and sometimes experience a deep sense of guilt and sinfulness. They blame themselves when something goes wrong and have a low opinion of their abilities and sometimes feel completely worthless. When things go wrong, they feel discouraged, bleak, and hopeless.
	Low (T < 45)	Individuals rarely feel lonely, sad, or depressed. They do not get discouraged and do not blame themselves when things go wrong. They have not experienced a deep sense of guilt or sinfulness.

(continued)

Table 10.4 (*Continued*)

Domain	Facet	Interpretation
N4 (Self-Consciousness)	High (T > 55)	Individuals are easily embarrassed, self-conscious, and feel inferior around other people. They fear making a social blunder and can hardly bear facing someone if they do make a blunder. They get embarrassed when people they know do foolish things.
	Low (T < 45)	Individuals are comfortable around other people. They seldom feel self-conscious and are not embarrassed if people tease them or if they do foolish things. They are not concerned about making social blunders.
N5 (Impulsiveness)	High (T > 55)	Individuals sometimes do things on impulse that they later regret and often give in to their impulses. They find it difficult to resist temptation or cravings and frequently overindulge. They have problems keeping their feelings under control. They eat too much of their favorite foods and sometimes eat themselves sick.
	Low (T < 45)	Individuals rarely overindulge and seldom give in to their impulses, cravings, or temptation. They are able to keep their feelings under control. They do not tend to eat too much of their favorite foods or eat themselves sick.
N6 (Vulnerability)	High (T > 55)	Individuals feel helpless, unstable emotionally, and at times as if they are going to pieces. They do not feel capable of dealing with most of their problems. They have a hard time making up their mind. They cannot handle themselves very well in a crisis or emergency.
	Low (T < 45)	Individuals can handle themselves pretty well in a crisis or emergency. They are pretty stable emotionally and can cope with most of their problems. They can make good decisions even when things are going wrong or they are under a great deal of stress.
E (Extraversion)	High (T > 55)	Individuals are known as warm, friendly persons who enjoy talking to people. They like to have a lot of people around them and enjoy parties with lots of people. They are dominant, forceful, and assertive, and often have been leaders of groups to which they belong. They often crave excitement and like to be where the action is. They are cheerful, high-spirited persons who laugh easily.
	Low (T < 45)	Individuals do not get much pleasure from chatting with people and they do not take a personal interest in the people with whom they work. They shy away from crowds of people and usually prefer to do things alone. They sometimes fail to assert themselves as much as they should and usually let others do the talking. They are not as quick and lively as other people, and their work is likely to be slow and steady. They seldom crave excitement, and they do not like to be where the action is. They are not cheerful optimists and do not consider themselves especially lighthearted.

Table 10.4   (*Continued*)

Domain	Facet	Interpretation
E1 (Warmth)	High (T > 55)	Individuals are known as warm, friendly persons who enjoy talking to people. They really like most people they meet and they find it easy to smile and be outgoing with strangers. They take a personal interest in the people with whom they work. They have strong emotional attachments to their friends.
	Low (T < 45)	Individuals do not get much pleasure from chatting with people and they do not take a personal interest in the people with whom they work. Many people think of them as cold and distant and they do not have strong emotional attachments to their friends.
E2 (Gregarious-ness)	High (T > 55)	Individuals like to have a lot of people around them and enjoy parties with lots of people. They really feel the need for other people if they are by themselves for long. They would rather vacation at a popular beach than at an isolated cabin.
	Low (T < 45)	Individuals shy away from crowds of people and usually prefer to do things alone. Social gatherings are usually boring to them. They would rather vacation at an isolated cabin rather than a popular beach. They prefer jobs that let them work alone without being bothered by other people.
E3 (Assertiveness)	High (T > 55)	Individuals are dominant, forceful, and assertive, and often have been leaders of groups to which they belong. Other people look to them to make decisions. In conversations, they tend to do most of the talking.
	Low (T < 45)	Individuals sometimes fail to assert themselves as much as they should and usually let others do the talking. They would rather go their own way than be a leader of others. They do not find it easy to take charge of a situation.
E4 (Activity)	High (T > 55)	Individuals are active and have a fast-paced life. When they do things, they do them vigorously. They often feel as if they are bursting with energy and usually seem to be in a hurry.
	Low (T < 45)	Individuals are not as quick and lively as other people, and their work is likely to be slow and steady. They have a leisurely style in work and play.
E5 (Excitement-Seeking)	High (T > 55)	Individuals often crave excitement and like to be where the action is. They have sometimes done things just for the thrill of it. They are attracted to bright colors and flashy styles. They like being part of the crowd at sporting events.
	Low (T < 45)	Individuals seldom crave excitement and they do not like to be where the action is. They tend to avoid movies that are shocking or scary and they would not enjoy vacationing in Las Vegas.

(*continued*)

Table 10.4 (*Continued*)

Domain	Facet	Interpretation
E6 (Positive Emotions)	High (T > 55)	Individuals are cheerful, high-spirited persons who laugh easily. They have sometimes experienced intense joy or ecstasy and sometimes bubble with happiness.
	Low (T < 45)	Individuals are not cheerful optimists and do not consider themselves especially lighthearted. They have never literally jumped for joy and rarely use words like "fantastic!" or "sensational!" to describe their experiences.
O (Openness)	High (T > 55)	Individuals have an active imagination and fantasy life. They are intrigued by the patterns they find in art and nature. They feel a wide range of emotions or feelings. They think that it is interesting to learn and develop new hobbies. They enjoy playing with theories or abstract ideas and solving problems or puzzles. They consider themselves to be broad-minded and tolerant of other people's lifestyles.
	Low (T < 45)	Individuals try to keep all their thoughts directed along realistic lines and avoid flights of fancy. They are bored watching ballet or modern dance and poetry has little effect on them. They rarely experience strong emotions and seldom pay attention to their feelings of the moment. They find philosophical arguments boring and sometimes lose interest when people talk about abstract, theoretical matters. They believe that letting students hear controversial speakers only confuses and misleads them.
O1 (Fantasy)	High (T > 55)	Individuals have an active imagination and fantasy life. They enjoy concentrating on a fantasy or daydream and exploring all its possibilities. As children, they enjoyed games of make-believe.
	Low (T < 45)	Individuals try to keep all their thoughts directed along realistic lines and avoid flights of fancy. They do not like to waste their time daydreaming. They have difficulty letting their mind wander without control or guidance. As children they rarely enjoyed games of make-believe.
O2 (Aesthetics)	High (T > 55)	Individuals are intrigued by the patterns they find in art and nature. They are sometimes completely absorbed in music to which they are listening, and certain types of music have an endless fascination for them. They enjoy reading poetry that emphasizes feelings and images more than story lines.
	Low (T < 45)	Individuals are bored watching ballet or modern dance, and poetry has little effect on them. Aesthetic and artistic concerns are not very important to them.

Table 10.4 *(Continued)*

Domain	Facet	Interpretation
O3 (Feelings)	High (T > 55)	Individuals feel a wide range of emotions or feelings. Without strong emotions, life would be uninteresting to them. They find it easy to empathize with others.
	Low (T < 45)	Individuals rarely experience strong emotions and seldom pay attention to their feelings of the moment. They seldom notice the moods or feelings that different environments produce.
O4 (Actions)	High (T > 55)	Individuals think that it is interesting to learn and develop new hobbies. They often try new and foreign foods. Sometimes they make changes around the house just to try something different.
	Low (T < 45)	Individuals are pretty set in their ways and prefer to spend their time in familiar surroundings. Once they find the right way to do something, they stick to it. They follow the same route when they go someplace. On a vacation, they prefer going back to a tried-and-true spot.
O5 (Ideas)	High (T > 55)	Individuals enjoy playing with theories or abstract ideas and solving problems or puzzles. They have a wide range of intellectual interests and a lot of intellectual curiosity.
	Low (T < 45)	Individuals find philosophical arguments boring and sometimes lose interest when people talk about abstract, theoretical matters. They have little interest in speculating on the nature of the universe or the human condition.
O6 (Values)	High (T > 55)	Individuals consider themselves broad-minded and tolerant of other people's lifestyles. They believe that laws and policies should change to reflect the needs of a changing world. The different ideas of right and wrong that people in other societies have may be valid for them.
	Low (T < 45)	Individuals believe that letting students hear controversial speakers only confuses and misleads them. They believe that we should look to our religious authorities for decisions on moral issues and that the "new morality" of permissiveness is no morality at all. They believe that being loyal to their ideals and principles is more important than being open minded.
A (Agreeableness)	High (T > 55)	Individuals believe that most people are basically well intentioned, honest, and trustworthy. They are not crafty or sly, and could not deceive anyone even if they wanted to. They try to be courteous, thoughtful, and considerate. Most people they know like them. They would rather cooperate with others than compete with them. They try to be humble and would rather not talk about themselves and their achievements. They believe that all human beings are worthy of respect and we can never do too much for the poor and elderly.

(continued)

Table 10.4   (*Continued*)

Domain	Facet	Interpretation
	Low (T < 45)	Individuals tend to be cynical and skeptical of others' intentions and believe that most people will take advantage of them if they let them. They are willing to manipulate people to get what they need and sometimes trick people into doing what they want. They are thought to be selfish, egotistical, cold, and calculating. They are hard-headed, tough-minded, and stubborn, and can be sarcastic and cutting when they need to be. They do not mind bragging about their talents and accomplishments.
A1 (Trust)	High (T > 55)	Individuals believe that most people are basically well intentioned, honest, and trustworthy. They have a good deal of faith in human nature and assume the best about people.
	Low (T < 45)	Individuals tend to be cynical and skeptical of others' intentions and believe that most people will take advantage of them if they let them. They are suspicious when someone does something nice for them.
A2 (Straightfor-wardness)	High (T > 55)	Individuals are not crafty or sly, and could not deceive anyone even if they wanted to. They would hate to be thought of as a hypocrite.
	Low (T < 45)	Individuals are willing to manipulate people to get what they need and sometimes trick people into doing what they want. Being perfectly honest is a bad way to do business. They pride themselves on their shrewdness in handling people.
A3 (Altruism)	High (T > 55)	Individuals try to be courteous, thoughtful, and considerate. Most people they know like them. They think of themselves as being charitable, and they go out of their way to help others.
	Low (T < 45)	Individuals are thought to be selfish, egotistical, cold, and calculating. They are not known for their generosity.
A4 (Compliance)	High (T > 55)	Individuals would rather cooperate with others than compete with them. They hesitate to express their anger even when it is justified. When they have been insulted, they just try to forgive and forget.
	Low (T < 45)	Individuals are hard-headed and stubborn, and can be sarcastic and cutting when they need to be. If they do not like people, they let them know it. If someone starts a fight, they are ready to fight back. They often get into arguments with their family and coworkers.
A5 (Modesty)	High (T > 55)	Individuals try to be humble and would prefer to not talk about themselves and their achievements. They would rather praise others than be praised. They think that they are no better than others, no matter what their condition.
	Low (T < 45)	Individuals do not mind bragging about their talents and accomplishments. They are better than most people and they know it. They have a high opinion of themselves.

Table 10.4   (*Continued*)

Domain	Facet	Interpretation
A6 (Tender-Mindedness)	High (T > 55)	Individuals believe that all human beings are worthy of respect and that we can never do too much for the poor and elderly. Human needs always should take priority over economic considerations. They have sympathy for others less fortunate than them.
	Low (T < 45)	Individuals are hard-headed and tough-minded. They have no sympathy for panhandlers. They would rather be known as "just" than "merciful."
C (Conscientiousness)	High (T > 55)	Individuals are competent and known for their prudence and common sense. They like to keep everything in its place so they know just where it is. They try to perform all the tasks assigned to them conscientiously. They have a clear set of goals and work hard to accomplish them in an orderly fashion. They think things through and always consider the consequences before making a decision or taking action.
	Low (T < 45)	Individuals often come into situations without being fully prepared and do not seem to be completely successful at anything. They are not very methodical and never seem to get organized. They are not as dependable or reliable as they should be. They are easygoing, lackadaisical, and do not feel driven to get ahead. They have trouble making themselves do what they should, and they waste a lot of time before settling down to work. They often do things on the spur of the moment and do not think things through before coming to a decision or taking action.
C1 (Competence)	High (T > 55)	Individuals are competent and known for their prudence and common sense. They keep themselves informed and usually make intelligent decisions. They pride themselves on their sound judgment. They are effective and efficient at their work. They are productive persons who always get the job done.
	Low (T < 45)	Individuals often come into situations without being fully prepared and do not seem to be completely successful at anything. They do not take their civic duties and voting very seriously.
C2 (Order)	High (T > 55)	Individuals like to keep everything in its place so they know just where it is. They tend to be somewhat fastidious and exacting. They keep their belongings neat and clean.
	Low (T < 45)	Individuals are not very methodical and never seem to be able to get organized. They spend a lot of time looking for things that they have misplaced. They would rather keep their options open than plan everything in advance.

(*continued*)

Table 10.4   (*Continued*)

Domain	Facet	Interpretation
C3 (Dutifulness)	High (T > 55)	Individuals try to perform all the tasks assigned to them conscientiously. They try to do jobs carefully so that they will not have to be done again. They adhere strictly to their ethical principles.
	Low (T < 45)	Individuals are not as dependable or reliable as they should be.
C4 (Achievement Striving)	High (T > 55)	Individuals have a clear set of goals and work hard to accomplish them in an orderly fashion. They strive to achieve all they can and are something of a "workaholic."
	Low (T < 45)	Individuals are easygoing, lackadaisical, and do not feel driven to get ahead. When they start a self-improvement program, they usually let it slide after a few days.
C5 (Self-Discipline)	High (T > 55)	Individuals are productive persons who always get the job done. They have a lot of self-discipline. They are pretty good at pacing themselves to get things done on time.
	Low (T < 45)	Individuals have trouble making themselves do what they should and they waste a lot of time before settling down to work. When a project gets too difficult, they are inclined to start a new one.
C6 (Deliberation)	High (T > 55)	Individuals think things through and always consider the consequences before making a decision or taking action. They plan ahead carefully when they go on a trip.
	Low (T < 45)	Individuals often do things on the spur of the moment and do not think things through before coming to a decision or taking action. Over the years, they have done some pretty stupid things.

Interpretation of the NEO PI-R starts with the domain scores that provide the broad framework of the person's personality. Five caveats must be kept in mind when interpreting the domain scales as well as the facet scales. First, the NEO PI-R is not a measure of psychopathology and consequently examiners who work primarily with clinical samples must be cautious about making too pathological an interpretation of a score. The easiest example of such a potential error in interpretation would be to conceive elevations on the Neuroticism (N) domain as a measure of psychopathology rather than as more general dissatisfaction with life.

Second, low scores (introversion) on the Extraversion (E) domain should not be considered to be the opposite of extraversion, but rather the absence of extraversion. Characterizing introversion as the absence of extraversion will assist the examiner in avoiding a pathological interpretation of low scores on this domain. Introverts are reserved, not unfriendly, independent individuals rather than followers, and may prefer to be alone without having social anxiety.

Your **NEO** Summary

Paul T. Costa, Jr., PhD, and Robert R. McCrae, PhD

The NEO inventory measures five broad domains, or dimensions, of personality. The responses that you gave to the statements about your thoughts, feelings, and goals can be compared with those of other adults to give a description of your personality.

For each of the five domains, descriptions are given below for different ranges of scores. The descriptions that are *checked* provide descriptions of *you*, based on your responses to the inventory items.

The NEO inventory measures differences among normal individuals. It is not a test of intelligence or ability, and it is not intended to diagnose problems of mental health

or adjustment. It does, however, give you some idea about what makes you unique in your ways of thinking, feeling, and interacting with others.

This summary is intended to give you a general idea of how your personality might be described. It is not a detailed report. If you completed the inventory again, you might score somewhat differently. For most individuals, however, personality traits tend to be very stable in adulthood. Unless you experience major life changes or make deliberate efforts to change yourself, this summary should apply to you throughout your adult life.

Compared with the responses of other people, your responses suggest that you can be described as:

☐ Sensitive, emotional, and prone to experience feelings that are upsetting.	☐ Generally calm and able to deal with stress, but you sometimes experience feelings of guilt, anger, or sadness.	☐ Secure, hardy, and generally relaxed even under stressful conditions.
☐ Extraverted, outgoing, active, and high-spirited. You prefer to be around people most of the time.	☐ Moderate in activity and enthusiasm. You enjoy the company of others but you also value privacy.	☐ Introverted, reserved, and serious. You prefer to be alone or with a few close friends.
☐ Open to new experiences. You have broad interests and are very imaginative.	☐ Practical but willing to consider new ways of doing things. You seek a balance between the old and the new.	☐ Down-to-earth, practical, traditional, and pretty much set in your ways.
☐ Compassionate, good-natured, and eager to cooperate and avoid conflict.	☐ Generally warm, trusting, and agreeable, but you can sometimes be stubborn and competitive.	☐ Hardheaded, skeptical, proud, and competitive. You tend to express your anger directly.
☐ Conscientious and well-organized. You have high standards and always strive to achieve your goals.	☐ Dependable and moderately well-organized. You generally have clear goals but are able to set your work aside.	☐ Easygoing, not very well-organized, and sometimes careless. You prefer not to make plans.

PAR **Psychological Assessment Resources, Inc.** · 16204 N. Florida Avenue · Lutz, FL 33549 · 1.800.331.8378 · www.parinc.com

9 8 7 6 5 4 3 2 1   Reorder #RO-2033   Printed in the U.S.A.

Figure 10.3   Standard Feedback form for the NEO PI-R. Reproduced by special permission of the Publisher, Psychological Assessment Resources, Inc., 16204 North Florida Avenue, Lutz, Florida 33549 from the Revised NEO Personality Inventory, by Paul T. Costa Jr., PhD, and Robert R. McCrae, PhD. Copyright 1978, 1985, 1989, 1991, 1992 by Psychological Assessment Resources, Inc. (PAR). Further reproduction is prohibited without permission of PAR.

Third, high scores on the Openness (*O*) domain are not equivalent to intelligence, but rather to divergent thinking and creativity. They also do not imply that persons are unprincipled or without values. They are willing to entertain new ideas and can apply these ideas conscientiously. In a similar manner, low scores on the *O* domain do not mean that persons are closed, defensive, or authoritarian, but rather that they have a narrower scope and intensity of interest. "Openness may sound healthier or more mature to many psychologists, but the value of openness or closedness depends on the requirement of the situation, and both open and closed individuals perform useful functions in society" (Costa & McCrae, 1992, p. 15).

Fourth, high scores on the Agreeableness (*A*) domain may seem to be more socially preferable and psychologically healthier, and such persons are generally easier with whom to interact. However, some situations require that the person be independent and skeptical of what is happening and being too agreeable can actually be a detriment. Dependent Personality Disorder would be characterized by a high score on the Agreeableness domain to illustrate that it is not necessarily psychologically healthy.

Finally, high scores on the Conscientiousness (C) domain reflect that the person is more active in planning and organized in carrying out their activities. These qualities may be expressed in academic and occupational achievement or in annoying, fastidious behaviors. Low scores on the Conscientious domain do not reflect that individuals are without principles to govern their behavior, but rather they are more lackadaisical in working toward their goals.

The six facet scores for each domain are intended to flesh out the general qualities that have been described by the parent domain scale. Important differences can be identified between individuals who have similar scores on the parent domain and a different pattern of scores on the facet scales for that domain. Two individuals with similar scores on the Extraversion (*E*) domain, one of whom has primary elevations on Activity (*E4*) and Excitement Seeking (*E5*), while the other has primary elevations on Assertiveness (*E2*) and Positive Emotions (*E6*), are very different persons.

The interpretation of the facet scales, in addition to the domain scales on the NEO PI-R, is recommended in most cases, and particularly in clinical, educational, and occupational assessments. It is conceivable in research applications that only the domain scales are relevant to the issue under study, and consequently, there is no reason to score and interpret the facet scales. It is very important to consider computer scoring the NEO PI-R when all the domain and facet scales are to be interpreted, because of the high probability of some scoring error in making that many calculations. Computer scoring also allows for the factor score for each domain to be computed directly rather than using the formulas presented in the *Manual* (Costa & McCrae, 1992, p. 8) to estimate them.

APPLICATIONS

As a self-report inventory, the NEO PI-R is easily administered in a wide variety of settings and for a variety of purposes. It is the most widely used self-report measure of personality in countries around the world. Costa and McCrae (2003) reported that there are 9 published translations, 25 validated translations, 8 research translations, and 3 more translations in progress. This 60-page, single-spaced, bibliography illustrates the variety of issues and research on the NEO PI-R and NEO-FFI. Any comprehensive review of this literature is beyond the scope of this *Handbook*.

There are numerous settings in which the NEO PI-R is appropriate for use: clinical, educational, medical, organizational, and research. The NEO PI-R is primarily used in educational, organizational, and research settings. The NEO PI-R is probably underutilized in clinical and medical settings and would seem worthy of wider usage in these settings. The NEO PI-R comes out of a long line of research on the five-factor model of personality described earlier (p. 315) and will not be reiterated. The use of the NEO PI-R is discussed for each of these other four settings in turn.

In clinical settings, the NEO PI-R can serve at least six useful purposes. First, it can provide a positive or nonpathological description of the person that can compensate for the heavy focus on psychopathology in most assessment tools and techniques. Most of the self-report inventories discussed in this *Handbook* have few, if any, positive statements to make about the person. Second, the focus on the more positive aspects of the person can help establish rapport and build the therapeutic alliance, and serves as an easy means of starting the feedback of the results of the assessment process before getting into the psychopathological issues. Third, there is a fairly extensive literature on the use of the NEO PI-R in the treatment of personality disorders (cf. Costa & Widiger, 2002). Fourth, the assessment of validity as described should be carried out routinely in clinical settings because of the higher probability of some type of response distortion. Fifth, knowledgeable others' ratings of the person using Form R can make an important contribution to understanding him or her, particularly when there is some reason to suspect that may be some type of response distortion. Finally, the NEO PI-R is neither a diagnostic instrument nor a measure of psychopathology and cannot be used as the sole assessment tool or technique in a clinical setting.

In educational settings, the NEO PI-R can be used in advising students about personality characteristics that will facilitate or impede their academic progress. There are areas of study, such as chemistry or accounting, where careful attention to detail is mandatory for success, and other areas, such as philosophy or literature, where the focus is on more abstract or larger conceptual issues, and careful attention to detail is much less necessary. Persons with high scores on the Conscientiousness (*C*) domain are more likely to be successful in chemistry or accounting, while persons with high scores on the Openness (*O*) domain are more likely to be successful in philosophy or literature. In neither example is academic success foreclosed in the other area, but these individuals may have to work harder to recognize how their natural personality style affects their academic performance and they may need to find methods for coping with them to increase the probability of success. The NEO PI-R also can be used in counseling students in academic settings, which would be considered a clinical setting and was discussed earlier.

In medical settings, the NEO PI-R can be used to identify personality characteristics that might facilitate or impede treatment. The NEO PI-R will be better accepted by medical patients than other self-report inventories that have a heavy focus on psychopathology. Medical patients, particularly pain patients, are frequently upset at the thought of psychological assessment because they think that it implies that the problem "is all in their head."

Medical patients with high scores on the Neuroticism (*N*) domain can alert the examiner to review their background and history for the potential impact of psychopathology on the medical treatment. Medical patients with high scores on the Conscientiousness (C) domain would be expected to be more likely to follow through on the recommended steps for treatment, particularly as the treatment process becomes more complex or long-term. An interesting line of research has used the NEO PI-R in predicting risk for coronary heart disease (cf. Costa, McCrae, & Dembroski, 1989), and Vollrath and Torgersen (2002) used the NEO PI-R to predict risky health behavior in college students. Costa and McCrae (2003) have listed the multiple areas in behavioral medicine in which the NEO PI-R is being used.

In occupational settings, the NEO PI-R can be used to identify personality characteristics that might facilitate or impede success in a specific occupation. As with educational settings, certain personality dimensions are more important in some occupations than others. These personality dimensions can be used in selecting candidates for specific occupations or in advising individuals on what occupations might be better suited for them. When the NEO PI-R is used to select potential candidates for specific occupations, the examiner must be aware that because examinees may simulate their scores on the appropriate domains, evaluating the validity of the NEO PI-R will be important (cf. Griffin et al., 2004).

When an occupation requires significant amounts of interpersonal interactions, individuals with higher scores on the Extraversion (E) and Agreeableness (A) domains will be more likely to be successful than individuals with lower scores on these same domains. Conversely, when an occupation requires a significant amount of time by oneself, individuals with lower scores on the Extraversion and Agreeableness domains will be more likely to be successful than individuals with higher scores on these same domains. Again, the examiner is reminded that when individuals do not have the optimal scores on the personality dimensions for a specific occupation, their success is not precluded, but they need to be aware of the potential impact these personality dimensions may have on their performance.

PSYCHOMETRIC FOUNDATIONS

Demographic Variables

Age

Specific norms are not provided by age for adults on the NEO PI-R. There are some differences in young adults (<20) and a separate profile form and norms are used for them. The items on the NEO PI-3 are easier to read than those on the NEO PI-R, and the NEO PI-3 can be used for adolescents 12 years of age and older. Further research currently is being conducted to determine whether the NEO PI-3 can be considered as a replacement for the NEO PI-R at all ages.

Terracciano, McCrae, Brant, and Costa (2005) examined age trends on the NEO PI-R in a sample of nearly two thousand adults in the Baltimore Longitudinal Study on Aging. There was a gradual curvilinear decline of slightly over one-half of a standard deviation in the Neuroticism (N) and Extraversion (E) domains from age 30 to age 90. There was a linear decline in the Openness (O) domain and linear increase in the Agreeableness (A) domain. There was a parabolic change in the Conscientiousness (C) domain with scores increasing until about age 70 and then slightly declining thereafter. All these changes in adulthood across the five domains were about one T score point per decade or slightly more than one-half of a standard deviation across the entire 60-year age span. A cross-sectional analysis of these data produced results that are similar to the longitudinal analysis. Terracciano et al. also provide similar information on all 30 of the facet scales on the NEO PI-R.

Gender

Gender does not create any general issues in NEO PI-R interpretation because separate norms (profile forms) are used for men and women. Any gender differences in how individuals responded to the items on each scale are removed when the raw scores are converted to T scores. Consequently, men and women with a T score of 60 (84th percentile) on Agreeableness (*A*) are one standard deviation above the mean, although women have a slightly higher raw score (~142) than men (~136; Costa & McCrae, 1992, Appendix C, p. 79). Costa, Terracciano, and McCrae (2001) analyzed gender differences in 26 cultures and found that these gender differences were typically less than one-half of a standard deviation (5 T points), and most were closer to one-quarter of a standard deviation, relative to variations within gender.

Education

The potential effects of education have not been investigated in any systematic manner on the NEO PI-R, It is not apparent that such research would yield any significant findings given the ease with which the NEO PI-R is read and the similar findings in factor structure across multiple cultures.

Ethnicity

The effects of ethnicity per se on NEO PI-R performance have not been studied, if ethnicity as construed as being different from culture. However, the prolific literature on the cross-cultural use of the NEO PI-R is discussed briefly in the next section.

Cross-Cultural Implementation

Costa and McCrae (2003) reported that there are 9 published translations, 25 validated translations, 8 research translations, and 3 more translations in progress of the NEO PI-R. The breadth of the use of the NEO PI-R across various cultures can be seen by the fact that there are 79 contributing members to the Personality Profiles of Cultures Project who represent 51 cultures from six continents (McCrae, Terracciano, et al., 2005). This project is looking at the aggregate personality profiles of different cultures to assess whether they can provide insight into cultural differences and the stereotypes of national character (McCrae & Terracciano, 2006). The robustness of the factor structure of the NEO PI-R across these various cultures not only speaks to the usefulness of the NEO PI-R cross-culturally, but it allows for comparisons to be made into the actual differences in aggregate personality profiles. As would be expected, stereotypes of national character are erroneous (McCrae & Terracciano, 2006), similar to the erroneous conceptualization that all patients within a specific diagnostic category are alike (pp. 60–61). There are small differences in these aggregate personality profiles across the different cultures, but much larger variability within cultures. These variations in aggregate personality profiles appear to reflect real differences that warrant further investigation.

In summary, it appears that demographic variables have minimal impact on the NEO PI-R profile in most individuals. The fact that the NEO PI-R can be read to individuals and is available in many different languages makes it applicability even broader.

Reliability

The *NEO PI-R Manual* (Costa & McCrae, 1992, table 5, p. 44) reports the reliability (coefficient alpha) data for 1,539 individuals for Form S. Coefficient alpha ranged from .56 to .81 for the facet scales and .86 to .92 for the domain scales. The reliability data are quite good for the domain scales that contain 48 items each. As expected, the reliability data are somewhat lower, though still very respectable, for the facet scales that only have eight items each.

A subset of the college students ($N = 208$) in the normative sample for the NEO PI-R were retested after an average of nearly 3 months with the NEO-FFI, which allowed determination of the reliability of the five domain scores. The test-retest correlations ranged from .75 to .83 across the five scales and averaged .79. The standard error of measurement is about 4 T points for the domain scales; that is, the individual's true score on the domain scales will be within ± 4 T points two-thirds of the time.

Stability

There is impressive research on the long-term stability of NEO PI-R scores. Costa and McCrae (1988) reported that the stability coefficients over a 6-year period in a large sample of adults for the domains of N (Neuroticism), E (Extraversion), and O (Openness) were .83, .82, and .83, respectively. The stability coefficients over a 3-year period for the domains of A (Agreeableness) and C (Conscientiousness) were .63 and .79, respectively. These stability coefficients are higher and over a longer time period than for any of the other self-report inventories reviewed in this *Handbook*.

CONCLUDING COMMENTS

The voluminous literature on the five-factor model of personality provides solid underpinnings for the NEO PI-R (Costa & McCrae, 1992). The Personality Profiles of Cultures Project that represents 51 cultures from six continents (McCrae, Terracciano, et al., 2005) shows how well regarded the NEO PI-R is internationally. More widespread use of the NEO PI-R in clinical and medical settings to provide a positive perspective on the person is warranted given the heavy bias toward psychopathology in virtually all other assessment tests and techniques. The existence of a parallel form for rating of the person by a knowledgeable other (Form R) is an invaluable source of information any time there is reason to suspect any type of response distortion that seems particularly helpful in clinical and medical settings.

REFERENCES

Bagby, R. M., Rector, N. A, Bindseil, K., Dickens, S. F., Levitan, R. D., & Kennedy, S. H. (1998). Self-reports and informant ratings of personalities of depressed outpatients. *American Journal of Psychiatry*, *155*, 437–438.

Ballenger, J. F., Caldwell-Andrews, A., & Baer, R. A. (2001). Effects of positive impression management on the NEO PI-R in a clinical population. *Psychological Assessment*, *13*, 254–260.

Berry, D. T. R., Bagby, R. M., Smerz, J., Rinaldo, J. C., Caldwell-Andrews, A., & Baer, R. A. (2001). Effectiveness of NEO PI-R research validity scales for discriminating analog malingering and genuine psychopathology. *Journal of Personality Assessment*, *76*, 496–516.

Caldwell-Andrews, A. (2001). *Relationships between MMPI-2 validity scales and NEO PI-R experimental validity scales in police candidates.* Unpublished doctoral dissertation, University of Kentucky.

Caldwell-Andrews, A., Baer, R. A., & Berry, D. T. R. (2000). Effects of response sets on NEO PI-R scores and their relation to external criteria. *Journal of Personality Assessment*, *74*, 472–488.

Costa, P. T., Jr., & McCrae, R. R. (1985). *The NEO Personality Inventory manual.* Odessa, FL: Psychological Assessment Resources.

Costa, P. T., Jr., & McCrae, R. R. (1988). Personality in adulthood: A six-year longitudinal study of self-reports and spouse ratings on the NEO PI. *Journal of Personality and Social Psychology*, *54*, 853–863.

Costa, P. T., Jr., & McCrae, R. R. (1992). *Revised NEO Personality Inventory (NEO PI-R) and NEO Five-Factor Inventory (NEO-FFI) professional manual.* Odessa, FL: Psychological Assessment Resources.

Costa, P. T., Jr., & McCrae, R. R. (2003). *Bibliography for the NEO PI-R and NEO FFI.* Lutz, FL: Psychological Assessment Resources. Available at www3.parinc.com/uploads/pdfs/NEO_bib.pdf.

Costa, P. T., Jr., McCrae, R. R., & Dembroski, T. M. (1989). Agreeableness vs. antagonism: Explication of a potential risk factor for CHD. In A. Siegman & T. M. Dembroski (Eds.), *In search of coronary-prone behavior: Beyond Type A* (pp. 41–63). Hillsdale, NJ: Erlbaum.

Costa, P. T., Jr., Terracciano, A., & McCrae, R. R. (2001). Gender differences in personality traits across cultures: Robust and surprising findings. *Journal of Personality and Social Psychology*, *81*, 322–331.

Costa, P. T., Jr., & Widiger, T. A. (2002). *Personality disorders and the five-factor model of personality* (2nd ed.). Washington, DC: American Psychological Association.

Fiedler, E. R., Oltmanns, T. F., & Turkheimer, E. (2004). Traits associated with personality disorders and adjustment to military life: Predictive validity of self and peer reports. *Military Medicine*, *169*, 32–40.

Finn, S. (1996). *Using the MMPI-2 as a therapeutic intervention.* Minneapolis: University of Minnesota Press.

Fischer, C. T. (1994). *Individualizing psychological assessment.* Hillsdale, NJ: Erlbaum.

Griffin, B., Hesketh, B., & Grayson, D. (2004). Applicants faking good: Evidence of bias in the NEO PI-R. *Personality and Individual Differences*, *36*, 1545–1558.

McCrae, R. R., Costa, P. T., Jr., & Martin, T. A. (2005). The NEO PI-3: A more readable revised NEO Personality Inventory. *Journal of Personality Assessment*, *84*, 260–270.

McCrae, R. R., Costa, P. T., Jr., Parker, W. D., Mills, C. J., Terracciano, A., De Fruyt, F., et al. (2002). Personality trait development from age 12 to age 18: Longitudinal, cross-sectional, and cross-cultural analyses. *Journal of Personality and Social Psychology*, *83*, 1456–1468.

McCrae, R. R., & Terracciano, A. (2006). National character and personality. *Current Directions in Psychological Science*, *15*, 156–161.

McCrae, R. R., Terracciano, A., & 79 Members of the Personality Profiles of Cultures Project. (2005). Personality profiles of cultures: Aggregate personality traits. *Journal of Personality and Social Psychology*, *89*, 407–425.

Morey, L. C. (1991). *Personality Assessment Inventory: Professional manual.* Odessa, FL: Psychological Assessment Resources.

Morey, L. C., Quigley, B. D., Sanislow, C. A., Skodol, A. E., McGlashan, T. H., Shea, M. T., et al. (2002). Substance or style? An investigation of the NEO PI-R validity scales. *Journal of Personality Assessment*, *79*, 583–599.

Pauls, C. A., & Crost, N. W. (2005). Effects of different instructional sets on the construct validity of the NEO PI-R. *Personality and Individual Differences, 39*, 297–308.

Piedmont, R. L., McCrae, R. R., Riemann, R., & Angleitner, A. (2000). On the invalidity of validity scales: Evidence from self-report and observer ratings in volunteer samples. *Journal of Personality and Social Psychology, 78*, 582–593.

Schinka, J. A., Kinder, B. N., & Kremer, T. (1997). Research validity scales for the NEO PI-R: Development and initial validation. *Journal of Personality Assessment, 68*, 127–138.

Terracciano, A., McCrae, R. R., Brant, L. J., & Costa, P. T., Jr. (2005). Hierarchical linear modeling analyses of the NEO PI-R scales in the Baltimore Longitudinal Study of Aging. *Psychology and Aging, 20*, 493–506.

Vollrath, M., & Torgersen, S. (2002). Who takes health risks? A probe into eight personality types. *Personality and Individual Differences, 32*, 1185–1198.

Wiggins, J. S. (Ed.). (1996). *The five-factor model of personality.* New York: Guilford Press.

Yang, J., Bagby, R. M., & Ryder, A. G. (2000). Response style and the NEO PI-R: Validity scales and spousal ratings in a Chinese psychiatric sample. *Assessment, 7*, 389–402.

Young, M. S., & Schinka, J. A. (2001). Research validity scales for the NEO PI-R: Additional evidence for reliability and validity. *Journal of Personality Assessment, 76*, 412–420.

Part III

PERFORMANCE-BASED MEASURES

Chapter 11

RORSCHACH INKBLOT METHOD

The preceding five chapters have presented the most commonly used self-report inventories for assessing personality functioning. As noted in Chapter 1, inventories of this kind differ in several respects from performance-based personality measures. Self-report inventories provide direct assessments of personality characteristics in which people are asked to describe themselves by indicating whether certain statements apply to them. Performance-based measures are an indirect approach in which personality characteristics are inferred from the way people respond to various standardized tasks. Self-report and performance-based methods both bring advantages and limitations to the assessment process, as discussed in Chapters 1 and 2, and there are many reasons personality assessments should ordinarily be conducted with a multifaceted test battery that includes both kinds of measures (see pp. 13–15 and 22–26).

This and the following three chapters address the most widely used performance-based measures of personality functioning: the Rorschach Inkblot Method (RIM), the Thematic Apperception Test (TAT), figure drawing methods, and sentence completion methods. These and other performance-based personality measures have traditionally been referred to as *projective* tests and are still commonly labeled this way. As pointed out in concluding Chapter 1, however, "projective" is not an apt categorization of these measures, and contemporary assessment psychologists prefer more accurate descriptive labels for them such as *performance-based*.

NATURE OF THE RORSCHACH INKBLOT METHOD

The Rorschach Inkblot Method (RIM) consists of 10 inkblots printed individually on $6\frac{3}{4}''$ by $9\frac{3}{4}''$ cards. Five of these blots are printed in shades of gray and black (Cards I and IV-VII); two of the blots are in shades of red, gray, and black (Cards II and III); and the remaining three blots are in shades of various pastel colors (Cards VIII-X). In what is called the *Response Phase* of a Rorschach examination, people are shown the cards one at a time and asked to say what they see in them. In the subsequent *Inquiry Phase* of the examination, persons being examined are asked to indicate where in the blots they saw each of the percepts they reported and what made those percepts look the way they did.

These procedures yield three sources of data. First, the manner in which people structure their responses identifies how they are likely to structure other situations in their lives. People who base most of their responses on the overall appearance of the inkblots and pay little attention to separate parts of them are likely to be individuals who tend to form global impressions of situations and ignore or overlook details of these situations. Conversely, people who base most of their responses on parts of the blots and seldom make use of an entire blot are often people who become preoccupied with the details of situations and fail to grasp their overall significance—as in "not being able to see the forest for the trees." As another example of response structure, people who report seeing objects that are shaped similarly to the part of the blot where they are seeing them are likely in general to perceive people and events accurately, and hence to show adequate reality testing. By contrast, people who give numerous perceptually inaccurate responses that do not resemble the shapes of the blots are prone in general to form distorted impressions of what they see, and hence to show impaired reality testing.

As a second source of data, Rorschach responses frequently contain content themes that provide clues to a person's underlying needs, attitudes, and concerns. People who consistently describe human figures they see in the inkblots as being angry, carrying weapons, or fighting with each other may harbor concerns that other people are potentially dangerous to them, or they may view interpersonal relationships as typified by competition and strife. Conversely, a thematic emphasis on people described as friendly, as carrying a peace offering, or as helping each other in a shared endeavor probably reveals a sense of safety in interpersonal relationships and an expectation that people will interact in collaborative ways. In similar fashion, recurrent descriptions of people, animals, or objects seen in the blots as being damaged or dysfunctional (e.g., "a decrepit old person"; "a wounded bug"; "a piece of machinery that's rusting away") may reflect personal concerns about being injured or defective in some way, or about being vulnerable to becoming injured or defective.

The third source of data in a Rorschach examination consists of the manner in which individuals conduct themselves and relate to the examiner, which provides behavioral indications of how they are likely to deal with task-oriented and interpersonal situations. Some of the behavioral data that emerge during a Rorschach examination resemble observations that clinicians can make whenever they are conducting interview or test assessments. Whether people being assessed seem deferential or antagonistic toward the examiner may say something about their attitudes toward authority. Whether they appear relaxed or nervous may say something about how self-confident and self-assured they are and about how they generally respond to being evaluated.

The RIM also provides some test-specific behavioral data in the form of how people handle the cards and how they frame their responses. Do they carefully hand each card back to the examiner when they are finished responding to it, or do they carelessly toss the card on the desk? Do they give definite responses and take responsibility for them (as in "This one looks to me like a bat"), or do they disavow responsibility and avoid commitment (as in "It really doesn't look like anything to me, but if I have to say something, I'd say it might look something like a bat")?

To summarize this instrument, then, the RIM involves each of the following three tasks:

1. A perceptual task yielding structural information that helps to identify personality states and traits
2. An associational task generating content themes that contain clues to a person's underlying needs and attitudes
3. A behavioral task that provides a representative sample of an individual's orientation to problem-solving and interpersonal situations

In parallel to these three test characteristics, Rorschach assessment measures personality functioning because the way people go about seeing things in the inkblots reflects how they look at their world and how they customarily make decisions and deal with events. What they see in the inkblots provides a window into their inner life and the contents of their mind, and how they conduct themselves during the examination provides information about how they usually respond to people and to external demands.

By integrating these structural, thematic, and behavioral features of the data, Rorschach clinicians can generate comprehensive personality descriptions of the people they examine. These descriptions typically address adaptive strengths and weaknesses in how people manage stress, how they attend to and perceive their surroundings, how they form concepts and ideas, how they experience and express feelings, how they view themselves, and how they relate to other people. Later sections of this chapter elaborate the codification, scoring, and interpretation of Rorschach responses and delineate how Rorschach-based descriptions of personality characteristics facilitate numerous applications of the instrument. As a further introduction to these topics and to the psychometric features of the RIM, the next two sections of the chapter review the history of Rorschach assessment and standard procedures for administering the instrument.

HISTORY

Of the personality assessment instruments discussed in this text, the Rorschach Inkblot Method has the longest and most interesting history because it was shaped by diverse personal experiences and life events. The inkblot method first took systematic form in the mind of Hermann Rorschach, a Swiss psychiatrist who lived only 37 years, from 1885 to 1922. As a youth, Rorschach had been exposed to inkblots in the form of a popular parlor game in turn-of-the-century Europe called *Klecksographie. Klecks* is the German word for "blot," and the Klecksographie game translates loosely into English as "Blotto." The game was played by dropping ink in the middle of a piece of paper, folding the paper in half to make a more or less symmetrical blot, and then competing to see who among the players could generate the most numerous or interesting descriptions of the blots or suggest associations to what they resembled. According to available reports, Rorschach's enthusiasm for this game, which appealed to adolescents as well as adults, and his creativity in playing it led to his being nicknamed "Klex" by his high school classmates (Exner, 2003, chap. 1).

From 1917 to 1919, while serving as Associate Director of the Krombach Mental Hospital in Herisau, Switzerland, Rorschach pursued a notion he had formed earlier in his career that patients with different types of mental disorders would respond to inkblots differently from each other and from psychologically healthy people. To test this notion, he constructed and experimented with a large number of blots, but these were not the accidental ink splotches of the parlor games. Rorschach was a skilled amateur artist who left behind an impressive portfolio of drawings that can be viewed in the Rorschach Archives and Museum in Bern, Switzerland. The blots with which he experimented were carefully drawn by him, and over time he selected a small set that seemed particularly effective in eliciting responses and reflecting individual differences.

Rorschach then administered his selected set of blots to samples of 288 mental hospital patients and 117 nonpatients, using a standard instruction, "What might this be?" Rorschach published his findings from this research in a 1921 monograph titled *Psychodiagnostics* (Rorschach, 1921/1942). The materials and methods described by Rorschach in *Psychodiagnostics* provided the basic foundation for the manner in which Rorschach assessment has been most commonly practiced since that time, and the standard Rorschach plates used today are the same 10 inkblots that were published with Rorschach's original monograph.

Rorschach's monograph was nevertheless a preliminary work, and he was just beginning to explore potential refinements and applications of the inkblot method when he succumbed a year after its publication to peritonitis, following a ruptured appendix. The monograph itself did not attract much attention initially, and the method might have succumbed along with its creator were it not for the efforts of a few close friends and colleagues of Rorschach who were devoted to keeping the method alive. Their efforts were facilitated by the fact that Switzerland in the 1920s was a Mecca for medical scientists and researchers, who visited from many parts of the world to study with famous physicians at Swiss hospitals and medical schools. Some of these visiting scholars and practitioners heard about Rorschach's method while they were in Switzerland and took copies of the inkblots home with them. As a result, articles on the Rorschach were published during the 1920s in such diverse countries as Russia, Peru, and Japan.

Turning to how the Rorschach came to the United States, an American psychiatrist named David Levy went to Zurich in the mid-1920s to study for a year with Emil Oberholzer, a prominent psychoanalyst who had been one of Rorschach's good friends and supporters. Levy returned to the United States with several copies of the inkblots, and that is how the Rorschach came to America. Levy's interests lay elsewhere, and the Rorschach materials languished for a time in his desk at the New York Institute of Guidance. Then, in 1929, Samuel Beck, a graduate student at Columbia University who was doing a fellowship at the Institute, mentioned to Levy that he was looking for a dissertation topic. Levy told Beck about the Rorschach materials he had brought back from Switzerland and suggested that Beck might do a research project with them. Acting on this suggestion, Beck earned his doctorate with a Rorschach standardization study of children. While collecting his data, Beck published the first two English language articles on the method in 1930 (Beck, 1930a, 1930b). He followed these articles 7 years later with *Introduction to the Rorschach Method,* which was the first English language monograph on the Rorschach, and in 1944 with the first edition of his basic text, *Rorschach's Test: I. Basic Processes* (Beck, 1937, 1944). Throughout a long, productive career, Beck remained an influential figure in Rorschach assessment, and his contributions became internationally known and respected.

In 1934, Beck went to Switzerland for a year's study with Oberholzer, and his departure coincided with the arrival from Zurich of another Rorschach pioneer, Bruno Klopfer. Klopfer had received a doctorate in educational psychology in 1922 and by 1933 had advanced to a senior staff position at the Berlin Information Center for Child Guidance. He also had become interested in Jungian psychoanalytic theory and was in the final phases of completing training as a Jungian analyst. However, the restrictions being placed on Jews in Adolf Hitler's Germany at that time led Klopfer to an advisedly dim view of his future professional prospects in Berlin, and he decided to move to Zurich. Without a job in Zurich, he was helped by Carl Jung to obtain a position as a technician at the Zurich

Psychotechnic Institute. Klopfer's responsibilities at the Institute included psychological testing of applicants for various jobs, and the Rorschach was among the tests he was required to use for this purpose. He had no previous interest or experience in testing, but he soon became intrigued with the ways in which Rorschach responses could reveal the underlying thoughts and feelings of the people he was testing.

Klopfer was dissatisfied with his low status as a technician and soon began looking for other opportunities. His search resulted in his being appointed as a research associate in the Department of Anthropology at Columbia University, where he began working in 1934. Having learned of his arrival on campus, a group of psychology graduate students asked their department to arrange for Klopfer to give them some Rorschach training. Unimpressed with Klopfer's credentials, the department declined to hire him for this purpose. The students were not deterred, however, and they approached Klopfer privately about offering some evening seminars for them in his home, which he agreed to do.

Giving these seminars for this and subsequent groups of students and professionals produced a network of Klopfer-trained psychologists who were eager to keep in touch with each other and continue exchanging ideas about the Rorschach. In response to this interest, Klopfer in 1936 founded the *Rorschach Research Exchange,* which has been published regularly since that time and evolved into the contemporary *Journal of Personality Assessment.* In 1938, Klopfer founded the Rorschach Institute, a scientific and professional organization that continues to function actively today, and more broadly than Klopfer envisioned, as the Society for Personality Assessment. Klopfer's first Rorschach book, *The Rorschach Technique,* appeared in 1942, but it was not until 1954 that he published his definitive basic text, *Developments in the Rorschach Technique: Volume 1. Technique and Theory* (Klopfer, Ainsworth, Klopfer, & Holt, 1954; Klopfer & Kelley, 1942).

Because one of them needed a dissertation topic and the other needed a job, then, these two Rorschach pioneers were drawn into a lifetime engagement with the inkblot method. Like Beck, Klopfer gained international acclaim for his teaching and writing about Rorschach assessment. Regrettably for the development of the instrument, Beck and Klopfer approached their work from very different perspectives. Having been educated in an experimentally oriented department of psychology, Beck was interested in describing personality characteristics and was firmly committed to advancing knowledge through controlled research designs and empirical data collection. He stuck closely to Rorschach's original procedures for administration and coding, and he favored a primarily quantitative approach to Rorschach interpretation. With respect to the distinction between nomothetic and idiographic approaches in personality assessment discussed in Chapters 1 (pp. 12–13) and 2 (p. 34), Beck was very much in the nomothetic camp.

Klopfer, on the other hand, was a Jungian analyst at heart and an enthusiast for idiography. He had a strong interest in symbolic meanings and with unraveling the phenomenology of each person's human experience. He employed qualitative approaches to interpretation that Beck considered inappropriate, and he added many new response codes and summary scores on the basis of imaginative ideas rather than research data, which Beck found unacceptable.

These differences in perspective led Beck and Klopfer to formulate and promulgate distinctive Rorschach systems that involved dissimilar approaches to administering, scoring, and interpreting the test. Divergence in method did not stop with these two pioneers, however. In the early 1930s, Beck talked about his Rorschach research with Marguerite Hertz, the wife of an old friend of his, who was working on her doctorate in psychology at Western Reserve University in Cleveland. Hertz became an ardent enthusiast for the value of Rorschach assessment, especially in working with children. She developed some distinctive variations of her own in Rorschach administration, scoring, and interpretation, and, in the course of a long and productive life as a university professor, she taught her approach to many generations of graduate students and workshop participants.

Klopfer's first seminar group included several psychology graduate students and a friend of one of these students who had encouraged him to sit in. This friend was Zygmunt Piotrowski, who at the time was a postdoctoral fellow at the Neuropsychiatric Institute in New York. Piotrowski had received a doctorate in experimental psychology in Poland in 1927 and was in the United States for advanced study in neuropsychology. Aside from curiosity, he had little interest in Rorschach assessment when he joined Klopfer's seminar group. However, he soon began to contemplate the possibility that persons with various kinds of neurological disorders might respond to the inkblots in ways that would help identify their condition. Piotrowski subsequently pioneered in conducting Rorschach research with brain-injured patients, and he developed many creative ideas about how the inkblot method should be conceived, coded, and interpreted. These new ideas coalesced into a Rorschach system that Piotrowski called *Perceptanalysis* (Piotrowski, 1957). Like Beck, Klopfer, and Hertz, Piotrowski worked productively throughout a long life during which his courses, publications, and lectures introduced a loyal following to his particular Rorschach system.

This early history of the Rorschach in America came to a close with the arrival in the United States of another refugee from Europe, David Rapaport, a psychoanalytically oriented doctoral-level psychologist who fled his native Hungary in 1938. In 1940, Rapaport joined the staff of the Menninger Foundation in Topeka, Kansas, where 2 years later he became head of the psychology department His responsibilities at the Foundation included mounting a research project to evaluate the utility of a battery of psychological tests for describing people and facilitating differential diagnosis. The Rorschach was part of this test battery, and Rapaport's collaborators in the project included Roy Schafer, who was an undergraduate psychology student at the time and completed his doctoral studies several years later at Clark University, after moving from the Menninger Foundation to the Austen Riggs Center in Massachusetts (see Schafer, 2006).

Rapaport's psychoanalytic perspectives and many original ideas that he and Schafer formed about how to elicit and interpret Rorschach responses resulted in their using a modified inkblot method that differed substantially from any of the previous methods. Publication of a 2-volume treatise based on the Menninger research project and subsequent influential books by Schafer established the Rapaport/Schafer system as another alternative for practitioners and researchers to consider in their work with the Rorschach (Rapaport, Gill, & Schafer, 1946/1968; Schafer, 1948, 1954).

By 1950, then, there were five different Rorschach systems in the United States, each with its own adherents. Moreover, even though the Beck and Klopfer systems had become well-known abroad, the Rorschach landscape also included distinctive systems developed in other countries and popular among psychologists in Europe, South America, and Japan. This diversity of method made it difficult for Rorschach practitioners to communicate with each other and almost impossible for researchers to cumulate systematic data concerning the reliability of Rorschach findings and their validity for particular purposes. This problem persisted until the early 1970s, when John Exner undertook to resolve it by standardizing the Rorschach method in a conceptually reasonable and psychometrically sound manner. Having conducted a detailed comparative analysis of the five American systems (Exner, 1969), Exner instituted a research program to measure the impact of the different methods of administration used in the systems and to identify which of their response codes could be explained clearly and coded reliably. Drawing on what appeared to be the best features of each of the five American systems, Exner combined them into a Rorschach *Comprehensive System* (CS) that he published in 1974 (Exner, 1974).

The Rorschach CS provides specific and detailed instructions for administration and coding that are to be followed in exactly the same way in every instance. Now in its fourth edition (Exner, 2003), the CS has become by far the most frequently used Rorschach system in the United States as well as in many other countries of the world. Widespread adoption of the CS standardization has made possible the development of large sample normative standards and international collaboration in examining cross-cultural similarities and differences in Rorschach responses. The cross-cultural applicability of Rorschach assessment has provided a unique large-scale opportunity to compare and understand different cultures from all over the world (see Shaffer, Erdberg, & Meyer, 2007).

Standard Rorschach procedures have also fostered systematic collection and comparison of data concerning intercoder agreement, retest reliability, and criterion, construct, and incremental validity, both in the United States and abroad, which are reviewed later in the chapter. The advent of the CS has additionally allowed clinicians who use it to exchange information about Rorschach findings with confidence that these findings are based on the same method of obtaining and codifying the data. The next two sections of the chapter provide an overview of the CS administration and coding procedures.

ADMINISTRATION

To preserve standardization for the reasons just mentioned, Rorschach examiners should follow as closely as possible the administration and coding procedures delineated for the CS by Exner (2003). Prior to beginning the testing, as discussed in Chapter 2, the examiner should have discussed with the person being evaluated such matters as the purposes of the assessment and how and to whom the results will be communicated. People are entitled to information about these matters, and even a brief discussion of them can be helpful in establishing rapport, reducing concerns the person may have about being examined, and clarifying misconceptions about the testing process. Typically, the RIM is part of a test battery that can be introduced in general terms such as the following: "As for the tests we're going to do, I'll be asking you questions about various matters and giving you some tasks to do; let's get started, and I'll show you what each of these tests is like as we do them."

In preparing to administer the RIM, the examiner should have the cards face down in a single pile where they can be seen but not easily reached by the examinee. The examiner should also sit alongside the person or at an angle that is at least slightly behind the examinee and out of the person's direct line of vision. This arrangement makes it easy for people to show the examiner where on the blots they are seeing their percepts. Avoiding face-to-face administration also minimizes the possible influence on test responses of an examiner's facial expressions or other bodily movements. The Rorschach administration should begin with the following type of explanation:

> The next test we're going to do is one you may have heard of. It's often referred to as the inkblot test, and it's called that because it consists of a series of cards with blots of ink on them. The blots aren't anything in particular, but when people look at them, they see different things in them. There are 10 of these cards, and I'm going to show them to you one at a time and ask you what kinds of things you see in them and what they look like to you.

No further explanation should routinely be given of Rorschach procedures or of what can be learned from Rorschach responses. Should examinees ask, "How does this test work?" they can be told the following: "The way people look at things says something about what they are like as a person, and this test will give us information about your personality that should be helpful in ... [some reference to the purpose of the examination]." Should examinees say something on the order of "So this will be a test of my imagination" or "You want me to tell you what they remind me of?" the perceptual elements of the Rorschach task should be emphasized by indicating otherwise: "No, this is a test of what you see in the blots, and I want you to tell me what they look like to you." If there are no such questions or comments that examiners must answer first, they should proceed directly after their explanation by handing the person Card I and saying, "What might this be?"

People will usually take Card I when it is handed to them and should be asked to do so if necessary. Having people hold the cards promotes their engagement in the Rorschach task, and, as mentioned, the manner in which they handle the cards can be a source of useful behavioral data. In other respects, the individual's task during the Response Phase of the administration should be left as unstructured as possible. In response to questions ("How many responses should I give?" "Can I turn the card?" "Do I use the whole thing or parts of it as well?"), examiners should provide noncommittal replies ("It's up to you"; "Any way you wish"). Should the person begin by saying "It's an inkblot," the examiner should restate the basic instruction: "Yes, that's right, but what you need to do is tell me what it looks like to you, what kinds of things you see in it."

Occasionally, some additional procedures may be necessary to obtain a record of sufficient but manageable length. A minimum of 14 responses is required to ensure the validity of a Rorschach protocol. Records with fewer than 14 responses are too brief to be entirely reliable and rarely support valid interpretations. To decrease the risk of ending up with a record of insufficient length, persons who give only one response to Card I should be prompted by saying, "If you look at it some more, you'll see other things as well." If the person still does not produce more than one response, the single response should be accepted and the card taken back. However, individuals who have given just one or two responses to Card I, and then handed back or put down Cards II, III, or IV after only a single response, can be offered the following indirect encouragement, should they seem disengaged from their task and on their way to producing a brief record with fewer than 14 responses: "Wait, don't hurry through these; we're in no hurry, take your time." Should the Response Phase for all 10 cards yield fewer than 14 responses, despite such prompting and encouragement, the examiner should implement the following instructions:

> Now you know how it's done. But there's a problem. You didn't give enough answers for us to learn very much from the test. So let's go through them again, and this time I'd like you to give me more responses. You can include the same ones you've already given, if you like, but give me more answers this time through.

There is also a standard procedure for not taking more responses than are necessary for interpretive purposes. If a person has given five responses to Card I and appears about to give more, the examiner should take the card back while saying, "Okay, that's fine, let's go on to the next one." This procedure can be repeated on each subsequent card, should the person continue to give five responses and appear ready to give more. However, if on any card the person gives fewer than five responses, the limiting procedure should be discontinued and not resumed, even if the person later on gives more than five responses to some card. Exner (2003, pp. 52–56) identifies some unusual circumstances that might warrant departing from these standard guidelines for increasing or curtailing response total, but the procedures presented here suffice with few exceptions to direct the Response Phase of the administration.

Of additional importance in conducting both the Response Phase and the subsequent Inquiry Phase is verbatim recording of whatever the examiner and the examinee say. Accurate coding and thorough interpretation depend on having a complete account of exactly how people expressed themselves and precisely what they were told or asked by the examiner. Most examiners rely on a system of abbreviations to simplify the task of recording a verbatim protocol; for example, using "ll a bfly" for "Looks like a butterfly" or "enc" to indicate when they have used the encouragement prompt after getting only one response on Card I. Some examiners tape-record Rorschach administrations to ensure preservation of the verbatim record. Whatever means is used, adequate Rorschach administration demands maintaining the integrity of the raw data. To this end, examiners should write down how examinees behave during the administration as well as what they say (e.g., "laughed," "big sigh," "detached, looking at ceiling") to provide the behavioral data that enrich Rorschach interpretation.

Following completion of the Response Phase, the examiner should introduce the Inquiry Phase of the administration as follows:

> Now I want to take a moment to go through these cards with you again, so that I can see the things you saw. I'll read back each of the things you said, and for each one I'd like you to tell me where you saw it and what made it look like that to you.

The examiner should then hand the cards to the person one at a time, say for each response something on the order of "On this one you saw ..." or "Then you said ..." or "Next there was ...," and then complete this statement with a verbatim reading of the person's exact words. Nondirective prompts should then be used as necessary to help people comply with the inquiry instructions by clarifying what they have seen, where on the blot they saw it, and why it looked as it did to them. With respect to what the person has seen, appropriate prompts would include such statements and questions as "I'm not sure what it is you're seeing there," "Is it the whole person or just part of the person?" or "You said it could be a butterfly or a moth—which does it look more like to you?"

To inquire about where the person has seen a percept, the examiner might ask, "How much of the blot is included in it?" or say, "You mentioned a head and a tail, and I'm not clear which part of the blot is which." Should the response to such questions or statements leave unclear where a percept has been seen, examinees should be asked to outline with their finger the area of the blot they were using for it. Inquiry about what made a percept look as it did can take the form of such questions as "What made it look like that to you?" "What helped you see it that way?" or "What about the blot suggested that to you?" In each of these aspects of the Inquiry Phase, examiners should strive as much as possible to eliminate ambiguity concerning the what, where, and why of a response, because such ambiguities in responses are the main source of uncertainty in deciding how to code them.

As these nondirective questions and statements illustrate, a paramount principle of conducting a Rorschach inquiry is to avoid leading the examinee or providing clues to what may be expected or desired. For example, "Are the people doing anything?" and "Did the color help you see it that way?" are inappropriate questions, because they can convey that movement and color are important for the person to note. Such messages can influence individuals to articulate more movement or color determinants during the course of an inquiry than they would have otherwise. As a similar precaution against conveying unintended messages, examiners should avoid the question "Anything else?" Asking "Anything else?" can suggest that more is expected from the person, or that something has been left out, either of which can lead individuals to say more than they would have otherwise and thereby detract from the standardization of the administration.

A second guiding principle in conducting the Inquiry Phase concerns its basic purpose, which is to enable accurate coding of the response. With this principle in mind, examiners should stop inquiring about a response once they have obtained enough information to code it. For example, "Two people standing there" is clearly a human movement response that, as indicated in the next section, warrants coding an *M*. It is neither necessary nor appropriate to ask, "What makes it look like two people standing there?" The additional question in this instance would not generate any information necessary to code an *M*. Asking such unnecessary questions violates CS standardization and may have the unwanted consequence of eliciting response elaborations that, however interesting, would not have occurred if standard procedures had been followed.

Should a person report, "Two funny-looking people picking up a basket," there is no need to inquire about the human movement, but two other inquiry questions would be called for: "What suggests that the people are funny-looking?" and "What helped you see this part as a basket?" The first question illustrates the importance of inquiring about key words in an individual's responses, particularly nouns, adjectives, verbs, and adverbs that give responses a potentially distinctive flavor. Consider the following examples, with the key words shown in italics: "Two *witches* dancing" [Inquiry: What suggests they are witches?]; "Two *old* people dancing" [Inquiry: What makes them look like old people?]; "Two people *arguing* or *fighting*" [Inquiry: What helps you see them as arguing or fighting?]; "Two people walking along *slowly*" [Inquiry: What gave you the idea that they're walking slowly?]. The second question illustrates the importance of inquiring about each part of a complex response. Thus "Animals climbing a tree" requires clarifying the where and the why for both the animals and the tree, "A jet plane with exhaust coming out the back" must be inquired sufficiently to code both the plane and the exhaust, and so on.

CODING AND SCORING

The scoring of a Rorschach protocol is a two-step process. The first step consists of assigning each response a set of codes that identify various features of how the response has been formulated and expressed. The second step consists of combining these response codes in various ways to generate several totals, ratios, percentages, and indices that are known as *summary scores*. These scores are typically arrayed in what is called a *Structural Summary*. The Rorschach Structural Summary, like the profile of scales on a self-report inventory, plays a key role in the interpretive process and can be computer generated (see Exner & Weiner, 2003). To arrive at a Structural Summary, the examiner must first code the individual responses for their basic, supplementary, and elaborative aspects.

Basic Codes: Location, Determinants, and Contents

Every Rorschach response is coded for three basic aspects of how it is formulated: (1) where it was seen (Location), (2) what made it look as it did (Determinants), and (3) what it consists of (Contents).

Location

The location of a response is the part of the blot that has been used for a percept. Location is determined in the Inquiry Phase by instructing people, "Show me where you saw it" or asking them, "Where did you see it?" If the whole blot has been used for a percept, it is coded as *W*. If a commonly used detail has been used, the Location is coded as *D*. If the percept has been given to an infrequently used detail, it is coded as *Dd*. The *D* (common) and *Dd* (unusual) details for each blot are indicated in location charts that are reproduced in Exner's (2001, 2003) CS textbook and workbook. The criterion for identifying common details was their occurrence in 5% or more of 7,500 test protocols in the CS standardization database. Location choices occurring in fewer than 5% of these protocols were considered infrequently used details.

In addition to being coded as *W, D,* or *Dd* for its location, some responses involve the white space as well as the inked space on a card. These white space responses are coded by adding *S* to the location code to produce the combined codes of *WS, DS,* and *DdS*. The CS location codes and their descriptions are listed in Table 11.1.

Determinants

Determinants are characteristics of the inkblot that have given rise to a response. Determinants are elicited in the Inquiry Phase with the instruction, "Tell me what made it look like that" and by asking such questions as "What helped you see it that way?" and "What suggested that to you?" There are five basic categories of determinants: form, movement, chromatic color, achromatic color, and shading.

Table 11.1   Comprehensive System location codes

Code	Description
W (Whole)	Responses to an entire blot
D (Common Detail)	Responses to frequently used blot areas
Dd (Unusual Detail)	Responses to infrequently used blot areas
WS (Space/Whole)	Responses using white space in a Whole location
DS (Space/Common)	Responses using white space in Common Detail areas
DdS (Space/Uncommon)	Responses using white space in Uncommon Detail areas

Responses based solely on the form of a location area are coded as *F*. Use of form is indicated when individuals articulate its influence ("It's shaped like one") or identify parts of an object they have seen ("Here are the head, the arms, and the legs"), and *F* is also coded by default when no other determinants are reported ("It just looks like that"). When any of the other four types of determinants are reported as the basis for a response, *F* is typically not coded separately, even when shape or object parts are mentioned.

People sometimes attribute movement to their Rorschach percepts. If they see people moving ("Two women lifting something") or animals engaged in human activities ("Dogs playing patty-cake"), the response is coded *M*. If they see animals engaged in movement appropriate to their species ("A lion walking along"), the response is coded *FM*. If they see inanimate objects in motion ("A leaf falling"), the response is coded *m*.

Individuals may articulate having used chromatic colors in the blots in formulating a percept. If the chromatic color is secondary to the form of an object ("It's round, like an apple, and it's red"), the response is coded *FC*. If chromatic color takes precedence over the form of an object ("It's different colors here, maybe like some flowers"), the response is coded *CF*. If chromatic color is used without any form ("The sky, because it's blue, no shape to it"), the response is coded *C*.

The achromatic colors black, gray, and white may also be reported by people as the basis for a percept ("A black bat," "Gray, like storm clouds," "Snow, because it's white"). Parallel to the coding for chromatic color use, achromatic color is coded as *FC'* ("A black bat"), *FC'* ("Gray, like storm clouds"), or *C'* ("White, like snow"), depending on the relative prominence of form or achromatic color in determining the percept.

Shading as a determinant involves a reaction to variations in the saturation of the hues in a blot, most commonly with respect to contrasts among the shades of gray and black. If the shading is used as a basis for inferring a three-dimensional perspective ("The colors are fainter here, so it looks farther away"), the response is coded *V* for Vista. If shading is used as a basis for inferring some tactile quality of an object ("It looks soft and furry because of the way it's shaded"), the response is coded *T* for Texture. If shading is used as a basis for describing darker or lighter coloration in a percept, without Vista or Texture ("The darker and lighter parts are shaded, like a moth's wings"), the response is coded *Y* for Diffuse Shading. *V, T,* and *Y,* like the chromatic and achromatic color codes, allow for designation of the role of form in determining the response (e.g., *FT, TF,* or *T*).

In addition to these five basic categories of determinants, two other possibilities may occur. The first of these is Form Dimension, which is coded with *FD* when a response involves a 3-dimensional perspective but does not include an articulated use of shading. The two most common types of responses coded *FD* involve something seen in the distance ("A man leaning backward, with his head farther away than his feet"; "An aerial view of an island") or one object seen behind another ("Someone hiding behind a bush"; "An animal with its tail sticking out behind").

The second additional possibility is Reflection, which is coded as *Fr* or *rF* when one part of a blot is identified specifically as a reflection of another identically shaped part of the blot. The *Fr* code is used when a reflected object has a definite form (e.g., "Here's an animal on this side, and on the other side is its reflection in the water"), and *rF* is coded when reflected content has no specific form (e.g., "This looks like a landscape reflected in the water").

People may at times articulate more than one determinant in explaining the basis for a particular percept. In these instances, the determinants are coded together in what is called a *Blend* response. For example, "A rocket ship taking off, and the exhaust is here, because of the red" involves a blend of inanimate movement and color-form, and the determinant would be coded as *m.CF.* A response of "Here's a red butterfly, with different shades of color on it's wings" blends form-color and shading and would be coded as *FC.FY.* The CS determinant codes and their descriptions are listed in Table 11.2.

Contents

Every response is assigned a code to designate the content of what a person has reported seeing. On the average, approximately 75% of an individual's Rorschach responses involve percepts of human or animal figures (see Exner & Erdberg, 2005, table 22.1). Human figures are coded as *H* for whole persons, *Hd* for partial figures ("Head of a person"; "A person's legs"), and *(H)* or *(Hd)* for mythical or fictitious figures ("An angel"; "A clown's face"; "The upper torso of the abominable snowman"). Animal figures are coded as *A, Ad, (A),* or *(Ad)* on the same basis.

For designating other contents, the CS provides 17 specific content categories from which to choose, as shown in Table 11.3. Contents that do not fit into any of these established categories are coded as *Id,* for Idiographic. Some responses may have multiple contents, in which case each of them is coded. For example, the content coding for "A man wearing a hat and with some blood on him" would be *H, Cg, Bl.*

Supplementary Codes

In addition to being coded for location, determinants, and contents, every Rorschach response is given one or more supplementary codes to identify its form quality *(FQ)* and whether it involves a pair of objects (2), a popular percept *(P),* or organizational activity *(Z).*

Form Quality

Form quality codes are assigned to indicate whether responses represent an accurate and conventional perception of the inkblot shapes to which they are given. This coding is facilitated by form-quality tables that list responses given to each whole blot and common detail by 2% or more of a large standardization sample comprising 9,500 nonpsychotic persons, and to unusual details by at least two-thirds of persons responding to that area (see Exner, 2003, chap. 8). These responses and responses similar to them are coded as *ordinary* form *(o)* and are considered to indicate accurate and conventional perception, that is, seeing things the way other people see them. Occasionally, individuals elaborate an ordinary form percept with considerable specification of details (e.g., "A head of a person, and here are the eyes, ears, nose, and mouth, with thin lips and bushy eyebrows"), in which case the form level is coded as *ordinary-elaborated* (+).

Most people also report some percepts that do not occur with sufficient frequency to be considered ordinary, but are nevertheless easy to see. Responses of this kind are perceptually accurate but not conventional, and they are coded as *unusual* (*u*) rather than ordinary. As a final possibility, responses that are neither common nor easily seen, but instead indicate

Table 11.2   Comprehensive System determinant codes

Code	Description
F (Form)	Responses based solely on the form of a blot area
M (Human movement)	Responses in which people or animals are engaged in human activities
FM (Animal movement)	Responses in which animals are engaged in movement appropriate to their species
m (Inanimate movement)	Responses in which inanimate objects are in motion
FC (Form-color)	Responses in which chromatic color is used secondary to the form of an object
CF (Color-form)	Responses in which chromatic color takes precedence over the form of an object
C (Pure color)	Responses based solely on the chromatic color of a blot area
FC′ (Form-achromatic color)	Responses in which achromatic color is used secondary to the form of an object
C′F (Achromatic color-form)	Responses in which achromatic color takes precedence over the form of an object
C′ (Pure achromatic color)	Responses based solely on the achromatic color of a blot area
FV (Form-vista)	Responses in which shading used to infer a three-dimensional perspective secondary to the form of an object
VF (Vista/form)	Responses in which shading used to infer a three-dimensional perspective takes precedence over the form of an object
V (Pure vista)	Responses based solely on the use of shading to infer a three-dimensional perspective
FT (Form-texture)	Responses in which shading is used to infer some tactile quality of an object
TF (Texture-form)	Responses in which shading used to infer some tactile quality takes precedence over the form of an object
T (Pure texture)	Responses based solely on the use of shading to infer a tactile quality
FY (Form-shading)	Responses in which shading is used to describe lighter or darker coloration of an object, without Vista or Texture
YF (Shading-form)	Responses in which shading is used to describe lighter or darker coloration takes precedence over the form of an object, without Vista or Texture
Y (Pure shading)	Responses based solely on the use of shading to describe lighter or darker coloration, without Vista or Texture
FD (Form dimension)	Responses involving a three-dimensional perspective without the use of shading
Fr (Form-reflection)	Responses in which a blot area is identified as a reflection of another identically shaped blot area
rF (Reflection-form)	Responses in which identically shaped blot areas are identified as reflecting a content that has no specific form

Table 11.3   Comprehensive System content categories

Category	Description
H	Entire person
Hd	Part of a person
(H)	Entire mythical or fictitious person
(Hd)	Part of a mythical or fictitious person
Hx	Human experience of emotion (e.g., anger) or sensation (e.g., smell)
A	Entire animal
(A)	Entire mythical or fictitious animal
Ad	Part of an animal
(Ad)	Part of a mythical or fictitious animal
An	Internal anatomy (skeletal, muscular, organ systems)
Art	Artistic creations or decorative products (e.g., painting, jewelry)
Ay	Items of cultural, or historical, or anthropological interest
Bl	Blood
Bt	Botany (any form of plant life)
Cg	Any article of clothing
Ex	Explosion (including fireworks)
Fi	Fire or smoke
Fd	Any edible item of food
Ge	Geography (including maps)
Hh	Any household item
Ls	Description of landscape or underwater scene
Na	Features of the natural environment not coded as Bt or Ls (e.g., sun, snow, storm); Na responses containing Bt or Ls content are coded only for Na
Sc	Scientific or science fiction items or products (telescope, spaceship, bridge, skyscraper)
Sx	Sex organs or activities
Xy	Any kind of X-ray

distorted or inaccurate perception of the inkblot shapes, are coded as *minus* form (−). Whereas there is a finite number of *o* and + responses (those with a 2% or more frequency in the standardization sample), there is no limit to how many different kinds of *u* or − responses people can produce. For guidance in form-level coding, however, examples of unconventional or inaccurate percepts are also included in the CS form quality tables. The form quality codes and their descriptions are shown in Table 11.4.

Pair (2)

Responses are coded with *2,* for *Pair,* when they involve two of the same object seen in exactly the same-shaped detail on opposite sides of a blot. Two of the same objects seen in dissimilar blot locations are not coded *Pair,* and *Pair* is not coded for essentially single objects that naturally occur in pairs (e.g., "a person's lungs").

Table 11.4   Comprehensive System form quality codes

Code	Description
+ (Ordinary-elaborated)	Accurate and conventional responses, given by 2% or more of a standardization sample to *W* and *D* locations and 25% or more of the sample to *Dd* locations, that are elaborated with considerable detail
o (ordinary)	Accurate and conventional responses, given by 2% or more of a standardization sample to *W* and *D* locations and at least two-thirds of the sample to *Dd* locations, that do not include unusual specification of detail
u (unusual)	Accurate but unconventional responses that do not occur with sufficient frequency to be coded ordinary
–(minus)	Inaccurate responses involving distorted perception of the inkblot shapes

Popular (P)

Among the responses given by the CS standardization sample of nonpsychotic persons, 13 were notable for being given by at least one-third of the respondents. These 13 responses, shown in Table 11.5, are designated as *Popular (P)* in the Comprehensive System. They are coded as *P* whenever they occur in a record.

Organizational Activity (Z-Score)

Rorschach responses may involve some meaningful organization of separate portions of an inkblot. Such integrative effort is apparent when the whole blot is used for a percept, although relatively little effort is required to integrate a solid blot like Card I into a single percept (e.g., "A bat"), compared with integrating the diverse and scattered portions of a broken blot like Card X into a single percept (e.g., "An underwater scene with different fish and some coral," "A bouquet of daffodils and other types of flowers"). Blot details can also be organized into meaningful relationships, without using the whole blot, as in seeing the black portions of Card II as "Bears touching noses." However, this type of Card II integration of adjacent blot details does not require as much organizational effort as

Table 11.5   Comprehensive System popular responses

Card I: Entire blot seen as a bat or butterfly
Card II: Side black details seen as a bear, dog, elephant, or lamb
Card III: Side black details seen as human figures
Card IV: Entire blot, or entire blot except for the bottom center detail, seen as a human or humanlike figure
Card V: Entire blot seen as a bat or butterfly
Card VI: Entire blot or entire lower portion seen as an animal skin, hide, pelt, or rug
Card VII: Upper-side details seen as a human head or face (often seen as part of a human figure)
Card VIII: Side pink details seen as an animal figure
Card IX: Upper-side orange details seen as human or humanlike figures
Card X: Outer blue details seen as a spider or crab

integrating details that are distant from each other, as in seeing the top side details of Card VII as "The heads of two people, looking at each other." If these Card VII details were seen only as "The heads of two people," without any mention of their interacting in some way, the response would not be regarded as involving organizational activity.

With these considerations in mind, meaningful integrations of blot portions in forming a response are assigned a numerical Z-score ranging from 1 to 6. The specific value of the Z-score assigned to an integrated response depends on whether it involves a W, adjacent details, distant details, or use of the white space, and each of these types of integration has different values for each card. The appropriate Z-score is indicated by a table of values that is printed on the CS Structural Summary test form and also appears in the previously referenced Exner text and workbook. Examiners need only to identify the type of integration that has occurred and then consult the table to determine the Z-score value for it on the card where it occurred.

Code Elaborations

The Location, Determinant, and Content codes can each be elaborated in ways that enrich the interpretive yield of Rorschach responses. These elaborations consist of a Developmental Quality (DQ) coding for locations, an active/passive (a/p) designation for movement determinants, and some Special Scores for content characteristics.

Developmental Quality (DQ)

Coding for Developmental Quality expands the utility of the Z-score by providing additional information concerning the quality of the organizational effort reflected in a response. To this end, each location code is designated as representing a synthesis (DQ+), an ordinary (DQo), or a vague (DQv) approach to articulating what the blot might be. A DQ+ response involves two or more separate objects that have some integral relationship to each other. The previously mentioned whole responses of "underwater scene" and "bouquet of flowers" are both synthesis responses that would be given a location code of W+. However, a whole response of "bat" to Card I, although qualifying for a Z-score, involves a single object without any synthesis and would be coded Wo, not W+. The DQ codes and their descriptions are listed in Table 11.6.

Table 11.6   Comprehensive System developmental quality codes

Code	Description
+ (synthesized)	Two or more separate objects, at least one of which has some specific form, are seen as related to each other
o (ordinary)	A single object having some specific form is identified
v (vague)	An object having no specific form is identified (e.g., clouds)
v/+ (vague synthesis)	Two or more separate objects, none of which has any specific forms, are seen as related to each other (e.g., clouds moving toward each other)

Table 11.7   Comprehensive System content special scores

Code	Description
Abstract (AB)	Responses containing Human Experience (*Hx*) content or articulation of a symbolic representation
Aggressive Movement (AG)	Movement responses (*M, FM,* or *m*) involving aggressive action
Cooperative Movement (COP)	Movement responses (*M, FM,* or *m*) involving collaborative interactions
Color Projection (CP)	Responses in which chromatic color is attributed to an achromatic blot or blot area
Good/Poor Human Representation (GHR/PHR)	Human and human movement response showing or quality representations, as identified by other codes assigned to the response and automatically scored by the RIAP computer program
Morbid (MOR)	Responses involving objects identified as dead, damaged, destroyed, dysfunctional, and the like, or to which dysphoric feelings are attributed
Personal (PER)	Responses in which personal experience or knowledge is articulated as a basis for what is seen
Perseverative (PSV)	Responses that are almost identical to the response preceding it on a card, or are referred to again in responding to a subsequent card

Active/Passive (a/p)

Each human movement (*M*), animal movement (*FM*), and inanimate movement (*m*) response is additionally coded for whether it involves active (*a*) or passive (*p*) movement. Benchmarks for passive movement are "talking," "sitting," "standing," "falling," and "resting." Active movement is coded for movements that involve expending more energy than these benchmarks, for example, "arguing," "running," "climbing," and "working."

Special Scores

The CS includes two types of special scores that have a rich interpretive yield when they are present. The first type, called *Content Special Scores*, consists of eight codes that are assigned to responses with certain kinds of content characteristics. The second type, called *Cognitive Special Scores*, involves six codes for responses that are expressed in certain unusual ways. The Content Special Scores provide clues to a person's attitudes, concerns, and coping style and are listed alphabetically in Table 11.7. The Cognitive Special Scores identify loose associations or illogical reasoning and are listed in Table 11.8 in order of the degree of thinking disorder they are likely to suggest, from least to most. The DV, INC, DR, and FABCOM codes in Table 11.8 are additionally specified as Level 1 or Level 2 in severity. A Level 1 code is used to designate a mild degree of cognitive slippage that could be produced by almost anyone from time to time. A Level 2 code is assigned for a severe degree of cognitive slippage that is unlikely to be produced by anyone who does not have a thinking disorder.

For the coding of each response, then, there are five necessary elements and five possible elements to record. The five elements that must be coded for each response are its location,

Table 11.8   Comprehensive System cognitive special scores

Code	Description
Deviant Verbalization (DV)	Responses involving a redundancy (e.g., "A *tiny little* person"), a neologism (e.g., "A *fanciful* picture"), or some other misnomer (e.g., "A *telescopic* view of an amoeba") (Level 1 = 1 point; Level 2 = 2 points)
Incongruous Combination (INCOM)	Responses in which a single object is seen as having some features or engaging in some activities that are implausible or impossible (e.g, "A person with two heads"; "A green spider"; "A dog singing a song") (Level 1 = 2 points; Level 2 = 4 points)
Deviant Response (DR)	Responses that are fluid, rambling, disconnected, or elaborated in ways that are irrelevant to the task of specifying location, determinants, and content (e.g., "A bat or a moth or whatever it is, I could care less, because I don't care about the animal kingdom"; "People in love, and the world would be a better place if more people loved each other") (Level 1 = 3 points: Level 2 = 6 points)
Fabulized Combination (FABCOM)	Responses in which two or more separate objects are seen in some relationship to each other that is implausible or impossible (e.g., "Two bears sitting on a butterfly"; "Two people fighting over someone's lungs") (Level 1 = 4 points; Level 2 = 8 points)
Autistic Logic (ALOG)	Responses in which some circumstantial or illogical reason is articulated as the basis of an impression (e.g., "There are two of them, so they must be husband and wife"; "Because it's at the bottom of everything, this part represents Hell") (5 points)
Contamination (CONTAM)	Responses in which two or more impressions of the same blot area are condensed or fused into a single unrealistic percept, often involving a neologism (e.g., "A butterflower"; "An island, and it's red like blood, so it's a bleeding island") (7 points)

its developmental quality, its determinants, its form level, and its contents. The five response elements that might be coded, if they are present, include whether any movement responses are active or passive, whether there is a pair, whether the response is a popular, whether there is organizational activity calling for a Z score, and whether there are any content or cognitive special scores to be noted. These codes are written out in a standard sequence: location, developmental quality, determinant(s), active/passive, form level, content(s), popular, Z-score, and special scores. To illustrate the appearance of the code for a response containing all 10 of these elements, the code for all of Card VII seen as "Two women with skirts on doing a dance together" would be *W+ Mao (2) H,Cg P 2.5 COP*.

Structural Summary

The coding of the individual Rorschach responses is followed by tabulating various summary scores that constitute the CS Structural Summary and provide a basis for interpreting the structural data in a protocol. These summary scores consist of the frequency with which each of the basic, supplementary, and elaborative codes have been assigned and also various ratios, percentages, and indices that are calculated from these total scores. The formulas for these calculations are included for information purposes in the following discussion of structural interpretation, but readers are recommended to use the Rorschach Interpretation Assistance Program (RIAP; Exner & Weiner, 2003) for these calculations, to save time and avoid arithmetical errors. An illustrative copy of the Structural Summary as it appears in the RIAP computer printout is shown in Table 11.9. A sample interpretive report based on this Structural Summary appears in Appendix F.

As a final comment on administration and coding, it is important to stress that accurate summary scores are essential for adequate interpretation of the structural data. Errors and oversights in coding can lead to mistaken inferences and flawed decisions based on these inferences. Conducting a competent inquiry and assigning correct codes in a Rorschach administration are acquired skills that, once acquired, can be maintained only with continued practice and consultation. Clinicians new to Rorschach assessment should regularly have their coding checked by a knowledgeable colleague, and experienced examiners should at times discuss coding ambiguities and uncertainties with other Rorschach clinicians, to keep their skills sharp and avoid falling into bad coding habits.

INTERPRETATION: STRUCTURAL VARIABLES

Rorschach interpretation involves integrating the structural, thematic, and behavioral features of the test data into a comprehensive description of personality characteristics. The following overview of the interpretive significance of the structural variables in a Rorschach protocol is organized around the six previously mentioned dimensions of personality functioning that they assess: how people attend to and perceive their surroundings, how they form concepts and ideas, how they experience and express feelings, how they manage stress, how they view themselves, and how they relate to other people. The discussion focuses in particular on the relevance of these six personality dimensions to whether people are likely to be successful in adapting to their life circumstances or are instead at risk for adjustment difficulties (see also Exner, 2003, chaps. 14–21; Weiner, 2003b, chap. 5).

Attending to and Perceiving Surroundings

Successful adaptation is promoted by openness to experience, efficient organization of information, and realistic and conventional perception of events. Conversely, people who have difficulty attending to their surroundings openly, efficiently, realistically, and conventionally are susceptible to adjustment difficulties. Rorschach summary scores can be helpful in measuring each of these personality characteristics.

Being Open to Experience (Lambda)

Openness to experience is measured by *Lambda,* which is calculated by dividing the number of pure form (*F*) responses by the number of responses with determinants other than *F* (*R-F*). People whose *Lambda* ranges between .30 and .99 generally show an adaptively balanced focus of attention. A *Lambda* > .99 usually identifies lack of adequate openness to experience, a narrow frame of reference, and little tolerance for ambiguity or uncertainty. High *Lambda* people feel most comfortable in clearly defined and well-structured situations,

Table 11.9   Rorschach Comprehensive System Structural Summary

RIAP™ Structural Summary

Location Features		
Zf	=	12
ZSum	=	34.5
ZEst	=	38.0
W	=	9
(Wv	=	0)
D	=	13
W+D	=	22
Dd	=	0
S	=	2

DQ			
			(FQ-)
+	=	4	(0)
o	=	16	(4)
v/+	=	1	(0)
v	=	1	(0)

Form Quality				
		FQx	MQual	W+D
+	=	0	0	0
o	=	14	2	14
u	=	4	0	4
-	=	4	0	4
none	=	0	0	0

Determinants

Blends	Single	
M.FD	M	= 1
FM.m	FM	= 2
	m	= 0
	FC	= 2
	CF	= 0
	C	= 0
	Cn	= 0
	FC'	= 0
	C'F	= 0
	C'	= 0
	FT	= 1
	TF	= 0
	T	= 0
	FV	= 1
	VF	= 0
	V	= 0
	FY	= 2
	YF	= 0
	Y	= 0
	Fr	= 0
	rF	= 0
	FD	= 0
	F	= 11
	(2)	= 7

Contents	
H	= 1
(H)	= 1
Hd	= 0
(Hd)	= 0
Hx	= 0
A	= 10
(A)	= 0
Ad	= 1
(Ad)	= 0
An	= 1
Art	= 0
Ay	= 2
Bl	= 0
Bt	= 2
Cg	= 1
Cl	= 0
Ex	= 0
Fd	= 0
Fi	= 0
Ge	= 4
Hh	= 0
Ls	= 0
Na	= 0
Sc	= 0
Sx	= 0
Xy	= 3
Idio	= 0

S-Constellation

☐		FV+VF+V+FD > 2
☐		Col-Shd Blends > 0
☐		Ego < .31 or > .44
☐		MOR > 3
☐		Zd > ±3.5
☑		es > EA
☐		CF + C > FC
☑		X+% < .70
☐		S > 3
☐		P < 3 or > 8
☑		Pure H < 2
☐		R < 17
3		Total

Special Scores

		Lvl-1	Lvl-2
DV	=	0 x1	0 x2
INC	=	0 x2	0 x4
DR	=	0 x3	0 x6
FAB	=	2 x4	0 x7
ALOG	=	0 x5	
CON	=	0 x7	
Raw Sum6	=	**2**	
Wgtd Sum6	=	**8**	

AB	= 0		GHR	= 2
AG	= 0		PHR	= 0
COP	= 1		MOR	= 0
CP	= 0		PER	= 2
			PSV	= 1

RATIOS, PERCENTAGES, AND DERIVATIONS

R = 22		L = 1.00

EB	= 2 : 1.0	EA = 3.0	EBPer = N/A
eb	= 4 : 4	es = 8	D = -1
		Adj es = 7	Adj D = -1

FM = 3	SumC' = 0	SumT = 1
m = 1	SumV = 1	SumY = 2

AFFECT

FC:CF+C	= 2 : 0
Pure C	= 0
SumC' : WSumC	= 0 : 1.0
Afr	= 0.47
S	= 2
Blends:R	= 2 : 22
CP	= 0

INTERPERSONAL

COP = 1		AG	= 0
GHR:PHR			= 2 : 0
a:p			= 4 : 2
Food			= 0
SumT			= 1
Human Content			= 2
Pure H			= 1
PER			= 2
Isolation Index			= 0.27

IDEATION

a:p	= 4 : 2	Sum6	= 2
Ma:Mp	= 1 : 1	Lvl-2	= 0
2AB+(Art+Ay)	= 2	WSum6	= 8
MOR	= 0	M-	= 0
		M none	= 0

MEDIATION

XA%	= 0.82
WDA%	= 0.82
X-%	= 0.18
S-	= 0
P	= 7
X+%	= 0.64
Xu%	= 0.18

PROCESSING

Zf	= 12
W:D:Dd	= 9:13:0
W : M	= 9 : 2
Zd	= -3.5
PSV	= 1
DQ+	= 4
DQv	= 1

SELF-PERCEPTION

3r+(2)/R	= 0.32
Fr+rF	= 0
SumV	= 1
FD	= 1
An+Xy	= 4
MOR	= 0
H:(H)+Hd+(Hd)	= 1 : 1

PTI = 0	☐ DEPI = 4	☑ CDI = 5	☐ S-CON = 3	☐ HVI = No	☐ OBS = No

and they favor simple solutions even to complex problems. They tend to manage daily events in a detached, uninvolved, and matter-of-fact way that maximizes closure and minimizes loose ends. When *Lambda* falls below .30, by contrast, people tend to show an excessive openness to experience and an overly broad focus of attention. Low *Lambda* people welcome and even seek out ambiguous and complex situations; and they typically feel most comfortable in environments that are relatively unstructured and open-ended. Instead of dealing with situations in a simple, detached, or objective manner, they are inclined to make situations more complicated than they need to be and to become overly involved in contemplating the underlying significance of events or sorting out their feelings about them.

Organizing Information Efficiently (Zd)

Efficiency in organizing information is measured by the Processing Efficiency variable, *Zd*. The calculation of *Zd* is accomplished by adding all the *Z*-scores assigned to the responses in a record, which provides a *Zsum,* and then subtracting from this *Zsum* an estimated total *Z* (*Zest*) for the record. The values to use for a *Zest* are indicated by a table that provides *Zest* values for the number of responses having a *Z*-score. For example, a record containing 10 responses with a *Z*-score would have a *Z*-frequency (*Zf*) of 10, and the *Zest* shown by the table for a *Zf* of 10 is 31.0. The *Zest* tables as noted are printed on the structural summary forms used in administering the CS Rorschach.

Individuals with a normal range *Zd,* which runs from −3.0 to +3.0, tend to be taking in just about as much information as they can process adequately. Such people are likely to form conclusions, solve problems, and complete tasks in an efficient manner and with a degree of success consistent with their abilities. When *Zd* falls below −3.0, which is taken to indicate an inclination to *underincorporate,* people tend to absorb too little information and examine their experiences less thoroughly than would be desirable. Underincorporators are likely to come to conclusions hastily, without paying sufficient attention to relevant information, and to perform tasks quickly but carelessly, without putting much effort into quality control.

When *Zd* exceeds +3.0, by contrast, people are showing overincorporation, which involves taking in more information than they can organize efficiently and examining their experience more thoroughly than is necessary. Overincorporators tend to be careful and conscientious in whatever they do, but sometimes to a fault. Although very thorough in their work, they may have difficulty completing tasks in a timely fashion because of concerns that their efforts have not been thorough enough. They may similarly be hesitant and uncertain in making decisions, as a result of excessive concerns about not having enough information on which to base opinions and conclusions.

Perceiving Events Realistically (X-%, XA%, WDA%)

The ability of people to form accurate impressions of themselves and their experiences, and thus perceive events realistically, is measured on the RIM by three form quality variables expressed in percentages: Distorted Form (*X-%*), Form Appropriate (*XA%*), and Form Appropriate-Common Areas (*WDA%*). *X-%* is the percentage of the total number of responses (*R*) that have minus form quality. People whose *X-%* is no greater than .20 can generally be expected to show adequate reality testing. The more *X-%* exceeds .20, however, the more frequently people are likely to perceive events incorrectly, to form mistaken impressions of themselves, to misinterpret the actions and intentions of others, to fail to anticipate the consequences of their own actions, and to misconstrue the boundaries of appropriate behavior.

XA% is the percentage of total responses with ordinary, ordinary-elaborated, or unusual form quality. As such, *XA%* is merely the reciprocal of *X-%*, provided that all the responses in a record are coded for form quality. Occasionally, a record may contain one or more responses with no form at all (e.g., "blue sky," which would be coded as a pure *C* without any form quality code). In these instances the *XA%* is a more dependable index of an individual's level of reality testing than the *X-%*. Normally functioning individuals tend to have an *XA%* in the upper .80s, but an *XA%* of .70 or more (or .65 or more for children age 10 or younger) ordinarily indicates at least fairly good ability to perceive people and events realistically. However, as the *XA%* decreases toward .70, people become increasingly prone to instances in which they misperceive events and form mistaken impressions of other persons and what their actions signify. An *XA%* below .70 usually identifies a substantial impairment of reality testing capacities, although the interpretive significance of such a finding may be qualified by an adequate *WDA%*.

WDA% is the percentage of responses to *W* or *D* locations (the common areas) that are coded with appropriate form quality (+, *o*, or *u*). As such, *WDA%* measures the accuracy of persons' perceptions when they are attending to the usual and apparent shapes in the blots. Hence this variable has implications for the adequacy of reality testing when people are dealing with situations that provide clear and obvious clues to what constitutes appropriate behavior. With respect to *WDA%* qualifying a low *XA%*, an apparently poor level of reality testing indicated by numerous minus form responses may be offset by an adequate *WDA%*, defined as .80 or higher (.75 or higher in children age 10 or less). A low *XA%* combined with an adequate *WDA%* indicates that people can perceive the world accurately when their attention is focused on the usual and ordinary aspects of everyday life (as represented by the *W* and *D* responses). However, people with a low *XA%* but adequate *WDA%* are prone to misperceptions, false impressions, and poor judgment when their attention is drawn to unusual, peripheral, and relatively inconsequential matters (when their inaccurate forms cluster in *Dd* locations).

Perceiving Events Conventionally (W:D:Dd, Xu%, P)

The relative number of *W*, *D*, and *Dd* responses constitutes the Economy Index and helps to identify whether people pay attention to situations in a conventional way. Ordinarily, about half the responses in a record are given to usual details (*D*), one-third to one-half to the whole blot (*W*), and the remaining one-sixth or fewer to unusual details (*Dd*). A marked predominance of *D* responses at the expense of relatively few *W* or *Dd* responses indicates excessively conventional examination of situations. A predominance of either *W* or *Dd* responses at the expense of relatively few *D* responses indicates inordinate attention to global or unusual aspects of experience rather than to what is ordinary and commonplace, and this pattern of focusing is likely to be associated with unconventional attitudes or behavioral tendencies.

As for *Xu* responses, percentages falling below .10 of the total responses are likely to indicate a strong commitment to conventionality in what people choose to think and do, especially when a low *Xu%* is accompanied by a high *XA%*. The farther the *Xu%* rises above .25, especially in the company of numerous minus form responses, the more likely it is to identify distaste for conformity, or rejection of conformity, sometimes manifest in risk-taking or sensation-seeking behavior. The number of P responses people give has similar implications, with $P > 7$ identifying more than average endorsement of conformity and $P < 4$ suggesting notable idiosyncrasy in a person's preferences and view of the world.

$Xu\%$ and P can combine with $W{:}D{:}Dd$ to provide a usually dependable clue to whether a person is more or less likely than most people to attend to experience in a conventional manner. High $Xu\%$ and low P together with infrequent D and numerous Dd are especially likely to identify nonconformity, whereas low $Xu\%$ and high P occurring along with numerous D typically identify a firm commitment to conventionality.

Forming Concepts and Ideas

Forming concepts and ideas is an ideational function that consists of how people think about the experiences they have and the types of impressions they form. People adapt best when they can think logically, coherently, flexibly, constructively, and to a moderate but not excessive extent. Conversely, illogical, incoherent, inflexible, overly fanciful, and excessively preoccupying ways of thinking constitute liabilities that are likely to interfere with a person's psychological adjustment.

Thinking Logically and Coherently (WSum6)

Logical and coherent thinking are reflected on the RIM by *WSum6,* which is the sum of weighted values of the Special Scores for unusual forms of expression. As indicated in Table 11.8, INCOM, FABCOM, ALOG, and CONTAM are coded for instances of arbitrary thinking in which various objects, ideas, and impressions are integrated, combined, or assumed to interrelate in unlikely or bizarre ways. DV and DR are coded for instances of dissociated thinking in which ideas emerge out of sequence or intrude on each other to produce strange, rambling, tangential, and sometimes incomprehensible verbalizations. Table 11.8 also indicates the weighted Level 1 and Level 2 values for instances of DV, INCOM, DR, and FABCOM and a single value for instances of ALOG and CONTAM, which have no Level 2 designation.

The larger their *WSum6,* the more likely people are to display arbitrary and circumstantial reasoning and to think in loose and scattered ways that confuse them and are confusing to others. Among adults, a *WSum6* exceeding 17 often indicates the presence of a formal thought disorder, and somewhat higher criterion scores, as specified by Exner (2003, p. 525), have similar implications for children and adolescents at different ages. The lower their *WSum6,* on the other hand, the more likely people are to form concepts and ideas in a logical and coherent fashion. As an exception to this interpretive guideline, individuals with a high *Lambda* score, which was discussed in relation to openness to experience, may produce short, guarded, and generally unrevealing records in which underlying thought disturbance does not come to light.

Thinking Flexibly (a:p)

Flexible thinking is indicated on the RIM by a balanced tendency to attribute active and passive movements to figures seen in motion, as reflected in the *a:p* (active:passive) ratio. People who give approximately the same number of active and passive movement responses tend to be cognitively flexible in making decisions, solving problems, and adapting to new and unfamiliar situations. However, if there are at least five movement responses in a record (which is a sufficiently large sample for the *a:p* ratio to provide reliable information) and either the *a* or the *p* is more than twice the size of the other, there is an imbalance that usually identifies cognitive inflexibility. Unlike people who think flexibly, cognitively inflexible individuals tend to be closed-minded people who seldom change their opinions and rarely consider modifying their beliefs.

Thinking Constructively (Ma:Mp)

M (human movement) responses provide a good index of a person's capacity to think purposefully about how best to deal with situations and move through life by design rather than accident, especially when the movements attributed to human figures are active. However, individuals whose number of passive human movements (*Mp*) responses exceeds the number of active human movement (*Ma*) responses are likely to be making excessive use of fantasy as an alternative to constructive problem solving. Whereas $Ma => Mp$ indicates normative capacity for thinking constructively, then, $Mp > Ma$ identifies a predilection for escapist fantasy in which people deal with situations in their lives not by thinking through what they could or should do about them, but instead by imagining how other people or a fortunate turn of events will make their decisions and solve their problems for them.

Thinking in Moderation (EBPer, INTELL, FM+m)

Thinking in moderation allows people to use ideation effectively without allowing thoughts to disrupt their peace of mind or dominate their lives at the expense of an adaptive emotional side. People who think excessively rather than to a moderate extent are susceptible to becoming preoccupied with disturbing thoughts or distracted by intrusive ideation, and they often lack adequate capacities to experience and express feelings. Three Rorschach variables that help distinguish between moderate and excessive thinking are the Pervasive Experience Balance (*EBPer*), the Intellectualization Index (INTELL), and the sum of the animal and inanimate movement responses (*FM+m*).

The Rorschach Experience Balance (*EB*) shows the ratio of the number of *M* in a record to the weighted sum of the chromatic color responses (*WSumC*), which is calculated by summing 0.5 points for each *FC* in a record, 1.0 points for each *CF,* and 1.5 points for each pure *C* ($WSumC = .5FC + 1CF + 1.5C$). The *M* responses involve ideational, deliberative ways of dealing with experience, whereas *WSumC* represents an emotional, intuitive way of responding to situations. People whose *M* exceeds their *WSumC* by 2 points or more (2.5 points or more if $EA > 10$) are displaying a clear preference for solving problems and making decisions more on the basis of what they think than on the basis of how they feel; such individuals are described in Rorschach terms as having an *introversive EB* style. Being introversive is associated with being a thoughtful and contemplative person, which are qualities that can contribute to good psychological adjustment. However, *M* exceeding *WSumC* by a ratio of more than 2.5:1 identifies a pervasively introversive coping style (*EBPer*) and suggests that people are not giving the emotional side of their life its just due. Pervasively introversive people tend to be deep thinkers to the point of becoming ruminative, to have limited channels for affective expression, and to have difficulty dealing comfortably and effectively with emotionally charged situations.

INTELL is scored from three response characteristics that constitute an ideational effort by people to impose some distance between themselves and a real encounter with whatever feelings may have been elicited by their Rorschach responses or associations. These characteristics include the number of Art and Anthropology contents, which are given one point each, and the number of Abstract special scores, which are given two points each. When the sum of these points results in an INTELL > 3, an individual is more likely than most people to deal with feelings in an intellectual manner. Excessive reliance on intellectualization in processing affective experience constitutes an immoderate use of ideation that can interfere with showing one's feelings in a direct and genuine manner.

FM responses are thought to be associated with a disconcerting awareness of needs that are not being met, and *m* responses typically indicate worrisome thoughts about being helpless to prevent other people or events from determining one's destiny. Taken together, *FM+m* represents ideas that come unbidden into one's mind and that, unlike the intentional ideation associated with *M* responses (e.g., planning ahead, thinking through a problem) cannot be turned on and off at will. In this sense, then, *FM+m* indicates intrusive ideation that causes distress and serves no apparent purpose. People normally experience some distress of this kind, unless they are less motivated by everyday needs or less concerned about losing control of their destiny than they should be. Accordingly, *FM+m* ordinarily ranges from 4 to 6. An *FM+m* > 6 is likely to identify a maladaptive excess of distracting or troubling ideas that often contributes to people being anxious or having difficulty concentrating.

Experiencing and Expressing Feelings

The manner and comfort with which people experience and express their feelings has considerable bearing on how they get along in life. Good psychological adaptation is fostered by well-developed capacities to process affect sufficiently, pleasurably, and in moderation. A deficiency or impairment in these capacities tends to result in constricted, dysphoric, or overly intense ways of modulating affect.

Modulating Affect Sufficiently (Afr, WSumC:SumC')

Sufficient modulation of affect consists of engaging in emotionally charged situations and exchanging feelings with others. This capacity for affective engagement and exchange of feelings allows people to feel comfortable in situations that involve moderate levels of emotional expression or arousal. Being able to modulate affect sufficiently fosters tolerance for having one's feelings aroused and adaptive skills in recognizing and responding to feelings expressed by others. The capacity for sufficient modulation of affect is reflected on the RIM by an adequate Affective Ratio (*Afr*) and a *WSumC* equal to or larger than the number of achromatic color (*SumC'*) responses in a record.

The *Afr* is calculated by dividing the number of responses given to the last three cards (VIII–X) by the number of responses given to the first seven cards (I–VII). *Afr* is an index of receptivity to emotional stimulation, and persons with *Afr* > .49 tend to be at least as willing as most people to become involved in emotionally arousing situations and to exchange affect with others. The farther their *Afr* falls below .50, the more likely people are to feel uncomfortable in and avoid situations that call for emotional expression or exchange. Because close relationships between people usually involve exchanging feelings, low *Afr* individuals tend to be socially as well as emotionally withdrawn.

As distinct from *Afr,* which indicates a person's receptivity or aversion to becoming emotionally involved, *WSumC* provides an index of basic capacity to experience and express feelings, independent of whether the person chooses to do so. A *WSumC* of 2.5 or more indicates at least average ability to become aware of one's feelings and to describe them to others. *WSumC* < 2.5, on the other hand, suggests limited capacity to process emotional experience. A low *WSumC* becomes particularly problematic for adjustment when its value is exceeded by the number of *SumC'*. *SumC'* indicates the extent to which a person's affective experience is being internalized rather than expressed, and *WSumC:SumC'* is labeled the Constriction Ratio in the CS. People with *SumC'* $>$ *WSumC* are likely to be experiencing an emotional blockage and to be painfully aware of having feelings bottled up inside that they have difficulty expressing or making known to others.

Modulating Affect Pleasurably (SumC', Col-Shd Bld, SumShd, S)

Pleasurable modulation of affect consists of sustaining a positive emotional tone that promotes feeling happy and enjoying oneself. The likelihood of a positively toned affective life is increased when an adequate level of *WSumC* occurs in combination with a low frequency of determinants and locations that identify dysphoria, anhedonia, ambivalence, and anger. Hence adaptive capacities for pleasurable processing of affect is ordinarily indicated by a low *SumC'*, the absence of Color Shading Blends (*Col-Shd Bld*), a Sum Shading (*SumShd*) equal to or less than *FM+m*, and infrequent White Space (*S*) answers.

As just noted, *SumC'* is an index of internalized affect, and the unpleasant connotations commonly associated with black (as in "a black mood") and gray (as in "a gray day") suggest that the internalized affect indicated by *C'* responses, most of which involve black or gray objects, has a distinctly unpleasurable affective tone. With few exceptions, an elevated *C'*, defined as *SumC'* > 2, identifies feelings of sadness, gloom, and unhappiness.

Col-Shd Bld is coded for responses that have both a chromatic (*FC, CF,* or *C*) and an achromatic or shading (*C', T, V,* or *Y*) determinant. Persons whose records show *Col-Shd Bld* > 0 tend to be confused and uncertain about how they feel, and they often imbue people and events in their lives with positive (the color) and negative (the shading) emotional characteristics at the same time. They may consequently have difficulty sorting out their feelings, and their proclivity to attach both pleasant and unpleasant connotations to experiences in their lives may contribute to anhedonia by limiting their prospects for enjoying themselves. For some emotionally expressive individuals, as reflected in a high *Afr* and a large *WSum6,* a more conservative criterion of *Col-Shd Bld* > 1 may be necessary to identify a maladaptive elevation on this variable.

SumShd is the total number of *C', T, V,* and *Y* determinants in a record and constitutes the right side of the *eb* (experience base) ratio on the CS. The left side of the *eb* consists of *FM+m,* which as previously noted indicates the demands being made on people by intrusive ideation. *SumShd* is an index of stress or demand that is experienced as a consequence of painful or unwelcome emotions over which people cannot exert conscious control. People of all ages normatively have some *SumShd* as well as some *FM+m* in their record, but emotionally well-adjusted persons typically show more of the latter than the former. A finding of *SumShd* $>$ *FM+m* is likely to identify a maladaptive extent of depressing, troubling, or otherwise unpleasant affect.

S responses occur when people do just the opposite of what they have been asked to do. The standard Rorschach instructions ask people to look at the inkblots and say what they might be. If people respond instead to the empty space on a card, they are in effect countermanding the instructions and defining the task in their own terms. Showing some autonomy and self-determination in this way may indicate adaptive capacity to be one's own person. However, an excessive frequency of white space responses, defined as $S > 3$, is likely to reflect generalized oppositional tendencies that go beyond adaptive autonomy and are associated with underlying feelings of anger or resentment. Individuals with an elevation in S typically harbor more than ordinary amounts of anger and resentment, either toward people in their lives whom they regard as having failed to meet their needs, or toward situations they view as having prevented them from achieving their goals.

Modulating Affect in Moderation (EBPer, FC:CF + C, CP)

Modulating affect in moderation consists of maintaining an adaptive balance between emotional and ideational channels of expression, between reserved and expansive patterns of emotional discharge, and between natural and forced efforts to process affective experience in a positive manner. Balance in these respects is reflected on the RIM by sufficient but not preoccupying attention to the chromatic features of the blots (*EBPer*), an age-appropriate Form-Color Ratio (*FC:CF:C*), and avoidance of Color Projection (*CP*) responses.

EBPer (Experience Balance Pervasive) has previously been identified in terms of an excessively ideational coping style, described as being pervasively introversive and identified by an M more than 2.5 times larger than *WSumC*. *EBPer* can also involve an excessively emotional coping style, indicated by a *WSumC* more than 2.5 time larger than M and described as being pervasively extratensive. Moderately extratensive people are ordinarily capable of recognizing and responding to their feelings and the feelings of others without losing sight of the constructive purposes of thoughtful reflection. Being pervasively extratensive, on the other hand, points to a maladaptive preference for dealing with experience primarily through affective channels and giving short shrift to the ideational side of one's life. Pervasively extratensive people tend to be highly expressive and action-oriented individuals who typically make decisions intuitively, without thoughtful planning and analysis, and attempt to solve problems by trial and error, without reflection and conceptualization.

FC responses are associated with relatively well-modulated and reserved processing of emotion. *FC*-type feelings tend to emerge and dissipate slowly and are deeply felt but mild to moderate in their intensity. *CF* and *C* responses, by contrast, are associated with relatively unmodulated and spontaneous processing of emotion in which feelings come and go quickly and tend to be superficial but often quite intense while they last. Among adults, an age-appropriate balance in $FC:CF + C$, which is known as the Form-Color Ratio, ranges from a slight preponderance of $CF + C$ responses to a substantial preponderance of FC responses. Outside these approximate limits, adults with $(CF + C) > (FC + 1)$ or $FC > (CF + C + 3)$ are likely to be having difficulty modulating their affect at an adaptive level of moderation. Adults showing an age-inappropriate emphasis on $CF + C$ tend to be emotionally immature individuals who experience and express affect dramatically and with intensity, but whose affects are also shallow and superficial. Adults with $FC > (CF + C + 3)$ tend to be emotionally reserved individuals whose affects run deep and long but who typically experience and express feelings in a relatively cool and calm manner.

The interpretive significance of color responses is the same for children as for adults. However, because young people are normatively more intense and less reserved than adults in how they modulate affect, the Form-Color Ratio criteria for inferring adjustment difficulties are different as well. The criterion for excessive emotional exuberance or intensity is $CF + C > FC + 2$ in young people aged 11 to 16 and $CF + C > FC + 3$ for children aged 10 and under. Maladaptive emotional reserve is suggested for persons aged 14 or less by $FC > (CF + C) + 1$ and for 15- and 16-year-olds by $FC > (CF + C) + 2$. For further information concerning the typical color responses of young people, readers are referred to the detailed reference data for 5- to 16-year-olds provided by Exner (2003, chap. 12).

CP responses constitute a forced effort to transform a potentially dysphoric feature of a blot (black or gray) into a bright and appealing feature (chromatic color). As such, any instance of $CP > 0$ identifies tendencies to deny unpleasant affect by attributing attractive qualities to situations and events that are in fact quite otherwise. People with one or more CP in their record are usually individuals who strain to keep themselves in good spirits by using denial to ward off potentially depressing feelings or concerns.

Managing Stress

People regularly find it necessary in their daily lives to make decisions and solve problems. Having to make decisions and solve problems imposes demands that a person must meet in some way to feel comfortable and function effectively. The more adequately people can handle the demands they experience, the more likely they are to manage stress successfully and reap the benefits of good psychological adjustment. The likelihood of success or failure in stress management is measured by Rorschach indices of whether people can muster adequate resources for meeting the demands they are facing, can minimize their level of subjectively felt distress, and can maintain consistency and flexibility in their coping style.

Mustering Adequate Resources (EA, CDI)

Capacities for using ideation effectively and modulating affect sufficiently and pleasurably, as previously discussed, capture the essential components of being a psychologically competent and resourceful person. In addition to what can be learned from ideational and affective variables considered separately, the Experience Actual (EA) variable provides a combined ideational/affective index of adaptive capacities that serves as a useful barometer of psychological competence. As a companion variable, the Coping Deficit Index (CDI) measures several aspects of the amount and kind of adaptive resources on which people can draw in meeting their experienced demands.

EA is calculated by adding the left (M) and right (WSumC) sides of the EB. As such, EA represents an individual's preferred and self-selected ways of dealing with experience, whether in an ideational and contemplative manner (M) or in an emotional, expressive manner (WSumC). It is characteristic of M-type and WSumC-type behaviors that people have considerable control over them and can initiate and discontinue them as they choose. The nature of these behaviors makes the sum of $M + WSumC$ a useful index of how much resource people have available for planning and implementing deliberate strategies of coping with decision-making and problem-solving situations.

Should people give a guarded record (i.e., one with $R < 17$ and $Lambda > .99$), a low EA may not be a dependable finding. A guarded record represents a decision to withhold rather than an ability to produce, and the data it contains may not reveal the full measure of an individual's personality strengths or limitations. Otherwise, with $R > 16$, EA should reach at least 6 to indicate adaptive capacity within the average range. Individuals with

EA < 6 usually have limited coping resources, as a consequence of which they are more likely than most people to meet life's demands in an inept and ineffective manner that limits their accomplishments, gives them little gratification, and earns them limited success. This criterion applies to adults and to most adolescents as well. Early adolescents and younger children normatively show somewhat less *EA* than older people, and the criterion score for insufficient adaptive capacities must accordingly be scaled down for this age group.

CDI is a multifactor variable that is coded positive when four or more of the following five conditions are met:

1. *EA* < 6 or *AdjD* < 0
2. *COP* < 2 and *AG* < 2
3. *WSumC* < 2.5 or *Afr* < .46
4. $p > a + 1$ or *H* < 2
5. *T* < 1 or *ISOL* > .24 or Food > 0.

A *CDI* < 4 does not indicate any special personality assets or preclude adjustment difficulties, but unguarded people at all ages with an elevated *CDI* of 4 or 5 are likely to show inept and ineffective ways of attempting to cope with ordinary aspects of everyday living. Like the indications of disordered thinking mentioned earlier, this *CDI* guideline may not apply in the interpretation of guarded, high *Lambda* records. The point for examiners to keep in mind is that individuals who give short and relatively unrevealing records may not be showing the full extent of their functioning limitations (e.g., as in having a misleadingly low *WSum6*) or of their adaptive capacities (e.g., by having a misleadingly high *CDI*).

Minimizing Subjectively Felt Distress (D, AdjD)

Having sufficient adaptive resources to manage the stresses in their lives allows individuals to minimize their experiences of subjectively felt distress and maintain a sense of comfort, composure, and satisfaction. Being able to meet the demands in one's life without becoming unduly upset by them fosters peace of mind, a psychological equilibrium that is stable over time, and the ability to tolerate frustrations and maintain self-control. The adequacy of coping capacities in relation to the level of demand people are experiencing is measured on the RIM by two closely related indices, the *D*-Score (*D*) and the Adjusted *D*-Score (*AdjD*).

The *D*-Score is calculated by subtracting from *EA* the sum of the left (*FM* + *m*) and right (*SumShd*) sides of the *eb* to produce the *es* (experienced stimulation). *EA-es* ranges normatively from +2.5 to –2.5, and results within this range are given a *D*-Score of 0. For every 2.5 points beyond this normative range, one point is assigned. Hence, an *EA-es* of +3.0 would yield a *D*-Score of +1, an *EA-es* of –5.5 would yield a *D*-Score of –2, and so on. Persons with *D* = 0 are usually relatively free from overt anxiety, tension, nervousness, and irritability. They tend to be self-satisfied individuals who feel no particular need to change the way they are or the circumstances they are in, and they tend to be fairly stable individuals who, other things being equal, present a psychological picture today that closely resembles how they appeared yesterday and will appear tomorrow. They have at least average capacities to tolerate frustration and to persevere in the face of obstacles, and they ordinarily are as capable as most people of controlling their behavior and avoiding impulsive episodes of intense emotionality or ill-advised actions.

People with $D > 0$ have an abundance of coping capacities and considerable resources in reserve on which to call when they need it. *D-plus* people usually display impressive stress tolerance and admirable talent for remaining calm, cool, and collected in dangerous or troubling circumstances. On the other hand, otherwise capable *D-plus* people commonly lack sufficient sensitivity to deal with people and situations effectively. Able to remain calm and unflustered because they do not let events bother them, they sometimes ignore or minimize the implications of events that should capture their attention and cause them concern.

A summary score of $D < 0$ indicates the extent to which people are likely to be feeling anxious, tense, nervous, and irritable. It typically represents a stress overload and is associated with limited tolerance for frustration, concerns about losing self-control, and a resulting proclivity for impulsiveness. The specific implications of *D-minus* vary with its magnitude. The larger it becomes, the more likely a person is to be incapacitated by stress, susceptible to losing self-control, and notably agitated and distraught.

The *AdjD*-Score is calculated by reducing the *es* by the number of *m* responses greater than one and by the number of *Y* responses greater than one, which are the normative expectations for these variables, before subtracting it from the *EA* (*adjusted es = es −* $(m - 1) - (Y - 1)$). This adjustment removes elevations in situational stress (as measured by the more than one *m* and *Y* responses) from the *D*-Score formula, leaving mainly those stress indicators associated with persistent or chronic demands that a person is facing. *AdjD* accordingly indicates the extent of subjective distress a person is experiencing beyond what appears attributable to situational stress. These calculations additionally make it possible to identify $D < AdjD$ as a Rorschach index of situational distress. People showing $D < 0$ but $AdjD = 0$ are likely to be basically stable and psychologically comfortable individuals who are presently experiencing the ill effects of more situational stress than they can manage adequately, but who will return to a customary state of psychological equilibrium as soon as the situational demands on them abate. Like $D = 0$, then, $AdjD = 0$, especially when *EA* is at least average, generally points to having sufficient psychological resources to cope adequately with the ongoing demands in one's life.

Maintaining Consistency and Flexibility (*EB* style)

People manage stress most adaptively when they can call on consistent and flexible patterns of dealing with decision-making and problem-solving situations in their lives. Consistency and flexibility in preferred patterns of coping are indicated on the RIM by the nature of the *EB* style. Having an introversive or extratensive style, as previously defined, identifies a consistent pattern of preference for either ideational or expressive ways of dealing with experience. By contrast, persons whose difference between *M* and *WSumC* is less than 2.0 (or less than 2.5 when $EA > 10$) do not meet the criterion for being introversive or extratensive and are instead showing an *ambient EB* style. The lives of individuals with an ambient *EB* style tend to be marked by inconsistent coping efforts, unpredictable behavior, and an uncertain self-image. These persons are likely to have difficulty making decisions, because they vacillate between following the dictates of their minds and the murmurings of their hearts. They tend to solve problems neither by concerted efforts to conceptualize them nor by sustained trial-and-error experimentation, but instead by alternating between these methods in an inefficient manner.

The previously discussed pervasively introversive and pervasively extratensive *EB* styles are both indicators of inflexibility in responding to one's experiences. On the other hand, persons with a clearly defined but not pervasively introversive or extratensive *EB* style are typically capable of modifying their behavior as circumstances change. At times, they make decisions by contemplating alternative possibilities in a deliberate manner, whereas at other times they allow their actions to be guided by how they feel rather than what they think. Sometimes they solve problems conceptually, by mulling over possible solutions in their minds, whereas at other times they seek solutions by trying out various courses of action. In either instance, introversive and extratensive individuals employ a preference for either a primarily ideational or primarily expressive coping style and fairly consistently approach similar situations in similar ways.

Viewing Oneself

Psychological adjustment is enhanced by capacities to view oneself in favorable ways that maintain adequate self-esteem and promote positive self-regard. Limited or impaired capacities to view themselves favorably and thoroughly make people susceptible to negative self-attitudes and an insufficient grasp of the kind of person they are. Several Rorschach variables provide information about these positive and negative aspects of viewing oneself.

Maintaining Adequate Self-Esteem [Fr + rF, 3r + (2)/R]

The purposes of good adjustment are best served when people can maintain an adequate level of self-esteem that steers a broad middle ground between self-denigration and self-glorification. Individuals with adequate self-esteem do not underrate their attractiveness to other people or their ability to succeed in various undertakings, nor do they overrate how appealing and talented they are. They consequently can usually avoid being either displeased with themselves and their efforts or enchanted with themselves and what they have done. People with adequate self-esteem can typically strike an adaptive balance between being preoccupied with themselves at the expense of adequate attention to the needs and interests of others and being totally absorbed in what other people want and enjoy, at the cost of sufficient regard for their own preferences and individuality. Balanced attention to self and others and seeing oneself as being a worthy person are measured on the RIM by Reflections ($Fr + rF$) and the Egocentricity Index [$3r + (2)/R$].

Reflection responses are associated with marked tendencies to overvalue one's personal worth and become preoccupied with one's own needs at the expense of attention to the needs of others. With few exceptions, people with $Fr + rF > 0$ in their records are self-centered individuals who have an inflated sense of their importance and an exalted estimate of their attributes. They may seek attention and admiration from others in ways that make them interpersonally appealing, or they may show a sense of entitlement, a tendency to externalize responsibility, and a degree of selfishness and self-admiration that other people find disagreeable.

The Egocentricity Index [$3r + (2)/R$] is calculated by multiplying the number of Reflections by 3, adding the number of Pairs, and dividing this sum by R. This index provides a measure of the balance people strike between focusing on themselves and paying attention to others. In adults, an Egocentricity Index ranging from .33 to .44 indicates an adaptive inclination to attend to oneself sufficiently but not excessively. People with a moderate

Egocentricity Index do not avoid focusing on themselves, nor do they become so self-absorbed as to ignore what is going on in the lives of other people.

Adults in whom $3r + (2)/R < .33$ are usually not paying sufficient attention to themselves and may even be purposefully avoiding self-focusing. Low Egocentricity individuals tend to compare themselves unfavorably with other people and to have difficulty maintaining adequate self-esteem. An elevated Egocentricity Index of $3r + (2)/R > .44$, in combination with $Fr + rF > 0$, usually identifies an unusual degree of preoccupation with oneself and a high level of self-esteem. However, an elevated Egocentricity Index in the absence of Reflection responses may signify that individuals are not taking any special pleasure in their self-focusing. This may be the Rorschach equivalent of paying a lot of attention to oneself but not enjoying it very much. Like the Form-Color ratio, the Egocentricity Index is age related, and the moderate range for this variable must be determined by consulting the reference data for 5- to 16-year-olds (see Exner, 2003, chap. 12).

Promoting Positive Self-Regard (V, MOR)

Whereas self-esteem consists of the general value people place on themselves and is typically a stable characteristic that persists at a similar level time, self-regard can be conceived as comprising numerous specific attitudes people have toward themselves, some more favorable than others, that fluctuate in response to changing circumstances (e.g., a success or failure in some endeavor). For use in concert with Reflections and the Egocentricity Index as measures of self-esteem, the Rorschach Vista (V) and Morbid (MOR) variables monitor aspects of self-regard.

A finding of $V = 0$ has no particular significance as an index of high self-regard, but $V > 0$ is typically associated with self-critical attitudes that become increasingly negative as the number of V increases. The more V in a record, the more likely it is that persons' attitudes toward some aspects of themselves or their actions have progressed from displeasure and dissatisfaction to disgust and loathing. However, the implications of $V > 0$ must be weighed in light of the Reflections and Egocentricity Index in individuals' records and recent events in their lives. $V > 0$ combined with $Fr + rF = 0$ and either a low or high Egocentricity Index suggests chronic self-criticism and persistently poor self-regard as well as low self-esteem. Evidence of recent events that could have evoked self-recriminations, especially when $Fr + rF > 0$ and the Egocentricity Index is high, usually identifies $V > 0$ as a sign of situationally related self-critical attitudes.

MOR responses typically identify negative attitudes toward one's body and its functions. Like $V = 0$, a low frequency of MOR has no implications for personality assets other than freedom from the negative self-attitudes indicated when MOR are frequent. A finding of $MOR > 2$ is likely to indicate difficulty maintaining an adaptive level of self-esteem, particularly with regard to viewing one's body as unappealing, damaged, or dysfunctional.

Enhancing Self-Awareness (FD)

The FD variable provides a Rorschach index of interest in and capacity for being introspective. An FD of 1 or 2 identifies a moderate level of self-awareness and is usually associated with recognizing one's needs, appreciating how one's actions affect other people, and considering the alteration of one's self-view. $FD = 0$ suggests little interest in critical self-examination and minimal capacity to appreciate one's impact on other people. At the other end of this dimension, individuals with $FD > 2$ tend to be excessively self-aware, unusually self-conscious, and given to considerable soul-searching.

Forming a Stable Sense of Identity [H:Hd + (H) + (Hd)]

Forming a stable sense of identity is facilitated when people have had opportunities to form identifications with real persons in their lives after whom they have modeled themselves in some appropriate fashion. The capacity to identify with real persons and the likelihood of having done so are reflected in the RIM by the number of whole and real human figures seen (H) and the ratio of this number to the number of partial or fictitious human figures [$Hd + (H) + (Hd)$]. Adaptive identifications are indicated by the presence of at least two H responses and a total number of H that exceeds the number of $Hd + (H) + (Hd)$. Persons with a sufficient frequency of H to meet these criteria typically have adequate capacity to identify comfortably with people who are a real part of their lives and with whom they have had opportunities to form such identifications. This combination of capacity to form identifications and opportunity to do so provides a foundation for developing a clear and stable sense of one's personal identity. $H < [Hd + (H) + (Hd)]$ often indicates maladaptive tendencies to identify with partial objects or with people who do not participate in an individual's everyday real world.

Relating to Others

Adaptive interpersonal relationships are characterized by the abilities (a) to sustain a reasonable level of interest, involvement, and comfort in interacting with other people; (b) to anticipate intimacy and security in interpersonal interactions; (c) to balance collaboration and acquiescence with competitiveness and assertiveness in relating to other people; and (d) to perceive people and social situations in an accurate and empathic manner.

Sustaining Interpersonal Interest, Involvement, and Comfort
(SumH, [H:Hd + (H) + Hd]), ISOL

Interest in being around people and comfort in interacting with others are measured on the RIM by the Interpersonal Interest variable (*SumH*), the previously mentioned [$H:Hd + (H) + (Hd)$] ratio, and the Isolation Index (*ISOL*). *SumH,* which is the total number of all types of human content in a record, indicates a person's level of attentiveness to others. *SumH > 3* usually identifies at least average interpersonal interest, whereas a *SumH* falling below 4 begins to indicate limited interest in people. A surplus of [$Hd + (H) + (Hd)$] over H responses suggests not only the deficiencies in identification previously noted, but also some social discomfort. Individuals with this imbalance in their human contents tend to feel uneasy when dealing, not with partial or fictitious objects, but people who are real, live, and fully functional—who literally have all of their parts in place and in working order.

    ISOL is calculated by assigning 2 points for every Nature and Cloud content in a record and 1 point for every Botany, Geography, and Landscape content, and then dividing this sum by R. *ISOL* has no particular implications for personality strengths when it is low, but when elevated it is typically associated with limited interpersonal interest, minimal social interaction, and a dearth of persons with whom one can share companionship and confidences. *ISOL > .25* usually indicates social withdrawal and interpersonal isolation. Even while in the company of an apparently ample number of acquaintances or family members, high *ISOL* individuals usually do not have many people playing an important part in their lives.

Anticipating Interpersonal Intimacy and Security (*SumT, HVI*)

Close interpersonal relationships define the nature of intimacy, which can occur on either a physical or psychological basis. People who hold and touch each other in a fond, caressing manner are involved in an intimate relationship, as are those who feel spiritually at one and share their innermost secrets with each other. Looking forward to opportunities for intimacy defines the nature of security in interpersonal relationships, which leads people to reach out for interpersonal relationships, to prefer engaging others up close rather than at arm's length, and to regard intimacy as an opportunity to be cherished rather than as a danger to be avoided. Two Rorschach variables that often provide useful information concerning interpersonal intimacy and security are the number of Texture responses in a record (*SumT*) and the Hypervigilance Index (*HVI*).

The presence of *T* indicates capacity to anticipate and establish close, intimate, and mutually supportive relationships with other people. Generally speaking, people who give *T* responses are likely not only to enjoy but to need, want, and reach out for physical and/or emotional closeness to others. $T = 0$, by contrast, often identifies limited capacity to form close attachments to other people. Individuals who have no *T* in their record do not necessarily avoid interpersonal relationships, but the relationships they form tend to be distant and detached, rather than close and intimate, and their friendships tend to be with people who share their preference for relating at arm's length rather than up close. On the other end of this personality characteristic, $T > 1$ is likely to indicate more needs for closeness than are currently being met in a person's life, and multiple *T* responses may be a clue to a person feeling emotionally deprived, interpersonally unfulfilled, and lonely.

HVI is a multivariable index that is coded as positive when $T = 0$ is combined with four or more of the following seven findings:

1. $Zf > 12$
2. $Zd > +3.5$
3. $SumH > 6$
4. $[(H) + (Hd) + (A) + (Ad)] > 3$
5. $[H{:}Hd + (H) + (Hd)] > 4{:}1$
6. $Cg > 3$
7. $S > 3$

Individuals who are positive on *HVI* tend to be highly alert to potential sources of danger or threat in their environment, usually because they feel unable to trust the motives of others or to depend on the safety of their surroundings. *HVI* people are likely to view close relationships with alarm and to avoid them in favor of keeping their distance from others, guarding carefully the boundaries of their personal space, and taking pains to preserve their privacy. They tend to approach and assess people and situations cautiously, often suspiciously, before making any commitments to them.

Balancing Interpersonal Collaboration and Acquiescence with Competitiveness and Assertiveness (COP, AG, a:p)

The balance people strike between being cooperative and acquiescent in their relationships with others or being competitive and assertive is reflected in the RIM by the Cooperative Movement (*COP*), Aggressive Movement (*AG*), and previously mentioned *a:p* variables. *COP* responses identify an interest in collaborative engagement with others. Generally speaking, persons with one or two *COP* responses tend to view interactions among people in positive ways and to participate in them willingly. Persons with more than an average number of *COP* responses tend to be notably successful in their social lives, other things being equal, and *COP* > 2 is commonly associated with being regarded as likable and outgoing and being sought after as a friend or companion. The absence of *COP*, by contrast, suggests a deficiency in the capacity to anticipate and engage in collaborative activities with others. Unlike the positive interpersonal messages communicated by people who give *COP*, individuals with *COP* = 0 typically convey to others a disinterest in or even a distaste for doing things together in cooperative ways. In combination with an elevated *ISOL* and a low *SumH*, *COP* = 0 often points to interpersonal avoidance and withdrawal.

AG responses identify an expectation that interactions in the real world are likely to be assertive or at least competitive, rather than collaborative or acquiescent. The presence of more than two *AG* responses in a record is associated with a more than usual likelihood of behaving toward others in a verbally or physically assertive fashion. However, this implication of frequent *AG* responses may be offset by the presence as well of numerous *COP*, or by a preference for passivity, as discussed next. Of further note, the absence of *AG* responses does not have any known interpretive significance, and *AG* = 0 does not contraindicate aggressiveness or violence risk potential.

The *a:p* ratio is interpretively significant for interpersonal relatedness when the number of passive movements in a record exceeds the number of active movements by more than one. People who show $p > a + 1$ are likely to be behaviorally passive in their interactions with others. Such persons are typically more comfortable being followers than leaders. They are inclined to shrink from taking initiative or responsibility and to defer to the preferences and wishes of others.

Remaining Interpersonally Empathic (accurate M)

The form level of responses involving human movement (*M*) usually provides information about the accuracy of persons' social perception and their ability to form realistic impressions of people and interpersonal events. The presence of two or more accurately seen *M* responses (*M+*, *Mo*, or *Mu*) usually identifies adequate empathic capacity, whereas individuals with more than one perceptually distorted *M* responses (*M-* > 1) are likely to have some impairment of this capacity. The more frequent the *M-* responses in a record, the more severely a person is likely to show faulty perception of people and social interactions.

Additional Global Indices

In addition to the structural variables related to specific dimensions of personality functioning, the Rorschach CS includes three global indices that have important implications in the clinical assessment of psychopathology: the Perceptual Thinking Index (*PTI*), the Depression Index (*DEPI*), and the Suicide Constellation (*S-CON*).

The *PTI* is considered positive when at least four of the following five indicators of impaired reality testing or disordered thinking are present:

1. *XA%* < .70 and *WDA%* < .75
2. *X-%* > .29
3. Level 2 Special Scores > 2 and FAB2 > 0
4. *R* < 17 and *WSum6* > 12 or *R* > 16 and *WSum6* > 17
5. *M-* > 1 or *X-%* > .40.

An elevated *PTI* is likely to indicate a schizophrenia-spectrum disorder, although neither this nor any other specific condition should ever be inferred solely on the basis of Rorschach findings. Moreover, in light of various circumstances that can produce false negative findings on this index, the possibility of a schizophrenia-spectrum disorder should never be ruled out on the basis of a *PTI* < 4 (see Dao & Prevatt, 2006; Exner, 2003, pp. 524–525; Ritsher, 2004; Smith, Baity, Knowles, & Hilsenroth, 2001).

The *DEPI* is considered positive when five or more of the following seven conditions are met:

1. *V* > 2 or *FD* > 2
2. *Col-Shd Bld* > 0 or *S* > 2
3. *[3r + (2)/R]* > .44 and *Fr + rF* > 0, or *[3r + (2)/R]* < .33)
4. *Afr* < .46 or *Blends* < 4
5. *SumShd* > *FM + m* or *C'* >2
6. *MOR* > 2 or *2AB + Art + Ay* > 3
7. *COP* < 2 or *ISOL* > .24

A *DEPI* = 5 is likely to suggest that a person is experiencing some depressive symptoms, and *DEPI* > 5 is often associated with a diagnosable mood disorder or a chronic disposition to recurrent depressive episodes. Like the *PTI* and all other Rorschach variables, the *DEPI* is never by itself sufficient basis for drawing diagnostic conclusions with respect to mood disorder. Moreover, although false positive findings are infrequent on this index, false negative findings are not uncommon, and depression is never contraindicated by a *DEPI* < 5 (see Exner, 2003, pp. 310–314; Ilonen et al., 1999).

The *S-CON* is coded by determining how many of the following 12 findings are present:

1. *V + FD* > 2
2. *Col-Shd Bld* > 0
3. *(3r + 2)/R* < .31 or > .44
4. *MOR* > 3
5. *Zd* > + 3.5 or *Zd* < −3.5
6. *es* > *EA*

7. $CF + C > FC$
8. $X + \% < .70$
9. $S > 3$
10. $P < 3$ or > 7
11. $Pure\ H < 2$
12. $R < 17$

An *S-CON* of 8 or more has been found to occur commonly in the records of persons who committed suicide within 60 days after taking the Rorschach and should accordingly be considered indicative of suicidal risk. *S-CON* scores of 7 or more have been found to predict serious, near lethal suicide attempts during a 60-day posttest period. Scores below 7 on this index, like low scores on *PTI* and *DEPI,* have little or no interpretive significance, and they should never be used as a basis for ruling out suicidal or self-injurious potential (see Exner, 2003, pp. 523–524; Fowler, Piers, Hilsenroth, Holdwick, & Padawer, 2001; Ganellen, 2005).

INTERPRETATION: THEMATIC VARIABLES

As noted in discussing the nature of the RIM (see pp. 345–347), the way people structure their response process provides information primarily about structural features of their personality functioning, whereas the thematic imagery they produce is valuable mainly for providing clues to their personality dynamics or inner life. Interpretation of the content themes in a Rorschach protocol proceeds through four sequential steps: (1) identifying the responses in a record that are most likely to be rich in thematic imagery, (2) reading these thematically rich responses and generating associations to them, (3) drawing on these associations to form hypotheses concerning an individual's personality dynamics, and (4) determining the plausibility of these hypotheses on the basis of general considerations for judging the likely accuracy of thematic interpretations.

Identifying Responses Rich in Thematic Imagery

Rorschach responses differ in the extent to which their thematic imagery is likely to reveal aspects of a person's inner life, that is, the underlying needs, attitudes, conflicts, and concerns that influence how people are likely to think, feel, and act, sometimes with but more often outside their conscious awareness. Generally speaking, the responses that are most likely to be rich in thematic imagery are those in which characteristics are attributed to a percept beyond the stimulus characteristics of the inkblots. Such attributions typically appear in responses involving form distortion, movement, or various embellishments.

In the case of form distortion, the coding of a minus form quality indicates that the blot does not closely resemble what it has been said to look like. Hence the idea of the perceived object cannot have come from the actual shape of the blot, but must instead have come from inside the individual and have some special meaning for that person. Likewise, the blots are static and do not move, which means that any actions that are attributed to them, resulting in coding for movement, have come from the mind of the examinee and are likely to say something about that person's inner life. Embellishments include the kinds of content elaborations for which Special Scores (e.g., *MOR, FABCOM*) are coded, and they also include uncoded elaborations of the characteristics of objects (e.g., seeing people not just as "people," but as "witches," "soldiers," or "fat sloppy people," and seeing animals not just as "animals," but as "friendly dogs," or "dangerous creatures").

The first step in content interpretation, then is to identify those responses that, by virtue of distorted form, movement, or embellishments, involve elements that are based more on a person's attributions than on the stimulus characteristics of the blots and accordingly promise to be revealing with respect to that person's inner life.

Generating Associations and Formulating Interpretive Hypotheses

The next two steps in Rorschach content interpretation consist of reading those responses that are likely to be rich in thematic imagery and generating associations to what the imagery in these responses might signify, and then using these associations as a basis for formulating interpretive hypotheses. This process differs in two important respects from the interpretation of structural variables. First, the interpretive significance of a thematic image typically involves more alternative possibilities and is more speculative than the likely meaning of how responses are structured. For example, a low *XA%* quite probably indicates inaccurate perception of people and events as well as of the inkblots. By contrast, "a woman with her back turned" could indicate some underlying concerns about being rejected by women, or possibly some woman in particular (e.g., mother); or about confronting anatomical differences between the sexes, which are more apparent when viewed from the front than from the rear; or perhaps about something entirely different, the meaning of which is unique to the individual's psyche.

Because of this diversity in the possible meanings of thematic images, there are few hard-and-fast guidelines for generating interpretively meaningful associations to them. Skill in this task requires a solid grasp of personality dynamics, familiarity with various approaches used in the interpretation of thematic material, and good access to one's own association process. The more skilled examiners are in these respects, the better able they will be to generate sensible speculations about the implications of examinees' thematic imagery for their dynamic personality characteristics.

The second key difference between thematic and structural interpretation involves the particular relevance of thematic imagery to aspects of object relatedness—how people view themselves, how they regard other people, and how they conceive interpersonal relationships. As reviewed in discussing structural variables in the previous section, these variables provide information across a broad spectrum of personality dimensions. Thematic variables, on the other hand, are informative mainly with respect to the self-perception and interpersonal perception dimensions of an individual's personality functioning.

To illustrate thematic interpretation along these lines, consider the possible self-image and needs of a woman who reports, "Some little birds in a nest, waiting for their mother to come feed them." The imagery in this movement response seems fairly clearly to suggest that this woman sees herself as a small, relatively helpless person with strong and perhaps unmet dependent needs to be fed, nurtured, and cared for. The response might also suggest some disappointment or resentment with respect to being kept waiting. Suppose this woman elsewhere in her record sees "Two people here, one is sort of mean-looking and the other one is leaning on her." Now there would be a further suggestion of dependent needs, but also the implication that the person or people on whom one depends cannot be counted on to be nice, nurturant, and responsive.

As an apparently simpler but in fact more complex example, consider a man who gives as his first response to Card I a minus form (perceptually distorted) "Battleship." What might identifying himself as a "battleship" mean to this man? Does being a battleship signify to him being a big, powerful, indestructible object that wins wars and defeats the enemy? Or does he think of a battleship as an oversized, ponderous craft that is easily outflanked by smaller and swifter vessels, has outlasted its usefulness, and should be put in mothballs? Or could it be that battleship has both meanings to this man because he is experiencing strong needs to see and portray himself as strong and capable but has underlying concerns about becoming inept and outmoded and being put out to pasture?

Such multiple possibilities illustrate the importance of not rushing to judgment concerning the accuracy or value of any one interpretive meaning of a thematic image. Instead, all possibilities should be considered carefully to determine which if any seem credible, as discussed next. Additional discussion of generating associations to the thematic imagery in Rorschach responses can be found in books by Aronow, Reznikoff, and Moreland (1994, chaps. 9–12), Lerner (1998, chap. 11), Schafer (1954, chap. 4), and Weiner (2003b, chap. 6).

Determining the Plausibility of Thematic Interpretations

Examiners should never place faith in their impressions of what content themes signify without first subjecting these impressions to close scrutiny based on two types of criteria for judging the adequacy of such impressions. To specify these criteria, content interpretations are most likely to be dependable when they are (a) derived from particularly compelling thematic imagery and (b) limited to conservative inferences about the meaning of this imagery.

The particularly compelling themes in a record are the ones that are most repetitive, most dramatic, most original, and most spontaneous. With respect to repetition, the Rorschach literature has traditionally stressed the considerable likelihood that recurrent themes in people's records say more about their inner life than occasional themes (Klopfer et al., 1954, chap. 13; Phillips & Smith, 1953, chap. 6; Schafer, 1954, chap. 5). Drama as a marker of compelling content themes is inferred from the ways in which responses are elaborated and expressed, as illustrated by the difference between the following two structurally similar responses to Card III: "Two people picking up a basket" (a bland response); "Two big guys struggling with all their might to pick up some heavy object, and I think they are succeeding" (an embellished response). Such drama increases the likely significance of a content theme, even if it occurs only infrequently. The same can be said for originality, which is inferred from the extent to which a response elaboration differs from how a particular blot or blot detail is commonly seen or described.

With respect to spontaneity, the import of content themes is usually a function of how early in the response process they are elaborated. For example, consider a response to the upper side details of Card IX of "Two sorcerers casting spells at each other." Assuming this response has some implications for concerns about aggressive interpersonal interactions or perhaps an underlying wish to possess the magical powers of a sorcerer, these implications are more compelling if all of this imagery is reported during the Response Phase of the administration, as opposed to its emerging only during inquiry of an original response limited to "Two human figures." Similarly, thematic imagery emerging immediately after the examiner has begun the inquiry by reading back a person's original response should be regarded as more compelling than imagery that does not appear until late in the inquiry, after the examiner has invited further comment (e.g., as by saying, "I'm not sure how you're seeing it").

Conservative inferences from content themes are those that give most credence to meanings involving the most clarity, the least ambiguity, the readiest rationale, and the most limited scope. Inferences based on remote, uncertain, vague, and sweeping associations to the possible significance of content themes, on the other hand, run considerable risk of suggesting personality features that do not in fact characterize a particular individual. To illustrate these elements of thematic interpretation, some responses are more clearly and less ambiguously suggestive of a particular meaning than others. Thus a percept of *spear* is very likely to have some significance related to spears falling within the class of objects called *weapons*. Although spears could be conceived as being something other than weapons or as being used for nonweaponry purposes, these would be remote possibilities. The basic associative link between "spear" and "weapon," as objects that are dangerous and potentially harmful, is both fairly obvious and relatively unambiguous, in that there are few, if any, reasonable alternatives.

By contrast, consider the center detail of Card I seen as "A woman with her arms up." What does having her arms up signify? Is she waving hello, waving goodbye, gesturing in supplication ("Help me"), gesturing in despair ("I give up"), or doing something else entirely? In the absence of further elaboration from the examinee, there is no easy way to choose among these alternative possibilities, and the meaning of the response is neither clear nor unambiguous. Deciding that any one of the possible alternative meanings of seeing a woman with her arms up is a reliable clue to the person's underlying needs or attitudes would fall short of satisfying criteria for conservative content interpretation.

As for the rationale of content interpretations, inferred meanings should be taken seriously only when they are easy to justify with a few steps of logical reasoning. Inferring that an individual who sees numerous spears may have some concerns about being a victim or perpetrator of violence can readily be explained, once spear is identified as a potentially dangerous weapon. The less tortuous the logic necessary to translate a content theme into an association, the more likely it is that the association will lead to a valid and useful personality description.

Conservatism in the scope of content interpretations calls for limiting them mainly to inferences concerning a person's underlying needs, attitudes, conflicts, and concerns at the present time. A firm grasp of personality dynamics combined with informed Rorschach interpretation allows knowledgeable clinicians to formulate many reasonable hypotheses concerning how past events may have shaped individuals' lives, how they responded to those events when they occurred, and how they are likely to conduct themselves in various kinds of future situations. In terms of judging the adequacy of content interpretations, those that focus most narrowly on current personality dynamics merit most credence. The more sweeping content interpretations are, and the farther they look into the past or the future, the more speculative and unreliable they become. To put this important interpretive guideline into other terms, Rorschach inferences are typically more dependable when they address what people are like than when they postdict what they are likely to have done or experienced, or when they predict how they are likely to feel or act (see Weiner, 2003a).

INTERPRETATION: BEHAVIORAL VARIABLES

As also indicated in introducing this chapter, a Rorschach administration is likely to elicit certain kinds of behavior that contribute hypotheses to the interpretive process. Types of behavior that can be particularly revealing with respect to an individual's personality characteristics include (a) whether and how they turn the cards, (b) any comments or personalized remarks they make during the response process, and (c) the expressive style they use in giving their responses. The interpretive value of these behavioral clues derives from the relatively unstructured nature of the Rorschach situation. Because of the limited information examinees are given concerning what is expected of them, the behavior they show while performing the Rorschach task is largely determined by the kind of person they are, and not by the test. It is for this reason that observable and easily identifiable variations in examinee behavior, especially if repetitive and sustained during the examination, contribute useful information to the interpretive process.

Card Turning

Whether and how people turn the cards is an ever-present feature of Rorschach examinations and can provide a representative sample of how they are generally inclined to conduct themselves, as well as how they may be feeling at the moment. With respect to personality traits, individuals who are rigid and authoritarian by nature may hold the cards in the position in which they are handed to them and not even consider turning them. Among persons who are sufficiently flexible to consider turning the cards, those who are relatively autonomous and self-assured may just go ahead and do so, whereas those who are relatively submissive or concerned about staying within the rules may first ask for permission ("Can I turn the card?").

Following a standard response to such requests for permission ("If you like"; "It's up to you"), people who are dependent by nature, lacking in self-confidence, or fearful of doing the wrong thing may ask for further clarification of the rules ("Is it all right to look at it from any direction?"). Such persons may also continue on subsequent cards to ask for permission ("Can I turn this one?"). As further examples of the influence of personality traits on card-turning behavior, compulsive individuals may be inclined to examine the cards carefully in each of the four possible positions, whereas those who generally attend to their experience superficially may limit their card turning to an occasional casual glance at one or two of the blots in an alternate position.

As for people's attitudinal and emotional states at the time they are being examined, those who take being tested seriously and feel positively toward the examiner and the evaluation process tend to become sufficiently involved in the response process to consider looking at the cards in various positions. Conversely, individuals who are disinterested in being tested or skeptical about the purpose of the examination may not bother to turn the cards, as a manifestation of their limited involvement in seeing things in them. As another possibility, disinterested or skeptical persons who are also overtly hostile and defiant may show an oppositional pattern of test behavior in which they turn each card upside down immediately on being handed it, as if to say, "You want me to look at it this way, but I'm going to look at it in just the opposite way."

Numerous other personality states and traits are likely to influence card-turning behavior. None of these characteristics necessarily or inevitably leads to particular patterns of card turning, nor does the way in which individuals turn the cards or ask about doing so always identify some specific personality state or trait. Nevertheless, because people's personal general dispositions and current attitudes and affects are likely to influence whether and how they turn the cards, card-turning behavior provides clues to these personality characteristics. As in interpreting thematic imagery, examiners need to ponder alternative possibilities in considering the possible significance of particular patterns of card turning and formulate hypotheses concerning personality characteristics that might contribute to and are therefore revealed by these behavior patterns.

Comments and Personals

The interpretive significance of Rorschach responses is often enriched by comments and personalized remarks that accompany them. Comments consist of remarks that are not an integral part of reporting what certain parts of the inkblots might be and why. Sometimes comments are *response-referential,* in that they consist of evaluative statements about responses the person has given. Such evaluative comments often include some indication that a response pleases or displeases them ("I like that response:" "I don't think that's a very good response"). Responses that elicit expressions of pleasure may contain elements bearing on aspects of their lives in which people correspondingly take pleasure, whereas expressly displeasing responses may furnish clues to the nature or extent of distressing concerns in their lives.

At other times, evaluative comments are *self-referential* and have general implications for people's attitudes toward themselves, especially if such comments are repetitive. Frequent positive comments about their responses suggest that people are generally inclined to be pleased with themselves and their products, even to the point of informing others of what a good job they think they have done (e.g., "I did pretty well on that card, didn't I?"). Conversely, individuals who repeatedly criticize their performance (e.g., "I don't think I'm very good at this") may be revealing a generally negative view of their efforts to function effectively.

Personalized remarks attribute the basis of a response entirely or in part to some experience in an individual's life and, as previously noted, are coded as Personal (*PER*) in the CS (see Table 11.7). Some Personals simply state a resemblance to something an individual has seen elsewhere and serve mainly to justify why the percept was seen in the blot ("I recognize them as cartoon figures because they're like the ones I see on television"). Persons who frequently resort to such self-justification are likely to be insecure people who lack self-confidence and frequently feel compelled to inform others of the basis of their actions and conclusions.

Other Personals go beyond merely mentioning prior knowledge or experience to justify a percept and elaborate in addition how much an individual knows or has done ("A native symbol, like I remember seeing in my travels to the South Seas"; "A jet airplane, which I know all about from my flying days"). People who give many such self-aggrandizing

Personals tend to be insecure, as are those who give numerous self-justifying Personals, but they are inclined to defend against their insecurity quite differently. Instead of apologetically attempting to prove themselves adequate and respectable, they attempt to prove themselves superior and admirable by immodestly touting their talents and accomplishments.

In a third type of Personal, people talk about themselves not to show off, but merely to share information about themselves ("It looks just like my dog at home; I've had different kinds of pets, but I like dogs best"). Self-revealing Personals of this kind often indicate an effort by an examinee to reach out to the examiner, as if to say, "I want you to know more about me as a person." These Personals are accordingly less likely than self-justifying and self-aggrandizing Personals to suggest insecurity and defensiveness, and more likely to identify a genuine interest in sharing experiences with other people.

Expressive Style

The manner in which people express themselves in delivering Rorschach responses provides an additional rich source of interpretive hypotheses concerning their personality character-istics. Particularly useful in this regard are three aspects of an examinee's language usage that are specific to the Rorschach task: wordiness, qualifiers, and sign-offs.

Wordiness in Rorschach responses refers simply to how many words people use in framing their responses. The same basic percept can be expressed in "bare bones" fashion ("A black bat flying around") or at considerable length ("It looks to me like some sort of bat, like it's flying, because here's the body in the middle, and these outer parts look like wings stretched out, big wings, and they're all black, and bats are black, of course, and the head is up here and the tail is down here, and is there anything else you would like me to tell you about it?" These two responses would be coded identically—*Wo ma.FC'o A P 1.0*)—but their verbiage suggests different attitudes, emotional states, and personality characteristics in the persons who gave them.

With respect to a person's attitudes, numerous unusually short responses may indicate a lack of engagement in the Rorschach task or an effort to avoid revealing information, whereas unusually long responses usually identify considerable involvement in the task and a cooperative spirit with respect to providing information. Emotionally, people who can give only a few words when more would be appropriate may be feeling depressed or lethargic, whereas those who give many words when fewer would suffice may be feeling euphoric or energized. As for personality characteristics, being long-winded during an examination may reflect a general disposition to being expansive and forthcoming in communicating with others, whereas being terse or cryptic in giving Rorschach responses may identify a generally circumspect person of few words.

Qualifiers consist of ways of introducing responses that indicate the extent of a person's commitment to them. People most commonly begin their Rorschach responses with rela-tively noncommittal phrases like "It looks like . . . ," "It might be . . . ," "It resembles . . . ," or "It reminds me of . . ." Sometimes, however, people qualify their responses well beyond being normally noncommittal, as by prefacing their percepts with statements like "Well, I suppose it might possibly could be . . ." or "If I really have to say something, and if I stretch my imagination, recognizing that it's really not anything, I could say . . ." Repeated use of such noncommittal qualifiers in introducing responses usually indicates an effort to minimize in advance the implications of any conclusions drawn from the test results. In addition, pervasive tentativeness in delivering responses may reflect a general personality style characterized by limited self-assurance, reluctance to take a definite stand on anything, and aversion to commitment. By contrast, some people may show an unusual degree of certainty in expressing their responses, with phrases like "That's definitely . . . ," "No doubt about this one, it's . . . ," or "I'm sure this is . . ." Such certainty may at times point to an assertive nature on the part of individuals, or perhaps to pressing needs to minimize ambiguity in their lives and avoid distress by emphasizing what is safe and certain.

Sign-offs are phrases that people often use in concluding their final responses to a card. Most people after giving their last response to a card hand it back to the examiner, put it down, or say something like "That's all I see" or "I can't think of anything else on this one." Such common sign-off behaviors rarely have any interpretive significance. Occasionally, however, people conclude a card with unusual statements that may have special meaning for them. Consider the possible implications of the following sign-offs, each delivered emphatically: "There's nothing more on this card!" or "That's all I'm going to tell you about this one!" or "I have no idea what else it could be!" Concluding statements of this kind suggest that there may in fact be something further on this card that the individual sees and could report, if willing to do so. Such statements also convey a tone of assertiveness, certainty, and self-assurance that provides clues to similar characteristics in an individual's personality style.

For contrast, consider the possible implications of a person frequently signing off with statements like, "I'm afraid that's all I see," "I'm sorry I can't tell you more about it," or "I wish I could do a better job for you." Although perhaps also serving as excuses for not being fully responsive, these comments differ sharply from the previous examples with respect to their implications for personality characteristics, by suggesting in this instance an apologetic, self-denigrating, self-effacing way of presenting oneself to others.

INTERPRETATION: CARD PULL

Appreciation for what the Rorschach blots are likely to signify to most people, which is known as "card pull," facilitates the interpretive process in two ways. First, knowing what each card is likely to pull with respect to structural, thematic, and behavioral aspects of responses helps to identify deviations from common expectations. The more closely responses resemble what the cards ordinarily pull, the more they reveal about ways in which individuals resemble other people. Conversely, the more responses deviate from ordinary expectations concerning the kinds of percepts, associations, and test behavior pulled by each card, the more clearly they point to idiographic and personally meaningful features of persons' psychological nature. Exner and Erdberg (2005, chap. 23) provide detailed information concerning the expected frequency among nonpatient adults for the various location choices, determinants, and other codes on each of the 10 cards.

Second, familiarity with what the blots are likely to signify helps to clarify which aspects of their psychological lives people are managing comfortably and which are causing them distress. When people deal effectively with a particular card, they are likely to be managing the issues and challenges associated with that card in an adaptive fashion. On the other hand, people who respond ineffectively on a card may be having difficulty coping comfortably and constructively with issues and challenges signified by those cards.

Several criteria can help to judge whether people are displaying adaptive strengths or coping limitations in how they deal with the individual cards. Dealing effectively with a card usually consists of proceeding calmly and with little hesitation to articulate clearly defined, perceptually accurate, and logically organized responses that are free from distressing content. Difficulty dealing with cards is indicated when people show an unusually long reaction time, express themselves in an uncharacteristically halting manner, or make negative comments about them (e.g., "I don't like this one"; "This one is hard to see anything in"). Other indicators are vague, minus form, dissociated, or arbitrarily reasoned responses, or direct statements that the cards or their responses to them are disturbing or upsetting ("I don't want to look at this one any more").

Each of the 10 Rorschach inkblots can be described in terms of the perceived objects, associated themes, and evaluative comments it tends to elicit and the ease or difficulty of formulating responses to it. The following comments on the 10 cards are based on empirical findings concerning Comprehensive System variables and theoretically based speculations advanced by Aronow and Reznikoff (1976, pp. 248–263), Aronow et al. (1994, pp. 34–38), and Klopfer et al. (1954, pp. 320–327).

Card I

As the first card shown, Card I commonly elicits questions from people about how they should proceed. People who are inclined to seek structure and ascertain the rules before they commit themselves in a new situation are especially likely to ask such questions. Because of their frequency, questions like how many responses to give, whether the whole blot must be used, and if the card can be turned usually have little significance on Card I, unless the person emphasizes them in some way. As the administration proceeds, requests for structure take on increasing implications for idiographic characteristics or concerns. People who are asking on Card VI whether they are allowed to turn the card may be revealing something noteworthy about themselves, such as sexual concerns prompted by the clear resemblance of the upper-center detail on this card to a penis. Similarly, asking on Card X about how many responses they should give may indicate difficulty dealing with many different matters at the same time, as represented in this blot by its large number of separate details.

Card I nevertheless occupies a special place in the order of the 10 cards. Coming first, it presents people with a new and usually unfamiliar task. The comfort, style, and effectiveness with which people approach Card I may accordingly provide clues to how they generally respond to new and stressful situations in their lives. Card I also gives people their first Rorschach opportunity to communicate something about who they are and what is important to them. Hence the initial response, especially when it contains idiographic elements that go beyond the *W F A* popular bat or butterfly, often serves as a revealing "sign in" response. Consider the likelihood that an individual who begins on Card I with "A black bat with drooping wings, looking sad" is depressed, discouraged, or feeling weak and helpless.

Although causing some people to experience initial uncertainty or uneasiness, Card I does not ordinarily pose a difficult task. The ready availability of the "bat" and "butterfly" *Populars,* in combination with the many other winged or flying creatures often seen to the whole card and the easily identifiable human figure in the center detail, provide numerous opportunities for people to select bland and untroubling responses. On the other hand, there is some evidence that the shape and darkness of Card I convey to some people a negative emotional tone and an impression of something ugly and unattractive. Accordingly, depressed individuals who are struggling with feelings of dysphoria, guilt, and pessimism may find Card I and the four other gray-black cards more upsetting than the chromatic cards and more difficult to manage effectively.

Card II

The most distinctive feature of Card II is its areas of bright red color. The upper-red and lower-center details are easily and readily seen as blood, which for many people elicits associations to anger and to being physically damaged or harmed. For this reason, dealing with Card II may prove difficult for persons who are struggling to keep control over feelings of hostility and resentment or who are concerned about being vulnerable to bodily damage or dysfunction. How people respond to the red areas of this card, or decline to respond to them ("I'm not using the red parts"; "The red doesn't suggest anything"), can therefore provide clues to how they are likely to manage such feelings and concerns.

Also noteworthy on Card II is the number of accurately perceived Sex responses that can be given to it. Seven different Sex responses, more than on any other card, are coded as ordinary or unusual form quality on Card II, meaning that they can be easily seen. These easily seen Sex responses include both male and female sexual anatomy, as illustrated by the appearance of a penis in the upper-center black detail and a vagina in the lower-center red detail or in the inner pale red detail in the lower-center red. How people respond to Card II and what if anything they say about these three areas may accordingly be influenced by what these areas connote sexually and whatever concerns they may have about sexual matters.

Card III

Card III derives its card pull primarily from the very common percept on this blot of two people involved in some kind of interaction. Possible implications of the particular kind of interaction that is attributed to human figures are codified in part by the scores for Aggressive Movement (*AG*) and Cooperative Movement (*COP*). Moreover, the interpersonal significance of Card III provides reason to believe that how people respond to this card reveals their attitudes and concerns about relating to other people, even if they do not attribute movement to the popular figures or fail to report them at all. In particular, the more difficulty people have in responding to Card III, the more likely they are to be struggling with negative and aversive attitudes toward social interactions.

Although Card III is less likely than Card II to elicit Sex responses, its popular human figures include one unusual detail area that is coded ordinary form quality for "breast" and another unusual detail that is ordinary form for "penis." For people who are uncertain about their gender-role identity, this feature of the blot may make it difficult for them to decide whether the human figures are male or female. As an alternative possibility, gender-role uncertainty may lead to their describing the figures as having both masculine and feminine sexual characteristics, or to their being reluctant to say anything at all about the black details on this card.

Card IV

Although Card IV is not and should not be referred to as the "father card," it has been demonstrated to evoke associations to big, strong, massive, heavy, powerful, authoritarian, and sometimes threatening figures. Such impressions of Card IV are compounded by the frequently mentioned experience of "looking up" at the figure seen, which places the observing examinee in a weak and inferior position. In this same vein, the figures seen on this card are commonly giants, monsters, gorillas, or very large people, and they are almost always men rather than women. Hence there is good reason to regard Card IV as conveying a sense of authority or an authority figure, usually male but possible female, to whom one is responsible and subordinate.

Moreover, although Card IV is not *the* father card, because many persons other than one's father can function as an authority figure and because attitudes toward father figures can be expressed on many other cards as well, Card IV can certainly serve on occasion as *a* father card. Additionally, because the qualities conveyed by Card IV are also frequently associated with masculinity rather than femininity, Card IV responses may reveal something about attitudes toward men in general and perhaps toward important particular men in a person's life (e.g., father, husband, lover, boss, or supervisor).

Card IV is also notable for its dark color and heavy shading, both of which make an impression on most examinees. Like Card I, this card may consequently pose difficulties for people who are depressed or are trying to avoid dealing with gloomy affect. Because it is even darker than Card I and does not have as obvious a Popular to ease the person's task, Card IV may prove particularly difficult in this respect. Some people may in fact respond comfortably to each of the first three cards and show their first indications of distress on Card IV, perhaps because of its implications for dominant authority but perhaps also because of the depressive tone of its achromatic color.

As for the shading in Card IV, research findings concerning T indicate as mentioned that articulation of the tactile quality of shading is associated with capacities for forming physically and psychologically intimate attachments to other people—literally being close enough to touch each other. For this reason, the percepts and associations people report in response to heavily shaded blot areas often provide information concerning their openness to, attitudes toward, and need for close relationships. In particular, difficulty dealing comfortably with heavily shaded blot areas suggests aversion, uncertainty, and distress in the context of contemplating such relationships. Card IV is less potent in signifying shading-related concerns than Card VI, which is even more heavily shaded and elicits the popular "animal skin" response that often involves shading. Nevertheless, the impact of this card on examinees is likely to derive at least in part from its shading features.

Card V

Aside from being dark in color and therefore potentially depressing, Card V contains relatively few features that arouse concerns; complicate the response process; or suggest a variety of percepts, associations, or affects. To the contrary, the solid and unbroken appearance of this blot and its commonly seen resemblance to the popular bat or butterfly, as well as other winged creatures, make it the easiest blot in the series for which to formulate a good-quality response. Because Card V lacks any impact comparable to the newness of

Card I, the red of Card II, the interpersonal interaction of Card III, and the dominant authority figure of Card IV, it often provides welcome relief from any distress prompted by Cards I–IV.

People commonly verify that Card V is a "breather" by giving more adequate and less revealing responses than they have on the previous cards, and some individuals may comment to this effect. People who have shown uncertainty and distress while responding to the first four cards may greet Card V with comments like "Now this one I *know* is a bat," or "I don't have any trouble seeing this one as a butterfly." When people do struggle with Card V, their difficulty is usually less likely to result from what this blot signifies to them than from some carryover of concerns aroused by their encounter with Card IV.

Card VI

With respect to the meaning it is likely to convey, the dominant characteristic of Card VI is the textural quality suggested by its black and gray shadings. Even more than Card IV, as has been noted, Card VI tends to arouse percepts and associations related to interpersonal closeness. The manner in which people elaborate responses in which they articulate *T,* together with what they say about the whole blot or the lower detail of Card VI even without articulating *T,* often reveal some of their attitudes toward intimate relationships. Indications of difficulty dealing effectively with this card often identify concerns about reaching out to touch other people or being touched by them, whether physically or psychologically.

Card VI also has considerable sexual significance for many people. Like Card II, Card VI provides clear resemblances to both male and female sexual anatomy, with "penis" to the upper-center detail and "vagina" to the lower-center detail being accurately perceived responses. Although Cards II and III both have more numerous easily seen sexual contents, Card VI appears to elicit reported sexual percepts and themes more frequently than any of the other cards. For these reasons, the interpretive process can be enriched in many cases by attending to the possible sexual significance of how people describe Card VI and whether they have difficulty formulating responses to it.

Card VII

The meanings typically associated with Card VII contrast sharply with those usually conveyed by Card IV. Compared with Card IV, Card VII is likely to be seen as attractive rather than threatening, soft rather than hard, weak rather than strong, and passive rather than active. Allowing for individual differences and ever mindful of the pitfalls of gender-role stereotypes, these characterizations of Card VII embrace many features traditionally associated with femininity, just as typical impressions of Card IV consist of traits associated mainly with masculinity. As with Card IV, these conjectures accord with empirical data concerning the types of figures usually seen on Card VII. Whereas Card IV is rarely seen as a female figure, Card VII is hardly ever seen as a male figure, at least not as an adult male. With few exceptions, the partial or whole human figures commonly seen on Card VII are described as being women or children.

Accordingly, individuals' percepts, associations, and test behaviors on Card VII often have a bearing on their feelings and attitudes toward women. However, no assumptions can be made concerning whether these feelings and attitudes are held toward women in general or toward a person's mother, wife, grandmother, aunt, sister, teacher, friend, or some other female or feminized figure. In parallel with the interpretation of responses to Card IV, feelings and attitudes expressed in Card VII responses can be tracked to particular people only on the basis of additional information specific to the individual person being examined. For the same reasons discussed with respect to a father card, then, Card VII does not function universally as *the* mother card although, for some persons, it may serve as *a* mother card.

Because of the femininity often associated with Card VII, difficulties in responding to it may point to troubling or unresolved concerns individuals have in relation to female figures in their lives. Of further importance in this regard, the lower-center detail of Card VII is ordinary form level for "vagina." Hence this card may elicit associations to or concerns not only about femininity, but about feminine sexuality as well.

Card VIII

Card VIII often constitutes a change-of-pace point during a Rorschach administration, much as Card V does earlier. As already mentioned, Card V is a relatively nonthreatening and easily articulated inkblot that many people experience as a welcome relief following the previous four more difficult or challenging blots. Card VIII follows four cards (IV–VII) that are darkly colored in shades of gray and black, and it presents people instead with a softly colored card in pastel hues that is usually experienced as attractive and that contains an easily seen popular animal figure in its side details. Like Card V, then, Card VIII provides many people a breathing space in which they relax a bit and respond more effectively than they have on Cards IV–VII. Not uncommonly, people express relief on being handed Card VIII, with comments on the order of "I like this one," or "Finally, a pretty one," or "This one's easy."

For some individuals, Card VIII may present new difficulties. It is more complex than the preceding seven cards with respect to its broken appearance and number of loosely connected large details, and it is also the first multicolored card in the series. People who generally have difficulty when asked to sort out and integrate the components of complex situations may find Card VIII an unwelcome challenge and struggle to form responses other than the obvious Popular. People who become uncomfortable in affect-arousing situations or who prefer to avoid emotional stimulation may display avoidance and distress rather than pleasure and relief as they begin to look at Card VIII.

Card IX

With respect to what it conveys to examinees, Card IX is distinctive mainly for its vague and diffuse quality. Because the colors on Card IX are somewhat muted, the chromatic features of this blot do not appear to be particularly affect arousing. The shapes on the blot are less definite than those on the other cards, and the Card IX Popular of human or humanlike figures for the upper side details occurs less frequently than any of the other 12 *Populars* in the Comprehensive System (see Table 11.5). Consequently, this card is the least likely in the series to suggest any particular percepts or specific concerns on a regular basis. Difficulty responding to it usually reflects inability or disinclination to come to grips effectively with complex, unstructured situations.

This guideline does not preclude person-specific features of card pull that may influence a person's behavior or responses on Card IX. The popular human figures may in some instances pull an impression that they are fighting, in which case Card IX could arouse some concerns about aggression. Similarly, the resemblance of the lower middle red detail of Card IX to female genitals could evoke some sexual concerns that affect a person's manner and responses while looking at this card. Neither of these possible Card IX pulls is as strong or common as the other card pulls identified in this section.

Card X

The broken appearance of Card X and its array of loosely connected but rather sharply defined and colored details give it a close structural resemblance to Card VIII. At the same time, the sheer number of variegated shapes and colors on Card X imbue it with the same type of uncertainty and complexity posed by Card IX. Although Card X is usually seen as a pleasant stimulus and offers examinees many alternative possibilities for easily seen percepts, the challenge of organizing it effectively makes it the second most difficult card to manage, after Card IX. Particularly for people who feel overwhelmed or overburdened by having to deal with many things at once, responding to Card X, despite its pleasant appearance and bright colors, may be a disconcerting experience that they dislike and are happy to complete.

Finally of note is the position of Card X as the final card. Just as the initial response in a record may be a way for people to sign in and introduce what they feel is important about themselves, the last response may serve as an opportunity to sign out by indicating, in effect, "When all is said and done, this is where things stand for me and what I want you to know about me." As a parallel to the example given earlier of a sign-in response, consider the contrasting implications of the following responses for the present status of two depressed persons. The first one concluded Card X by saying, "And it looks like everything is falling apart"; the second one concluded, "And it's brightly colored, like the sun is coming up."

APPLICATIONS

In common with the self-report inventories presented in Chapters 6 through 10, the RIM is an omnibus personality assessment instrument, in the sense that it provides information about a broad range of personality characteristics. As elaborated in discussing the interpretive significance of Rorschach findings, these data shed light on the adequacy of a person's adaptive capacities in several key respects, on the types of psychological states and traits that define what the person is like, and on the underlying needs, attitudes, conflicts, and concerns that may be influencing the person's behavior. Such information about personality functioning serves practical purposes by helping to identify (a) the presence and nature of psychological disorder, (b) whether a person needs and is likely to benefit from various kinds of treatment, and (c) the probability of a person's functioning effectively in certain kinds of situations.

By serving these purposes, the RIM frequently facilitates making decisions that are based in part on personality characteristics. Such personality-based decisions commonly characterize the practice of clinical, forensic, and organizational psychology, the three contexts in which Rorschach assessment finds its most frequent applications.

Clinical Practice

Rorschach assessment contributes to clinical practice by assisting in differential diagnosis and treatment planning and outcome evaluation. With respect to differential diagnosis, many states and traits identified by Rorschach variables are associated with particular forms of psychopathology. Schizophrenia is usually defined to include disordered thinking and poor reality testing, and Rorschach evidence of these cognitive impairments (low $XA\%$ and $WDA\%$, an elevated $WSum6$) accordingly indicates the likelihood of a schizophrenia spectrum disorder. Similarly, because paranoia involves being hypervigilant and interpersonally aversive, a positive HVI suggests the presence of paranoid features in how people look at their world. Depressive disorder is suggested by Rorschach indices of dysphoria (elevated C', Col-$Shd\,Blds$) and negative self-attitudes (elevated V, low $3r + 2/R$), obsessive-compulsive personality disorder is suggested by indices of pedantry and perfectionism (positive OBS), and so on. To learn more about these and other applications of Rorschach findings in differential diagnosis, readers are referred to articles and books by Hartmann, Norbech, and Grønnerød (2006), Huprich (2006), Kleiger (1999), and Weiner (2003b).

The applications to which the RIM contributes by measuring personality characteristics identify its limitations as well. In assessing psychopathology, Rorschach data are of little use in determining the particular symptoms a person is manifesting. Someone with Rorschach indications of an obsessive-compulsive personality style may be a compulsive hand washer, an obsessive prognosticator, or neither. Someone with depressive preoccupations may be having crying spells, disturbed sleep, or neither. There is no isomorphic relationship between the personality characteristics of disturbed people and their specific symptoms. Accordingly, the nature of these symptoms is better determined from observing or asking directly about them than by speculating about their presence on the basis of Rorschach data.

Likewise, Rorschach data do not provide dependable indications concerning whether a person has had certain life experiences (e.g., been sexually abused) or behaved in certain ways (e.g., abused alcohol or drugs). Only when there is a substantial known correlation between specific personality characteristics and the likelihood of certain experiences or behavior having occurred can Rorschach findings provide reliable postdictions, as mentioned. The predictive validity of Rorschach findings are similarly limited by the extent to which personality factors determine whatever is to be identified or predicted.

As for treatment planning, Rorschach findings measure personality characteristics that have a bearing on numerous decisions that must be made prior to and during an intervention process. The degree of disturbance or coping incapacity reflected in Rorschach responses assists in determining whether a person requires inpatient care or is functioning sufficiently well to be treated as an outpatient. Considered together with the person's preferences, the personality style and severity of distress or disorganization revealed by Rorschach findings help indicate whether treatment needs will best be met by a supportive approach oriented to relieving distress, a cognitive-behavioral approach designed to modify symptoms or behavior, or an exploratory approach intended to enhance self-understanding. Whichever treatment approach is implemented, the maladaptive personality traits and the underlying concerns identified by the Rorschach data can help therapists determine, in consultation with their patients, what the goals for the treatment should be and in what order these treatment targets should be addressed (see Weiner, 2005b).

Some predictive utility derives from the fact that certain personality characteristics measured by Rorschach variables are typically associated with ability to participate in and benefit from psychological treatment. These personality characteristics include being open to experience (*Lambda* not elevated), cognitively flexible (balanced *a:p*), emotionally responsive (adequate *WSumC* and *Afr*), interpersonally receptive (presence of *T,* adequate *SumH*), and personally introspective (presence of *FD*), each of which facilitates engagement and progress in psychotherapy. By contrast, having an avoidant or guarded approach to experience, being set in one's ways, having difficulty recognizing and expressing one's feelings, being interpersonally aversive or withdrawn, and lacking psychological mindedness are often obstacles to progress in psychotherapy (Clarkin & Levy, 2004; Weiner, 1998, chap. 2).

In a research project relevant to the utility of the RIM in guiding therapist activity once treatment is underway, Blatt and Ford (1994) used Rorschach variables to assist in categorizing patients as having problems primarily with forming satisfying interpersonal relationships (called *anaclitic*) or primarily with maintaining their own sense of identity, autonomy, and self-worth (called *introjective*). In the course of their subsequent psychotherapy, the anaclitic patients studied by Blatt and Ford were initially more involved in and responsive to relational aspects of the treatment than the introjective patients, who were more attuned to and influenced by their therapist's interpretations than by attention to the treatment relationship.

By helping to identify treatment goals and targets, Rorschach assessment can also be helpful in monitoring treatment progress and evaluating treatment outcome. Suppose that a RIM is administered prior to beginning therapy and certain treatment targets can be identified in Rorschach terms (e.g., reducing subjectively felt distress, as in changing $D < 0$ to $D = 0$; increasing receptivity to emotional arousal, as in bringing up a low *Afr;* promoting more careful problem solving, as in reducing a $Zd < -3.5$). Retesting after some period of time can then provide quantitative indications of how much progress has been made toward achieving these goals and how much work remains to be done on them. Rorschach evidence concerning the extent to which the goals of the treatment have been achieved can guide therapists in deciding if and when termination is indicated. Similarly, comparing Rorschach findings at the point of termination or in a later follow-up evaluation with those obtained in a pretreatment evaluation will provide a useful objective measure of the effects of the treatment, for better or worse.

Both research findings and case reports have demonstrated how Rorschach assessment can be applied in treatment outcome evaluation. In studies reported by Weiner and Exner (1991) and Exner and Andronikof-Sanglade (1992), patients in long-term, short-term, and brief psychotherapy were examined at several points during and after their treatment. The data analysis focused on 27 structural variables considered to have implications for a person's overall level of adjustment. The results of both studies showed significant positive changes in these Rorschach variables over the course of therapy, consistent with expectation, and the amount of improvement was associated with the length of the therapy. These findings were considered to demonstrate both the effectiveness of psychotherapy in promoting positive personality change and the validity of the RIM in measuring such change.

In a study with similar implications, Fowler et al. (2004) monitored the progress of a group of previously treatment-refractory patients who entered a residential treatment center and were engaged in psychodynamically oriented psychotherapy. After a treatment duration averaging 16 months, these patients showed significant improvement in their average behavior ratings on scales related to social and occupational functioning, and these improvements were matched by significant changes for the better in their average scores on three Rorschach scales based on response content. With its thematic imagery as well as its structural variables, then, Rorschach assessment has been shown to provide valid measurement of treatment progress, while helping to demonstrate the effectiveness of the treatment. Readers are referred to Weiner (2004a, 2005a) for additional discussion of Rorschach monitoring of psychotherapy and a detailed case study that illustrates positive Rorschach changes accompanying successful psychotherapy.

Forensic Practice

In the clinical applications just discussed, diagnostic inferences derive from linkages between personality characteristics that typify certain disorders and Rorschach variables that measure these characteristics. In similar fashion, forensic applications of Rorschach assessment in criminal, civil, and family law cases derive from a translation of legal concepts into psychological terms.

In criminal law, the two questions most commonly addressed to consulting psychologists concern whether an accused person is competent to proceed to trial and whether the person can or should be held responsible for the alleged criminal behavior. Being competent in this context consists of having a rational and factual understanding of the legal proceedings one is facing and being able to participate effectively in one's own defense. These principal components of competency are commonly translated into specific questions such as (a) whether defendants appreciate the nature of the charges and possible penalties they are facing, (b) whether they understand the adversarial process and the roles of the key people in it, (c) whether they can disclose pertinent facts in their case to their attorney, and (d) whether they are capable of behaving appropriately in the courtroom and testifying relevantly in their own behalf (Stafford, 2003; Zapf & Roesch, 2006).

With respect to dimensions of personality functioning, these aspects of competence are most closely related to being able to think logically and coherently and to perceive people and events accurately. Disordered thinking and impaired reality testing, in combination with the poor judgment and inappropriate behavior typically associated with them, can interfere with a person's ability to demonstrate competence. Accordingly, the same Rorschach indices of disordered thinking and impaired reality testing just mentioned in connection with differential diagnosis (low *XA%*, low *WDA%*, elevated *WSum6*), although not sufficient evidence of incompetence, serve two purposes in this regard. They alert the examiner to a distinct likelihood that the defendant will have difficulty satisfying customary criteria for competency to stand trial, and if a defendant appears incompetent with respect to the applicable criteria, these Rorschach findings help the examiner explain to the court why the person is having this difficulty.

Criminal responsibility refers in legal terms to whether an accused person was legally sane at the time of committing an alleged offense. In some jurisdictions, insanity is defined as a cognitive incapacity that prevented the accused person from recognizing the criminality of his or her actions or appreciating the wrongfulness of this conduct. Insanity in other jurisdictions is defined either as this type of cognitive incapacity or as a loss of behavioral control, such that the person was unable to alter or refrain from the alleged criminal conduct at the time (Goldstein, Morse, & Shapiro, 2003; Zapf, Golding, & Roesch, 2006).

With respect to personality functioning, cognitive incapacity is measured on the RIM by the previously mentioned indices of disordered thinking and poor reality testing. Behavioral dyscontrol is suggested by Rorschach indices of acute and chronic stress overload (minus D-score, minus $AdjD$-score), which are commonly associated with limited frustration tolerance, intemperate outbursts of affect, and episodes of impulsive behavior. However, because legal sanity is defined by the person's state of mind at the time of an alleged offense, and not at the time of a present examination, Rorschach findings suggesting cognitive impairment or susceptibility to loss of control must be supplemented by other types of information (e.g., observations of defendants' behavior by witnesses to their alleged offense and by the law enforcement officers who arrested them) to serve adequately as a basis for drawing conclusions about criminal responsibility.

In civil law cases involving allegations of personal injury, personality assessment helps to determine the extent to which a person has become emotionally distressed or incapacitated as a consequence of irresponsible behavior on the part of another person or some entity. As prescribed by tort law, this circumstance exists when the potentially liable person or entity has, by omission or commission of certain actions, been derelict in a duty or obligation to the complainant, thereby causing the aggrieved person to experience psychological injury that would otherwise not have occurred (see Greenberg, 2003).

Emotional distress caused by the irresponsible actions of others is often likely to be reflected in Rorschach responses, most commonly in indications of generalized anxiety, stress disorder, depressive affect and cognitions, and psychotic loss of touch with reality.

Persons with Posttraumatic Stress Disorder tend to produce one of two types of Rorschach protocols. Those whose disorder is manifest primarily in the reexperiencing of distressing events and mental and physical hyperarousal tend to produce a flooded protocol that is notable for the incursions of anxiety on comfortable and effective functioning. The implications of the minus D-score and minus Adj D-score for stress overload can be particularly helpful in identifying such incursions, as can a high frequency of content codes suggesting concerns about bodily harm (e.g., $AG, An, Bl, MOR, Sx;$ see Armstrong & Kaser-Boyd, 2004; Kelly, 1999; Luxenberg & Levin, 2004). Those anxious or traumatized persons whose disorder is manifest primarily in efforts to avoid or withdraw from thoughts, feelings, or situations that might precipitate psychological distress tend to produce a constricted Rorschach protocol that is notably guarded or evasive. Such hallmarks of a guarded record as a low R, high $Lambda$, low $WSumC$, and $D = 0$ tend to increase the likelihood that a person who has been exposed to a potentially traumatizing experience is experiencing a stress disorder characterized by defensive avoidance.

However, neither flooded nor constricted Rorschach protocols are specific to anxiety and stress disorder, nor do they provide conclusive evidence that such a disorder is present. Given historical and other clinical or test data to suggest such a disorder, they merely increase its likelihood. Moreover, as in the case of evaluating sanity, the results of a present personal injury examination are useful only if they can be interpreted in the context of past events. Personal injury cases require examiners to determine whether any currently observed distress predated the alleged misconduct by the defendant and whether this distress constitutes a decline in functioning capacity from some previously higher level prior to when the misconduct occurred.

Similar considerations apply in the assessment of depressive or psychotic features in plaintiffs seeking personal injury damages. As noted, the *DEPI* and its several components are helpful in identifying the presence of dysphoric affect and negative cognitions, but they do not provide a dependable basis for ruling out these features of depression. A psychotic impairment of reality testing is indicated by a low *XA%* and low *WDA%*, and psychosis can usually be ruled out if these variables fall within a normal range. Lack of evidence of psychosis would counter a plaintiff's claim to have suffered psychological injury, but present indications of psychosis would give little support to such a claim unless other reliable data (e.g., previous testing, historical indications of sound mental health) gave good reason to believe that this person was not psychotic prior to the alleged harmful conduct by the defendant.

Personality assessment also enters into family law cases, in the context of disputed child custody and visitation rights. In determining how a child's time and supervision should be divided between separated or divorced parents, judges frequently make their determination partly on the basis of information about the personality characteristics of the child and the parents. Similarly, in deciding whether persons should have their parental rights terminated, courts often seek information about their personality strengths and weaknesses as identified by a psychological examination. There are no infallible guidelines concerning which of two persons would be the better parent for a particular child, nor is there any perfect measure of suitability to parent. However, certain personality characteristics as measured by the RIM are likely to enhance or detract from parents' abilities to meet the needs of their children. These characteristics pertain to the presence or absence of serious psychological disturbance, the adequacy of the person's coping skills, and the person's degree of interpersonal accessibility.

Although having a psychological disorder does not necessarily prevent a person from being a good parent, being seriously disturbed or psychologically incapacitated is likely to interfere with a person's having sufficient judgment, impulse control, energy, and peace of mind to function effectively in a parental capacity. As indicated in presenting interpretive guidelines for the RIM and as previously mentioned in this section on applications, several Rorschach variables help identify such serious disturbance. These include indices of significant thinking disorder and substantially impaired reality testing (elevated *PTI*), pervasive dysphoria and negative cognitions (elevated *DEPI*), overwhelming anxiety (a large minus *D*-score), and marked suicide potential (elevated *S-CON*).

As for coping skills, good parenting is facilitated by capacities for good judgment, careful decision making, a flexible approach to solving problems, and effective stress management. Conversely, poor judgment, careless decision making, inflexible problem solving, and inability to manage stress without becoming unduly upset are likely to interfere with effective parenting. Rorschach findings often cast light on the adequacy of a person's skills in each of these respects, as noted in discussing interpretive guidelines: *XA%* with respect to judgment; *Zd* with respect to decision making; *a:p* with respect to problem-solving approach; and *D*-score with respect to stress management. This is by no means a definitive or exhaustive list of coping skills relevant to quality of parenting or of Rorschach variables that might prove helpful in evaluating parental suitability. The list nevertheless illustrates important respects in which Rorschach assessment can be applied in family law consultation.

Finally, with respect to interpersonal accessibility, the quality of child care that parents can provide is usually enhanced by their being a person who is interested in people and comfortable being around them, a person who is nurturing and caring in his or her relationships with others, and a person who is sufficiently empathic to understand what other people are like and recognize their needs and concerns. Conversely, interpersonal disinterest and discomfort are likely to detract from parental effectiveness, as is being a detached, self-absorbed, or insensitive person. In Rorschach terms, then, the likelihood of a person's being a good parent is measured in part by the interpersonal cluster of variables discussed earlier, which means that good parenting is often, though not always, associated with the following seven Rorschach findings:

1. $SumH > 3$
2. $H > Hd + (H) + (Hd)$
3. $ISOL < .25$
4. $p < a + 2$
5. $T > 0$
6. $COP > 1$
7. Accurate $M > 2$ and $M- < 2$

In drawing these inferences about interpersonal accessibility, examiners must always keep in mind that such Rorschach findings may suggest how parents are likely to interact with their children, but they are never conclusive. The test data identify probable parental strengths or limitations in interpersonal accessibility that should be considered as evaluators proceed to observe and obtain reports of how parents are functioning. Integration of Rorschach indications of adjustment level and coping skills with these behavioral observations and reports should always precede coming to conclusions about a person's effectiveness as a parent. Further elaboration of these and other substantive guidelines in forensic Rorschach assessment is provided by Erard (2005), Gacono, Evans, Kaser-Boyd, and Gacono (in press), Johnston, Walters, & Olesen (2005), and Weiner (2005a, 2006, 2007, in press).

Whatever the nature of a forensic case, attention must be paid not only to the substantive interpretation of Rorschach findings, but also to whether testimony based on these findings is admissible into evidence in courtroom proceedings. Applicable criteria for admissibility vary, depending on the particular federal or state jurisdiction in which a case is being tried, and judges have considerable discretion in determining what types of testimony are allowed. As established by published guidelines and case law, the criteria used in individual cases involve some combination of the following considerations: whether the testimony is relevant to the issues in the case and will help the judge or jury arrive at their decision (Federal Rules of Evidence); whether the testimony is based on generally accepted methods and procedures in the expert's field (Frye standard); and whether the testimony is derived from scientifically sound methods and procedures (Daubert standard; see Ewing, 2003; Hess, 2006).

The RIM satisfies criteria for admissibility in all three of these respects. The usefulness of Rorschach-based testimony in facilitating legal decisions is demonstrated by the frequency with which this testimony is in fact welcomed in the courtroom. In a survey of almost 8,000 cases in which forensic psychologists offered the court Rorschach-based testimony, the appropriateness of the instrument was challenged in only six instances, and in only one of these cases was the testimony ruled inadmissible (Weiner, Exner, & Sciara, 1996). Among the full set of 247 cases in which Rorschach evidence was presented to a federal, state, or military court of appeals during the half-century from 1945 to 1995, the admissibility and weight of the Rorschach data were questioned in only 10.5% of the hearings. The relevance and utility of Rorschach assessment was challenged in only two of these appellate cases, and the remaining criticisms of the Rorschach testimony were directed at the interpretation of the data, not the method itself (Meloy, Hansen, & Weiner, 1997).

More recently Meloy (in press) has examined the full set of 150 published cases in which Rorschach findings were cited in federal, state, and military appellate court proceedings during the 10-year period from 1996 to 2005. These 150 cases over a 10-year period indicate an average of 15 Rorschach citations per year in appellate cases, which is three times the annual rate of citation found by Meloy et al. (1997) for the preceding 50 years. Along with this greatly increased use of the RIM in appellate courts, the percentage of cases in which these courts recorded criticisms of Rorschach testimony decreased from 10.5% during 1945 to 1995 to just 2% during 1996 to 2005. In not one of these 1996 to 2005 appellate cases was the Rorschach method ridiculed or disparaged by opposing counsel.

The general acceptance of the Rorschach method is reflected in data concerning how frequently it is used, taught, and studied. Surveys over the past 40 years have consistently shown substantial endorsement of Rorschach testing as a valuable skill to teach, learn, and practice. Among clinical psychologists, the RIM has been the fourth most widely used test, exceeded in frequency of use only by the Wechsler Adult Intelligence Scale (WAIS), the Minnesota Multiphasic Personality Inventory (MMPI), and the Wechsler Intelligence Scale for Children (WISC), in that order (Hogan, 2005). Surveys also indicate that over 80% of clinical psychologists engaged in providing assessment services use the RIM in their work and believe that clinical students should be competent in Rorschach assessment; that over 80% of graduate programs teach the RIM; and that students usually find this training helpful in improving their assessment skills and their understanding of the patients and clients with whom they work (see Camara, Nathan, & Puente, 2000; Viglione & Hilsenroth, 2001).

With respect to assessment of young people, 162 child and adolescent practitioners surveyed by Cashel (2002) reported that the RIM was their third most frequently used personality assessment measure, following sentence completion and figure drawing methods. Among 346 psychologists working with adolescents in clinical and academic settings, Archer and Newsom (2000) found the RIM to be their most frequently used personality test and second among all tests only to the Wechsler scales.

Surveys of training directors in predoctoral internship sites have also identified widespread endorsement of the value of Rorschach testing. Training directors report that the RIM is one of the three measures most frequently used in their test batteries (along with the WAIS/WISC and the MMPI-2/MMPI-A), and they commonly express the hope or expectation that their incoming interns will have had a Rorschach course or at least arrive with a good working knowledge of the instrument (Clemence & Handler, 2001; Stedman, Hatch, & Schoenfeld, 2000).

Survey findings confirm that Rorschach assessment has gained an established place in forensic as well as clinical practice. Data collected from forensic psychologists by Ackerman and Ackerman (1997), Boccaccini and Brodsky (1999), Borum and Grisso (1995), and Quinnell and Bow (2001) showed 30% using the RIM in evaluations of competency to stand trial, 32% in evaluations of criminal responsibility, 41% in evaluations of personal injury, 44% to 48% in evaluations of adults involved in custody disputes, and 23% in evaluations of children in custody cases. Consistent with these earlier surveys, a more recent report by Archer, Buffington-Vollum, Stredny, and Handel (2006) indicated Rorschach usage for all purposes combined by 36% of the forensic psychologists participating in their survey.

As for study of the instrument, the scientific status of the RIM has been attested over many years by a steady and substantial volume of published research concerning its nature and utility. Buros (1974) *Tests in Print II* identified 4,580 Rorschach references through 1971, with an average yearly rate of 92 publications. In the 1990s, Butcher and Rouse (1996) found an almost identical trend continuing from 1974 to 1994. An average of 96 Rorschach research articles appeared annually during this 20-year period in journals published in the United States, and the RIM was second only to the MMPI among personality assessment instruments in the volume of research it generated. For the 3-year period 2004 to 2006, PsycINFO lists 350 scientific articles, books, book chapters, and dissertations worldwide concerning Rorschach assessment.

There is in fact a large international community of Rorschach scholars and practitioners whose research published abroad has for many years made important contributions to the literature (see Weiner, 1999). The international presence of Rorschach assessment is reflected in a survey of test use in Spain, Portugal, and Latin American countries by Muniz, Prieto, Almeida, and Bartram (1999) in which the RIM emerged as the third most widely used psychological assessment instrument, following the Wechsler scales and versions of the MMPI. The results of surveys in Japan, as reported by Ogawa (2004), indicate that about 60% of Japanese clinical psychologists use the RIM in their daily practice. An International Rorschach Society was founded in 1952, and triennial congresses sponsored by this society typically attract participants from over 30 countries and all parts of the world.

With respect to the scientific soundness of Rorschach assessment, the final section of this chapter reviews extensive research findings that document the adequate intercoder agreement and retest reliability of the instrument, its validity when used appropriately for its intended purposes, and the availability of normative reference data for representative samples of children and adults. Significantly in this regard, Meloy (2007) reported in his previously mentioned review, "There has been no Daubert challenge to the scientific status of the Rorschach in any state, federal, or military court of appeal since the U.S. Supreme Court decision in 1993 set the federal standard for admissibility of scientific evidence" (p. 85).

Despite widespread dissemination of this information, some authors have contended that Rorschach assessment does not satisfy contemporary criteria for admissibility into evidence and have discouraged forensic examiners from using the RIM, even to the point of calling for a moratorium on its use in forensic settings (Garb, 1999; Grove & Barden, 1999). These Rorschach critics have not presented any data to refute previous surveys in this regard or to support their contention that the RIM is unwelcome in the courtroom. The ways in which Rorschach assessment has been demonstrated to assist in forensic decision making are amplified further in contributions by McCann (1998, 2004), McCann and Evans (in press), Ritzler, Erard, and Pettigrew (2002), and Hilsenroth and Stricker (2004).

Organizational Practice

Rorschach assessment in organizational practice is concerned primarily with the selection and evaluation of personnel. Personnel selection typically consists of determining whether a person applying for a position in an organization is suitable to fill it, or whether a person already in the organization is qualified for promotion to a position of increased responsibility. Standard psychological procedure in making such selection decisions consists of first identifying the personality requirements for success in the position being applied or aspired to, and then determining the extent to which a candidate shows these personality characteristics.

A leadership position requiring initiative and rapid decision making would probably not be filled well by a person who is behaviorally passive and given to painstaking care in coming to conclusions, as would be suggested by Rorschach findings of $p > a + 1$ and $Zd > +3.0$. A position in sales or public relations that calls for extensive and persuasive interaction with people is unlikely to be a good fit for a person who is emotionally withdrawn and socially uncomfortable, as would be suggested by a low Afr and $H < Hd + (H) + (Hd)$. Among persons being considered for hire as an air traffic controller or a nuclear power plant supervisor, it would support their candidacy to find evidence on personality testing of good coping capacities and the ability to remain calm and exercise good judgment even in highly stressful situations—in Rorschach terms, a person with a high EA, $D > = 0$, and $XA\%$ in the normal range.

Personnel evaluations may also involve assessing the current fitness for duty of persons whose ability to function has become impaired by psychological disorder. Most common in this regard is the onset of an anxiety or depressive disorder that prevents people from continuing to perform their job or practice their profession as competently as they had previously. Impaired professionals seen for psychological evaluation may also have had difficulties related to abuse of alcohol, drugs, or prescription medicine. Because Rorschach data can help identify the extent to which people are anxious or depressed and whether they are struggling with more stress than they can manage, the RIM can often contribute to determining fitness for duty and assessing progress toward recovery in persons participating in a treatment or rehabilitation program.

Violence in the workplace has also given rise in recent years to frequent referrals for fitness-for-duty evaluations, usually in the wake of an employee's making verbal threats or acting aggressively on the job. Estimation of violence potential is a complex process that requires careful consideration of an individual's personality characteristics, interpersonal and sociocultural context, and previous history of violent behavior (Monahan, 2003). Personality characteristics do not by themselves provide sufficient basis for concluding that someone poses a danger to the safety and welfare of others. However, there is reason to believe that certain personality characteristics increase the likelihood of violent behavior in persons who have behaved violently in the past and are currently confronting annoying or threatening situations that on previous occasions were likely to provoke aggressive reactions on their part. Following is a list of personality characteristics and Rorschach findings identified earlier in the chapter that help identify them (see also Gacono, 2000; Gacono & Meloy, 1994).

1. Being a selfish and self-centered person with a callous disregard for the rights and feelings of other people and a sense of entitlement to do and have whatever one wants (e.g., $Fr + rF > 0$ and $3r + (2)/R$ elevated).

2. Being a psychologically distant person who is generally mistrustful of others, avoids intimate relationship, and either ignores people or exploits them to one's own ends (e.g., HVI, $T = 0$, low $SumH$, $COP = 0$ with $AG > 2$).

3. Being an angry and action-oriented person inclined to express this anger directly (e.g., $S > 3$, $a > p$, extratensive EB).

4. Being an impulsive person with little tolerance for frustration, or a psychologically disturbed person with impaired reality testing and poor judgment (e.g., $D < 0$, $AdjD < 0$, $XA\%$ and $WDA\%$ low).

Neither these personality characteristics nor the Rorschach variables associated with them are specific to persons who show violent behavior. Even among people who exhibit all these characteristics and Rorschach findings, moreover, many or most may never consider physically assaulting another person. However, in persons with a history of violent behavior who are exposed to violence-provoking circumstances, each of these characteristics and findings increases violence potential risk. The more numerous these characteristics and findings, and the more pronounced they are, the greater is the violence risk they suggest.

PSYCHOMETRIC FOUNDATIONS

As mentioned in discussing the history of Rorschach assessment, the blossoming of various Rorschach systems in the United States and abroad enriched the instrument for clinical purposes, but at a cost to its scientific development. The many Rorschach variations created by gifted and respected clinicians limited cumulative research on the psychometric properties of the instrument prior to Exner's 1974 standardization of coding and administration procedures in the Comprehensive System (CS). Subsequent widespread use of the CS in research and practice has fostered substantial advances in knowledge concerning the psychometric soundness of the RIM, particularly with respect to its intercoder agreement, retest reliability, validity, and normative reference base.

Intercoder Agreement

In constructing the Rorschach CS, Exner included only variables on which his coders could achieve at least 80% agreement, and subsequent research confirmed that the CS variables can be reliably coded with at least this level of agreement. However, measuring intercoder reliability by percentage of agreement is a questionable procedure, because this method does not take account of agreement occurring by chance. With this consideration in mind, Rorschach researchers began in the late 1990s to assess intercoder reliability with two statistics that correct for chance agreements, kappa and intraclass correlation coefficients

(ICC). This later research yielded the same positive results as the earlier work. Meta-analytic reviews and studies with patient and nonpatient samples have identified mean kappa coefficients ranging from .79 to .88 across various CS coding categories, which for kappa coefficients is generally regarded as being in the good to excellent range (Acklin, McDowell, Verschell, & Chan, 2000; Meyer, 1997a, 1997b).

Two other studies exemplify the positive results that consistently emerge from intercoder agreement research with the RIM. Meyer et al. (2002), examining four different patient samples involving 219 protocols and 4,761 responses, found median and mean ICCs of .92 and .90, respectively, for intercoder agreement across 164 structural summary variables. Of these 164 variables, 156 (95%) showed a level of agreement that would be classified as "excellent" by customary ICC standards. Of the other eight variables, seven could be classified as showing "good" agreement on the basis of their ICC level and one as showing "fair" agreement, and none of the 164 ICCs fell in the range of "poor" agreement. When Meyer et al. limited their data analysis to 138 structural summary variables that occur with some regularity, the percentage showing excellent intercoder agreement increased to 97% (134 of the 138). In the other illustrative study, Viglione and Taylor (2003) examined coder concurrence for 84 Rorschach protocols containing 1,732 responses and obtained a median ICC of .92 for 68 variables considered to be of central significance in interpreting Rorschach findings.

Even while remaining in the excellent range, Rorschach variables tend to differ somewhat in their level of intercoder agreement. These differences are no doubt associated with the relative ease or difficulty examiners experience in making various coding decisions. The Meyer et al. (2002) data show that coders achieve almost perfect agreement in deciding whether a response involves a pair of objects (2) and whether it is located in the whole blot (W), in a common detail (D), or in an unusual detail (Dd). Among the determinants, coding agreement is nearly perfect for pure form (F) and reflections (Fr + rF), a little less perfect for movement (M, FM, m), lower still for chromatic color (FC, CF, C), and lowest for shading and achromatic color (C', T, Y, and V), with shading and achromatic color being the determinants most likely to cause coding uncertainty.

Agreement on form quality is almost perfect in assigning codes for ordinary (o) and minus (−) form quality, but less so in coding responses as having ordinary-elaborated (+) or unusual (u) form. Content categories show relatively high ICC levels, consistent with the relative ease of coding them, whereas the critical special scores (DV, INC, DR, FAB, ALOG, CON) show relatively low ICC levels and are often the most challenging response feature to code with confidence.

Despite the kappa and ICC evidence of substantial intercoder agreement for Rorschach structural variables, some authors have expressed concern about a lack of field studies to demonstrate that examiners in practice can code the instrument reliably (Hunsley & Bailey, 1999; Lilienfeld, Wood, & Garb, 2000). Field reliability is an important matter, because it bears on whether practitioners are using personality assessment instruments properly and basing their conclusions and recommendations on accurately coded test protocols. As noted in Chapter 5, there have been reports from clinical settings of frequent errors in the hand scoring of self-report inventories, including the Minnesota Multiphasic Personality Inventory (MMPI), the Beck Depression Inventory, and the State-Trait Anxiety Inventory (see Allard & Faust, 2000). With respect to the RIM, however, there has been no published evidence that coding inconsistencies are widespread. To the contrary, research results give good reason to believe that the RIM can be coded reliably in field settings.

One of the samples in the Meyer et al. (2002) study of intercoder reliability and a sample reported by McGrath et al. (2005) consisted of patient protocols that were initially coded in clinical practice, without any anticipation of their becoming part of a research project, and then independently coded at a later time to assess intercoder agreement. In both samples, the obtained correlation coefficients were more than adequate to demonstrate the potential of the RIM to show field reliability. In the only other published study to date bearing on field reliability of Rorschach coding, Guarnaccia, Dill, Sabatino, and Southwick (2001) compared the codes assigned by Rorschach users to a series of responses for which a correct coding had previously been established. Guarnaccia et al. concluded from their findings that the level of agreement they found was unacceptable. However, in a departure from usual procedures for judging coding accuracy, these investigators deducted credit for errors of omission. This methodological idiosyncracy prevents any meaningful comparison of the Guarnaccia et al. results with usual guidelines for judging the adequacy of coder agreement rates.

Two additional considerations should be noted concerning accurate scoring of the RIM and other assessment instruments. First, as elaborated by McGrath (2003), research findings indicate that coding errors can be reduced in clinical settings by an emphasis on correct scoring and recourse to detailed coding guidelines. The relative complexity of Rorschach coding, compared with other personality assessment instruments, has proved energizing in this respect. Although challenging with respect to achieving intercoder agreement, this complexity has fostered considerable attention to the teaching and learning of Rorschach coding, considerable discussion about coding criteria among Rorschach examiners, and publication of detailed coding manuals. These manuals include Exner's (2001) scoring workbook for the CS and an even more detailed elaboration of this workbook by Viglione (2002), both of which are recommended as supplementary reading for this chapter.

Second, although field studies are important in assessing the quality of clinical practice, they are not ordinarily considered to play a role in establishing the scoring reliability of an assessment instrument. Scoring reliability is established by showing that examiners who are familiar with the coding criteria for an instrument and have had some basic training in applying these criteria can achieve adequate agreement. Should practitioners in the field fail to code the RIM or any other personality assessment instrument accurately, the fault lies with their not being adequately informed and trained in using the measure, not with flaws inherent in the measure.

As an extension of the research on coding agreement, Meyer, Mihura, and Smith (2005) investigated whether clinicians could reach agreement on the interpretations they assigned to Rorschach protocols. A set of 29 characteristics (e.g., "This person feels distant or isolated from others"; "This person oversimplifies situations as a basic way of coping") were independently rated by several experienced clinicians for their degree of applicability to 55 patients whose CS structural summaries they were given to review. In their data analysis, 550 independently paired judgments concerning the 29 items yielded a reliability coefficient of .71. Pending replication, these findings appear to demonstrate that experienced clinicians presented with the same Rorschach data are likely to draw similar conclusions from them.

Reliability

As summarized by Exner (2003, chap. 11), Grønnerød (2003, 2006), Viglione and Hilsenroth (2001), and Meyer and Viglione (in press), the reliability of Rorschach summary scores and indices has been demonstrated in a series of retest studies with both children and adults over intervals ranging from 7 days to 3 years. Almost all the variables coded in the CS that are conceptualized as relating to trait characteristics show substantial short-term and long-term stability in adults. Retest correlations for most of these variables exceed .75, and some approach .90 (the Affective Ratio and the Egocentricity Index). Only two Rorschach variables—inanimate movement (m) and diffuse shading (Y)—show consistently low retest correlations among adults, and both of these variables, as noted in the section of this chapter on interpretation of structural variables, are considered to signify situational stress. Meta-analysis of these and other retest findings for Rorschach variables as reported by Meyer (2004) indicate a degree of reliability that compares favorably with psychometric findings for other frequently used and highly regarded personality assessment measures, including the self-report inventories discussed in Chapters 6 through 10.

As for children, 3-week retest studies identify stability coefficients in young people similar to those found in adults. Over a 2-year retest interval, younger children initially fluctuate considerably in their Rorschach scores, but as the years pass, they show steadily increasing long-term consistency, just as would be expected in light of the gradual consolidation of personality characteristics that occurs during the developmental years. By the time they reach age 14, adolescents are likely to display the same level of 2-year retest stability as adults (Exner, Thomas, & Mason, 1985).

These Rorschach retest data have important implications not only for the reliability of the instrument, but for its intercoder agreement and validity as well. With respect to intercoder agreement, the substantial stability coefficients shown by most Rorschach variables attest good reliability among the many persons who did the coding for these retest studies. The size of the correlation between two sets of scores is limited by the reliability of each set, and substantial correlations can emerge from a retest study only when the measure has been scored reliably on both occasions. As for validity, the finding of high retest correlations for Rorschach variables believed to identify trait characteristics and low retest correlations for variables considered to measure situational or state characteristics lends construct validity to interpreting these variables as indices of trait or state dimensions of personality, respectively. Similarly, the gradual increase in 2-year retest correlations for most Rorschach variables during the developmental years validates the RIM as a measure of developmental progression in personality consolidation from childhood into adolescence.

Some critics of Rorschach assessment, noting that only a portion of the CS variables have traditionally been included in reports of retest studies, have contended that its reliability is yet to be demonstrated (Garb, Wood, Nezworski, Grove, & Stejskal, 2001). However, most of the retest correlations identified as missing by these critics relate to composite scores for which reliability data have been published for their component parts. Garb et al. listed EB as a variable for which there are no reliability data, which overlooks that EB merely expresses the number of M and the size of $WSumC$, both of which have shown retest correlations above .85 (Exner, Armbruster, & Viglione, 2001). Other missing retest correlations mentioned by Garb et al. (2001) involve codes that do not occur with sufficient frequency to support meaningful statistical treatment without extremely large samples. A rarely coded variable like *CP*, which was given by only two of 600 and five of 450 adult nonpatients in two CS reference samples presented later in this section, may not occur at all in samples of 100 or fewer persons tested twice. In such a case, the first test score of zero would exactly predict the retest score of zero, but this perfect correlation would have little meaning as a reliability estimate.

Viglione and Hilsenroth (2001) provide additional detail concerning the issues to be considered in examining the temporal stability of Rorschach variables and the flawed allegations that Rorschach reliability has not yet been demonstrated. These authors include in their presentation a more detailed listing of retest correlations for CS structural variables than has previously been available and that lends considerable weight to their statement: "The empirical data support the conclusion that the great majority of CS central interpretive ratios, percentages, and derivations possess impressive temporal consistency" (p. 453). As Viglione and Hilsenroth (2001) note further, the relatively few CS variables for which published retest correlations are not available tend to have limited interpretive significance by themselves and enter into the calculation of summary scores that show at least adequate temporal stability. For example, there are no separate retest data for the content categories *Bt, Cl, Ge, Ls,* and *Na,* but these structural variables acquire interpretive significance by constituting the Isolation Index, which has shown a 1-year retest reliability coefficient of .84 in 50 adult nonpatients.

Validity

As elaborated by Weiner (2001a, 2004b), researchers evaluating the validity of the RIM should take account of three critical considerations. First, the validity of personality measures that yield multiple scores and indices resides in the correlations of their individual scales with personality characteristics that these scales are intended to measure. Rorschach variables should accordingly be expected to correlate with phenomena or events that are determined in substantial part by personality characteristics; they should not be expected to predict complex behaviors in which personality characteristics play little part, nor should their validity be judged by how well or poorly they do in this regard.

Second, the validity of Rorschach variables for various purposes should be determined from their correlations with observed rather than inferred variables. Observed variables consist of directly noted features of how people think, feel, and act; inferred variables are hypotheses, derived from indirect sources of information, about how people might be likely to think, feel, and act. Personality assessment instruments are themselves inferential measures, not direct observations, and their correlations with each other consequently provide only modest indications of how valid they are for explaining or predicting aspects of observed behavior. For this reason, validity research with the RIM should focus on correlations of Rorschach variables with observed behavioral manifestations of personality characteristics, not with the summary scores of other personality assessment instruments.

Third, Rorschach validation studies should be conceptually based. In conceptually based personality assessment research, expectations are formulated in terms of particular personality characteristics that are believed to account both for particular test scores that measure these characteristics and for particular behaviors that reflect these characteristics. If a minus *D*-score is conceptualized as an indicator of subjectively felt distress, as is done in this chapter (see p. 375), then this score should be larger among persons with a diagnosed stress disorder, which is conceptualized as involving considerable subjectively felt distress, than among nonpatient comparison groups, which is in fact the case (see Sloan, Aresnault, & Hilsenroth, 2002; Weiner, 1996). In this example, being in a state of distress can thus be seen as contributing both to a minus D-score and to manifestations of a stress disorder. In nonpatient individuals, a minus D-score has been found to correlate significantly with the degree to which they express concern about being able to control their internal states and report difficulty doing so (Greenway & Milne, 2001).

As a further example involving the conceptualization of a minus D-score as an index of stress overload, Elfhag, Barkeling, Carlsson, and Rössner (2003) studied eating behavior in 32 obese persons and hypothesized that stress would cause these persons to increase how rapidly they are eating when beginning a meal. Consistent with their hypothesis, they found a correlation of .39 between the Rorschach D-score and initial eating rate, as measured by a computerized eating monitor. Hence the construct of stress overload could account both for these persons eating rapidly and for their showing a minus D-score.

Significant correlations emerging from validation research based on such conceptual frames of reference identify not only the co-occurrence of certain test and nontest variables, which demonstrates criterion validity, but also the reasons for this co-occurrence, which demonstrates construct validity. The advantage of construct over criterion validity in psychological assessment is the understanding it provides of why observed relationships exist and hypothesized expectations prove true.

The most extensive source of information concerning Rorschach validity in studies taking account of these three considerations is a meta-analysis reported by Hiller, Rosenthal, Bornstein, Berry, and Brunell-Neuleib (1999; see also Rosenthal, Hiller, Bornstein, Berry, & Brunell-Neuleib, 2001). These investigators analyzed a random sample of RIM and MMPI studies published from 1977 to 1997 in which there was at least one external (nontest) variable and in which some reasonable basis had been put forward in advance for expecting associations between the test and nontest variables.

In Hiller et al.'s analysis of these studies, which included 2,276 RIM and 5,007 MMPI protocols, the validity of the RIM and the MMPI, as measured by their average effect sizes, proved almost identical. The unweighted mean validity coefficients were .29 for RIM variables and .30 for MMPI variables, with there being no significant difference between these two validity estimates. Hiller et al. concluded that these obtained effect sizes are sufficiently large to warrant confidence in using both the RIM and the MMPI for their intended purposes, and furthermore that the validity of these instruments "is about as good as can be expected for personality tests" (p. 291).

Hiller et al. (1999) also reported some noteworthy differences between RIM and MMPI variables in the strength of their relationship to different types of dependent variables. On the one hand, Rorschach variables proved somewhat superior (mean validity coefficient of .37) to MMPI variables (mean validity coefficient of .20) in predicting behavioral outcomes, such as whether patients remain in or drop out of therapy. On the other hand, the MMPI showed higher effect sizes than the RIM in correlating with psychiatric diagnosis and self-reports (.37 versus .18). These differences probably reflect a particular sensitivity of the RIM to persistent behavioral dispositions, consistent with the primarily trait implications of most of its variables, and the self-report nature of MMPI, which resembles the methodology of other self-report measures and the basis on which psychiatric diagnoses are made. For a summary of the Hiller et al. (1999) and other meta-analytic comparisons of the global validity of Rorschach, MMPI, and WAIS assessment, readers are referred to Meyer and Archer (2001).

Two other meta-analytic studies have illustrated the types of validity shown by specific Rorschach scales when they are used appropriately to measure personality characteristics that are likely to foster certain kinds of behavior. In one of these studies, Meyer and Handler (1997) examined the effectiveness of the Rorschach Prognostic Rating Scale (RPRS) in predicting treatment response. The RPRS, introduced over 50 years ago by Klopfer, Kirkner, Wisham, and Baker (1951), draws on several Rorschach variables that measure reality testing, emotional integration, and self-realization to generate a composite score conceptualized as a measure of ego strength. Good ego strength is in turn generally considered to facilitate progress in psychotherapy. For 20 sets of data obtained from a total of 752 persons tested at the beginning of therapy, Meyer and Handler found an average effect size of .44 between the RPRS and independent ratings of psychological treatment outcomes 1 year later.

In the other study, Bornstein (1999) analyzed the validity of the Rorschach Oral Dependency scale (ROD), which combines several structural variables and content themes to yield an index conceived to measure a dependent personality orientation. Examining 21 studies, Bornstein found an average validity coefficient of .37 for effect sizes in relating ROD scores in 538 test protocols to independently observed dependency-related behaviors. More recently, the ROD has been demonstrated to predict such diverse behaviors as weight loss among obese persons being treated with behavior modification and both positive attachment behavior and excessive isolation among female inpatients diagnosed with borderline personality disorder (Elfhag, Rössner, Lindgren, Andersson, & Carlsson, 2004; Fowler, Brunnschweiler, Swales, & Brock, 2005).

Extending well beyond the boundaries of published meta-analyses, an extensive research base has documented the validity of Rorschach assessment when the instrument is used for its intended purposes. As described in the previously cited reviews by Viglione (1999), Viglione and Hilsenroth (2001), and Weiner (2001a, 2004b), this validation research has also demonstrated that Rorschach findings can show incremental validity as well, by contributing diagnostic and predictive information in addition to what can be gleaned from self-report and interview methods. As examples of this incremental validity, readers are referred to Rorschach research studies by Blais, Hilsenroth, Castlebury, Fowler, and Baity (2001), Hartmann, Sunde, Kristensen, and Martinussen (2003), Janson and Stattin (2003), Meyer (2000), and Perry (2001).

Readers should also be aware that the validity of Rorschach assessment has been demonstrated for a variety of reliable and useful scales that are not currently part of the CS. Some of these scales, like the previously mentioned RPRS, are based primarily on structural variables (see Handler & Clemence, 2005). Others, like the previously mentioned ROD scale, draw largely or in part on coding of thematic imagery as well (see Bornstein & Masling, 2005). Prominent among well-validated structural Rorschach scales currently in use, primarily for research purposes, are two measures of thinking disorder, the Thought Disorder Index (TDI) developed by Holzman and Johnston (see Holzman, Levy, & Johnston, 2005) and the Ego Impairment Index developed Perry and Viglione (see Auslander, Perry, & Jeste, 2002; Viglione, Perry, & Meyer, 2003). Frequently used and well-validated Rorschach research scales based largely on thematic imagery include the Mutuality of Autonomy (MOA), a measure of object relations developed by Urist (1977; see also Fowler &

Erdberg, 2005; Stricker & Gooen-Piels, 2004); the Primary Process scoring system (Pripro), a measure of psychological drives and defenses developed by Holt (see Holt, 2005); and the Lerner Defense Scale (see Lerner, 2005).

Based on a review of these and other research findings concerning the reliability and validity of Rorschach assessment, the Society for Personality Assessment issued in 2005 a formal statement that included the following conclusion:

> Overall, meta-analytic reviews and individual studies show the Rorschach possesses adequate psychometric properties. The research literature consistently demonstrates that the Rorschach can be scored reliably, has scores that measure important psychological functions, and has scores that provide unique information that cannot be obtained from other relevant instruments or clinical interviews. (Society for Personality Assessment, 2005, p. 220)

Normative Reference Data

As in the case of validating the RIM and other personality assessment instruments in appropriate ways against appropriate criteria, the accumulation of normative reference data for Rorschach scales and scores should proceed according to certain guidelines. First, the population that is sampled should be adequately representative of the persons with whom the instrument is likely to be used and sufficiently large to minimize error variance. Second, particularly for performance-based as opposed to self-report instruments, the data should be collected by experienced examiners who have been thoroughly trained in proper administration and coding. With specific respect to the RIM, summary scores emerging from an inadequate inquiry are highly likely to misrepresent the scores persons would have shown if their answers had been inquired properly. Third, participation in normative studies should be voluntary and anonymous, but efforts should be made to promote serious involvement on the part of the participants by stressing the importance of what they are being asked to do (see Weiner, 2001b).

The development of the Rorschach CS included the compilation of descriptive statistics for each of its codes and summary scores for a sample of 600 nonpatient adults age 19 to 69 (Mean of 31.7). As described by Exner (2003, chap. 12), this sample was randomly selected from a larger group of volunteer participants who were informed of the importance of what they were doing—helping to standardize a widely used personality test—and were examined by well-trained professional psychologists and research technicians. The sample was stratified to include an equal number of males and females and 120 persons from each of five geographic areas across the United States (Northeast, South, Midwest, Southwest, and West). This normative sample is also generally representative of United States demographic patterns of marital status, socioeconomic status, and urban-suburban-rural residence, and it includes 18% of African American, Latino, and Asian American individuals.

Two-thirds of the 600 persons in the nonpatient reference sample were recruited through their place of employment and were given time off from work to participate in the data collection. Another one-fourth were recruited through social or interest organizations (e.g., PTA groups, bowling leagues), and the remaining 8% through social service agencies. These 600 persons averaged 13.4 years of education, with 68% having attended college, and none of them had any significant history of mental health problems. As such, this nonpatient sample is representative of people who are relatively well-educated and appear to be functioning reasonably well socially and vocationally. Additional reference data are available for 1,390 nonpatient young people, ages 5 to 16, and for three groups of adult psychiatric patients: 328 first admission inpatients with schizophrenia, 279 patients hospitalized for depression, and 535 outpatients presenting a diversity of symptoms (Exner, 2001, chap. 11). Taken together, then, the CS reference data identify the frequency with which each of the Rorschach structural variables is likely to occur in nonpatient groups, in persons with various kinds of psychological disorder, and in young people at different ages.

Because Exner's reference data were collected mainly from 1973 to 1986, questions may be raised whether they remain adequately representative in the twenty-first century. Assessment instruments are commonly renormed after a generation has passed, and some late twentieth century data collected in California from samples of nonpatient adults ($n = 123$) and children ($n = 100$) appeared to show some differences from Exner's reference data and have received considerable attention in the literature (Hamel, Shaffer, & Erdberg, 2000; Shaffer, Erdberg, & Haroian, 1999).

However, in addition to involving rather small samples for a normative study, the California research fell short as well of the other just mentioned criteria for collecting reference data. The participants were recruited exclusively in California, with over 70% of the adult sample consisting of donors at a blood bank, and the Rorschach administrations were conducted entirely by graduate students in a research seminar. As also elaborated by Meyer (2001), the modest size and demographically unrepresentative nature of the California study samples and the collection of the data by inexperienced examiners limit the confidence that can be placed in the results. Moreover, the published results of the California studies do not describe any steps that were taken to promote serious test-taking attitudes in the participants.

A further source of concern about the current adequacy of the CS norms emerged from a 12-country collaborative international study of Rorschach structural data in nonpatient samples. As reported by Erdberg and Shaffer (2001), these studies have demonstrated many striking cross-cultural similarities in patterns of Rorschach responses, but also some notable differences from the U.S. norms published by Exner. More recently, the report by Shaffer et al. (2007) mentioned earlier in this chapter has expanded these international Rorschach reference data to include 20 adult samples involving 4,080 participants. Although this expanded data set continues to show considerable homogeneity for many Rorschach variables, there continue to be some differences among countries and from the CS data that call for some explanation. These differences have thus far suggested the following three possibilities, as elaborated by Eprhaim (2000) and Allen and Dana (2004).

First, the differences may be artifacts of variation in such sample characteristics as average level of education, which tends to be less in the international samples than in the CS nonpatient reference group. Second, if the cross-cultural differences are real and not artifactual, it may be that personality characteristics are manifest differently in different cultures. Should this be the case, the interpretive criteria for inferring these characteristics will have to be adjusted on the basis of culture-specific norms. For example, a Rorschach variable associated with dysphoric mood in one country when its frequency exceeds two (e.g., $C' > 2$ in the United States) may not become a marker for dysphoria in some other country until it exceeds three.

As the third possibility, Rorschach criterion scores for inferring personality characteristics may be universal and not culture specific. In this case, observed differences in normative Rorschach summary scores from one culture to another would reflect actual differences between them in modal personality patterns. For example, a relatively high average frequency of C' in one country could indicate that its people are on the average sadder or less happy than the people of another country in which the C' average is found to be lower. In other words, could there be "national character" patterns that would contribute to some actual cross-cultural differences in Rorschach responses? Interestingly in this regard, McCrae and Terracciano (2006) have concluded from international assessment findings with the Revised NEO Personality Inventory (see Chapter 10) that personality differences within cultural groups are larger than the differences between them and that perceptions of national character are unfounded stereotypes.

However this may be, Ritzler (2001, 2004) has pointed out that the RIM is a *culture-free* method, because research evidence indicates that its stimulus properties and standardized administration and coding generate relatively culture-free data, and also a *culture-sensitive* method, in that the differences in Rorschach findings between cultures are likely to be consistent with otherwise observed psychological differences between these cultures. Whatever future research may indicate about cross-cultural differences, however, the fact remains that Rorschach assessment is widely practiced and has proved useful in many different countries around the world.

These cross-cultural considerations aside, the current applicability of the CS reference data collected in 1973 through 1986 is an empirical question that must be answered by contemporary data. With this in mind, Exner in 1999 undertook a new normative data collection project for the purpose of updating the CS reference information. Following closely the procedures of the earlier work, participants were solicited to provide a demographically representative U.S. sample of 450 nonpatient adults, age 19 to 86, and these individuals were examined by experienced professional examiners according to a uniform and carefully formulated set of instructions. With just a few minor exceptions, the new CS reference data, as reported by Exner and Erdberg (2005, chap. 22), are strikingly similar to the older data and do not call for any major alterations in interpretive criteria.

Critics of the Rorschach have nevertheless alleged that the available CS reference data are outdated, inaccurate, and likely to overpathologize by identifying people as psychologically disturbed when they are functioning normally (Wood, Nezworski, Garb, & Lilienfeld, 2001). In support of this last allegation, Wood et al. (2001) cited an elevated frequency of indices of psychopathology in two participant samples: the previously mentioned California study of nonpatient adults, which suffers from serious methodological shortcomings; and a pool of control groups participating in 32 separate Rorschach studies, none of which had been designed for the purposes of collecting normative reference data. Quite the contrary, the sample characteristics and testing procedures in many of these studies make it unlikely that the control groups provided representative findings for adult nonpatients.

In particular, 16 of the 32 Wood et al. (2001) control samples consisted of college students or elderly persons, who commonly produce atypical test responses when used as volunteer participants in research studies. Five of the Wood et al. samples included current or former psychiatric patients, and 11 other samples were collected without any mental health screening. Participants in some of the Wood et al. samples were given the RIM under unusual conditions, which included being told to remain motionless during the testing, instructed not to touch the cards, or asked to wear electrodes on their heads. Rorschach findings obtained under such conditions from participant samples of this kind have little bearing on whether the CS norms are adequately representative of well-functioning nonpatient adults, nor can any scale elevations found in these circumstances be taken as evidence of overpathologizing under standard circumstances.

As for data collected under standard circumstances, the 450 nonpatient adults in the contemporary CS reference sample, like the 600 persons in the older reference sample, show little indication of being overpathologized by Rorschach assessment. The data in this regard are quite clear with respect to five major Rorschach indices of psychological disorder discussed earlier in this chapter. Among the 450 participants in the new normative sample, an elevated Perceptual Thinking Index ($PTI > 3$) occurred in just 1 (0%); an elevated Depression Index ($DEPI > 5$) occurred in just 18 (4%); an elevated Coping Deficit Index ($CDI > 3$) occurred in just 39 (9%); a positive Hypvervigilance Index (HVI) occurred in just 20 (4%); and a D-score < -1 occurred in just 28 (6%). In other words, it is extremely unusual and far from commonplace for reasonably well-functioning nonpatients to show Rorschach indications of psychopathology, and elevations in the indices just mentioned are much more likely to reflect significant adjustment difficulties than errors of measurement.

In addition to allegations of overpathologizing, which the contemporary normative data prove to be groundless, Rorschach critics have also questioned the appropriateness of Rorschach assessment in multicultural settings. According to Wood and Lilienfeld (1999), "Blacks, Hispanics, Native Americans, and non-Americans score differently on important Rorschach variables" (p. 342). Without reporting any specific data in support of this allegation, these authors concluded, "Because there are important cross-cultural differences, and because appropriate norms have not been developed, it is doubtful whether the Comprehensive System should be used to evaluate members of American minority groups" (p. 341).

The facts of the matter are quite different. In the first place, as noted, cross-cultural differences in obtained personality test scores, if demonstrated to be real rather than artifactual, may reflect actual cultural differences in personality characteristics and have no necessary implications for the appropriateness of using a test with diverse cultures. Second, recent studies with American minority groups indicate that there are no substantial CS differences among them. Presley, Smith, Hilsenroth, and Exner (2001) found a clinically significant difference on only 1 of 23 core Rorschach variables between 44 African Americans and 44 demographically matched Caucasian Americans from the CS nonpatient reference sample. In a multicultural patient sample of 432 consecutive persons evaluated in a hospital-based psychological testing program, Meyer (2002) found no association between ethnicity and 188 Rorschach summary scores among demographically matched European American, African American, Hispanic American, Asian American, and Native American individuals. Meyer concluded from his findings that "the available data clearly support the cross-ethnic use of the Comprehensive system" (p. 127).

Finally, with respect to the CS reference data, like the retest reliability findings they provide implicit evidence of the construct validity associated with Rorschach assessment. As an example related to indications of psychological disorder, the nonpatient, outpatient, inpatient depressive, and inpatient schizophrenic samples for which CS reference data are available can reasonably be considered to represent increasing severity of disturbance.

Major Rorschach indices of psychological disturbance include the X-% (an index of impaired reality testing) and the *WSum6* (an index of disordered thinking). If X-% and *WSum6* are valid measures of disturbance, they should increase in linear fashion across these four reference groups—and they do, as shown by the Exner (2001, chap. 11) reference data.

A second example of construct validity demonstrated by the normative reference data concerns developmental changes in young people. The previously noted increasing stability of Rorschach structural variables from childhood into adolescence, consistent with the gradual consolidation of personality characteristics, is a case in point. Among specific changes occurring with maturation, young people are known to become less self-centered (less egocentric) and increasingly capable of moderating their affect (less emotionally intense). The RIM Egocentricity Index is conceptualized as a measure of self-centeredness, and the balance between presumed indices of relatively mature emotionality (*FC*) and relatively immature emotionality (*CF*) is conceptualized as an indication of affect moderation.

If these variables are valid measures of what they are posited to measure, their average values should change in the expected direction among children and adolescents at different ages—and they do. In the CS reference data, the mean Egocentricity Index of .67 at age 6 decreases in almost linear fashion to .43 at age 16, which is just slightly higher than the adult mean of .40. The mean for *FC* increases steadily over time from 1.11 at age 6 to 3.43 at age 16 (compared with an adult mean of 3.56), while the mean for *CF* decreases from 3.51 to 2.78 between age 6 and 16 (the adult mean is 2.41).

The present chapter has been concerned mainly with the Rorschach assessment of adults and older adolescents. In closing the chapter, it is important to note that the RIM can also be used to good effect in evaluating children and early adolescents. Assessors working with young people will profit from consulting Erdberg (2007), Exner and Weiner (1995), and Leichtman (1996) in this regard.

REFERENCES

Ackerman, M. J., & Ackerman, M. C. (1997). Custody evaluations in practice: A survey of experienced professionals (revisited). *Professional Psychology, 28,* 137–145.

Acklin, M. W., McDowell, C. J., Verschell, M. S., & Chan, D. (2000). Interobserver agreement, intraobserver agreement, and the Rorschach Comprehensive System. *Journal of Personality Assessment, 74,* 15–57.

Allard, G., & Faust, D. (2000). Errors in scoring objective personality tests. *Assessment, 7,* 119–129.

Allen, J., & Dana, R. H. (2004). Methodological issues in cross-cultural and multicultural Rorschach research. *Journal of Personality Assessment, 82,* 189–206.

Archer, R. P., Buffington-Vollum, J. K., Stredny, R. V., & Handel, R. W. (2006). A survey of psychological test use patterns among forensic psychologists. *Journal of Personality Assessment, 87,* 84–94.

Archer, R. P., & Newsom, C. R. (2000). Psychological test usage with adolescent clients: Survey update. *Assessment, 7,* 227–235.

Armstrong, J., & Kaser-Boyd, N. (2004). Projective assessment of psychological trauma. In M. J. Hilsenroth & D. L Segal (Eds.), *Comprehensive handbook of psychological assessment: Vol. 2. Personality assessment* (pp. 500–512). Hoboken, NJ: Wiley.

Aronow, E., & Reznikoff, M. (1976). *Rorschach content interpretation.* New York: Grune & Stratton.

Aronow, E., Reznikoff, M., & Moreland, K. L. (1994). *The Rorschach technique*. Boston: Allyn & Bacon.

Auslander, L. A., Perry, W., & Jeste, D. V. (2002). Assessing disturbed thinking and cognition using the Ego Impairment Index in older schizophrenic patients: Paranoid vs. nonparanoid distinction. *Schizophrenia Research, 53*, 199–207.

Beck, S. J. (1930a). Personality diagnosis by means of the Rorschach test. *American Journal of Orthopsychiatry, 1*, 81–88.

Beck, S. J. (1930b). The Rorschach test and personality diagnosis. *American Journal of Psychiatry, 10*, 19–52.

Beck, S. J. (1937). *Introduction to the Rorschach method: American Orthopsychiatric Association Monograph I*. New York: American Orthopsychiatric Association.

Beck, S. J. (1944). *Rorschach's test: Vol. I. Basic processes*. New York: Grune & Stratton.

Blais, M. A., Hilsenroth, M. J., Castlebury, F., Fowler, J. C., & Baity, M. R. (2001). Predicting DSM-IV Cluster B personality disorder criteria from MMPI-2 and Rorschach data: A test of incremental validity. *Journal of Personality Assessment, 76*, 150–168.

Blatt, S. J., & Ford, R. Q. (1994). *Therapeutic change*. New York: Plenum Press.

Boccaccini, M. T., & Brodsky, S. L. (1999). Diagnostic test usage by forensic psychologists in emotional injury cases. *Professional Psychology, 30*, 253–259.

Bornstein, R. F. (1999). Criterion validity of objective and projective dependency tests: A meta-analytic assessment of behavioral prediction. *Psychological Assessment, 11*, 48–57.

Bornstein, R. F., & Masling, J. M. (2005). The Rorschach Oral Dependency scale. In R. F. Bornstein & J. M. Masling (Eds.), *Scoring the Rorschach: Seven validated systems* (pp. 135–158). Mahwah, NJ: Erlbaum.

Borum, R., & Grisso, T. (1995). Psychological test use in criminal forensic evaluations. *Professional Psychology, 26*, 465–473.

Buros, O. K. (Ed.). (1974). *Tests in print II*. Highland Park, NJ: Gryphon.

Butcher, J. N., & Rouse, S. V. (1996). Personality: Individual differences and clinical assessment. *Annual Review of Psychology, 47*, 87–111.

Camara, W., Nathan, J., & Puente, A. (2000). Psychological test usage: Implications in professional psychology. *Professional Psychology, 31*, 141–154.

Cashel, M. L. (2002). Child and adolescent psychological assessment: Current clinical practices and the impact of managed care. *Professional Psychology: Research and Practice, 33*, 446–453.

Clarkin, J. F., & Levy, K. N. (2004). The influence of client variables on psychotherapy. In M. J. Lambert (Ed.), *Bergin and Garfield's handbook of psychotherapy and behavior change* (5th ed., pp. 194–226). Hoboken, NJ: Wiley.

Clemence, A., & Handler, L. (2001). Psychological assessment on internship: A survey of training directors and their expectations for students. *Journal of Personality Assessment, 76*, 18–47.

Dao, T. K., & Prevatt, F. (2006). A psychometric evaluation of the Rorschach Comprehensive System's Perceptual Thinking Index. *Journal of Personality Assessment, 86*, 180–189.

Elfhag, K., Barkeling, B., Carlsson, A. M., & Rössner, S. (2003). Microstructure of eating behavior associated with Rorschach characteristics in obesity. *Journal of Personality Assessment, 81*, 40–50.

Elfhag, K., Rössner, S., Lindgren, T., Andersson, I., & Carlsson, A. M. (2004). Rorschach personality predictors of weight loss with behavior modification in obesity treatment. *Journal of Personality Assessment, 83*, 293–305.

Eprhaim, D. (2000). Culturally relevant research and practice with the Rorschach Comprehensive System. In R. H. Dana (Ed.), *Handbook of cross-cultural and multicultural personality assessment* (pp. 303–328). Mahwah, NJ: Erlbaum.

Erard, R. E. (2005). What the Rorschach can contribute to child custody and parenting time evaluations. *Journal of Child Custody, 2*, 119–142.

Erdberg, P. (2007). Using the Rorschach with children. In S. R. Smith & L. Handler (Eds.), *The clinical assessment of children and adolescents* (pp. 139–147). Mahwah, NJ: Erlbaum.

Erdberg, P., & Shaffer, T. W. (2001, March). *International Symposium on Rorschach nonpatient data: Worldwide findings.* Symposium conducted at the annual meeting of the Society for Personality Assessment, Philadelphia.

Ewing, C. P. (2003). Expert testimony: Law and practice. In I. B. Weiner (Editor-in-Chief) & A. M. Goldstein (Vol. Ed.), *Handbook of psychology: Vol. 11. Forensic psychology* (pp. 55–66). Hoboken, NJ: Wiley.

Exner, J. E., Jr., (1969). *The Rorschach systems.* New York: Grune & Stratton.

Exner, J. E., Jr., (1974). *The Rorschach: A comprehensive system.* New York: Wiley.

Exner, J. E., Jr., (2001). *A Rorschach workbook for the comprehensive system* (5th ed.). Asheville, NC: Rorschach Workshops.

Exner, J. E., Jr., (2003). *The Rorschach: A comprehensive system: Vol. I. Basic foundations and principles of interpretation* (4th ed.). Hoboken, NJ: Wiley.

Exner, J. E., Jr., & Andronikof-Sanglade, A. (1992). Rorschach changes following brief and short-term therapy. *Journal of Personality Assessment, 59,* 59–71.

Exner, J. E., Jr., Armbruster, G. L., & Viglione, D. (2001). The temporal stability of some Rorschach features. *Journal of Personality Assessment, 42,* 474–482.

Exner, J. E., Jr., & Erdberg, P. (2005). *The Rorschach: A comprehensive system: Vol. 2. Advanced interpretation* (3rd ed.). Hoboken, NJ: Wiley.

Exner, J. E., Jr., Thomas, E. A., & Mason, B. (1985). Children's Rorschachs: Description and prediction. *Journal of Personality Assessment, 49,* 13–20.

Exner, J. E., Jr., & Weiner, I. B. (1995). *The Rorschach: A comprehensive system: Vol. 3. Assessment of children and adolescents* (2nd ed.). New York: Wiley.

Exner, J. E., Jr., & Weiner, I. B. (2003). *Rorschach interpretation assistance program, Version 5(RIAP5).* Lutz, FL: Psychological Assessment Resources.

Fowler, J. C., Ackerman, S. J., Speanburg, S., Bailey, A., Blagys, M., & Conklin, A. C. (2004). Personality and symptom change in treatment-refractory inpatients: Evaluation of the phase model of change using Rorschach, TAT, and DSM-IV Axis V. *Journal of Personality Assessment, 83,* 306–322.

Fowler, J. C., Brunnschweiler, B., Swales, S., & Brock, J. (2005). Assessment of Rorschach dependency measures in female inpatients diagnosed with borderline disorder. *Journal of Personality Assessment, 85,* 146–153.

Fowler, J. C., & Erdberg, P. (2005). The Mutuality of Autonomy scale: An implicit measure of object relations for the Rorschach Inkblot Method. *South African Rorschach Journal, 2,* 3–10.

Fowler, J. C., Piers, C., Hilsenroth, M. J., Holdwick, D. J., Jr., & Padawer, J. R. (2001). The Rorschach Suicide Constellation: Assessing various degrees of lethality. *Journal of Personality Assessment, 76,* 333–351.

Gacono, C. B. (Ed.). (2000). *The clinical and forensic assessment of psychopathy.* Mahwah, NJ: Erlbaum.

Gacono, C. B., Evans, F. B., Kaser-Boyd, N., & Gacono, L. (Eds.). (in press). *Handbook of forensic Rorschach psychology.* Mahwah, NJ: Erlbaum.

Gacono, C. B., & Meloy, J. R. (1994). *Rorschach assessment of aggressive and psychopathic personalities.* Hillsdale, NJ: Erlbaum.

Ganellen, R. J. (2005). Rorschach contributions to assessment of suicide risk. In R. I. Yufit & D. Lester (Eds.), *Assessment, treatment, and prevention of suicidal behavior* (pp. 93–119). Hoboken, NJ: Wiley.

Garb, H. N. (1999). Call for a moratorium on the use of the Rorschach Inkblot Test in clinical and forensic settings. *Assessment, 6,* 311–318.

Garb, H. N., Wood, J. M., Nezworski, M. T., Grove, W. M., & Stejskal, W. J. (2001). Toward a resolution of the Rorschach controversy. *Psychological Assessment, 13*, 433–448.

Goldstein, A. M., Morse, S. J., & Shapiro, D. L. (2003). Evaluation of criminal responsibility. In I. B. Weiner (Editor-in-Chief) & A. M. Goldstein (Vol. Ed.), *Handbook of psychology: Vol. 11. Forensic psychology* (pp. 381–406). Hoboken, NJ: Wiley.

Greenberg, S. A. (2003). Personal injury examinations in torts for emotional distress. In I. B. Weiner (Editor-in-Chief) & A. M. Goldstein (Vol. Ed.), *Handbook of psychology: Vol. 11. Forensic psychology* (pp. 233–257). Hoboken, NJ: Wiley.

Greenway, P., & Milne, L. C. (2001). Rorschach tolerance and control of stress measures *D* and *AdjD:* Beliefs about how well subjective states and reactions can be controlled. *European Journal of Psychological Assessment, 17*, 137–144.

Grønnerød, C. (2003). Temporal stability in the Rorschach method: A meta-analytic review. *Journal of Personality Assessment, 80*, 272–293.

Grønnerød, C. (2006). Reanalysis of the Grønnerød. (2003). Rorschach temporal stability meta-analysis set. *Journal of Personality Assessment, 86*, 222–225.

Grove, W. M., & Barden, R. C. (1999). Protecting the integrity of the legal system: The admissibility of testimony from mental health experts under *Daubert/Kumho* analysis. *Psychology, Public Policy, and Law, 5*, 224–242.

Guarnaccia, V., Dill, C. A., Sabatino, S., & Southwick, S. (2001). Scoring accuracy using the Comprehensive System for the Rorschach. *Journal of Personality Assessment, 77*, 464–474.

Hamel, M., Shaffer, T. W., & Erdberg, P. (2000). A study of nonpatient preadolescent Rorschach protocols. *Journal of Personality Assessment, 75*, 280–294.

Handler, L., & Clemence, A. J. (2005). The Rorschach Prognostic Rating scale. In R. F. Bornstein & J. M. Masling (Eds.), *Scoring the Rorschach: Seven validated systems* (pp. 1–24). Mahwah, NJ: Erlbaum.

Hartmann, E., Norbech, P. B., & Grønnerød, C. (2006). Psychopathic and nonpsychopathic violent offenders on the Rorschach: Discriminative features and comparisons with schizophrenic inpatient and university student samples. *Journal of Personality Assessment, 86*, 291–305.

Hartmann, E., Sunde, T., Kristensen, W., & Martinussen, M. (2003). Psychological measures as predictors of military training performance. *Journal of Personality Assessment, 80*, 87–98.

Hess, A. K. (2006). Serving as an expert witness. In I. B. Weiner & A. K. Hess (Eds.), *Handbook of forensic psychology* (3rd ed., pp. 652–700). Hoboken, NJ: Wiley.

Hiller, J. B., Rosenthal, R., Bornstein, R. F., Berry, D. T. R., & Brunner-Neuleib, S. (1999). A comparative meta-analysis of Rorschach validity. *Psychological Assessment, 11*, 278–296.

Hilsenroth, M. J., & Stricker, G. (2004). A consideration of attacks upon psychological assessment instruments used in forensic settings: Rorschach as exemplar. *Journal of Personality Assessment, 83*, 141–152.

Hogan, T. P. (2005). 50 widely used psychological tests. In G. P. Koocher, J. C. Norcross, & S. S. Hill III (Eds.), *Psychologists' desk reference* (2nd ed., pp. 101–104). New York: Oxford University Press.

Holt, R. R. (2005). The Pripro scoring system. In R. F. Bornstein & J. M. Masling (Eds.), *Scoring the Rorschach: Seven validated systems* (pp. 191–236). Mahwah, NJ: Erlbaum.

Holzman, P. S., Levy, D. L., & Johnston, M. H. (2005). The use of the Rorschach technique for assessing formal thought disorder. In R. F. Bornstein & J. M. Masling (Eds.), *Scoring the Rorschach: Seven validated systems* (pp. 55–96). Mahwah, NJ: Erlbaum.

Hunsley, J., & Bailey, J. M. (1999). The clinical utility of the Rorschach: Unfulfilled promises and an uncertain future. *Psychological Assessment, 11*, 266–277.

Huprich, S. K. (Ed.). (2006). *Rorschach assessment of the personality disorders.* Mahwah, NJ: Erlbaum.

Ilonen, T., Taiminen, T., Karlsson, H., Lauerma, H., Leinonen, K.-M., Wallenius, E., et al. (1999). Diagnostic efficiency of the Rorschach schizophrenia and depression indices in identifying first-episode schizophrenia and severe depression. *Psychiatry Research, 87*, 183–193.

Janson, H., & Stattin, H. (2003). Predictions of adolescent and adult delinquency from childhood Rorschach ratings. *Journal of Personality Assessment, 81*, 51–63.

Johnston, J. R., Walters, M. G., & Olesen, N. W. (2005). Clinical ratings of parenting capacity and Rorschach protocols of custody-disputing parents: An exploratory study. *Journal of Child Custody, 2*, 159–178.

Kelly, F. D. (1999). *The psychological assessment of abused and traumatized children*. Mahwah, NJ: Erlbaum.

Kleiger, J. H. (1999). *Disordered thinking and the Rorschach*. Hillsdale, NJ: Analytic Press.

Klopfer, B., Ainsworth, M. D., Klopfer, W. G., & Holt, R. R. (1954). *Developments in the Rorschach technique: Vol. I. Technique and theory*. Yonkers-on-Hudson, NY: World Books.

Klopfer, B., & Kelley, D. M. (1942). *The Rorschach technique*. Yonkers-on-Hudson, NY: World Books.

Klopfer, B., Kirkner, F., Wisham, W., & Baker, G. (1951). Rorschach Prognostic Rating scale. *Journal of Projective Techniques and Personality Assessment, 15*, 425–428.

Leichtman, M. (1996). *The Rorschach: A developmental perspective*. Hillsdale, NJ: Analytic Press.

Lerner, P. M. (1998). *Psychoanalytic perspective on the Rorschach*. Hillsdale, NJ: Analytic Press.

Lerner, P. M. (2005). Defense and its assessment: The Lerner Defense scale. In R. F. Bornstein & J. M. Masling (Eds.), *Scoring the Rorschach: Seven validated systems* (pp. 237–270). Mahwah, NJ: Erlbaum.

Lilienfeld, S. O., Wood, J. M., & Garb, H. N. (2000). The scientific status of projective techniques. *Psychological Science in the Public Interest, 1*, 27–66.

Luxenberg, T., & Levin, P. (2004). The role of the Rorschach in the assessment and treatment of trauma. In J. P. Wilson & T. M. Keane (Eds.), *Assessing psychological trauma and PTSD* (2nd ed., pp. 190–225). New York: Guilford Press.

McCann, J. T. (1998). Defending the Rorschach in court: An analysis of admissibility using legal and professional standards. *Journal of Personality Assessment, 70*, 125–144.

McCann, J. T. (2004). Projective assessment of personality in forensic settings. In M. Hersen (Editor-in-Chief), M. J. Hilseroth, & D. L. Segal (Vol. Eds.), *Comprehensive handbook of psychological assessment: Vol. 2. Personality assessment* (pp. 562–572). Hoboken, NJ: Wiley.

McCann, J. T., & Evans, F. B. (in press). Admissibility of the Rorschach. In C. B. Gacono, F. B. Evans, N. Kaser-Boyd, & L. Gacono (Eds.), *Handbook of forensic Rorschach psychology*. Mahwah, NJ: Erlbaum.

McCrae, R. R., & Terracciano, A. (2006). National character and personality. *Current Directions in Psychological Science, 15*, 156–161.

McGrath, R. E. (2003). Enhancing accuracy in observational test scoring: The Comprehensive System as a case example. *Journal of Personality Assessment, 81*, 104–110.

McGrath, R. E., Pogge, D. L., Stokes, J. M., Cragnolino, A., Zaccario, M., Hayman, J., et al. (2005). Field reliability of Comprehensive System scoring in an adolescent inpatient sample. *Assessment, 12*, 199–209. [11]

Meloy, J. R. (2007). The authority of the Rorschach: An update. In C. B. Gacono, F. B. Evans, N. Kaser-Boyd, & L. Gacono (Eds.), *Handbook of forensic Rorschach psychology* (pp. 79–87). Mahwah, NJ: Erlbaum.

Meloy, J. R., Hansen, T., & Weiner, I. B. (1997). Authority of the Rorschach: Legal citations in the past 50 years. *Journal of Personality Assessment, 69*, 53–62.

Meyer, G. J. (1997a). Assessing reliability: Critical corrections for a critical examination of the Rorschach Comprehensive System. *Psychological Assessment, 9*, 480–489.

Meyer, G. J. (1997b). Thinking clearly about reliability: More critical corrections regarding the Rorschach Comprehensive System. *Psychological Assessment, 9*, 495–598.

Meyer, G. J. (2000). The incremental validity of the Rorschach Prognostic Rating scale over the MMPI Ego Strength scale and IQ. *Journal of Personality Assessment, 74*, 356–370.

Meyer, G. J. (2001). Evidence to correct misperceptions about Rorschach norms. *Clinical Psychology: Science and Practice, 8*, 389–396.

Meyer, G. J. (2002). Exploring possible ethnic differences and bias in the Rorschach Comprehensive System. *Journal of Personality Assessment, 78*, 104–129.

Meyer, G. J. (2004). The reliability and validity of the Rorschach and Thematic Apperception Test (TAT) compared to other psychological and medical procedures: An analysis of systematically gathered evidence. In M. Hersen (Editor-in-Chief), M. Hilsenroth, & D. Segal (Vol. Eds.), *Comprehensive handbook of psychological assessment: Vol. 2. Personality assessment* (pp. 315–342). Hoboken, NJ: Wiley.

Meyer, G. J., & Archer, R. P. (2001). The hard science of Rorschach research: What do we know and where do we go? *Psychological Assessment, 13*, 486–502.

Meyer, G. J., & Handler, L. (1997). The ability of the Rorschach to predict subsequent outcome: Meta-analysis of the Rorschach Prognostic Rating scale. *Journal of Personality Assessment, 69*, 1–38.

Meyer, G. J., Hilsenroth, M. J., Baxter, D., Exner, J. E., Jr., Fowler, J. C., Pers, C. C., et al. (2002). An examination of interrater reliability for scoring the Rorschach Comprehensive System in eight data sets. *Journal of Personality Assessment, 78*, 219–274.

Meyer, J. G., Mihura, J. L., & Smith, B. L. (2005). The interclinician reliability of Rorschach interpretation in four data sets. *Journal of Personality Assessment, 84*, 296–314.

Meyer, G. J., & Viglione, D. J. (in press). Scientific status of the Rorschach. In C. B. Gacono, F. B. Evans, N. Kaser-Boyd, & L. Gacono (Eds.), *Handbook of forensic Rorschach psychology*. Mahwah, NJ: Erlbaum.

Monahan, J. (2003). Violence risk assessment. In I. B. Weiner (Editor-in-Chief) & A. M. Goldstein (Vol. Ed.), *Handbook of psychology: Vol. 11. Forensic psychology* (pp. 527–540). Hoboken, NJ: Wiley.

Muniz, J., Prieto, G., Almeida, L., & Bartram, D. (1999). Test use in Spain, Portugal, and Latin American countries. *European Journal of Psychological Assessment, 15*, 151–157.

Ogawa, T. (2004). Developments of the Rorschach in Japan: A brief introduction. *South African Rorschach Journal, 1*, 40–45.

Perry, W. (2001). Incremental validity of the Ego Impairment Index: A reexamination of Dawes (1999). *Psychological Assessment, 13*, 403–407.

Phillips, L., & Smith, J. G. (1953). *Rorschach interpretation: Advanced technique*. New York: Grune & Stratton.

Piotrowski, Z. A. (1957). *Perceptanalysis*. New York: Macmillan.

Presley, G., Smith, C., Hilsenroth, M., & Exner, J. (2001). Clinical utility of the Rorschach with African Americans. *Journal of Personality Assessment, 78*, 104–129.

Quinnell, F. A., & Bow, J. N. (2001). Psychological tests used in child custody evaluations. *Behavioral Sciences and the Law, 19*, 491–501.

Rapaport, D., Gill, M., & Schafer, R. (1968). *Diagnostic psychological testing* (Rev. ed.). New York: International Universities Press. (Original work published 1946)

Ritsher, J. B. (2004). Association of Rorschach and MMPI psychosis indicators and schizophrenia-spectrum diagnoses in a Russian clinical sample. *Journal of Personality Assessment, 38*, 46–63.

Ritzler, B. (2001). Multicultural usage of the Rorschach. In L. Suzuki, J. Ponterotto, & P. Meller (Eds.), *Handbook of multicultural assessment* (pp. 237–252). San Francisco: Jossey-Bass.

Ritzler, B. (2004). Cultural applications of the Rorschach, apperception tests, and figure drawings. In M. Hersen (Editor-in-Chief), M. J. Hilsenroth, & D. L. Segal (Vol. Eds.), *Comprehensive handbook of psychological assessment: Vol. 2. Personality assessment* (pp. 573–585). Hoboken, NJ: Wiley.

Ritzler, B., Erard, R., & Pettigrew, T. (2002). Protecting the integrity of Rorschach expert witnesses: A reply to Grove and Barden (1999) re: The admissibility of testimony under Daubert/Kumho analysis. *Psychology, Public Policy, and the Law, 8*(2), 201–215.

Rorschach, H. (1942). *Psychodiagnostics: A diagnostic test based on perception.* Bern, Switzerland: Hans Huber. (Original work published 1921)

Rosenthal, R., Hiller, J. G., Bornstein, R. F., Berry, D. T. R., & Brunell-Neuleib, S. (2001). Meta-analytic methods, the Rorschach, and the MMPI. *Psychological Assessment, 13*, 449–451.

Schafer, R. (1948). *Clinical application of psychological tests.* New York: International Universities Press.

Schafer, R. (1954). *Psychoanalytic interpretation in Rorschach testing.* New York: Grune & Stratton.

Schafer, R. (2006). My life in testing. *Journal of Personality Assessment, 86*, 235–241.

Shaffer, T. W., Erdberg, P., & Haroian, J. (1999). Current nonpatient data for the Rorschach, WAIS, and MMPI-2. *Journal of Personality Assessment, 73*, 305–316.

Shaffer, T. W., Erdberg, P., & Meyer, G. J. (Eds.). (2007). International reference sample for the Rorschach comprehensive system [Special issue]. *Journal of Personality Assessment, 89* (Suppl. 1).

Sloane, P., Arsenault, L., & Hilsenroth, M. (2002). Use of the Rorschach in the assessment of war-related stress in military personnel. *Rorschachiana, 25*, 86–122.

Smith, S., Baity, M. R., Knowles, E. S., & Hilsenroth, M. J. (2001). Assessment of disordered thinking in children and adolescents: The Rorschach Perceptual-Thinking Index. *Journal of Personality Assessment, 77*, 447–463.

Society for Personality Assessment. (2005). The status of the Rorschach in clinical and forensic practice: An official statement by the Board of Trustees of the Society for Personality Assessment. *Journal of Personality Assessment, 85*, 219–237.

Stafford, K. P. (2003). Assessment of competence to stand trial. In I. B. Weiner (Editor-in-Chief) & A. M. Goldstein (Vol. Ed.), *Handbook of psychology: Vol. 11. Forensic psychology* (pp. 359–380). Hoboken, NJ: Wiley.

Stedman, J., Hatch, J., & Schoenfeld, L. (2000). Preinternship preparation in psychological testing and psychotherapy: What internship directors say they expect. *Professional Psychology, 31*, 321–326.

Stricker, G., & Gooen-Piels, J. (2004). Projective assessment of object relations. In M. Hersen (Editor-in-Chief), M. J. Hilsenroth, & D. L. Segal (Vol. Eds.), *Comprehensive handbook of psychological assessment: Vol. 2. Personality assessment* (pp. 449–465). Hoboken, NJ: Wiley.

Urist, J. (1977). The Rorschach test and the assessment of object relations. *Journal of Personality Assessment, 41*, 3–9.

Viglione, D. J. (1999). A review of recent research addressing the utility of the Rorschach. *Psychological Assessment, 11*, 251–265.

Viglione, D. J. (2002). *Rorschach coding solutions: A reference guide for the comprehensive system.* San Diego, CA: Author.

Viglione, D. J., & Hilsenroth, M. J. (2001). The Rorschach: Facts, fictions, and future. *Psychological Assessment, 11*, 251–265.

Viglione, D. J., Perry, W., & Meyer, G. (2003). Refinements in the Rorschach Ego Impairment Index incorporating the human representational variable. *Journal of Personality Assessment, 81*, 149–156.

Viglione, D. J., & Taylor, N. (2003). Empirical support for interrater reliability of Rorschach comprehensive system coding. *Journal of Clinical Psychology, 59*, 111–121.

Weiner, I. B. (1996). Some observations on the validity of the Rorschach Inkblot Method. *Psychological Assessment, 8*, 206–213.

Weiner, I. B. (1998). *Principles of psychotherapy* (2nd ed.). New York: Wiley.

Weiner, I. B. (1999). Contemporary perspectives on Rorschach assessment. *European Journal of Psychological Assessment, 15*, 78–86.

Weiner, I. B. (2001a). Advancing the science of psychological assessment: The Rorschach Inkblot Method as exemplar. *Psychological Assessment, 13*, 423–432.

Weiner, I. B. (2001b). Considerations in collecting Rorschach reference data. *Journal of Personality Assessment, 77*, 122–127.

Weiner, I. B. (2003a). Prediction and postdiction in clinical decision making. *Clinical Psychology, 10*, 335–338.

Weiner, I. B. (2003b). *Principles of Rorschach interpretation* (2nd ed.). Mahwah, NJ: Erlbaum.

Weiner, I. B. (2004a). Monitoring psychotherapy with performance-based measures of personality functioning. *Journal of Personality Assessment, 83*, 323–331.

Weiner, I. B. (2004b). Rorschach assessment: Current status. In M. Hersen (Editor-in-Chief), M. J. Hilsenroth, & D. L. Segal (Vol. Eds.), *Comprehensive handbook of psychological assessment: Vol. 2. Personality assessment* (pp. 343–355). Hoboken, NJ: Wiley.

Weiner, I. B. (2005a). Rorschach assessment in child custody cases. *Journal of Child Custody, 2*, 99–120.

Weiner, I. B. (2005b). Rorschach Inkblot Method. In M. Maruish (Ed.), *The use of psychological testing in treatment planning and outcome evaluation* (3rd ed., Vol. 3, pp. 553–588). Mahwah, NJ: Erlbaum.

Weiner, I. B. (2006). The Rorschach Inkblot Method. In R. P. Archer (Ed.), *Forensic uses of clinical assessment instruments* (pp. 181–207). Mahwah, NJ: Erlbaum.

Weiner, I. B. (2007). Rorschach assessment in forensic cases. In A. M. Goldstein (Ed.), *Forensic psychology: Emerging topics and expanding roles* (pp. 127–153). Hoboken, NJ: Wiley.

Weiner, I. B. (in press). Presenting and defending Rorschach testimony. In C. B. Gacono, F. B. Evans, N. Kaser-Boyd, & L. Gacono (Eds.), *Handbook of forensic Rorschach psychology*. Mahwah, NJ: Erlbaum.

Weiner, I. B., & Exner, J. E., Jr. (1991). Rorschach changes in long-term and short-term psychotherapy. *Journal of Personality Assessment, 56*, 453–465.

Weiner, I. B., Exner, J. E., Jr., & Sciara, A. (1996). Is the Rorschach welcome in the courtroom? *Journal of Personality Assessment, 67*, 422–424.

Wood, J. M., & Lilienfeld, S. O. (1999). The Rorschach Inkblot Tests: A case of overstatement? *Assessment, 6*, 341–349.

Wood, J. M., Nezworski, M. T., Garb, H. N., & Lilienfeld, S. O. (2001). The misperception of psychopathology: Problems with the norms of the comprehensive system. *Clinical Psychology: Science and Practice, 8*, 360–373.

Zapf, P. A., Golding, S. L., & Roesch, R. (2006). Criminal responsibility and the insanity defense. In I. B. Weiner & A. K. Hess (Eds.), *Handbook of forensic psychology* (3rd ed., pp. 332–364). Hoboken, NJ: Wiley.

Zapf, P. A., & Roesch, R. (2006). Competency to stand trial. In I. B. Weiner & A. K. Hess (Eds.), *Handbook of forensic psychology* (3rd ed., pp. 305–331). Hoboken, NJ: Wiley.

Chapter 12 ———————————————————————

THEMATIC APPERCEPTION TEST

Like the Rorschach Inkblot Method (RIM) discussed in the preceding chapter, the Thematic Apperception Test (TAT) is a performance-based measure of personality. This means that TAT data consist of how people respond to a task they are given to do, not what they may say about themselves. In further contrast to self-report measures, the TAT resembles the RIM in providing an indirect rather than a direct assessment of personality characteristics, which makes it particularly helpful in identifying characteristics that people do not fully recognize in themselves or are reluctant to disclose.

The TAT is a storytelling technique in which examinees are shown pictures of people or scenes and asked to make up a story about them. The TAT differs from the RIM in three key respects. First, being real pictures rather than blots of ink, the TAT stimuli are more structured and less ambiguous than the Rorschach cards. Second, the TAT instructions are more open-ended and less structured than those used in administering the RIM. Rorschach examinees are questioned specifically about where they saw their percepts and what made them look as they did. On the TAT, as elaborated in the present chapter, people are asked only in general terms to expand on the stories they tell (e.g., "What is the person thinking?"). Third, the TAT requires people to exercise their imagination, whereas the RIM is a measure of perception and association. Rorschach examinees who ask whether to use their imagination should be told, "No, this is not a test of imagination; just say what the blots look like and what you see in them." By contrast, TAT takers who say "I'm not sure what the people in the picture are doing," or "I don't know what the outcome will be," can be told, "This is a test of imagination; make something up."

This distinction between the RIM and the TAT accounts for the TAT having been called an *apperceptive* test. As elaborated in Chapter 11, the RIM was originally designed as a test of perception that focused on what people see in the test stimuli, where they see it, and why it looks as it does. The TAT was intended to focus instead on how people interpret what they see and the meaning they attach to their interpretations, and the term "apperception" was chosen to designate this process. The development of the TAT is discussed further following the description of the test.

NATURE OF THE THEMATIC APPERCEPTION TEST

The Thematic Apperception Test (TAT) consists of 31 achromatic cards measuring $9\frac{1}{4} \times 11$ inches. Fourteen of the cards show a picture of a single person, 11 cards depict two or more people engaged in some kind of relationship, three are group pictures of three or four people, two portray nature scenes, and one is totally blank. The cards are numbered from

1 to 20, and nine of the cards are additionally designated by letters intended to indicate their appropriateness for boys (B) and girls (G) aged 4 to 14, males (M) and females (F) aged 15 or older, or some combination of these characteristics (as in 3BM, 6GF, 12BG, and 13MF). Twenty cards are designated for each age and gender group.

People are asked to tell a story about each of the cards they are shown. They are told that their stories should have a beginning, a middle, and an end and should include what is happening in the picture, what led up to this situation, what the people in the picture are thinking and feeling, and what the outcome of the situation will be. When people have finished telling their story about a picture, they are asked to add story elements they have omitted to mention (e.g., "How did this situation come about?" "What is on this person's mind?" "How is she feeling right now?" "What is likely to happen next?"). In common with a Rorschach administration, these TAT procedures generate structural, thematic, and behavioral data that provide a basis for drawing inferences about an individual's personality characteristics.

Structural Data

All TAT stories have a structural component that is defined by certain objective features of the test protocol. The length of the stories people tell can provide information about whether they are approaching this task—and perhaps other situations in their lives as well—in a relatively open and revealing fashion (long stories) or in a relatively guarded manner that conceals more than it reveals (short stories). Story length can also provide clues to a person's energy level, perhaps thereby identifying depressive lethargy in one person (short stories) and hypomanic expansiveness in another person (long stories), and clues to whether the individual is by nature a person of few or many words. Shifts in the length of stories from one card to the next, or in the reaction time before the storytelling begins, may identify positive or negative reactions to the typical themes suggested by the cards, which are described later in the chapter.

The amount of detail in TAT stories provides another informative structural element of a test protocol. Aside from their length in words, TAT stories can vary in detail from a precisely specified account of who is doing what to whom and why (which might reflect obsessive-compulsive personality characteristics), to a vague and superficial description of people and events that suggests a shallow style of dealing with affective and interpersonal experience. A related structural variable consists of the number and type of stimulus details that are noted in the stories. Most of the TAT pictures contain (a) some prominent elements that are almost always included in the stories people tell; (b) some minor figures or objects that are also included from time to time; and (c) many peripheral details that are rarely noted or mentioned. Card 3BM, for example, depicts a person sitting on the floor (almost always mentioned), a small object on the floor by the person's feet (frequently but not always mentioned), and a piece of furniture on which the person is leaning (seldom mentioned). Divergence from these common expectations can have implications for how people generally pay attention to their surroundings, particularly with respect to whether they tend to be inattentive to what is obvious and important, or whether instead they are likely to become preoccupied with what is obscure or of little relevance.

Also of potential interpretive significance is the extent to which TAT stories revolve around original themes or common themes. A preponderance of original themes may reflect creativity and openness on the part of the examinee, whereas consistently common themes often indicate conventionality or guardedness. As additional structural variables, the coherence and rationality of stories can provide clues to whether people are thinking clearly and logically, and the quality of the vocabulary usage and grammatical construction in people's stories usually says something about their intellectual level and verbal facility.

Thematic Data

All TAT stories have a thematic as well as a structural component. Like the thematic imagery that often emerges in Rorschach responses, the content of TAT stories provides clues to a person's underlying needs, attitudes, conflicts, and concerns. Because they depict real scenes, the TAT cards provide more numerous and more direct opportunities than the Rorschach inkblots for examinees to attribute characteristics to human figures in various circumstances. Typical TAT stories are consequently rich with information about the depicted characters' aspirations, intentions, and expectations that will likely reveal aspects of how people feel about themselves, about other people, and about their future prospects.

These kinds of information typically derive from four interpretively significant aspects of the imagery in TAT stories:

1. How the people in a story are identified and described (e.g., "young woman," "president of a bank," "good gymnast") and whether examinees appear to be identifying with these people or seeing them as representing certain other people in their lives (e.g., parent, spouse).
2. How the people in a story are interacting; for example, whether they are helping or hurting each other in some way.
3. The emotional tone of the story, as indicated by the specific affect attributed to the depicted characters (e.g., happy, sad, angry, sorry, enthused, indifferent).
4. The plot of the story, with particular respect to outcomes involving success or failure, gratification or disappointment, love gained or lost, and the like.

Behavioral Data

As when they are responding to the RIM and other performance-based measures of personality, the way people behave and relate to the examiner during a TAT administration provides clues to how they typically approach task-oriented and interpersonal situations. Whether they appear self-assured or tentative, friendly or surly, assertive or deferential, and detached or engaged can characterize individuals while they are telling their TAT stories, and these test behaviors are likely to reflect general traits of a similar kind.

Unlike the situation in Rorschach assessment, the structural, thematic, and behavioral sources of data in TAT assessment are not potentially equivalent in their interpretive significance. As discussed in Chapter 11, either the structural, the thematic, or the behavioral features of Rorschach responses may turn out to be the most revealing and reliable source of information about an individual's personality functioning, and it cannot be determined in advance which one it will be. On the TAT, by contrast, the thematic imagery in the stories almost always provides more extensive and more useful data than the structural and behavioral features of a test protocol.

Moreover, because the TAT pictures portray real-life situations, and because test takers are encouraged to embellish their responses, TAT stories are likely to generate a greater number of specific hypotheses than the thematic imagery in Rorschach responses concerning an individual's underlying needs, attitudes, conflicts, and concerns. TAT stories tend to help identify particular persons and situations with whom various motives, intentions, and expectations are associated. With respect both to the inner life of people and the nature of their social relationships, then, the TAT frequently provides more information than the RIM.

HISTORY

As befits a storytelling technique, the TAT emerged as the outcome of an interesting and in some respects unlikely story. Like the history of Rorschach assessment, the TAT story dates back to the first part of the twentieth century, but it is an American rather than a European story. The tale begins with Morton Prince, a Boston born and Harvard-educated neurologist who lectured at Tufts Medical College and distinguished himself as a specialist in abnormal psychology. Along with accomplishments as a practitioner, teacher, and author of the original work on multiple personality disorder (Prince, 1906), Prince founded the *Journal of Abnormal Psychology* in 1906 and served for many years as its editor. By the mid-1920s, he had come to believe that a university setting would be more conducive to advances in psychopathology research than the traditional locus of such research in medical schools, where patient care responsibilities often take precedence over scholarly pursuits. In 1926, Prince offered an endowment to Harvard University to support an academic center for research in psychopathology. The university accepted his offer and established for this purpose the Harvard Psychological Clinic, with Prince as its first director.

On assuming the directorship of the Harvard Psychological Clinic, Prince looked to hire a research associate who would plan and implement the programs of the new facility. Acting on the recommendation of an acquaintance, but apparently without benefit of a search committee or consultation with the Harvard psychology faculty, he hired an ostensibly unqualified person for the job—a surgically trained physician and PhD biochemist named Henry Murray. Two years later, Prince retired, and in 1928 Murray succeeded him as Director of the Clinic, a position for which, according to his biographer, Murray "was the first person to admit that he was unqualified . . . though he had done a good bit of reading" (Robinson, 1992, p. 142).

Henry Murray was to become one of the best-known and highly respected personality theorists in the history of psychology. He remains recognized today for his pioneering emphasis on individual differences rather than group tendencies, which as noted in Chapter 1 (see pp. 12–13) became identified in technical terms as an *idiographic* approach to the study of persons (as distinguished from a *nomothetic* approach emphasizing characteristics that differentiate groups of people). The main thrust of what Murray called "personology" was attention to each person's unique integration of psychological characteristics, rather than to the general nature of these characteristics. For Murray, then, the study of personality consisted of exploring individual experience and the kinds of lives that people lead, rather than exploring the origins, development, and manifestations of specific personality characteristics like dependency, assertiveness, sociability, and rigidity (see Barenbaum & Winter, 2003; Hall, Lindzey, & Campbell, 1998, chap. 5). Most of all, however, Murray is known for having originated the Thematic Apperception Test.

When Murray ascended to the directorship of the Harvard Psychological Clinic in 1928, there was little basis for anticipating his subsequent contributions to psychology. Born and reared in New York City, he had studied history as an undergraduate at Harvard, received his medical degree from Columbia in 1919, done a 2-year surgical internship, and then devoted himself to laboratory research that resulted in 21 published articles and a 1927 doctorate in biochemistry (Anderson, 1988, 1999; Stein & Gieser, 1999). As counterpoint to Murray's limited preparation for taking on his Harvard Clinic responsibilities, two personal events in the mid-1920s had attracted him to making this career change. One of these events was reading Melville's *Moby Dick* and becoming fascinated with the complexity of the characters in the story, particularly the underlying motivations that influenced them to act as they did.

The second event was meeting and beginning a lifelong friendship with Christiana Morgan, an artist who was enamored of the psychoanalytic conceptions of Carl Jung. Morgan encouraged Murray to visit Jung in Switzerland, which he did in 1925. He later stated that, in 2 days of conversation with Jung, "enough affective stuff erupted to invalid a pure scientist" (Murray, 1940, p. 153). These events and his subsequent extensive reading in the psychological and psychoanalytic literature, combined with his background in patient care and laboratory research, made him far better prepared to head up the Harvard Psychological Clinic than his formal credentials would have suggested. He later furthered his own education by entering a training program in psychoanalysis, which he completed in 1935.

During his tenure as Director from 1928 to 1943, Murray staffed the Harvard Psychological Clinic with a highly talented group of young scholars and clinicians, many of whom went on to distinguished careers of their own. Under his direction, the clinic gained worldwide esteem for its theoretical and research contributions to the literature in personality and psychopathology. As his first major project, Murray orchestrated an intensive psychological study of 50 male Harvard students, each of whom was assessed individually with over 20 different procedures. Included among these procedures was a picture-story measure in which Murray had become interested in the early 1930s. A conviction had formed in his mind that stories told by people can reveal many aspects of what they think and how they feel, and that carefully chosen pictures provide a useful stimulus for eliciting stories that are rich in personal meaning. In collaboration with Morgan, he experimented with different pictures and eventually selected 20 that seemed particularly likely to suggest a critical situation or at least one person with whom an examinee would identify. These 20 pictures constituted the original version of the TAT, first described in print by C. D. Morgan and Murray (1935) as "a method for investigating fantasies."

The results of Murray's Harvard study were published in a classic book, *Explorations in Personality,* which is best known for presenting his idiographic approach to studying people and his model of personality functioning (Murray, 1938). In Murray's model, each individual's personality is an interactive function of "needs," which are the particular motivational forces emerging from within a person, and "presses," which are environmental forces and situations that affect how a person expresses these needs. Less well-known or recalled is that the 1938 book was subtitled *A Clinical and Experimental Study of Fifty*

Men of College Age. After elaborating his personality theory in terms of 29 different needs and 20 different presses in the first half of the book, Murray devoted the second half to presenting the methods and results of the 50-man Harvard study. The discussion of this research included some historically significant case studies that illustrated for the first time how the TAT could be used in concert with other assessment methods to gain insight into the internal pressures and external forces that shape each individual's personality.

The original TAT used in the Harvard Clinic Study was followed by three later versions of the test, as C. D. Morgan and Murray continued to examine the stimulus potential of different kinds of paintings, photographs, and original drawings. The nature and origins of the pictures used in four versions of the test are reviewed by W. G. Morgan (1995, 2002, 2003). The final 31-card version of the test was published in 1943 (Murray, 1943/1971) and remains the version in use today. Ever the curious scientist, Murray might have continued trying out new cards, according to Anderson (1999), had he not left Harvard for Washington, D.C., in 1943 to contribute to the World War II effort. Murray was asked to organize an assessment program in the Office of Strategic Services (OSS), the forerunner of the CIA, for selecting men and women who could function effectively as spies and saboteurs behind enemy lines. A fascinating account of how Murray and his colleagues went about this task and the effectiveness of the selection procedures they devised was published after the war by the OSS staff (Office of Strategic Services, 1948), and Handler (2001) has more recently prepared a summary of this account.

As Rorschach had done with his inkblots, Murray developed a scheme for coding stories told to the TAT pictures. Also in common with Rorschach's efforts, but for different reasons, Murray's coding scheme opened the door for modification in the hands of others. Rorschach's system was still sketchy at the time of his death and left considerable room for additions and revisions by subsequent systematizers (see Chapter 11). By contrast, Murray (1943/1971) presented in his manual a detailed procedure for rating each of 28 needs and 24 presses on a 5-point scale for their intensity, duration, frequency, and importance whenever they occur in a story. This complex scoring scheme proved too cumbersome to gain much acceptance among researchers and practitioners who took up the TAT after its 1943 publication made it widely available. Consequently, as elaborated by Murstein (1963), many other systems for interpreting the TAT emerged over the next 15 to 20 years; some them followed Murray in emphasizing content themes, and others attended as well to structural and thematic features of stories.

Several of these new systems were proposed by psychologists who had worked with Murray at the Harvard Psychological Clinic, notably Leopold Bellak (1947), William Henry (1956), Edwin Shneidman (1951), Morris Stein (1948), and Silvan Tomkins (1947). Shneidman (1965) later wrote that the TAT had quickly become "everybody's favorite adopted baby to change and raise as he wished" (p. 507). Of these and other TAT systems that were devised in the 1940s and 1950s, only variations of an "inspection technique" proposed by Bellak became widely used. Currently in its sixth edition, Bellak's text recommends an approach to TAT interpretation in which an individual's stories are examined for repetitive themes and recurring elements that appear to fall together in meaningful ways (Bellak & Abrams, 1997). This inspection technique is described further in the coding and interpretation sections of the present chapter.

Aside from proposing different systems for interpreting TAT stories, assessment psychologists have at times suggested four reasons for modifying the TAT picture set that

Murray published in 1943. The first of these reasons concerns whether the standard TAT pictures are suitable for use with young children or the elderly. Young children may identify more easily with animals than with people, some said, and the situations portrayed in the standard picture set do not adequately capture the life experiences of older persons. In light of these possibilities, Bellak developed two alternative sets of pictures: the Children's Apperception Test (CAT), intended for use with children aged 3 to 10 and portraying animal rather than human characters, and the Senior Apperception Test (SAT), which depicts primarily elderly people in circumstances they are likely to encounter (Bellak, 1954, 1975; Bellak & Abrams, 1997). Little has been written about the utility of the SAT, however, and the development of the CAT appears to have been unnecessary. Research reviewed by Teglasi (2001, chap. 8) has indicated that children tell equally or even more meaningful stories to human cards than they do to animal cards.

A second reason for questioning the appropriateness of the standard TAT set is that all the figures in them are Caucasian. Efforts to enhance multicultural sensitivity in picture-story assessment, particularly in the evaluation of children and adolescents, led to the development of the Tell-Me-A-Story test (TEMAS; Costantino, Malgady, & Rogler, 1988). The TEMAS is a TAT-type measure for use with young people aged 5 to 18 in which the stimulus cards portray conflict situations involving African American and Latino characters. Research with the TEMAS pictures has confirmed that they are likely to elicit fuller and more revealing stories from minority individuals than the all-Caucasian TAT pictures (Costantino & Malgady, 1999; Costantino, Malgady, Rogler, & Tusi, 1988), and there are also indications that the TEMAS has cross-culture applicability in Europe as well as within the United States (see Dana, 2006).

As a third concern, there has been little standardization of which of the 20 TAT cards are administered and in what order to a person of a particular age and gender, which has made it difficult to assess the reliability and validity of the instrument. Considerations in card selection and the psychometric foundations of the TAT are discussed later in the chapter. However, dissatisfaction with widespread variation in these aspects of TAT administration influenced the development of two new TAT-type measures.

One of these newer measures, the Roberts Apperception Test for Children (RATC), was designed for use with young people aged 5 to 16 and portrays children and adolescents engaged in everyday interactions (McArthur & Roberts, 1990). There are 27 RATC cards, 11 of which are alternate versions for males or females, and each youngster taking the test is administered a standard set of 16 cards in a set sequence, using male or female versions as appropriate. A revision of the RATC, called the Roberts-2 (Roberts, 2006) extends the age range for the test to 18 and includes three parallel sets of cards for use with White, Black, and Hispanic children and adolescents. The second alternative standard set of cards, which also includes multiethnic pictures, is the Apperceptive Personality Test (APT; Holmstrom, Silber, & Karp, 1990; Karp, Holstrom, & Silber, 1989). The APT consists of just eight stimulus pictures, each of which is always administered and in a fixed sequence.

Fourth and finally, some users of the TAT have found fault with the generally dark, gloomy, achromatic nature of the pictures and with the old-fashioned appearance of the people and scenes portrayed in them. It may be that these features of the cards make it difficult for people to identify with the figures in them or to tell lively stories about them. The TEMAS, by contrast, features brightly colored pictures and contemporary situations. Colored photographs have also been used to develop an alternative picture set for use with adults, called the Picture Projective Test (PPT), and some research has suggested that the relatively bright PPT cards may generate more active and more emotionally toned stories than the relatively dark TAT cards (Ritzler, Sharkey, & Chudy, 1980; Sharkey & Ritzler, 1985).

As alternative picture sets for use with young and elderly individuals, the CAT, SAT, TEMAS, and RATC have enjoyed some popularity in applied practice. Each of these measures also remains visible as the focus of occasional research studies published in the literature. However, none of them appears to have detracted very much from clinical applications and research studies of the original 1943 version of the TAT. With respect to alternative picture sets for adults, neither the APT, the PPT, or any other proposed revision in the TAT picture set has attracted much attention from practitioners or researchers, despite their apparent virtues with respect to standardization and stimulus enhancement.

ADMINISTRATION

As spelled out in his 1943 *Manual*, Murray intended that persons taking the TAT would be asked to tell stories to all 20 of the pictures appropriate to their age (child/adult) and gender (male/female). The 20 pictures were to be shown in two 50-minute sessions, with a 1-day interval between sessions, and people would be instructed to devote about 5 minutes to each story. In actual practice over the years, TAT examiners have typically administered 8 to 12 selected cards in a single session. Most commonly, cards are selected on the basis of whether they are expected to elicit stories that are rich in meaning and relevant to specific concerns of the person being assessed. With respect to eliciting interpretively rich stories, the most productive cards are usually those that portray a person in thought or depict emotional states or interpersonal relationships. The selection of cards specifically relevant in the individual case involves matching the content themes commonly pulled by the various cards with what is known or suspected about a person's central issues, such as aggressive or depressive concerns, problematic family relationships, or heterosexual or homosexual anxieties.

In selecting which cards to use, then, examiners need to consider the content themes typically associated with each of them. A description of the TAT cards and the story lines they usually pull follows in the interpretation section of the chapter. With respect to common practice in card selection, Teglasi (2001, p. 38) has reported a consensus among TAT clinicians that the most useful TAT cards are 1, 2, 3BM, 6BM, 7GF, 8BM, 9GF, 10, and 13MF. According to Teglasi's report, each of these 9 cards appears to work equally well across ages and genders, despite their male, female, boy, or girl designation. Bellak (1999) recommends using a standard 10-card sequence consisting of these 9 cards plus Card 4, with the possible addition of other cards that pull for particular themes. In the individual case, then, the selected set should comprise all or most of these 9- or 10-card sets, with replacement or additional cards chosen on the basis of specific issues that are evaluated.

Two research findings relevant to TAT card selection should also be noted. In an analysis by Keiser and Prather (1990) of 26 TAT studies, the 10 cards used most frequently were 1, 2, 3BM, 4, 6BM, 7BM, 8BM, 10, 13MF, and 16. In the other study, Avila-Espada (2000) used several variables, including the number of themes in the stories each card elicited, to calculate a stimulus value for each of them. On this basis, he chose two 12-card sets that he considered equivalent in stimulus value to the full 20-card TAT set: one set for males (1, 2, 3BM, 4, 6BM, 7BM, 8BM, 10, 13MF, 14, 15, and 18BM) and one set for females (1, 2, 3GF, 4, 6GF, 7GF, 8GF, 9GF, 10, 13MF, 17GF, and 18GF).

Turning now to the actual administration of the test, many of the general considerations discussed in Chapter 11 with respect to administering the RIM apply to the TAT as well. Test takers should have had an opportunity to discuss with the examiner (a) the purpose of their being tested (e.g., "The reason for this examination is to help in planning what kind of treatment would be best for you"); (b) the types of information the test will provide (e.g., "This is a measure of personality functioning that will give us a clearer understanding of what you're like as an individual, the kinds of concerns you have, and what might be helpful to you at this point"); and (c) how the results will be used (e.g., "When the test results are ready, I will be reviewing them with you in a feedback session and then sending a written report to your therapist").

In preparation for giving the formal TAT instructions, the cards that have been selected should be piled face down on the table or desk, with Card I on the top and the rest of the selected cards beneath it in the order in which they are to be presented. To minimize inadvertent influence of the examiner's facial expressions or bodily movements, it is advisable for the examiner to sit beside or at an angle from the person taking the test, rather than directly in front of the person. Once the test begins, whatever the examinee says should be recorded verbatim. Examiners can word-process the protocol with a computer instead of writing it longhand, should they prefer to do so, and a person's stories can also be tape-recorded and transcribed later on. There is no evidence to indicate that the examiner's writing out the record, using a computer, or tape-recording the protocol makes any difference in the stories that are obtained.

Examiners should begin the TAT administration by informing people of the nature of their task. The following instructions, based on Murray's (1943/1971) original procedures and modifications suggested by Bellak and Abrams (1997), will serve this purpose well with adolescents and adults of at least average intelligence:

I am going to show you some pictures, one at a time, and your task will be to make up as dramatic a story as you can for each. Tell what has led up to the event shown in the picture, describe what is happening at the moment, what the characters are feeling and thinking, and then give the outcome. Speak your thoughts as they come to your mind. Do you understand?

When the TAT is being administered to adolescents and adults of limited intelligence, to children, or to seriously disturbed persons, the following simplified version of the instructions is recommended:

This is a storytelling test. I have some pictures here that I am going to show you, and for each picture I want you to make up a story. Tell what has happened before and what is happening now. Say what the people are feeling and thinking and how it will come out. You can make up any kind of story you please. Do you understand?

Following whichever of set of instructions is given, the examiner should say, "Here is the first picture" and then hand Card 1 to the examinee. Each of the subsequent cards can be presented by saying, "Here is the next one" or merely handing it to the person without further comment. The story told to each picture should be recorded silently, without interruption, until the person has finished with it. Immediately following the completion of each story, the examiner should inquire about any of the requested story elements that are missing. Depending on the content of the story, this inquiry could include questions about what is happening, what led up to this situation, what the people are thinking and feeling, or what the outcome will be.

If a story as first told is missing most of these elements, a gentle reminder of the test instructions and a request to tell the story again may be preferable to asking each of the individual questions concerning what has been omitted. If only some of the requested story elements are missing and individual inquiries about them are answered with "Don't know" or "Can't say," examinees as previously indicated should be encouraged to "Use your imagination and make something up." Should this encouragement fail to generate any further elaboration of the story element being inquired, the examiner should desist without pressing the person further. Putting excessive pressure on test takers rarely generates sufficient additional information to justify the distress it may cause them, and doing so can also generate negative attitudes that limit cooperation with the testing procedures that follow. To the contrary, because adequately informative TAT protocols are so dependent on individuals being willing to fantasize and share the products of their fantasy, it can be helpful to encourage them with occasional praise (e.g., "That's an interesting story"). As Murray (1943/1971, p. 4) said about a little praise from time to time, "There is no better stimulant to the imagination."

The examiner's inquiry questions should be limited to requests for information about missing story elements and should not include any other kinds of discussion or questions. For example, direct questions about the character's motives (e.g., "Why are they doing this?") should be avoided. Motivations that emerge in response to such leading questions lack the interpretive significance of motivations that people report spontaneously, and leading questions that go beyond the basic instructions may encourage examinees to report motivations and other kinds of information on subsequent cards when they would not otherwise have done so. Similarly, people should not be asked to talk about any person or object in a picture that they omitted from their story. This kind of question can influence the thoroughness with which individuals attend to subsequent pictures and thereby dilute the potential information value of total or selective attention to certain parts of certain pictures.

Certain kinds of responses may at times call for the examiner to interrupt an examinee during the spontaneous phase of a TAT administration. Should the person be telling a rambling, extremely detailed story that contains all the requisite story elements but seems endless, the examiner should break in with something on the order of, "That's fine; I think I have the gist of that story; let's go on to the next picture." If a rambling and detailed story covers all the requisite elements except an outcome, the interruption can be modified to, "That's fine; just tell me how the story ends, and we'll go on to the next one." Long stories rarely provide more information than a briefer version that covers all the required story elements, and endless stories are seldom worth the time and energy they consume in a testing session.

A second kind of response that calls for interruption is a drawn-out description of what a person sees in the picture with little or no attention to developing a story line with a plot. In this circumstance, the appropriate intervention is to remind the individual of the instructions: "That's fine so far, but let me remind you that what we need for this test is for you to tell a story about each picture, with a beginning and an end, and to say what the people are thinking and feeling." A third problematic circumstance arises when people say that they can think of two or three different possibilities in a picture and set out to relate more than one story. Once more, to minimize any dilution of the interpretive significance of the data, examinees should not be allowed to tell alternative stories. If they indicate that such is their intent, they should be interrupted with words to this effect: "For each of these pictures I want you to tell just one story; if you have more than one idea about a picture, choose the one that you think is the best story for it."

Finally, the nature of the test makes it suitable for group as well as individual assessments. In group administration, the selected cards are shown on a screen, the instructions are given in written form as well as orally by the person conducting the administration, and people are asked to write out their stories for each picture. Although group administration sacrifices the opportunity for examiners to inquire about missing story elements, this shortcoming can be circumvented in large part by mentioning the story requirements in the instructions. Based on recommendations by Atkinson (1958, Appendix III), who was a leading figure in developing procedures for large sample research with the TAT, the following written instructions can be used for group administration:

> You are going to see a series of pictures, and your task is to tell a story that is suggested to you by each picture. Try to imagine what is going on in each picture. Then tell what the situation is, what led up to the situation, what the people are thinking and feeling, and what they will do. In other words, write a complete story, with a plot and characters. You will have four minutes to write your story about each picture, and you will be told when it is time to finish your story and get ready for the next picture. There are no right or wrong stories or kinds of stories, so you may feel free to write whatever story is suggested to you when you look at a picture.

Together with these written instructions, group test takers can be given a sheet of paper for each picture they will be shown, with the following four sets of questions printed on each sheet and followed by space for writing in an answer:

1. What is happening? Who are the persons?
2. What led up to this situation? What has happened in the past?
3. What is being thought and felt? What do the persons want?
4. What will happen? What will be done?

CODING

As noted, the cumbersome detail of the TAT coding scheme originally proposed by Murray (1943/1971) discouraged its widespread adoption in either clinical practice or research. The only comprehensive procedure for coding TAT stories that has enjoyed even mild popularity is an "Analysis Sheet" developed by Bellak (Bellak & Abrams, 1997, chap. 4) for use with his inspection method. Bellak's Analysis Sheet calls for examiners to describe briefly several features of each story, including its main theme, the needs and intentions of its characters, the kinds of affects that are being experienced, and the nature of any conflicts that are described or defended against. Each story is additionally rated for the degree to which it appears to reflect strengths or weaknesses in an individual's personality integration (e.g., a relatively good or poor sense of reality, high or low tolerance for frustration).

Because Bellak's Analysis Sheet for rating story content is not widely used, despite being the best known comprehensive TAT scoring system, it will not be presented in further detail. Likewise, numerous efforts over the years to develop scoring systems based on objective structural features of TAT stories have fallen short of generating consistently useful data or gaining even a modicum of acceptance in the professional community. As a contemporary example of such efforts, Avila-Espada (2000) has used ratios among the word count, reaction time, and total time of TAT stories to construct some indices of cognitive ability and productivity. The validity and utility of these indices remains to be demonstrated, however. Earlier work on coding of objective TAT variables was reviewed by Vane (1981), and Jenkins (in press) provides information about a broad range of more recently developed approaches to scoring the instrument.

In the absence of any well-established comprehensive coding procedures for the TAT comparable to Exner's Comprehensive System for the RIM, and in contrast to the limited information yield from the coding of objective TAT variables, three notable content rating scales have been developed for measuring specific dimensions of personality with the TAT. Each of these scales has been empirically validated as a fruitful measure of the personality characteristics it addresses, and this validation research, as elaborated later in the chapter, has proved central in demonstrating the potential psychometric adequacy of the TAT. Two of these scales—the Social Cognition and Object Relations Scale (SCORS), developed by Westen and his colleagues (Westen, 1991; Westen, Lohr, Silk, Gold, & Kerber, 1990), and the Defense Mechanism Manual (DMM), developed by Cramer (1991)—can be used to enrich clinical evaluations as well as for research purposes. The third scale, the Need for Achievement (n-Ach) scale developed by McClelland and his colleagues (McClelland, Atkinson, Clark, & Lowell, 1953; McClelland, Clark, Roby, & Atkinson, 1958), has found applications mainly as a research tool.

Social Cognition and Object Relations Scale (SCORS)

Westen, Lohr, Silk, Kerber, and Goodrich (1989) constructed the Social Cognition and Object Relations Scale (SCORS) to codify TAT imagery in ways that would tap persons' underlying attitudes toward themselves, toward other people, and toward social relationships. Westen et al. initially identified four dimensions of object relationships that could be evaluated in TAT stories, and Westen (1995) later expanded this number to the following eight SCORS dimensions, each of which is coded on a 7-point scale for the maturity level reflected in the actions and attitudes of the characters in a story:

1. *Complexity of representation of people,* which ranges from making little distinction between one's own thoughts and feelings and the thoughts and feelings of others (least mature) to clear distinction between oneself and others with good insight into both (most mature).

2. *Affective quality of relationships,* which ranges from expecting hostile and abusive relationships with people (least mature) to generally positive expectations and a favorable view of relationships (most mature).

3. *Emotional investment in relationships,* which ranges from focusing primarily on one's own needs in relationships and having few or only tumultuous relationships (least mature) to having deeply committed relationships characterized by mutuality, interdependence, and respect (most mature).

4. *Emotional investment in values and moral standards,* which ranges from selfish, inconsiderate, and self-indulgent behaviors unaccompanied by remorse (least mature) to thoughtful, compassionate behaviors and a willingness to challenge or question convention (most mature).

5. *Understanding of social causality,* which ranges from confused, distorted, extremely sparse, or largely incoherent accounts of interpersonal experiences (least mature) to coherent narratives of interpersonal events that reflect keen understanding of people and the impact of their actions on each other (most mature).

6. *Experience and management of aggressive impulses,* which ranges from assaultive, destructive, sadistic, or poorly controlled actions (least mature) to appropriate self-assertion and adequately modulated expression of anger and aggression (most mature).

7. *Self-esteem,* which ranges from viewing oneself as an evil, rotten, loathsome, or globally bad person (least mature) to having realistic and positive self-regard (most mature).

8. *Identity and coherence of oneself,* which ranges from a fragmented sense of self with little conception of permanence or stability (least mature) to an integrated sense of identity and commitment to long-term goals and aspirations (most mature).

The numerical ratings from 1 (least mature) to 7 (most mature) are assigned for the content of each of a person's stories, and these ratings are averaged over the number of cards administered to give a summary score for each of the eight dimensions. Further guidelines for coding SCORS are available in the Westen publications and in a research report by S. J. Ackerman, Clemence, Weatherill, and Hilsenroth (1999) and a case study by Kelly (2007). A meta-analysis by Meyer (2004) of studies involving 653 pairs of SCORS coding judgments has shown an overall correlation coefficient of .86 for interrater reliability in determining these summary scores. In a study by Peters, Hilsenroth, Eudell-Simmons, Blagys, and Handler (2006) of 90 patients participating in short-term dynamic psychotherapy, the SCORS scales showed a medium to large degree of convergent validity with independent ratings of social, occupational, and interpersonal functioning and a mild to moderate relationship to symptomatic distress. Additional validating data for the SCORS are summarized by Kelly (2007), Huprich and Greenberg (2003), and Stricker and Gooen-Piels (2004).

Defense Mechanism Manual (DMM)

Cramer (1991, 1996, chap. 7, 2006) based the Defense Mechanism Manual (DMM) on a fairly traditional definition of defense mechanisms as efforts to ward off feelings of anxiety and guilt and by so doing to protect one's self-esteem and sense of well-being. Some of the psychological defenses are relatively mature and adaptive, Cramer noted, whereas others are childish or infantile. The less mature a person's defenses are, the more likely they are to detract from rather than safeguard the individual's ability to feel comfortable and function effectively. Research findings have confirmed that the developmental level of their preferred defense mechanisms has implications for how much happiness and success people find in their lives and their susceptibility to particular kinds of psychopathology (Vaillant, 1977, 1994).

In constructing the DMM, Cramer selected three mechanisms customarily considered to represent different levels of maturity. The least mature of these three mechanisms is *denial,* which involves failing to see or ignoring something that is really there, or constructing unrealistic fantasies that change an unpleasant situation into its opposite. Denial is likely to be in evidence when people remain unshakably optimistic in the face of overwhelming obstacles or unremittingly elated despite grievous circumstances. A less immature but also usually maladaptive mechanism is *projection,* which consists of attributing characteristics to people and situations in the absence of adequate justification. Because such projected attributes often consist of angry feelings and hostile intentions, they contribute to unwarranted mistrust of others and excessive concerns about being in danger and needing protection. The third and most mature mechanism in Cramer's DMM scale is *identification,* which is occurring when a person adopts certain characteristics of other people in an attempt to become like them.

For each of these three mechanisms, Cramer identified seven characteristics of TAT stories that are likely to reflect them. Denial is coded when people omit to mention a major figure in a picture or go to great lengths to minimize the possibility of a negative story outcome. Projection is coded for such story characteristics as attribution of aggressive intent to figures that are not usually seen as hostile or threatening, and also for story lines that involve themes of entrapment and escape. Identification is coded when characters are described as emulating each other or as gaining self-esteem through sharing a relationship. The number of times a person's stories reflect any of these defenses provides an index of the individual's level of defensiveness, and the relative magnitude of the subtotal scores for denial, projection, and identification indicates the maturity and likely adaptiveness of his or her defense preferences. In Meyer's (2004) previously mentioned meta-analysis, the interrater reliability coefficient for 713 pairs of DMM coding judgments was .80. Porcerelli and Hibbard (2004) provide a summary of the DMM validating data.

Need for Achievement (n-Ach)

Unlike the SCORS and DMM, which developed from clinical perspectives on the maturity level and adaptability of certain personality characteristics, the Need for Achievement (n-Ach) scale emerged from the experimental psychology of motivation. McClelland and his colleagues (McClelland et al., 1953, 1958) hypothesized that TAT stories would reflect the strength of a person's psychological needs and could be used to measure it. To test their hypothesis, they considered first the need to achieve and constructed a scoring scheme for identifying six presumably achievement-related features of stories: (1) a stated desire to reach some goal; (2) activity intended to reach that goal; (3) anticipation of success or failure in reaching the goal; (4) obstacles that impede goal-directed activity; (5) assistance from someone else in achieving the goal; and (6) an affective state associated with success or failure in attaining an achievement goal.

Early success in demonstrating the utility of the n-Ach scale as a conceptually rich and empirically sturdy research tool stimulated numerous experimental applications of the TAT and the construction of several companion scales for measuring needs for affiliation, power, intimacy, and responsibility. Good overviews of this experimental work and of the construction of these companion scales are provided by Cramer (1996, chap. 15), McClelland (1999), Smith (1992), and Winter (1998). Winter (1999) has also noted that high interscorer reliability, with total score correlations of .85 or higher, "has been a consistent hallmark of research with all measures developed in the McClelland-Atkinson tradition" (p. 117). Readers interested in contemporary refinements and cross-cultural application of n-Ach and other needs assessment with TAT-type pictures are referred to research reports by Blankenship et al. (2006), Lanagan-Fox and Grant (2006), Pang and Schultheiss (2005), and Tuerlinks, De Boeck, and Lens (2002).

INTERPRETATION: CARD PULL

Like the Rorschach inkblots, the TAT cards tend to draw certain patterns of response that constitute their "card pull." As mentioned, most people take note of certain features of each card (e.g., the violin in Card 1), but rarely mention certain other features (e.g., the horse in Card 2). In addition, the TAT pictures commonly suggest certain themes or plots in the stories that are told to them. As a third aspect of TAT card pull, many of the pictures remind people of issues in their lives (e.g., parent-child relationships) or particular concerns they have (e.g., managing anger). Familiarity with the frequently noted features, commonly elicited story lines, and issues often tapped for each card provides a backdrop for grasping the meaning of the stories people tell. The following information draws in part on previous contributions by Bellak and Abrams (1997, chap. 3) and Henry (1956, chap. 12) and on normative data collected by Eron (1950, 1953; see also Zubin, Eron, & Schumer, 1965, chap. 12).

Card 1

Frequently Noted Features

Card 1 shows a boy sitting at a table and looking at a violin lying on the table in front of him. People almost always note the boy and the violin in their story, and they may mention the table as well. They rarely call attention to a bow lying next to the violin, to what appears to be a cloth or sheet of music under the violin, or to a vague outline of the chair in which the boy is sitting.

Common Story Lines

The stories told to Card 1 revolve mostly around two basic plots. In one plot, a boy is being compelled by his parents or some other authority figure to practice the violin. Because he would rather be doing something else more to his liking (e.g., playing outside with his friends), he is just sitting and looking at the instrument. In the other common plot, the boy is an ambitious and self-motivated student of the violin who enjoys music and is either daydreaming about becoming a famous violinist or is destined to become one.

Issues Tapped

Despite its simplicity, Card 1 taps a broad range of potential issues in people's lives. Its interpretive richness and nonthreatening nature account for its being almost universally recommended as the first TAT card to administer; Bellak and Abrams (1997) regard it as "the single most valuable picture in the T.A.T." The stories elicited by Card 1 usually have implications for the tenor of parent-child relationships. Are parents seen as reasonable, supportive, and sympathetic, or as demanding, dictatorial, or indifferent? Card 1 stories are also likely to touch on modes of dealing with unwelcome authority, whether with compliance and obedience or with resistance and rebellion.

A third issue commonly raised by Card 1 and reflected in stories told to it concerns the balance that is struck between having fun and doing what one wants to do, on the one hand, and doing what one is supposed to do, on the other hand. Card 1 stories accordingly often reveal a person's attitudes toward achievement, particularly whether goal-directed striving is viewed as a worthwhile endeavor likely to bring gratification and rewards, or as a frustrating effort likely to end in disappointment and failure.

Card 2

Frequently Noted Features

Card 2 shows a country scene with a young woman in the foreground who is holding some books in her arms. The background depicts a shirtless man working in the fields and an older woman who appears to be leaning against a tree and watching him. Most examinees identify these three figures, describe some kind of relationship among them, and refer to their being in the country or on a farm. People also often note that the young woman is carrying books, the man is working, and the older woman is leaning against a tree. Occasionally noted is the possibility that the older woman is pregnant, as inferred from the outline of her figure. Details in the picture that are clearly depicted but seldom mentioned include a horse, some buildings in the background, furrows in the ground where the man is working, and the man's muscular physique. Also in the distant background and hardly ever noticed, is the dim outline of another worker and horse.

Common Story Lines

Card 2 typically elicits two alternative plots. One of these plots focuses on the young woman seen as seeking to become better educated and find a fuller life for herself than she will have if she stays on the farm. The other plot centers on the family, which is typically seen as working strenuously to sustain themselves and often as having to contend with the hardships and economic strains of small-scale independent farming.

Issues Tapped

The scene in Card 2 raises concerns about several kinds of family and interpersonal issues. Primary among these are feelings about children growing up and leaving home to pursue ambitions and possibly reap rewards that have been beyond the reach of the parents. Are the children delighted with this opportunity, or are they fearful of giving up the support of a familiar environment? Are the parents happy about having upwardly mobile children, or are they saddened by the prospect of their children moving away, or resentful at not having had such opportunities, or angry about being deserted by children who have turned their back on family values?

Interpersonal attitudes that may be revealed in stories told to Card 2 vary with how the three figures are paired. Stories about a daughter seeking to better herself, for example, with a pairing between the man and woman in the background, usually touch on parent-child interactions and on sources of pleasure or conflict between parents and their children. A pairing in which the two women are linked in some way provide a clue to a mother-daughter relationship that is perceived as close (e.g., if the mother supports the daughter's continuing in school, whereas the father objects to her doing so) or as competitive (e.g., if the daughter envies the attention her mother receives from her father, especially if the mother is seen as being pregnant).

As another possibility, the man in the picture is sometimes seen not as the father in the family, but instead as a hired hand working on the farm. Then the story may contain clues to heterosexual relationships and the pleasures and problems they can cause. The man could be linked with the younger woman, who is sexually attracted to him but stymied by her mother's keeping close watch on them and preventing any relationship from developing. Or the mother could be romantically involved with the hired hand, to her satisfaction but to her daughter's envy or dismay.

Card 3BM

Frequently Noted Features

This card was originally described by Murray (1943/1971) as follows: "On the floor against a couch is the huddled form of a boy with his head bowed on his right arm. Beside him on the floor is a revolver." However, the figure is seen from the back, and the object on the floor is not sharply defined. Also of note in grasping the impact of the picture, the figure is leaning forward against the couch on which his or her arm rests. This figure is typically identified as a young person, either male or female, together with some account of why the person is "huddled" in this way. People who identify the figure as opposite in gender to themselves may be conveying a wish or need to minimize their identification with whatever the figure is described as thinking, feeling, or doing. Thus a female examinee who describes the figure as "A man thinking about shooting somebody" could be attempting to deny or otherwise avoid coming to grips with distressing aggressive impulses of her own. The unspoken message in such instances would be, "This is something a man might think about doing, but I as a woman would never have such a thought."

The object on the floor is often but not always noted, and some significance may attach to its being ignored, especially if people have seen it as a gun and keep it out of their story because of concerns aroused by its violent connotations. Instead of seeing this object as a dangerous weapon, examinees may at times identify it as a set of keys or as a toy pistol. The couch is also commonly mentioned, but it rarely plays a part in whatever story is told.

Common Story Lines

Like Card 1, Card 3BM is a simple picture that nevertheless elicits story lines with considerable interpretive significance. The figure is most commonly described as being in acute distress, usually with intense feelings of depression or guilt. In one set of variations on this theme, the person has been attacked by some assailant, has been wounded in a suicide attempt, or is contemplating inflicting harm on himself or herself. In another set of variations, the person has recently attacked someone else or is considering doing so. These aggressive themes are most common when the object on the floor is seen as a revolver. Even when the object is ignored or seen as something nonthreatening, stories involving themes of depression, guilt, and suicide are still likely to occur. As a possibility in this latter regard, the object may be identified as a syringe or hypodermic needle and the person's perceived mental state or emotional distress as related to drug use.

Issues Tapped

As transparently reflected by its common story lines, Card 3BM arouses concerns related to depression and aggression. With respect to depression, the origins of the figure's distress will have implications for circumstances that are most likely to precipitate depressive episodes in the individual's life, or may have done so if the person is currently depressed. The common origins of depression that may be suggested by story lines include an actual or anticipated loss of some relationship, disappointment following some failed quest, and guilt over some perceived misdeed.

The outcome of a tale of depression is often informative with respect to a person's coping style, general outlook on life, and future prospects, particularly when suicidality is part of the tale. Consider the possible implications of three contrasting Card 3BM stories about a depressed and suicidal man. In one story, the man continues to feel sad and worthless, is unable to solve any of his problems, and goes ahead with his plan to shoot himself. Such a story would suggest persistent susceptibility to depression, a pessimistic outlook, limited coping capacities, and suicidal potential. In another story, the man starts to feel better in a week or two, gets some ideas about how to improve aspects of his life, and stops thinking of killing himself. This story would suggest adaptive ability to avoid or recover from depression, an optimistic outlook, capacity for constructive problem solving, and minimal suicide risk. In a third alternative story, the man gets over his depression by the end of the day, decides that he has nothing to worry about, and will live a happy life from now on. Now the pendulum has perhaps swung too far, resulting in a story that suggests forced gaiety and unbridled optimism of a type that often reveals denial of depression, rather than adaptive efforts to resolve it, and identifies continuing susceptibility to depressive episodes and suicidal thoughts.

Stories to Card 3BM tend to reflect the kinds of events that are likely to anger an individual, the ways in which the person manages anger when it becomes aroused, and whether people view themselves as more likely to be victims or perpetrators of aggression. Does the anger persist indefinitely or pass quickly? Does it lead mainly to hostile attitudes or does it foster aggressive impulses as well? Are hostile attitudes directed toward other people (which could indicate externalization of blame or responsibility) or toward the self (thus fostering feelings of guilt and worthlessness)? Are aggressive impulses other-directed (which would put the person in the role of a perpetrator) or self-directed (which would put the person in the roles of both perpetrator and victim). Are these aggressive impulses resisted (thus showing self-control) or acted on (thus increasing the individual's violence potential)?

Card 3GF

Frequently Noted Features

In Card 3GF, a woman is standing in a doorway with her head downcast and her right hand covering her face. With her left hand, she is holding onto the edge of the door. Most commonly, people mention the woman and comment on the way she is standing and holding her face in her hand. On occasion, the door is noted as well, but it rarely enters the plot of the story.

Common Story Lines

The woman in Card 3GF is commonly seen as sad and distraught, often as crying or in pain. Her distress is usually attributed to some interpersonal loss, like death of a loved one, or to remorse over something she has done. Often she is described as despondent and, when depression is a prominent theme, as contemplating harming herself.

Issues Tapped

Like Card 3BM, Card 3GF taps depressive concerns, guilt feelings, and suicidal tendencies. Why the woman feels as badly as she does and how she will deal with her distress are likely to say something about the sources of distress in an individual's life and the person's ways of coping with them. The woman's fairly obvious anguish limits the possibility for realistic alternative interpretations of this card, however, which reduces individual variability in the stories that are told to it. Because of this strong single card pull, themes of depression and suicide tend to have less idiographic significance on 3GF than they do on the multithematic 3BM. As a further difference between these two pictures in their card pull, 3GF depicts a clearly feminine figure with whom women can more easily identify than men. Card 3GF is accordingly suitable mainly for female examinees, whereas the previously noted gender ambiguity of Card 3BM makes it equally useful with both genders.

Card 4

Frequently Noted Features

Card 4 shows a woman with her hand on the shoulder of a man who is turned away from her, as if trying to pull away. People typically give some identity to these two figures and some explanation of why they are positioned as they are. Also noted on occasion is a vague image in the background of a partially clad woman, usually seen either as a real person or as a picture or poster on the wall.

Common Story Lines

In the most common plot of Card 4 stories, the woman in the picture is attempting to restrain the man or dissuade him from doing something dangerous or foolish. In this scenario, the woman is often portrayed as a pillar of morality, wisdom, or self-control, and the man as being on the irrational, impulsive side. As an alternative to the woman's being perceived as beseeching the man in some well-intended way, she may be described as consoling him about some disappointment or bad news he has received. In still a different scenario, the man is sometimes seen as a decent and righteous person contending with a domineering and intrusive woman who is trying to prevent him from doing something that he wants to do or should do, or who may be demanding an explanation for something he has already done. If the background figure of the woman is included in the story, the plot is likely to involve some kind of triangular relationship among the three people, as in a wife having returned home unexpectedly to discover her husband in a romantic tryst with another woman.

Issues Tapped

Card 4 is a rich stimulus picture that is likely to capture a person's attitudes toward men and women and toward marital or live-in relationships. Positive attitudes toward women can be reflected in describing the main female figure as kind, caring, concerned, sympathetic, level headed, or in other ways admirable; negative attitudes can be reflected in describing her as self-centered, insensitive, excitable, demanding, unreasonable, or in other ways unappealing. Likewise, admirable or unappealing characteristics attributed to the man in the picture can reveal corresponding perceptions of men on the part of the test taker. As for marital or live-in relationships, the interaction between the two main figures often elicits a person's perspectives on whether such relationships are more likely to constitute a collaboration, in which the partners help and console each other, or a confrontation, in which they disappoint and find fault with each other.

When Card 4 stories include the partially clad woman in the background, they are likely to reflect concerns about betrayal and guilt, particularly if the man is perceived as having behaved improperly. Should the presence of the other woman be rationalized in some way (e.g., seeing her as a painter's model and a wife as unjustly accusing her artist husband of infidelity) the examinee may be revealing concerns about mistrust and suspiciousness rather than about betrayal and guilt.

Card 5

Frequently Noted Features

Card 5 shows a middle-aged woman who is standing on the threshold of a half-opened door and looking into a room. Typical responses to this card note the woman and include some explanation of why she acting as she is. Various objects in the room, including a table in the foreground with a lamp and a flower vase on it, are often mentioned but rarely play a part in the story.

Common Story Lines

The woman in Card 5 is commonly seen as a maternal figure who is looking in on her children to make sure that they are safe and behaving properly. In an occasional alternative, the story tells about a woman who is concerned that there may be an intruder in the house and is checking to see if the room is empty. It is not unusual for a nonpictured character in the room to be introduced into the story.

Issues Tapped

This card typically arouses people's attitudes and feelings toward their mother or toward being mothered, particularly how closely they were supervised and how strictly they were controlled by maternal figures. How they describe the woman in the picture is likely to provide clues to whether persons view their mother as having been, or as still being, caring or indifferent, concerned or oblivious, harshly judgmental or liberally accepting, overly restrictive or excessively permissive, and the like.

This picture may also arouse attitudes toward watching and being watched. Should that occur, a person's stories may reflect an investment in keeping a close eye on what people are doing or, alternatively, an aversion to looking at things closely, lest one see something one is not supposed to see. As for being watched, Card 5 stories may reveal concerns about being under the scrutiny of others, being caught in the act of misbehaving, or being made to feel guilty for having committed wrongful acts. Both heightened watchfulness and preoccupation with being watched may in turn identify excessive concerns about being attacked or victimized, especially if story themes involve a break-in by a burglar or rapist.

Card 6BM

Frequently Noted Features

In Card 6BM, a gray-haired woman is looking out a window, and behind her stands a younger, taller man holding his hat in his hands and looking down with a troubled expression on his face. Stories typically include mention of the woman and the man and some account of the relationship between them. The hat and the window are rarely noted.

Common Story Lines

In the story usually told to Card 6BM, the man in the picture is giving his mother some unwelcome news. This news commonly consists of the son's decision to depart for some distant place or his report of something unfortunate having befallen another person close to them, both of which sadden his mother. A nonpictured father or husband is often introduced into the story.

Issues Tapped

Card 6BM taps a broad range of issues in mother-son relationships. These include how men view their mothers and maternal figures (e.g., whether as kindly or mean-spirited, as nurturing or rejecting), and how women view their sons and children (e.g., whether as caring and respectful or as undependable and ungrateful). Stories involving the son's imminent departure are also likely to reflect perspectives on parent-child independence. Although saddened, is the mother nevertheless pleased about her son's having new opportunities, or is she angry at him for ignoring her wish to have him remain close by? Although troubled, is the son nevertheless eager to wean himself from his mother's control, or does he have mixed feelings about giving up the support she provides? Does the mother feel justified in insisting that her son not leave, or does she regret having been a burden to him? Does the son feel justified in wanting to have a life of his own, or does he feel guilty about abandoning her?

Card 6GF

Frequently Noted Features

Card 6GF depicts a young woman sitting on the edge of a sofa and looking back over her shoulder at an older man, who has a pipe in his mouth and appears to be saying something to her. Examinees typically note these two people and comment on the relationship between them. The sofa and the pipe are also commonly mentioned, but rarely as part of the story line. A table visible in the foreground is seldom noted.

Common Story Lines

Card GF typically elicits plots involving a heterosexual interaction between a younger woman and an older man in which the man is introducing himself or suggesting some kind of activity, and the woman is responding to his overture or reacting to his proposition. In common variations of this story line, the man is seen as asking for a date or a sexual encounter, or even as proposing marriage, and the woman is described a showing various shades of pleasure or dismay at having thus been approached.

Issues Tapped

According to Bellak and Abrams (1997), Card 6GF was originally intended as a companion stimulus to Card 6BM that would reflect father-daughter issues. However, although 6GF may pull some attitudes of women toward older men, and hence toward their father or father figures, the people in the picture are rarely identified as a father and daughter. Instead, Card 6GF is useful mainly as a source of attitudes and concerns about interpersonal relationships and heterosexuality. As on most of the TAT cards, the terms in which people describe the man and the woman are likely to reveal attitudes they have toward men and women and toward themselves. How the characters in the story manage their interaction usually reflects examinees' level of comfort and confidence in social situations and whether they anticipate handling such situations clumsily or skillfully. When a sexual proposition is part of the story, Card 6GF is also likely to tap issues and concerns related to an individual's sexual needs, anxieties, and code of conduct.

Card 7BM

Frequently Noted Features

Card 7BM shows the head and shoulders of two men, one a young man who is staring sullenly into space and the other a gray-haired older man who is looking at the younger man. Both men and the relationship between them are almost always noted, and there are no other stimulus elements in the picture.

Common Story Lines

Card 7BM is most frequently seen as a father and son or as a professional relationship (both men are wearing jackets and ties) in which the older man is giving advice to the younger man or commenting on his behavior. The older man is often noted to be the wiser and more experienced of the two, and the younger man as able to benefit from listening to him. As pulled by the younger man's unhappy expression, the older man's evaluative comments are more frequently negative than positive.

Issues Tapped

In parallel to the mother-son issues raised by Card 6BM, Card 7BM typically stimulates father-son attitudes and concerns. The father may be seen as stern and hypercritical or as wise and helpful. The son may be described as surly and rebellious or as dutiful and appreciative. Attribution of such characteristics to the two figures will provide clues to people's underlying beliefs about what fathers and sons are like and how they are likely to relate to each other.

In addition, especially when the figures are seen in a professional rather than familial relationship (e.g., a boss and an apprentice), the picture often elicits attitudes toward authority. How the younger man in the story responds to advice or criticism can be particularly revealing with respect to whether he resents having to meet the standards of people senior to him or is comfortable complying with their demands.

Card 7GF

Frequently Noted Features

In Card 7GF, a young girl is sitting on a couch, holding a doll on her lap, and looking away from a woman who is seated behind her and appears to be reading to her from a book. People almost always identify the woman and the girl and comment on what they are doing. The doll is also frequently mentioned, and the book somewhat less so. Neither the couch, a table on which the woman is resting her arm, nor a doily under her arm on the table is likely to be noted.

Common Story Lines

Most often the figures in Card 7GF are seen as a mother and her child, usually with the mother reading to her daughter. Occasionally, the book is omitted from the story, and the mother is described as giving her daughter some guidance, attempting to soothe her feelings about an upsetting event, or rebuking her for having misbehaved in some way. Whether she is being read or talked to, the girl's being turned away tends to pull story lines in which she is bored, disinterested, and disengaged from whatever connection her mother is trying to make with her. It is also not unusual for attention to be paid to the relationship between the girl and her doll.

Issues Tapped

As a companion to the compelling mother-son and father-son stimuli presented by Cards 6BM and 7BM, Card 7GF arouses issues related to mother-daughter relationships. In contrast to 6BM and 7BM, which show interactions between young adults and gray-haired older persons, however, 7GF depicts an apparently preadolescent girl and a woman most likely of an age consistent with her being the girl's mother. The woman in Card 7GF is thus likely to elicit attitudes toward youthful mothers and toward being a mother of young children, and the girl in the picture tends to draw corresponding impressions of what children are like and what it is like to be a child. Their attitudes toward each other, together with whatever positive or negative features characterize their interaction, then, provide a rich source of information about concerns and expectations they attach to mothering and being mothered. The thoughts and feelings of the girl may be especially revealing in the assessment of children and adolescents, for whom the perceived meaning of the girl's experience will have more currency than the reminiscences of adult examinees.

Card 8BM

Frequently Noted Features

Card 8BM is a complex picture in which the foreground shows an adolescent boy looking straight ahead and, at his side, the barrel of a rifle. The background is a somewhat hazy image of two men, one with a knife in his hand, who appear to be performing surgery on a third man who is lying on a cot. Typical stories to this card mention the boy and the image in the background, with some explanation of how they relate to each other. The rifle and the participants in the surgical scene are also frequently noted, and the knife less so. Neither the cot in the background on which the "patient" is lying, nor what appears to be a window or bookcase in the corner, is regularly noted.

Common Story Lines

Because of its complexity, Card 8BM generates several common story lines. Most often, the picture is construed as a fantasy in which the surgical scene in the background is a figment of the boy's imagination, perhaps a daydream related to his aspiring to study medicine and become a physician. As an alternative, the boy may be identifying with the patient rather than the doctor and having a worrisome fantasy about being under the knife himself. The picture is also frequently interpreted in real terms, usually with a plot in which the surgical patient has been injured in an accident, either on the highway or, if the rifle is noted, by gunshot. Sometimes the boy is a bystander in this type of story, but at other times he is seen as having been responsible for the accident. As a final twist of importance, the accident victim is sometimes identified as a stranger and at other times as someone the boy knows, most often his father.

Issues Tapped

Card 8BM typically generates stories rich in information about ambition and aggression. Daydreams about becoming a physician may reveal hopes of being successful, acquiring wealth and status, and helping people, as well as urgent needs in these respects. Stories concerning ambition are also likely to arouse either expectations of accomplishment or fears of failing in attempting to attain one's goals. These stories frequently reflect the circumstances people anticipate as being likely to facilitate or impede their efforts to achieve.

Interpreted as an accident scene, Card 8BM usually taps concerns about being harmed or victimized in some way. The image of a man going under the knife may arouse specific anxieties about being cut or mutilated, particularly in male examinees, and for some, the subjection of the patient to the surgical procedures of an older man may stimulate childhood fears of being abused or damaged by their father. Similarly, perception of the patient as the boy's father may be an expression of unresolved father-son conflict, with anger toward the father leading to his being injured in the story. Arousal of anger toward the father is likely to be especially intense when the boy is perceived as having fired the accidental shot that wounded his father. In this latter scenario, the picture may stimulate prominent guilt feelings as well.

Card 8GF

Frequently Noted Features

Card 8GF shows a young woman sitting on a chair, her arms resting on the back of the chair and her chin in her hand, looking off into space. The woman is the only frequently noted feature in this card. Neither the chair, some material draped over the back of the chair, or what appears to be a large picture in the background is likely to be mentioned.

Common Story Lines

Card 8GF is almost always described as a woman who is deep in thought about some past or possible future events in her life. There are few clues to the possible content of her daydream, and the picture accordingly elicits a broad range of themes, no one of which is sufficiently common to note.

Issues Tapped

By reflecting an individual's own daydreams, stories told to Card 8GF may have some interpretive significance. However, because of its lack of notable detail, the picture does not consistently tap any particular psychological issues and for this reason is rarely administered.

Card 9BM

Frequently Noted Features

In Card 9BM, four men dressed in working clothes are lying on the grass. Two of the men have their head resting on the back of one of the other men, and the fourth man is in the foreground, somewhat separated from the other three, and appears to be watching them. People typically note the presence of the men in the picture and attempt to account for their prone position on the ground. The number of men is frequently noted, along with some characterization of them (e.g., as laborers). Less often, mention may be made of their clothing, position of their body parts (e.g., heads, arms, legs), and the apparent youthfulness of the man in the foreground compared with the other three men.

Common Story Lines

The scene in Card 9BM is commonly described as a group of workmen who are taking a break and resting from their labors, or perhaps as homeless men who have nothing else to do.

Issues Tapped

Card 9BM may arouse attitudes toward working-class men or toward what it means to work long hours for low pay in a menial job. Their seemingly relaxed position can suggest that the men are lazy and goofing off, or that they are totally exhausted from the physically demanding nature of their work. If the men are seen as unemployed, the story that is told may reflect how individuals feel about homeless people or about being willing to work but unable to find a job. In addition, this picture touches on how men relate to each other, whether comfortably and in collaboration or whether uneasily and in competition. The physical proximity of three of the men may also elicit attitudes and concerns related to homosexuality. Should that occur, the stance of the younger man in the foreground—whether he is looking on with envy and wishing he were part of the close group, or instead observing with distaste and hoping he is not invited to move in closer—can provide additional information about whether examinees are attracted by or averse to homosexual involvements.

Card 9GF

Frequently Noted Features

In the foreground of Card 9GF, a young woman is standing behind a tree, holding a magazine and a purse in her hand. She appears to be looking at another young woman down below her who is running along a beach. People typically take note of the two women and give some account of why they are behaving as they are. The beach, the water, and the tree are also frequently mentioned, but not the magazine and the purse in the woman's hand.

Common Story Lines

The stories most commonly told to Card 9GF concern two women in conflict or competition, often in relation to a man in whom they are both interested. The women may be seen as friends, or even as siblings, but even then, the woman behind the tree is often described as hiding there and spying on the woman on the beach, who may be seen as running because she has done something wrong, or is about to, and therefore bears watching. Alternatively with respect to placing blame, the woman on the beach is sometimes perceived as distressed and running away as a consequence of something bad done by the woman in hiding.

Issues Tapped

Card 9GF is a good source of information about peer relationships among young women, particularly with respect to stresses and strains that such relationships may involve. With each of the women commonly seen as intent on pursuing her own interests, the picture tends to arouse concerns about rivalry, jealousy, mistrust, and betrayal that are rarely muted by associations to altruism or empathy. The hidden observer and the unaware person being observed in the scene may tap concerns that individuals have about being watched or needing to keep a watchful eye on others.

Card 10

Frequently Noted Features

Card 10 shows the heads of two people, with the head and hand of a shorter person appearing to rest on the shoulder of a taller person. The gender of the two people is not clearly defined, but the taller person on the left is almost always seen as male and the shorter person on the right as female. Stories typically include mention of the heads of both persons, but rarely the hand.

Common Story Lines

Stories to Card 10 usually portray the two people in a mutual embrace. Most often they are seen as comforting or nurturing each other, often purely for the pleasure of doing so, and at other times because they are about to spend some time apart or have just been reunited after separation.

Issues Tapped

Card 10 conveys to most people a sense of contentment and is accordingly likely to identify expectations or concerns people have about enjoying such contentment in their own lives. Stories are also likely to reveal persons' level of comfort with sensuality and intimacy in male-female relationships and their attraction or aversion to close physical contact between men and women. In those rare instances in which both figures are seen as men or as women, this picture may tap attitudes toward gay and lesbian relationships.

Card 11

Frequently Noted Features

Card 11 shows a vaguely defined and surrealistic scene of a narrow pathway on the edge of a deep chasm. In the distance, several obscure figures appear to be approaching a bridge over the chasm, while above them the long head and neck of a dragon-like figure protrude from the rocky side of a cliff. People commonly note the pathway, the dragon, and the obscure figures, which are variously identified as people, bugs, or perhaps a pack animal. The bridge and some rocks strewn alongside the cliff are less frequently mentioned, and a small humanlike figure on the far end of the bridge who appears to be in flight is rarely noted. Typical stories also include some accounting for the fantasy or prehistoric nature of the scene.

Common Story Lines

Card 11 most often elicits stories about the obscure figures being perilously perched on the edge of the cliff and at risk for being attacked by the dragon. Reflecting the influence of cartoon portrayals of benign dragons, the long-necked creature is also seen at times as providing protection for the figures as they wend their way in dangerous territory.

Issues Tapped

Card 11 typically arouses concerns about being vulnerable to harm in an unsafe world in which uncontrollable forces of nature and risk of assault by aggressive creatures combine to threaten people's well-being. Hence the stories told often reveal how people are inclined to react in situations they are helpless to control and how they customarily deal with fears of being attacked. Should the story cast the dragon as a protector, it may reflect needs to seek out people who are viewed as more powerful and resourceful than oneself and to rely on these people to assure one's safety.

Card 12M

Frequently Noted Features

In Card 12M, a young man is lying on a couch and an older man is standing over him, leaning forward with his knee on the couch and his hand stretched out over the younger man's face. Stories typically include mention of the two figures and some explanation of their positioning. The older man's hand is also frequently noted, but neither his knee, the couch, nor a cushion under the younger man's head is likely to be mentioned.

Common Story Lines

Stories to Card 12M typically depict the older man as doing something to the younger man, who is the passive recipient of whatever the older man is doing to him. In some common scenarios, the younger man is ill and the older man is a physician treating him or a clergyman performing some religious rite on his behalf. In other frequent scenarios, the younger man is seen as being hypnotized or as reclining on a psychoanalyst's couch, with the older man being his therapist. As an occasional alternative to stories describing the older man as helpful and well-intentioned, he is seen as attacking or taking advantage of the younger man in some way.

Issues Tapped

Card 12M tends to tap anticipations of relationships that are likely to arise between younger and older men. Like Card 7BM, then, it touches on issues of respect and authority in such relationships. In addition, Card 12M is noteworthy for its portrayal of passivity in the younger man, who is lying prone with his eyes closed. Stories to this card are accordingly likely to reflect male examinees' attitudes toward being passive, concerns they may have about controlling or being under the control of another man, and perhaps their perspectives on homosexual encounters as well. Whether the intentions of the older man are kindly or sinister and whether the young man is a willing or conscripted participant in what is going on are likely in particular to reflect a person's perspectives in these respects.

Card 12F

Frequently Noted Features

Card 12F shows the head and shoulders of an adult woman and just behind her the head and shoulders of an older, gray-haired woman. The older woman has a shawl over her head and is holding her chin in her hand. Stories to the picture typically identify both figures and comment on the relationship between them. The shawl, the older woman's holding her chin in her hand, and the older woman's rather unusual facial expression are also occasionally noted.

Common Story Lines

In a common line of stories to Card 12F, the older woman is seen as a mother or maternal figure giving advice to the younger woman or being critical of her. Alternatively, the figure of the older woman is frequently construed as a figment of the younger woman's imagination, most often as a vision of how she might look when she grows old or as a representation of her conscience remonstrating with her for things she has done or failed to do.

Issues Tapped

Card 12F arouses issues related to mother-daughter relationships. Unlike the Card 7GF scene, in which the mother figure is an adult woman and the daughter figure a young girl, the figures in Card 12F are likely to bring out attitudes toward being the adult daughter of an aging mother or the elderly mother of an adult daughter. In common with the other TAT depictions of parent-child or older person-younger person relationships, the interactions attributed to the figures in Card 12F may also reveal attitudes and concerns about such matters as authority, caring, control, and respect. The interactions in Card 12F stories are also likely to shed light on whether a person anticipates finding help, support, sympathy, and reassurance in adult parent-child relationships or expects instead to encounter disinterest, distaste, criticism, and rejection. When Card 12F stories focus on the younger woman, with the figure of the older woman seen as symbolizing part of the younger woman's self, concerns about the aging process are likely to come to the fore, as are guilt feelings and the anticipation about being either deservedly or unfairly punished.

Card 12BG

Frequently Noted Features

Card 12BG is a woodland scene with a tree on the left and on the right a rowboat pulled up on the bank of a stream. There are no human figures in the picture. Stories typically mention the boat and its being in the woods, and examinees are also likely to offer some explanation of why there is no one in the boat or nearby. Neither the tree, the stream, nor other details of the surrounding flora are commonly noted.

Common Story Lines

Perhaps more than any of the other TAT cards, Card 12BG is likely to be perceived as a picture in which nothing much is happening. Spontaneous stories told to this card often consist only of its being described as a pleasant and relaxing scene in the woods. When encouraged by the standard instructions to make up a story with a beginning and end, examinees often inject some people into their story and relate a tale of adventure in which the people have abandoned the boat for some reason, have wandered off temporarily for a stroll or a picnic, or have gone exploring and lost their way.

Issues Tapped

When the boat in Card 12BG is perceived as abandoned or the person or persons who brought it ashore as having met some bad end, this picture may suggest themes of abandonment, loneliness, depression, or danger. More commonly, however, the picture arouses positive connotations of peacefulness, serenity, being at one with nature, and having a welcome respite from the hurly-burly of everyday demands and responsibilities. Because of its typically calming effect and the infrequency with which it touches on conflict-laden issues, some examiners have found it useful to insert Card 12BG into their TAT administration when an examinee becomes unusually upset telling stories to some of the more potent cards.

Card 13MF

Frequently Noted Features

Card 13MF is a complex picture that shows a man standing in the foreground with his head downcast and his face buried in his arm. Behind the man is the figure of an apparently naked woman lying in bed and covered up to the waist with a blanket or sheet. Stories typically identify the man, the woman, and the perceived reason why they are together and positioned in this way. Also frequently mentioned are the bed, some books on a table, and the nudity of the woman. Other details in the picture that are rarely mentioned include a chair, a lamp on the table, and a picture on the wall.

Common Story Lines

Card 13MF commonly elicits three alternative story lines. In one of these plots, the man and woman have just had sexual intercourse, the man is overcome with guilt and remorse, and the woman is seen as a prostitute or person of easy virtue, and rarely as the man's wife. In a second frequent plot, the woman is ill or dead, and the man, usually seen as her husband, is in a state of shock or grief. The third alternative avoids the sexual and illness implications of the picture with description of a mundane domestic scene in which the man, still rubbing sleep from his eyes, is dressed and ready to go to work and trying not to wake up his wife, who remains sleeping in the bed.

Issues Tapped

Card 13MF, seen as a scene of sexuality, is usually revealing about attitudes toward heterosexual encounters. Moral perspectives on adultery, fidelity, and promiscuity are likely to be tapped by the picture, as are specific attitudes toward women who welcome sexual liaisons and toward men who seduce women into them. Is the woman seen as the seducer, and the man a sympathetic character to be pitied rather than blamed, or is the man a despicable attacker and the woman seen as a blameless victim who was powerless to resist him? These and other variations in sexual stories told to Card 13MF provide clues to a wide range of heterosexual conflicts and concerns in the lives of people who tell them.

As a scene of illness or death, Card 13MF is likely to tap feelings about marital relationships and anxieties people may have about losing the support and companionship of loved ones who become ill and die. The outcome of stories along this line may be predictive of how individuals will deal in their own lives with the inevitable passing of people close to them. By contrast with the usually significant meaning of the sexual and illness stories commonly told to Card 13MF, stories that interpret the picture in terms of routine daily events are likely to disguise more than they reveal about a person's inner experience.

Card 13B

Frequently Noted Features

In Card 13B, a little boy is sitting on the doorstep of a log cabin, with his hands held together and his elbows resting on his knees. He is barefoot and fills only a small part of the large doorway in which he sits. Frequently noted features include the boy, some description of the cabin, and an explanation for his being by himself. The boy's hands and feet are rarely mentioned, although he is sometimes seen as holding something in his hands.

Common Story Lines

The boy in 13B is usually described as having been left alone and as waiting for his parents to return, or as being deep in thought. Because the generally drab appearance of the boy's clothing and surroundings suggest that he is living in disadvantaged circumstances, stories about introspection sometimes have him thinking or fantasizing about his prospects for enjoying a more prosperous life in a more appealing environment.

Issues Tapped

Card 13B tends to touch on parent-child relationships, particularly with respect to childhood concerns about being deserted or abandoned by one's parents. Related worries about being lonely, perhaps rejected by peers as well as neglected by parents, may surface in stories told to this picture. Finally, this picture may remind people of childhood fantasies they had about finding solutions to their problems and having a future life better than their current one.

Card 13G

Frequently Noted Features

In Card 13G, a little girl is climbing a winding flight of stairs. Like the little boy in Card 13B who occupies only a small part of a large doorway, the little girl is overshadowed by vast surrounds, stationed at the bottom of a massive staircase that towers over her. Stories usually include mention of the girl, the staircase, and her reason for being on it. Clearly defined latticework in the staircase and a cap that covers most of the girl's head are rarely noted.

Common Story Lines

Stories to Card 13G usually depict the girl as climbing the stairs to explore an unknown or unfamiliar situation. As a potentially significant variant of this story line, she may be enjoying and excited by an adventure she has chosen for herself, or she may be fearful and apprehensive as she undertakes a climb that has been required of her, against her wishes.

Issues Tapped

Like Card 13B, Card 13G portrays a lone, small figure dwarfed by large surrounds. However, the figure of the girl in this card is not clearly defined and has no visible facial features. Card 13G consequently lacks the rich and varied card pull of less obscure and multiperson TAT pictures, and it is less likely than 13B to tap interpersonal issues. For some individuals, this card may nevertheless tap concerns about having to contend with overpowering or overwhelming environmental obstacles or anxieties associated with being in strange, unrecognizable, or unpredictable situations.

Card 14

Frequently Noted Features

Card 14 shows the outline of a figure usually, but not always, seen as a man, silhouetted in bright light against a window frame. The rest of the picture is solid black. People typically note the figure and the window frame and comment on what the person is doing or thinking.

Common Story Lines

Typical Card 14 stories describe the figure as standing in the window, either at nighttime or early in the morning, and being deep in thought, usually about future plans or prospects. In a positively toned version of this story line, the person is welcoming the new day while reflecting on the good things in his or her life and the appealing possibilities that lie ahead. In a negatively toned alternative version, the person is dreading the new day (or, if a nighttime scene, regretting events in the previous day), envisions little likelihood of happiness or success, and may even be contemplating jumping from the window in a suicide attempt.

Issues Tapped

Because of its pull for future events and its equivalent stimulus value for events turning in either positive or negative directions, Card 14 often provides a barometer of people's underlying sense of self-worth and their hopes and fears about what lies ahead for them. Ambitions and aspirations are particularly likely to come to the fore in stories told to this card, as are discouragement, despair, and self-destructive tendencies. In stories that skirt affective components, the ruminations of the figure in the window are still likely to be revealing about an individual's worldview and philosophy of life.

Card 15

Frequently Noted Features

In Card 15, a gaunt, gray-haired man dressed in black is standing amid some tombstones with his hands held together in front of him. The man and the tombstones are typically noted in Card 15 stories, along with some explanation for his presence among them. The man's hands are also frequently noted, but the man's unusual clothing and the varied sizes and shapes of the numerous tombstones in the picture are rarely mentioned.

Common Story Lines

Because of its clearly delineated content and heavy dark shading, Card 15 exerts perhaps the strongest card pull of any of the TAT pictures. Stories told to this card almost always involve a man in a cemetery grieving over the loss of a loved one. These stories may vary with respect to such matters as whether the loved one's passing was recent or long ago and how the man is coping with his grief. Exceptions to the basic cemetery theme are rare and likely to reveal strained efforts to deny depressive concerns.

Issues Tapped

Because of the strong Card 15 card pull for depressing stories about loss and loneliness and about death and dying, these themes rarely have interpretive significance. However, details of the stories people tell can reveal underlying attitudes toward people who have died, such as anger for having been deserted by them, guilt for having survived them, or remorse for having treated them badly while they were alive. Story elaborations may also provide clues to expectations or fears people have concerning their own mortality and how their life might end.

Card 16

Frequently Noted Features

Card 16 is the totally blank card in the series. As such, it has no frequently noted features, other than being totally white, and any other descriptions will be based on what people create in their mind when they are asked to imagine a picture as well as a story to go with it.

Common Story Lines

Having no descriptive characteristics, Card 16 does not elicit any common story lines.

Issues Tapped

In the absence of any card pull, Card 16 cannot be identified as arousing any particular issues or revealing any psychological characteristics. Highly verbal individuals who have a vivid imagination and are comfortably engaged in the examination process may produce varied and detailed Card 16 stories that are rich in meaning. On the other hand, reticent and resistive individuals who lack a creative bent or who are uneasy about being tested are likely to relate skimpy and superficial stories that document their avoidant approach to the testing situation but make little additional contribution to the interpretive process.

Card 17BM

Frequently Noted Features

In card 17BM, a naked man is hanging onto a rope and is climbing either up or down. People typically include the man and the rope in their stories and describe the direction he is taking. His nakedness is also frequently mentioned, as is his muscular physique, and the flat surface behind him is sometimes identified as a wall or the side of a structure. The man's facial features are clearly defined in the picture, but are rarely mentioned

Common Story Lines

Card 17BM commonly suggests two alternative story lines. In one of these frequent scenarios, the action takes place in a gymnasium, and the man is displaying his athletic prowess, perhaps in a competition of some kind. In the alternate common scenario, the man is using the rope to escape from prison or from some other inhospitable place where his safety and security have been threatened.

Issues Tapped

Stories to Card 17BM are likely to reflect attitudes toward achievement and accomplishment. Both the gymnast and the escapist in the common 17B story lines are making an attempt that can end in success or failure, and the hopes, fears, and expectations people have about challenging or competitive situations are likely to surface in these narratives. The picture can also arouse attitudes toward exhibitionistic displays of one's prowess and, especially among male examinees, self-perceptions of one's physical capabilities. The exhibitionistic pull of Card 17BM is heightened by the man's nudity, which can also stimulate homosexual interests or anxieties in male examinees.

Card 17GF

Frequently Noted Features

In Card 17GF, the small figure of a woman is leaning over the railing of a bridge and looking down at the water. A large building towers above her, and behind it the sun is shining through some clouds. Below the bridge are small figures of men unloading a boat. Stories typically mention the woman and what is happening in the scene, and the bridge, the water, and the men are frequently included in the story. Other details that are seldom noted in this complex picture include not only the boat, the large building, the sun, and the clouds, but windows in the large building, a smaller building under the bridge where the men are unloading, and the bundles being carried by the men on their shoulders.

Common Story Lines

Card 17GF tends to elicit a wide variety of stories, none of which is especially common. Within this variety, the story line most likely to appear has the woman in the picture eagerly awaiting the arrival of a loved one or sadly observing a loved one's departure. Occasionally the picture is described as the scene of a crime, with the men stealing or smuggling goods and the woman serving as their lookout. Also, the woman may be perceived as distraught for some reason and contemplating jumping from the bridge.

Issues Tapped

When the woman in the picture is perceived as the sole focus of the story, Card 17GF often arouses feelings and anticipations related to experiences of attachment and reunion or separation and loss. When the woman in the picture is seen as involved with the men in some way, instead of the men being peripheral figures in the scene, this card may tap perspectives on the obligations and rewards of being an accepted group member. When the woman's position on the bridge, like the position of the figure in the window on Card 14, stimulates thoughts about jumping, Card 17GF can be one of the TAT cards that helps identify suicidal ideation.

Card 18BM

Frequently Noted Features

Card 18BM shows a man wearing a long coat and being grabbed from behind by three hands. The figures of whoever may be doing the grabbing are not visible. People can be expected to take note of the man, the hands, and the unusual nature of a picture in which the owners of the hands cannot be seen. A pained look on the man's face and his disheveled clothing are also frequently mentioned.

Common Story Lines

People responding to Card 18BM commonly color their stories with themes either of attack or support. In stories of attack, the man is being grabbed by unknown assailants intent on beating, robbing, or even killing him. In stories of support, the man is seen as ill, inebriated, or overdosed with drugs and is being helped by friends or passersby who have come to his aid.

Issues Tapped

Card 18BM is likely to tap fears of being vulnerable to injury and abuse at the hands of unknown aggressors, as well as fears of falling ill or becoming incapacitated by substance abuse. Either way, being helpless to control regrettable events and incapable of functioning effectively are typically reflected in stories to this card. The distressing thoughts and feelings aroused by this card may be eased somewhat by perceiving the man as in the hands of supportive friends. Even then, issues related to being dependent on others and unable to take care of oneself are likely to make an appearance. When the man is perceived as under the influence of substances, attitudes toward drunkenness and addiction and toward people who fall prey to them may also emerge.

Card 18GF

Frequently Noted Features

Care 18GF shows a woman holding another woman by the throat and apparently pushing her backward across the banister of a flight of stairs. Typically noted are the two women and some account of why one of the women has her hands around the other woman's neck. The banister is also frequently mentioned

Common Story Lines

Card 18GF is most often described as an aggressive interaction in which one woman is for some reason choking another woman. Nevertheless, there is variability as to whether the two women are friends or enemies, siblings, or a mother and daughter. Not infrequently, the woman being held by the neck is described as being consoled by the other woman, or perhaps being helped up from the floor or up the stairs. Because of the strong pull of this card for an aggressive interaction, stories of consolation and help are likely to indicate efforts to deny hostility and avoid dealing with the causes and consequences of aggression.

Issues Tapped

As just suggested, stories to Card 18GF tend to reflect attitudes and expectations about how anger between women becomes aroused and expressed. Either mother-daughter or sibling conflicts may be reflected in these stories, and the interaction between the women may be particularly likely to bring forward feelings of envy, jealousy, or resentment.

Card 19

Frequently Noted Features

Like Card 12BG, Card 19 is a nature scene with no animate figures, and like Card 11, it is a surrealistic picture, in this instance of some oddly shaped clouds hanging over a strangely shaped, snow-covered cabin, with windswept snow in the foreground. People usually take note of the cabin and the snow and comment on the apparently inclement weather or on the forces of nature. Other frequently noted details include windows in the cabin and a vague black figure hovering above the back of the cabin. Also obvious but rarely mentioned is a black chimney sticking up from the roof of the cabin.

Common Story Lines

Card 19 tends to pull stories in which the cabin is in harm's way from potentially dangerous forces of nature (e.g., wind, snow, storms) or sometimes from ghosts, witches, extraterrestrials, or abstractions of evil. In both contexts, the cabin is seen either as being at risk for being battered by whatever surrounds it or as a sturdy and safe haven that will provide refuge from the battering for whoever is fortunate enough to be inside.

Issues Tapped

The picture in Card 19 tends to arouse concerns about being isolated and cut off from sources of support while having to contend with frightening elements of nature or the supernatural. Stories to this card are likely to reflect how individuals may react to uncertain, threatening, or potentially dangerous situations. A story line may identify confidence in finding shelter and escaping harm even in terrifying situations, or it may instead convey a sense of hopelessness and impending doom in the face of danger.

Card 20

Frequently Noted Features

Card 20 is a nighttime scene in which a dimly lit figure, usually seen as a man, is leaning against a lamppost. Stories typically note the man and the lamppost and include some reference to the dim light. Also visible in the picture, but rarely mentioned, are a coat and hat the man is wearing, his position with his hand in his coat pocket, and a tree in the background.

Common Story Lines

The picture in Card 20 most commonly elicits stories about being alone and waiting. In a pleasant variation of this common theme, the man is waiting for a friend or a date to arrive, although sometimes pleasant anticipation may have given way to impatience with having been kept waiting or disappointment with a "no show." In a less pleasant variation, the man is seen as a dangerous person up to no good, perhaps a mugger or rapist on the prowl for a victim.

Issues Tapped

Like many of the other TAT cards portraying a single figure, especially figures that are only dimly visible, Card 20 tends to arouse concerns related to loneliness and isolation. Stories to this card can also reflect interpersonal attitudes and expectations, should the figure be seen as waiting for an acquaintance to arrive on the scene. When the figure is perceived in more sinister ways, perspectives on perpetrators of aggression are likely to be aroused, as well as fears of being victimized by aggression.

INTERPRETATION: STORY MEANING

The stories people tell to the TAT pictures typically reflect many of their attitudes, intentions, and expectations, both those they recognize in themselves and some that have not been in their conscious awareness. TAT stories also contain clues to a person's affective disposition, preferred coping style, and cognitive integrity. This section of the chapter illustrates how these personality characteristics can be assessed by reading through a person's stories with close attention to how the characters in the stories are described and interact, how the story plots begin and end, the emotional tone that characterizes the stories, and the manner in which the stories are expressed. This approach to interpretation closely resembles Bellak's inspection method, which was identified earlier as the most commonly used interpretive procedure in clinical practice.

As a further general consideration, the TAT interpretive process shares with the interpretation of other personality assessment instruments the necessity of a two-step sequence. The first step consists of generating hypotheses about the implications of the test data. The second step calls for gauging the validity of these hypotheses in light of information available from other test findings and from the background and case history of the person being examined. Suppose a TAT story appears to suggest that a male examinee is inclined to express anger directly and to feel justified in perpetrating violence on others. This suggestion would be strengthened by Rorschach indications that he is an impulsive and action-oriented individual, an MMPI-2 with a 49/94 codetype and an elevated Antisocial Practices scale (ASP), and a history of assaultive behavior.

But suppose that this man's Rorschach responses indicate a contemplative nature and good capacities for self-control, his MMPI-2 scores on Scales 4 and 9 and ASP are unremarkable, and he has no history of harming other people physically. Then a TAT-based inference that he is a potentially violent person should probably be replaced with an alternative hypothesis, perhaps that the anger and violence in his TAT stories reflect seeing himself as a victim rather than a perpetrator, and fearing harm rather than being disposed to inflict harm. An admonition by Murray (1943/1971) in this regard remains as relevant today as it was over 60 years ago: "In any event, the conclusions that are reached by an analysis of TAT stories must be regarded as good 'leads' or working hypotheses to be verified by other methods, rather than as proved facts" (p. 13).

Of further help in gauging the accuracy of TAT interpretations, apparent meanings are most likely to be dependable when they are inferred from compelling story lines and formulated at low levels of inference. The compelling story lines in a TAT protocol, like the richest elements of Rorschach imagery (see Chapter 11), are those that are repetitive, dramatic, original, and spontaneous. Recurring themes of love or hate, happiness or despair, conflict or collaboration, and any other sort of attitude, affect, or interaction tend to reveal more about a person's inner life than single instances of such themes. With respect to drama, however, even occasional themes gain interpretive weight when they are expressed with intensity rather than in bland fashion (e.g., "She'll never fall in love again, and she'll be terribly unhappy for the rest of her life" versus "That will be the end of her relationship with this man, end of story"). Themes that are both recurrent and presented dramatically are particularly likely to convey reliable information about a person's concerns and expectations.

The originality of a story refers to whether its features diverge from common attributions to a picture. As noted, Card 13B (figure of a boy sitting in a doorway) usually elicits single-person themes of being lonely, alone, or in deep thought. A story to this picture about "A boy sitting there on the stoop because his mother threw him out of the house, and she's standing back there in the house still yelling at him" includes a figure (the mother), an interaction (rejection), and an emotional tone (anger) that are not ordinarily elicited by Card 13B. The originality of such a story would add weight to its possible implications for a boy's feeling undeservedly punished by a rejecting mother, or perhaps seeing himself as a bad person who deserves to be punished for his misdeeds. As for spontaneity, a story element is likely to have more definite implications for whatever personality characteristics it suggests when it appears in an examinee's original story than when it emerges in response to the examiner's subsequent questions about the story as originally told.

As for formulating impressions of TAT stories at low levels of inference, Bellak and Abrams (1997, p. 84) make a useful distinction between "observation-near" and "observation-distant" interpretations. An observation-near interpretation sticks closely to what is actually seen in the pictures and said in telling stories about them. A Card 1 story about a boy being compelled to practice the violin against his wishes can generate observation-near hypotheses about individuals' attitudes toward being required to do something they would rather not. By contrast, an alternative interpretation suggested by Bellak and Abrams (1977, p. 63), in which playing of the violin is conceived as symbolic of playing with oneself, and a Card 1 story as reflecting attitudes toward masturbation, would be an observation-distant interpretation involving a high level of inference.

Generally speaking, the more clearly and directly interpretations are based on what is depicted in the cards and on the content of the stories told to them, the more likely they are to capture accurately some characteristics of an individual's mental and emotional life. Conversely, to the extent that interpretations are based on such symbolic associations as equating the playing of a musical instrument with masturbation, the more room there is for them to be off the mark, like artillery fired from a great distance.[1]

Attitudes, Intentions, and Expectations

The characteristics that people attribute to the characters and events in their TAT stories often reflect some of their own attitudes, intentions, and expectations. A Card 1 story about a "talented" boy who wants to master the violin, practices diligently, and becomes a world-famous performer suggests positive attitudes of confidence in one's capabilities, intent to work hard toward ambitious goals, and expectations of success in what one tries to accomplish. By contrast, a Card 17BM story about a "feeble" man who is attempting to climb a rope but "isn't strong enough to pull himself up" suggests negative attitudes (perhaps seeing oneself as a weak or ineffectual person) and limited expectations (perhaps expecting a future fraught with failure and little to be gained from trying hard).

Should stories of the first type (successful violinist) accumulate in a person's protocol, the individual is probably giving evidence of solid self-esteem, a strong work ethic, and a generally optimistic outlook on the future. Should repetitive stories of the second type

---

[1] It is of historical interest to note that the conceptual basis for this interpretive guideline was anticipated by Freud (1910/1957), who asserted that the accuracy and effectiveness of interpretations in psychoanalytic psychotherapy will be related to whether a patient's self-awareness has "reached the neighborhood" (p. 226) of what they suggest (see also Busch, 1995, chap. 2).

(unsuccessful rope-climber) predominate, a person is likely to be giving evidence of low self-esteem, feelings of frustration about unrewarded effort, and a pessimistic perspective on life. As a third possibility, stories may seem silent with respect to success and failure, and they may be peopled with inactive characters who show little interest in pursuing clearly defined goals. Then the data may be reflecting neither enthusiasm nor discouragement in competitive pursuits, but rather lack of ambition, avoidance of commitment, and distaste for energetic striving.

In drawing inferences about an individual's self-perceptions from characteristics attributed to a story figure, the possibility should also be considered that the figure represents an ideal rather than an actual image in the person's mind. Thus the way figures are described may reveal how people wish they were, or dream of being, rather than how they actually see themselves. Suppose that the man leaning against a lamppost in Card 20 is described by a male examinee as "A guy who has his act together—he looks relaxed, he feels good about himself, he knows what he wants to do, and he thinks he can do it." This story could indicate the same kind of positive self-image that is suggested by a purposeful and eventually successful violin student in Card 1. Alternatively, however, the man telling this feel-good Card 20 story could be engaging in wishful thinking about how he would like things to be, when in truth they are quite otherwise. The distinction between actual and ideal self-representations in TAT stories must often rest on other sources of information. Knowing from his past history that the man telling this Card 20 story has been chronically indecisive and unsure of himself would be helpful in identifying the effectively functioning figure portrayed in the story as an ideal rather than an actual self-image.

Along with providing clues to people's attitudes toward themselves and their future prospects, the characteristics attributed to figures in their TAT stories may also identify images they have of other people. The woman apparently reading or talking to the girl in Card 7GF could be described as a caring and devoted mother, or as an indifferent parent who takes no notice of her daughter's seeming disinterest or boredom. The older woman in Card 6BM could be described as the helpful and sympathetic mother of the troubled younger man in the picture, or as a self-centered and demanding mother who is the source of her son's difficulties. These alternative descriptions would suggest parallel differences in persons' attitudes toward their own mothers or their expectations from maternal figures in general. Likewise, the older man in Card 7BM might be described as the kindly and supportive father of the younger man in the picture, or as the younger man's autocratic and rejecting father, and these images could reflect similar perceptions of fathers in general or of the examinee's father in particular.

Thematic elements of TAT stories can shed light as well on the attitudes individuals have toward males and females and on how they expect people to relate to each other. Consider the following possible alternative themes for Card 4: (a) the woman in the picture is a concerned and devoted wife who is consoling her despondent husband following some disappointment or failure he has experienced; (b) the man in the picture is a frazzled and frustrated husband who is fed up with his wife's nagging, selfishness, and unreasonable demands and is thinking of leaving her; (c) the couple in the picture are a husband and wife who love each other deeply and rarely disagree, but are expressing opposite opinions about whether to visit her parents or his parents during a coming holiday. Such themes can indicate whether a person views women and wives as comforting or demanding; views men and husbands as dependent or undependable; and views marital relationships as smooth or stormy.

TAT stories may also have implications for how people feel about sexuality and aggression in interpersonal relationships. Perhaps the older man in Card 6GF has just asked the younger woman in the picture for a date, or made an explicit sexual overture, and she has found his proposition offensive and ridiculous, or flattering and welcome, depending on how the individual tells the story. Is the man characterized in undesirable ways, as clumsy, presumptuous, and amoral, or in appealing ways, as suave, self-confident, and adventurous? Is the woman promiscuous, flirty, lonely, flustered, or uncertain how to respond? Is the outcome of this interaction pleasant, fulfilling, embarrassing, or disappointing? These and similarly denotative elements in a Card 6GF story can be a rich source of clues to a female examinee's attitudes and expectations in heterosexual interactions.

With respect to attitudes and expectations in aggressive interactions, how does the man in Card 18BM respond in a story in which he is being rudely grabbed from behind? Does he become fearful of being harmed, humiliated by his inability to fight back, and resigned to taking a beating? Does he become angry, rather than fearful, and fight off his attackers with a display of martial arts, or talk his way out of the situation with a glib use of his wits? Is he spared any of these outcomes by the arrival of another party who disperses the attackers? The course the story takes is likely to have implications for whether the storytellers tend to see themselves as inept or as resourceful people, whether their preference runs to fight or flight in the face of aggression, and whether they are given to rescue fantasies as a way of dealing with threatening situations.

Affective Disposition

The emotional tone of the TAT stories people tell, together with the emotions they display while telling their stories, usually provides clues to how they feel. Pronounced or recurrent tendencies to describe characters in stories as being happy or sad, anxious or comfortable, or angry or at peace with the world suggest that a person may be experiencing similar affects. Additionally, events in the story that are seen as having elicited these affects may provide clues to the kinds of life situations that are likely to result in the person's feeling this way.

Familiarity with the previously presented card pull information is often helpful in evaluating the implications of story tone for a person's affective state. Sad stories told to pictures that rarely elicit sad stories (e.g., Card 12B, woodland scene) may be particularly indicative of despondency or depression. Conversely, strained efforts to ascribe happiness and gaiety to people and scenes that contain little indication of either (e.g., Card 11, surrealistic scene; Card 15, man in cemetery) may be a clue to the pattern of denial and forced euphoria that often characterizes hypomania. In some instances, especially for people who say very little about how the characters in their stories are feeling, the emotional tone they ascribe to scenes and situations in general (e.g., pleasant, gloomy, scary) may provide the main TAT clue to their affective state (e.g., a corresponding sense of well-being, despondency, or fearfulness).

Clues to persons' affective disposition may also emerge in the manner in which they express their stories. A lighthearted, bemused recounting of stories, accompanied by positive comments about the task ("This is interesting; I like these better than those inkblots") has different implications from a tearful engagement with the stories being told ("These are all so sad; it's really hard for me to talk about them"). Such differences in expressive style suggest corresponding differences in how people generally respond to emotionally arousing situations, particularly with respect to whether their tendencies run to intellectual detachment ("This is interesting") or affective involvement ("These are all so sad").

Coping Style

Just as the feelings attributed to the figures in TAT stories are likely to reflect the affective disposition of the storyteller, the ways in which story characters deal with their circumstances often provide clues to a person's preferred coping style. Suppose that the characters in a person's stories typically respond to situations by deferring action, avoiding decisions, and hoping or expecting that the passage of time or the intervention of others will provide solutions to problems (e.g., "He's not sure what to do next, so he'll just sit tight and see what happens"; "She usually lets her mother make her decisions for her"). Suppose, by contrast, that another person's story characters typically display initiative, self-reliance, and constructive problem solving (e.g., "She'll figure out what has to be done, and she'll do it"; "He's listening to the advice he's getting, but he's already made up his mind").

The stories told by the first of these two persons suggest that he or she is a somewhat passive individual, more of a follower than a leader, who tends to defer to the judgment and wishes of others and prefers to let other people take responsibility. The stories of the second person suggest an active coping style characterized by preferences to be in charge, to seek and accept responsibility, and to shape events rather than be shaped by them. This active/passive dimension of coping style parallels the dilemma of Shakespeare's (1604/1947) Hamlet, who muses whether "to take arms against a sea of troubles and by opposing end them" or "by a sleep to say we end the heart-ache and the thousand natural shocks that flesh is heir to" (*Tragedy of Hamlet*, Act III, Scene 1).

To illustrate another dimension of coping style that is often illuminated by the TAT, the structure and content of stories and the demeanor of examinees while telling them sometimes suggest a preference on their part for either ideational or expressive ways of dealing with situations. Some people elaborate comfortably and at length on what the characters in their stories are thinking, but have little to say about how the characters are feeling. Asked about characters' feelings, these individuals may become uneasy, answer haltingly and with reluctance, and even try to dismiss the topic altogether (as in "I have no idea what their feelings might be"—to which, by the way, the examiner should respond with "Use your imagination and make up something"). Other people may show the opposite pattern, by describing spontaneously and in detail how their characters feel, while paying little attention to what the characters are thinking and becoming uncomfortable and unresponsive when asked to imagine what these thoughts might be.

This difference in storytelling is likely to identify a corresponding difference in an ideational/expressive dimension of coping style. People who are more comfortable with thoughts than feelings on the TAT may be the kind of person who is known as a thinker rather than a doer. Such people tend to be contemplative individuals who make decisions by considering alternative possibilities in a deliberate manner before taking action, and who solve problems conceptually, by mulling over possible solutions in their minds before trying them out. By contrast, individuals who appear more comfortable with feelings than thoughts in their TAT performance are likely to be doers who decide what actions to take on the basis of intuition rather than reflection, are guided more by how they feel than what they think, and solve problems by trying out various possible solutions to them.

As these brief descriptions indicate, coping preferences along the active/passive and ideational/expressive dimensions have substantial implications for how people are likely to conduct themselves in various situations. These dimensions illustrate just two of many ways in which TAT findings can reflect coping style, including application of the DMM described earlier to identify an affinity for specific defense mechanisms. As always in the interpretation of thematic imagery, inferences along these lines are best taken as clues to consider and hypotheses to pursue, not as conclusions that by themselves provide sufficient basis for applied decision making.

Cognitive Integrity

The structural characteristics of TAT stories and the manner in which they are expressed frequently contain clues to the integrity of people's cognitive functioning—particularly their attention, perception, and thinking. Regarding attention, persons who are functioning well cognitively tend to notice and comment on the obvious and commonly noted stimulus elements of the pictures, as identified in the earlier discussion in this chapter on card pull, and they avoid becoming distracted by or preoccupied with minor or rarely mentioned details. Accordingly, failure to take account of central stimulus features of the pictures and excessive emphasis on peripheral features are likely to identify an unbalanced and potentially maladaptive focus of attention. Such faulty focusing could reflect obsessive-compulsive disorder, attention deficit or dissociative disorder, or anxiety reactions to particular cards, or perhaps other possible etiologies. When deciding which is the most likely among alternative possibilities, clinicians must be guided by the direction in which general trends in the assessment data appear to point.

As for perception, cognitively intact examinees typically perceive the people in their TAT stories realistically and construct plots that reflect likely relationships among events. By contrast, describing the man in Card 2 (farm scene) as drilling for oil, the people in Card 6BF (elderly woman and young man) as husband and wife, and the woman in Card 8GF (woman with chin in her hand) as a man would constitute instances of inaccurate perception of the cards' stimulus characteristics. Even if considered merely improbable, and not totally impossible, highly unusual impressions of such kinds usually identify limited capacity to perceive and endorse conventional reality. Nevertheless, unusual stories may sometimes reflect the eccentricity of creative people, whom the test instructions have asked to use their imagination, rather than poor reality testing.

Impaired reality testing is almost always indicated by stories in which unlikely outcomes reflect faulty judgment concerning how one event leads to another. Examples of such unrealistic judgments that stretch the boundaries of reality or seem excessively fanciful would be a story to Card 8BM (boy with rifle) in which the boy has killed someone "but he'll get away with it, because no one cares," or a story to Card 13G (girl climbing a staircase) in which the girl is rewarded for reaching the top by "being made into an angel." Because the TAT pictures are more structured than the Rorschach inkblots, unrealistic judgments of this kind do not have to occur as frequently on the TAT as on the RIM to indicate cognitive disorder. Even one such distorted story may warrant considering the possibility that an individual has a loose hold on reality.

Turning to their thinking, people whose cognitive integrity is intact typically produce coherent TAT stories that are easy to follow and exemplify logical reasoning. Disjointed stories that do not flow smoothly, and confusing stories that lack a sensible sequence, give reason for concern that a person's thought processes may be similarly scattered and incoherent. Narratives characterized by strained and circumstantial reasoning also raise questions about the clarity of an individual's thought processes. Illogical reasoning consists of drawing definite conclusions on the basis of minimal or irrelevant evidence and expressing these conclusions with absolute certainty when alternative inferences would be equally or more likely. The following examples illustrate what people who are thinking illogically might say in telling their TAT stories.

To Card 9BM (men lying on the ground): "These men are probably a barbershop quartet, because there are four of them, and the little guy would be the tenor, because he's the smallest" [being four in number is a highly circumstantial and far from compelling basis for inferring that the men are a vocal group, and there is no necessary or exclusive relationship between small stature and tenor voice].

To Card 12M (young man lying on couch with older man leaning over him): "The boy has a tie on, which means that he's a college student" [this is possible, but far from being a necessary meaning; perhaps the young man is wearing a tie because his mother made him wear it, or because he is going to get his picture taken today].

To Card 13MF (man standing in front of a woman lying in bed): "I think she must be dead, because she's lying down" [seeing the woman in this picture as dead is not unusual, but inferring certain death from lying down overlooks the possibility that she might be sleeping or resting].

APPLICATIONS

In common with the other assessment measures presented in this *Handbook*, the TAT derives its applications from the information it provides about an individual's personality characteristics. The TAT was described in the introduction to this chapter as a performance-based measure that, like the RIM, generates structural, thematic, and behavioral sources of data. As also noted, however, these data sources are not of potentially equivalent significance in TAT interpretation as they are in Rorschach interpretation. Instead, the TAT, with few exceptions, is most useful by virtue of what can be learned from the thematic imagery about a person's inner life.

Because the TAT functions best as a measure of underlying needs, attitudes, conflicts, and concerns, its primary application is in clinical work, mostly in planning psychotherapy and monitoring treatment progress. TAT findings may at times provide some secondary assistance in differential diagnosis, as illustrated in some of the examples presented in discussing story interpretation. Nevertheless, TAT stories are more helpful in understanding the possible sources and implications of adjustment difficulties than in distinguishing among categories of psychological disorder. For this reason, forensic and organizational applications of TAT assessment have also been limited, although attention is paid in the discussion that follows to the general acceptance of the TAT in the professional community and its potential utility in personnel selection. Other aspects of TAT assessment that enhance its utility are its suitability for group administration, its value in cross-cultural research, and its resistance to impression management.

Treatment Planning and Monitoring

The interpretive implications of TAT stories often prove helpful in planning, conducting, and evaluating the impact of psychological treatment. Especially in evaluating people who are seeking mental health care but are unable to recognize or disinclined to reveal very much about themselves, TAT findings typically go well beyond interview data in illuminating issues that should be addressed in psychotherapy. Inferences based on TAT stories are particularly likely to assist in answering the following four central questions in treatment planning:

1. What types of conflicts need to be resolved and what concerns need to be eased for the person to feel better and function more effectively?
2. What sorts of underlying attitudes does the person have toward key figures in his or her life, toward certain kinds of people in general, and toward interpersonal relatedness?
3. What situations or events are likely to be distressing or gratifying to the person, and how does this person tend to cope with distress and respond to gratification?
4. Which of these unresolved conflicts, underlying attitudes, or distressing experiences appears to be a root cause of the emotional or adjustment problems that brought the person into treatment?

By providing such information, TAT findings can help guide therapists plan their treatment strategies, anticipate obstacles to progress, and identify adroit interventions. Having such knowledge in advance about elements of a person's inner life gives therapists a head start in conducting psychotherapy. This advantage can be especially valuable in short-term or emergency therapy, when the time spent obtaining an in-depth personality assessment is more than compensated by the time saved with early identification of the issues and concerns that need attention.

Three research studies with the SCORS and DMM scales have demonstrated the potential utility of TAT stories for anticipating the course of psychotherapy and monitoring treatment progress. In one of these studies, S. J. Ackerman, Hilsenroth, Clemence, Weatherill, and Fowler (2000) found significant relationships between the pretherapy SCORS levels for affective quality of representations and emotional investment in relationships and the continuation in treatment of 63 patients with a personality disorder, as measured by the number of sessions they attended.

Also working with the SCORS, Fowler et al. (2004) followed 77 seriously disturbed patients receiving intensive psychotherapy in a residential setting who were administered the TAT prior to beginning treatment and a second time approximately 16 months later. Behavioral ratings indicated substantial improvement in the condition of these patients, and four of the SCORS scales showed corresponding significant changes for the better (Complexity of Representations, Understanding Social Causality, Self-esteem, and Identity and Coherence of the Self).

Cramer and Blatt (1990) were similarly successful in demonstrating the utility of the DMM in monitoring treatment change. In the Cramer and Blatt study, 90 seriously disturbed adults in residential treatment were tested on admission and retested after an average of 15 months of therapy. Reduction of psychiatric symptoms in these patients was accompanied by significant decline in total use of defenses, as measured with the DMM.

Diagnostic Evaluations

Contemporary practice in differential diagnosis distinguishes among categories or dimensions of disorder primarily on the basis of a person's manifest symptomatology or behavior, rather than the person's underlying attitudes and concerns (see American Psychiatric Association, 2000). For this reason, what the TAT does best—generate hypotheses about a person's inner life—rarely plays a prominent role in clinical diagnostic evaluations. Nevertheless, certain thematic, structural, and behavioral features of a TAT protocol may be consistent with and reinforce diagnostic impressions based on other sources of information. Examples of this diagnostic relevance include suspicion-laden story plots that suggest paranoia, disjointed narratives that indicate disordered thinking, and a slow rate of speech that points to depressive lethargy.[2]

In addition, research with the SCORS and DMM scales has demonstrated that objectified TAT findings can identify personality differences among persons with different types of problem. Patients with borderline personality disorder differ significantly on some SCORS variables from patients with major depressive disorder (Westen et al., 1990), and SCORS variables have been found to distinguish among patients with borderline, narcissistic, and antisocial personality disorders (S. J. Ackerman et al., 1999). Young people who have been physically or sexually abused display quite different interpersonal attitudes and expectations on the SCORS scales from the attitudes and expectations of children and adolescents who have not experienced abuse (Freedenfeld, Ornduff, & Kelsey, 1995; Kelly, 1999; Ornduff, Freedenfeld, Kelsey, & Critelli, 1994; Ornduff & Kelsey, 1996).

Sandstrom and Cramer (2003) found that elementary schoolchildren whose DMM scores indicate use of identification are better adjusted psychologically, as measured by parent and self-report questionnaires, than children who rely on denial. In particular, the children in this study who showed identification reported less social anxiety and depression than those who showed denial, were less often described by their parents as having behavior problems, and were more likely to perceive themselves as socially and academically competent. Adolescents with conduct disorder show less mature defenses on the DMM than adolescents with adjustment disorder, with the conduct disorder group being more likely to use denial than the adjustment disorder group, and less likely to use identification (Cramer & Kelly, 2004). Frequency of resorting to violence for resolution of interpersonal conflicts, as

---

[2]Note should be taken of the recent publication of the *Psychodynamic Diagnostic Manual* (PDM Task Force, 2006), which is intended to supplement the *Diagnostic and Statistical Manual* (*DSM;* American Psychiatric Association, 2000) as a guideline for differential diagnosis. The diagnostic framework formulated in the *PDM* encourages attention to each person's profile of mental functioning, which includes "patterns of relating, comprehending, and expressing feelings, coping with stress and anxiety, observing one's own emotions and behaviors, and forming moral judgments" (p. 2). Should such considerations come to play a more formal part in differential diagnosis than has traditionally been the case, TAT findings may become increasingly relevant in determining diagnostic classifications.

self-reported by a sample of college student men, has shown a significant negative correlation with DMM use of identification and a significant positive correlation with use of projection (Porcerelli, Cogan, Kamoo, & Letman, 2004).

These and similar TAT findings can help clinicians understand psychological disturbances and appreciate the needs and concerns of people with adjustment problems. However, these findings do not warrant using the SCORS, the DMM, or any other TAT scale as a sole or primary basis for diagnosing personality disorders or identifying victims of abuse. Differential diagnosis should always be an integrative process drawing on information from diverse sources, and for reasons already mentioned, the information gleaned from TAT stories usually plays a minor role in this process. Moreover, neither the TAT nor any other performance-based measure of personality provides sufficient basis for inferring whether a person has been abused or had any other particular type of past experience. The following caution in this regard should always be kept in mind: "Psychological assessment data are considerably more dependable for describing what people are like than for predicting how they are likely to behave or postdicting what they are likely to have done or experienced" (Weiner, 2003, p. 335).

Forensic and Organizational Applications

Like the imagery in Rorschach responses, stories told to TAT pictures are better suited for generating hypotheses to be pursued than for establishing the reasonable certainties expected in the courtroom. On occasion, thematic preoccupations may carry some weight in documenting a state of mind relevant to a legal question, as in a personal injury case in which the TAT stories of a plaintiff seeking damages because of a claimed posttraumatic stress disorder reflect pervasive fears of being harmed or damaged. By and large, however, the psycholegal issues contended in the courtroom seldom hinge on suppositions about a litigant's or defendant's inner life. In terms of the criteria for admissibility into evidence discussed in the previous chapter, then, TAT testimony has limited likelihood of being helpful to judges and juries. As discussed in the final section of this chapter, moreover, TAT interpretation does not rest on a solid scientific basis, except for conclusions based on objectified scales for measuring specific personality characteristics.

Nevertheless, forensic psychologists report using the TAT in their practice, and TAT assessment easily meets the general acceptance criterion for admissibility into evidence. Among forensic psychologists responding to surveys, over one-third report using the TAT or CAT in evaluations of children involved in custody disputes, and 24% to 29% in evaluating adults in these cases, with smaller numbers using the TAT in evaluations of personal injury (9%), criminal responsibility (8%), and competency to stand trial (5%; M. J. Ackerman & Ackerman, 1997; Boccaccini & Brodsky, 1999; Borum & Grisso, 1995; Quinnell & Bow, 2001). In a more recent survey of forensic psychologists by Archer, Buffington-Vollum, Stredny, and Handel (2006), 29% reported using the TAT for various purposes in their case evaluations. In clinical settings, the TAT has consistently been among the four or five most frequently used tests, and it has been the third most frequently used personality assessment method, following the MMPI and RIM with adults and the RIM and sentence completion tests with adolescents (Archer & Newsom, 2000; Camara, Nathan, & Puente, 2000; Hogan, 2005; Moretti & Rossini, 2004).

A majority (62%) of internship training directors report a preference for their incoming trainees to have had prior TAT coursework or at least a good working knowledge of the instrument (Clemence & Handler, 2001). Over the years, the TAT has been surpassed only by the MMPI and the RIM in the volume of published personality assessment research it has generated (Butcher & Rouse, 1996). As judged from its widespread use, its endorsement as a method that clinicians should learn, and the extensive body of literature devoted to it, TAT assessment appears clearly to have achieved general acceptance in the professional community.

With respect to potential applications of the TAT in personnel selection, two meta-analytic studies have identified substantial relationships between McClelland's n-Ach scale and achievement-related outcomes. In one of these meta-analyses, Spangler (1992) found a statistically significant average affect size for n-Ach in predicting such outcomes as income earned, occupational success, sales success, job performance, and participation in and leadership of community organizations. This TAT measure of achievement motivation showed higher correlations with outcome criteria in these studies than self-report questionnaire measures of motivation to achieve.

In the other meta-analysis, Collins, Hanges, and Locke (2004) examined 41 studies of need for achievement among persons described as entrepreneurs. Entrepreneurship in these studies consisted of being a manager responsible for making decisions in the business world or a founder of a business with responsibility for undertaking a new venture. The n-Ach scale in these studies was significantly correlated with choosing an entrepreneurial career and performing well in it, and Collins et al. concluded, "Achievement motivation may be particularly potent at differentiating between successful and unsuccessful groups of entrepreneurs" (p. 111). Hence there is reason to expect that TAT assessment may be helpful in identifying individuals who are likely to be adept at recognizing and exploiting entrepreneurial opportunities in the marketplace.

Group Administration, Cross-Cultural Relevance, and Resistance to Impression Management

As mentioned, three other aspects of the TAT are likely to enhance its applications for various purposes. First, the suitability of the TAT for group administration facilitates large-scale data collection for research purposes and creates possibilities for using the instrument as a screening device in applied settings.

Second, since early in its history, the TAT has been used as a clinical and research instrument in many different countries and has proved particularly valuable in studying cultural change and cross-cultural differences in personality characteristics. Contributions by Dana (1999) and Ephraim (2000) provide overviews of these international applications of the TAT, and the particular sensitivity of TAT stories to cultural influences is elaborated by Ritzler (2004) and by Hofer and Chasiotis (2004).

Third, as a performance-based measure, the TAT is somewhat resistant to impression management. People who choose to conceal their inner life by telling brief and unelaborated stories can easily defeat the purpose of the examination. In so doing, however, they make it obvious that they are delivering a guarded protocol that reveals very little about them, other than the fact of their concealment. For examinees who are being reasonably open and cooperative, the ambiguity of the task and their limited awareness of what their stories might signify make it difficult for them to convey any intentionally misleading impression of their attitudes and concerns.

Nevertheless, telling stories is a more reality-based enterprise than saying what inkblots might be, and for this reason, the TAT is probably not as resistant as the RIM to impression management. Moreover, research reported in the 1960s and 1970s showed that college students could modify the TAT stories they told after being instructed to respond in certain ways (e.g., as an aggressive and hostile person). Schretlen (1997) has concluded from these early studies that they "clearly demonstrate the fakability of the TAT" (p. 281).

To take issue with Schretlen's conclusion, however, the ability of volunteer research participants to shape their TAT stories according to certain instructions may have little bearing on whether people being examined for clinical purposes can successfully manage the impression they give on this measure. Moreover, it is reasonable to hypothesize that experienced examiners, working with the benefit of case history information and data from other tests as well, would have little difficulty identifying in TAT stories the inconsistencies and exaggerations that assist in detecting malingering. However, the sensitivity of clinicians to attempted impression management in real-world TAT assessment has not yet been put to adequate empirical test.

PSYCHOMETRIC FOUNDATIONS

The nature of the TAT and the ways in which it has most commonly been used have made it difficult to determine its psychometric properties. Aside from a widely used and fairly standard set of instructions based on Murray's original guidelines for administration, research and practice with the TAT has been largely unsystematic. Certain sets of cards have been recommended by various authorities on the test, but there has been little consistency with respect to which cards are used and in what sequence they are shown (Keiser & Prather, 1990). Moreover, the primarily qualitative approach that typifies TAT interpretation in clinical practice does not yield the quantitative data that facilitate estimating the reliability of an assessment instrument, determining its validity for various purposes, and developing numerical reference norms.

This lack of systematization and the resultant shortfall in traditional psychometric verification have fueled a long history of controversy between critics who have questioned the propriety of using the TAT in clinical practice and proponents who have endorsed the value of the instrument and refuted criticisms of its use. Commentaries by Conklin and Westen (2001), Cramer (1999), Garb (1998), Hibbard (2003), Karon (2000), and Lilienfeld, Wood, and Garb (2000) provide contemporary summaries of these opposing views. Without rehashing this debate, and with the psychometric shortcomings of traditional TAT assessment having already been noted, the following discussion calls attention to four considerations bearing on how and why this instrument can be used effectively for certain purposes.

First, criticisms of the validity of the TAT have frequently been based on low correlations between impressions gleaned from TAT stories and either clinical diagnosis or self-report data. However, correlations with clinical diagnoses and self-report measures are conceptually irrelevant to the validity of TAT for its intended purposes, and criticisms based on such correlations accordingly lack solid basis. The TAT was designed to explore the personal experience and underlying motives of people, not to facilitate a differential diagnosis based primarily on manifest symptomatology (which is the basis of psychiatric classification in the *Diagnostic and Statistical Manual* [*DSM-IV-TR*]; American Psychiatric Association, 2000). Should some TAT scales show an association with particular psychological disorders, as they in the SCORS and DMM research, the test may help identify personality characteristics associated with these disorders. Failure to accomplish differential diagnosis, although important to recognize as a limitation of TAT applications, does not invalidate use of the instrument for its primary intended purposes.

As for correlations with self-report measures, there is little to gain from attempting to validate performance-based personality tests against self-report questionnaires, or vice versa for that matter. These are two types of test that are constructed differently, ask for different kinds of responses, provide different amounts of structure, and tap different levels of self-awareness, as discussed in concluding Chapter 1. Hence they may at times yield different results when measuring similar constructs, and in such instances they are more likely to complement than to contradict each other (see pp. 24–26; see also Weiner, 2005). Meyer et al. (2001) drew the following conclusions in this regard from a detailed review of evidence and issues in psychological testing:

> Distinct assessment methods provide unique information.... Any single assessment method provides a partial or incomplete representation of the characteristics it intends to measure.... Cross-method correlations cannot reveal...how good a test is in any specific sense.... Psychologists should anticipate disagreements when similarly named scales are compared across diverse assessment methods. (p. 145)

Because both self-report and performance-based personality tests are inferential measures, furthermore, substantial correlations between them usually have only modest implications for their criterion validity. Two tests that correlate perfectly with each other can be equally invalid, with no significant relationship to any meaningful criterion. Compelling evidence of criterion validity emerges when personality test scores correlate not with each other, but with external (nontest) variables consisting of what people are like and how they are observed to behave.

Second, the traditionally qualitative TAT methods have been supplemented with quantitative scales that are readily accessible to psychometric verification. The previously mentioned research with the SCORS, DMM, and n-Ach scoring demonstrates that TAT assessment can be objectified to yield valid and reliable scales for measuring dimensions of personality functioning. Additional research has demonstrated the internal consistency of SCORS and its validity in identifying developmental differences in the interpersonal capacities of children (e.g., Hibbard, Mitchell, & Porcerelli, 2001; Niec & Russ, 2002).

The DMM has been validated as a measure of maturity level in children and adolescents, of developmental level of maturity in college students, and of long-term personality change and stability in adults (Cramer, 2003; Hibbard & Porcerelli, 1998; Porcerelli, Thomas, Hibbard, & Cogan, 1998). Support for the validity of these scales is acknowledged by critics as well as proponents of the TAT, although in the former case with the qualification that these "promising TAT scoring systems...are not yet appropriate for routine clinical use" (Lilienfeld et al., 2000, p. 46). Even if this qualification is warranted, the point has been made that TAT assessment has the potential to generate valid and reliable findings.

Research with other picture-story measures, notably the RATC and the TEMAS, has provided additional evidence of the potential psychometric soundness of assessing personality with this method. As reviewed by Weiner and Kuehnle (1998), quantitative scores generated by both measures have valid and meaningful correlates and have shown adequate levels of interscorer agreement and either internal consistency or retest stability.

Third, not having systematically gathered quantitative normative data to guide TAT interpretations does not mean that the instrument lacks reference points. As reviewed in the section of this chapter on card pull, cumulative clinical experience has established expectations concerning the types of stories commonly elicited by each of the TAT cards. Hence examiners are not in the position of inventing a new test each time they use the TAT. Instead, similarities and differences between a person's stories and common expectations can and should play a prominent role in the interpretive process, as they did in many of the examples presented in this chapter.

The fourth consideration pertains to the primary purpose of TAT assessment, which is to explore an individual's personal experience and generate hypotheses concerning the individual's underlying needs, attitudes, conflicts, and concerns. The value of the TAT resides in generating hypotheses that expand understanding of a person's inner life. If a TAT story suggests three alternative self-perceptions or sources of anxiety, and only one of these alternatives finds confirmation when other data sources are examined, then the test has done its job in useful fashion. It is not invalidated because two-thirds of the suggested alternatives in this instance proved incorrect. This is the nature of working with a primarily qualitative assessment instrument, which shows its worth, not through quantitative psychometric verification, but by clinicians finding it helpful in understanding and treating people who seek their services. Psychologists who may be concerned that this qualitative perspective detracts from the scientific status of assessment psychology should keep in mind that generating hypotheses is just as much a part of science as confirming hypotheses.

REFERENCES

Ackerman, M. J., & Ackerman, M. C. (1997). Custody evaluations in practice: A survey of experienced professionals (revisited). *Professional Psychology, 28*, 137–145.

Ackerman, S. J., Clemence, A. J., Weatherill, R., & Hilsenroth, M. J. (1999). Use of the TAT in the assessment of DSM-IV Custer B personality disorders. *Journal of Personality Assessment, 73*, 422–448.

Ackerman, S. J., Hilsenroth, M. J., Clemence, A. J., Weatherill, R., & Fowler, J. C. (2000). The effect of social cognition and object representation on psychotherapy continuation. *Bulletin of the Menninger Clinic, 64*, 386–408.

American Psychiatric Association. (2000). *Diagnostic and statistical manual of mental disorders* (4th ed., text rev.). Washington, DC: Author.

Anderson, J. W. (1988). Henry Murray's early career: A psychobiographical exploration. *Journal of Personality, 56*, 139–171.

Anderson, J. W. (1999). Henry A. Murray and the creation of the Thematic Apperception Test. In L. Gieser & M. I. Stein (Eds.), *Evocative images: The Thematic Apperception Test and the art of projection* (pp. 23–38). Washington, DC: American Psychological Association.

Archer, R. P., Buffington-Vollum, J. K., Stredny, R. V., & Handel, R. W. (2006). A survey of psychological test use patterns among forensic psychologists. *Journal of Personality Assessment, 87*, 84–94.

Archer, R. P., & Newsom, C. R. (2000). Psychological test usage with adolescent clients: Survey update. *Assessment, 7*, 227–235.

Atkinson, J. W. (Ed.). (1958). *Motives in fantasy, action, and society.* Princeton, NJ: Van Nostrand.

Avila-Espada, A. (2000). Objective scoring for the TAT. In R. H. Dana (Ed.), *Handbook of cross-cultural and multicultural personality assessment* (pp. 465–480). Mahwah, NJ: Erlbaum.

Barenbaum, N. R., & Winter, D. G. (2003). Personality. In I. B. Weiner (Editor-in-Chief) & D. K. Freedheim (Vol. Ed.), *Handbook of psychology: Vol. 1. History of psychology* (pp. 177–302). Hoboken, NJ: Wiley.

Bellak, L. (1947). *A guide to the interpretation of the Thematic Apperception Test.* New York: Psychological Corporation.

Bellak, L. (1954). *The Thematic Apperception Test and the Children's Apperception Test in clinical use.* New York: Grune & Stratton.

Bellak, L. (1975). *The TAT, CAT, and SAT in clinical use* (3rd ed.). New York: Grune & Stratton.

Bellak, L. (1999). My perceptions of the Thematic Apperception Test in psychodiagnosis and psychotherapy. In L. Gieser & M. I. Stein (Eds.), *Evocative images; The Thematic Apperception Test and the art of projection* (pp. 133–141). Washington, DC: American Psychological Association.

Bellak, L., & Abrams, D. M. (1997). *The TAT, CAT, and SAT in clinical use* (6th ed.). Boston: Allyn & Bacon.

Blankenship, V., Vega, C. M., Ramos, E., Romero, K., Warren, K., Keenan, K., et al. (2006). Using the multifaceted Rasch model to improve the TAT/PSE measure of need for achievement. *Journal of Personality Assessment, 86*, 100–114.

Boccaccini, M. T., & Brodsky, S. L. (1999). Diagnostic test usage by forensic psychologists in emotional injury cases. *Professional Psychology, 30*, 253–259.

Borum, R., & Grisso, T. (1995). Psychological test use in criminal forensic evaluations. *Professional Psychology, 26*, 465–473.

Busch, F. (1995). *The ego at the center of clinical technique.* Northvale, NJ: Aronson.

Butcher, J. N., & Rouse, S. V. (1996). Personality: Individual differences and clinical assessment. *Annual Review of Psychology, 47*, 87–111.

Camara, W., Nathan, J., & Puente, A. (2000). Psychological test usage: Implications in professional use. *Professional Psychology, 31*, 141–154.

Clemence, A. J., & Handler, L. (2001). Psychological assessment on internship: A survey of training directors and their expectations for students. *Journal of Personality Assessment, 76*, 18–47.

Collins, C. J., Hanges, P. J., & Locke, E. A. (2004). The relationship of achievement motivation to entrepreneurial behavior: A meta-analysis. *Human Performance, 17*, 95–117.

Conklin, A., & Westen, D. (2001). Thematic apperception test. In W. I. Dorfman & M. Hersen (Eds.), *Understanding psychological assessment* (pp. 107–133). Dordrecht, The Netherlands: Kluwer Academic.

Costantino, G., & Malgady, R. G. (1999). The Tell-Me-A-Story Test: A multicultural offspring of the Thematic Apperception Test. In L. Gieser & M. I. Stein (Eds.), *Evocative images: The Thematic Apperception Test and the art of projection* (pp. 177–190). Washington, DC: American Psychological Association.

Costantino, G., Malgady, R. G., & Rogler, L. H. (1998). *Technical manual: TEMAS Thematic Apperception Test.* Los Angeles: Western Psychological Services.

Costantino, G., Malgady, R. G., Rogler, L. H., & Tusi, E. C. (1998). Discriminant analysis of clinical outpatients and public school children by TEMAS: A thematic apperception test for Hispanics and Blacks. *Journal of Personality Assessment, 52*, 670–678.

Cramer, P. (1991). *The development of defense mechanisms: Theory, research and assessment*. New York: Springer-Verlag.

Cramer, P. (1996). *Storytelling, narrative, and the Thematic Apperception Test*. New York: Guilford Press.

Cramer, P. (1999). Future directions for the Thematic Apperception Test. *Journal of Personality Assessment, 72*, 74–92.

Cramer, P. (2003). Personality change in later adulthood is predicted by defense mechanism use in early adulthood. *Journal of Research in Personality, 37*, 76–104.

Cramer, P. (2006). *Protecting the self: Defense mechanisms in action*. New York: Guilford Press.

Cramer, P., & Blatt, S. J. (1990). Use of the TAT to measure change in defense mechanisms following intensive psychotherapy. *Journal of Personality Assessment, 54*, 236–251.

Cramer, P., & Kelly, F. D. (2004). Adolescent conduct disorder and adjustment reaction. *Journal of Nervous and Mental Diseases, 192*, 139–145.

Dana, R. H. (1999). Cross-cultural—multicultural use of the Thematic Apperception Test. In L. Gieger & M. I. Stein (Eds.), *Evocative images: The Thematic Apperception Test and the art of projection* (pp. 177–190). Washington, DC: American Psychological Association.

Dana, R. H. (2006). TEMAS among the Europeans: Different, complementary, and provocative. *South African Rorschach Journal, 3*, 17–28.

Ephraim, D. (2000). A psychocultural approach to TAT scoring and interpretation. In R. H. Dana (Ed.), *Handbook of cross-cultural and multicultural personality assessment* (pp. 427–446). Mahwah, NJ: Erlbaum.

Eron, L. D. (1950). A normative study of the Thematic Apperception Test. *Psychological Monographs, 64*(Whole No. 315).

Eron, L. D. (1953). Responses of women to the Thematic Apperception Test. *Journal of Consulting Psychology, 17*, 269–282.

Fowler, J. C., Ackerman, S. J., Speanburg, S., Bailey, A., Blagys, M., & Conklin, A. C. (2004). Personality and symptom change in treatment refractory inpatients: Evaluation of the phase model of change using Rorschach TAT and DSM-IV Axis V. *Journal of Personality Assessment, 83*, 306–322.

Freedenfeld, R. N., Ornduff, S. R., & Kelsey, R. M. (1995). Object relations and physical abuse: A TAT analysis. *Journal of Personality Assessment, 64*, 552–568.

Freud, S. (1957). "Wild" psychoanalysis. In J. Strachey (Ed. & Trans.), *The standard edition of the works of Sigmund Freud* (Vol. *11*, pp. 221–227). London: Hogarth Press. (Original work published 1910)

Garb, H. N. (1998). Recommendations for training in the use of the Thematic Apperception Test (TAT). *Professional Psychology, 29*, 621–622.

Hall, C. S., Lindzey, G., & Campbell, J. B. (1998). *Theories of personality* (4th ed.). New York: Wiley.

Handler, L. (2001). Assessment of men: Personality assessment goes to war by the Office of Strategic Services Assessment staff. *Journal of Personality Assessment, 76*, 558–578.

Henry, W. E. (1956). *The analysis of fantasy: The thematic apperception technique in the study of personality*. New York: Wiley.

Hibbard, S. (2003). A critique of Lilienfeld et al.'s (2000) "The scientific status of projective techniques." *Journal of Personality Assessment, 80*, 260–271.

Hibbard, S., Mitchell, D., & Porcerelli, J. (2001). Internal consistency of the Object Relations and Social Cognition scales for the Thematic Apperception Test. *Journal of Personality Assessment, 77*, 408–419.

Hibbard, S., & Porcerelli, J. (1998). Further validation for the Cramer Defense Mechanisms manual. *Journal of Personality Assessment, 70*, 460–483.

Hofer, J., & Chasiotis, A. (2004). Methodological considerations of applying a TAT-type picture-story test in cross-cultural research. *Journal of Cross-Cultural Psychology, 35*, 224–241.

Hogan, T. P. (2005). 50 widely used psychological tests. In G. P. Koocher, J. C. Norcross, & S. S. Hill III (Eds.), *Psychologists' desk reference* (2nd ed., pp. 101–104). New York: Oxford University Press.

Holmstrom, R. W., Silber, D. E., & Karp, S. A. (1990). Development of the Apperceptive Personality Test. *Journal of Personality Assessment, 54*, 252–264.

Huprich, S. K., & Greenberg, R. P. (2003). Advances in the assessment of object relations in the 1990s. *Clinical Psychology Review, 23*, 665–698.

Jenkins, S. R. (in press). *Handbook of clinical scoring systems for Thematic Apperception techniques.* Mahwah, NJ: Erlbaum.

Karon, B. P. (2000). The clinical interpretation of the Thematic Apperception Test, Rorschach, and other clinical data: A reexamination of statistical versus clinical prediction. *Professional Psychology, 31*, 230–233.

Karp, S. A., Holstrom, R. W., & Silber, D. E. (1989). *Manual for the Apperceptive Personality Test (APT).* Orland Park, IL: International Diagnostic Services.

Keiser, R. E., & Prather, E. N. (1990). What is the TAT? A review of ten years of research. *Journal of Personality Assessment, 55*, 800–803.

Kelly, F. D. (1999). *The psychological assessment of abused and traumatized children.* Mahwah, NJ: Erlbaum.

Kelly, F. D. (2007). The clinical application of the Social Cognition and Object Relations scale with children and adolescents. In S. R. Smith & L. Handler (Eds.), *The clinical assessment of children and adolescents* (pp. 169–182). Mahwah, NJ: Erlbaum.

Lanagan-Fox, J., & Grant, S. (2006). The Thematic Apperception Test: Toward a standard measure of the big three motives. *Journal of Personality Assessment, 87*, 277–291.

Lilienfeld, S. O., Wood, J. M., & Garb, H. N. (2000). The scientific status of projective techniques. *Psychological Science in the Public Interest, 1*, 27–66.

McArthur, D. S., & Roberts, G. E. (1990). *Roberts Apperception Test for Children manual.* Los Angeles: Western Psychological Services.

McClelland, D. C. (1999). How the test lives on: Extensions of the Thematic Apperception Test approach. In L. Gieser & M. I. Stein (Eds.), *Evocative images: The Thematic Apperception Test and the art of projection* (pp. 163–175). Washington, DC: American Psychological Association.

McClelland, D. C., Atkinson, J. W., Clark, R. A., & Lowell, E. L. (1953). *The achievement motive.* New York: Appleton-Century-Crofts.

McClelland, D. C., Clark, R. A., Roby, T. B., & Atkinson, J. W. (1958). The effect of the need for achievement on thematic apperception. In J. W. Atkinson (Ed.), *Motives in fantasy, action, and society* (pp. 64–82). Princeton, NJ: Van Nostrand.

Meyer, J. G. (2004). The reliability and validity of the Rorschach and Thematic Apperception Test (TAT) compared to other psychological and medical procedures: An analysis of systematically gathered evidence. In M. Hersen (Editor-in-Chief), M. Hilsenroth, & D. Segal (Vol. Eds.), *Comprehensive handbook of psychological assessment: Vol. 2. Personality assessment* (pp. 315–342). Hoboken, NJ: Wiley.

Meyer, J. G., Finn, S. E., Eyde, L. D., Kay, G. G., Moreland, K. L., Dies, R. R., et al. (2001). Psychological testing and psychological assessment: A review of evidence and issues. *American Psychologist, 56*, 128–165.

Moretti, R. J., & Rossini, E. D. (2004). The Thematic Apperception Test (TAT). In M. Hersen (Editor-in-Chief), M. J. Hilsenroth, & D. L. Segal (Vol. Eds.), *Comprehensive handbook of psychological assessment: Vol. 2. Personality assessment* (pp. 356–371). Hoboken, NJ: Wiley.

Morgan, C. D., & Murray, H. A. (1935). A method for investigating fantasies: The Thematic Apperception Test. *Archives of Neurology and Psychiatry, 34*, 289–306.

Morgan, W. G. (1995). Origin and history of Thematic Apperception Test images. *Journal of Personality Assessment, 65*, 237–254.

Morgan, W. G. (2002). Origin and history of the earliest Thematic Apperception Test pictures. *Journal of Personality Assessment, 79*, 422–445.

Morgan, W. G. (2003). Origin and history of the "Series B" and "Series C" TAT pictures. *Journal of Personality Assessment, 81*, 133–148.

Murray, H. A. (1938). *Explorations in personality: A clinical and experimental study of fifty men of college age.* New York: Oxford University Press.

Murray, H. A. (1940). What should psychologists do about psychoanalysis? *Journal of Abnormal and Social Psychology, 35*, 150–175.

Murray, H. A. (1971). *Thematic Apperception Test: Manual.* Cambridge, MA: Harvard University Press. (Original work published 1943)

Murstein, B. I. (1963). *Theory and research in projective techniques (Emphasizing the TAT).* New York: Wiley.

Niec, L. N., & Russ, S. W. (2002). Children's internal representations, empathy, and fantasy play: A validity study of the SCORS-Q. *Psychological Assessment, 14*, 331–338.

Office of Strategic Services Assessment Staff. (1948). *Assessment of men.* New York: Rinehart.

Ornduff, S. R., Freedendeld, R. N., Kelsey, R. M., & Critelli, J. W. (1994). Object relations of sexually abused female subjects: A TAT analysis. *Journal of Personality Assessment, 63*, 223–238.

Ornduff, S. R., & Kelsey, R. M. (1996). Object relations of sexually and physically abused female children: A TAT analysis. *Journal of Personality Assessment, 66*, 91–105.

Pang, J. S., & Schultheiss, O. C. (2005). Assessing implicit motives in U.S. college students effects of picture type and position, gender, and ethnicity, and cross-cultural comparisons. *Journal of Personality Assessment, 85*, 280–294.

PDM Task Force. (2006). *Psychodynamic diagnostic manual.* Silver Spring, MD: Alliance of Psychoanalytic Organizations.

Peters, E. J., Hilsenroth, M. J., Eudell-Simmons, E. M., Blagys, M. D., & Handler, L. (2006). Reliability and validity of the Social Cognition and Object Relations scale in clinical use. *Psychotherapy Research, 16*, 617–616.

Porcerelli, J. H., Cogan, R., Kamoo, R., & Leitman, W. (2004). Defense mechanisms and self-reported violence toward partners and strangers. *Journal of Personality Assessment, 82*, 317–320.

Porcerelli, J. H., & Hibbard, S. (2004). Projective assessment of defense mechanisms. In M. Hersen (Editor-in-Chief), M. J. Hilsenroth, & D. L. Segal (Vol. Eds.), *Comprehensive handbook of psychological assessment: Vol. 2. Personality assessment* (pp. 466–475). Hoboken, NJ: Wiley.

Porcerelli, J. H., Thomas, S., Hibbard, S., & Cogan, R. (1998). Defense mechanism development in children, adolescents, and late adolescents. *Journal of Personality Assessment, 71*, 411–420.

Prince, M. (1906). *The dissociation of a personality: A biographical study in abnormal psychology.* New York: Longmans.

Quinnell, F. A., & Bow, J. N. (2001). Psychological tests used in child custody evaluations. *Behavioral Sciences and the Law, 19*, 491–501.

Ritzler, B. A. (2004). Cultural applications of the Rorschach, Apperception Tests, and figure drawings. In M. Hersen (Editor-in-Chief), M. J. Hilsenroth, & D. L. Segal (Vol. Eds.), *Comprehensive handbook of psychological assessment: Vol. 2. Personality assessment* (pp. 573–585). Hoboken, NJ: Wiley.

Ritzler, B. A., Sharkey, K. J., & Chudy, J. F. (1980). A comprehensive projective alternative to the TAT. *Journal of Personality Assessment, 44*, 358–362.

Roberts, G. E. (2006). *Roberts-2 manual.* Los Angeles: Western Psychological Services.

Robinson, F. G. (1992). *Love's story told: A life of Henry A. Murray.* Cambridge, MA: Harvard University Press.

Sandstrom, M. J., & Cramer, P. (2003). Defense mechanisms and psychological adjustment in childhood. *Journal of Nervous and Mental Diseases, 191*, 487–495.

Schretlen, D. J. (1997). Dissimulation on the Rorschach and other projective measures. In R. Rogers (Ed.), *Clinical assessment of malingering and deception* (2nd ed., pp. 208–222). New York: Guilford Press.

Shakespeare, W. (1947). *The tragedy of Hamlet, Prince of Denmark.* New Haven, CT: Yale University Press. (Original work published 1604)

Sharkey, K. J., & Ritzler, B. A. (1985). Comparing diagnostic validity of the TAT and a new Picture Projective Test. *Journal of Personality Assessment, 49*, 406–412.

Shneidman, E. S. (1951). *Thematic test analysis.* New York: Grune & Stratton.

Shneidman, E. S. (1965). Projective techniques. In B. B. Wolman (Ed.), *Handbook of clinical psychology* (pp. 498–521). New York: McGraw-Hill.

Smith, C. P. (Ed.). (1992). *Motivation and personality: Handbook of thematic content analysis.* New York: Cambridge University Press.

Spangler, W. D. (1992). Validity of questionnaire and TAT measures of need for achievement: Two meta-analyses. *Psychological Bulletin, 112*, 140–154.

Stein, M. I. (1948). *The Thematic Apperception Test.* Reading, MA: Addison-Wesley.

Stein, M. I., & Gieser, L. (1999). The zeitgeists and events surrounding the birth of the Thematic Apperception Test. In L. Gieser & M. I. Stein (Eds.), *Evocative images: The Thematic Apperception Test and the art of projection* (pp. 15–22). Washington, DC: American Psychological Association.

Stricker, G., & Gooen-Piels, J. (2004). Projective assessment of object relations. In M. Hersen (Editor-in-Chief), M. J. Hilsenroth, & D. L. Segal (Vol. Eds.), *Comprehensive handbook of psychological assessment: Vol. 2. Personality assessment* (pp. 449–465). Hoboken, NJ: Wiley.

Teglasi, H. (2001). *Essentials of TAT and other storytelling techniques assessment.* New York: Wiley.

Tomkins, S. S. (1947). *The Thematic Apperception Test: The theory and technique of interpretation.* New York: Grune & Stratton.

Vaillant, G. E. (1977). *Adaptation to life.* Boston: Little, Brown.

Vaillant, G. E. (1994). Ego mechanisms of defense and personality psychopathology. *Journal of Abnormal Psychology, 105*, 44–50.

Vane, J. R. (1981). The Thematic Apperception Test: A review. *Clinical Psychology Review, 1*, 319–336.

Weiner, I. B. (2003). Prediction and postdiction in clinical decision making. *Clinical Psychology: Science and Practice, 10*, 335–338.

Weiner, I. B. (2005). Integrative personality assessment with self-report and performance-based measures. In S. Strack (Ed.), *Handbook of personology and psychopathology* (pp. 317–331). Hoboken, NJ: Wiley.

Weiner, I. B,, & Kuehnle, K. (1998). Projective assessment of children and adolescents. In A. S. Bellack & M. Hersen (Eds.), *Comprehensive clinical psychology: Vol. 4. Assessment* (pp. 432–458). New York: Pergamon Press.

Westen, D. (1991). Social cognition and object relations. *Psychological Bulletin, 109*, 429–455.

Westen, D. (1995). *Social Cognition and Object Relations Scale: Q-Sort for Projective Stories (SCORS-Q).* Unpublished manuscript, Harvard Medical School, Cambridge, MA.

Westen, D., Lohr, N. E., Silk, K., Gold, L., & Kerber, K. (1990). Object relations and social cognition in borderlines, major depressives, and normals: A Thematic Apperception Test analysis. *Psychological Assessment, 2*, 355–364.

Westen, D., Lohr, N. E., Silk, K., Kerber, K., & Goodrich, S. (1989). *Object relations and social cognition TAT scoring manual* (4th ed.). Unpublished manuscript, University of Michigan, Ann Arbor.

Winter, D. G. (1998). Toward a science of personality psychology: David McClelland's development of empirically derived TAT measures. *History of Psychology, 1*, 130–153.

Winter, D. G. (1999). Linking personality and "scientific" psychology: The development of empirically derived Thematic Apperception Test measures. In L. Gieser & M. I. Stein (Eds.), *Evocative images: The Thematic Apperception Test and the art of projection* (pp. 106–124). Washington, DC: American Psychological Association.

Zubin, J., Eron, L. D., & Schumer, F. (1965). *An experimental approach to projective techniques.* New York: Wiley.

Chapter 13

FIGURE DRAWING METHODS

Figure drawing methods are performance-based measures in which persons being examined draw pictures of people or objects. The use of figure drawings in personality assessment is based on the assumption that how people approach this task and the way they draw the figures reflect some of their basic dispositions and concerns and their attitudes toward themselves and other people. This assumption derives from the widely acknowledged extent to which the works of creative artists tend to mirror their moods and personal preoccupations.

In literature, the chronic melancholia of Edgar Allan Poe infused his poems and short stories with gloom and despair, notable examples being "The Raven" and "The Fall of the House of Usher." The music of Chopin varied from the lovely, lighthearted waltzes he wrote during moments of relative calm in his life to dramatic and stirring compositions that expressed his fervor as a Polish patriot, including his Revolutionary Etude and his Military Polonaise. As for the graphic arts, Van Gogh's mood swings and probable manic-depressive disorder are captured in the contrast between such loud canvases as *The Starry Night* and such quiet ones as *Vincent's Bedroom in Arles*. Van Gogh is reputed to have said, "Real artists paint things not as they are, but as they feel to them" (Hammer, 1986, p. 240). Munch's *The Scream* would be a vivid case in point.

Unlike the inkblot and picture-story assessment methods described in Chapters 11 and 12, figure drawing methods do not involve any test stimuli. The test materials consist of only a pencil and blank sheets of paper on which examinees are instructed to make certain kinds of drawings. The drawings are usually followed by an inquiry in which people are asked to tell a story about their drawings or answer questions about them.

This chapter elaborates the nature, history, administration, scoring, interpretation, application, and psychometric foundations of the three figure drawing methods that are most widely used in clinical practice: the Draw-A-Person test (DAP), the House-Tree-Person test (HTP), and the Kinetic Family Drawing test (KFD). According to surveys of clinical psychologists, the HTP is the fourth most frequently used personality or behavioral assessment measure, following the Minnesota Multiphasic Personality Inventory (MMPI), the Rorschach Inkblot Method (RIM), and the Thematic Apperception Test (TAT). The DAP ranks seventh among such measures in frequency of use, and the KFD is the fourteenth most frequently used (Camara, Nathan, & Puente, 2000; Hogan, 2005).

Because figure drawing methods are particularly helpful in evaluating children and adolescents, and are brief and easy to administer, psychologists working with young people or in school settings are especially likely to use them. Survey data indicate that the DAP is the fifth most frequently used personality assessment instrument in examinations of children and adolescents, with the HTP ranking sixth and the KFD eighth or ninth in frequency of use (Archer & Newsom, 2000; Cashel, 2002). In school settings, the DAP, HTP, and KFD are the three most frequently used personality tests, and among psychological tests of all kinds used in schools, they are exceeded in frequency of use only by the Wechsler Intelligence Scale for Children, the Peabody Individual Achievement Test, and the Development Test of Visual-Motor Integration (Hogan, 2005). As might be expected from these survey findings, some texts on figure drawing interpretation are devoted entirely to the graphic productions of young people (e.g., DiLeo, 1973; Schildkrout, Shenker, & Sonnenblick, 1972), although texts addressed specifically to the interpretation of drawings by adults have appeared as well (e.g., Leibowitz, 1999).

Finally of note with respect to the status of figure drawing methods are survey data obtained by Clemence and Handler (2001) from 382 directors of psychology internship training programs. Among training directors from child care facilities, community mental health centers, and private psychiatric and general hospitals, from 52% to 64% preferred their interns to have had some DAP/HTP/KFD coursework prior to entering their program, or at least a good working knowledge of these measures.

NATURE AND HISTORY OF FIGURE DRAWING METHODS

As mentioned, figure drawing methods consist of blank sheets of paper on which people make drawings of various kinds: human figures on the DAP; a house, a tree, and a person on the HTP; and a family "doing something" on the KFD. Characteristics of these drawings and what people say about them during an inquiry yield structural, thematic, and behavioral data, in much the same way as RIM and TAT assessments.

The structural data in figure drawings consist of objective features of what people draw. The core structural features of drawings include their line quality (heavy or light, continuous or broken), the size of the figures (large or small), the placement of figures on the page (middle, top, bottom, side), and any emphasis on or omission of basic parts (e.g., person with disproportionately small head or big ears, person with no hands or feet, house with a tiny door, tree with no branches, family with no father).

Thematic imagery emerges in figure drawing assessment when people are asked to talk about what they have drawn. An examinee may describe a human figure as being "sad" or "not able to do much" and a tree as "not growing as tall as most trees do," in which case the imagery might reflect such depressive phenomena as dysphoric mood, a sense of helplessness, and low self-esteem. Similarly, comments that a person who has been drawn "looks worried about what might happen to him" and that a house "looks like it wouldn't stand up very well if a hurricane came along" might reveal anxiety or insecurity about unwelcome events occurring outside one's control.

The behavioral data in figure drawing tests, as in other performance-based personality assessment measures, consist of how people approach their task and how they interact with the examiner. Examinees may draw slowly or rapidly, carefully or carelessly, eagerly or grudgingly. They may accompany their drawing with comments that are compliant and ingratiating ("I'll be happy to do whatever you ask me to do") or depreciatory and resistive ("This seems like a silly thing to do"). These and other types of behavior and commentary are likely to mirror aspects of individuals' problem-solving style and their test-taking and interpersonal attitudes.

Historically, no one knows when it was first suggested that what people choose to draw and how they draw it might shed light on features of their personality, whether the drawing is a prehistoric sketch found on the wall of a cave, a painting by a great master, or the doodles of an ordinary citizen. It is known, however, that the formal application of figure drawings in psychological assessment began with Florence Goodenough, a child psychologist who completed her doctoral studies at Stanford University in 1924, under the mentorship of Lewis Terman, and later served for many years as Professor of Child Welfare at the University of Minnesota. Terman is well known for publishing an English language revision and standardization of the French Binet-Simon scales for measuring mental abilities, which subsequently became known as the Stanford-Binet Intelligence Scale (Terman, 1916).

As Terman's student, Goodenough became interested in supplementing the Stanford-Binet with a nonverbal measure of intellectual maturity in young people. From her observations of children, she concluded that the amount of accurate detail they include in their drawing of a human figure can provide such a measure. Goodenough's pursuit of this belief led her to develop the Draw-A-Man test, which was published in 1926 (Goodenough, 1926). The Draw-A-Man test soon became a popular assessment instrument and was widely used in its original form for many years. Harris (1963) later revised the Draw-A-Man by expanding Goodenough's scoring system and enlarging the standardization sample for the test, and he suggested that children should be asked to draw not only a man, but also a woman and a picture of themselves. The current version of the Goodenough-Harris method was published in 1988 by Naglieri, who clarified aspects of the scoring criteria and provided new normative guidelines for assessing cognitive development in young people aged 6 to 17 (Naglieri, 1988).

Shortly after the Draw-A-Man test came into use, psychologists began considering the possibility that children's figure drawings could reveal differences among them in their personality characteristics as well as their intellectual maturity. Interestingly, the inaugural volume of the *American Journal of Orthopsychiatry*, which is noted in Chapter 11 as containing the first English language article on Rorschach assessment, also included a pioneering article titled "Drawings by Children as Aids to Personality Studies" (Appel, 1931). It was not until 1949, however, that Karen Machover, then a senior psychologist at Kings County Psychiatric Hospital in New York, published the first formal method for assessing personality with a figure drawing task that she called the *Draw-A-Person* test (Machover, 1949).

Draw-A-Person (DAP)

Based on her experience in examining the drawings of disturbed adolescents and adults, Machover recommended using the DAP with persons of all ages, not just children, and obtaining drawings of both male and female figures. In her 1949 book and a subsequent book chapter (Machover, 1951), she elaborated the notion that structural features of the human figures people draw are likely to reflect their underlying attitudes and concerns and many of their personality traits. Machover suggested that the drawing of small figures might indicate low self-esteem or timidity, whereas the drawing of large figures could be a sign of self-confidence or grandiosity. The placement of figures high on the page might reflect high levels of aspiration and achievement striving, she hypothesized, whereas placement low on the page could identify insecurity and feelings of inadequacy.

Machover also formulated numerous hypotheses concerning the specific meaning of various features of how the head, eyes, nose, ears, hair, mouth, neck, and other body parts are drawn and of how the figures are dressed. It was also Machover's suggestion to include an inquiry procedure in which examinees are asked "to make up a story about this person as if he were a character in a play or novel" (Machover, 1951, p. 345). For use with people who are having difficulty generating a spontaneous story about the figures they have drawn, Machover provided two lists of questions that examiners could ask, one list for children and the other one for adults. These questions concern such matters as the age, education, occupation, and ambitions of the figures; how the figures feel about themselves, their family, and their friends; and what attitudes the figures have toward school, sex, and marriage.

Machover proposed a qualitative approach to figure drawing interpretation in which a broadly based personality description is constructed from the hypothesized meaning of various individual drawing characteristics, each considered in its own right. Some later clinicians recommended instead a quantitative, more global, and more narrowly focused interpretive approach in which the overall frequency of selected figure drawing character-istics provides an index of adjustment difficulty.

The best known of these quantitative approaches is a list of "emotional indicators" developed by Koppitz (1966, 1968, 1984). Koppitz used Machover's interpretive hypotheses and some comparisons between the drawings of public school children and child guidance clinic patients as a basis for identifying 30 drawing characteristics that she considered likely to indicate emotional disturbance in young people aged 5 to 12. These proposed emotional disorder indicators included aspects of how the figures are drawn (e.g., a tiny figure 2 inches high or less; a slanting figure with its axis tilted by 15 degrees or more), omissions of certain body parts (e.g., no eyes, mouth, nose, arms, or legs), and several "special features" (e.g., eyes are crossed, legs are pressed together, arms cling to the sides of the body). The total number of these indicators in a drawing is calculated to provide a quantitative index of the likely extent of a child's emotional disturbance.

Another noteworthy quantitative scheme for coding human figure drawings is the Draw-A-Person Screening Procedure for Emotional Disturbance (DAP:SPED), which was con-structed by Naglieri and his colleagues as an enhancement of Koppitz's work (McNeish & Naglieri, 1993; Naglieri, McNeish, & Bardos, 1991; Naglieri & Pfeiffer, 1992). Concerned that the Koppitz system had not been adequately standardized, Naglieri et al. (1991) used data from a nationally representative sample of 2,355 young people aged 6 to 17 to construct the DAP:SPED, which consists of 55 characteristics that seldom appear in the drawings of normal children and adolescents. Naglieri et al. recommended their measure as a screening procedure for helping to identify whether a young person is having adjustment difficulties that call for further evaluation. Because neither the Koppitz 30-item list nor the 55-item DAP:SPED has become widely used in clinical practice, their full item list is not included here. Research with these two scoring systems is considered later in the chapter in discussing the application and psychometric properties of figure drawing methods.

In a further significant development, Tharinger and Stark (1990) proposed a DAP scoring system focused on an examiner's general impressions of a drawing, instead of on objective drawing features like the size and placement of figures. Called the Integrated System, Tharinger and Stark's approach calls for rating each drawing on a scale from 1 (absence of psychopathology) to 5 (severe psychopathology). This overall rating for level of adjustment is based on the prominence of four undesirable drawing qualities: (1) inhumanness, as suggested by drawings that strike the examiner as incomplete, grotesque, or monstrous; (2) lack of agency, as conveyed to the examiner by a sense of powerlessness in the drawing; (3 lack of well-being, as reflected in negative facial expressions; and (4) lack of capacity to interact, as inferred from a drawing's having a hollow, vacant, or stilted quality. Like the Koppitz and DAP:SPED interpretive systems, the Integrated System has not become widely used but has generated some research work that is discussed later in the chapter.

House-Tree-Person (HTP) and Kinetic Family Drawing (KFD)

Both the HTP and the KFD, in common with Goodenough's Draw-A-Man test, were developed primarily to facilitate the assessment of young people. The HTP was devised by John Buck (1948) and elaborated by Emmanuel Hammer (1960, 1985) to tap the concerns, interpersonal attitudes, and self-perceptions of children and adolescents more fully than is usually possible with human figure drawings alone. The HTP can be used with persons of all ages, beginning as early as the preschool years, but Buck and Hammer regarded its special value as residing in the potential of a house, a tree, and a person drawings to symbolize important aspects of a child's world.

Drawing a house was expected to arouse children's feelings about their home life and family relationships. Buck and Hammer hypothesized, for example, that a tiny door in relation to the size of the windows or windows with shutters over them could indicate withdrawal from interpersonal relationships and reluctance to make contact with the environment outside the home. Drawing a tree was expected to elicit feelings about the self and to do so in a less anxiety-provoking manner than drawing a person, inasmuch as a tree is less obvious than a human figure as a self-portrait. Among numerous possibilities, Buck and Hammer suggested, the way the trunk of the tree is drawn (e.g., whether thick or thin, sturdy or flimsy looking) could reflect a person's basic feeling of inner strength or weakness, or of power or fragility; branches drawn with thorns rather than leaves on them could identify concerns about anger or hostility. The drawing of the person was believed to reveal additional aspects of how people view themselves (a self-image), as well as how they would like to be (an ideal image) and what they think about significant other people in their lives.

The KFD was foreshadowed by Machover (1949) and other figure drawing pioneers who suggested that valuable information could be obtained by asking children to draw members of their family (Appel, 1931; Reznikoff & Reznikoff, 1956). Robert Burns and S. Harvard Kaufman (1970, 1972) formalized this suggestion by developing the KFD, in which examinees are asked to draw a picture that includes everyone in their family, including themselves, doing something. The drawing is examined both for structural features of the individual family members (e.g., omission or exaggeration of body parts) and for relationships among them, including their relative size, the way they are grouped, and how they are behaving toward each other. These drawing characteristics are expected to provide clues to the intensity and emotional tone of family members' attitudes toward each other and how they are likely to interact. Special note is taken of any barriers between family members that would interfere with their interacting at all, such as drawing one of them within a circle or a box or at a distance from the others.

As a variation of the KFD, Prout and Phillips (1974) proposed a kinetic school drawing (KSD), in which children are asked to draw a school picture of themselves, their teacher, and a friend or two, with everyone doing something. The KSD was intended to provide information about peer relationships and about attitudes and concerns related to school in the same manner as the KFD does for family relationships and feelings about the home. Knoff and Prout (1985) later recommended combining the KFD and the KSD and administering both measures for purposes of analysis and comparison. This combined approach, which they called the Kinetic Drawing System, is expected to identify adjustment difficulties both at home and in the school, to clarify causal or reciprocal relationships between family and school-related issues, and to indicate which people in a child's life (e.g., father, sister, teacher) are sources of support or tension. As one further extension of the kinetic approach, Burns (1987) proposed a kinetic version of the HTP, in which respondents are instructed to draw on a single page a picture of a house, a tree, and a person, "all in the same picture, with the person doing something."

ADMINISTRATION AND SCORING

The materials to administer the DAP, HTP, and KFD figure drawing tests consist of blank pieces of $8^1/_2 \times 11$-inch paper and some well-sharpened #2 pencils with erasers. People taking the test should be seated comfortably at a table or desk that provides a smooth, flat surface on which to draw, and they should have ample room to rest their arms on the drawing surface. The specific instructions that are given vary with which test is being used.

DAP

Examiners administering the DAP should place one sheet of paper and a pencil in front of the person being assessed and say, "I would like you to draw a picture of a person." To maximize the person's role in deciding how to proceed, no additional guidance should be given. If examinees ask for further structure (e.g., "What kind of person should I draw?" "Can it be a picture of someone I know?" "With or without clothes on?"), they should be told, "It's up to you; you can do it any way you like." Some examinees, more commonly adults than children and adolescents, may express concern about their drawing ability, as by saying, "I'm not much of an artist" or "I don't think this test will work for me, because I don't know how to draw." The appropriate reply to such comments is "This is not a test of artistic ability, and it doesn't matter how well you can draw; just go ahead and do the best you can."

If examinees respond to these initial instructions by drawing a stick figure, they should be given another sheet of paper and told, "This time I would like you to draw a regular person, not a stick figure." If the first drawing consists only of the head or head and shoulders of a person, a second sheet of paper should be provided with the additional instruction, "This time I would like you to draw a whole person." Following satisfactory completion of this first drawing, the examiner should replace it with a new sheet of paper and say, "Now I would like you to draw a person of the opposite sex from the one you have just drawn." If the respondent is a child, this request for a second drawing can be stated alternatively as,

"You drew a boy (man) before; now draw a girl or a woman" or "You drew a girl (woman) before; now draw a boy or a man" (see Handler, 1996).

The two human figure drawings obtained in this way constitute the basic DAP protocol. As mentioned, a supplementary inquiry usually enriches the test protocol with valuable additional data. Although no particular inquiry procedure has been standardized or universally adopted, the method described next combines fairly common practices and is recommended as a useful way of generating thematic as well as structural DAP findings.

Following completion of the two drawings, one of each gender, the examiner in this recommended method shows the person the first drawing and says, "I'd like you to look at the first drawing you did and make up a story about the person you've drawn." The examinee's story should be recorded verbatim. Just as in a Rorschach or TAT protocol, the way people express themselves in words frequently provides information about the kind of person they are, which calls for an exact transcription of DAP stories. When the examinee has finished telling a story about the first drawing, the procedure is repeated for the second one: "Next, I'd like you to look at the second drawing you did and make up a story about this person."

After obtaining the stories to these two drawings, the examiner gives the person a third sheet of paper and asks for a self-portrait: "Now on this page I'd like you to draw a picture of yourself." Completion of the self-portrait is then followed by asking, "What kind of person are you?"

This procedure for administering the DAP can also be adapted for self-administration or group administration using a 5-page booklet of $8^{1}/_{2} \times 11$-inch sheets of paper. In this version of the test, the first and second pages of the booklet contain the following printed instructions:

[First page] In the blank space below, draw a person. Any kind of person will do. Be sure to draw a *whole* person. This is not a test of drawing skill. Just draw a person as best you can.

[Second page] Now please draw another person. This one should be different from your first drawing. If you drew a man first, now draw a woman. If you drew a woman first, now draw a man.

The third page of the booklet is divided into two parts, with the first of the following instructions printed in the upper half and the second instruction printed in the lower half:

[Third page, upper half] THE MAN—In the space below, make up a short story about the man you drew. Tell how old he is, about his job, his family, the kind of person he is, his best points and his worst points.

[Third page, lower half] THE WOMAN—Now make up a short story about the woman you drew. Try to include as much information as you can make up about her. Describe her as if she were a real person.

The fourth page of the booklet says at the top, "Now draw a picture of yourself," and the fifth page has the heading, "What kind of person are you?"

Self-administration of the DAP with a booklet form limits examiner-examinee interaction during the test and restricts this source of information, but it does not prevent examiners from observing how people go about drawing their figures. Moreover, examinees who are uncomfortable interacting with the examiner may express themselves more fully in writing about their drawings than in talking about them. Additional potential advantages of using a booklet include helping to ensure a verbatim record of what examinees say about their drawings and providing indications not only of their vocabulary skills, but also of their command of grammar, spelling, and punctuation.

As for the scoring of human figure drawings, what was said previously in recounting the development of the DAP tells much of the story about approaches to codifying this measure. The Koppitz emotional indicators and the DAP:SPED have existed in their present form since 1968 and 1991, respectively, and the Tharinger and Stark Integrated System since 1990. Although numerous other DAP scoring systems have been proposed from time to time—for example, a 21-item sign list proposed by Handler (1967) for rating anxiety level and a Human Figure Drawing Test (HFDT) scoring manual developed by Mitchell, Trent, and McArthur (1993) for assessing cognitive impairment—no systems other than the Koppitz, the DAP:SPED, and the Integrated System have attracted much attention from either practitioners or researchers.

HTP

Administration of the HTP begins in the same manner as the DAP, by giving the examinee a pencil and a blank sheet of $8^1/_2 \times 11$-inch paper. Following procedures recommended by Handler (1996), the paper for the first drawing should be placed in front of the examinee in a horizontal rather the usual vertical position, with the following instruction: "I want you to draw as good a picture of a house as you can. You may draw any kind of house you wish; it's entirely up to you." After this drawing is finished, the person should be given a second piece of paper, this time placed in a vertical position, and told, "Next I would like you to draw as good a picture as you can of a tree." For the third drawing, also with the paper placed vertically, the instruction should be, "And now I want you to draw as good a picture of a person as you can." Hesitation on the part of examinees or expressed concern about not being good at drawing should be handled as in administering the DAP, by indicating that this is not a test of artistic ability and that they should just do the best job they can.

Also in common with the DAP, the HTP can be enriched by inquiry. After the three drawings have been completed, this inquiry can begin with open-ended questions like "What can you tell me about this house?" "What do you think about this tree?" and "What is this person like?" Open-ended inquiry can be supplemented with specific questions designed to help examinees define, describe, and elaborate on their drawings. Numerous authors, including Buck (1985, 1992) and Handler (1996), have provided lists of questions for this purpose, of which the following are some examples:

What kinds of activities go on in this house?

What does this house need?

What are the weakest and strongest parts of this tree?

What does this tree remind you of or make you think of?

What does this person like most or least to do?

What sorts of things make this person angry or sad?

Along with qualitative guidelines for interpretation, Buck (1948) originally proposed a quantitative scoring system for the HTP in which points are given for such features as the presence or absence of various details and the relative size of certain parts of the figures. These HTP scoring procedures have not become well known or widely used in clinical practice, nor have they been systematically evaluated for their psychometric properties. An effort by Jolles (1971) to condense Buck's scoring system into a more attractive version has also met with little success, and no other HTP scoring systems have become visible in the literature.

KFD

The KFD is administered with a pencil and a single sheet of blank paper, with the following instructions, as recommended by Burns and Kaufman (1972, p. 5):

> Draw a picture of everyone in your family, including you, *doing* something. Try to draw whole people, not cartoons or stick people. Remember, make everyone doing something—some kind of actions.

As in administering the other figure drawing tests, examiners should give as little structure as possible in responding to questions about the procedure. Examinees should follow the instructions and can be reminded as necessary (a) that it is up to them to do the drawing however they wish, (b) that they should do the best they can, and (c) that this is not a test of artistic ability. Examiners should otherwise keep silent about the nature of the test, the types of drawings that are expected, and how the drawings will be interpreted.

As with the other figure drawing methods, including an inquiry in the KFD administration usually proves worthwhile. Following suggestions by Knoff and Prout (1985) and McConaughy and Achenbach (1994), three types of questions can be recommended as particularly likely to enrich a KFD protocol. First, examiners can inquire about the name and age of each person in the drawing, each person's relationship to the examinee, and each person's noteworthy attributes (e.g., "What are three words that describe this person?" "What are this person's good and bad points?"). Second, people can be asked to imagine what each person in their drawing is thinking and feeling at the moment. Third, questions can be asked about the family unit, including "What was happening to this family just before this picture?" "How does this family get along with each other?" "Who do you get along with best?" "Who do you get along with least?" "What will happen to this family in the future?"

Burns and Kaufman (1970, 1972) proposed a scoring system for the KFD, as have several other assessment psychologists who believed that an objective scoring method would facilitate KFD interpretation in clinical practice (e.g., Meyers, 1978; O'Brien & Patton, 1974; Reynolds, 1978). Burns (1982) subsequently presented a revised and detailed KFD scoring scheme that emphasized four features of the drawing: the physical characteristics of the figures, the types of actions attributed to each figure, the distances between and positions relative to each other of each pair of family members, and various stylistic features that might indicate emotional disturbance (e.g., drawing all the figures in a rectangle along the edges of the paper). None of these efforts to score and quantify KFD characteristics has become well known or widely used, either in research or practice.

INTERPRETATION

As noted, the sources of data in figure drawing methods comprise structural variables consisting of what examinees draw, thematic variables consisting of what examinees say about their drawings, and behavioral variables consisting of how examinees perform the drawing task and interact with the examiner. Interpretation of these three data sources proceeds according to the following separate sets of guidelines.

Structural Variables

The structural variables in figure drawings are most commonly interpreted by inspecting the drawings for unusual or distinctive features that might reflect some personality characteristic. This inspection method, which is based largely on Machover's (1949) original proposals, focuses on the previously mentioned core structural characteristics of the DAP, HTP, and KFD: the line quality of the drawings, the size of the figures and their placement on the page, and any emphasis on or omission of basic parts. In addition, drawings should be inspected for the gender differentiation of human figures and for the possible role of artistic ability in accounting for this and other noteworthy drawing features.

Along with taking note of these core structural characteristics in each individual drawing, examiners should compare a person's drawings with each other. Are there differences in size or line quality between the male and female figures or between these figures and a drawing of the self? Do unusual features appear in a male, female, or self drawing but not in the other human figures? Is there any grouping or form of activity that involves some but not other members of a family?

After identifying striking, unusual, or distinctive features of a person's figure drawings, examiners should formulate hypotheses about what these features might signify for the person being examined. Like the thematic imagery in Rorschach responses and stories told to the TAT pictures (see Chapters 11 and 12), noteworthy features of figure drawings typically have alternative possible meanings, none of which necessarily applies to the individual who has drawn them. In weighing the plausibility of these alternatives, examiners should limit their inferences to those with a compelling rationale and be correspondingly wary of inferences that require an extensive stretch of the imagination. Even then, apparently reasonable inferences linking figure drawing characteristics to personality characteristics should be considered only conjectures, until they are reinforced by repetitive evidence in the structural and thematic data of the drawings and supplemented by congruent indications in interview findings, collateral reports, and other test data.

This interpretive caution does not mean that examiners should shrink from conjecture. To the contrary, even though the precise meaning of figure drawing features may initially be unclear, assessment psychologists should approach test data with the idea that everything means something. At times, this meaning may escape discovery, and sometimes an eventually determined meaning may prove of little consequence. Nonetheless, forming reasonable hypotheses is a necessary step in translating figure drawing features into accurate and useful personality descriptions. The examples that follow illustrate application of the inspection method in interpreting structural variables in figure drawings, with an emphasis on the importance of limiting inferences to what test signs *might* mean, while refraining from conviction about what they *must* mean.

Line Quality

Suppose a person draws a house in which there are gaps in the lines depicting the side walls and the roof of the dwelling. Then the person draws a tree trunk with broken rather than continuous lines and with branches disconnected from the trunk and leaves detached from the branches. Finally, the person draws people whose heads are not joined to their necks, whose arms hang disconnected from their shoulders, or whose legs are separated from their torsos.

Thoughts about what these drawing features might mean could well begin with associations to damage and fragmentation. The outer boundaries of the wall and the human bodies in this example are no longer intact, as they may once have been, but instead are incomplete and full of holes. As damaged goods, they may not provide much protection for what lies within, and hence they may convey a sense of weakness, fragility, and vulnerability to further damage. A broken wall may crumble and fall, and an incomplete person, like an argument that is full of holes, may not be able to stand up to challenges.

As for fragmentation, the disconnected parts of the tree and the human figures in this example could be seen as suggesting a sense of coming apart. People who draw fragmented figures may be worried about things going badly in their lives or the world around them; they may be fearful of losing their mind or having their body deteriorate ("I feel like I'm falling apart," troubled people sometimes say); or they may be finding it difficult to maintain a realistic grasp of their body boundaries and bodily functions. Neither these nor any other alternative hypotheses concerning the personal meaning of damage and fragmentation necessarily apply when a person produces drawings with broken lines. Each of the alternatives offered here is a reasonable possibility to consider, but the likely accuracy of each must be judged in light of its congruence with information from other data sources.

In considering the possible interpretive significance of line quality, it may be that drawing unusually heavy lines indicates a person who is by nature assertive, bold, forceful, self-confident, and perhaps quick to anger, whereas unusually light lines in drawings might reflect passivity, timidity, fearfulness, self-derogation, and an aversion to expressing anger. LaRoque and Obrzut (2006) administered the DAP to a group of fifty 6- to 11-year-old children and measured the pencil pressure with which they drew. Those children with relatively high state anxiety, as indicated by their scores on the State Trait Anxiety Inventory for Children, used significantly less pencil pressure in rendering their drawings than children who showed lower levels of trait anxiety. By itself, this finding does not warrant basing any definite conclusions on line quality, but it supports the likelihood that unusually heavy or light lines have some implications for personality characteristics and provides a basis for generating hypotheses about what these characteristics might be.

Placement of Figures

Suppose a 9-year-old girl draws a picture of a family in which the figures of a man, a woman, and two children are grouped closely together and engaged in some shared activity, while a third child is placed off in the distance, far removed from the others and not involved in what they are doing. Even before she is asked to identify the figures in the drawing, she prints "ME" directly above the spatially distant child. Little imagination is required to equate the spatial distance and disengagement in the drawing to feelings of separation, isolation, and alienation in real life. Hence this girl's family drawing gives reasonable grounds for hypothesizing that she feels lonely and alone, uninvolved in family activities or perhaps excluded from them, and possibly ignored, unappreciated, or even disliked by her parents and siblings.

Unless there is reasonable grounds for a hypothesis, as in this example, assessors should be circumspect in deriving inferences from it. To cite an example, Machover (1951, p. 360) originally suggested that placement of human figure drawings "corresponds to where the person places himself in the environment," with people who place their figures on the left side of the page being "self-oriented" and those who place their figures on the right side being "environment-oriented." She did not offer any rationale for this inference, nor does any association between left-right and self-environment come easily to mind. Hence this proposed interpretation of figure placement does not seem reasonable to consider.

By contrast, consider the familiarity of most people with common parlance concerning what it means to feel "on top of the world" or to describe someone as "a bottom-feeder." Perhaps, then, there is some rationale for hypothesizing that people who place their drawings near the top of a page are feeling more optimistic and better about themselves than those who locate their drawings on the bottom. The rationale in this instance would be more compelling than the uncertain basis for the left-right placement hypothesis from Machover, but it is not nearly as compelling as the inference about family distance in the example of the 9-year-old girl. In the absence of supporting empirical data, examiners should always distinguish among speculative hypotheses by attending to the soundness of the rationale for them, and as noted in Chapter 2 (see p. 42), they should frame their conclusions in language that reflects how certain they are. These considerations do not rule out instances in which empirical data support a test-based inference for which there is no apparent rationale. Empirical confirmation of hypotheses that lack a convincing rationale usually identifies a phenomenon that is being validly measured but is not yet fully understood.

Size of Figures

Suppose a male examinee draws a picture of a large, powerful looking man. This drawing could reflect the person's image of himself as a strong, capable, and important individual. Alternatively, this large male figure might reflect how this man wishes he were (an ideal self-image) instead of how he perceives himself (his actual self-image). In that case, any apparent grandiosity on his part could be veiling underlying feelings of inadequacy or inferiority. Suppose this same man also draws a large and imposing figure of a woman and then, when asked to produce a picture of himself, draws a small and ineffectual looking figure. Taken together, the three figures would support inferring that the large drawing of the man is an ideal or compensatory self-image and that, instead of being self-assured, this man is likely to have limited self-confidence and perceive himself as less capable and less worthy than other people.

Should the man in fact devalue himself, there are still other ways to interpret the size of his drawings. Perhaps the large, powerful man he drew is neither an actual nor an ideal self-image, but instead a representation of men in general, to whom he feels inferior, or of some particular man in his life by whom he has felt overwhelmed, whether his father, an older brother who bullied or surpassed him, or an employer or commanding officer who browbeat or ridiculed him. Perhaps for this man, the large woman he drew represents women in general, compared with whom he also feels weak and powerless, or some particular woman by whom he feels or felt dominated, such as his mother, an overbearing wife, or a harsh teacher who shamed and embarrassed him.

Showing that a figure drawing can represent the actual self, an ideal self, certain kinds of people in general, or certain people in particular demonstrates further the importance of generating alternative hypotheses about the possible meanings of figure drawing features. As noted by Handler (1996), a similar range of alternative possibilities must be considered in evaluating the structure of KFD drawings. Whether drawn by a child or an adult, a family depiction can represent the person's family as it actually is, or as the person believes it to be, or as the person wishes it were. Just as there are few if any universal symbols, there is seldom any invariant meaning associated with specific drawing characteristics. Instead, the structural features of drawings frequently have multiple meanings and can mean different things to different people.

As for the plausibility of the inferences in this example, common parlance provides a ready rationale for associating size with strength, power, authority, importance, and the like, even though large people may not necessarily possess these qualities. Napoleon Bonaparte is often described as having been a dominant commander despite his short stature, not because of it, and it is said of influential people that they "carry a lot of weight," and of people who have behaved admirably that they "stood tall," not that they "stood short."

This example also demonstrates that figure size, because of its alternative possible meanings, cannot serve as a barometer of self-esteem, as was originally suggested by Machover (1949). Research findings have in fact shown that there is no systematic relationship between figure drawing variables and level of self-esteem (Cummings, 1986; Groth-Marnat & Roberts, 1998). Findings of this kind do not disconfirm the validity of figure drawing methods, however. The absence of a systematic relationship does not signify absence of any relationship, nor does a test variable having more than one meaning equate to its meaning nothing at all. Moreover, a test variable having no clinical implications some of the time does not signify that it has no clinical implications at any time. To the contrary, the ready rationale for the possible significance of figure size gives good reason to consider that unusually large or small drawings indicate some type of concern or adjustment difficulty related to whether individuals compare themselves favorably or unfavorably to other people in general or to certain people in particular.

Emphasis on Parts

Suppose a person draws human figures with ears or eyes that are disproportionately large, unusually detailed, or heavily shaded. As sensory organs, ears and eyes are the primary means by which people attend to each other and take in information about what is going on in the world. The wolf in the fairy tale of Little Red Riding Hood tells her that he has big ears "The better to hear you with" and big eyes "The better to see you with." In actuality, the size of these organs has nothing to do with how well they function, but special attention to them may reflect heightened concern about being under the scrutiny of people who are listening closely to what one says or observing carefully what one does. Or, a notable emphasis on the ears and eyes in a drawing could reflect a person's felt urgency to be an attentive listener and alert observer.

This hypothesized association of emphasized ears with concerns about hearing or being heard involves only a short leap of inference, and there is a similarly ready rationale for linking emphasized eyes with concerns about seeing or being seen. Moreover, indications of feeling under scrutiny or needing to be a scrutinizer both have compelling implications for an overly cautious and perhaps suspicious or hypervigilant stance in interpersonal relationships. Even when such plausible and convergent inferences emerge from an emphasis on ears and eyes, however, examiners should not overlook other possible reasons for this or any other drawing characteristic. Among middle-aged people and the elderly, concerns about hearing loss or failing eyesight might contribute to their giving special attention to the ears and eyes in their drawings. In young people concerned with their physical appearance, preoccupation with what they perceive as unattractive features of their ears and eyes could contribute to unusual treatment of these body parts in their drawings.

Omission of Parts

Suppose a person draws a human figure with ordinary looking arms but no hands at the end of them, or with the hands concealed by being placed in pockets or held behind the back. Hands can reasonably be regarded as agents for doing things and for reaching out to touch and hold other people. As alternative possibilities, then, the omission or concealment of hands might reflect concerns about being helpless to take constructive action; or guilt about having behaved badly in some way, as captured in such common expressions as "having dirty hands" or "being caught with your hands in the cookie jar"; or fears of losing control and engaging in regrettable acts of some kind; or anxiety about close physical contact with others and an aversion to touching or being touched by people.

As a quite different possibility in this instance, some people avoid drawing hands because they are harder to draw than most other body parts. This possibility can be tested by asking examinees who have omitted or concealed the hands in their original drawings to draw a separate picture of just a hand. Should the person then show little difficulty in drawing a reasonably good representation of a hand, the original omission or concealment would be all the more likely to reflect some kind of concern related to what people do with their hands.

Omission or concealment of other body parts should be considered a basis for generating alternative hypotheses about the meaning of this drawing feature. As in the previous examples of the interpretive process, the accuracy of these possible meanings should then be considered in light of which, if any, are particularly compelling and supported by information from other sources.

Gender Differentiation

People with artistic talent are more likely than inferior artists to embellish their drawings of human figures with details that have potential interpretive significance, such as a dramatic facial expression (e.g., scowling, tearful), a particular type of clothing (e.g., bathing suit, evening gown), or engagement in some activity (e.g., reading a book, riding a motorcycle). Limited artistry is usually reflected in unelaborated drawings that contain only the essential characteristics of what is bring drawn. Poor artists seldom depict gender differences as clearly and thoroughly in their skimpy drawings as do skilled artists in their more elaborate drawings, particularly with respect to body shape, hairstyle, type of dress, and other distinctive accoutrements (e.g., man with a beard, woman wearing high-heeled shoes).

Nevertheless, scanty or cursory indications of gender in human figure drawings can and should be distinguished from complete absence of any gender differentiating characteristics. Basic indications of gender require little drawing skill to produce, and drawings that cannot easily be identified as male or female are unlikely to be solely the product of limited artistic ability. Instead, drawings that contain no clues of any kind to the gender of human figures usually suggest some concern or uncertainty on the part of examinees about their gender identity.

Artistic Ability

Examiners should generally avoid inferring personality characteristics from drawing features that could be attributed to a person's being a poor artist. As illustrated in the instance of inadequate gender differentiation, however, limited artistry does not necessarily invalidate otherwise warranted inferences. Like rudimentary gender differentiation, the basic structural dimensions of line quality, size and placement of drawings, and omission or exaggeration of parts are largely independent of drawing skill. Being a poor artist would not account for whether a person draws broken lines, for example, large or small figures, or faces without ears, eyes, or a mouth.

This last example is reminiscent of the familiar statue of the three monkeys with their hands clasped over their eyes, their ears, or their mouth to symbolize "See no evil, hear no evil, speak no evil." These would be intriguing possible meanings to pursue when ears, eyes, or a mouth are absent from a person's drawings of human figures or covered up in some way. Whatever its significance turned out to be, omission or concealment of these features would probably indicate some type of conflict or concern for the individual and should not be discounted as merely a consequence of poor drawing skill.

Limited artistry is also unlikely to account for gross distortions of reality in figure drawings. Instead, research findings reviewed by Handler (1996) indicate that the distorted body imagery and impaired reality sense frequently associated with severe psychopathology commonly diminish a disturbed person's capacity to represent the body accurately in figure drawings. With this consideration in mind, bizarre or impossible features of figure drawings should be regarded as probable indicators of psychological disturbance. As elaborated by Handler, Campbell, and Martin (2004), limited artistry is seldom a source of error in figure drawing interpretation, because it is usually not difficult to distinguish drawing characteristics that represent poor psychological differentiation from characteristics that are attributable to limited artistic ability.

Especially noteworthy is a transparency effect in which internal organs show through the body of a human figure or interior furniture is visible through the walls of a house. Such transparencies are unlikely to reflect poor drawing skills and are important to note, because they suggest some loss of touch with reality. The severity of the reality testing impairment suggested by transparencies depends on how bizarre a drawing is. A person's heart, stomach, or ovaries showing through the body should be considered a major transparency and would point to substantial or pervasively impaired reality sense. A relatively minor transparency would be adding clothing to human figures and then neglecting to erase the lines of their arms or legs under the clothing, which would suggest mild or transient lapses in reality sense.

As always in interpreting figure drawings, allowance must be made for exceptions and alternative possibilities. In the drawings of young children whose reality sense is not fully developed, minor and even major transparency effects may occur as a normative phenomenon. In older children and adults, major transparencies cannot be discounted as normative distortions, but minor transparencies can sometimes appear as a reflection of immaturity or carelessness rather than psychopathology. Examinees can temper the pathological significance even of major transparencies by attempting to account for their bizarre features, as by explaining that the drawing is an X-ray view of the body or a picture of a house with glass walls.

Thematic Variables

The stories that people tell about their figure drawings, together with answers they give to specific questions about what they have drawn, provide thematic data in much the same way as the TAT method discussed in Chapter 12. Thematic interpretation of figure drawing methods should accordingly proceed as in TAT interpretation, with attention to how the figures are described, the affective tone that is attributed to them, how the story plots evolve, and the manner in which the stories are expressed. As elaborated next, each of these story elements can contribute to deriving inferences from figure drawing imagery.

Figure Description

How people describe the figures they have drawn often provides clues to their attitudes toward themselves, toward other persons, and toward the world in general. Human figures can be described as intelligent, attractive, talented, kind, caring, diligent, or successful, or as dumb, homely, inept, mean, selfish, lazy, or doing poorly. Whatever form such characterizations take, their attribution to a self-portrait suggests similar perceptions by examinees of themselves or how they would like to be. As in the interpretation of figure size, the drawings of male and female figures other than the self can also provide clues to an actual or ideal self-image, and they may reflect as well attitudes toward people in general or toward certain people in particular.

Characterizations of the figures in a family drawing often reveal how young people view their parents and siblings, the roles they ascribe to family members, and how they experience their home life, as in the following story by an 11-year-old girl: "This is my Dad, he's the one who tells us what to do, and this is my Mom, she's pretty nice and not as mean as my Dad, and that's my little brother, who's a bit dorky sometimes, but we all get along pretty well." Neither this nor any other family drawing story constitutes conclusive evidence of any pattern of family relationships. Such stories nevertheless provide some fairly transparent clues to pursue in the assessment process, such as the implication of this girl's story for a somewhat bossy father but a reasonably agreeable family life.

Descriptions of trees as well as of human figures may suggest how people view themselves. Consider the contrasting implications for the self-image of a tree "that's growing strong and tall" and a tree "that's losing its leaves." The possible meaning of such descriptions can often be clarified by thinking of them as prefaced with the words "I am." It takes little imagination to translate "I am a tree that's growing strong and tall" into positive attitudes toward one's physical assets and progress in life. Similarly compelling is the implication of "I am a tree that's losing its leaves" for negative views of one's functioning capacities as limited and one's future prospects as diminishing.

As for drawings of a house, these too can be described in ways that suggest positive or negative attitudes toward one's home and family life. Is the drawing referred to as "a nice house" or "a crummy house"? Is it seen as a shabby, flimsy, or termite-infested dwelling, or as a structure that is well designed and solidly built? Is it located in a good neighborhood or in a slum? Is it referred to as comfortable, pleasant, and "a neat place to live," or as dark, dingy, and "not a house I'd like to spend much time in"? Such descriptions raise the possibility that examinees regard their own house in similar terms, although, like an ideal self-image, a house described in glowing terms can also represent an appealing way of life that a person wishes for but does not have.

Affective Tone

The affective tone ascribed to human figure drawings usually provides clues to a person's emotional state or how the person perceives other people as feeling. In the case of unwelcome affects that people usually prefer to avoid, such as feeling sad, angry, or afraid, their presence in DAP figures tends to be a direct reflection of similar feelings being experienced or perceived in others. A predominance of positive affects, especially when they receive considerable emphasis, suggests either similar feelings in a person or that they represent defensive efforts to ward off unpleasant affect. These defensive efforts can take the form of seeing all three DAP figures as "really very happy," "feeling good about everything," or as "always having a fun time," or making such comments as, "He's an easygoing guy, never gets angry or riled up," or "She is a very capable person who doesn't have to be afraid of anything." Generally speaking, emphatic protestations of positive affect may indicate denial of negative or disturbing emotions that lie beneath the surface or outside a person's conscious awareness.

With respect to distinguishing between self-experienced affects and affects attributed to other people, comparisons among the three DAP drawings may at times prove helpful. The combination of a male figure seen as an "angry man" with a female figure and a self-portrait who are not seen as angry might suggest a tendency to perceive anger in men more than in women or in oneself. Seeing the female figure but not the male figure or the self-portrait as fearful might suggest a perception applicable to women but not men or oneself. Combining an unhappy self-portrait with male and female figures who "feel pretty good" would tend to locate depressive affect in the examinee, along with the self-perception of being troubled in ways that other people are not experiencing.

Story Plot

The plot elements of stories and responses to questions about figure drawings may provide clues to a person's expectations in life, the person's aspirations and anticipated obstacles to realizing those aspirations, and the coping style the person brings to bear to get his or her needs met. The following excerpts illustrate how story plots can be translated into hypotheses concerning attitudes, aspirations, expectations, and coping styles that characterize people or that they attribute to others.

> [Female drawing] She's an intelligent woman, and she wanted for a long time to be a lawyer, and she worked hard and made it, and now she's in a good firm and doing well. [An optimistic story suggesting ambition, commitment to diligence, and anticipation of success as a reward for effort]

> [Male drawing] This guy was in the army, and he got wounded, and it's taken him a while to recover. He's working again, but he'd like to be his own boss and have his own shop. But he probably won't be able to get enough money together to start up his own business, and he'll be disappointed. [A pessimistic story suggesting aspiration, but also bad luck, frustrated progress, and a dim view of what the future will bring]

> [Self drawing] I'm an active person. I like to keep busy and do things. Sometimes I do things faster than I should, and I can get in trouble that way. But I don't like to sit around and twiddle my thumbs. Mostly people can count on me to get things done when they need to be done, and I like it that way. [Suggests satisfaction with a restless, unreflective, and action-oriented lifestyle, with insufficient attention to learning from past mistakes and thinking ahead about future consequences]

Plot elements in KFD stories are likely to contain numerous clues to how people view their family life. Family members may be described as engaging in a shared activity ("They're watching their favorite TV program") or as pursuing separate activities, each one independent of the others. Family interactions can be seen as pleasant ("They're talking about where they want to go for a vacation") or unpleasant ("They're having a big fight about who should help out around the house"), or as having a happy outcome ("They'll enjoy themselves wherever they go") or not so happy outcome ("I bet these parents end up in a divorce").

Manner of Expression

The manner in which people express themselves in telling stories or answering questions about figures they have drawn provides information about the integrity of their cognitive functioning, particularly with respect to whether they can think clearly, reason logically, and perceive people and situations realistically. As in interpretation of the TAT (see pp. 466–467), stories that flow in a continuous fashion and are easy to follow indicate that an examinee is thinking clearly and coherently. Disjointed and confusing stories suggest scattered thinking, difficulty in maintaining a relevant focus of attention, and corresponding tendencies to wander off into loosely connected trains of association.

Stories that are sensible and, even when fanciful, present a probable or at least conceivable sequence of events usually reflect ability to reason logically. People who tell stories that involve highly unlikely cause-and-effect relationships or unimaginable links between events may tend to think in a circumstantial and irrational manner. Consider, a young person who says about a female drawing, "This woman looks real angry, so her hair will probably fall out," or about a male drawing, "He likes to watch people riding bicycles, and this will put him on the football team." Examiners hearing such stories may well wonder what one of these things has to do with the other. When they find themselves pondering this question, they are probably examining a person who is prone to arbitrary reasoning and illogical inference.

As for being realistic, figure drawing stories ordinarily remain within the boundaries of actuality. A disturbed man said of his drawing of a male figure, "He's a hard man, a bad man, looking right at me like he wants to do something bad to me, and he scares me, he's making me feel afraid." Of his drawing of himself, he said, "I'm in a bad place, and I'm going to sprout wings and fly right out of here." Becoming fearful of one's own drawing on a piece of paper and expecting to sprout wings and fly away illustrate a loss of distance from reality that suggests a propensity for misperceiving people and events.

Possible thematic indications of impaired cognitive integrity need to be qualified in two ways. First, to apply the maturational consideration mentioned in discussing the interpretation of structural drawing variables, cognitively immature children may normatively tell inconceivable or unimaginable stories that in a more mature person would suggest disturbances in thinking or reality testing. Second, older children and adults, if given the opportunity, may account for unusual stories by identifying them as fictitious, metaphorical, or purely wishful, as in the following examples:

> But he's not a real person, he's a science fiction guy or one of those aliens, so that's how he can do that.

> When I said she was two people, I meant that there were two different sides to her, and she can't make up her mind which one she wants to be.

> I drew myself with fire coming out of my mouth, but it's just a fantasy I have sometimes of being able to get my anger out and scorch some of the people around me, so to speak.

The less effort that people make to explain unrealistic stories in one of these ways, the more serious are the implications of these stories for cognitive dysfunction. Similarly serious implications attach to unrealistic stories that would defy any such reasonable explanation. Stress or anxiety may result in hair falling out, for example, but it is difficult to conceive or rationalize any link between hair loss and anger.

Behavioral Variables

Like other performance-based measures, figure drawing methods provide opportunities to observe a representative sample of how people approach tasks, feel about themselves, and relate to others, particularly those in authority. Two main sources of information are the commitment of examinees to their task and whatever comments they may make about their participation and performance.

Commitment

People being examined tend to vary considerably in their commitment to the drawing task. Some approach the task diligently, work slowly and carefully in producing the figures, and appear intent on doing a good job. Others draw hastily and carelessly, as if disinterested in being examined or unconcerned about the quality of their performance. This difference in commitment can help identify whether people are being open and forthcoming in the examination, or instead are intent on not revealing very much about themselves. Additionally, persons who perform diligently on figure drawing tests are likely to approach other tasks in their lives with care and investment and to take pride in a job well done, whereas those who devote little effort or concern to their drawings often tend to deal with other tasks in a similarly uninvolved and superficial manner.

Figure drawing behavior also provides some information about how well individuals can sustain their attention. Whether drawing slowly or rapidly, people ordinarily work at a steady pace. Those who work unevenly, slowing down at times or perhaps stopping entirely and looking off into space, may be having difficulty sustaining their attention. Similarly, examinees who are easily distracted from their task by a telephone ringing in the next room or the examiner shuffling some papers may also have impaired concentration. Such lapses in concentration may be clues to an attention disorder or to some transient anxiety or intrusive ideation that is interfering with the person's ability to sustain attention.

Comments

Attitudes toward themselves and toward other people are sometimes reflected in comments people make while drawing their figures. Independently of whether they identify themselves as good or poor artists, working on the drawings may evoke expressions of satisfaction or dissatisfaction that have implications for how they value themselves. Self-critical comments like "I'm afraid I'm doing a poor job" or "I'm making a mess of things here, as I usually do" suggest low self-esteem, whereas self-congratulatory comments like "Making these drawings is easy for me because I have a sensitive nature and I'm very good at visualizing things" suggest positive self-regard. Suppose after completing the test, a person says, "Those aren't very good drawings, I know, but I'm not much of an artist; something I'm really good at is solving puzzles, like the ones we did before [reference to previously administered Wechsler performance subtests], and you'll be able to see that if we do some more of them." This person is probably more self-assured and more self-confident than a person who says, "You'll probably think this is a good picture, because I always was good at drawing; too bad I was never much good at anything else."

Comments made during the figure drawing administration can also provide information about an individual's interpersonal attitudes. A person who repeatedly requests structure (e.g., "Should I draw a man or a woman?" "How much time do I have?" "Can I do a profile?" "Will you tell me if I am doing it properly?") may be a passive-dependent individual who is excessively concerned about complying with the expectations of other people, overly reliant on getting guidance from them, and inclined to structure interpersonal situations in an authoritarian way. Examinees who grumble, "This doesn't make much sense to me," or "I don't see how you can get any useful information out of a test like this" are demonstrating resistance to the examination process (if the test is senseless and useless, there is no need to invest much energy in it and little reason to give credence to the results), and they are also displaying a provocative, belligerent, and depreciatory interpersonal style. Like other representative samples of behavior, such attitudes and styles emerging during the assessment often reflect a person's behavioral tendencies in other situations as well.

APPLICATIONS

Figure drawing methods bring certain advantages to the personality assessment process. The DAP, HTP, and KFD are brief, uncomplicated measures that can ordinarily be administered in 20 to 30 minutes with a full inquiry and in less than 10 minutes if only the drawings are requested. These measures can be used with persons of all ages, beginning as early as age 3 years, and they are often helpful in evaluating people who are anxious about being examined, have limited language skills, or are reluctant to talk. Young people in particular may find it easier to express their thoughts and feelings in drawings rather than in words, and drawing pictures tends to be a more familiar and less threatening task for children than most of what they are asked to do in a psychological examination. Braden (2003) has suggested that this familiarity of figure drawing tasks, together with their brevity, is what accounts for their frequent use by school psychologists.

Because figure drawing methods do not involve any test stimuli, they are not only easy to administer but also relatively culture free. Provided there is sufficient language communication for the person being examined to understand the instructions, figure drawings can be obtained in similar fashion and interpreted following the same procedures whatever a person's ethnicity, national origin, or sociocultural background (see Ritzler, 2004). Nevertheless, as in all psychological evaluations and psychosocial interventions, methods that involve relatively culture-free stimuli may nevertheless call for clinicians to interpret the data they obtain in light of cultural differences.

Consider a drawing of a woman whose clothing covers her body from the neck down to the wrists and ankles. A drawing of this kind in the general U.S. population might suggest maladaptive anxiety about or aversion to physical sexuality. Drawn by a member of an Amish, Islamic, or Orthodox Jewish community, however, the same drawing could represent a normative and adaptive sense of how women should dress. As this example illustrates, figure drawing methods despite being culture-free with respect to their stimulus properties are culturally sensitive with respect to their interpretive significance, and persons from different backgrounds are likely to differ in the kinds of drawings they produce.

Along with being relatively brief, nonverbal, nonthreatening, and culture-free, figure drawing methods also allow for self-administration. As mentioned in describing a booklet form for these tests, self-administration helps some examinees feel more comfortable and express themselves more fully than they would during a question-and-answer interaction with an examiner. Use of a booklet makes group administration possible as well, which facilitates large-scale screening for indications of emotional disturbance. However, group administration sacrifices both an opportunity to observe how people go about drawing their figures (which is still possible with individual administration using the booklet form) and any information that would have come from interacting with examinees as they perform their task.

The brevity and simplicity of figure drawing methods also come at a price, because they restrict the number and scope of interpretive hypotheses that can be generated from the data, especially compared with the interpretive yield of more complex and extensive assessment procedures. As for being relatively nonverbal, nonthreatening, and culture-free, these advantages apply mainly to the basic drawing task and may dissipate when people are asked to tell stories or answer questions about the figures they have drawn.

Turning to applications of figure drawing methods, cumulative clinical experience and available research data indicate that these measures serve two main purposes: as a screening procedure for identifying possible psychological disturbance or adjustment difficulty, and as a source of information about personality characteristics and underlying concerns that have implications for planning psychotherapy and monitoring its progress.

Screening for Psychological Disturbance

The previous discussion of interpreting DAP, HTP, and KFD protocols illustrated several ways that figure drawings can suggest psychological disturbance or adjustment difficulties. Drawings that are bizarre (e.g., with major transparencies) probably indicate an impaired sense of reality. Incoherent and irrational stories about drawings often identify disordered thinking. A dramatic emphasis in the structure or description of drawings can reveal distressing preoccupations or troubling affects, as in the case of someone who draws people with tears on their cheeks and says about each of them, "This person is very unhappy."

The Koppitz indicators of emotional disturbance were selected for their low frequency of occurrence in the drawings of normally functioning children and adolescents and were expected to serve this diagnostic screening purpose. Research with the Koppitz list, however, has not provided any consistent evidence that it can effectively differentiate emotionally disturbed from well-adjusted young people. In one frequently cited study, Tharinger and Stark (1990) compared anxiety and mood-disordered children in grades 4 through 7 with normally functioning children and found no significant difference between the groups in either their mean total score on the Koppitz list or the frequency of any of its 30 individual items.

There is empirical support for screening young people for psychological disturbance with the 55-item DAP:SPED developed by Naglieri and his colleagues as an enhancement of the Koppitz list. Significantly higher mean DAP:SPED scores have been found (a) among children and adolescents being treated for conduct or oppositional-defiant disorders than among nonpatient youngsters and (b) among schoolchildren in special education classes for the severely emotionally disturbed than among students in regular class placements (McNeish & Naglieri, 1993; Naglieri & Pfeiffer, 1992). Other studies have shown significant correlations between DAP:SPED scores and parent and teacher ratings of children's behavior problems, together with indications that these scores can predict internalizing as well as externalizing disorders (Bardos & Powell, 2001; Matto, 2002; Matto, Naglieri, & Clausen, 2005).

The Integrative System of Tharinger and Stark, in which emotional disturbance is inferred from ratings of examiners' impressions of figure drawings rather than from sign lists, has also received some empirical support as a screening device for use with children. In Tharinger and Stark's (1990) negative outcome study with the Koppitz indicators, their DAP and KFD examiner ratings successfully discriminated the mood- and anxiety-disordered children from the normally functioning group of children. In related work, Yama (1990) found significant relationships between three impressionistic ratings of DAP figures—for artistic quality, bizarreness, and estimated level of adjustment—and the number of foster home placements that a group of children had experienced, but no predictive significance for the Koppitz indicators.

Although these findings are promising, the utility of the DAP:SPED and Integrated System approaches in screening for psychological disturbance has not yet been studied extensively. Even when helpful in identifying probable adjustment difficulty, moreover, these screening systems do not shed light on the nature of these difficulties, nor do they distinguish among patterns of psychopathology. As a further limitation of figure drawing methods in general, they have little value as a sole criterion for inferring the occurrence of specific past events in person's lives. This limited utility of figure drawings in postdicting previous events is particularly important because of the frequency with which psychologists are asked to evaluate children who may have been physically or sexually abused.

Mental health professionals have on occasion endorsed using drawings to help determine whether a young person has been an abuse victim (e.g., Burgess & Hartman, 1993). As reviewed by Handler (1996) and Kuehnle (1996, chap. 9), however, there is no compelling clinical rationale to support the use of children's drawings as a diagnostic tool for identifying abuse, nor are there any consistent research findings that would warrant applying figure drawings in this way. Psychological assessors must recognize that no figure drawing characteristics serve adequately as a marker of abuse in the individual case.

Abused children as a group do show more indications of emotional distress in their figure drawings than nonabused children (Hibbard & Hartman, 1990). Given that children who have been abused are expected on the average to be more distressed than their nonabused peers, this congruence of expectation with test findings constitutes a validation of figure drawing assessment. However, emotional distress can result from many kinds of disturbing or unpleasant experience, and becoming distressed is not unique to having been abused. Even though heightened distress commonly characterizes abuse victims, such distress lacks specificity to having been abused, which means that test indices of distress cannot reliably differentiate abuse victims from children who are distressed for other reasons.

Although children's figure drawings cannot dependably identify whether they have been abused, specific features of a drawing may sometimes suggest this possibility. For example, drawings of naked figures with unusually emphasized genitals warrant concern that a child may have been exposed to excessive sexual stimulation. Blatantly sexualized drawings are quite rare, however, even among children who are known to have been sexually abused (Hibbard, Roghmann, & Hoekelman, 1987), and the concern they raise calls only for further investigation, not for concluding that a young person has been abused. Some reports of work with abused children indicate that making and talking about drawings can help them recall past events more clearly than while being interviewed, thereby facilitating their evaluation and treatment (Aldridge et al., 2004; Matto, 2007; Peterson, Hardin, & Nitsch, 2001; Veltman & Browne, 2001, 2002; see also Weiner, 2003).

The utility of figure drawing methods in screening young people for adjustment difficulties also gives them some part to play in the evaluation of children whose parents are contesting their custody. Survey data indicate that 19% of forensic psychologists include the HTP and 18% include the KFD in their test battery when they assess young people whose separated or divorced parents are disputing custody or visitation rights (Ackerman & Ackerman, 1997). Consistent with the generally more frequent use of figure drawing methods with young people than with adults, fewer than 10% of surveyed forensic psychologists report including them in their evaluations of parents in custody cases.

As for other forensic applications, the information provided by figure drawing methods is rarely relevant to the decision-making process in criminal or personal injury cases. Reflecting this limitation, forensic psychologists report using these methods in fewer than 4% of competency, criminal responsibility, and personal injury evaluations (Boccaccini &

Brodsky, 1999; Borum & Grisso, 1995). Examiners should also be aware that, because of their limited relevance to many issues in legal cases, and because of their uncertain psychometric foundations, as discussed in the final section of this chapter, figure drawing methods may not meet the courtroom standards for admissibility into evidence (see Chapter 11, p. 401).

With further regard to the admissibility into evidence of testimony based on figure drawings, Lally (2001) concluded in a review of forensic considerations that quantitative rating scales like the DAP:SPED could with additional validation satisfy generally accepted guidelines for bringing psychological tests into the courtroom. For linking individual test signs with specific diagnoses or personality characteristics or forming global impressions of what figure drawings might signify, he doubted that these approaches to interpretation provide an admissible basis for testimony: "These methods may arguably have a place in clinical practice, but they clearly do not belong in a courtroom" (Lally, 2001, p. 146).

Lally's argument echoes the attention paid in Chapter 2 to selecting test batteries with an eye to the referral question and the context in which the assessment findings will be presented. Whether figure drawing findings are in fact regularly excluded from courtroom proceedings is a matter to be determined by surveys of actual practice, not by arguments about what should be the case, however sound these arguments may seem. However, the kinds of information figure drawings provide rarely relate to psycholegal issues other than the adjustment level of children in custody cases, and forensic assessors seldom find them useful in criminal or personal injury cases.

Treatment Planning and Monitoring

As described in the interpretation section of this chapter, DAP, HTP, and KFD protocols can generate reasonable hypotheses about a broad range of personality characteristics and underlying concerns that may be contributing to adjustment difficulties. These characteristics and concerns touch on how people perceive themselves (self-image) and how they would like to be (ideal image); their attitudes toward themselves and other people and toward interpersonal engagement; their hopes and fears and their aspirations and expectations for the future; and their coping style, affective disposition, and capacities to think clearly and see the world realistically. Information of this kind, even when emerging as hypotheses to consider and not as firm conclusions or established fact, can prove valuable in planning psychological treatment and monitoring treatment change.

Advance knowledge about an individual's underlying concerns helps therapists recognize and focus on issues that are most central to whatever life problems have led a person to seek or be referred for psychotherapy. Along with other performance-based measures in a pretherapy test battery, figure drawings assist in bringing to light psychological needs and conflicts of which prospective patients have not been fully aware and that might otherwise become apparent only after many sessions of treatment. Hypotheses based on figure drawings can thus serve to focus the course of treatment and to shorten it as well. In addition, advance information can help therapists select a treatment approach with a high likelihood of benefiting the patient and phrase their interventions in ways that will minimize the person's discomfort or resistance and prevent premature termination. An extensive literature elaborates the advantages of selecting treatment approaches and intervention styles that are tailored to the needs of the individual patient (see Beutler & Harwood, 2000; Beutler, Malik, Talebi, Fleming, & Moleiro, 2004; Clarkin & Levy, 2004).

Figure drawings are also useful in assessing progress and change in psychotherapy. Structural and thematic indications of psychological disturbance and troubling concerns can be expected to abate or disappear over time in persons who are benefiting from psychotherapy. Should figure drawing suggestions of adjustment difficulty persist on retesting, it may be that the patient is resistant or refractory to psychological intervention, or that the particular treatment approach or the particular therapist is not attuned to the patient's needs, or that the treatment has not continued long enough to bring about a positive response.

Despite this potential application of figure drawings in monitoring treatment progress, there are few published reports of their being used in this way. A notable exception is a study by Robins, Blatt, and Ford (1991) in which 32 seriously disturbed young adults were administered the DAP on admission to an inpatient facility and retested after 1 year or more of intensive treatment. As measured by a quantified and reliable coding scheme, the drawings of these patients showed substantial positive change over this period, as measured by the apparent stability of the depicted figures and the degree of articulation and differentiation of body details and clothing in them. Robins et al. (1991) concluded that their DAP variables can provide a valuable measure of therapeutic change in seriously disturbed persons. Numerous other clinical case examples have been presented in the literature to show how readministered figure drawings can reflect progress and change in psychotherapy (e.g., Hammer, 1958; Handler, 1996; Handler & Riethmiller, 1998; Harrower, 1965; Leibowitz, 1999).

PSYCHOMETRIC FOUNDATIONS

For figure drawing methods as for the Thematic Apperception Test (TAT) discussed in Chapter 12, the traditional and most common interpretive approach in clinical practice is an inspection method that is difficult to operationalize for research purposes and has not yet been substantiated with empirical data. As a further parallel to developments with the TAT, alternative approaches to figure drawing interpretation involving quantification of test signs and numerical ratings of global impressions have indicated potential for figure drawing findings to demonstrate psychometric adequacy as well as clinical utility. The evolution of the inspection method and the construction of sign lists and global impression scales provide separate sources of information concerning the clinical and scientific status of figure drawing assessment.

Inspection Methods

Just 1 year following publication of the book in which Machover (1949) introduced formal personality assessment with human figure drawings, Levy (1950) expressed the following opinion: "In order to avert cynicism and disillusion it is well to emphasize that the technique of analyzing drawings is without sufficient experimental validation, rarely yields unequivocal information, and frequently misleads the unwary into plausible misstatements about the personality of the person whose drawings are being studied" (p. 257). However, Levy added, "The lack of adequate information about validity does not negate the clinical utility of this technique. . . . If it is used with the same caution, artistry, and skill that are applied to other clinical instruments, it may frequently prove to be a fruitful and economical source of insights about the personality of the subject" (pp. 258, 288). Although much has been learned in the past half-century about the psychometric foundations and clinical utility of figure drawing methods, much of what Levy had to say remains an apt commentary.

With respect to empirical validation, figure drawing assessment as commonly practiced with an inspection method still lacks experimental verification. For 30 years following Machover's seminal contribution, research findings failed to confirm many of her proposed linkages between specific features of figure drawings and particular personality character-istics. Influential reviews of this early research by Swensen (1957, 1968), Roback (1968), and Kahill (1984) led many subsequent authors to question the utility and propriety of Machover's inspection method of figure drawing interpretation, sometimes to the point of asserting that figure drawing assessment of personality is a worthless and unethical prac-tice that clinicians should avoid (Joiner, Schmidt, & Barnett, 1996; Martin, 1983; Motta, Little, & Tobin, 1993). In response to such criticism, advocates of figure drawing assess-ment have called attention to the clinical value of figure drawing assessment in generating reasonable hypotheses, even in the absence of empirical confirmation, and attributed nega-tive research findings largely to ill-conceived or inappropriately implemented study designs (Bardos, 1983; Holtzman, 1983; Riethmiller & Handler, 1997a, 1997b).

For the most part, the apparently limited validity of Machover's original propositions has become a moot point. Most figure drawing specialists have long advised against at-tempting to relate individual signs to specific personality characteristics and have instead recommended formulating hypotheses on the basis of alternative possible meanings, global impressions, and constellations of indices (see Handler et al., 2004; Handler & Riethmiller, 1998; Knoff, 2003; Matto, 2007; Naglieri, McNeish, & Bardos, 1991; Tharinger & Stark, 1990).

Attention to alternative meanings, as anticipated in Levy's comment about the rarity of unequivocal information, has figured prominently in idiographic refinements of Machover's approach to figure drawing interpretation. The interpretive guidelines presented earlier in this chapter reflect an idiographic inspection of drawings and differ in four critical respects from Machover's nomothetic specification of invariant meanings:

1. The guidelines presented here emphasize not only that drawing characteristics typi-cally have alternative possible meanings for a person being examined, but also that the same drawing characteristics can have different meanings for different people.

2. The guidelines take into account that qualities projected into a figure drawing may represent elements of a person's self-image, the person's ideal image, or how the person views other people in general or certain people in particular.

3. The guidelines include examination not only of individual figures but also of simi-larities and differences between figures in how they are drawn.

4. The guidelines call for formulating interpretive hypotheses in light of information from other sources, including an examinee's sociocultural background and life cir-cumstances and the implications of other test findings.

Accordingly, the inspection approach to figure drawing interpretation presented in this chapter bears little resemblance to Machover's empirically challenged reliance on universal symbolism as a basis for assigning fixed meanings to drawing characteristics. Regrettably, these idiographic refinements in the inspection method have not been adequately operationalized for research purposes. Methodologically sound studies of figure drawing interpretations that take sufficient account of alternative meanings, of distinctions among self, ideal self, and other-attributed projections, and of similarities and differences between figures have yet to be conducted. Hence the contemporary inspection method, not having been adequately tested, lacks empirical verification at the present time, and its psychometric foundations must accordingly be considered uncertain.

Although contemporary inspection methods of interpreting figure drawings have not yet been adequately researched, this does not mean that psychologists must avoid using them. As Stricker (2006) has pointed out in discussing the interface between research and practice in clinical psychology, "The research-informed practitioner knows that the absence of evidence is not the same as the evidence of absence" (p. 7). The implications of the uncertain psychometric foundations of figure drawing interpretation by the inspection method are twofold. First, there is a need for clinical researchers to design and conduct appropriate evaluations of the reliability and validity of inferences based on idiographic inspection of figure drawings. Nomothetic studies of drawing characteristics presumed to have invariant meaning have not provided adequate assessments of the psychometric foundations of figure drawing interpretation and will not do so in the future.

The second implication of psychometric uncertainty in figure drawing interpretation, as highlighted in Levy's observations, is that the absence of experimental validation calls for examiners to exercise "caution, artistry, and skill" if they are to achieve useful applications of figure drawings. Caution in this context refers to recognizing that figure drawing inferences are hypotheses to be confirmed, not conclusions to be believed. Otherwise, as Levy notes, the "unwary" can be misled into misstatements about an examinee's personality characteristics.

Smith and Dumont (1995) confirmed Levy's concern by finding tendencies among a group of experienced psychologists to express confidence in some meanings of individual figure drawing characteristics that previous empirical studies had disconfirmed. There is considerable difference, on the one hand, between employing assessment methods that have proved useful in clinical practice but have not yet been validated in adequately designed research studies, and on the other hand, practicing in ways that have been demonstrated to be invalid or harmful. The Dumont and Smith findings would appear to be an instance of the latter and to reflect insufficient attention by the clinicians in their study to the limitations of figure drawing methods.

The artistry to which Levy referred consists of an examiner's psychological sensitivity in generating hypotheses about the possible meanings of figure drawing characteristics. As confirmed in a study by Burley and Handler (1997), this sensitivity is typically fostered by assessors being empathic individuals who understand personality dynamics, are open to ideas, and can tolerate ambiguity. Along with interpretive sensitivity, the skills necessary to conduct effective and useful figure drawing evaluations parallel the following four requisite skills for making good use of any personality assessment instrument:

1. Being able to establish productive rapport with the person being examined.
2. Knowing and implementing proper procedures for test administration and interpretation.

3. Having sufficient familiarity with personality processes, dimensions of psychopathology, and strategies of psychological intervention to integrate test findings with other relevant sources of information.

4. Being able to formulate and communicate helpful personality descriptions and treatment recommendations.

The preceding information concerning the uncertain psychometric foundations of the inspection method for inferring personality characteristics from figure drawings has emerged from attention by practitioners and researchers to the structural data of the DAP and, to a lesser extent, the KFD. As reviewed by Handler and Habenicht (1994), systematic relationships between specific drawing characteristics and particular personality characteristics have been as elusive in KFD studies as in DAP research. These authors are among figure drawing authorities who explicitly discourage the analysis of single signs or variables in clinical interpretation, while asserting that single sign research "is not a fair test of the validity of the KFD" (Handler & Habenicht, 1994, p. 447). As in the case of the DAP, however, available KFD research has not examined the reliability or validity of inferences based on idiographic inspection of the structural data.

Moreover, hypotheses based on idiographic inspection of the thematic data in figure drawing narratives, which often constitute the richest source of information in a DAP, HTP, or KFD protocol, have not been adequately examined for their psychometric properties, nor have test behavior clues to various traits or attitudes. In the absence of empirical support, interpretation of the thematic and behavioral data in figure drawings calls for proceeding with the same caution, artistry, and skill that characterize appropriate structural interpretation with an idiographic inspection method.

Sign Lists and Global Impression Scales

The contemporary idiographic inspection method of interpreting figure drawings is an atomistic approach in which examiners derive hypotheses about a broad array of personality characteristics from distinct structural, thematic, and behavioral features of the test data. By contrast, the other two main approaches to interpreting figure drawings—using sign lists and global impression scales to generate an overall index of emotional distress or adjustment difficulty—are holistic in nature. As holistic approaches, sign lists and global impression scales are easier to quantify than hypotheses based on inspecting drawings for their unique or unusual characteristics, and the single variable of adjustment level that these approaches use is easier to measure than the multiple idiographic characteristics inferred from figure drawing inspection. For these reasons, empirical investigations of the psychometric properties of these holistic approaches to figure drawing interpretation are less difficult to design and have been more plentiful than studies of contemporary inspection methods.

Research studies of holistic figure drawing interpretation have, for the most part, shown satisfactory reliability and validity for sign lists and global impression scales. For overall scores calculated from DAP sign lists, Kahill's (1984) literature review indicated interrater and retest reliabilities mostly over .80. Cummings (1986, pp. 213–214) has summarized studies showing interjudge agreement in human figure drawing scores ranging from .75 to .97 and retest stability ranging from .68 to .96 over intervals from 1 day to 3 months.

Lally (2001) concluded from his research review that the reliability of overall figure drawing scores is sufficient to meet criteria for admissibility into evidence in courtroom proceedings.

For the DAP:SPED sign list, Naglieri et al. (1991) reported internal consistency coefficients of 76, .77, and .71, respectively, for the 6- to 8-, 9- to 12-, and 13- to 17-year-olds in their standardization sample of children and adolescents. Naglieri and Pfeiffer (1992) have found interrater reliability of .91 for DAP:SPED total scores. Studies by Marsh, Linberg, and Smeltzer (1991) and Rae and Hyland (2001), among others, have demonstrated substantial interrater reliability for other Koppitz-type sign lists as well.

In their review of the KFD literature, Handler and Habenicht (1994) found that most of the scoring systems developed for use with this measure have also shown adequate interrater reliability, with percentages of agreement ranging from 87% to 95% . Repeat KFD examination of elementary school children over brief intervals, as exemplified in a 2-week retesting study by Mostkoff and Lazarus (1983), has indicated variable short-term stability for KFD characteristics. Some KFD characteristics (e.g., omission of body parts) have shown 70% to 90% similarity over brief intervals, whereas for other characteristics (e.g., omission of a family member) the obtained test-retest agreement has ranged from 46% to 60%.

Such findings call for caution in arriving at long-term expectations on the basis of what young children draw, but they do not necessarily indicate that the KFD is an unreliable instrument. Although some personality traits may become fairly well established at an early age, young children vary considerably in their feelings, attitudes, and perspectives on family life from one day or week to the next. For the KFD, then, as well as for other figure drawing tests and personality assessment measures in general, changes over time in test characteristics that are not expected to measure stable personality traits may reflect reliable measurement of changes in an examinee's situation or frame of mind.

In research on the validity of figure drawing sign lists, DAP:SPED has shown how well a holistic sign approach to interpretation can work when it is carefully constructed and cautiously applied. As reviewed in discussing the applications of figure drawing assessment, the DAP:SPED system for quantifying a constellation of signs to yield an index of psychological maladjustment can effectively discriminate emotionally disturbed from well-functioning young people. Other data reported by Matto and Naglieri (2005) have supported the cross-cultural applicability of the DAP:SPED. In a study of 138 pairs of Black and White students matched for gender, grade, and school classroom and 59 similarly matched pairs of Hispanic and White students, they found no statistically significant differences between groups in their DAP:SPED scores.

Two other studies with implications for the validity of figure drawing sign lists also merit mention. Marsh et al. (1991) used their Koppitz-type sign list of emotional distress indicators to compare adjudicated adolescent delinquents being held in a detention center with a group of public high school students who had never been placed outside their homes. Consistent with expectations based on delinquency research, the overall Marsh et al. (1991) figure drawing results showed greater psychosocial dysfunction in the adjudicated than in the nondelinquent adolescents.

In the other study of note, reported by Zalsman et al. (2000), a 27-item list of graphic indicators of suicide risk developed by Pfeffer and Richman (1991) was scored for the figure drawings of 90 consecutively admitted 12- to 18-year-old patients in a university hospital psychiatric unit. Twenty of these hospitalized adolescents had been admitted following a suicide attempt, 19 had reported serious suicidal ideation, and the remaining 51 were nonsuicidal youngsters with eating, depressive, or schizophrenic disorder. The Zalsman et al. (2000) sign list correlated significantly with severity of suicidal behavior in this sample, and a discriminant function developed from their indicators correctly classified 84.6% of the suicidal and 76.6% of the nonsuicidal adolescents. The findings of these authors appear to indicate that human figure drawings can effectively assist in the assessment of suicidal behavior among severely disturbed adolescent psychiatric patients.

Regrettably, the Marsh et al. and Zalsman et al. studies just described are not selections from an ample literature. Instead, contemporary studies concerned with the validity and application of figure drawing sign lists have been few and far between. Even with the promise shown by the DAP:SPED system, studies with it have appeared only infrequently in recent years, and research reports concerning other figure drawing methods or interpretive approaches have been similarly sparse. Perhaps the negative reviews from years past have discouraged investigators from investing themselves in designing studies that adequately reflect advances in concepts and methods of interpretation, including the DAP:SPED sign list as well as the idiographic inspection approach. However this may be, the studies that have been available to cite demonstrate that overall sign lists for structural features of figure drawings can be reliably scored and can provide valid measures of adjustment difficulty. These studies also negate any blanket assertion that figure drawing methods cannot contribute to reliable and valid personality assessments.

Finally, with respect to global impression scales for assessing extent of emotional disturbance from figure drawings, the validity of Tharinger and Stark's (1990) Integrated System for rating DAP and KFD drawings was noted in the earlier discussion of applying figure drawing assessment. Like the DAP:SPED, the Integrated System approach in screening for psychological disturbance, despite its initial promise, has received little attention from researchers who might have been in a position to conduct additional studies of its psychometric properties.

Summary

To summarize this final section of the chapter, the psychometric foundations of figure drawing methods are presently uncertain. Systematic inference of specific personality characteristics from individual structural features or drawings, as originally proposed by Machover (1949), received little research support in the first 35 years or so following publication of her book. Critical reviews of this early research did not dissuade clinicians from using figure drawing measures, but they evoked conviction in some quarters that figure drawing assessment is unreliable, invalid, and of little use.

For many years, however, figure drawing specialists have discouraged reliance on systematic single sign interpretation as proposed by Machover and have recommended instead an idiographic approach to the meaning of drawings. This individualized interpretive approach for inspecting drawings requires keeping in mind that drawing characteristics commonly have alternative possible meanings and can mean different things to different people, depending on their background, their life circumstances, and their frame of mind.

As elaborated in the interpretation section of this chapter, idiographic inspection of drawings for their unique or unusual structural features can generate hypotheses about a person's needs, concerns, and capacities that prove useful in treatment planning, even though they emerge as alternative possibilities rather than as certainties, and even though the psychometric foundations of this contemporary inspection method are yet to be examined in appropriately designed research studies. The thematic and behavioral data in figure drawing protocols likewise can provide therapeutically useful clues to the nature of a person's coping style and inner experience, particularly how people view themselves, other people, and interpersonal relationships, even in the absence of research studies adequately designed to assess their psychometric properties.

Dependable data are available concerning the psychometric properties of two holistic approaches to figure drawing interpretation that involve using total scores on sign lists or ratings based on global impressions as indicators of adjustment difficulty: the DAP:SPED for the DAP and the Integrated System for the DAP and the KFD, both of which have demonstrated adequate reliability and validity in appropriately designed studies. The apparently solid psychometric foundations of these two figure drawing interpretive systems has been acknowledged by figure drawing critics, including Lilienfeld, Wood, and Garb (2000), who in specific reference to the DAP:SPED and the Integrated System noted, "There is suggestive evidence that global approaches can achieve modest validity" (p. 49).

In conclusion, then, cautious and sensitive interpretation of figure drawings through idiographic inspection of their structural, thematic, and behavioral features can generate numerous hypotheses about a person's attitudes, concerns, and coping capacities, particularly their self-perceptions and interpersonal perspectives. Although such hypotheses have not yet been adequately examined for their psychometric properties, clinical experience indicates that they can prove valuable in planning psychotherapy and assessing treatment progress. In addition, certain overall figure drawing scores based on sign lists and global impressions can be helpful in screening persons for adjustment difficulty and have to some extent been empirically validated for this purpose, although additional research is needed.

REFERENCES

Ackerman, M. J., & Ackerman, M. C. (1997). Custody evaluations in practice: A survey of experience professionals (revisited). *Professional Psychology, 28*, 137–145.

Aldridge, J., Lamb, M. E., Sternberg, K. J., Orbach, Y., Esplin, P. W., & Bowler, L. (2004). Using a human figure drawing to elicit information from alleged victims of child sexual abuse. *Journal of Consulting and Clinical Psychology, 72*, 304–316.

Appel, K. (1931). Drawings by children as aids to personality studies. *American Journal of Orthopsychiatry, 1*, 129–144.

Archer, R. P., & Newsom, C. R. (2000). Psychological test usage with adolescent clients: Survey update. *Assessment, 7*, 227–235.

Bardos, A. N. (1983). Human figure drawings: Abusing the abused. *School Psychology Quarterly, 8*, 177–181.

Bardos, A. N., & Powell, S. (2001). Human figure drawings and the Draw-A-Person: Screening Procedure for Emotional Disturbance. In W. I. Dorfman & M. Hersen (Eds.), *Understanding psychological assessment* (pp. 275–294). Dordrecht, The Netherlands: Kluwer Academic.

Beutler, L. E., & Harwood, T. M. (2000). *Prescriptive psychotherapy: A practical guide to Systematic Treatment Selection.* New York: Oxford University Press.

Beutler, L. E., Malik, M., Talebi, H., Fleming, J., & Moleiro, C. (2004). Use of psychological tests/instruments for treatment planning. In M. Maruish (Ed.), *The use of psychological testing for treatment planning and outcomes assessment* (3rd ed., *Vol. 1*, pp. 111–146). Mahwah, NJ: Erlbaum.

Boccaccini, M. T., & Brodsky, S. L. (1999). Diagnostic test usage by forensic psychologists in emotional injury cases. *Professional Psychology, 30*, 253–259.

Borum, R., & Grisso, T. (1995). Psychological test use in criminal forensic evaluations. *Professional Psychology, 26*, 465–473.

Braden, J. P. (2003). Psychological assessment in school settings. In I. B. Weiner (Editor-in-Chief), J. R. Graham, & J. A. Naglieri (Vol. Eds.), *Handbook of psychology: Vol. 10. Assessment psychology* (pp. 261–290). Hoboken, NJ: Wiley.

Buck, J. N. (1948). The H-T-P technique, a qualitative and quantitative method. *Journal of Clinical Psychology, 4*, 317–396.

Buck, J. N. (1985). *The House-Tree Person technique: Revised manual.* Los Angeles: Western Psychological Services.

Buck, J. N. (1992). *The House-Tree-Person projective drawing technique: Manual and interpretive guide* (Rev. ed.). Los Angeles: Western Psychological Services.

Burgess, A. W., & Hartman, C. R. (1993). Children's drawings. *Child Abuse and Neglect, 17*, 161–168.

Burley, T., & Handler, L. (1997). Personality factors in the accurate interpretation of projective tests. In E. F. Hammer (Ed.), *Advances in projective drawing interpretation* (pp. 359–377). Springfield, IL: Charles C Thomas.

Burns, R. C. (1982). *Self-growth in families: Kinetic Family Drawings (K-F-D) research and application.* New York: Brunner/Mazel.

Burns, R. C. (1987). *Kinetic-House-Tree-Person drawings (K-H-T-P).* New York: Brunner/Mazel.

Burns, R. C., & Kaufman, S. H. (1970). *Kinetic Family Drawings (K-F-D) research and application.* New York: Brunner/Mazel.

Burns, R. C., & Kaufman, S. H. (1972). *Actions, styles, and symbols in Kinetic Family Drawings (K-F-D).* New York: Brunner/Mazel.

Camara, W., Nathan, J., & Puente, A. (2000). Psychological test usage: Implications in professional use. *Professional Psychology, 31*, 141–154.

Cashel, M. L. (2002). Child and adolescent psychological assessment: Current clinical practices and the impact of managed care. *Professional Psychology: Research and Practice, 33*, 446–453.

Clarkin, J. F., & Levy, K. N. (2004). The influence of client variables on psychotherapy. In M. J. Lambert (Ed.), *Bergin and Garfield's handbook of psychotherapy and behavior change* (5th ed., pp. 194–226). Hoboken, NJ: Wiley.

Clemence, A. J., & Handler, L. (2001). Psychological assessment on internship: A survey of training directors and their expectations for students. *Journal of Personality Assessment, 76*, 18–47.

Cummings, J. A. (1986). Projective drawings. In H. M. Knoff (Ed.), *The assessment of child and adolescent personality* (pp. 199–244). New York: Guilford Press.

DiLeo, J. H. (1973). *Children's drawings as diagnostic aids.* New York: Brunner/Mazel.

Goodenough, F. L. (1926). *Measurement of intelligence by drawings.* New York: Harcourt, Brace & World.

Groth-Marnat, G., & Roberts, L. (1998). Human figure drawings and house tree person drawings as indicators of self-esteem: A quantitative approach. *Journal of Clinical Psychology, 54*, 219–222.

Hammer, E. F. (1958). *The clinical application of projective drawings.* Springfield, IL: Charles C Thomas.

Hammer, E. F. (1960). The House-Tree-Person (H-T-P) drawings as a projective technique with children. In A. Rabin & M. Haworth (Eds.), *Projective techniques with children* (pp. 258–272). New York: Grune & Stratton.

Hammer, E. F. (1985). The House-Tree-Person test. In C. S. Newmark (Ed.), *Major psychological assessment instruments* (pp. 133–164). Boston: Allyn & Bacon.

Hammer, E. F. (1986). Graphic techniques with children and adolescents. In A. I. Rabin (Ed.), *Projective techniques for adolescents and children* (pp. 239–263). New York: Springer.

Handler, L. (1967). Anxiety indexes in projective drawings: A scoring manual. *Journal of Projective Techniques and Personality Assessment, 31*, 46–57.

Handler, L. (1996). The clinical use of drawings: Draw-A-Person, House-Tree-Person, and Kinetic Family Drawings. In C. S. Newmark (Ed.), *Major psychological assessment instruments* (pp. 206–293). Boston: Allyn & Bacon.

Handler, L., Campbell, A., & Martin, B. (2004). Use of graphic techniques in personality assessment: Reliability, validity, and clinical utility. In M. Hersen (Editor-in-Chief), M. J. Hilsenroth, & D. L. Segal (Vol. Eds.), *Comprehensive handbook of psychological assessment: Vol. 2. Personality assessment* (pp. 387–404). Hoboken, NJ: Wiley.

Handler, L., & Habenicht, D. (1994). The Kinetic Family Drawing technique: A review of the literature. *Journal of Personality Assessment, 62*, 440–464.

Handler, L., & Riethmiller, R. (1998). Teaching and learning the administration and interpretation of graphic techniques. In L. Handler & M. J. Hilsenroth (Eds.), *Teaching and learning psychological assessment* (pp. 267–294). Mahwah, NJ: Erlbaum.

Harris, D. B. (1963). *Children's drawings as a measure of intellectual maturity.* New York: Harcourt, Brace & World.

Harrower, M. (1965). *Psychological testing: An empirical approach.* Springfield, IL: Charles C Thomas.

Hibbard, R. A., & Hartman, G. (1990). Emotional indicators in human figure drawings of sexually victimized and nonabused children. *Journal of Clinical Psychology, 46*, 211–219.

Hibbard, R. A., Roghmann, K., & Hoekelman, R. A. (1987). Genitals in children's drawings: An association with sexual abuse. *Pediatrics, 79*, 129–137.

Hogan, T. P. (2005). 50 widely used psychological tests. In G. P. Koocher, J. C. Norcross, & S. S. Hill III (Eds.), *Psychologists' desk reference* (2nd ed., pp. 101–104). New York: Oxford University Press.

Holtzman, W. H. (1983). An unjustified, sweeping indictment by Motta et al. of human figure drawings for assessing psychological functioning. *School Psychology Quarterly, 8*, 189–190.

Joiner, T. E., Jr., Schmidt, K. L., & Barnett, J. (1996). Size, detail, and line heaviness in children's drawings as correlates of emotional distress: (More) negative evidence. *Journal of Personality Assessment, 67*, 127–141.

Jolles, I. (1971). *A catalog for the qualitative interpretation of the House-Tree-Person (HTP).* Los Angeles: Western Psychological Services.

Kahill, S. (1984). Human figure drawings in adults: An update of the empirical literature. *Canadian Psychology, 25*, 269–292.

Knoff, H. M. (2003). Evaluation of projective drawings. In C. R. Reynolds & R. W. Kamphaus. (Eds.), *Handbook of psychological and educational assessment of children* (pp. 91–125). New York: Guilford Press.

Knoff, H. M., & Prout, H. T. (1985). *The Kinetic drawing system: Family and school.* Los Angeles: Western Psychological Services.

Koppitz, E. M. (1966). Emotional indicators in Human Figure Drawings of young children. *Journal of Clinical Psychology, 22*, 313–315.

Koppitz, E. M. (1968). *Psychological evaluation of children's human figure drawings.* New York: Grune & Stratton.

Koppitz, E. M. (1984). *Psychological evaluation of human figure drawings by middle school pupils.* New York: Grune & Stratton.

Kuehnle, K. (1996). *Assessing allegations of child sexual abuse.* Sarasota, FL: Professional Resource Press.

Lally, S. E. (2001). Should figure drawings be admitted into court? *Journal of Personality Assessment, 76*, 125–149.

LaRoque, S. D., & Obrzut, J. E. (2006). Pencil pressure and anxiety in drawings: A techno-projective approach. *Journal of Psychoeducational Assessment, 38*, 381–393

Leibowitz, M. (1999). *Interpreting projective drawings.* New York: Brunner/Mazel.

Levy, S. (1950). Figure drawing as a projective test. In L. E. Abt & L. Bellak. (Eds.), *Projective psychology* (pp. 257–297). New York: Knopf.

Lilienfeld, S. O., Wood, J. M., & Garb, H. N. (2000). The scientific status of projective techniques. *Psychological Science in the Public Interest, 1,* 27–66.

Machover, K. (1949). *Personality projection in the drawing of the human figure.* Springfield, IL: Charles C Thomas.

Machover, K. (1951). Drawing of the human figure: A method of personality investigation. In H. H. Anderson & G. L. Anderson. (Eds.), *An introduction to projective techniques* (pp. 341–369). New York: Prentice Hall.

Marsh, D. T., Linberg, L. M. N., & Smeltzer, J. K. (1991). Human figure drawings of adjudicated and nonadjudicated adolescents. *Journal of Personality Assessment, 57,* 77–86.

Martin, R. P. (1983). The ethical issues in the use and interpretation of the Draw-A-Person test and other similar projective procedures. *School Psychologist, 38,* 6.

Matto, H. C. (2002). Investigating the validity of the Draw-A-Person: Screening Procedure for Emotional Disturbance: A measurement validation study with high-risk youth. *Psychological Assessment, 14,* 221–225.

Matto, H. C. (2007). Drawings in clinical assessment of children and adolescents. In S. R. Smith & L. Handler. (Eds.), *The clinical assessment of children and adolescents* (pp. 207–221). Mahwah, NJ: Erlbaum.

Matto, H. C., & Naglieri, J. A. (2005). Race and ethnic differences and human figure drawings: Clinical utility of the DAP:SPED. *Journal of Clinical Child and Adolescent Psychology, 34,* 706–711.

Matto, H. C., Naglieri, J. A., & Clausen, C. (2005). Validity of the Draw-A-Person: Screening Procedure for Emotional Disturbance (DAP:SPED) in strengths-based assessment. *Research on Social Work Practice, 15,* 41–46.

McConaughy, S. H., & Achenbach, T. M. (1994). *Manual for the semistructured clinical interview for children and adolescents.* Burlington: University of Vermont, Department of Psychiatry.

McNeish, T. J., & Naglieri, J. A. (1993). Identification of individuals with serious emotional disturbance using the Draw A Person: Screening Procedure for Emotional Disturbance. *Journal of Special Education, 27,* 115–121.

Meyers, D. V. (1978). Toward an objective procedure evaluation of the Kinetic Family Drawings (KFD). *Journal of Personality Assessment, 42,* 358–365.

Mitchell, J., Trent, R., & McArthur, R. (1993). *Human Figure Drawing Test (HFDT): An illustrated handbook for clinical interpretation and standardized assessment of cognitive impairment.* Los Angeles: Western Psychological Services.

Mostkoff, D., & Lazarus, P. (1983). The Kinetic Family Drawing: The reliability of an objective scoring system. *Psychology in the Schools, 20,* 16–20.

Motta, R. W., Little, S. G., & Tobin, M. I. (1993). The use and abuse of human figure drawings. *School Psychology Quarterly, 8,* 162–169.

Naglieri, J. A. (1988). *Draw-a-Person: A quantitative scoring system.* New York: Psychological Corporation.

Naglieri, J. A., McNeish, T. J., & Bardos, A. N. (1991). *Draw-A-Person: Screening Procedure for Emotional Disturbance.* Austin, TX: ProEd.

Naglieri, J. A., & Pfeiffer, S. I. (1992). Performance of disruptive behavior disordered and normal samples on the Draw A Person: Screening Procedure for Emotional Disturbance. *Psychological Assessment, 4,* 156–159.

O'Brien, R. P., & Patton, W. F. (1974). Development of an objective scoring method for the Kinetic Family Drawing. *Journal of Personality Assessment, 38,* 156–164.

Peterson, L. W., Hardin, M., & Nitsch, M. J. (2001). The use of children's drawings in the evaluation and treatment of child sexual, emotional, and physical abuse. *Trauma and Loss: Research and Intervention, 1*, 29–36.

Pfeffer, C. R., & Richman, J. (1991). Human figure drawings: An auxiliary diagnostic assessment of childhood suicidal potential. *Comprehensive Mental Health Care, 1*, 77–90.

Prout, H. T., & Phillips, P. D. (1974). A clinical note: The kinetic school drawing. *Psychology in the Schools, 11*, 303–396.

Rae, G., & Hyland, P. (2001). Generalisability and classical test theory analyses of Koppitz's scoring system for human figure drawings. *British Journal of Educational Psychology, 71*, 369–382.

Reynolds, C. R. (1978). A quick scoring guide to the interpretation of children's Kinetic Family Drawings (KFD). *Psychology in the School, 15*, 489–492.

Reznikoff, M., & Reznikoff, H. (1956). The Family Drawing Test: A comparative study of children's drawings. *Journal of Clinical Psychology, 12*, 167–169.

Riethmiller, R. J., & Handler, L. (1997a). The great figure drawing controversy: The integration of research and clinical practice. *Journal of Personality Assessment, 69*, 488–496.

Riethmiller, R. J., & Handler, L. (1997b). Problematic methods and unwarranted conclusions in DAP research: Suggestions for improved research procedures. *Journal of Personality Assessment, 69*, 459–475.

Ritzler, B. (2004). Cultural applications of the Rorschach, apperception tests, and figure drawings. In M. Hersen (Editor-in-Chief), M. J. Hilsenroth, & D. L. Segal (Vol. Eds.), *Comprehensive handbook of psychological assessment: Vol. 2. Personality assessment* (pp. 573–585). Hoboken, NJ: Wiley.

Roback, H. (1968). Human figure drawings: Their utility in the clinical psychologist's armamentarium for personality assessment. *Psychological Bulletin, 70*, 1–19.

Robins, C. E., Blatt, S. J., & Ford, R. Q. (1991). Changes in human figure drawings during intensive treatment. *Journal of Personality Assessment, 57*, 477–497.

Schildkrout, M. S., Shenker, I. R., & Sonnenblick, M. (1972). *Human figure drawings in adolescence*. New York: Brunner/Mazel.

Smith, D., & Dumont, F. (1995). A cautionary study: Unwarranted interpretations of the Draw-A-Person test. *Professional Psychology, 3*, 298–303.

Stricker, G. (2006). The local clinical scientist, evidence-based practice, and personality assessment. *Journal of Personality Assessment, 86*, 4–9.

Swensen, C. H. (1957). Empirical evaluations of human figure drawings. *Psychological Bulletin, 54*, 431–466.

Swensen, C. H. (1968). Empirical evaluation of human figure drawings: 1957–1966. *Psychological Bulletin, 70*, 20–44.

Terman, L. M. (1916). *The measurement of intelligence*. Boston: Houghton-Mifflin.

Tharinger, D. J., & Stark, K. (1990). A qualitative versus quantitative approach to the Draw-A-Person and Kinetic Family Drawing: A study of mood- and anxiety-disorder children. *Psychological Assessment, 2*, 365–375.

Veltman, M. W. M., & Browne, K. D. (2001). Identifying childhood abuse through favorite kind of day and kinetic family drawings. *Arts in Psychotherapy, 28*, 251–259.

Veltman, M. W. M., & Browne, K. D. (2002). The assessment of drawings from children who have been maltreated: A systematic review. *Child Abuse Review, 11*, 19–37.

Weiner, I. B. (2003). Prediction and postdiction in clinical decision making. *Clinical Psychology: Science and Practice, 10*, 335–338.

Yama, M. F. (1990). The usefulness of human figure drawings as an index of overall adjustment. *Journal of Personality Assessment, 54*, 78–86

Zalsman, G., Netanel, R., Fischel, T., Freudenstein, O., Landau, E., Orbach, I., et al. (2000). Human figure drawings in the evaluation of severe adolescent suicidal behavior. *Journal of the American Academy of Child and Adolescent Psychiatry, 39*, 1024–1031.

Chapter 14

SENTENCE COMPLETION METHODS

Sentence completion methods consist of words or phrases, usually referred to as *item stems,* that people are asked to extend into complete sentences. How individuals go about this task tends to reflect the kind of person they are, and their sentence completions often provide indirect clues to their underlying attitudes, affects, and concerns. Sentence completion methods function primarily as a performance-based measure of personality, although they may at times contain self-reports that identify personality characteristics fairly directly. A sentence completion response of "I FEEL depressed" is much the same as endorsing "I feel depressed" on a self-report inventory; unless there is reason to suspect dishonesty, both responses provide direct evidence that a person is in fact feeling depressed.

Sentence completions can also function in the same manner as self-reports when both give rise to slightly indirect inferences. The sentence completion "I WISH that I had never been born" would be taken by most clinicians as suggesting some depression, as would endorsement of the self-report statement, "I wish that I had never been born." In both instances, the evidence for depression is not as direct as a person's saying or endorsing "I feel depressed," but in both, the implications for depression are fairly compelling.

When sentence completions shift from self-descriptions to comments on other people or events, however, they become less direct in their implications than self-report endorsements. Consider a man who responded, "I WISH my father had been a different kind of person when I was growing up." This sentence completion is not a descriptive self-report, except as it may indicate this man does in fact wish that his father had been a different kind of person—which by itself is not a particularly useful piece of information. What is useful about the response is its indirect suggestion of possible interpersonal issues (e.g., a strained paternal relationship), certain underlying affects or attitudes (e.g., I hate my father; my father was a bad man), or tendencies to externalize blame (e.g., it's not my fault that I'm the way I am, it's because of how my father treated me).

As for commenting on an event, consider a woman who responded, "I WISH that I had waited longer to get married." Like the information that the man in the previous example wishes his father had been a different kind of person, knowing that this woman regrets not having waited longer to get married is not by itself very useful. Indirectly, however, her response provides clues to possible underlying concerns that could be important for her to recognize and a therapist to discuss with her. Does she regret her choice of a spouse and believe that she would have "married better" had she not married so young or too hastily? Or is she happily married but sorry about having become a wife and mother at an early age at the expense of a promising career or opportunities to travel?

Some sentence completion tests have been constructed with standard sets of items for use in general personality assessment; others comprise items selected to examine such specific characteristics as egocentricity (Exner, 1973), underachievement (Riedel, Grossman, & Burger 1971), moral attitudes (Musgrave, 1984), marital satisfaction (Inselberg, 1964), managerial motivation (Miner, 1978, 1984), and depression (Barton, Morley, Bloxham, Kitson, & Platts, 2005). Sherry, Dahlen, and Holaday (2004) list 47 sentence completion tests that have been described in the literature, and an unknown but probably large number of unpublished item sets have been used by personality assessors for various ad hoc purposes.

This chapter focuses on the nature, history, administration, scoring, interpretation, applications, and psychometric foundations of two standardized sentence completion measures for general personality assessment: the Rotter Incomplete Sentences Blank (RISB), which is by far the most widely used sentence completion method in clinical practice, and the Washington University Sentence Completion Test (WUSCT), which is the most widely studied and best validated sentence completion method currently available.

NATURE OF SENTENCE COMPLETION METHODS

Like other performance-based personality assessment instruments, sentence completion tests have the potential to generate three types of data: structural, thematic, and behavioral. The structural data in sentence completions consist of such objective response characteristics as the reaction times to individual items, the total time required to complete the test, the length of the responses, and the frequency of personal pronouns in the responses. Historically, however, little attention has been paid in the literature to the interpretive significance or possible valid correlates of such structural features of sentence completion tests. Instructions to record this structural information are not included in standard sentence completion test manuals, and it is not common practice for clinicians to take systematic note of them.

As for behavioral data, the manner in which people work on the sentence completion task (e.g., whether carefully or carelessly, energetically or wearily, seemingly relaxed or obviously edgy) and how they interact with the examiner (e.g., pleasant or grumpy, deferential or resistive) usually provide clues to their general nature, their current frame of mind, and their interpersonal attitudes. Survey results indicate, however, that sentence completion tests are much more commonly administered in written form than orally, which limits opportunities for examinees to display interpersonal attitudes (Holaday, Smith, & Sherry, 2000).

Written sentence completions, like the written TAT and figure-drawing stories described in Chapters 12 and 13, provide information about a person's handwriting, grasp of grammar and spelling, and language usage. Differences between how people use language when they write and when they respond orally, as during an interview or on other tests, can be a useful source of behavioral data. Is a person's written language formal or informal in style, coherent or convoluted, prissy or profane, bland or dramatic, or in some other respects suggestive of certain personality characteristics? If the person's written and oral language differ in such respects, what implications might these differences in self-expressive style have for how the individual adapts to the requirements of various situations?

The most extensive and informative data source in sentence completions is the thematic imagery they contain. The content of individuals' associations to the item stems typically provides a rich array of clues to their underlying feelings, attitudes, and concerns. In addition to eliciting general information in these respects, sentence completion stems can be phrased to evoke persons' attitudes toward specific individuals (e.g., "MEN___"; "A MOTHER___") and their perspectives on particular events and circumstances in their lives (e.g., "IN SCHOOL___"; "I FAILED___"). Unless indicated otherwise, these examples and the other item stems used for illustrative purposes in this chapter appear in the RISB.

The ease with which item stems can be formulated to serve certain purposes or pursue particular lines of inquiry has contributed to the previously noted abundance of general purpose and specific purpose sentence completion tests, and some additional information in this regard is included in the history section of this chapter. Historical considerations aside, the remaining discussion in this section on the nature of sentence completion methods focuses on the two most noteworthy sentence completion measures: the one that is most frequently used in clinical practice (RISB), and the one that has been most thoroughly researched and validated (WUSCT).

The RISB was originally published in 1950 and currently is in its second edition (Rotter, Lah, & Rafferty, 1992). It is a 40-item test printed on the front and back of a one-page, $8\frac{1}{2} \times 11$ inch form, with 15 items on the front and 25 items on the back. Eight of the 40 item stems consist of a single word (e.g., "PEOPLE___"; "SPORTS___"), 21 have two words (e.g., "I SUFFER___"; "MOST WOMEN___"), six have three words (e.g., "THE ONLY TROUBLE___"; "WHAT PAINS ME___"), and the remaining five are four or five words in length (e.g., "I AM BEST WHEN___"; "WHEN I WAS A CHILD___"). These examples are taken from the Adult Form of the test. There are two other 40-item forms of the RISB, a College Form for use in college and university settings and a High School Form intended for secondary school students. The College and High School Forms are printed in the same format as the Adult Form but differ slightly from it in their content.

The WUSCT has been published in several versions beginning in 1970, the most recent of which is Form 81 (Hy & Loevinger, 1996; Loevinger, 1998). The WUSCT consists of 36 item stems printed on two pages with 18 items per page. In common with the RISB stems, the WUSCT stems touch on aspects of how people perceive and respond to such matters as authority (e.g., "RULES ARE___"), frustration (e.g., "IF I CAN'T GET WHAT I WANT___"), relationships (e.g., "MY MOTHER AND I___"), and responsibilities (e.g., "RAISING A FAMILY___"). As a difference from the RISB, however, six of the WUSCT items have alternate forms for men and women (e.g., "SOMETIMES HE [SHE] WISHED THAT___"; "THE WORST THING ABOUT BEING A WOMAN [MAN]___").

There is also a Youth version of the WUSCT, the SCT-Y, which contains 32 items and is intended for use with young people aged 8 to 18 (Westenberg, Treffers, & Drewes, 1998). Of the 32 Y-SCT items, 21 are identical with WUSCT items, and the other 11 are new or revised items considered appropriate for younger people. Additional information on the adaptation of other sentence completion methods for personality assessment of children of elementary school age is available in contributions by Haak (1990) and Hart (1986).

HISTORY

Sentence completion methods of assessing psychological characteristics first appeared in the context of efforts to construct formal measures of intelligence in children. Herman Ebbinghaus, who was a pioneering figure in the experimental study of human memory, was also interested in how intellectual capacity and reasoning ability develop in young people. In pursuit of this interest, he devised what appears to have been the earliest sentence completion task (Ebbinghaus, 1897). Binet and Simon (1905) later included a version of Ebbinghaus's sentence completion task in their intelligence scale, which eventually became the Stanford-Binet Intelligence Scale and in which sentence completion items were retained through many revisions (see Roid, 2003). As noted by Lah (1989b), a wide variety of sentence completion tests continue to be used in assessing achievement, intelligence, and language skills in young people.

The notion that sentence completion methods could contribute to assessing personality characteristics as well as intellectual functioning originated with some observations by the Swiss psychoanalyst Carl Jung about the possible personal meanings of word associations. Jung (1916) popularized the notion that much could be learned about the inner life of people by eliciting their associations with various words. "Say the first word that comes into your mind," the person would be instructed, and alternative hypotheses could then be generated concerning the possible meaning of such associations as "MOTHER—good," "FATHER—scary," "SEX—dirty," and "WORK—proud."

The association method was formalized in the United States by Grace Kent and Aaron Rosanoff, who constructed a Free Association Test consisting of 100 ordinary, everyday words like "table," "dark," "music," "sickness," and "man." Kent and Rosanoff (1910) published frequency tables for the occurrence of various kinds of content in Free Association Test responses of 1,000 "normal" adults, 279 "insane" adults, and large groups of "normal" and "defective" children aged 4 to 15. Many other word association lists were published or used informally in subsequent years, probably the best known of which was a 60-item measure developed by David Rapaport, Merton Gill, and Roy Schafer for a seminal research study of the clinical diagnostic application of psychological tests conducted at the Menninger Foundation in the early 1940s (Rapaport, Gill, & Schafer, 1946/1968, chap. 8).

Rapaport et al. departed in two respects from Kent and Rosanoff's method. First, instead of limiting their list to ordinary and relatively neutral words, they included words with aggressive or sexual content (e.g., "fight," "gun," "penis," "vagina," "masturbation," "intercourse"). Second, instead of emphasizing the content of responses, they focused on the interpretive significance of structural features of a word association protocol, including reaction times, tendencies to use synonyms ("STREET—road") or antonyms ("GOOD—bad"), preference for single word or multiword associations, and such strange ways of responding as repeating stimulus words (e.g., "MOUTH—mouth") or giving nonsensical clang associations to them ("BEEF—weef").

Reviews by Daston (1968) and Rotter (1951) include the full list of words used in these and other word association tests, together with summaries of the early clinical and research applications of these tests. The word association technique gained some popularity in clinical practice and remains visible in parlor games and fictionalized re-creations of psychological evaluations. Over time, however, professional assessors concluded that single-word responses to one-word stimuli do not fully tap the potential of an association method to identify an individual's personality characteristics. Gradually the notion emerged that association tasks could be enriched by replacing the word-word format with brief phrases extended into full sentences, and by the late 1920s, contemporary sentence completion methods had begun to evolve. As for word association tests, survey data indicate that they are no longer among the 50 most widely used psychological tests (Hogan, 2005).

Three persons notable for their early work in developing sentence completion formats for assessing personality are Arthur Payne, Alexander Tendler, and Amanda Rohde. Payne (1928, 1930) constructed what appears to have been the first formal list of sentence completion items, which he designed for use in vocational counseling as a source of information about career-related personal traits. Tendler (1930) was interested primarily in emotionality and compiled a 20-item list of sentence stems each beginning with a first-person pronoun and intended to sample an affective state (e.g., "I LOVE___"; "I GET ANGRY WHEN___"). He described his measure as a test of "emotional insight" and recommended its use in clinical evaluations of emotional responsiveness.

Whereas the Payne and Tendler sentence completion tests were designed with specific purposes in mind, Rohde (1946, 1957) began working in the late 1930s to develop the sentence completion method into an instrument for general personality assessment. Originally published in 1940, the Rohde Sentence Completion Test was the first carefully constructed and validated measure of its kind, and its items covered a broad range of personal issues and experiences. The expressed purpose of the instrument was to "reveal latent needs, sentiments, feelings, and attitudes which subjects would be unwilling or unable to recognize or to express in direct communication" (Rohde, 1946, p. 170). Rohde was clear in her emphasis on the performance-based rather than the self-report aspects of sentence completion assessment.

Rohde's Sentence Completion Test served as a model for numerous similar instruments that were developed in the 1940s and 1950s. Three of these sentence completion tests from a half-century ago helped to shape the format of the method and still find some occasional use. The Sacks Sentence Completion Test consists of 60 item stems, most of which include a first-person pronoun (I, me, my) and were designed to elicit information about a person's family relations, interpersonal relations, sexual perspectives, and self-attitudes (Sacks & Levy, 1950).

The Forer Structured Sentence Completion Test comprises 100 relatively long and specifically focused structured items, such as "WHEN I FEEL THAT OTHERS DON'T LIKE ME, I___." The relatively structured nature of the Forer test, which he supplemented with an elaborate system for categorizing responses, was expected to facilitate treatment planning by identifying a broad spectrum of attitudes and behavioral tendencies (Forer, 1950, 1993). By contrast, the 73-item Miale-Holsopple Sentence Completion test consists mainly of brief, open-ended stems (e.g., "A WOMAN'S BODY___"; "BEHIND ONE'S BACK___") that are designed to maximize subjectivity in the response process. Interpretation of the Miale-Holsopple test emphasizes examiner impressions, rather than categorizations, with the aim of achieving global descriptions of people, especially their unconscious attitudes and concerns (Holsopple & Miale, 1954). Before turning to the history of the RISB and the WUCST, information about contemporary usage of sentence completion methods is relevant to note.

Usage of Sentence Completion Methods

Asked about their use of sentence completion tests in the survey by Holaday et al. (2000), members of the Society for Personality Assessment identified five such measures by name: the aforementioned Sacks, Forer, and Miale-Holsopple sentence completion tests, which 1% or 2% of the respondents reported using with adults or adolescents; the RISB, which was reported as being used by 28% of the respondents in their evaluations of adults and 19% in their evaluations of adolescents; and the WUSCT, reportedly used by 2% of respondents with adults and 1% with adolescents. Because of its previously mentioned extensive research base, the WUSCT was selected along with the relatively frequently used RISB for detailed presentation in this chapter.

As for the overall usage of sentence completion methods, 53% of clinical psychologists responding to a survey by Camara, Nathan, and Puente (2000) reported using some form of sentence completion test in their practice. This 53% usage frequency made sentence completions the fourth most commonly used personality assessment method instrument among these respondents, following the Minnesota Multiphasic Personality Inventory (MMPI), the Rorschach Inkblot Method (RIM), and the Thematic Apperception Test (TAT). Other surveys have indicated particularly wide use of sentence completion methods in evaluations of young people. In one sample of 162 child and adolescent clinical psychologists working in diverse settings, sentence completion methods were reported as being the most frequently used personality test and were exceeded in frequency of use among all tests only by the Wechsler Intelligence Scale for Children and the Child Behavior Checklist (Cashel, 2002). In another study of testing practices, 362 psychologists working with adolescents in a variety of settings reported using only Wechsler scales and the RIM more frequently than sentence completion methods (Archer & Newsom, 2000).

Sentence completion methods have held some appeal for forensic as well as clinical psychologists, especially in child custody cases. Among forensic psychologists surveyed by Ackerman and Ackerman (1997) and Quinnell and Bow (2001), 29% to 30% reported using sentence completion methods in their evaluations of children in custody cases, and 22% to 26% reported using them in evaluating the adults in such cases. These usage frequencies made sentence completions the second most frequently used performance-based personality assessment measure in these child evaluations, following the TAT/Children's Apperception Test, and the third most frequently used in the adult evaluations, following the RIM and the TAT. In a survey by Archer, Buffington-Vollum, Stredny, and Handel (2006), 27% of the responding psychologists reported using sentence completion methods in forensic evaluations of adults, a frequency exceeded among performance-based measures only by the RIM, at a 36% frequency of use.

Finally worth mentioning with respect to interest in sentence completion methods are survey data obtained by Clemence and Handler (2001) from 382 directors of psychology internship training programs. Among training directors from child care facilities, community mental health centers, and private psychiatric and general hospitals, from 59% to 78% preferred their interns to have had some coursework in sentence completion methods prior to entering their program, or at least a good working knowledge of these methods.

Rotter Incomplete Sentences Blank (RISB)

The history of the RISB begins with Julian Rotter, a clinical psychologist and prominent social learning theorist who spent most of his career as a faculty member and clinical training director at the Ohio State University (1946–1963) and at the University of Connecticut (1963–1987). Working in an army convalescent hospital in 1945, Rotter saw a need for a brief screening measure that could be administered to large groups of people, scored reliably to provide a quantitative index of adjustment level, and used to evaluate fitness to return to duty. He constructed a sentence completion task with items from various other sentence completion measures that had been used by army psychologists during World War II. This effort resulted in a 40-item Incomplete Sentences Test that Rotter, working in collaboration with Benjamin Willerman, administered to 200 army hospital patients. Rotter and Willerman (1947) subsequently published a description of this new measure, together with guidelines for administering and coding it and preliminary evidence of its reliability and validity.

Shortly thereafter, Rotter collaborated with Janet Rafferty to modify the army test for use with college students. This was done by retaining 32 item stems from the Incomplete Sentences Test used with the army personnel and revising the other eight stems to increase their suitability for a college population (e.g., "OVERSEAS___" and "COMBAT___" were replaced with "IN HIGH SCHOOL___" and "BOYS___"). The revised measure was renamed as the RISB and described by Rotter and his colleagues as a means of screening for maladjustment and obtaining diagnostic information for use in treatment planning (Rotter & Rafferty, 1950; Rotter, Rafferty, & Schachtitz, 1949). As noted, adult and high school forms for the RISB were constructed soon after the college form and published simultaneously with it. Construction of the RISB adult and high school forms involved some minor changes in wording to make them appropriate for these age groups. For example, an item on the college form that reads, "IN HIGH SCHOOL___" reads as "IN SCHOOL___" on the adult form and as "IN THE LOWER GRADES___" on the high school form.

Although Rotter and Rafferty (1950) described the RISB as useful in treatment planning as well as in determining adjustment level, they emphasized that the test is intended primarily for screening purposes and not for providing comprehensive assessments of personality characteristics or their "deep layers" (p. 6). Nevertheless, the minimal instructions and open-ended nature of its item stems create considerable potential for the test to reveal aspects of a person's inner life.

Washington University Sentence Completion Test (WUSCT)

The WUSCT was designed for research rather than applied purposes and was constructed to operationalize elements of a particular theoretical formulation, not to obtain general information about psychological adjustment or personality functioning. Its history begins with Jane Loevinger, who was educated first as a measurement psychologist at the University of Minnesota and later as a developmental psychologist at the University of California at Berkeley, where she received her PhD in 1944 and worked for a time as a research assistant to Erik Erikson. Like Erikson, Loevinger formulated a stage theory of development, which she based on conceptions of "ego level."

Ego level in Loevinger's formulation is a "master trait" that encompasses aspects of cognitive complexity, moral perspective, behavioral control, and interpersonal relatedness, and she viewed this trait as accounting for most of the ways in which people differ from each other. With respect to development, Loevinger described eight stages of maturation in ego formation, with each stage of personality growth characterized by distinctive ways of thinking, feeling, and interacting with others. Maturation in her theory consists of developmental advances in a person's characteristic manner of perceiving and responding to the social world (Loevinger, 1976).

Loevinger devoted much of a long career, which culminated in her appointment as Stuckenberg Professor of Human Values and Moral Development at Washington University in St. Louis, to examining the validity and implications of her theoretical formulations. Advancing her research agenda required an assessment instrument for identifying level of ego development, and she devised for this purpose a sentence completion measure that became known as the WUSCT. This instrument was first published in 1970, underwent some minor revisions over time, and appeared in its current form in 1996 (Hy & Loevinger, 1996; Loevinger, 1985, 1998; Loevinger & Wessler, 1970; Loevinger, Wessler, & Redmore, 1970). Loevinger's ego development stage theory has not become particularly well known or widely cited, compared with the more influential stage theories of Erikson, Piaget, and Kohlberg. Nevertheless, the WUSCT has gained respect as a useful measure of psychosocial maturity and, as elaborated by Westenberg, Hauser, and Cohn (2004), has been used in a substantial body of personality research.

ADMINISTRATION

The RISB is printed on both sides of a 1-page form, as previously noted, and the following instructions appear at the top of the front side:

> Complete these sentences to express *your real feelings*. Try to do every one. Be sure to make a complete sentence.

With these instructions in mind, examiners can introduce the test in the following way, varying their choice of words according to which if any measures have previously been administered during their evaluation:

> Next we're going to do [a test] [another test] that you will work on by yourself. This test consists of a list of words or phrases, and you're asked to complete each of them to make a sentence that expresses your feelings. As you will see, these instructions are printed on the front of the test form, and you should also notice that there are items on both the front and the back of the form.

Seated comfortably in a well-lighted room and with a flat writing surface in front of them, examinees should then be handed the RISB form and a pencil with an eraser. People who invest themselves in the RISB task, especially if they are struggling with uncertainty in their lives, often decide to change what they have written as they proceed through the items, and writing with a pencil and eraser rather than a pen facilitates their doing so.

In keeping with customary procedure in administering relatively unstructured performance-based personality assessment instruments, additional guidance to examinees should be kept to a minimum. Occasional factual questions can be answered directly, as in "Is there a time limit?" ("No") or "Do I have to answer every one?"("It will be helpful if you do them all"). Other requests for structure should for the most part be turned back to the person, as in "How long should the sentences be?" ("It's up to you") or "Should I put in people's names?" ("However you like"). Depending on the pace at which people work and the amount of detail they include in their responses, administration of the RISB has generally been observed to require from 10 to 40 minutes, with most people completing the task in 20 to 25 minutes (Lah, 1989b, 2001; Sherry et al., 2004).

As an alternative to the written form of the RISB, the sentence stems can be read aloud to people and their oral responses recorded by the examiner. Rotter et al. (1992) discourage proceeding this way, however, because taking oral rather than written responses can confound the obtained data by infusing the administration with an interpersonal component. This consideration is worth keeping in mind, especially when personal encounter with the examiner is likely to evoke a guardedness that leads people to limit the length of their responses or sanitize their content. Relatively silent or inarticulate people who dislike talking, have difficulty expressing themselves orally, or do not feel comfortable interacting with an examiner may be able and willing to say more about themselves when they are writing sentence completions than when they are asked to vocalize them.

The following is an example of the potential advantage of a written, as opposed to an oral, RISB protocol. A 16-year-old high school boy being evaluated was pleasant, socially appropriate, and seemingly relaxed during an initial clinical interview, but he was also tight-lipped and had little that he wanted to say. His answers to usual kinds of interview questions were bland and psychologically uninformative, and his Rorschach responses and oral TAT stories were sparse and mundane, providing some indications of his personality characteristics but few clues to any underlying concerns. On the RISB, however, he wrote the following revealing completions:

I WANT TO KNOW why my parents and I don't get along.

AT HOME my parents and I argue a lot.

WHAT ANNOYS ME most is when my parents bother me.

MY GREATEST FEAR is my parents not wanting me at the house.

WHEN I WAS YOUNGER I had a great relationship with my parents.

I NEED my parents to understand me.

I HATE when I get in fights with my parents.

I WISH that I had a better relationship with my parents.

I love my parents even though they think otherwise.

These sentence completions by a boy who could not unburden himself in direct conversation with a mental health professional, and who might otherwise have given the impression of being either untroubled or psychologically insensitive, provided compelling indications of perplexity and regrets in the face of dysfunctional family relationships and of deeply felt ambivalent feelings toward his parents.

Paralleling Rotter et al.'s (1992) recommendation for written rather than oral administration of the RISB, standard procedure for the WUCST also calls for a written format. Westenberg, Hauser, et al. (2004) have noted in this regard, "The written procedure fits best with the purpose of the test: to reveal the respondent's frame of reference without distortion that might arise from the presence of the administrator" (p. 596). Westenberg et al. express concern in particular that examinees' oral interaction with the examiner can lead them to respond in a socially desirable rather than a personally revealing manner.

Interestingly, research comparing oral and written administration has found no significant difference between them in the types of responses or ego-level scores they evoke, on either the WUSCT or the SCT-Y (McCammon, 1981; Westenberg, van Strien, & Drewes, 2001). Opting for written rather than oral administration of these measures may not prevent an uninformative protocol from a guarded examinee. Nevertheless, an oral administration may forgo the opportunity to obtain an especially revealing written protocol from a reticent and interpersonally aversive person, as in the case of the adolescent boy whose RISB was just discussed.

In the administration of the WUSCT, the instructions printed on the test form merely state, "Complete the following sentences." Hy and Loevinger (1996, p. 26) suggest accompanying distribution of the test with the following introduction:

> Now I would like you to fill out this sentence completion form. You see that these are incomplete sentences. Please finish each one. Notice that there are two pages; please make sure that you have finished both.

As in administering the RISB, examiners giving the WUSCT should respond to requests for additional guidance by indicating in a noncommittal way that there are no right or wrong answers and that people can write out their sentences however they wish. In addition, Hy and Loevinger (1996) stress that an examiner should always be present to monitor both individual and group test administrations. To maintain the security of test measures and obtain dependable data, this recommendation holds for all personality and mental tests that can be self-administered. Allowing people to take test forms out of the examining room and complete them without supervision opens the door to indiscriminant dissemination of their item content and to responses based on unknown sources of influence (as in a woman asking her husband, "How do you think I should answer this one?" or a man consulting a personality assessment textbook for clues to creating some impression). Firsthand monitoring of test administration to safeguard the integrity of test results is widely endorsed among assessment psychologists and is reflected in Standards 5.6 and 5.7 of the *Standards for Educational and Psychological Testing* developed by the American Educational Research Association, the American Psychological Association, and the National Council on Measurement in Education (1999).

SCORING

In keeping with his original interest in developing an objective quantitative index of adjustment, Rotter devised a scoring system for rating each of the RISB items on a 7-point scale from 0 (most positive adjustment) to 6 (most indication of conflict). Introduced in preliminary form in the original Rotter and Willerman (1947) publication, this scoring system remains in place and is elaborated with detailed guidelines and specific examples in the most recent RISB manual (Rotter et al., 1992).

Positive adjustment is scored from 0 to 2, depending on the extent to which sentence completions express such adaptive perspectives as an optimistic outlook (e.g., "THE FUTURE looks bright for me"), receptive attitudes toward people (e.g., "THE HAPPIEST TIME is when I'm with my friends"), and an upbeat affective state (e.g., "DANCING is something I enjoy doing"). Conflict is scored from 4 to 6, depending on the intensity with which negative attitudes, interpersonal strains, and various kinds of symptoms or concerns are expressed (e.g., "WHAT ANNOYS ME is how stupid people can be sometimes";

"I REGRET being by myself so much of the time"; "OTHER PEOPLE don't appreciate me"; "I CAN'T stand heights"; "MY NERVES are frazzled"). Neutral responses that have no personal reference or consist only of descriptions or catch phrases are given a score of 3 (e.g., "AT BEDTIME I watch TV and fall asleep"; "MEN are different from women"; "THIS PLACE is okay").

After adjustment/conflict ratings have been assigned for the 40 responses, they are totaled to provide an overall adjustment index, which can range from 0 to 240. Should any items be left blank, the total score is prorated to maintain comparability with scores for a full 40-response protocol. This scoring procedure generally requires 15 to 35 minutes, depending on the examiner's familiarity with the scoring criteria (Sherry et al., 2004), and it makes the RISB unusual among personality assessment instruments in paying as much attention to indications of good adjustment as to evidence of psychological difficulties. Despite this advantage of measuring both how well and how poorly people seem to be feeling and functioning, the RISB scoring system is seldom used in clinical practice. In the previously mentioned survey by Holaday et al. (2000), most of the clinicians who reported using sentence completion measures indicated that they rarely if ever score these measures as prescribed in the test manual.

Like the RISB, the WUSCT is scored in two phases, first at the item level and then for determination of an overall score, which is called the Total Protocol Rating (TPR). Each of the 36 sentence completions (or 32 on the SCT-Y) is given an independent rating from E2 to E9 according to which of Loevinger's eight ego levels it appears to reflect. There is no E1 in Loevinger's system because it would refer to a stage in early infancy during which ego development is not accessible "by our methods of study" (Hy & Loevinger, 1996, p. 4). There are four alternative procedures for determining the TPR, three of which are straightforward: summing the item scores that range from 2 to 9 for each item, calculating the mean value of these item scores, or taking the mode of the item ratings as representative of the ego level at which the person most frequently operates. Hy and Loevinger (1996, chap. 5) express reservations about all three of these approaches because none of them takes account of outliers in the distribution of item scores. Outliers in this context are extremely high or low item scores that distort the meaning of a person's total or average score and thereby generate an inaccurate or misleading indication of the developmental level at which the person generally functions.

To circumvent this problem, Hy and Loevinger (1996) developed a set of rules for considering both item scores and the distribution of these scores in determining the developmental level that a person has achieved. These rules for determining the TPR, which can be found in Table 5.1 on page 39 in their text, are not difficult to implement. However, the criteria for assigning developmental level scores to individual item responses are complex. Hy and Loevinger (1996) provide a detailed set of scoring guidelines, case examples, and practice exercises that examiners will find helpful in mastering this scoring system. In their opinion, becoming proficient at scoring the WUSCT correctly requires a minimum of 2 hours daily work with the practice exercises for a period of 2 to 3 weeks.

INTERPRETATION

In common with the TAT and the figure-drawing methods discussed in Chapters 12 and 13, sentence completion methods can be objectively scored, and they provide structural and behavioral data that enrich personality evaluations. As is true of the TAT and figure-drawing methods, however, sentence completion methods are rarely scored in clinical practice, and the richest and most useful information they provide usually comes from inspection of their content. Accordingly, this section of the chapter first presents some guidelines for interpreting the thematic imagery in sentence completion responses and then considers the interpretive significance of the RISB and WUSCT total scores and of certain structural features of the data in them.

Content Features

The inspection method for interpreting the content of sentence completion responses proceeds according to the same principles delineated in Chapters 11, 12, and 13 for interpreting thematic imagery. The completions should be read and pondered for their possible personal meanings, and the hypotheses that are generated in this way should then be evaluated for how compelling and plausible they are in the individual case.

In generating alternative hypotheses, examiners should rely on their understanding of personality development and dynamics, their familiarity with how different types of persons commonly respond on sentence completion measures, and their own associations to what certain responses might signify. As testimony to the particular value of the RISB and WUSCT, this phase of the interpretive process is generally less challenging than the interpretation of Rorschach and TAT imagery, because it requires a lesser level of inference and produces fewer alternative possibilities.

To reprise illustrations from Chapters 11 and 12, a Card I Rorschach response of "A woman with her arms up" could reflect persons' attitudes toward or perceptions of their mother, their wife, or women in general, and having her "arms up" could represent waving hello, waving goodbye, preparing to deliver a blow, or reacting to something with fear or surprise. The man leaning against a lamppost in Card 20 of the TAT who "feels good about himself, knows what he wants to do, and thinks he can do it" could reflect a positive self-image or some wishful thinking about how the person would like things to be when they are actually quite otherwise.

Unlike the Rorschach task, which calls for reporting what inkblots "might be," and the TAT, in which people are instructed to "use your imagination," the RISB asks people to "express your real feelings," and its stimulus stems include such specifications as "A MOTHER___" and "MOST WOMEN___." Hence, the possible interpretive significance of sentence completion responses is often fairly obvious and relatively unambiguous. A 51-year-old man who wrote "A MOTHER is someone very special" and "MY FATHER was a good man" could with reasonable confidence be inferred to have enjoyed good parent-child relationships, unless there were good reasons to question his veracity. To illustrate a somewhat less direct but still compelling interpretive hypothesis, the previously mentioned 16-year-old boy troubled by dysfunctional family relationships wrote, "MY FATHER travels a lot." This statement strongly suggested that growing up with a frequently absent father had contributed to adjustment difficulties he was having, which on further investigation turned out to be the case.

Whether sentence completion interpretations are compelling depends in part on how clear they are and how easy it is recognize their basis. Given the clarity and readily apparent basis of the illustrative interpretations in the previous paragraph, and in view of how little inference is required to arrive at them, they could be considered compelling. Along with being clear, sentence completion interpretations become compelling to the extent that the evidence for them is repetitive or dramatic. The more frequently an attitude or perspective is suggested by the completions in a protocol, the more likely it is to characterize the individual. The previously quoted 51-year-old man who expressed positive feelings toward his parents also gave compelling repetitive evidence of pleasure in family living, with the following responses: "I LIKE being a father and a family man"; "THE BEST thing that every happened to me is my family"; "MARRIAGE is very important to me").

Significantly, however, this same contented family man, who had a 3-year history of persistent depression, also gave repetitive indications of feeling (a) that his better days were in other respects behind him ("I REGRET the closure of my business"; "MY GREATEST FEAR is not gaining control of my life again"); (b) that he had not become the person he had hoped to be ("I SECRETLY wish I was as good as my dad"; "I FAILED to be the best I could be"); and (c) that he had little to look forward to ("I HATE growing old"; "I AM VERY worn out").

As for drama, a single sentence completion response can at times have compelling interpretive significance by virtue of the intensity with which it is expressed. To illustrate this possibility, consider first the response "IN SCHOOL I didn't do very well." This is a mildly stated and largely ambiguous sentence completion. It suggests some adjustment difficulty that could be important to investigate further, but by itself it gives little indication of just how badly the person did in school and no indication of whether the person's difficulties were primarily academic or primarily social, or possibly athletic or artistic, in a school in which these talents were highly valued.

By contrast, suppose a person gives an RISB protocol that is generally bland and uninformative with respect to interpersonal relationships (e.g., "PEOPLE come in all shapes and sizes"; "MARRIAGE is something you need a license for"), but contains the response, "IN SCHOOL things were rotten and I hated all of the kids—I couldn't stand them and they couldn't stand me." Such a dramatically intense response is sufficient by itself to warrant hypothesizing that this person experienced serious social problems as a student and may even have been developing an avoidant or antisocial personality disorder. Having this particular dramatic breakthrough in the context of guardedness suggested by an otherwise bland protocol makes its interpretive implications even more compelling.

Whether sentence completion interpretations are plausible as well as compelling in the individual case goes beyond their being clear, repetitive, or dramatic and depends on their confirmation by external data sources. Three types of external data in particular can help establish the plausibility of these interpretations: (1) findings from other tests suggesting personality characteristics or life experiences similar to those that have been hypothesized on the basis of sentence completion responses, (2) interview or case history information that is consistent with inferences drawn from a person's sentence completions, and (3) collateral reports or direct observations of a person that match the implications of the sentence completion data for certain behavior patterns. The more these external data sources confirm sentence completion interpretations, the more confident examiners can be that these interpretations accurately describe an individual's personality characteristics.

At times, on the other hand, apparent divergence among data sources may also provide valuable information. In one case, a woman gave the sentence completion response, "I FEEL very good about my life," which would seem to indicate that she was generally in good spirits. According to family members, however, she had been struggling with episodes of moodiness and trying hard to "put on a happy face." This collateral evidence suggested that "I FEEL very good about myself" represented a defensive effort to ward off depression and that this woman's reliance on denial might make her susceptible to such hypomanic characteristics as unwarranted optimism or exuberance. Instances of this kind illustrate how sentence completion responses can generate interpretive hypotheses with important treatment implications when they diverge from collateral reports as well as when they closely parallel them. The potential information value of divergent findings, and their implications for conducting psychological examinations with a multifaceted test battery, are elaborated in Chapter 2 (see pp. 24–26).

Total Scores

As indicated in describing the scoring of RISB and WUSCT protocols, both tests generate a total score. The RISB total score, ranging from 0 to 240, is intended to serve as an adjustment index. Based on the standardization data they obtained from college students, Rotter and Rafferty (1950) originally set 135 as the score for distinguishing people who should be categorized as "adjusted" (total score less than 135) from those who should be categorized as "maladjusted" (total score of 135 or more). This same cutting score was subsequently used for administrations of the adult and high school forms of the test as well, even though no additional normative data were obtained from adult or adolescent samples.

In three new samples of college students subsequently tested in 1965, 1970, and 1975, Lah and Rotter (1981) found that these groups did not differ significantly among themselves in their mean RISB total scores but showed significantly higher mean scores than the 1950 standardization sample. On the basis of two further studies, Lah (1989a) subsequently recommended increasing the adjusted/maladjusted cutting score from 135 to 145. In the first of these studies, he obtained mean RISB scores of 128.0 and 130.8 from groups of 64 female and 52 male college students, respectively.

In the second study, he examined the impact of alternative cutting scores ranging from 125 to 160 among 120 students being seen in the college campus mental health service and 120 control participants. An unacceptably high frequency (35%) of the control participants had scores of 135 or more, and 145 proved to be the most efficient cutting score for discriminating between the control participants (of whom 82.4% scored below 145) and the mental health service group (85.0% of whom received scores of 145 or more). In a similar vein, Ames and Riggio (1995) found a 40% frequency of maladjustment in a sample of 136 college students, as defined by the original RISB total score of 135 or more, and a 55% frequency of scores above 135 among 368 high school students.

These findings demonstrated that the original cutting score for adjustment problems was no longer appropriate for high school or college students, and Rotter et al. (1992) increased this cutting score to 145 in their second edition of the RISB. Like all cutting scores used in clinical practice, 145 should be regarded as the midpoint in a range, and not as an absolute index for inferring maladjustment or rendering opinions about a person's need for psychotherapy or fitness to return to work. In assessing psychopathology, there will inevitably be some false positive findings at scores above 145 and some false negative results at scores below 145. A score somewhat above 145 may not necessarily warrant referral for mental health services, depending on other considerations; and a score somewhat below 145 may not reflect sufficient peace of mind and emotional resiliency for a person to function effectively in a high-stress situation. Additionally, the Ames and Riggio (1995) finding of higher scores among high school than college students argues for particular caution in inferring maladjustment from RISB total scores on the High School form.

Turning to the WUSCT, the TPR on this measure serves to classify people as having on the average attained a particular developmental level of ego functioning. How people are classified on the basis of the WUSCT does not mean that they always and in every respect—cognitively, emotionally, and interpersonally—behave at their identified level of psychosocial maturity. It means only that they are likely to conduct themselves at this level most of the time and in most respects. The following descriptions of the eight levels of ego development in Loevinger's model, as elaborated by Hy and Loevinger (1996, chap. 1) and Westenberg, Hauser, et al. (2004), illustrate the types of personality characteristics commonly associated with each level.

Impulsive Stage (E2)

Individuals at the impulsive stage of development are self-centered, pleasure-seeking persons with propensities for impulsive aggressive and sexual behavior. They expect other people to cater to their needs and desires, and they have little tolerance for frustration. They tend to be oppositional and defiant and to regard other people as either all good or all bad, depending on whether these other people are meeting their needs. They typically see rules as arbitrary or unfair, and only external constraints may suffice to keep their impulses in check. This stage of development typifies young children, and persons who have not advanced beyond this stage by the time they enter school are likely to be diagnosed as having an impulse disorder.

Self-Protective Stage (E3)

The self-protective stage is characterized by a focus on being in control and finding ways to maximize one's own pleasure. Self-protective persons can control their impulses when they sense that doing so will benefit them, and they also begin to appreciate and follow rules if abiding by those rules will be to their advantage. Interpersonally, they tend to mistrust other people and to manipulate and exploit them to their own ends. They are creatures of the moment, lacking long-term goals and ideals. If their actions get them into trouble, they externalize blame by holding other people or unavoidable circumstances responsible. Older children and adults who remain at this stage of development are likely to become hostile, opportunistic individuals who often show psychopathic personality features.

Conformist Stage (E4)

This level of ego development involves a transition from the earlier egocentric self-protective stage to a group-centered conformist stage. Conformist individuals endorse social norms and are committed to gaining social approval. They pay close attention to what other people think and expect, they believe that the same rules and requirements should apply to everyone, and they regard individual differences in attitudes and codes of conduct as inappropriate and undesirable. People at this stage of development tend to describe interpersonal interactions mainly in terms of what people do, not how they feel, and to describe themselves and people close to them by referring to their socially acceptable behavior.

Self-Aware Stage (E-5)

In the self-aware stage of ego development, people begin to recognize being different from other people and having their own private feelings, ideas, and opinions. This increasing self-awareness and examination of one's distinctive inner life promotes a growing appreciation of differences among people. Individuals at this stage begin to distinguish between public and private aspects of themselves and to appreciate the importance of being true to one's self. People who mature to this level also begin to recognize that morality is not absolute and that exceptions to the rules may at times be acceptable.

Conscientious Stage (E-6)

The conscientious stage is marked by pursuit of self-evaluated standards and preoccupation with aspirations, accomplishments, ideals, and morality. Individuals who reach this level of psychosocial maturity tend to be self-critical and self-motivated; they are intent on defining their own goals and working toward these goals in their own way. Concurrently, they also become increasingly likely to take responsibility for their actions and for whatever choices they make in their lives.

Individualistic Stage (E7)

At the individualistic stage of development, people can be expected to show good comprehension of psychological development and causation and a clear sense of personal identity. They are likely to have gained an appreciation of the complexity of interpersonal relationships and of the multiple roles that people play in their lives (e.g., as a daughter, mother, spouse, and professional). No longer trying to change themselves and other people to fit an ideal image (which is a pursuit characteristic of the conscientious stage), people at the individualistic level recognize and take note of contradictory emotions, motivations, and inner conflicts in themselves and others. Whereas relationships with people have ordinarily become deeper and more intense with maturation from the conformist to the conscientious stage, interpersonal attachments are likely to be viewed at the individualistic stage as a potential obstacle to achievement striving and a source of excessive responsibility for others.

Autonomous Stage (E-8)

Should they reach the autonomous stage of development, people tend to become less concerned than before with issues of achievement and morality and less preoccupied with evaluating their own actions and the actions of other people. Instead, this stage is characterized by belief in the need for people to find their own way, wherever their roads may take them, and to make their own mistakes and reap their own rewards. Individuals at this stage may also display a bemused appreciation of life's paradoxes, contradictions, and inconsistencies, without a sense of resignation to them.

Integrated Stage (E-9)

The integrated stage of ego development as conceived by Loevinger is more of an ideal to which people should aspire than a reality they are apt to attain. She likens this stage to Maslow's (1954) concept of self-actualizing people, defined as those rare individuals who have fully realized their human potential. Loevinger estimates that fewer than 1% of adults reach this developmental milestone. Because of the infrequency with which persons at the integrated stage have been encountered in their research samples, Hy and Loevinger (1996) conclude that available data "do not suffice to describe fully this theoretical high point" (Hy & Loevinger, 1996, p. 6). For practical purposes in classifying people on the basis of their WUCST scores, Loevinger accordingly recommends collapsing the integrated stage of development with the autonomous stage.

For examiners who administer the WUSCT and determine its TPR, these descriptions provide some information about features of personality that are likely to characterize individuals who fall clearly into one of these eight ego stage categories. Although indicating a person's level of psychosocial maturity, the WUSCT PTR does not serve as an adjustment index. Unlike the RISB total score, which provides a numerical index along a continuum from relatively poor to relatively good adjustment, the PTR level is largely independent of adjustment. Persons at higher stages of ego development who are acutely self-aware may, as a consequence of inner conflicts and uncertainty, be more upset and less psychologically comfortable than persons at lower stages who rarely examine their own behavior or entertain self-doubts. In younger people, limited psychosocial maturity may be more adaptive than a high level of maturity that is unusual among persons of their age. Whether a person functions and feels better as a conformist or an individualist is likely to vary with what is expected of them in their particular life circumstances and by the people with whom they interact.

These and other considerations in inferring adjustment level from stage of ego development are elaborated by Hy and Loevinger (1996), who conclude that "ego maturity and adjustment must be described independently in order to ascertain the relation between them" (p. 7).

Structural Features

The interpretive significance of reaction time, word count, and other structural features of sentence completions has seldom received much attention from assessment psychologists, either in clinical practice or in research. Nevertheless, some observations by Kleiger (2004) are notable for describing sentence completion characteristics that can help identify disordered thinking. Drawing on guidelines proposed by Rapaport et al. (1946/1968) for inferring thought disorder from word associations, Kleiger described how sentence completions can sometimes point to thinking disorder by being expressed in peculiar ways or showing too little or too much distance from the content of the item stems.

Exemplifying peculier expressions, the sentence completions of persons whose thinking is disordered are sometimes marked by strange word usage, as in "I NEED more physicalness for sexuality." At other times, deviant verbalization may take the form of a rambling and illogical discourse on some matter of concern, as in "MY GREATEST WORRY is about the glaciers melting, which is going to cause a lot of war and disease, especially if people don't eat better." As Kleiger noted, the more incoherent, disorganized, or irrational people are in giving sentence completion responses, the more likely it is that their thought processes are similarly muddled, dissociated, and illogical.

As for their distance from the item stems, sentence completions with too little distance take the form of concrete responses that stick closely to the content or sound of the stems at the expense of appropriate attention to their meaning. Such loss of distance can result in responses that simply repeat all or part of a stem (e.g., "A MOTHER is a mother";

"I REGRET what I regret") or consist of a clang association to it, as in "PEOPLE steeple." Sentence completions involving too much distance take item stems as a springboard for nonsensical associations that have little or no apparent connection to the stem content. Such disconnected association was illustrated by a man who wrote, "THE ONLY TROUBLE is fear itself." Perhaps this man was associating "trouble" with the Great Depression of the 1930s and connecting it with Franklin Delano Roosevelt's exhortation at the time: "The only thing we have to fear is fear itself." The omission of such explanatory links makes overly distant completions difficult to follow and a likely manifestation of disordered thinking.

APPLICATIONS

On the one hand, sentence completion methods bring to a personality assessment battery an easily administered performance-based test that can be given to groups as well as individuals and can be completed by most people in 30 minutes or less. Barring a language or reading difficulty, people taking the test usually have no difficulty grasping the meaning of sentence completion stems, and they are not ordinarily asked by the examiner to explain, elaborate, or account for their responses. For this reason, sentence completion methods tend to be less anxiety provoking than the inkblot, picture-story, and figure-drawing methods discussed in Chapters 11 through 13. As a written measure involving little interaction with the examiner, moreover, sentence completions are less likely than oral measures to cause distress to people who are by nature untalkative or uncomfortable in social situations. Like the adolescent boy first mentioned on page 525, such people may be less guarded and more revealing about themselves in what they write than in what they say.

On the other hand, the relative lack of ambiguity in many sentence completion stems means that people are more aware of how they are presenting themselves than they are when describing inkblots, pictures, or drawings they have made. The clarity and directness of self-report of stems like "I FEEL," along with the obvious implications of completing such a stem with "happy" or "sad," make it easy for people to paint a deceptively positive picture of themselves or to exaggerate the extent of their distress or difficulties. Responding in a deceptive mode, a person whose life has been a showcase of failures to cope adequately might write, "I FEEL that I have managed my life very well," and a demonstrably well-functioning and psychologically stable person intent on malingering disorder might write, "I FEEL that I'm falling apart."

As reviewed by Schretlen (1997), there is some research evidence that presumed indices of malingering on sentence completion tests correlate modestly with MMPI validity scales. Additionally, some success has been reported in using features of sentence completion responses to identify misrepresentation among persons applying for disability status and defensiveness in a selection program for special assignments in the military (Lanyon, Almer, & Maxwell, 2002; Picano, Roland, Rollins, & Williams, 2002). However, no formal coding system for assessing impression management with sentence completion measures has been developed sufficiently to warrant its general use in clinical practice.

RISB

Turning now to specific measures, the RISB was developed to serve as a brief screening measure of adjustment, primarily for use in identifying persons in need of mental health intervention, and it serves this purpose well. With an RISB cutting score of 145, Lah (1989a) could distinguish with above 80% accuracy between college students receiving campus mental health serves and a nonpatient comparison group. In a separate sample of 116 college students, Lah (1989a) additionally found significant correlations between the RISB scores and sociometric ratings of several aspects of adjustment, including general happiness, sense of humor about oneself, and self-acceptance. In studies comparing delinquent adolescent boys in residential treatment with randomly selected high school boys, Fuller, Parmelee, and Carroll (1982) found significant differences between the groups in their RISB total score and developed a maladjustment score that correctly identified 80% of the delinquents and 75% of the high school boys.

Along with helping to identify persons with adjustment difficulties for which treatment may be indicated, sentence completion data can sometimes suggest a specific type of disorder. With respect to psychopathic personality features, Endres (2004) reported moderate positive correlations between scores on the Psychopathy Checklist-Revised (PCL-R) and certain cognitive and linguistic characteristics of sentence completions, including use of coarse language and a prominent focus on exerting power. Although not unique to psychopathy, these sentence completion characteristics were found by Endres (2004) to be highly sensitive to it.

In addition to suggesting patterns of possible personality disorder, sentence completions can give direct expression to manifestations of symptomatic disorders. The illustration of "I FEEL depressed" at the beginning of this chapter is a case in point. Similar examples would be "I FEEL afraid of heights" as an indicator of phobic disorder; "AT BEDTIME worrying about having a nightmare keeps me awake" as a clue to posttraumatic stress disorder; and "SOMETIMES my moods go from happy to sad all at once" as suggestive of bipolar or cyclothymic disorder.

Despite its potential for serving these diagnostic purposes, the RISB is rarely relied on for them. Most of the other commonly used assessment measures discussed in this *Handbook* provide more dependable indices of overall adjustment and differential diagnosis than the RISB. With respect to screening for adjustment difficulties, the previously noted infrequency with which practitioners calculate scores for sentence completion tests indicates how seldom the RISB is used in this way. As for differential diagnosis, there are no systematic guidelines in the literature for discriminating among types of disorder on the basis of sentence completions. It is not in these respects that RISB data prove particularly useful, then, but rather in providing clues to persons' underlying conflicts and concerns, their feelings about themselves and other people, and their attitudes toward various life situations and experiences. Information of this kind creates valuable applications of the RISB in clinical practice, forensic consultation, and personality research.

In clinical practice, RISB clues to a troubled person's conflicts, concerns, feelings, and attitudes can contribute to planning psychotherapy and evaluating treatment progress and outcome. In the planning phase, sentence completion reflections of a person's inner life help to identify issues to address in the course of therapy. The extent to which subsequent retesting indicates that these issues have been resolved helps to monitor progress in treatment and determine whether therapy has proved beneficial.

In the case of the adolescent boy who revealed more of himself on the RISB than on other tests in the battery, his initial sentence completions identified as treatment targets some resolution of his ambivalent feelings toward his parents and an easing of his conflicts with them. Suppose on retesting during the course of therapy he were to write, instead of "AT HOME my parents and I argue a lot," "AT HOME things are going pretty well." Suppose as other notable changes in his sentence completions he were to write, instead of "I NEED my parents to understand me," "I NEED to find a girlfriend," and instead of "I WISH that I had a better relationship with my parents," "I WISH that I could get my grades up." Then his sentence completions would strongly suggest positive change in treatment, with reduced family conflict and increased attention to normative age-related concerns.

In forensic consultations, the utility strength of the RISB in reflecting aspects of a person's inner life has only limited applications. The nature of a person's underlying conflicts, concerns, feelings, and attitudes has little bearing on the psycholegal issues with which courts are concerned in criminal and personal injury cases. Moreover, the limited availability of research findings that validate thematic interpretations of sentence completion responses may in some courtrooms prevent RISB-based testimony from being accepted into evidence. Still, as suggested by the previously mentioned frequency with which forensic psychologists have reported using sentence completion methods in custody cases (29% in evaluations of children, 22% in evaluations of parents), RISB data can at times be put to effective use in family law cases.

In particular, information concerning how parents feel about their children and about the responsibilities of parenthood is often sought and valued by family court judges. How children feel about their parents and about their home life, together with indications of family conflict, are also commonly of interest in family law hearings and mediations. As illustrated in this chapter, RISB responses can provide clues to such feelings and attitudes. There may also be instances in which sentence completions have face validity that the court might consider relevant. The adolescent boy who wrote "MY FATHER travels a lot" also gave the sentence completion, "A MOTHER helps guide their children in life." If this boy's parents were contesting custody or visitation rights, these contrasting responses might speak loudly to the court about who was the more important and available parent in his life.

In research applications, the RISB has proved useful not only in identifying personality characteristics, but also in providing an overall quantitative index of adjustment level. Whereas most personality assessment instruments measure adequate adjustment by the absence of indicators of maladjustment, the RISB item scores range from 0 (most positive) to 6 (most conflict). Hence the RISB total score provides a bipolar measurement with normality in the middle, superior adjustment at the low end, and severe psychopathology at the high end of the scale. This sensitivity of the RISB to both particularly good and markedly poor adjustment facilitates selection of adjusted and maladjusted samples for research purposes. Early research using the RISB for this purpose is summarized by Lah (1989a, 1989b), and interesting results have also been reported in more recent investigations in which the RISB total score was used as a criterion measure of adjustment. In a study of children of divorce, for example, Kouser and Najam (1992) used the RISB to demonstrate more maladjustment among adolescent girls whose parents were divorced than among girls from intact families.

WUSCT

The WUSCT was developed primarily for research purposes to measure level of ego development, and it has served this purpose often and well. Westenberg, Hauser, et al.

(2004) report that more than 300 empirical studies employing the WUCST had been published by the early 1990s. As an example of its research utility, the WUSCT has proved helpful in identifying developmental aspects of the personality dimensions measured by the NEO PI-R, which is discussed in Chapter 10, especially in relation to cognitive and interpersonal levels of functioning (Hogansen & Lanning, 2001; Kurtz & Tiegreen, 2005).

In other research, the WUCS has been used as a measure of psychosocial maturity in studies examining emotional complexity (Kang & Shaver, 2004), mothers' feelings about their maternal role (Luthar, Doyle, Suchman, & Mayes, 2001), attitudes toward athletics and academic achievement in high school students (Bursik & Martin, 2006; Takenouchi, Taguchi, & Okuda, 2004), developmental changes in childhood fears and vulnerability to social anxiety disorder (Westenberg, Drewes, Goedhart, Siebelink, & Treffors, 2004), gender and cross-cultural differences in levels of ego development (Bakken & Huber, 2005; Truluck & Courtenay, 2002), and self-regard in adolescent psychiatric inpatients (Evans, Brody, & Noam, 2001).

Research applications aside, the previously noted infrequent use of the WUSCT in clinical practice seems regrettable. In its format and content, the WUSCT is just as suitable as the RISB for generating thematic data that provide clues to a person's inner life. Moreover, placement at one of eight levels of psychosocial maturity coded with the WUSCT has implications for differential diagnosis and treatment planning. As noted, the level of ego development measured by the WUSCT is not necessarily related to the presence or absence of psychopathology (see Hy & Loevinger, 1996, chap. 1). Ego level, however, does have implications for the type of disorder people are likely to develop if they become disturbed.

As elaborated by Westenberg, Hauser, et al. (2004), there is evidence to suggest that behavioral and externalizing problems occur mostly among persons who are functioning at the Impulsive and Self-Protective levels of ego development and less so among persons who attain the Conformist and higher levels of psychosocial maturity. Emotional and internalizing problems like anxiety and depression can characterize people at all ego levels but tend to become most noticeable among persons functioning at the Conformist or higher levels of ego development.

In treatment planning, WUCST findings can assist in selecting a treatment approach appropriate to a patient's needs and capacities. Individuals at lower levels of ego development may be relatively likely to think about psychotherapy in concrete terms as a service that their therapist will provide for them and be responsible for making it helpful. Persons at higher ego levels, by contrast, may be more likely than psychosocially immature individuals to regard psychotherapy as a participatory process of learning about themselves in which they will bear primary responsibility for progress.

Stakert and Bursik (2006) reported some relevant findings in a study of 100 adult patients with serious psychological disturbance who were being treated in a community mental health center. Those patients who showed relatively high levels of ego development as measured by the WUSCT had more complex therapeutic goals and were more committed to those goals than patients with lower levels of ego development. Patients functioning at higher ego levels were also more likely than those at lower levels to include improved social relationships and increased self-understanding among their treatment goals, whereas a treatment focus limited to symptom relief and rehabilitation was more prevalent among patients at lower ego levels. To the extent that these distinctions apply in the individual case, the WUSCT Total Protocol Rating of persons seeking psychotherapy is likely to have implications for whether their treatment needs will be better met by a supportive and directive approach or by an expressive and relatively unstructured form of psychotherapy.

PSYCHOMETRIC FOUNDATIONS

In their psychometric foundations, as in their frequency of use for clinical purposes, the RISB and WUCST stand in sharp contrast. The RISB has been used frequently in research studies as a criterion measure of adjustment, as noted in discussing its applications, but its psychometric properties have rarely been examined directly. The WUSCT, despite its infrequent clinical use and in addition to its prominent research role as a measure of ego development, has been studied extensively to determine its reliability and validity. Both the overall adjustment score on the RISB and the total score on the WUSCT have shown good psychometric properties, although the evidence in this regard is much stronger for the WUCST than for the RISB. Loevinger's categorization of levels of ego development has also shown predictive and construct validity, but the clues to aspects of a person's inner life that can be inferred from the thematic information in sentence completions have not been the subject of any systematic validity studies.

RISB

Although limited, the available data have consistently demonstrated solid reliability for the RISB total score. With respect to interrater reliability, Rotter and Rafferty (1950) reported in their original test manual that examiners had achieved correlations for agreement of $r = .96$ in coding protocols of females and $r = .91$ for males. Lah (1989a) in his two previously mentioned research samples obtained coefficients for interrater agreement of $r = .94$ and $r = .90$. As summarized by Sherry et al. (2004), other studies over the years have shown similarly high levels of scoring reliability, with observed correlations for agreement ranging from .72 to .99 and falling mostly in the .90s. Split-half reliabilities for the RISB for its different forms have ranged from .83 to .86 for females and from .74 to .84 for males in various studies, and retesting over 1- to 2-week intervals has yielded reliability coefficients averaging in the low .80s (Sherry et al., 2004).

As for the validity of the RISB, the studies mentioned in discussing clinical applications of this test bear witness to the validity of its total score for identifying maladjustment, and the many research studies in which it has been used effectively as a criterion measure of adjustment level provide further indirect evidence of its validity. Regrettably, the validity of the RISB for drawing inferences either about observable personality characteristics or underlying thoughts and feelings has seldom been examined, and there is no body of accumulated empirical evidence in this area. Sherry et al. (2004) wrote in their 2004 review of the literature that they had not found any validity studies of the RISB published since Lah's (1989a) report.

In the absence of this validation, examiners need always to treat inferences drawn from the thematic content of sentence completions as clues to possible features of an individual's personality, and not as certain fact. Even so, as elaborated in this and the three preceding chapters, thematically based hypotheses can prove useful in clinical practice and merit careful consideration. As the distinguished psychologist Paul Meehl (1945) once wrote about personality assessment, "The final test of the adequacy of any technique is its utility in clinical work" (p. 302).

WUSCT

As reviewed by Westenberg, Hauser, et al. (2004) and Westen, Feit, and Zittel (1999), the WUSCT has shown excellent reliability in numerous studies. Obtained correlations for interrater agreement in scoring responses for their psychosocial maturity level ranges from $r = .80$ to $r = .90$, perfect agreement on item scoring averages about 85%, and disagreement by more than one level in categorizing stage of development is often less than 10%. The split-half reliability of the Total Protocol Rating on WUSCT and the SCT-Y is about .80, and most studies report a Cronbach alpha for internal consistency of .90 or higher.

An impressive body of research has also validated both Loevinger's theoretical formulations and her assessment method. With respect to her stage theory of ego development, empirical data have confirmed (a) that ego development exists on a continuum of stages; (b) that individuals pass through an invariant sequence of these stages as they mature, from the initial E2 (Impulsivity) up to the highest level of maturity they can attain; and (c) that ego level of development is a personality typology in which there are individual differences among people at every chronological age. As for Loevinger's assessment method, the WUSCT and SCT-Y have been extensively validated as measures of ego development. They have shown expected age changes in longitudinal studies of children and adolescents, they have predicted delinquent behavior and academic achievement in adolescents, and they are associated with behavior patterns reflecting such personality characteristics as altruism, responsibility, and conformity (see Bursik & Martin, 2006; Loevinger, 1998, chap. 5; Noam, Young, & Jilnina, 2006; Stakert & Bursik, 2006; Westen et al., 1999; Westenberg, Hauser, et al., 2004).

These abundant validating data have earned considerable praise in the literature for the psychometric soundness of the WUSCT. Garb, Lilienfeld, Wood, and Nezworski (2002) have described the WUSCT as an extensively validated measure of personality that can be "used to evaluate a range of traits, including impulse control, moral development, cognitive style, interpersonal styles, and conscious preoccupations" p. 463). Manners and Durkin (2001) concluded in a critical review of ego development theory and its measurement, "There is substantial empirical support for the conceptual soundness of ego development theory and the WUSCT" (p. 541).

REFERENCES

Ackerman, M. J., & Ackerman, M. C. (1997). Custody evaluations in practice: A survey of experienced professionals (revisited). *Professional Psychology, 28,* 137–145.

American Educational Research Association, American Psychological Association, and National Council on Measurement in Education. (1999). *Standards for educational and psychological testing.* Washington, DC: American Educational Research Association.

Ames, P. C., & Riggio, R. E. (1995). Use of the Rotter Incomplete Sentences Blank with adolescent populations: Implications for determining maladjustment. *Journal of Personality Assessment, 64,* 159–167

Archer, R. P., Buffington-Vollum, J. K., Stredny, R. V., & Handel, R. W. (2006). A survey of psychological test usage among forensic psychologists. *Journal of Personality Assessment, 87,* 84–94.

Archer, R. P., & Newsom, C. R. (2000). Psychological test usage with adolescent clients: Survey update. *Assessment, 7,* 227–235.

Bakken, L., & Huber, T. (2005). Ego development at the crossroads: Identity and intimacy among Black men and White women in cross-racial relationships. *Journal of Adult Development, 12,* 63–73.

Barton, S., Morley, S., Bloxham, G., Kitson, C., & Platts, S. (2005). Sentence completion test for depression (SCD): An idiographic measure of depressive thinking. *British Journal of Clinical Psychology, 44,* 29–46.

Binet, A., & Simon, T. (1905). Methodes nouvelles pour le diagnostic du niveau intellectual des anormaux [New methods for the diagnosis of abnormal intellectual level]. *L'Annee Psychologique, 11,* 193–244.

Bursik, K., & Martin, T. A. (2006). Ego development and adolescent academic achievement. *Journal of Research on Adolescence, 16,* 1–18.

Camara, W., Nathan, J., & Puente, A. (2000). Psychological test usage: Implications in professional use. *Professional Psychology, 31,* 141–154.

Cashel, M. L. (2002). Child and adolescent psychological assessment: Current clinical practices and the impact of managed care. *Professional Psychology: Research and Practice, 33,* 446–453.

Clemence, A., & Handler, L. (2001). Psychological assessment on internship: A survey of training directors and their expectations for students. *Journal of Personality Assessment, 76,* 18–47.

Daston, P. G. (1968). Word association and sentence completion methods. In A. I Rabin (Ed.), *Projective techniques in personality assessment* (pp. 264–289). New York: Springer.

Ebbinghaus, H. (1897). Über eine neue methode zur prüfung geistiger fähigkeiten und ihre anwendung bei schulkindern [On a new method for the testing of intellectual capacity and its application by school children]. *Zeitschrift fur Psychologie und Physiologie der Sinnesorgane, 13,* 451–457.

Endres, J. (2004). The language of the psychopath: Characteristics of prisoners' performance in a sentence completion test. *Criminal Behavior and Mental Health, 14,* 214–226.

Evans, D. W., Brody, L., & Noam, G. G. (2001). Ego development, self-perception, and self-complexity in adolescence: A study of female psychiatric inpatients. *American Journal of Orthopsychiatry, 71,* 79–86.

Exner, J. E., Jr. (1973). The Self Focus Sentence Completion: A study of egocentricity. *Journal of Personality Assessment, 37,* 437–455.

Forer, B. (1950). A structured sentence completion test. *Journal of Projective Techniques, 14,* 15–30.

Forer, B. (1993). *The Forer Structured Sentence Completion Test.* Los Angeles: Western Psychological Services.

Fuller, G. B., Parmelee, W. M., & Carroll, J. L. (1982). Performance of delinquent and nondelinquent high school boys on the Rotter Incomplete Sentences Blank. *Journal of Personality Assessment, 46,* 506–510.

Garb, H. N., Lilienfeld, S. O., Wood, J. M., & Nezworski, M. T. (2002). Effective use of projective techniques in clinical practice: Let the data help with selection and interpretation. *Professional Psychology: Research and Practice, 33,* 454–463.

Haak, R. A. (1990). Using the sentence completion to assess emotional disturbance. In C. R. Reynolds & R. W. Kamphaus (Eds.), *Handbook of psychological and educational assessment of children* (*Vol. 2,* pp. 147–167). New York: Guilford Press.

Hart, D. H. (1986). The sentence completion techniques. In H. M. Knoff (Ed.), *The assessment of child and adolescent personality* (pp. 245–272). New York: Guilford Press.

Hogan, T. P. (2005). 50 widely used psychological tests. In G. P. Koocher, J. C. Norcross, & S. S. Hill III. (Eds.), *Psychologists' desk reference* (2nd ed., pp. 101–104. New York: Oxford University Press.

Hogansen, J., & Lanning, K. (2001). Five factors in Sentence Completion Test categories: Toward rapprochement between trait and maturational approaches to personality. *Journal of Research in Personality*, *35*, 449–462.

Holaday, M., Smith, D. A., & Sherry, A. (2000). Sentence completion tests: A review of the literature and results of a survey of members of the Society for Personality Assessment. *Journal of Personality Assessment*, *74*, 371–383.

Holsopple, J. Q., & Miale, F. R. (1954). *Sentence completion: A projective method for the study of personality*. Springfield, IL: Thomas.

Hy, L. X., & Loevinger, J. (1996). *Measuring ego development* (2nd. ed.). Mahwah, NJ: Erlbaum.

Inselberg, R. M. (1964). The sentence completion technique in the measurement of marital satisfaction. *Journal of Marriage and the Family*, *26*, 339–341.

Jung, C. G. (1916). The association method. *American Journal of Psychology*, *21*, 219–269.

Kang, S.-M., & Shaver, P. R. (2004). Individual differences in emotional complexity: Their psychological implications. *Journal of Personality*, *72*, 687–726.

Kent, G. H., & Rosanoff, A. (1910). A study of association in insanity. *American Journal of Insanity*, *67*, 317–390.

Kleiger, J. H. (2004). Projective assessment of disordered thinking. In M. Hersen (Editor-in-Chief), M. J. Hilsenroth, & D. L. Segal (Vol. Eds.), *Comprehensive handbook of psychological assessment: Vol. 2. Personality assessment* (pp. 526–537). Hoboken, NJ: Wiley.

Kouser, S., & Najam, N. (1992). Children of divorce: A comparative study of adolescent girls of divorced and intact families. *Journal of Behavioral Sciences*, *3*, 11–20.

Kurtz, J. E., & Tiegreen, S. B. (2005). Matters of conscience and conscientiousness: The place of ego development in the five-factor model. *Journal of Personality Assessment*, *85*, 312–317.

Lah, M. I. (1989a). New validity, normative, and scoring data for the Rotter Incomplete Sentences Blank. *Journal of Personality Assessment*, *53*, 607–620.

Lah, M. I. (1989b). Sentence completion tests. In C. S. Newmark. (Ed.), *Major psychological assessment instruments* (*Vol. 2*, pp. 133–163). Boston: Allyn & Bacon.

Lah, M. I. (2001). Sentence completion test. In W. I. Dorfman & M. Hersen. (Eds.), *Understanding psychological assessment* (pp. 135–143). New York: Kluwer Academic.

Lah, M. I., & Rotter, J. B. (1981). Changing college student norms on the Rotter Incomplete Sentences Blank. *Journal of Consulting and Clinical Psychology*, *49*, 985.

Lanyon, R. I., Almer, E. R., & Maxwell, B. M. (2002). Validation and norms for sentence completion: Task scales to assess misrepresentation during disability assessment. *American Journal of Forensic Psychology*, *20*, 39–52.

Loevinger, J. (1976). *Ego development: Conceptions and theories*. San Francisco: Jossey Bass.

Loevinger, J. (1985). Revision of the Sentence Completion Test for ego development. *Journal of Personality and Social Psychology*, *48*, 420–427.

Loevinger, J. (Ed.). (1998). *Technical foundations for measuring ego development: The Washington University Sentence Completion Test*. Mahwah, NJ: Erlbaum.

Loevinger, J., & Wessler, R. (1970). *Measuring ego development: Vol. 1. Construction and use of a sentence completion test*. San Francisco: Jossey-Bass.

Loevinger, J., Wessler, R., & Redmore, C. (1970). *Measuring ego development: Vol. 2. Scoring manual for women and girls test*. San Francisco: Jossey-Bass.

Luthar, S. S., Doyle, K., Suchman, N. E., & Mayes, L. (2001). Developmental themes in women's emotional experiences of motherhood. *Development and Psychopathology*, *13*, 165–182.

Manners, J., & Durkin, K. (2001). A critical review of the validity of ego development theory and its measurement. *Journal of Personality Assessment*, *77*, 541–567.

Maslow, A. H. (1954). *Motivation and personality*. New York: Harper.

McCammon, E. P. (1981). Comparison of oral and written forms of the Sentence Completion Test for Ego Development. *Developmental Psychology*, *17*, 233–235.

Meehl, P. E. (1945). The dynamics of "structured" personality tests. *Journal of Clinical Psychology*, *1*, 296–303.

Miner, J. B. (1978). Twenty years of research on role-motivation theory of managerial effectiveness. *Personnel Psychology*, *31*, 739–760.

Miner, J. B. (1984). The Miner Sentence Completion Scale: A reappraisal. *Academy of Management Journal*, *21*, 283–294.

Musgrave, P. W. (1984). Adolescent moral attitudes: Continuities in research. *Journal of Moral Education*, *13*, 133–136.

Noam, G. G., Young, C. H., & Jilnina, J. (2006). Social cognition, psychological symptoms, and mental health: The model, evidence, and contribution of ego development. In D. Cicchetti & D. J. Cohen. (Eds.), *Developmental psychopathology: Vol. 1. Theory and method* (2nd ed., pp. 750–794). Hoboken, NJ: Wiley.

Payne, A. F. (1928). *Sentence completions*. New York: New York Guidance Clinic.

Payne, A. F. (1930). Experiment in human engineering at the College of the City of New York. *School and Society*, *32*, 292–294.

Picano, J. J., Roland, R. R., Rollins, K. D., & Williams, T. J. (2002). Development and validation of a sentence completion test measure of defensive responding in military personnel assessed for nonroutine missions. *Military Psychology*, *14*, 279–298.

Quinnell, F. A., & Bow, J. N. (2001). Psychological tests used in child custody evaluations. *Behavioral Sciences and the Law*, *19*, 491–501.

Rapaport, D., Gill, M., & Schafer, R. (1968). *Diagnostic psychological testing (Rev. ed.)*. New York: International Universities Press. (Original work published 1946)

Riedel, R. G., Grossman, J. H., & Burger, G. (1971). Special Incomplete Sentence Test for Underachievers: Further research. *Psychological Reports*, *29*, 251–257.

Rohde, A. R. (1946). Explorations in personality by the sentence completion method. *Journal of Applied Psychology*, *30*, 169–181.

Rohde, A. R. (1957). *The sentence completion method*. New York: Ronald Press.

Roid, G. H. (2003). *The Stanford Binet Intelligence Scales* (5th. ed.). Tasca, IL: Riverside.

Rotter, J. B. (1951). Word association and sentence completion methods. In H. H. Anderson & G. L. Anderson. (Eds.), *An introduction to projective techniques* (pp. 279–311). Englewood Cliffs, NJ: Prentice-Hall.

Rotter, J. B., Lah, M. I., & Rafferty, J. E. (1992). *Rotter Incomplete Sentences Blank* (2nd. ed.). Orlando, FL: Psychological Corporation.

Rotter, J. B., & Rafferty, J. E. (1950). *Manual for the Rotter Incomplete Sentences Blank: College form*. New York: Psychological Corporation.

Rotter, J. B., Rafferty, J. E., & Schachtitz, E. (1949). Validation of the Rotter Incomplete Sentences Blank for college screening. *Journal of Consulting Psychology*, *13*, 348–356.

Rotter, J. B., & Willerman, B. (1947). The Incomplete Sentences Test as a method of studying personality. *Journal of Consulting Psychology*, *11*, 42–48.

Sacks, J. M., & Levy, S. (1950). The sentence completion test. In L. E. Abt & L. Bellak. (Eds.), *Projective psychology: Clinical approaches to the total personality* (pp. 357–402). New York: Knopf.

Schretlen, D. J. (1997). Dissimulation on the Rorschach and other projective measures. In R. Rogers. (Ed.), *Clinical assessment of malingering and deception* (2nd ed., pp. 208–222). New York: Guilford Press.

Sherry, A., Dahlen, E., & Holaday, M. (2004). The use of sentence completion tests with adults. In M. Hersen (Editor-in-Chief), M. J. Hilsenroth, & D. L. Segal (Vol. Eds.), *Comprehensive handbook of psychological assessment: Vol. 2. Personality assessment* (pp. 372–386). Hoboken, NJ: Wiley.

Stakert, R. A., & Bursik, K. (2006). Ego development and the therapeutic goal-setting capacities of mentally ill adults. *American Journal of Psychotherapy*, *60*, 357–371.

Takenouchi, T., Taguchi, T., & Okuda, A. (2004). Relationship of sports experience and ego development of adolescent Japanese athletes. *Psychological Reports*, *95*, 13–26.

Tendler, A. D. (1930). A preliminary report on a test for emotional insight. *Journal of Applied Psychology*, *14*, 122–136.

Truluck, J. E., & Courtenay, B. C. (2002). Ego development and the influence of gender, age, and educational level among older adults. *Educational Gerontology*, *28*, 325–336.

Westen, D., Feit, A., & Zittel, C. (1999). Methodological issues in research using projective methods. In P. C. Kendall, J. N. Butcher, & G. N. Holmbeck. (Eds.), *Handbook of research methods in clinical psychology* (pp. 224–240). New York: Wiley.

Westenberg, P. M., Drewes, M. J., Goedhart, A. W., Siebelink, B. M., & Treffers, P. D. A. (2004). A developmental analysis of self-reported fears in late childhood through mid-adolescence: Social-evaluative fears on the rise? *Journal of Child Psychology and Psychiatry*, *45*, 481–495.

Westenberg, P. M., Hauser, S. T., & Cohn, L. D. (2004). Sentence completion measurement of psychosocial maturity. In M. Hersen (Editor-in-Chief), M. J. Hilsenroth, & D. L. Segal (Vol. Eds.), *Comprehensive handbook of psychological assessment: Vol. 2. Personality assessment* (pp. 595–616). Hoboken, NJ: Wiley.

Westenberg, P. M., Treffers, P. D. A., & Drewes, M. J. (1998). A new version of the WUSCT: The Sentence Completion Test for Children and Youths (SCT-Y). In J. Loevinger. (Ed.), *Technical foundations for measuring ego development: The Washington University Sentence Completion Test* (pp. 81–89). Mahwah, NJ: Erlbaum.

Westenberg, P. M., van Strien, S. D., & Drewes, M. J. (2001). Revised description and measurement of ego development in early adolescence: An artifact of the written procedure. *Journal of Early Adolescence*, *22*, 470–493.

Appendixes

COMPUTER-GENERATED INTERPRETIVE REPORTS

As discussed in Chapter 2 (see pp. 34–36), software programs that generate interpretive reports are available for most widely used personality assessment instruments, including the six measures discussed in Chapters 6–11 of this *Handbook*. To acquaint readers with the format of these computer-generated reports and the types of statements they include, this Appendix provides a sample report for each measure. These sample reports also illustrate the breadth and depth of useful information about personality functioning that can be gleaned from personality assessment procedures.

Appendix A

MINNESOTA MULTIPHASIC PERSONALITY INVENTORY-2

Many computerized interpretive reports are available for the MMPI-2, and only a representative sample will be provided here. Because of the long history of usage of the MMPI and MMPI-2, there has been ample time for the development of these various interpretive reports, the first of which appeared in the 1960s. These computerized interpretive reports were developed initially for clinical settings, and in the past decade have been extended to a variety of additional settings. The Minnesota report also is available for criminal justice and correctional settings, a variety of forensic settings, and personnel settings. The Caldwell report also is available for child-custody settings. The Caldwell child-custody report is the only one of these interpretive reports that is written specifically for the psycholegal issue being addressed.

These computerized interpretive reports are written to describe the *group* of individuals that this specific individual is most like. They are not stand-alone products that can be used without change. Each of these reports needs to be adapted to fit the clinical history and current behavior and symptoms of this specific individual. As such, the computerized interpretive report provides the general framework for beginning the process of understanding this specific individual.

A sample of three computerized interpretive reports for clinical settings using the MMPI-2 follows. Readers should pay special attention to the caveats that precede these reports.

MMPI-2 ADULT INTERPRETIVE SYSTEM

developed by
Roger L. Greene, PhD
and PAR Staff

Client Information

Name:	Sample Client
Client ID:	12345-67890
Gender:	Female
Date Of Birth:	01/31/1959
Age:	47
Education:	High School Grad.
Ethnicity:	Hispanic
Test Date:	01/31/2006

The interpretive information contained in this report should be viewed as only one source of hypotheses about the individual being evaluated. No decisions should be based solely on the information contained in this report. Specific scale(s) and/or item(s) referenced by interpretive statements may not have been endorsed or elevated by the individual being evaluated. This material should be integrated with all other sources of information in reaching professional decisions about this individual. This report is confidential and intended for use by qualified professionals only. It should not be released to the individual being evaluated.

PROFILE MATCHES AND SCORES

Best 2 Point Matches with Client's Profile
Based on Validity and Clinical Scales (using All Profiles)

Discriminant Function		Cohen's Index			Deviation Squared		
Codetype	Prob.	Codetype	rc	%ile	Codetype	DSq	%ile
Spike 9	0.399	2-9/9-2	0.832	40	2-9/9-2	657	71
2-3/3-2	0.140	1-9/9-1	0.753	27	1-9/9-1	919	50
3-9/9-3	0.120	3-9/9-3	0.773	23	3-9/9-3	875	47

Best 3 Point Matches with Client's Profile
Based on Validity and Clinical Scales (using All Profiles)

Cohen's Index			Deviation Squared		
Codetype	rc	%ile	Codetype	DSq	%ile
2-3/3-2-(9)	0.881	57	2-3/3-2-(9)	546	55
1-9/9-1-(2)	0.830	39	1-9/9-1-(2)	783	61
2-7/7-2-(9)	0.812	31	1-2/2-1-(9)	808	58

Best Fit 2 or 3 Point Codetype: 2-3/3-2-(9)

Validity and Clinical Scales

Scale	Client T Score	Best Fit Prototype
L	61	58
F	58	58
K	44	48
Hs	57	65
D	69	73
Hy	69	75
Pd	48 -	58
Mf	39 -	49
Pa	68	59
Pt	56	63
Sc	58	63
Ma	69	71
Si	55	48

Profile Characteristics

	Client	Best Fit Prototype
Mean Scale	59	62
Scatter	10	9
Client Age	47	42
Male Percent		32
Female Percent	X	68

Potential Impact of Demographic Variables

Her ethnicity, and particularly her level of acculturation, should be considered in the interpretation of responses to individual MMPI-2 items. The MacAndrew Alcoholism Scale (*MAC-R*) should be interpreted cautiously, if at all.

Dangerousness to Self/Others Items
Age Group: 40 - 49

Her responses (either "True" or "Omitted") to the dangerousness to self items (150, 303, 506, 520, 524, 530) should be documented in writing in her clinical record.

Dangerousness to Self - Responses		
Test Item Number	Client Response	Typical Percent Endorsed TRUE
150	FALSE	9.98
303	FALSE	12.54
506	FALSE	16.62
520	FALSE	11.31
524	FALSE	8.41
530	FALSE	3.34

Dangerousness to Self - Item Count		
Number of Items Endorsed TRUE	Number Endorsed by This Client	Typical Percent Endorsing This Number
0	X	73.89
1		11.23
2		5.28
3		4.10
4		3.05
5		1.77
6		0.67

Her responses (either "True" or "Omitted") to the dangerousness to others items (150, 540, 542, 548) should be documented in writing in her clinical record.

Dangerousness to Others - Responses		
Test Item Number	**Client Response**	**Typical Percent Endorsed TRUE**
150	FALSE	9.98
540	FALSE	4.73
542	FALSE	49.15
548	FALSE	5.83

Dangerousness to Others - Item Count		
Number of Items Endorsed TRUE	**Number Endorsed by This Client**	**Typical Percent Endorsing This Number**
0	X	47.76
1		39.53
2		9.79
3		2.42
4		0.51

Test-Taking Behaviors

Omissions

She omitted no items.

Consistency of Item Endorsement

She endorsed the items consistently (*VRIN* 38-61, TRIN <= 84).

Accuracy of Item Endorsement

She has endorsed the items accurately (*L* < 62, *F* < 99, *K* 36-58). There are no indications of either a very positive or negative self-description that would impact the interpretation of the MMPI-2.

Clinical Interpretation for Best Fit Prototype

2-3/3-2-(9)

Clinical Presentation:

Moods

She reports that she is experiencing a mild to moderate level of emotional distress (*A*, *NEGE*, *RCd*[*dem*]) characterized by dysphoria (*2[D]*, *DEP*) and worrying (*7[Pt]*, *ANX*). She frequently has spells of the blues (**388F**), she broods a great deal (215T), and her daily life has few things that keep her interested (**9F**), yet she is happy most of the time (95T). Her worries seem to disappear when she gets into a crowd of lively friends (363T). She has difficulty expressing her feelings, describing herself as feeling bottled up (*2[D]*, *3[Hy]*). She has had long periods of time when she could not take care of things because she could not get going (38T). She is overcontrolled and fearful of losing control (*2[D]*, *3[Hy]*). She is likely to experience increases in depression, fatigue, and physical symptoms in response to stress (*3[Hy]*). It makes her angry when people hurry her (461T), and she lets them know how she feels about it (481T). She has become so angry that she feels as though she will explode (542T). When she gets bored she likes to stir up some excitement (169T). She has periods when she feels unusually cheerful without any special reason (267T).

Cognitions

She reports that she has problems with attention, concentration (31T, 299T, 325T), and memory (**165F**, 533T). She certainly thinks she is useless at times (130T).

At times her mind seems to work more slowly than usual (341T) and at other times she can make up her mind with unusually great ease (206T). Her judgment is not as good as it was in the past (**43F**). She sometimes thinks that she is about to go to pieces (469T).

She does not analyze the motives for her own or others' behavior (*3[Hy]*, *CYN*, *RC3*[*cyn*]). She is not happy with herself the way she is (377T) and wishes she could be as happy as others seem to be (56T).

Interpersonal Relations

She reports that she is somewhat introverted (*0[Si]*, *SOD*, *SOD1*), yet she is very sociable and makes friends quickly (49T, 280T, 360T). She likes making decisions and assigning jobs to others (521T) and believes, if given the chance, she would make a good leader of people (350T). She enjoys social gatherings and parties (353T, 370T) and the excitement of a crowd (359T, **367F**). She reports good relations with her family (*Pd₁*, *FAM*). It is not hard for her to ask for help from her friends even though she cannot return the favor (200T). She is alienated from herself (*Pd₅*, *Si₃*) and others (*Pd₄*, *Sc₁*, *Si₃*).

Client: Sample Client
ID#: 12345-67890

Test Date: 01/31/2006
Page 8 of 32

Other Problem Areas

She reports that she has a number of physical (*1*[*Hs*], *HEA*, *Hy₄*, *RC1*[*som*]) and neurologic symptoms (*Sc₆*, *HEA2*). She worries about her health (**33F**). She has difficulty going to sleep because she is excited (304T) or thoughts or ideas are bothering her (**140F**), her sleep is fitful and disturbed (39T), and she does not wake up fresh and rested most mornings (**3F**). She is easily awakened by noise (5T). She tires quickly (**152F**) and feels tired a good deal of the time (464T). She does not feel weak all over much of the time (**175F**). At times she is all full of energy (330T). She usually has enough energy to do her work (561T), but she is not as able to work as she once was (**10F**). Her history and background should be reviewed to determine whether a medical or neurologic evaluation is warranted. She is a very conventional individual who is unlikely to have behavioral problems (*ASP*) or to abuse substances (*AAS*).

Treatment:

Her prognosis is generally poor because she sees little chance for significant change in her life (*2*[*D*], *3*[*Hy*]). Short-term, behavioral therapy that focuses on her reasons for entering treatment may be beneficial and may allow for the development of a therapeutic alliance that would be necessary for long-term therapy (*2*[*D*], *3*[*Hy*]). She will prefer to discuss her physical symptoms rather than focus on her psychological processes (*1*[*Hs*]).

She is not naturally introspective, and that will complicate the therapeutic process (*3*[*Hy*]). There are no specific issues that must be kept in mind when establishing and maintaining the therapeutic alliance.

Possible Diagnoses:

Axis I
R/O Mood Disorders
    300.4 Dysthymic Disorder
    301.13 Cyclothymic Disorder
    311   Depressive Disorder NOS
R/O Somatoform Disorders
    300.81 Somatoform Disorder NOS
R/O Adjustment Disorders
    309.0 Adjustment Disorder with Depressed Mood
    309.3 Adjustment Disorder with Disturbance of Conduct

Axis II
R/O Personality Disorders
    301.50 Histrionic Personality Disorder
    301.81 Narcissistic Personality Disorder
    301.83 Borderline Personality Disorder

Validity and K Corrected Clinical Scales

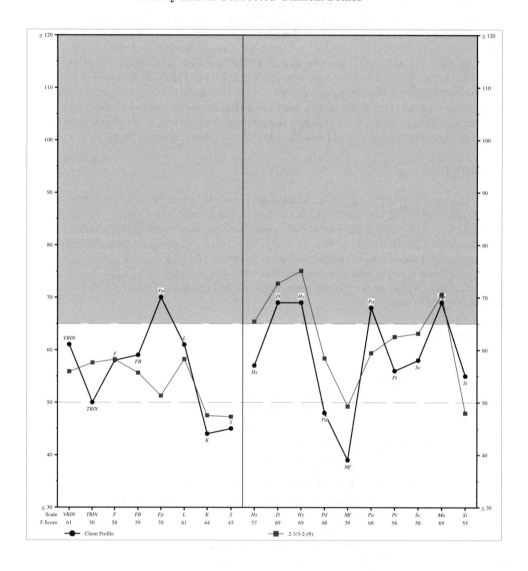

Scale	VRIN	TRIN	F	FB	Fp	L	K	S	Hs	D	Hy	Pd	Mf	Pa	Pt	Sc	Ma	Si
T-Score	61	50	58	59	70	61	44	45	57	69	69	48	39	68	56	58	69	55

●— Client Profile   ■— 2-3/3-2-(9)

Validity and Non-K Corrected Clinical Scales

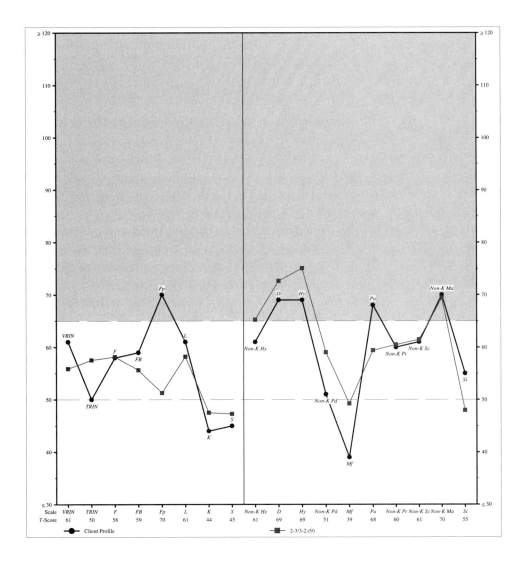

Scale	VRIN	TRIN	F	FB	Fp	L	K	S	Non-K Hs	D	Hy	Non-K Pd	Mf	Pa	Non-K Pt	Non-K Sc	Non-K Ma	Si
T-Score	61	50	58	59	70	61	44	45	61	69	69	51	39	68	60	61	70	55

● Client Profile   ■ 2-3/3-2-(9)

Client: Sample Client
ID#: 12345-67890

Test Date: 01/31/2006
Page 11 of 32

Restructured Clinical Scales

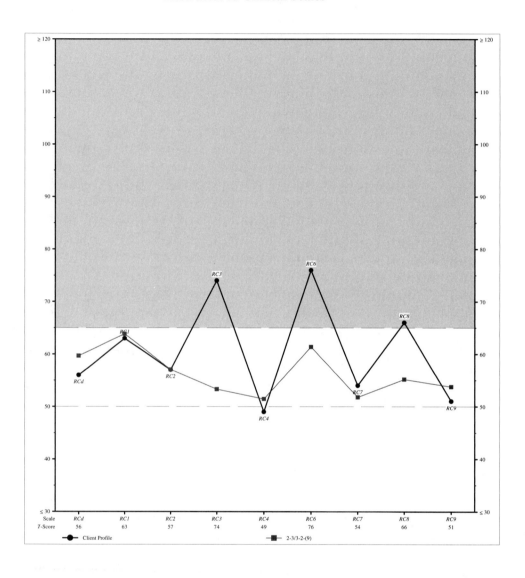

Scale	RCd	RC1	RC2	RC3	RC4	RC6	RC7	RC8	RC9
T-Score	56	63	57	74	49	76	54	66	51

●— Client Profile   ■— 2-3/3-2-(9)

Client: Sample Client
ID#: 12345-67890

Test Date: 01/31/2006
Page 12 of 32

Content Scales

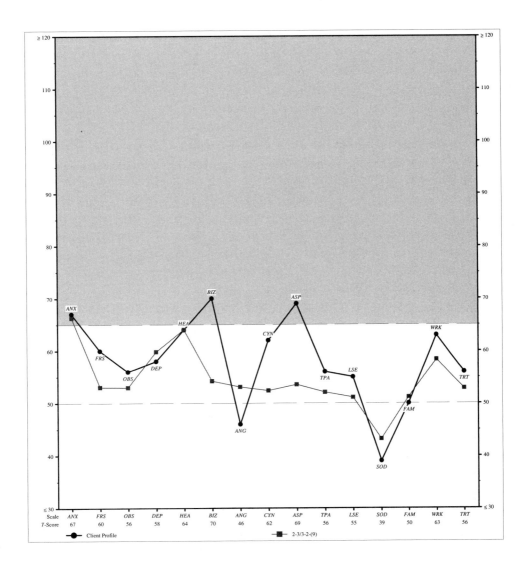

Scale	ANX	FRS	OBS	DEP	HEA	BIZ	ANG	CYN	ASP	TPA	LSE	SOD	FAM	WRK	TRT
T-Score	67	60	56	58	64	70	46	62	69	56	55	39	50	63	56

● Client Profile   ■ 2-3/3-2-(9)

Client: Sample Client
ID#: 12345-67890

Test Date: 01/31/2006
Page 13 of 32

Supplementary Scales

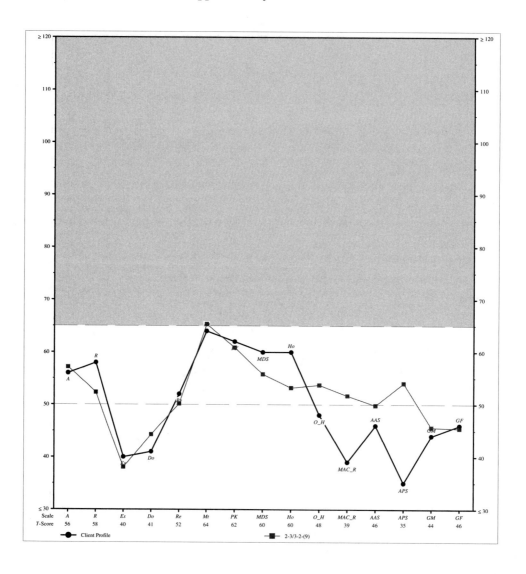

Scale	A	R	Es	Do	Re	Mt	PK	MDS	Ho	O_H	MAC_R	AAS	APS	GM	GF
T-Score	56	58	40	41	52	64	62	60	60	48	39	46	35	44	46

●— Client Profile   ■— 2-3/3-2-(9)

Client: Sample Client
ID#: 12345-67890

Psy-5 Scales

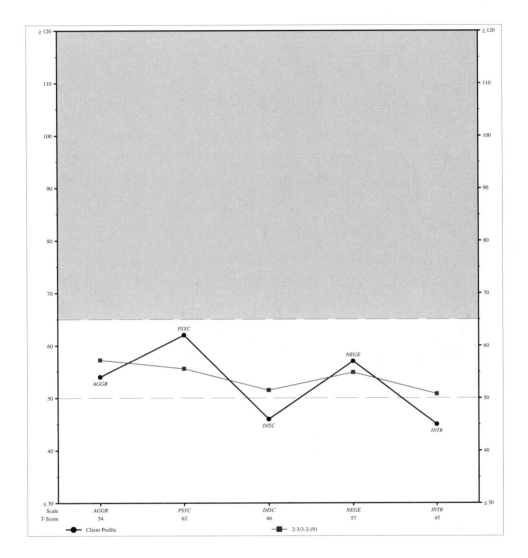

Scale	AGGR	PSYC	DISC	NEGE	INTR
T-Score	54	62	46	57	45

●— Client Profile   ■— 2-3/3-2-(9)

Client: Sample Client
ID#: 12345-67890

Test Date: 01/31/2006
Page 15 of 32

Harris-Lingoes and Social Introversion Subscales

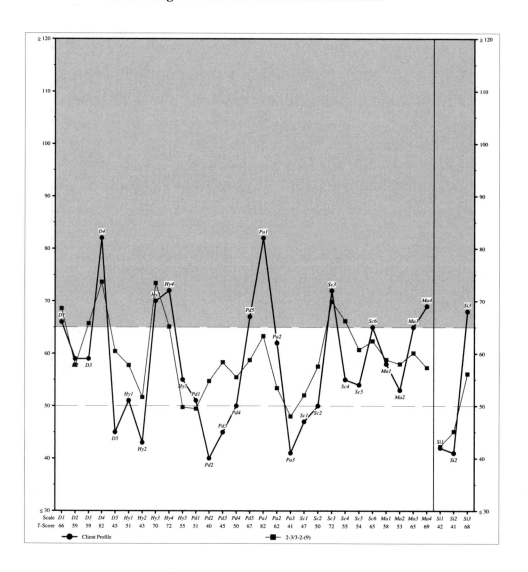

Scale	D1	D2	D3	D4	D5	Hy1	Hy2	Hy3	Hy4	Hy5	Pd1	Pd2	Pd3	Pd4	Pd5	Pa1	Pa2	Pa3	Sc1	Sc2	Sc3	Sc4	Sc5	Sc6	Ma1	Ma2	Ma3	Ma4	Si1	Si2	Si3
T-Score	66	59	59	82	45	51	43	70	72	55	51	40	45	50	67	82	62	41	47	50	72	55	54	65	58	53	65	69	42	41	68

●——● Client Profile   ■——■ 2-3/3-2-(9)

Content Component Scales

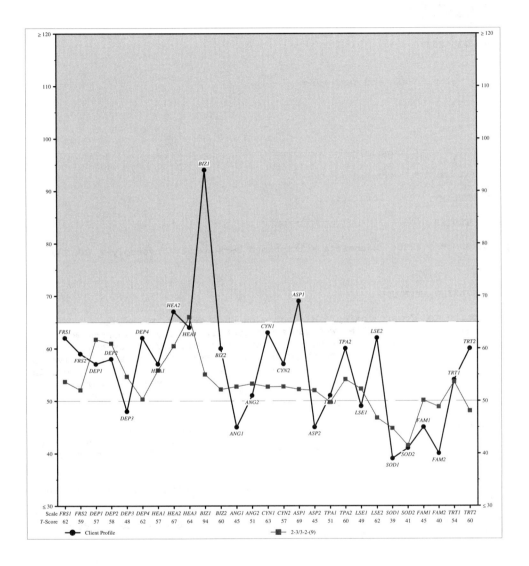

Scale	FRS1	FRS2	DEP1	DEP2	DEP3	DEP4	HEA1	HEA2	HEA3	BIZ1	BIZ2	ANG1	ANG2	CYN1	CYN2	ASP1	ASP2	TPA1	TPA2	LSE1	LSE2	SOD1	SOD2	FAM1	FAM2	TRT1	TRT2
T-Score	62	59	57	58	48	62	57	67	64	94	60	45	51	63	57	69	45	51	60	49	62	39	41	45	40	54	60

●——— Client Profile   ■——— 2-3/3-2-(9)

CALDWELL REPORT
5839 Green Valley Circle
Suite 203
Culver City, CA 90230
310-670-2874
FAX 310-670-7907

June 13, 2007

NAME: Sample Pain and Suffering

AGE: 39

SEX: Male

EDUCATION: 17 years

MARITAL STATUS: Married

REFERRED BY: ----------------

DATE TESTED:

TEST ADMINISTERED: Minnesota Multiphasic Personality Inventory-2 (MMPI-2)

TEST TAKING ATTITUDE

<u>Attention and Comprehension</u>: His score on the Variable Response
Inconsistency scale (VRIN) was quite unelevated; his item responses were
highly self-consistent throughout the inventory. This suggests that he was
clearly able to read and comprehend the test items, that he was attentive in
considering his responses, and that he carefully matched the item numbers in
the booklet to the corresponding numbers on the answer sheet. He does not
appear to have had any difficulties in understanding the content or
responding to the format of the inventory.

<u>Attitude and Approach</u>: Considering scales L, F, and K, he tended to be self-
favorable and moderately minimizing of emotional problems in his approach to
the inventory. The profile appears valid by the usual criteria for these
scales.

     He made almost no atypical and rarely given responses to the items in
the second half of the inventory (scale F-back). This was consistent with
the relative absence of such rare answers to the earlier MMPI-2 items (scale
F). The profile clearly does not appear to be of questionable validity
because of atypical responding.

<u>Socio-cultural Influences vs. Conscious Distortion</u>: The supplemental
validity scales showed an above average score on the scale (Ss) measuring
his level of currently attained, recently experienced, or self-perceived
socioeconomic status. He also showed a mild amount of conscious

---

defensiveness. It appears that most of his moderate elevation on scale K
was due to an authentic sophistication in his self-presentation, and only a
small amount of his self-favorableness on K was due to a deliberate slanting
of his responses.

SYMPTOMS AND PERSONALITY CHARACTERISTICS

The profile indicates a vulnerability to become preoccupied with his
physical pain and suffering. At least some aspects of localized pain,
general malaise, weakness, and fatigue are apt to be seen as beyond medical
expectations for his current physical status. Such symptoms as G.I. pain or
other G.I. complaints, hypertension, vasomotor instability, and headache are
often associated with this profile. Obesity or any of a variety of issues
involving his eating habits would also be typical. At times he may deny his
depression and show some indifference about his physical symptoms or about
their consequences in his life. However, the secondary depression appears
only partly expressed through the physical concerns and as only limitedly
covered over. Depressive qualities would color the clinical picture with
occasional breakthroughs of open distress. Nevertheless, the current level
of organization of his immediate personal coping and practical self-
sufficiency tests as basically adequate and at times as reasonably good.

Talkative about his current situation and concerns, he tests as
repressive of internal feelings, as inhibited and avoiding of his conflicts
and as poorly facing his personal problems. His symptoms may gain him
reassuring attention and consideration, or effectively allow him to avoid or
to say "no" to unwanted demands. He tests as naive and lacking in insight,
and his acceptance of his angry feelings and sexual wishes appears poor.
Others are apt to see him as much more self-centered, demanding, irritable,
and emotional than he sees himself. He is also prone to frustration with
his place in life, but he would have serious difficulties in facing this.

His efforts to be contented, cooperative, friendly, and cheerful would
reflect his ideals but cover over his strong emotional reactions to
rejections, to frustrations of his demands and wishes, and to losses of
emotional support. He would be especially vulnerable to the death of a
family member or other separation from an emotionally supporting person,
tending to idealize the lost person and to reject criticism of them. His
family ties appear reasonably firm so that family and marital problems are
apt to be poorly faced or indirectly expressed through irritability. He
would be seen as stereotyped and inflexible in his handling of emotional
problems. He tests as mildly extroverted. His overall balance of interests
appears quite masculine, such as mechanical and outdoor activities along
with some disinterest in cultural and esthetic pursuits.

Similar patients have been described as being at a "throw in the
sponge" phase of their lives at the time of testing. Multiple childhood
rejections and deprivations were reported, including poor or alcoholic
fathers, emotionally ill parents, fathers or mothers who had died during the
patient's childhood, and families that lacked affection either because of

strict and rigid attitudes or through an immoral and disorganized pattern. As children these patients handled stresses by repressiveness and by learning passive and dependent roles. However, their emotional reactions became attached to strong psychophysiologic reaction patterns as well as being expressed through symbolic conversions of their anxiety. It has been speculated that these life-long conditioned autonomic reactions directly contributed to their high incidence of organic breakdowns and psychophysiologic disorders. They tended to marry adaptable and well-liked wives on whom they depended in subtle if not open ways, but they rejected their children's demands rather as they had been rejected in their own childhoods. The onset of symptoms then appeared to follow an upheaval of their balance of negative input over positive gratifications, especially if such an upheaval coincided with physical symptoms that produced a large increase in the person's sense of vulnerability.

DIAGNOSTIC IMPRESSION

Diagnoses of hysterical neurosis, conversion type, of hypochondriacal neurosis, and of psychophysiologic disorders are the most common with this pattern.

TREATMENT CONSIDERATIONS

The hysterical trends indicate a vulnerability to difficulties with dependency fostering drugs, particularly to barbiturates and analgesics. Medications and other medical interventions are apt to be short-lived in their effects; he appears suggestible and prone to develop side-effects. A serious polysurgical risk is indicated, and in many similar cases surgeries were followed by temporary benefits and persisting postoperative pain. Similar patients have often had prolonged and complicated surgical recoveries with needs for extended postoperative pushing in order to resume functioning; a great deal of caution would be indicated in hospitalizing him for medical treatment or in arranging extensive physical workups if the indications were unclear and equivocal.

Psychotherapeutic intervention is difficult where the patient is so strongly oriented toward physical illnesses and somatic explanations of his difficulties. Family consultation can be quite beneficial to evaluate the secondary gains and to arrange to minimize them. It can also be beneficial to inform them fully as to his current physical status, treatment needs, and capacity for work and activity. Stresses should be minimized if feasible, and work with the family may improve currently frustrating or rejecting relationships even if he does not identify them as such.

His mild tendencies to be self-protective in responding to the inventory may have involved both an element of conscious defensiveness and some more internalized or preconscious denial. This suggests considering how he expected the test results to be used. That is, he appears to have had some concerns lest the results reflect poorly on him or perhaps end up being hurtful to his self-interests. At the same time, the scores suggest a

hesitation to admit genuine personal problems to himself. How to respond to
his needs to so moderate his responses and to present a socially desirable
image of himself depends, of course, on the context and circumstances of the
testing. In general his emotional constrictions and his tendency to declare
certain topics "off limits" could necessitate careful handling and patience
in therapy.

Similar patients have frequently benefitted from the release of stored-
up emotions. Often their personal conflicts were identified in part by what
they specifically denied to be problems. Emotional catharsis is apt to
relate to past rejections, hurt feelings, and unsatisfied needs for care and
protection. Frequently this opened up around a loss of emotional support
through separation from a loved one or unresolved grief over a loss such as
the potentially permanent defeat of a crucial personal goal or the death of a
parent or other family member. Similar patients had great difficulties in
working through the anger phases of grief processes. An increased
acceptance of his self-centered wishes, inhibited impulses, and intense
emotions is apt to be the main benefit of treatment. Termination typically
has involved some "face-saving" against the implication that his problems
were all psychological; efforts to make such a face-saving adaptive rather
than surgically self-destructive or otherwise self-defeating have been
reported as beneficial.

Thank you for this referral.

Alex B. Caldwell, Ph.D.
Diplomate in Clinical Psychology

ABC/ps

The preceding analysis is basically actuarial and probabilistic in
nature in that the symptoms and personality characteristics presented in the
report have been identified as disproportionately frequent among individuals
obtaining similar scores and patterns of scores on the MMPI-2 (tm). The
diagnosis of any individual, however, needs to be based on the integration
of information from personal contacts, the person's history, other test
results, and whatever independent data are relevant and available.

This report has an overall focus on psychotherapy intake, differential
diagnosis, treatment planning, and related personality-dependent
determinations. It provides assistance in the diagnostic process by
providing an extended set of clinical hypotheses, the largest part of the
basis for which is data from traditional psychiatric settings. The
application of these hypotheses to an individual requires independent

confirmation of them by the clinician and an allowance for the specific
context of testing if it differs substantially from the primarily
psychotherapeutic database.

This report was prepared for our professional clientele. In most cases
this is confidential information and legally privileged. The ongoing
protection of this privilege becomes the responsibility of the professional
person receiving the attached material from Caldwell Report.

THE ADAPTATION AND ATTACHMENT HYPOTHESES SUPPLEMENT:

     The following paragraphs present my current hypotheses as to etiologic
and developmental factors that likely contribute to the behaviors associated
with the codetype to which this profile best conforms. The following
description characterizes a relatively serious if not severe level of
disturbance. Typically an individual with a moderate although not severely
elevated profile will show an intermediate level of sensitization so that
the adaptive responses to the aversive shaping experiences described below
are demanding of but not overwhelming of the person's attentional energy and
somewhat less disruptive of day-to-day functioning. THIS DESCRIPTION IS NOT
MODIFIED OR ADJUSTED TO THE LEVEL OF DISTURBANCE OR SECONDARY VARIATIONS OF
THIS PERSON'S PROFILE: IT IS AN ETIOLOGIC PROTOTYPE FOR ANYONE WITH THIS
GENERAL PATTERN TYPE. It is intended to generate hypotheses as to how the
individual "got this way". This prototype material will always be the same
for any profile corresponding to his code type. At least three fourths of
the reports currently processed will have these paragraphs--the other
quarter are of more or less rarely occurring codes, and for want of code-
specific data they will not have these paragraphs at this time.

     My belief is that all behaviors are adaptive given the person's
biologic/constitutional makeup and life experiences. An awareness of
adaptational benefits is potentially helpful: (1) in understanding the
origins and adaptive self-protections of the person's present behaviors, (2)
in providing test-result feedback to the client as well as in explaining the
person's conduct to judges and any other parties appropriately involved, and
(3) in guiding psychotherapeutic intervention. These inductive hypotheses
are based on an extensive searching for developmental information on pattern-
matched cases. Some interpretations are supported by published data (e.g.,
Gilberstadt & Duker, 1965, Hathaway & Meehl, 1951, Marks & Seeman, 1963),
etc., and others are based on clinically examining any cases I have been
able to access on whom pertinent information has been available. Your
feedback to me will be much appreciated regarding: (1) whatever in the
material that follows is clearly a misfit to this individual, (2) more
precisely targeted word choices, phrasing, and especially the person's own
words for crucial experiences, and (3) behavioral characteristics that are
likely to generalize to the code type but are missing here. For everyone's
sakes, don't hesitate to send me a note.

PROPOSED DIAGNOSIS: INTENSIFIED PAIN-FEAR CONDITIONING
ADAPTATION TO: experiences of simultaneous intense fear and acute bodily
pain and suffering
TRADITIONAL DIAGNOSIS: pain and conversion disorders (which latter
clinically have been mainly complaints of pain, much less often other more
esoteric, "classical" symptoms)
PROTOTYPIC CHARACTERISTICS: persisting physical distress concerns with a
related focus on personal hopes as well as on potential medical and
emotional sources of pain and distress relief. Especially when emotionally
upset, the range of physical discomforts and/or the intensity of reported

distress are greater than medically expected, even though there may be well-defined and understandably distressing organic medical disorders from which the person is suffering.

The individual frequently presents as very trusting: "I am a very friendly, reasonable person to whom this painful malady has befallen. I've had to be so brave". Pollyanna attitudes mark the avoidance of the pain of face-to-face anger. Always being "nice" increases the hope for solace when suffering. Failures to anticipate or "see" interpersonal conflicts or other imminently negative and upsetting outcomes can become a sort of "emotional blindness". At the extreme, e.g., 3-Hy over 85 or 90, this blindness seems unbelievable to many observers, who then think it must be faked, "nobody could be that unaware!" But the shifts of attention described below can be quite total. At age 12 my own mother lost her mother; she could never understand my sister's enjoyment of mystery programs on TV: "Somebody always dies".

CONTRIBUTORY SHAPING HISTORY: In those cases with health issues dating back to early age levels (perhaps minimized or denied by the person but confirmed by family members), such factors as multiple rejections and deprivations, poor families, rigid family values, and emotionally disorganized families can set the stage for the inhibiting of any negative emotional expressions, of always "looking the other way" in order not to make a painful situation worse. Note the incidence of pre-pubertal parental deaths in Marks & Seeman (1963): 60% of their 13/31 patients reported a "parent death" which was more than any other code type (the related 231 was at 55%; all of their other codes were at least somewhat less). My hypothesis is that familial inhibition of open expressions of emotional anguish (e.g., your father just died and you are told, "Be quiet--You must be brave") would tend to orient attention onto how badly your body feels, perhaps establishing or considerably enhancing a fear/distress to body pain association.

The intense fear can also be contiguous with bodily sensations. Repeated or extreme associations of fear with a specific sensory input can lead to an alteration of the perception of that input. For example, repeated exposure to terrifying sounds can lead to a reduction of hearing and "hysterical deafness". Caldwell Report will soon have available CD copies of a radio dramatization of Starke Hathaway's treatment of hysterical deafness in an adolescent girl (on a isolated Minnesota farm, the other three family members were all deaf but could lipread, and a suggestible 15 year old girl was the only source of warning and alarm for dangerous sounds during the night). A conditioned activation, night after night, of the olivocochlear bundle that inhibits transmission from the cochlea to the central nervous system would offer a potential explanatory mechanism for a valid perceptual reduction of what is heard. A selective deafness (what activated her fears and hence the neural bundle) eventually spread, and she "discovered" that she was deaf but could "lipread". Thus the conversion metaphor, her fears "converted" her desperate need not to hear into hysterical deafness. Note that hypothesizing the same distress-fear

conditioning etiology for pain disorders as for conversion disorders makes
the DSM separation seems a superficial if not arbitrarily symptomatic
distinction.

    In adult onset cases this profile pattern is often seen after a
terrifying injury or other bodily trauma. This is usually physically
dramatic to the individual, e.g., a large object falls, crashing down on
one's head (with little more than a momentary loss of consciousness), or a
soldier falls ill or is in acute physical pain in the midst of horrifying
combat. THE SIMULTANEOUS EXPERIENCING OF ACUTE BODILY PAIN WITH AN EXTREME
FRIGHT CONDITIONS THE ASSOCIATION OF THE TWO, i.e., UNEXPECTED PAIN AROUSES A
STRONG SENSE OF FEAR, AND OCCASIONS OF FEAR ACTIVATE DISTRESSING BODILY
SENSATIONS. For example, the threat of a tragic loss or of an angry
confrontation, when one has become acutely pain-fear sensitized, can quickly
arouse fear-associated physical symptoms and thus an immediate sense of
danger to the person's sense of physical well-being. Conversely, an
increment of pain or other somatic distress can arouse a heightened if not
intense level of fear; so much fear can generate a misattribution of the
perceived seriousness and the cause of the pain or an increased sensitivity
and awareness of any concurrent and previously mild or unnoticed
discomforts. For example, fear due to the experience of an unexpected
increase in a particular pain can set the stage for an at least transitory
"conversion" symptom (e.g., an accelerated heartbeat when threatened with a
major loss or someone's sharp attack, "Oh, my heart doesn't feel right. Did I
have some kind of a heart attack? I don't know if the tests the doctor made
were good enough"). Toward the extreme, some who are strongly pain-
sensitized seem to lose the basic ability to distinguish emotional pain from
bodily pain, so that an acute or potentially overwhelming emotional pain is
only experienced and expressed as physical anguish.

    The longer-term impact of such conditioning is the suppression of the
healthily normal range of emotional expressions of anguish and grief at the
time of an emotional upset as well as the confounding of subsequently self-
owned anger (consider, "That hurt me, and I am p..... off. I don't want you
to say that to me again". In contrast to, "What you said wasn't real nice;
it wasn't as sensitive as I know you can be"). Focusing on points of hope
operates to mitigate or inhibit upsets. I believe the shift of attention
toward a focus of hope (however faint and tenuous) is reinforced not only by
reduced annoyance and social avoidance by others at an interpersonal level
but also at a neurophysiologic level by conditioned metenkephalin/opioid
synthesis. Especially strong or autonomically dominant peripheral
vasoconstriction responses may have a significant connecting effect between
fear and the somatic focus, that is, peripheral vasoconstriction in response
to a fear threatening stimulus would focus the attention on "what is
happening in my body". To my awareness, whether injuries enhance subsequent
peripheral vasoconstriction is not known.

    I believe these heightened sensitivities to any perceived threats to
the person's hopes or sense of well-being lead to automatic shifts of
attention lest a surge of pain become overwhelming. Over time these shifts

become so automatic and smooth as not to be noticed by the person (nor even
by many professional observers if not attuned to watch for them).
Specifically, I consider REPRESSION be the outcome of innumerably repeated
shifts of attention away from some painful memory whenever a cue of that
memory is even remotely approached. The repetitive opioid reinforcements of
these shifts of attention away from the threat of the painful memory can
progressively make that memory inaccessible and hence "repressed". For
example, a woman in her early 70's presented with complaints of declining
memory and impaired attention, which did not test as neuropsychologically
nor neurologically explainable. A year or so earlier, a bit before the time
of the onset of her symptoms, her husband had choked to death at the dinner
table. She had not recalled that, at age 5 she was looking out a window of
her home and saw her father run over and killed by a truck, for many decades
until the too-similar tragedy precipitated obtaining treatment for her
symptoms; treatment eventually led to the memory. Thus, her distress
appeared to have been sharply intensified by the prior unresolved but
inaccessible grief, and successful treatment focused on resolving that
accumulated grief.

     A persisting CONVERSION symptom is the outcome of a repetitive shifting
of attention away from a distressing threat onto a familiar and habituated
physical pain, e.g., pressure to do something stressful is seen as somehow a
danger to physical systems such as an undue strain on one's vulnerable
heart. Belle indifference is the absence of emotional/fear arousal due to
the habituation together with the effectiveness of the automatic shifting of
attention in blocking the distress response to an imminent interpersonal
threat.

     DENIAL is the shift of attention away from an immediately distressing
input. A postoperative patient was asked about her husband who rarely
visited her in the hospital. Without a pause she said, "Oh, he was here two
days ago. Look at those beautiful flowers over there. Mrs. Freund brought
those from her garden. Aren't they gorgeous!" Or, after a noticeable
pause, another 31/13 patient reacted to Rorschach card VIII, "Such beautiful
colors! What do other people see in them"? It can be instructive to be
alert to such shifts in an interview, and possibly in therapy to immediately
ask, "You just made a shift in what we are talking about. Did something
just cross your mind?" Thus, the person adapts to the threat of a surge of
pain by reflexive and classically conditioned shifts of attention that
mitigate or avoid hope-breaking inputs.

     The Hy scale readily partitions into two limitedly correlated halves.
The degree of emphasis can vary widely from one person to another. Some can
have high elevations on the somatic part (Hy Obvious or Hy3 + Hy4) without
much elevation on the interpersonal part: the person is body suffering-
focused and consolation--and care--needy. Others can have high elevations
on the interpersonal trust part (Hy Subtle or Hy1 + Hy2 + Hy5) and be
problem-denying, Pollyanna, and approval-needy; a singular conversion
symptom can emerge in a period of intense stress and perceived threat. In
the preceding, I have attempted to illuminate the underlying connections

Sample Pain and Suffering   Page 10

between these halves. The subscales give us this balance.

        For codetype information see Gilberstadt and Duker, 1965; Gynther,
Altman, and Sletten, 1973; Marks and Seeman, 1963; Marks, Seeman, and
Haller, 1974; Prokop, 1988.

Name: Sample Pain and Suffering

Date:

MMPI-2 CRITICAL ITEMS

Only the items shown in boldface were answered in the critical direction.

Distress and Depression

5. I am easily awakened by noise. (True)
24. Evil spirits possess me at times. (True)
73. I am certainly lacking in self-confidence. (True)
130. I certainly feel useless at times. (True)
140. Most nights I go to sleep without thoughts or ideas bothering me. (False)
146. I cry easily. (True)
165. My memory seems to be all right. (FALSE)
170. I am afraid of losing my mind. (True)
180. There is something wrong with my mind. (TRUE)
233. I have difficulty in starting to do things. (True)
299. I cannot keep my mind on one thing. (TRUE)
301. I feel anxiety about something or someone almost all the time. (True)

Suicidal Thoughts

71. These days I find it hard not to give up hope of amounting to something. (True)
75. I usually feel that life is worthwhile. (False)
150. Sometimes I feel as if I must injure either myself or someone else. (True)
215. I brood a great deal. (True)
234. I believe I am a condemned person. (True)
246. I believe my sins are unpardonable. (True)
303. Most of the time I wish I were dead. (True)
454. The future seems hopeless to me. (True)
506. I have recently considered killing myself. (True)
520. Lately I have thought a lot about killing myself. (True)
524. No one knows it but I have tried to kill myself. (True)

Ideas of Reference, Persecution, and Delusions

42. If people had not had it in for me, I would have been much more successful. (True)
99. Someone has it in for me. (True)
138. I believe I am being plotted against. (True)
144. I believe I am being followed. (True)
162. Someone has been trying to poison me. (True)
228. There are persons who are trying to steal my thoughts and ideas. (True)
314. I have no enemies who really wish to harm me. (False)
333. People say insulting and vulgar things about me. (True)
336. Someone has control over my mind. (True)
361. Someone has been trying to influence my mind. (True)
466. Sometimes I am sure that other people can tell what I am thinking. (True)

Peculiar Experiences and Hallucinations

32. I have had very peculiar and strange experiences. (True)
60. When I am with people, I am bothered by hearing very queer things. (True)
96. I see things or animals or people around me that others do not see. (True)
198. I often hear voices without knowing where they come from. (True)
298. Peculiar odors come to me at times. (True)
311. I often feel as if things were not real. (True)
316. I have strange and peculiar thoughts. (True)
319. I hear strange things when I am alone. (True)
355. At one or more times in my life I felt that someone was making me do things by hypnotizing me. (True)

Aggressive Impulses

37. At times I feel like smashing things. (True)
85. At times I have a strong urge to do something harmful or shocking. (True)
134. At times I feel like picking a fist fight with someone. (True)
213. I get mad easily and then get over it soon. (True)
389. I am often said to be hotheaded. (True)

Authority Problems and Poor Control

35. Sometimes when I was young I stole things. (True)
50. I have often had to take orders from someone who did not know as much as I did. (True)
84. I was suspended from school one or more times for bad behavior. (True)
105. In school I was sometimes sent to the principal for bad behavior. (True)
240. At times it has been impossible for me to keep from stealing or shoplifting something. (True)
266. I have never been in trouble with the law. (False)

Sexual Difficulties

12. My sex life is satisfactory. (False)
34. I have never been in trouble because of my sex behavior. (False)
62. I have often wished I were a girl. (or if you are a girl) I have never been sorry that I am a girl. Male: (True) Female: (False)
121. I have never indulged in any unusual sex practices. (False)
166. I am worried about sex. (True)
268. I wish I were not bothered by thoughts about sex. (True)

Name: Sample Pain and Suffering

Date:

MMPI-2 CRITICAL ITEMS

Only the items shown in boldface were answered in the critical direction.

Alcohol and Drugs

168. I have had periods in which I carried on activities without knowing later what I had been doing. (True)
229. I have had blank spells in which my activities were interrupted and I did not know what was going on around me. (True)
264. I have used alcohol excessively. (True)
487. I have enjoyed using marijuana. (True)
489. I have a drug or alcohol problem. (True)
511. Once a week or more I get high or drunk. (True)
527. After a bad day, I usually need a few drinks to relax. (True)
540. I have gotten angry and broken furniture or dishes when I was drinking. (True)

Family Discord

21. At times I have very much wanted to leave home. (True)
83. I have very few quarrels with members of my family. (False)
125. I believe that my home life is as pleasant as that of most people I know. (False)
190. My people treat me more like a child than a grown-up. (True)

195. There is very little love and companionship in my family as compared to other homes. (True)
217. My relatives are nearly all in sympathy with me. (FALSE)
288. My parents and family find more fault with me that they should. (True)

Somatic Concerns

2. I have a good appetite. (False)
10. I am about as able to work as I ever was. (FALSE)
18. I am troubled by attacks of nausea and vomiting. (True)
47. I am almost never bothered by pains over the heart or in my chest. (False)
101. Often I feel as if there were a tight band about my head. (True)
111. I have a great deal of stomach trouble. (True)
141. During the past few years I have been well most of the time. (FALSE)
164. I seldom or never have dizzy spells. (FALSE)
175. I feel weak all over much of the time. (True)
176. I have very few headaches. (False)
224. I have few or no pains. (False)

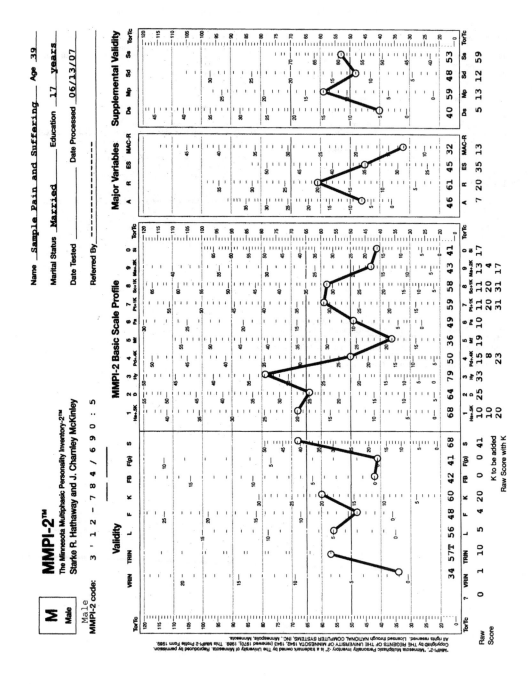

Name: Sample Pain and Suffering   Page 1 (MMPI-2)
Referred by: ----------------   Subscales
Date Tested:

2-D and Subscales

		RAW	T
D	(full scale)	25	64
D1	Subjective depression	8	53
D2	Indecision-retardation	6	54
D3	Health pessimism	5	67
D4	Mental dullness	7	72
D5	Brooding, loss of hope	1	45

6-Pa and Subscales

		RAW	T
Pa	(full scale)	10	49
Pa1	Persecutory ideas	0	40
Pa2	Poignant sensitivity	1	41
Pa3	Moral righteousness	8	65

3-Hy and Subscales

		RAW	T
Hy	(full scale)	33	79
Hy1	Denies social anxiety	6	61
Hy2	Need for affection	11	67
Hy3	Lassitude - malaise	8	75
Hy4	Somatic complaints	4	57
Hy5	Inhibits aggression	2	40

8-Sc and Subscales

		RAW	T
Sc	(full scale)	11	58
Sc1	Social alienation	1	43
Sc2	Emotional alienation	0	40
Sc3	Ego defect, cognitive	5	72
Sc4	Ego defect, conative	4	60
Sc5	Defective inhibition	1	47
Sc6	Sensorimotor dissociation	2	51

4-Pd and Subscales

		RAW	T
Pd	(full scale)	15	50
Pd1	Family discord	1	45
Pd2	Authority problems	2	40
Pd3	Social disinhibition	5	57
Pd4	Social alienation	3	45
Pd5	Self-alienation	1	38

9-Ma and Subscales

		RAW	T
Ma	(full scale)	13	43
Ma1	Opportunism	0	35
Ma2	Psychomotor acceleration	6	53
Ma3	Imperturbability	3	47
Ma4	Ego inflation	2	43

5-Mf and Subscales

		RAW	T
Mf	(full scale)	19	36
GM	Gender masculine	43	61
GF	Gender feminine	26	46

0-Si and Subscales

		RAW	T
Si	(full scale)	17	41
Si1	Shyness and self-consciousness	2	42
Si2	Social avoidance	1	41
Si3	Alienation - self and others	3	44

Name: Sample Pain and Suffering   Page 2 (MMPI-2)
Referred by: ----------------   Subscales
Date Tested:

Major Clinical Variables

		RAW	T
ES	Ego strength	35	45
MAC-R	Potential alcoholism	13	32
SAP	Teen drugs/alcohol	8	46
AAS		0	36
Mt	College maladjustment	15	56
N-P	Neurotic-psychotic profile balance		25

Interpersonal Style Variables

		RAW	T
ER-S	Ego resiliency	26	67
EC-5	Ego control	14	60
ORIG	Need novelty	11	38
INT	Abstract interests	54	55
Do	Need for autonomy	17	51
Dy	Need reassurances	10	44
Pr	Intolerance	3	37
Re	Value rigidity	26	65
Et	Ethnocentrism	5	38
St	Status mobility	20	57
R-S	Repression-sensitization	29	47
Lbp	Low back pain	13	69
O-H	Overcontrolled hostility	14	55
Ho	Cynical hostility	4	33
Ba	Good teamworker	50	60

Distress-Control

		RAW	T
A	Level of distress	7	46
R	Emotional constriction	20	61
Ca	Caudality-distress	6	45
Cn	Control-facade	17	40
So-r	Life as desirable	32	54
Th-r	Tired housewife	12	52
Wb-r	Worried breadwinner	10	46
PK	PTSD	4	43

Validity & Stability

		RAW	T
VRIN	Response inconsistency	1	34
TRIN	T-F inconsistency	10	57T
F-back	Rare answers - back	0	42
F(p)	Psychiatric infrequency	0	41
S	Superlative self-presentation	41	68
Ds	Overemphasize-fake sick	5	40
Mp	Consciously fake good	13	59
Sd	Consciously fake good	12	48
Ss	SES identification	59	53
Ch	Correction for H	10	42
Rc	Retest-consistency	28	59
Ic	Retest-item change	15	47
Tc	Retest-score change	12	48

Content Scales

		RAW	T
HEA	Health concerns	10	62
DEP	Depression	2	45
FAM	Family problems	1	37
ASP	Antisocial practices	0	30
ANG	Anger	4	46
CYN	Cynicism	0	32
ANX	Anxiety	7	53
OBS	Obsessiveness	2	41
FRS	Fears - phobias	5	54
BIZ	Bizarre mentation	0	39
LSE	Low self-esteem	0	35
TPA	Type A	8	48
SOD	Social discomfort	2	39
WRK	Work interference	8	52
TRT	Negative treatment indicators	1	39

Outpatient Mental Health Interpretive Report

MMPI-2™

The Minnesota Report™: Adult Clinical System-Revised, 4th Edition
James N. Butcher, PhD

Name:	William S.
ID Number:	2511
Age:	32
Gender:	Male
Marital Status:	Separated
Years of Education:	18
Date Assessed:	12/06/2004

MMPI-2™ Outpatient Mental Health Interpretive Report
12/06/2004, Page 2

ID: 2511
William S.

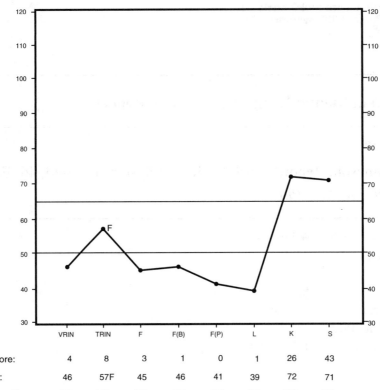

MMPI-2 VALIDITY PATTERN

	VRIN	TRIN	F	F(B)	F(P)	L	K	S
Raw Score:	4	8	3	1	0	1	26	43
T Score:	46	57F	45	46	41	39	72	71
Response %:	100	100	100	100	100	100	100	100

				Raw Score	T Score	Resp. %
Cannot Say (Raw):	0					
Percent True:	26	S1 - Beliefs in Human Goodness		14	67	100
Percent False:	74	S2 - Serenity		10	64	100
		S3 - Contentment with Life		6	60	100
		S4 - Patience/Denial of Irritability		8	68	100
		S5 - Denial of Moral Flaws		4	58	100

MMPI-2 CLINICAL AND SUPPLEMENTARY SCALES PROFILE

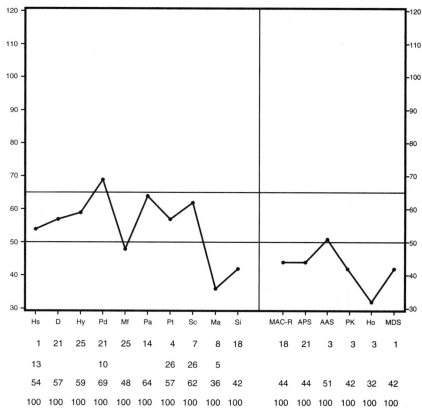

	Hs	D	Hy	Pd	Mf	Pa	Pt	Sc	Ma	Si	MAC-R	APS	AAS	PK	Ho	MDS
Raw Score:	1	21	25	21	25	14	4	7	8	18	18	21	3	3	3	1
K Correction:	13			10			26	26	5							
T Score:	54	57	59	69	48	64	57	62	36	42	44	44	51	42	32	42
Response %:	100	100	100	100	100	100	100	100	100	100	100	100	100	100	100	100

Welsh Code: 4+68-3271/50:9# K'+-/F:L#

Profile Elevation: 57.3

MMPI-2 CONTENT SCALES PROFILE

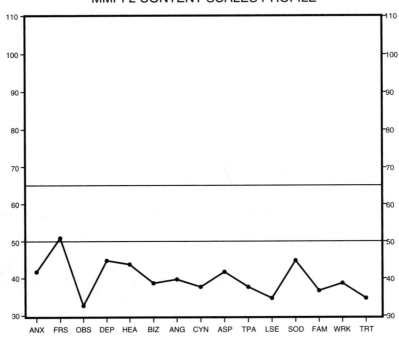

	ANX	FRS	OBS	DEP	HEA	BIZ	ANG	CYN	ASP	TPA	LSE	SOD	FAM	WRK	TRT
Raw Score:	2	4	0	2	3	0	2	2	4	3	0	5	1	2	0
T Score:	42	51	33	45	44	39	40	38	42	38	35	45	37	39	35
Response %:	100	100	100	100	100	100	100	100	100	100	100	100	100	100	100

PROFILE VALIDITY

This clinical profile has marginal validity because the client attempted to place himself in an overly positive light by minimizing faults and denying psychological problems. This defensive stance is characteristic of individuals who are trying to maintain the appearance of adequacy and self-control. This client tends to deny problems and is not very introspective or insightful about his own behavior.

His efforts to deny problems and present himself in a superlative manner might be understood more clearly by looking at the type of content he endorsed in a defensive manner. He approached the test items with a motivation to have others view him as a very well controlled person who never loses his temper or becomes irritated (as shown by his high score on S4, Patience or Denial of Irritability and Anger). In addition, he approached the test items with a desire to show that he has very positive views of other people. He endorsed a number of items on the Beliefs in Human Goodness subscale.

The clinical profile is likely to be an underestimate of the individual's psychological problems. He is likely to have little awareness of his difficulties. The client is likely to be rigid and inflexible in his approach to problems and may not be open to psychological self-evaluation. He is likely to project an excessively positive self-image and to be somewhat arrogant and intolerant of others' failings. He is unlikely to seek psychological treatment or to cooperate fully with treatment if it is suggested to him.

SYMPTOMATIC PATTERNS

The clinical scale prototype used in the development of this narrative included a prominent elevation on Pd. The client is somewhat immature and impulsive, a risk-taker who may do things others do not approve of just for the personal enjoyment of doing so. He is likely to be viewed as rebellious. He tends to be generally oriented toward thrill seeking and self-gratification. He may occasionally show bad judgment and tends to be somewhat self-centered, pleasure-oriented, narcissistic, and manipulative. He is not particularly anxious and shows no neurotic or psychotic symptoms.

PROFILE FREQUENCY

Profile interpretation can be greatly facilitated by examining the relative frequency of clinical scale patterns in various settings. The client's high-point clinical scale score (Pd) occurred in 9.1% of the MMPI-2 normative sample of men. However, only 3.3% of the normative men had Pd as the peak score equal to or greater than a T score of 65, and only 1.9% had well-defined Pd spikes.

The relative frequency of this profile in various outpatient settings is useful information for clinical interpretation. In the NCS Pearson male outpatient sample, this was the most frequent high-point clinical scale score (Pd), occurring in 17.8% of the sample. Additionally, 10.9% of the male outpatients had the Pd spike at or above a T score of 65, and 7.0% had well-defined Pd spikes.

PROFILE STABILITY

The relative elevation of the highest scales in his clinical profile reflects high profile definition. His high-point score on Pd is likely to remain stable over time. Short-term test-retest studies have shown a correlation of 0.81 for this high-point score. Spiro, Butcher, Levenson, Aldwin, and Bosse (2000) reported a moderate test-retest stability index of 0.67 in a large study of normals over a five-year test-retest period.

INTERPERSONAL RELATIONS

Individuals with this profile pattern tend to be rather likable and personable and may make a good first impression. His tendency to take personal risks and to act out at times may make it somewhat difficult to maintain close relationships.

Quite outgoing and sociable, he has a strong need to be around others. He is gregarious and enjoys attention. Personality characteristics related to social introversion-extraversion tend to be stable over time. The client is typically outgoing, and his sociable behavior is not likely to change if he is retested at a later time. His personal relationships are likely to be somewhat superficial. He appears to be rather spontaneous and expressive and may seek attention from others, especially to gain social recognition.

DIAGNOSTIC CONSIDERATIONS

This pattern is consistent with those of individuals whose personality traits predispose them to problems resulting from nonconformity.

TREATMENT CONSIDERATIONS

Individuals with this profile are generally not self-referred for therapy because they typically feel that they have few problems. They may be seen in mental health assessment settings as a result of court referral or at the insistence of a family member. They are usually not very motivated to change their behavior and may leave treatment prematurely.

Psychological treatment with this person may not be very successful because he tends to blame others for his problems.

Appendix B

MINNESOTA MULTIPHASIC PERSONALITY INVENTORY—ADOLESCENT

Only two computerized interpretive reports are available for the MMPI-A because the limited age range for which the MMPI-A is appropriate creates a smaller market. These computerized interpretive reports were developed for clinical settings. Both the Minnesota Report for the MMPI-A and the MMPI-A Interpretive System have been specialized for six additional settings.

These computerized interpretive reports are written to describe the *group* of adolescents that the adolescent who is being examined is most like. They are not stand-alone products that can be used without change. Each of these reports needs to be adapted to fit the clinical history and current behavior and symptoms for this adolescent. As such, the computerized interpretive report provides the general framework for beginning the process of understanding the adolescent.

Two samples of computerized interpretive reports for clinical settings using the MMPI-A follow. Readers should pay special attention to the caveats that precede these reports.

MMPI-A Interpretive System

developed by
Robert P. Archer, PhD
and
PAR Staff

Client Information

Name:	Sample Client
Client ID:	12345-67890
Gender:	Male
Date Of Birth:	11/26/1988
Age:	16
Grade Level:	11
Setting:	Drug/Alcohol
Test Date:	04/12/2005

The following MMPI-A interpretive information should be viewed as only one source of hypotheses about the adolescent being evaluated. No diagnostic or treatment decision should be based solely on these data. Instead, statements generated by this report should be integrated with other sources of information concerning this client, including additional psychometric test findings, mental status results, psychosocial history data, and individual and family interviews, to reach clinical decisions. The information contained in this report represents combinations of actuarial data derived from major works in the MMPI and MMPI-A literatures. This report is confidential and intended for use by qualified professionals only. It is recommended that clinicians do not release reports generated with this software to adolescents or their family members or guardians. This report should be released only if it is edited to incorporate information obtained from a comprehensive psychological evaluation about the adolescent. Clinicians should adhere to applicable ethical guidelines as well as state and federal regulations in handling computer-generated reports.

Client: Sample Client
ID#: 12345-67890

Test Date: 04/12/2005
Page 2

Profile Matches and Scores

	Client Profile	Highest Scale Codetype	Best Fit Codetype
Codetype match:		2-8/8-2	2-8/8-2
Coefficient of Fit:		0.884	0.884
Scores			
F (Infrequency)	60	67	67
L (Lie)	50	53	53
K (Correction)	40	55	55
Hs (Scale 1)	60	58	58
D (Scale 2)	90	67	67
Hy (Scale 3)	50	57	57
Pd (Scale 4)	50	57	57
Mf (Scale 5)	60	56	56
Pa (Scale 6)	55	52	52
Pt (Scale 7)	56	58	58
Sc (Scale 8)	95	67	67
Ma (Scale 9)	50	48	48
Si (Scale 0)	40	46	46
Codetype Definition in T Score Points:	30	9	9
Mean Clinical Scale Elevation:	63.0	58.0	58.0
Mean Excitatory Scale Elevation:	65.0	57.6	57.6
Mean Age - Females:		17.0	17.0
Mean Age - Males		14.7	14.7
Percent of Cases:		0.1	0.1

Configural clinical scale interpretation is provided in the report for the following codetype(s):
2-8/8-2

Unanswered (?) Items:	9
Welsh Code:	82*"'+1576349/0: F-L/K:

Client: Sample Client
ID#: 12345-67890

Test Date: 04/12/2005
Page 3

Validity and Clinical Scales

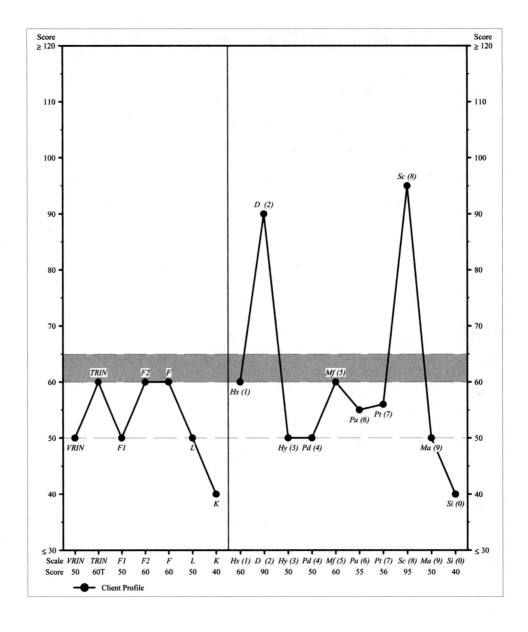

Scale	VRIN	TRIN	F1	F2	F	L	K	Hs (1)	D (2)	Hy (3)	Pd (4)	Mf (5)	Pa (6)	Pt (7)	Sc (8)	Ma (9)	Si (0)
Score	50	60T	50	60	60	50	40	60	90	50	50	60	55	56	95	50	40

—●— Client Profile

Client: Sample Client   Test Date: 04/12/2005
ID#: 12345-67890   Page 4

Content and Supplementary Scales

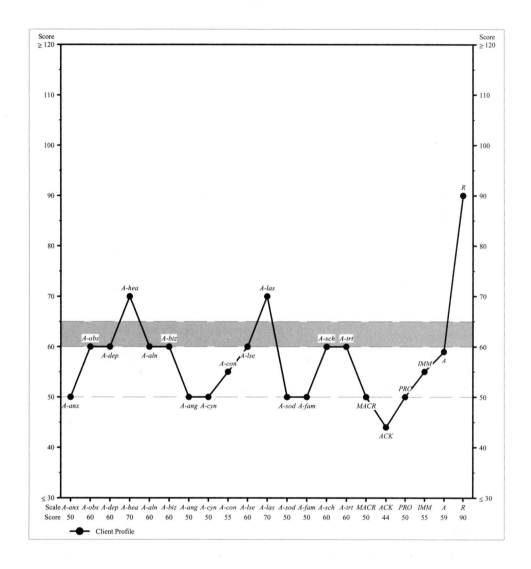

Scale	A-anx	A-obs	A-dep	A-hea	A-aln	A-biz	A-ang	A-cyn	A-con	A-lse	A-las	A-sod	A-fam	A-sch	A-trt	MACR	ACK	PRO	IMM	A	R
Score	50	60	60	70	60	60	50	50	55	60	70	50	50	60	60	50	44	50	55	59	90

—●— Client Profile

Client: Sample Client
ID#: 12345-67890

Test Date: 04/12/2005
Page 5

Harris – Lingoes and Si Subscales

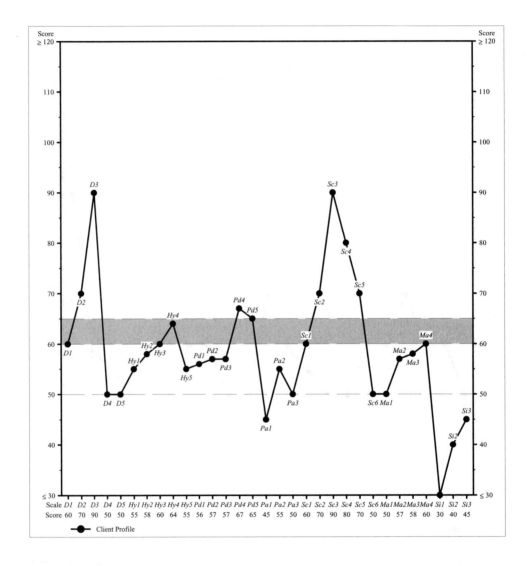

Scale	D1	D2	D3	D4	D5	Hy1	Hy2	Hy3	Hy4	Hy5	Pd1	Pd2	Pd3	Pd4	Pd5	Pa1	Pa2	Pa3	Sc1	Sc2	Sc3	Sc4	Sc5	Sc6	Ma1	Ma2	Ma3	Ma4	Si1	Si2	Si3
Score	60	70	90	50	50	55	58	60	64	55	56	57	57	67	65	45	55	50	60	70	90	80	70	50	50	57	58	60	30	40	45

━●━ Client Profile

Client: Sample Client
ID#: 12345-67890

Test Date: 04/12/2005
Page 6

Specified Setting

This adolescent was reported to have been in a drug and alcohol treatment setting at the time the MMPI-A was administered.

Configural Validity Scale Interpretation

This adolescent has produced a consistent MMPI-A response pattern reflected in acceptable values on validity scales *VRIN* and *TRIN*.

No configural hypotheses are available for this *F-L-K* scale pattern of scores.

Both *F1* and *F2* are below *T*-score values of 90. *T*-score values of 90 or greater on either *F1* or *F2* are likely to indicate problems with profile validity.

Validity Scales

Raw (?) = 9

There were a few items omitted in completing this MMPI-A. These omissions may represent areas of limitation in the adolescent's life experience which rendered certain items unanswerable, or limitations in the adolescent's reading ability. There is little probability of profile distortion as a result of these few item omissions.

Variable Response Inconsistency (*VRIN*) = 50

VRIN scores in this range suggest that the adolescent responded to test items with an acceptable level of consistency.

True Response Inconsistency (*TRIN*) = 60T

TRIN scores in this range suggest that the adolescent responded to test items with an acceptable level of consistency.

Infrequency 1 (*F1*) = 50

Scores in this range suggest that the adolescent has responded in a valid manner to items which appear in the first stage of the MMPI-A test booklet.

Infrequency 2 (*F2*) = 60

Scores in this range reflect a marginal or moderate elevation on unusual psychiatric symptomatology which appears in the latter stage of the MMPI-A test booklet.

Infrequency (*F*) = 60

Scores in this range are considered to be moderately elevated and indicate the possibility of significant psychological and emotional problems. This adolescent appears to be acknowledging unusual or infrequently endorsed symptomatology to a degree characteristically reported by teenagers receiving psychiatric treatment.

Lie (L) = 50

Scores in this range suggest an appropriate balance between the admission and denial of common social faults. These adolescents are often viewed as flexible and psychologically sophisticated.

Correction (K) = 40

Scores in this range are often produced by adolescents with poor self-concepts and limited resources for coping with stress. Adolescents in acute distress may produce similar scores, as may teenagers who are attempting to "fake bad" or exaggerate their degree of psychopathology.

Client: Sample Client
ID#: 12345-67890

Test Date: 04/12/2005
Page 8

Configural Clinical Scale Interpretation

2-8/8-2 Codetype

The MMPI-A profile may be classified as a 2-8/8-2 codetype which occurs in less than 1% of adolescent assessments in psychiatric settings.

Adolescents who obtain this profile type are characterized by fearfulness, timidity, anxiety, and social awkwardness. They appear to prefer a large degree of emotional distance from others, and are uncomfortable and anxious in interpersonal relationships. Teenagers with the 2-8/8-2 codetype often exhibit poor self-concept and poor self-esteem, and perceive themselves as awkward and inadequate. In both the adolescent and adult literature, this codetype has been associated with a higher frequency of suicidal behavior and more serious psychiatric symptomatology. Adolescents with this profile have been found to display a higher than average frequency of such symptoms as hallucinations, preoccupation with bizarre or unusual ideas, and unusual sexual beliefs.

Psychiatric diagnoses associated with this codetype include Schizoid Personality Disorder (301.20), Schizotypal Personality Disorder (301.22), Schizophreniform Disorder (295.40), Schizoaffective Psychosis, Depressed Type (295.70), and Major Depressive Disorder with Psychotic Features (296.X4). Isolation and repression have been reported as the primary defense mechanisms manifested by these adolescents. *Repression* scale results support the view that this is a significant defense for this adolescent. Given the association between suicidal behavior and this codetype, careful clinical evaluation of suicidal potential is indicated. The potential for engaging in suicidal behavior and the severity of psychopathology can be markedly exacerbated by substance use. The adolescent's substance use history should be taken into account when making a determination about his suicide risk. It would be expected that the development of a therapeutic relationship for adolescents with this codetype would be a relatively slow process, given these teenagers' interpersonal awkwardness and fearfulness. Finally, adolescents with this codetype might be evaluated for potential benefit from antipsychotic medications for the management of schizophrenic or thought-disordered symptomatology.

Clinical Scales

Scale 1 (*Hs*) = 60

The *T*-score value obtained for this basic MMPI-A scale is within a marginal or transitional level of elevation. Some of the following descriptors, therefore, may not be applicable for this adolescent.

Scores in this range are frequently obtained by adolescents who manifest a history of symptoms associated with hypochondriasis, including vague physical complaints and a preoccupation with body functioning, illness, and disease. Such elevated scores may also be obtained, however, by adolescents who are experiencing actual physical illness. The possibility of organic dysfunction should be carefully ruled out. High scores for adolescents on this scale often indicate the increased likelihood of neurotic diagnoses and the development of somatic responses to stress. These adolescents are typically seen by others as self-centered, dissatisfied, pessimistic, and demanding. The prognosis for psychological intervention is typically guarded, and these adolescents often display little insight in psychotherapy.

Scale 2 (*D*) = 90

Scores in this range are typically found for adolescents who are depressed, dissatisfied, hopeless, and self-depreciatory. They often experience apathy, loss of interest in daily activities, loss of self-confidence, and feelings of inadequacy and pessimism. Additionally, these adolescents often experience substantial feelings of guilt, worthlessness, and self-criticism, and may experience suicidal ideation. However, this degree of distress may serve as a positive motivator for psychotherapy efforts. The depressive affects and cognitions experienced by this adolescent may be exacerbated by his substance use, particularly if he abuses alcohol and/or sedatives. His level of disinhibition and depression may also significantly increase the potential for suicidal or other self-damaging behavior.

Scale 3 (*Hy*) = 50

The obtained score is within normal or expected ranges and this adolescent probably has the capacity to acknowledge unpleasant issues or negative feelings.

Scale 4 (*Pd*) = 50

The obtained score is within normal or expected ranges. This adolescent has a typical or average capacity to adhere to standard rules of social conduct and does not express or exhibit excessive problems with authority.

Scale 5 (*Mf*) = 60

The obtained score is within normal or expected ranges and indicates standard interest patterns in the traditional masculine activities.

Scale 6 (*Pa*) = 55

The obtained score is within normal or expected ranges, and this adolescent appears to be capable of engaging in interpersonal exchanges without excessive suspiciousness or distrust.

Scale 7 (*Pt*) = 56

The obtained score is within normal or expected ranges and this adolescent appears to be capable of meeting current life experiences without excessive worry or apprehension.

Scale 8 (*Sc*) = 95

Adolescents who score in this range are typically described as confused, disorganized, withdrawn, and alienated. They have strong feelings of inferiority, incompetence, and dissatisfaction, and are often reluctant to engage in interpersonal relationships. They are vulnerable to stress, easily upset, and may have poor reality testing ability. The possibility of schizophrenic symptoms should be investigated. It is very possible that the disorganization and impaired reality testing is, at least partially, the result of his substance abuse. Some substances, such as amphetamines and hallucinogens, may produce experiences such as these and efforts should be made to determine if the individual's pattern of drug or alcohol use is likely to have contributed to the noted problems with reality testing and disorganization.

Scale 9 (*Ma*) = 50

The obtained score is within normal or expected ranges and reflects a typical energy or activity level for normal adolescents.

Scale 0 (*Si*) = 40

Adolescents who score in this range are extroverted and gregarious. They appear to have strong needs for affiliation and are interested in social status and social recognition. Although socially competent and confident, these adolescents are often viewed by others as superficial and insincere in interpersonal relationships. Although often intellectually gifted, these teenagers frequently have a history of academic underachievement.

Outpatient Mental Health Interpretive Report

MMPI-A™

The Minnesota Report™: Adolescent System

James N. Butcher, PhD & Carolyn L. Williams, PhD

Name:	Rachel Sample
ID Number:	2611
Age:	15
Gender:	Female
Date Assessed:	01/22/2005

MMPI-A VALIDITY PATTERN

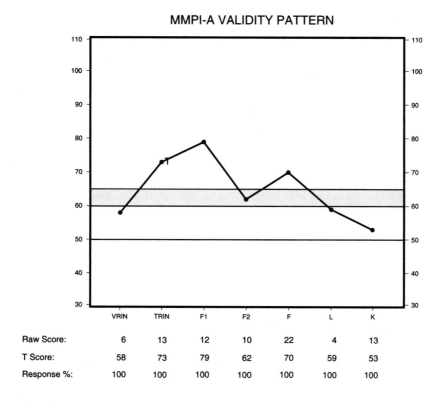

	VRIN	TRIN	F1	F2	F	L	K
Raw Score:	6	13	12	10	22	4	13
T Score:	58	73	79	62	70	59	53
Response %:	100	100	100	100	100	100	100

Cannot Say (Raw):	0
Percent True:	54
Percent False:	46

VALIDITY CONSIDERATIONS

She had a tendency to inconsistently respond True without adequate attention to item meaning. Although her TRIN score is not elevated enough to invalidate her MMPI-A, caution is suggested in interpreting and using the resulting profiles.

SYMPTOMATIC BEHAVIOR

This adolescent is immature, impulsive, and hedonistic, and she frequently rebels against authority. She may be hostile, aggressive, and frustrated. She seems unable to learn from punishing experiences and repeatedly gets into the same type of trouble. Many young people with this clinical profile develop severe acting-out problems and have legal, family, or school difficulties. This individual's nonconforming and impulsive lifestyle probably includes alcohol or drug problems.

Many externalizing behavior problems are likely. Her friends are frequently in trouble. They may cheat others and lie to avoid problems. They show little remorse for their misbehavior. If their difficulties pile up, they may run away.

The highest clinical scale in her MMPI-A clinical profile, Pd, occurs with very high frequency in adolescent alcohol/drug or psychiatric treatment units. Over 24% of girls in treatment settings have this well-defined peak score (i.e., with the Pd scale at least 5 points higher than the next scale). The Pd scale is among the least frequently occurring peak elevations in the normative girls' sample (about 3%).

Her MMPI-A Content Scales profile reveals important areas to consider in her evaluation. She endorsed a number of very negative opinions about herself. She reported feeling unattractive, lacking self-confidence, feeling useless, having little ability and several faults, and not being able to do anything well. She may be easily dominated by others.

She reported numerous problems in school, both academic and behavioral. She has limited expectations of success in school and is not very interested or invested in succeeding. She reported several symptoms of anxiety, including tension, worries, and difficulties sleeping. Symptoms of depression were reported.

INTERPERSONAL RELATIONS

She may appear charming and tends to make a good first impression, but she is selfish, hedonistic, and untrustworthy in interpersonal relations. She seems interested only in her own pleasure and is insensitive to the needs of others. She seems unable to experience guilt over causing others trouble.

Because she is unable to form stable, warm relationships, her current relationships are likely to be quite strained. In addition, she is likely to be openly hostile and resentful at times.

Some interpersonal issues are suggested by her MMPI-A Content Scales profile. Family problems are quite significant in this person's life. She reports numerous problems with her parents and other family members. She describes her family in terms of discord, jealousy, fault finding, anger, serious disagreements, lack of love and understanding, and very limited communication. She looks forward to the day when she can leave home for good, and she does not feel that she can count on her family in times of trouble. Her parents and she often disagree about her friends. She indicates that her parents treat her like a child and frequently punish her without cause. Her family problems probably have a negative effect on her behavior in school.

She feels considerable emotional distance from others. She may believe that other people do not like, understand, or care about her. She reports having no one, including parents or friends, to rely on.

BEHAVIORAL STABILITY

The relative elevation of the highest scale (Pd) in her clinical profile shows very high profile definition. Her peak scores are likely to remain very prominent in her profile pattern if she is retested at a later date. Her clinical profile tends to be associated with long-standing behavior problems.

DIAGNOSTIC CONSIDERATIONS

A diagnosis of one of the disruptive behavior disorders is highly likely given her elevations on Pd and A-con.

Given her elevation on the School Problems scale, her diagnostic evaluation could include assessment of possible academic skills deficits and behavior problems. Academic underachievement, a general lack of interest in any school activities, and low expectations of success are likely to play a role in her problems. Her endorsement of a significant number of depressive symptoms should be considered when arriving at a diagnosis.

She appears to be having difficulties that may involve the use of alcohol or other drugs. Adolescents with high scores on the PRO scale are usually involved with a peer group that uses alcohol or other drugs. This individual's involvement in an alcohol- or drug-using lifestyle should be further evaluated. Her use of alcohol or other drugs may be contributing to problems at home or in school. However, she has not acknowledged through her item responses that she has problems with alcohol or other drugs.

TREATMENT CONSIDERATIONS

Her serious conduct disturbance should figure prominently in any treatment planning. Her clinical scales profile suggests that she is a poor candidate for traditional, insight-oriented psychotherapy. A behavioral strategy is suggested. Clearly stated contingencies that are consistently followed are important for shaping more appropriate behaviors. Punishment techniques seem to have more limited success than positive rewards for appropriate behaviors. Treatment in a more controlled setting may need to be considered if there is no improvement in her behavior.

Her very high potential for developing alcohol or drug problems requires attention in therapy if important life changes are to be made. However, her relatively low awareness of or reluctance to acknowledge problems in this area might impede treatment efforts.

She should be evaluated for the presence of suicidal thoughts and any possible suicidal behaviors. If she is at risk, appropriate precautions should be taken.

Her family situation, which is full of conflict, should be considered in her treatment planning. Family therapy may be helpful if her parents or guardians are willing and able to work on conflict resolution. However, if family therapy is not feasible, it may be profitable during the course of her treatment to explore her considerable anger at and disappointment in her family. Alternate sources of emotional support from adults (e.g., foster parent, teacher, other relative, friend's parent, or neighbor) could be explored and facilitated in the absence of caring parents.

There are some symptom areas suggested by the Content Scales profile that the therapist may wish to consider in initial treatment sessions. Her endorsement of internalizing symptoms of anxiety and depression could be explored further.

She endorsed some items that indicate possible difficulties in establishing a therapeutic relationship. She may be reluctant to self-disclose, she may be distrustful of helping professionals and others, and she may believe that her problems cannot be solved. She may be unwilling to assume responsibility for behavior change or to plan for her future.

This adolescent's emotional distance and discomfort in interpersonal situations must be considered in developing a treatment plan. She may have difficulty self-disclosing, especially in groups. She may not appreciate receiving feedback from others about her behavior or problems.

MMPI-A CLINICAL AND SUPPLEMENTARY SCALES PROFILE

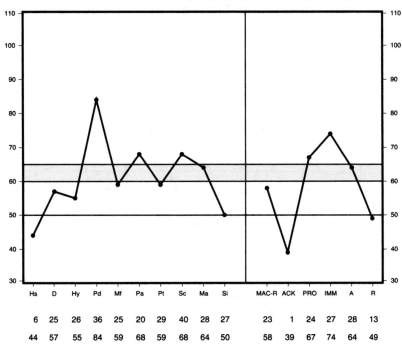

	Hs	D	Hy	Pd	Mf	Pa	Pt	Sc	Ma	Si	MAC-R	ACK	PRO	IMM	A	R
Raw Score:	6	25	26	36	25	20	29	40	28	27	23	1	24	27	28	13
T Score:	44	57	55	84	59	68	59	68	64	50	58	39	67	74	64	49
Response %:	100	100	100	100	100	100	100	100	100	100	100	100	100	100	100	100

Welsh Code: 4"68+9-57230/1: F'+-LK/

Mean Profile Elevation: 62.4

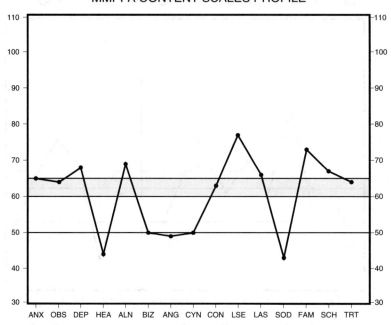

MMPI-A CONTENT SCALES PROFILE

	ANX	OBS	DEP	HEA	ALN	BIZ	ANG	CYN	CON	LSE	LAS	SOD	FAM	SCH	TRT
Raw Score:	15	12	18	5	12	4	9	14	13	14	10	4	23	11	15
T Score:	65	64	68	44	69	50	49	50	63	77	66	43	73	67	64
Response %:	100	100	100	100	100	100	100	100	100	100	100	100	100	100	100

SUPPLEMENTARY SCORE REPORT

	Raw Score	T Score	Resp %
Depression Subscales			
Subjective Depression (D1)	18	68	100
Psychomotor Retardation (D2)	4	46	100
Physical Malfunctioning (D3)	2	39	100
Mental Dullness (D4)	10	73	100
Brooding (D5)	7	65	100
Hysteria Subscales			
Denial of Social Anxiety (Hy1)	5	60	100
Need for Affection (Hy2)	5	50	100
Lassitude-Malaise (Hy3)	8	62	100
Somatic Complaints (Hy4)	3	44	100
Inhibition of Aggression (Hy5)	3	51	100
Psychopathic Deviate Subscales			
Familial Discord (Pd1)	7	66	100
Authority Problems (Pd2)	5	65	100
Social Imperturbability (Pd3)	6	67	100
Social Alienation (Pd4)	12	80	100
Self-Alienation (Pd5)	9	67	100
Paranoia Subscales			
Persecutory Ideas (Pa1)	12	79	100
Poignancy (Pa2)	5	57	100
Naivete (Pa3)	3	46	100
Schizophrenia Subscales			
Social Alienation (Sc1)	17	83	100
Emotional Alienation (Sc2)	7	76	100
Lack of Ego Mastery, Cognitive (Sc3)	7	67	100
Lack of Ego Mastery, Conative (Sc4)	11	75	100
Lack of Ego Mastery, Defective Inhibition (Sc5)	3	44	100
Bizarre Sensory Experiences (Sc6)	4	46	100

	Raw Score	T Score	Resp %
Hypomania Subscales			
Amorality (Ma1)	3	55	100
Psychomotor Acceleration (Ma2)	8	54	100
Imperturbability (Ma3)	5	64	100
Ego Inflation (Ma4)	6	58	100
Social Introversion Subscales (Ben-Porath, Hostetler, Butcher, & Graham)			
Shyness / Self-Consciousness (Si1)	3	40	100
Social Avoidance (Si2)	1	45	100
Alienation--Self and Others (Si3)	12	60	100

Uniform T scores are used for Hs, D, Hy, Pd, Pa, Pt, Sc, Ma, and the content scales; all other MMPI-A scales use linear T scores.

SUGGESTED ITEMS FOR FOLLOW-UP

The following item level indicators suggest symptoms for further evaluation.

Suicidal Behaviors
283. Omitted Item (True)

End of Report

Special Note:
The content of the test items
is included in the actual reports.
To protect the integrity of the test,
the item content does not appear
in this sample report.

NOTE: This MMPI-A interpretation can serve as a useful source of hypotheses about adolescent clients. This report is based on objectively derived scale indexes and scale interpretations that have been developed with diverse groups of clients from adolescent treatment settings. The personality descriptions, inferences, and recommendations contained herein need to be verified by other sources of clinical information because individual clients may not fully match the prototype. The information in this report should most appropriately be used by a trained, qualified test interpreter.

This and previous pages of this report contain trade secrets and are not to be released in response to requests under HIPAA (or any other data disclosure law that exempts trade secret information from release). Further, release in response to litigation discovery demands should be made only in accordance with your profession's ethical guidelines and under an appropriate protective order.

Appendix C

MILLON CLINICAL MULTIAXIAL INVENTORY-II/III

Only one computerized interpretive report is available for the MCMI-II/III that was developed initially for clinical settings. The MCMI-II/III Correctional Report was developed subsequently because of the frequency with which the MCMI-II/III is used in correctional settings.

This computerized interpretive report is written to describe the *group* of individuals that the individual who is being examined is most like. It is not a stand-alone product that can be used without change. The report needs to be adapted to fit the clinical history and current behavior and symptoms for this individual. As such, the computerized interpretive report provides the general framework for beginning the process of understanding the individual.

A sample of the computerized interpretive report for clinical settings with the MCMI-II/III follows. Readers should pay special attention to the caveats that precede this report.

Millon Clinical Multiaxial Inventory II/III

Narrative Report

by

Robert J. Craig, PhD
and
PAR Staff

Client Information

Client Name:	Sample
Client ID:	
Date of Evaluation:	03/13/2006
Age:	43
Gender:	Male
Education:	12
Marital Status:	Single
Setting:	Inpatient

The MCMI (as revised) was normed on individuals being evaluated or treated in mental health settings. Thus, the test should only be used with individuals who are in similar clinical settings for problems that are defined as psychological/psychiatric. Administering this test to people without clinical symptoms is inappropriate and will result in inaccurate descriptions of their functioning. Because this test is focused on personality disorders and clinical symptoms, the report is necessarily focused on these problematic behaviors, and cannot describe a person's strengths and competencies.

The interpretive information contained in this report should be viewed as only one source of hypotheses about the individual being evaluated. No decisions should be based solely on the information contained in this report. This material should be integrated with all other sources of information in reaching professional decisions about this individual. This report is confidential and intended for use by qualified professionals only. It should not be released to the individual being evaluated.

Client: Sample
ID#:

Test Date: 03/13/2006
Page 2

MCMI – II/III Profile

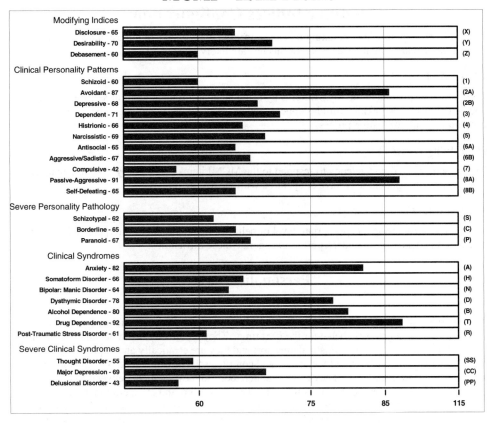

Client: Sample
ID#:

Test Date: 03/13/2006
Page 3

Modifier Indices Configurations

This patient's response style in taking this test appeared to be open and honest and no response distortions appear evident. The results of this test are likely to be valid.

Disclosure Level (X)

This patient responded to the MCMI items by using an appropriate amount of self-disclosure, and no defensive test-taking attitudes appear evident. This suggests that the patient was cooperative with the testing process.

Desirability Gauge (Y)

This patient showed no tendency to respond to the MCMI items in a socially desirable manner. This suggests the patient may have cooperated with the testing process.

Debasement (Z)

This patient is reporting an appropriate level of behavioral, emotional, or interpersonal problems and shows no tendency to underreport or exaggerate those difficulties.

Personality Style

8A2A'

These patients display a mixture of passive compliance and obedience at one time and then oppositional and negativistic behavior the next time. They are moody, irritable, and hostile; they manifest a grumbling and pessimistic demeanor; and they are erratically and explosively angry and stubborn at one moment and feel guilty and contrite at the next moment. Disillusionment seems to permeate their lives. They feel misunderstood, so they vacillate between passive dependency and stubborn contrariness that provokes discomfort and exasperation in those around them. They expect disappointment and maintain an unstable and conflictual role in relations with others. They sulk, feel unappreciated and/or feel they are being treated unfairly, constantly complain, and are persistently petulant and discontented. They often have problems with authority and, if employed, have job difficulties.

This patient presents as socially awkward, withdrawn, introverted, and self-conscious. Because people such as this patient are hypersensitive to rejection and fear negative evaluations, they either try to maintain a good social appearance despite their underlying fear or they withdraw from social contacts. Tension, anxiety, and anger also may be present but all stemming from the same issue--a desire for social acceptance and a fear of rejection. Most often, they maintain a social distance in order to avoid any further experience of being rejected. They are devastated by perceived signs of disapproval and tend to withdraw, thus reducing the chance to enhance relationships. This circumstance results in social isolation despite a very strong need for social relatedness. These patients can put on a pleasant appearance to mask their underlying social anxiety, but they have a pervasive belief that others will be disparaging of them. Their essential conflict is a strong desire to relate but an equally strong expectation of disapproval, depreciation, and rejection. This conflict results in keeping others at a distance but also in loneliness, isolation, and continued shyness and timidity. These people are at risk for social phobias.

Commentary: Elevations in Scale 8A are a good indicator of problems with authority and with criminal behaviors or potential for criminal behavior. Also, clinical elevations on this scale appear in a number of profile codes involving psychiatric patients. Patients with elevations on Scale 8A warrant close clinical evaluation.

Possible Diagnosis: Personality Disorder Not Otherwise Specified, Passive-Aggressive (negativistic) and Avoidant Personality Disorder.

Additional Personality Disorder Scales

This section provides narrative statements covering scales that were not considered primary in the profile code. However, this section may contain important information on additional personality traits. In some cases, information in these scales may appear inconsistent or contradictory to statements made in the main report. The clinician needs to determine which statements are applicable to the individual patient.

Schizoid (1)

This patient is likely to be viewed as a wallflower. Interpersonal relationships are generally absent but, if present, they do not seem central to the patient's personal happiness. Traits that describe scores at this level include introverted, quiet, dependent, self-sacrificing, passive, timid, and uncommunicative. Such people appear emotionally bland and even indifferent to events in their lives. These patients may lack affective expression with deficiencies in social communication. They prefer a simple life and defer to someone else in the management of their day-to-day life. They have little drive or ambition and prefer isolated activities to group involvement. If this patient is in a committed relationship, the spouse may complain about this person's lack of affection and, perhaps, reduced interest in sex.

Depressive (2B)

This patient has reported some traits associated with a depressive personality style but not in sufficient quantity to be diagnostically significant.

Dependent (3)

This patient has mild dependency needs that seem to drive many aspects of behavior. Timidity, some withdrawal tendencies, passivity, and perhaps demureness may be part of the personality constellation. Personal needs are sometimes sacrificed in order for the patient to please others. The patient does not take a dominant role in relationships and may take on too many tasks in order to please significant others. The patient is unlikely to erupt in emotional outbursts. These traits are not at sufficient intensity to warrant a personality disorder diagnosis and are more stylistic in nature than pathological.

Histrionic (4)

This patient has high needs for attention, recognition, and praise, and has a gregarious and extroverted personality style. Rather than acting seductively, dramatically, or in a manipulative manner, which characterizes patients who score at higher levels on this scale, the patient uses a natural charm and wit to have these needs met. When the patient becomes overly demanding, it usually is with close family relationships or within a work setting. Rarely is this style a cause of interpersonal disruption.

Narcissistic (5)

This patient shows some evidence of narcissistic-like traits. It is not possible to determine exactly which ones are manifest, and a clinical interview would be needed for more exact characterization. This patient probably does have high self-esteem.

Antisocial (6A)

This patient shows some evidence of antisocial-like traits. It is not possible to determine exactly which ones are manifest, and a clinical interview would be needed for more exact characterization.

Aggressive/Sadistic (6B)

This patient shows some evidence of aggressive traits. It is not possible to determine exactly which ones are manifest, and a clinical interview would be needed for more exact characterization.

Compulsive (7)

Millon does not provide information on nor does he interpret low scale scores. However, a low score on Compulsive might suggest a lack of conformity and low impulse control.

Self-Defeating (8B)

This patient shows some evidence of self-defeating traits. It is not possible to determine exactly which ones are manifest and a clinical interview would be needed for more exact characterization.

Schizotypal (S)

This patient shows few, if any, symptoms, behaviors, or traits associated with a schizotypal personality disorder.

Borderline (C)

This patient shows some evidence of borderline traits. It is not possible to determine exactly which ones are manifest and a clinical interview would be needed for more exact characterization.

Paranoid (P)

This patient shows few, if any, symptoms, behaviors, or traits associated with a paranoid personality disorder.

Client: Sample   *Test Date: 03/13/2006*
ID#:   *Page 6*

Clinical Syndromes

Anxiety (A)

This patient has reported many symptoms associated with anxiety. High scores on this scale are often seen in patients who are restless, anxious, apprehensive, edgy, and jittery. These patients tend to have a variety of somatic complaints associated with physiological overarousal. These complaints could include insomnia, headaches, nausea, cold sweats, undue perspiration, clammy hands, and palpitations. These symptoms appear to be experienced by the patient at a moderate degree of intensity.

Somatoform Disorder (H)

This patient shows only mild tendencies toward somatization.

Bipolar: Manic Disorder (N)

This patient reports some manic-like symptoms. The cause may be related to substance abuse, or the patient may have a recently developed Bipolar Affective Disorder and is self-medicated with substance abuse. A closer clinical evaluation is suggested.

Dysthymic Disorder (D)

This patient is reporting many problems and symptoms associated with depression. These problems and symptoms may include apathy, social withdrawal, guilt, pessimism, low self-esteem, feelings of inadequacy and worthlessness, self-doubts, and a diminished sense of pleasure. Generally, such patients can meet their day-to-day responsibilities but continue to experience a chronic dysphoria. A diagnosis associated with depression is usually associated with scores at this level, with Dysthymic Disorder being the most prevalent diagnosis. However, this depression may be secondary to substance abuse, particularly alcoholism or alcohol abuse. A more thorough clinical evaluation is recommended to determine if there are vegetative signs of depression and to determine which disorder, depression or substance abuse, is primary.

Possible Diagnosis: Rule out Dysthymic Disorder; Rule out Alcohol Abuse or Dependence; Rule out Drug Abuse or Dependence.

Alcohol Dependence (B)

This patient has reported symptoms and traits commonly associated with alcohol abuse and/or alcohol dependence. It also is possible that the patient has endorsed personality traits often seen in patients who subsequently develop problematic drinking. It also is possible that the patient has had problems with alcohol and is in recovery. A more thorough evaluation of the patient's drinking history, pattern and problems is recommended.

Drug Dependence (T)

This patient has reported symptoms and traits commonly associated with drug abuse and/or drug dependence. It also is possible that the patient has endorsed personality traits often seen in patients who subsequently develop problems associated with drug abuse. It also is possible that the patient has had problems with drugs and is in recovery. A more thorough clinical evaluation should be conducted to determine the presence of any specific problems that may be associated with this condition (e.g., medical, social, legal, psychological, psychiatric, vocational, spiritual). Scores at this level almost always reflect a diagnosis associated with drug abuse.

Possible Diagnosis: Drug Abuse/Dependence.

Post-Traumatic Stress Disorder (R)

This patient reports no symptoms associated with post-traumatic stress disorder.

Thought Disorder (SS)

This patient reports no abnormalities consistent with a thought disorder.

Major Depression (CC)

This patient is reporting some mild signs of depression, but not of sufficient severity to impair daily functioning.

Delusional Disorder (PP)

This patient reports no symptoms associated with a delusional disorder.

Research

The following studies have found this codetype among the populations indicated below:

8A2A'

(1) 25 Vietnam veterans with PTSD (Robert, J. A., Ryan, J. J., McEntyre, W. L., McFarland, R. S., Lips, O. J., & Rosenberg, S. J. [1985]. MCMI characteristics of *DSM-III*: Posttraumatic stress disorder in Vietnam veterans. *Journal of Personality Assessment, 49*, 226-230.)

(2) 144 depressed alcoholics (McMahon, R. C., & Davidson, R. S. [1986]. An examination of depressed vs. nondepressed alcoholics in inpatient treatment. *Journal of Clinical Psychology, 42*, 177-184.)

(3) 189 Vietnam veterans with PTSD (Sherwood, R. J., Funari, D. J., & Piekarski, A. M. [1990]. Adapted character styles of Vietnam veterans with posttraumatic stress disorder. *Psychological Reports, 66*, 623-631.)

(4) 100 Vietnam veterans with PTSD (Hyer, L. A., Albrecht, J. W., Boudewyns, P. A., Woods, M. G., & Brandsma, J. [1993]. Dissociative experiences of Vietnam veterans with chronic posttraumatic stress disorder. *Psychological Reports, 73*, 519-530.)

(5) 34 angry, nonpsychotic, black, psychiatric inpatients (Greenblatt, R. L., & Davis, W. E. [1992]. Accuracy of MCMI classification of angry and psychotic Black and White patients. *Journal of Clinical Psychology, 48*, 59-63.)

(6) Cluster analysis Type I Vietnam veterans with PTSD (sample size not indicated) (Hyer, L., Davis, H., Albrecht, W., Boudewyns, P. A., & Woods, G. [1994]. Cluster analysis of MCMI and MCMI-II of chronic PTSD victims. *Journal of Clinical Psychology, 50*, 502-515.) (MCMI-II)

(7) 69 patients treated in a military mental hygiene clinic (Rudd, M. D., & Orman, D. T. [1996]. Millon Clinical Multiaxial Inventory profiles and maladjustment in the military: Preliminary findings. *Military Medicine, 161*, 349-351.)

(8) 182 male and 73 female substance abusers (Nadeau, L., Landry, M., & Racine, S. [1999]. Prevalence of personality disorders among clients in treatment for addiction. *Canadian Journal of Psychiatry, 44*, 592-596.)

References

Additional interpretive material and test information is available in the following resources. The reader is encouraged to consult these sources for more specific test information.

Choca, J. P. (2003). *Interpretive guide to the Millon Clinical Multiaxial Inventory* (3rd ed.). Washington, DC: American Psychological Association.

Craig, R. J. (1993). *Psychological assessment with the Millon Clinical Multiaxial Inventory (II): An interpretive guide*. Odessa, FL: Psychological Assessment Resources.

Craig, R. J. (Ed.) (1993). *The Millon Clinical Multiaxial Inventory: A clinical research information synthesis*. Hillsdale, NJ: Erlbaum.

Craig, R. J. (Ed.). (2005). *New directions in interpreting the Millon Clinical Multiaxial Inventory-III (MCMI-III)*. New York: Wiley.

Millon, T., Davis, R., & Millon, C. (1997). *Millon Clinical Multiaxial Inventory-III (MCMI-III) manual*. Bloomington, MN: Pearson Assessments.

Appendix D

PERSONALITY ASSESSMENT INVENTORY

Only one computerized interpretive report is available for the PAI that was developed initially for clinical settings. Subsequently interpretive reports have been developed for correctional settings and personnel screening of safety officers because of the frequency with which the PAI is used in these settings.

This computerized interpretive report is written to describe the *group* of individuals that the individual who is being examined is most like. It is not a stand-alone product that can be used without change. The report needs to be adapted to fit the clinical history and current behavior and symptoms for this individual. As such, the computerized interpretive report provides the general framework for beginning the process of understanding the individual.

A sample of the computerized interpretive report for a clinical setting using the PAI follows. Readers should pay special attention to the caveats that precede this report.

PERSONALITY ASSESSMENT INVENTORY™

Clinical Interpretive Report

by

Leslie C. Morey, PhD
and PAR Staff

Client Information

Client Name	:	Sample A. Client
Client ID	:	12-3456789
Age	:	28
Gender	:	Male
Education	:	12
Marital Status	:	Single
Test Date	:	07/12/2000
Prepared For	:	-Not Specified-

The interpretive information contained in this report should be viewed as only one source of hypotheses about the individual being evaluated. No decisions should be based solely on the information contained in this report. This material should be integrated with all other sources of information in reaching professional decisions about this individual.

This report is confidential and intended for use by qualified professionals only. It should not be released to the individual being evaluated.

Full Scale Profile

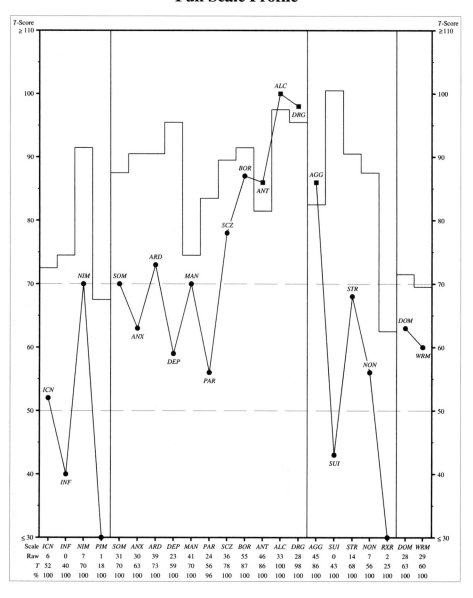

Scale	ICN	INF	NIM	PIM	SOM	ANX	ARD	DEP	MAN	PAR	SCZ	BOR	ANT	ALC	DRG	AGG	SUI	STR	NON	RXR	DOM	WRM
Raw	6	0	7	1	31	30	39	23	41	24	36	55	46	33	28	45	0	14	7	2	28	29
T	52	40	70	18	70	63	73	59	70	56	78	87	86	100	98	86	43	68	56	25	63	60
%	100	100	100	100	100	100	100	100	100	96	100	100	100	100	100	100	100	100	100	100	100	100

Plotted *T* scores are based upon a census matched standardization sample of 1,000 normal adults.
■ indicates that the score is more than two standard deviations above the mean for a sample of 1,246 clinical patients.
◆ indicates that the scale has more than 20% missing items.

Personality Assessment Inventory™ Clinical Interpretive Report   Page 3
Client ID   :   12-3456789
Test Date   :   07/12/2000

Subscale Profile

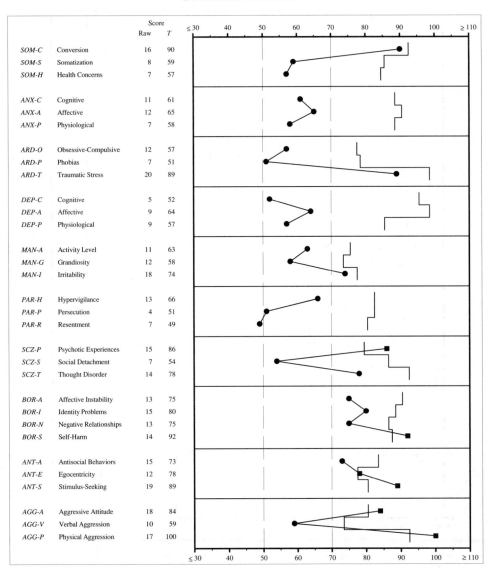

		Score Raw	T
SOM-C	Conversion	16	90
SOM-S	Somatization	8	59
SOM-H	Health Concerns	7	57
ANX-C	Cognitive	11	61
ANX-A	Affective	12	65
ANX-P	Physiological	7	58
ARD-O	Obsessive-Compulsive	12	57
ARD-P	Phobias	7	51
ARD-T	Traumatic Stress	20	89
DEP-C	Cognitive	5	52
DEP-A	Affective	9	64
DEP-P	Physiological	9	57
MAN-A	Activity Level	11	63
MAN-G	Grandiosity	12	58
MAN-I	Irritability	18	74
PAR-H	Hypervigilance	13	66
PAR-P	Persecution	4	51
PAR-R	Resentment	7	49
SCZ-P	Psychotic Experiences	15	86
SCZ-S	Social Detachment	7	54
SCZ-T	Thought Disorder	14	78
BOR-A	Affective Instability	13	75
BOR-I	Identity Problems	15	80
BOR-N	Negative Relationships	13	75
BOR-S	Self-Harm	14	92
ANT-A	Antisocial Behaviors	15	73
ANT-E	Egocentricity	12	78
ANT-S	Stimulus-Seeking	19	89
AGG-A	Aggressive Attitude	18	84
AGG-V	Verbal Aggression	10	59
AGG-P	Physical Aggression	17	100

Missing Items = 1

Plotted *T* scores are based upon a census matched standardization sample of 1,000 normal adults.
■ indicates that the score is more than two standard deviations above the mean for a sample of 1,246 clinical patients.
◆ indicates that the scale has more than 20% missing items.

Additional Profile Information

Supplemental PAI Indexes

Index	Value	*T* Score	
Defensiveness Index	1	38	
Cashel Discriminant Function	129.91	44	
Malingering Index	2	71	
Rogers Discriminant Function	-4.09	21	
Suicide Potential Index	13	81	
Violence Potential Index	13	102	
Treatment Process Index	9	91	
ALC Estimated Score	---	84	($16T$ lower than *ALC*)
DRG Estimated Score	---	89	($9T$ lower than *DRG*)
Mean Clinical Elevation	---	76	

Coefficients of Fit with Profiles of Known Clinical Groups

Database Profile	Coefficient of Fit
Drug abuse	0.806
Mania	0.796
Alcoholic	0.781
Antisocial Personality Disorder	0.776
Rapists	0.773
Current aggression	0.772
Prisoners	0.751
Assault history	0.742
Spouse abusers	0.694
Cluster 4	0.677
PIM Predicted	0.673
Cluster 9	0.661
NIM Predicted	0.626
All "Very True"	0.545
Self-Mutilation	0.506
All "Mainly True"	0.491

Database Profile	Coefficient of Fit
Cluster 6	0.485
Posttraumatic Stress Disorder	0.447
Cluster 3	0.442
Schizoaffective Disorder	0.433
Auditory hallucinations	0.419
Borderline Personality Disorder	0.419
Fake Bad	0.412
Anxiety Disorder	0.412
Suicide history	0.399
Paranoid delusions	0.393
Random responding	0.382
Dysthymic Disorder	0.379
Cluster 5	0.375
Cluster 1	0.371
Major Depressive Disorder	0.347
Antipsychotic medications	0.339
Cluster 2	0.315
Adjustment reaction	0.306
Schizophrenia	0.294
Current suicide	0.242
Cluster 7	0.218
All "Slightly True"	0.191
Cluster 8	0.157
Somatoform Disorder	0.155
Cluster 10	0.053
All "False"	-0.315
Fake Good	-0.480

Validity of Test Results

The PAI provides a number of validity indices that are designed to provide an assessment of factors that could distort the results of testing. Such factors could include failure to complete test items properly, carelessness, reading difficulties, confusion, exaggeration, malingering, or defensiveness. For this protocol, the number of uncompleted items is within acceptable limits.

Also evaluated is the extent to which the respondent attended appropriately and responded consistently to the content of test items. The respondent's scores suggest that he did attend appropriately to item content and responded in a consistent fashion to similar items.

The degree to which response styles may have affected or distorted the report of symptomatology on the inventory is also assessed. The scores for these indicators fall in the normal range, suggesting that the respondent answered in a reasonably forthright manner and did not attempt to present an unrealistic or inaccurate impression that was either more negative or more positive than the clinical picture would warrant.

Clinical Features

The PAI clinical profile is marked by significant elevations across several scales, indicating a broad range of clinical features and increasing the possibility of multiple diagnoses. Profile patterns of this type are usually associated with marked distress and severe impairment in functioning. The configuration of the clinical scales suggests a person with a history of polysubstance abuse, including alcohol as well as other drugs. When disinhibited by the substance use, other acting-out behaviors may become apparent as well. The substance abuse is probably causing severe disruptions in his social relationships and his work performance, with these difficulties serving as additional sources of stress and perhaps further aggravating his tendency to drink and use drugs.

The respondent reports that his use of alcohol has had a negative impact on his life to an extent that is higher than average even among individuals in treatment for alcohol problems. Such a pattern indicates that his use of alcohol has had a number of adverse consequences on his life. Numerous alcohol-related problems are probable, including difficulties in interpersonal relationships, difficulties on the job, and possible health complications. He is likely to be unable to cut down on his drinking despite repeated attempts at sobriety. Given this pattern, it is increasingly likely that he is alcohol-dependent and has suffered the consequences in terms of physiological signs of withdrawal, lost employment, strained family relationships, and financial hardship.

The respondent indicates that his use of drugs has had many negative consequences on his life at a level that is above average even for individuals in specialized treatment for drug problems. Such a pattern indicates that his use of drugs has had numerous ill effects on his functioning. Problems associated with drug abuse are probably found across several life areas, including strained interpersonal relationships, legal difficulties, vocational failures, financial hardship, and/or possible medical complications resulting from prolonged drug use. He reports having little ability to control the effect that drugs are having on his life. With this level of problems it is increasingly likely that he is drug-dependent and withdrawal symptoms may be a part of the present clinical picture. The withdrawal syndrome will vary according to the substance of choice, but such syndromes can include many psychopathological phenomena such as concentration problems, anxiety, and depression.

The respondent describes a number of problematic personality traits. He reports problems of many different types. He is likely to be quite emotionally labile, manifesting fairly rapid and extreme mood swings and, in particular, probably experiences episodes of poorly controlled anger. He appears uncertain about major life issues and has little sense of direction or purpose in his life as it currently stands. It is likely that he has a history of involvement in intense and volatile relationships and tends to be preoccupied with consistent fears of being abandoned or rejected by those around him. He is also quite impulsive and prone to behaviors likely to be self-harmful or self-destructive, such as those involving spending, sex, and/or substance abuse; he may also be at increased risk for self-mutilation or suicidal behavior. This pattern of behaviors is consistent with a diagnosis of Borderline Personality Disorder.

He describes a personality style with numerous antisocial character features to a degree that is unusual even in clinical samples. Such a pattern is typically associated with prominent features of Antisocial Personality Disorder; he is likely to be unreliable and irresponsible and has probably sustained little success in either the social or occupational realm. His responses suggest that he has a history of antisocial behavior and may have manifested a conduct disorder during adolescence. He may have been involved in illegal occupations or engaged in criminal acts involving theft, destruction of property, and physical aggression toward others. He is likely to be egocentric, with little regard for others or the opinions of the society around him. In his desire to satisfy his own impulses, he may take advantage of others and have little sense of loyalty, even to those who are close to him. Although he may describe feelings of guilt over past transgressions, he likely feels little remorse of any lasting nature. He would be expected to place little importance on his social role responsibilities. His behavior is also likely to be reckless; he can be expected to entertain risks that are potentially dangerous to himself and to those around him.

A number of aspects of the respondent's self-description suggest noteworthy peculiarities in thinking and experience. It is likely that he experiences unusual perceptual or sensory events (perhaps including full-blown hallucinations) as well as unusual ideas that may include magical thinking or delusional beliefs. His thought processes are likely to be marked by confusion, distractibility, and difficulty concentrating, and he may experience his thoughts as blocked, withdrawn, or somehow influenced by others. He may have some difficulty establishing close interpersonal relationships.

The respondent indicates that he is experiencing specific fears or anxiety surrounding some situations. The pattern of responses reveals that he is likely to display significant symptoms related to traumatic stress. He has likely experienced a disturbing traumatic event in the past-an event that continues to distress him and produce recurrent episodes of anxiety. Whereas the item content of the PAI does not address specific causes of traumatic stress, possible traumatic events involve victimization (e.g., rape, abuse), combat experiences, life-threatening accidents, and natural disasters.

The respondent describes significant problems frequently associated with aspects of a manic episode. It appears that his clinical picture is primarily characterized by irritability. Others are likely to view him as impatient and hostile. As a result, his relationships with others are probably under stress due to his frustration with the inability or unwillingness of those around him to keep up with his plans and possibly unrealistic demands. At its extreme, this irritability may result in accusations that significant others are attempting to thwart his plans for success and achievement. Grandiosity and abnormal levels of activity do not appear to be prominent features of the clinical picture at this time.

The respondent demonstrates an unusual degree of concern about physical functioning and health matters and probable impairment arising from somatic symptoms. He is likely to report that his daily functioning has been compromised by one or more physical problems. While he may feel that his health is good in general, he is likely to report that the health problems that he does have are complex and difficult to treat successfully. Physical complaints are likely to focus on symptoms of distress in neurological and musculoskeletal systems, such as unusual sensory or motor dysfunction. In psychiatric populations, such symptoms are often associated with conversion disorders, although they may be a result of numerous neurological conditions as well.

The respondent mentions that he is experiencing some degree of anxiety and stress; this degree of worry and sensitivity is still within what would be considered the normal range.

According to the respondent's self-report, he describes NO significant problems in the following areas: undue suspiciousness or hostility; unhappiness and depression.

Self-Concept

The self-concept of the respondent appears to be imperfectly established, with considerable uncertainty about major life issues and goals. Although outwardly he may appear to have adequate self-esteem, this self-esteem is likely to be fragile and he may be self-critical and self-doubting. His self-esteem may be particularly vulnerable to slights or oversights by other people, arising from a self-image that depends unduly upon the current status of his close relationships.

Interpersonal and Social Environment

The respondent's interpersonal style seems best characterized as friendly and extraverted. He will usually present a cheerful and positive picture in the presence of others. He is able to communicate his interest in others in an open and straightforward manner. He usually prefers activities that bring him into contact with others, rather than solitary pursuits, and he is probably quick to offer help to those in need of it. He sees himself as a person with many friends and as one who is comfortable in most social situations.

In considering the social environment of the respondent with respect to perceived stressors and the availability of social supports with which to deal with these stressors, his responses indicate that he is likely to be experiencing a mild degree of stress as a result of difficulties in some major life area. He reports that he has a number of supportive relationships that may serve as some buffer against the effects of this stress. The respondent's current level of distress appears to be related to these situational stressors, and the relatively intact social support system is a favorable prognostic sign for future adjustment.

Treatment Considerations

Treatment considerations involve issues that can be important elements in case management and treatment planning. Interpretation is provided for three general areas relevant to treatment: behaviors that may serve as potential treatment complications, motivation for treatment, and aspects of the respondent's clinical picture that may complicate treatment efforts.

With respect to anger management, the pattern of responses suggests considerable problems with temper and aggressive behavior. Such behaviors are likely play a prominent role in the clinical picture; these behaviors represent a potential treatment complication that should receive careful attention in treatment planning. His responses suggest that he is an individual who is easily angered, has difficulty controlling the expression of his anger, and is perceived by others as having a hostile, angry temperament. When he loses control of his anger, he is likely to respond with more extreme displays of anger, including damage to property and threats to assault others. However, some of these displays may be sudden and unexpected, as he may not display his anger readily when it is experienced. It is likely that those around him are intimidated by his potentially explosive temper and the potential for physical violence. It should also be noted that his risk for aggressive behavior is further exacerbated by the presence of a number of features, such as psychotic symptoms, agitation, and a limited capacity for empathy, that have been found to be associated with increased potential for violence.

With respect to suicidal ideation, the respondent is not reporting distress from thoughts of self-harm.

The respondent appears to have substantial interest in making changes in his life and he appears motivated for treatment. His responses indicate an acknowledgement of important problems, a perception of a need for help in dealing with these problems, and a positive attitude towards his responsibility in pursuing treatment. Despite this favorable sign, the combination of problems that he is reporting suggests that treatment is likely to be quite challenging and that the treatment process is likely to be arduous, with many reversals.

If treatment were to be considered for this individual, particular areas of attention or concern in the early stages of treatment could include:
- He may be somewhat defensive and reluctant to discuss personal problems, and as such he may be at-risk for early termination.
- He may have initial difficulty in placing trust in a treating professional as part of his more general problems in close relationships.
- He may currently be too disorganized or feel too overwhelmed to be able to participate meaningfully in some forms of treatment.
- He is likely to have difficulty with the treating professional as an authority figure, and he may react to the therapist in a hostile or derogatory manner.

DSM-IV Diagnostic Possibilities

Listed below are *DSM-IV* diagnostic possibilities suggested by the configuration of PAI scale scores. The following are advanced as hypotheses; all available sources of information should be considered prior to establishing final diagnoses.

Axis I Diagnostic Considerations:

303.90	Alcohol Dependence
304.90	Other (or Unknown) Substance Dependence (Psychoactive substance dependence)
309.81	Posttraumatic Stress Disorder
300.11	Conversion Disorder

Axis I Rule Out:

296.40	Bipolar I Disorder, Most Recent Episode Manic, Unspecified
312.34	Intermittent Explosive Disorder
294.9	Cognitive Disorder NOS
295.90	Schizophrenia, Undifferentiated Type

Axis II Diagnostic Considerations:

301.83	Borderline Personality Disorder
301.7	Antisocial Personality Disorder

Critical Item Endorsement

A total of 27 PAI items reflecting serious pathology have very low endorsement rates in normal samples. These items have been termed critical items. Endorsement of these critical items is not in itself diagnostic, but review of the content of these items with the respondent may help to clarify the presenting clinical picture. Significant items with item scores of 1, 2, or 3 are listed below.

Delusions and Hallucinations

90.	[Item text was removed from this report for sample purposes.]	(VT, 3)
130.		(VT, 3)

Potential for Aggression

21.	[Item text was removed from this report for sample purposes.]	(MT, 2)
61.		(VT, 3)
101.		(VT, 3)
181.		(VT, 3)

Substance Abuse

55.   [Item text was removed from this report for sample purposes.](VT, 3)
222.   (VT, 3)

Potential Malingering

129.   [Item text was removed from this report for sample purposes.](ST, 1)
249.   (VT, 3)

Unreliability / Resistance

31.   [Item text was removed from this report for sample purposes.](VT, 3)
71.   (ST, 1)

Traumatic Stressors

34.   [Item text was removed from this report for sample purposes.](VT, 3)
114.   (VT, 3)
194.   (VT, 3)
274.   (VT, 3)

Appendix E

REVISED NEO PERSONALITY INVENTORY

Only one computerized interpretive report is available for the NEO PI-R that was developed for normal adults. The NEO PI-R Professional Report (NEO PDR) was developed subsequently because of the frequency with which the NEO PI-R is used in business and industry. The NEO PDR addresses those personal characteristics that have the highest potential for yielding job-relevant information. It was specifically designed to function as a tool both for management planning and for promoting individual growth and development. Two reports are generated for each individual who takes the test—the Management Planning Report and the Individual Planning Report.

This computerized interpretive report is written to describe the *group* of individuals that the individual who is being examined is most like. It is not a stand-alone product that can be used without change. As such, the computerized interpretive report provides the general framework for beginning the process of understanding the individual.

A sample of the computerized interpretive report available on the NEO PI-R follows. Readers should pay special attention to the caveats that precede this report.

Revised NEO Personality Inventory™

Interpretive Report

Developed By

**Paul T. Costa, Jr., PhD,
Robert R. McCrae, PhD,
and PAR Staff**

Client Information

Results For :	Sample Client
Client ID :	123456789
Age :	40
Birthdate :	02/03/1960
Gender :	Male
Test Form :	S
Test Date :	07/26/2000

The following report is based on research using normal adult samples and is intended to provide information on the basic dimensions of personality. The interpretive information contained in this report should be viewed as only one source of hypotheses about the individual being evaluated. No decisions should be based solely on the information contained in this report. This material should be integrated with all other sources of information in reaching professional decisions about this individual. This report is confidential and intended for use by qualified professionals only; it should not be released to the individual being evaluated. "Your NEO PI-R™ Summary" provides a report in lay terms that may be appropriate for feedback to the client.

Client: Sample Client
Client ID: 123456789

Test Date: 07/26/2000
Page 2 of 18

NEO PI-R™ *T*-Score Profile

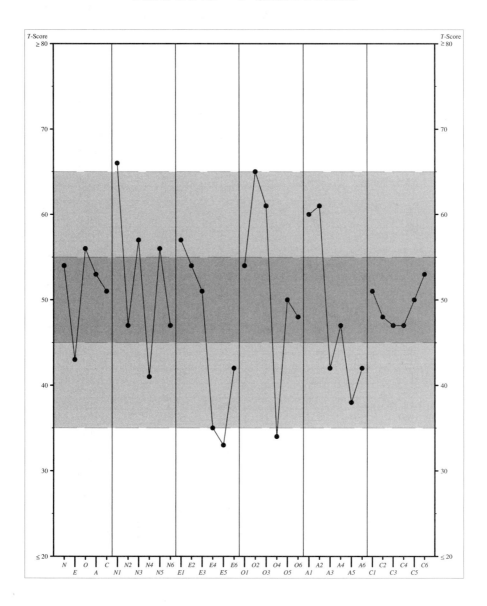

NEO PI-R™ Data Table

Scale		Raw Score	T Score	Range
Factors				
(N)	Neuroticism	---	54	Average
(E)	Extraversion	---	43	Low
(O)	Openness	---	56	High
(A)	Agreeableness	---	53	Average
(C)	Conscientiousness	---	51	Average
Neuroticism Facets				
(N1)	Anxiety	21	66	Very High
(N2)	Angry Hostility	11	47	Average
(N3)	Depression	15	57	High
(N4)	Self-Consciousness	10	41	Low
(N5)	Impulsiveness	18	56	High
(N6)	Vulnerability	8	47	Average
Extraversion Facets				
(E1)	Warmth	25	57	High
(E2)	Gregariousness	18	54	Average
(E3)	Assertiveness	17	51	Average
(E4)	Activity	11	35	Low
(E5)	Excitement-Seeking	9	33	Very Low
(E6)	Positive Emotions	16	42	Low
Openness Facets				
(O1)	Fantasy	19	54	Average
(O2)	Aesthetics	25	65	High
(O3)	Feelings	24	61	High
(O4)	Actions	10	34	Very Low
(O5)	Ideas	20	50	Average
(O6)	Values	20	48	Average
Agreeableness Facets				
(A1)	Trust	25	60	High
(A2)	Straightforwardness	25	61	High
(A3)	Altruism	20	42	Low
(A4)	Compliance	17	47	Average
(A5)	Modesty	13	38	Low
(A6)	Tender-Mindedness	17	42	Low
Conscientiousness Facets				
(C1)	Competence	23	51	Average
(C2)	Order	18	48	Average
(C3)	Dutifulness	22	47	Average
(C4)	Achievement Striving	18	47	Average
(C5)	Self-Discipline	22	50	Average
(C6)	Deliberation	19	53	Average

Validity Indices

Validity indices (i.e., A and C questions, total number of items missing, and response set) are within normal limits.

Because the NEO PI-R™ Scored Data Entry option was used, no checks for missing items, acquiesence, nay-saying, or random responding could be made.

Basis of Interpretation

This report compares the respondent to other adult men. It is based on self-reports of the respondent.

At the broadest level, personality can be described in terms of five basic dimensions or factors. NEO PI-R domain scores provide good estimates of these five factors by summing the six facets in each domain. Domain scores can be calculated easily by hand and are therefore used on the (hand-scored) Profile Form. More precise estimates of standing on the five factors, however, are provided by factor scores, which are a weighted combination of scores on all 30 facets (see Table 2 in the NEO PI-R™ Professional Manual). Factor scores are best calculated by computer.

Because factor scores have somewhat higher convergent and discriminant validity, they are used as the basis of this report. In general, domain T scores and factor T scores are very similar; occasionally, however, they differ. In these cases, the factor T score, which incorporates information from all 30 facets, is usually a more accurate description of the individual.

Factor scores are used to describe the individual at a global level, based on a composite of facet scale scores. To the extent that there is wide scatter among facet scores within a domain, interpretation of that domain and factor becomes more complex. Interpretive statements at the factor level may occasionally conflict with interpretive statements at the facet level. In these cases, particular attention should be focused on the facet scales and their interpretations.

Global Description of Personality: The Five Factors

The most distinctive feature of this individual's personality is his standing on the factor of Extraversion. Such people are somewhat introverted, preferring to do many things alone or with a small group of people. They avoid large, noisy parties and tend to be quiet and reserved in social interactions. Those who know such people would probably describe them as retiring and serious. The fact that these individuals are introverted does not necessarily mean that they lack social skills--many introverts function very well in social situations, although they might prefer to avoid them. Note also that introversion does not imply introspection; these individuals are likely to be thoughtful and reflective only if they are also high in Openness.

This person is high in Openness. High scorers like him are interested in experience for its own sake. They enjoy novelty and variety. They are sensitive to their own feelings and have a greater than average ability to recognize the emotions of others. They have a high appreciation of beauty in art and nature. They are willing to consider new ideas and values, and may be somewhat unconventional in their own views. Peers rate such people as original and curious.

Next, consider the individual's level of Neuroticism. Individuals scoring in this range are average in terms of their emotional stability. They experience a normal amount of psychological distress and have a typical balance of satisfactions and dissatisfactions with life. They are neither high nor low in self-esteem. Their ability to deal with stress is as good as the average person's.

This person is average in Agreeableness. People who score in this range are about as good-natured as the average person. They can be sympathetic, but can also be firm. They are trusting but not gullible, and ready to compete as well as to cooperate with others.

Finally, the individual scores in the average range in Conscientiousness. Men who score in this range have a normal level of need for achievement. They are able to set work aside in pursuit of pleasure or recreation. They are moderately well organized and fairly reliable, and have an average amount of self-discipline.

Detailed Interpretation: Facets of N, E, O, A, and C

Each of the five factors encompasses a number of more specific traits, or facets. The NEO PI-R measures six facets in each of the five factors. An examination of the facet scores provides a more detailed picture of the distinctive way that these factors are seen in this person.

Neuroticism

This individual is anxious, generally apprehensive, and prone to worry. He sometimes feels frustrated, irritable, and angry at others and he is prone to feeling sad, lonely, and dejected. Embarrassment or shyness when dealing with people, especially strangers, is not a problem for him. He reports being poor at controlling his impulses and desires, but he is able to handle stress as well as most people.

Extraversion

This person is very warm and affectionate toward others and he sometimes enjoys large and noisy crowds or parties. He is as assertive as most men when the circumstances require. The individual has a low level of energy and prefers a slow and steady pace. Excitement, stimulation, and thrills have little appeal to him and he is less prone to experience feelings of joy and happiness than most men.

Openness

In experiential style, this individual is generally open. He has an average imagination and only occasionally daydreams or fantasizes. He is particularly responsive to beauty as found in music, art, poetry, or nature, and his feelings and emotional reactions are varied and important to him. He seldom enjoys new and different activities and has a low need for variety in his life. He has only a moderate level of intellectual curiosity and he is generally middle-of-the-road in his social, political, and moral beliefs.

Agreeableness

This person easily trusts others and usually assumes the best about anyone he meets. He is very candid and sincere and would find it difficult to deceive or manipulate others, but he tends to put his own needs and interests before others'. This individual holds his own in conflicts with others, but he is also willing to forgive and forget. He is quite proud of himself and his accomplishments, and happy to take credit for them. Compared to other people, he is hard-headed and tough-minded, and his social and political attitudes reflect his pragmatic realism.

Client: Sample Client
Client ID: 123456789

Test Date: 07/26/2000
Page 6 of 18

Conscientiousness

This individual is reasonably efficient and generally sensible and rational in making decisions. He is moderately neat, punctual, and well organized, and he is reasonably dependable and reliable in meeting his obligations. He has a moderately high need for achievement, but he can also set work aside for recreation. He is average in self-discipline and generally finishes the tasks he starts. He is reasonably cautious, and generally thinks things through before acting.

Personality Correlates: Some Possible Implications

Research has shown that the scales of the NEO PI-R™ are related to a wide variety of psychosocial variables. These correlates suggest possible implications of the personality profile, because individuals who score high on a trait are also likely to score high on measures of the trait's correlates.

The following information is intended to give a sense of how this individual might function in a number of areas. It is not, however, a substitute for direct measurement. If, for example, there is a primary interest in medical complaints, an inventory of medical complaints should be administered in addition to the NEO PI-R™ .

Coping and Defenses

In coping with the stresses of everyday life, this individual is not very likely to react with ineffective responses, such as hostile reactions toward others, self-blame, or escapist fantasies. He is more likely than most adults to use humor and less likely to use faith in responding to threats, losses, and challenges. In addition, he is somewhat less likely to use positive thinking and direct action in dealing with problems.

Somatic Complaints

This person likely responds in a normal fashion to physical problems and illness. He is prone neither to exaggerate nor to minimize physical symptoms and is fairly objective in assessing the seriousness of any medical problems that he might have.

Psychological Well-being

Although his mood and satisfaction with various aspects of his life will vary with the circumstances, in the long run this individual is likely to experience the normal course of positive and negative feelings and be generally content with life. Because he is open to experience, his moods may be more intense and varied than those of the average man.

Cognitive Processes

This individual is likely to be more complex and differentiated in his thoughts, values, and moral judgments than others of his level of intelligence and education. He would also probably score higher on measures of ego development. Because he is open to experience, this individual is likely to perform better than average on tests of divergent thinking ability; that is, he can generate fluent, flexible, and original solutions to many problems. He may be considered creative in his work or hobbies.

Interpersonal Characteristics

Many theories propose a circular arrangement of interpersonal traits around the axes of Love and Status. Within such systems, this person would likely be described as modest, submissive, cold, unfeeling, and especially aloof and reserved. His traits are associated with low standing on the interpersonal dimensions of Love and Status.

Needs and Motives

Research in personality has identified a widely used list of psychological needs. Individuals differ in the degree to which these needs characterize their motivational structure. The respondent is likely to show high levels of the following needs : affiliation, harm avoidance (avoiding danger), nurturance, sentience (enjoyment of sensuous and aesthetic experiences), and understanding (intellectual stimulation). The respondent is likely to show low levels of the following needs : abasement, change, and play.

Clinical Hypotheses: Axis II Disorders and Treatment Implications

The NEO PI-R™ is a measure of personality traits, not psychopathology symptoms, but it is useful in clinical practice because personality profiles can suggest hypotheses about the disorders to which patients are prone and their responses to various kinds of therapy. This section of the NEO PI-R™ Interpretive Report is intended for use in clinical populations only. The hypotheses it offers should be accepted only when they are supported by other corroborating evidence.

Psychiatric diagnoses occur in men and women with different frequencies, and diagnoses are given according to uniform criteria. For that reason, information in this section of the Interpretive Report is based on Combined Gender norms.

Since Same Gender Norms were used for the Interpretive Report, there may be some apparent inconsistencies in score levels and interpretations.

Axis II Disorders

Personality traits are most directly relevant to the assessment of personality disorders coded on Axis II of the DSM-IV. A patient may have a personality disorder in addition to an Axis I disorder, and may meet criteria for more than one personality disorder. Certain diagnoses are more common among individuals with particular personality profiles; this section calls attention to diagnoses that are likely (or unlikely) to apply.

Borderline Personality Disorder. The most common personality disorder in clinical practice is Borderline, and the mean NEO PI-R™ profile of a group of patients diagnosed as having Borderline Personality Disorder provides a basis for evaluating the patient. Profile agreement between the patient and this mean profile neither suggests nor rules out a diagnosis of Borderline Personality Disorder; it is comparable to agreement seen in normal individuals.

Other Personality Disorders. Personality disorders can be conceptually characterized by a prototypic profile of NEO PI-R™ facets that are consistent with the definition of the disorder and its associated features. The coefficient of profile agreement can be used to assess the overall similarity of the patient's personality to other DSM-IV personality disorder prototypes.

It is unlikely that the patient has Paranoid Personality Disorder, Schizotypal Personality Disorder, Histrionic Personality Disorder, or Dependent Personality Disorder because the patient's coefficients of profile agreement are lower than 50% of the subjects' in the normative sample.

Treatment Implications

This patient scores relatively low in Neuroticism, compared to other psychotherapy patients. His problems are likely to be due to a recent stressor or a difficult situation, and treatment may focus on dealing with those specific issues.

Because he is introverted, this patient probably finds it difficult to talk about his problems, and may be uncomfortable interacting with others. He may prefer more direct therapy that requires less spontaneous verbalization, and would probably prefer individual to group therapy.

This patient is open to experience, probably including the novel experience of psychotherapy. He tends to be introspective and psychologically-minded, and will probably be willing to try a variety of psychotherapeutic techniques. Free association, dream interpretation, and imaging techniques are likely to be congenial. Focusing on concrete solutions to problems may be more difficult for extremely open individuals.

Stability of Profile

Research suggests that the individual's personality profile is likely to be stable throughout adulthood. Barring catastrophic stress, major illness, or therapeutic intervention, this description will probably serve as a fair guide even in old age.

Personality Style Graphs

Broad personality factors are pervasive influences on thoughts, feelings, and actions, and combinations of factors provide insight into major aspects of people's lives, defining what can be called *personality styles*. For example, for many years psychologists have known that interpersonal interactions can be conceptualized in terms of a circular ordering or circumplex, defined by the two axes of Dominance and Love, or by the alternative axes of Extraversion and Agreeableness. These two factors define a *Style of Interactions*.

The nine other pairs of factors also define styles, and all ten are represented in NEO Style Graphs. An "X" is placed on each graph to indicate where the respondent falls; the description of that quadrant applies to the respondent. Descriptions are likely to be most accurate if (1) the "X" is far from the center; (2) the "X" is near the diagonal passing through the center of the quadrant; and (3) all the facets in each domain show similar levels. If the "X" is placed in the central circle, then none of the descriptions is especially relevant. If the "X" is located near the horizontal or vertical axis, then both quadrants on that side of the circle may be descriptive. If there is marked scatter among the facets in a domain, then interpretation should focus on these facets rather than the domain and its combinations in Style Graphs.

Appendix F

RORSCHACH INKBLOT METHOD

As noted in Chapter 11, the Rorschach Interpretation Assistance Program (RIAP) generates structural summary data that provide a basis for inferring a broad range of personality characteristics. In its current version, the RIAP5 also generates two narrative reports. One of these reports, called the *Interpretive Report*, presents a detailed set of interpretive hypotheses and their possible implications and is intended for examiner use. The other report, called the *Client Report*, summarizes the major test findings in a personalized and nontechnical manner and is intended to be given to examinees and reviewed with them. There is also a Forensic Edition of the RIAP (the RIAP5-FE) that, in addition to an Interpretive Report and a Client Report, can print out three types of forensic reports. These three separate forensic reports address personality characteristics relevant to psycholegal issues in criminal cases, personal injury litigations, and child custody disputes, and examiners using the RIAP5-FE have the option of printing any one or all three of these forensic reports.

A case sample of the Interpretive Report and Client Report follows. Readers should pay special attention to the caveats that precede the Interpretive Report and indicate the sources of the interpretive statements, how these statements can best be used, and the nature of their limitations.

Rorschach Interpretation Assistance Program™ Interpretive Report

by

John E. Exner, Jr., PhD, and Irving B. Weiner, PhD

Client Information

Name:	Hypothetical	**Gender:**	Male
Client ID:	123456789	**Ethnicity:**	Caucasian
Birthdate:	11/21/1954	**Age (years):**	52
Marital Status:	Married	**Education (years):**	12

Protocol Information

Test Date:	12/15/2006	**Examiner ID :**	Psychologist

Caveats

The Rorschach Interpretive Assistance Program (RIAP) Version 5 for Windows® provides computer-generated quantitative data and narrative statements that are based on the Comprehensive System. The scoring guidelines and interpretive strategies were primarily derived from the following sources: *The Rorschach: A Comprehensive System, Volume 1: Basic Foundations, Fourth Edition* (Exner, 2003); *A Rorschach Workbook for the Comprehensive System, Fifth Edition* (Exner, 2000); *The Rorschach: A Comprehensive System, Volume 3, Assessment of Children and Adolescents, Second Edition* (Exner & Weiner, 1995); and *Principles of Rorschach Interpretation* (Weiner, 2003). The RIAP5 incorporates the new Comprehensive System variables included in *A Rorschach Workbook for the Comprehensive System, Fifth Edition* (Exner, 2001). Additional interpretive information about the Comprehensive System is also presented in *A Primer for Rorschach Interpretation* (Exner, 2000). The quantitative data include a Sequence of Scores, a Structural Summary, a Constellations Table, and a Summary of Response Contents. The narrative statements consist of interpretive hypotheses derived mainly from the structural features of a Rorschach protocol and take only modest account of the thematic imagery contained in individual responses. These computer-based interpretive hypotheses identify various personality characteristics associated with quantitative aspects of Rorschach data and can contribute to forming valid and comprehensive impressions of an individual's psychological functioning. However, the narrative statements produced by the RIAP5 for Windows describe the implications of Rorschach findings among people in general, and do not necessarily apply in all respects to the functioning of any one person. To ensure a thorough and accurate description of a particular individual's personality characteristics and behavioral tendencies, examiners should consider qualitative as well as quantitative features of the person's Rorschach protocol, and they should also judge the applicability of RIAP5 interpretive hypotheses in light of information from other sources concerning the person's clinical status and past and present life circumstances. This interpretive assistance program is intended for use by or under the supervision of qualified professional persons with training and experience in Rorschach assessment. Utilization of the RIAP5 in the absence of such qualifications may violate ethical guidelines for providing services only within the boundaries of one's competence.

Sequence of Scores

Card	Resp. No	Location and DQ	Loc. No.	Determinant(s) and Form Quality	(2)	Content(s)	Pop	Z Score	Special Scores
I	1	Wo	1	Fo		A	P	1.0	
	2	Wo	1	Fo		A	P	1.0	PSV
II	3	Do	3	Fo		A			
	4	D+	6	Mao	2	H		3.0	FAB, COP, GHR
	5	Do	2	FCu	2	A			PER
III	6	Dv	2	Fu	2	Ge			
	7	Do	3	Fo		A			
	8	D+	9	FMpo	2	A,Cg		4.0	FAB
	9	Do	7	FY-		An			
IV	10	Wo	1	Mp.FDo		(H)	P	2.0	GHR
	11	Wo	1	FVu		Ge		2.0	
V	12	Wo	1	Fo		A	P	1.0	
VI	13	Wo	1	FTo		Ay,Ad	P	2.5	
VII	14	WSv/+	1	Fo		Ge		4.0	
	15	DSo	10	Fu		Ay			
VIII	16	W+	1	FMa.mao	2	A,Bt	P	4.5	PER
IX	17	Wo	1	FC-		Xy		5.5	
X	18	Do	14	FYo		Xy			
	19	Do	1	Fo	2	A	P		
	20	Do	9	F-		Ge			
	21	D+	15	FMao	2	A,Bt		4.0	
	22	Do	10	F-		Xy			

Structural Summary

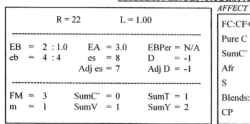

Location Features

Zf	=	12
ZSum	=	34.5
ZEst	=	38.0
W	=	9
(Wv	=	0)
D	=	13
W+D	=	22
Dd	=	0
S	=	2

DQ

			(FQ-)
+	=	4	(0)
o	=	16	(4)
v/+	=	1	(0)
v	=	1	(0)

Form Quality

		FQx	MQual	W+D
+	=	0	0	0
o	=	14	2	14
u	=	4	0	4
-	=	4	0	4
none	=	0	0	0

Determinants

Blends
M.FD
FM.m

Single		
M	=	1
FM	=	2
m	=	0
FC	=	2
CF	=	0
C	=	0
Cn	=	0
FC'	=	0
C'F	=	0
C'	=	0
FT	=	1
TF	=	0
T	=	0
FV	=	1
VF	=	0
V	=	0
FY	=	2
YF	=	0
Y	=	0
Fr	=	0
rF	=	0
FD	=	0
F	=	11
(2)	=	7

Contents

H	=	1
(H)	=	1
Hd	=	0
(Hd)	=	0
Hx	=	0
A	=	10
(A)	=	0
Ad	=	1
(Ad)	=	0
An	=	1
Art	=	0
Ay	=	2
Bl	=	0
Bt	=	2
Cg	=	1
Cl	=	0
Ex	=	0
Fd	=	0
Fi	=	0
Ge	=	4
Hh	=	0
Ls	=	0
Na	=	0
Sc	=	0
Sx	=	0
Xy	=	3
Idio	=	0

S-Constellation

☐	FV+VF+V+FD > 2	
☐	Col-Shd Blends > 0	
☐	Ego < .31 or > .44	
☐	MOR > 3	
☐	Zd > ±3.5	
☑	es > EA	
☐	CF + C > FC	
☑	X+% < .70	
☐	S > 3	
☐	P < 3 or > 8	
☑	Pure H < 2	
☐	R < 17	
3	Total	

Special Scores

			Lvl-1		Lvl-2
DV	=	0	x1	0	x2
INC	=	0	x2	0	x4
DR	=	0	x3	0	x6
FAB	=	2	x4	0	x7
ALOG	=	0	x5		
CON	=	0	x7		

Raw Sum6	=	2
Wgtd Sum6	=	8

AB	= 0		GHR	= 2	
AG	= 0		PHR	= 0	
COP	= 1		MOR	= 0	
CP	= 0		PER	= 2	
			PSV	= 1	

RATIOS, PERCENTAGES, AND DERIVATIONS

R = 22		L = 1.00

EB	=	2 : 1.0	EA	= 3.0	EBPer	= N/A		
eb	=	4 : 4	es	= 8	D	= -1		
			Adj es	= 7	Adj D	= -1		

FM	=	3	SumC'	= 0	SumT	= 1	
m	=	1	SumV	= 1	SumY	= 2	

AFFECT

FC:CF+C	= 2 : 0	
Pure C	= 0	
SumC' : WSumC	= 0 : 1.0	
Afr	= 0.47	
S	= 2	
Blends:R	= 2 : 22	
CP	= 0	

INTERPERSONAL

COP = 1		AG = 0	
GHR:PHR		= 2 : 0	
a:p		= 4 : 2	
Food		= 0	
SumT		= 1	
Human Content		= 2	
Pure H		= 1	
PER		= 2	
Isolation Index		= 0.27	

IDEATION

a:p	=	4 : 2	Sum6	= 2	
Ma:Mp	=	1 : 1	Lvl-2	= 0	
2AB+(Art+Ay)	=	2	WSum6	= 8	
MOR	=	0	M-	= 0	
			M none	= 0	

MEDIATION

XA%	= 0.82
WDA%	= 0.82
X-%	= 0.18
S-	= 0
P	= 7
X+%	= 0.64
Xu%	= 0.18

PROCESSING

Zf	= 12
W:D:Dd	= 9:13:0
W : M	= 9 : 2
Zd	= -3.5
PSV	= 1
DQ+	= 4
DQv	= 1

SELF-PERCEPTION

3r+(2)/R	= 0.32
Fr+rF	= 0
SumV	= 1
FD	= 1
An+Xy	= 4
MOR	= 0
H:(H)+Hd+(Hd)	= 1 : 1

PTI = 0	☐ DEPI = 4	☑ CDI = 5	☐ S-CON = 3	☐ HVI = No	☐ OBS = No

CONSTELLATIONS TABLE

S-Constellation (Suicide Potential)

☐ Positive if 8 or more conditions are true:
    NOTE: Applicable only for subjects over 14 years old.

☐ FV+VF+V+FD [2] > 2
☐ Col-Shd Blends [0] > 0
☐ Ego [0.32] < .31 *or* > .44
☐ MOR [0] > 3
☐ Zd [-3.5] > ±3.5
☑ es [8] > EA [3.0]
☐ CF + C [0] > FC [2]
☑ X+% [0.64] < .70
☐ S [2] > 3
☐ P [7] < 3 or > 8
☑ Pure H [1] < 2
☐ R [22] < 17

3   Total

PTI (Perceptual-Thinking Index)

☐ (XA% [0.82] < 0.70) *and* (WDA% [0.82] < 0.75)
☐ X-% [0.18] > 0.29
☐ (Sum Level 2 Special Scores [0] > 2)
     and (FAB2 [0] > 0)
☐ ((R [22] < 17) *and* (WSum6 [8] > 12)) *or*
     ((R [22] > 16) *and* (WSum6 [8] > 17))
☐ (M- [0] > 1) *or* (X-% [0.18] > 0.40)
0   Total

DEPI (Depression Index)

☐ Positive if 5 or more conditions are true:

☑ (FV + VF + V [1] > 0) *or* (FD [1] > 2)
☐ (Col-Shd Blends [0] > 0) *or* (S [2] > 2)
☑ (3r + (2)/R [0.32] > 0.44 *and* Fr + rF [0] = 0)
     or (3r + (2)/R [0.32] < 0.33)
☑ (Afr [0.47] < 0.46) *or* (Blends [2] < 4)
☐ (SumShading [4] > FM + m [4])
     or (SumC' [0] > 2)
☐ (MOR [0] > 2) *or* (2xAB + Art + Ay [2] > 3)
☑ (COP [1] < 2)
     or ([Bt+2xCl+Ge+Ls+2xNa]/R [0.27] > 0.24)
4   Total

CDI (Coping Deficit Index)

☑ Positive if 4 or more conditions are true:

☑ (EA [3.0] < 6) *or* (AdjD [-1] < 0)
☑ (COP [1] < 2) *and* (AG [0] < 2)
☑ (Weighted Sum C [1.0] < 2.5)
     or (Afr [0.47] < 0.46)
☑ (Passive [2] > Active + 1 [5])
     or (Pure H [1] < 2)
☑ (Sum T [1] > 1)
     or (Isolate/R [0.27] > 0.24)
     or (Food [0] > 0)
5   Total

HVI (Hypervigilance Index)

☐ Positive if condition 1 is true and at least 4 of the others
are true:

☐ (1) FT + TF + T [1] = 0
- -
☐ (2) Zf [12] > 12
☐ (3) Zd [-3.5] > +3.5
☐ (4) S [2] > 3
☐ (5) H + (H) + Hd + (Hd) [2] > 6
☐ (6) (H) + (A) + (Hd) + (Ad) [1] > 3
☐ (7) H + A : Hd + Ad [12:1] < 4 : 1
☐ (8) Cg [1] > 3

OBS (Obsessive Style Index)

☐ (1) Dd [0] > 3
☐ (2) Zf [12] > 12
☐ (3) Zd [-3.5] > +3.0
☐ (4) Populars [7] > 7
☐ (5) FQ+ [0] > 1
- -
☐ Positive if one or more is true:

☐ Conditions 1 to 5 are all true
☐ Two or more of 1 to 4 are true *and* FQ+ [0] > 3
☐ 3 or more of 1 to 5 are true
     and X+% [0.64] > 0.89
☐ FQ+ [0] > 3 *and* X+% [0.64] > 0.89

NOTE: '*' *indicates a cutoff that has been adjusted for age norms.*

Interpretive Hypotheses

This record contains a sufficient number of responses to provide reliable information and to support valid interpretations.

Capacity for Control and Tolerance for Stress

EB = 2 : 1.0	EA = 3.0		D = -1
eb = 4 : 4	es = 8	Adj es = 7	Adj D = -1
FM = 3 C' = 0 T = 1			☑ CDI = 5
m = 1 V = 1 Y = 2			

1. This person appears to be in a state of mild but chronic stimulus overload resulting from persistent difficulty in mustering adequate psychological resources to cope with the demands being imposed on him by internal and external events in his life. This finding is not surprising in light of other indications that his adaptive capacities are below average for an adult. Therefore, he is likely to have difficulty managing even ordinary ideational and emotional stresses of everyday life without becoming unduly upset by them. He is consequently at risk for recurrent episodes of overt anxiety, tension, nervousness, and irritability. People with this pattern of stimulus overload tend to have limited tolerance for frustration and less than average ability to persevere in the face of obstacles; they may consequently show a tendency toward emotional outbursts and impulsive actions. Because the level of his chronic stimulus overload is only mild, the usual extent of his subjectively felt distress is unlikely to result in any serious adjustment problems. In fairly structured situations in which he knows what is expected of him, he may even function in a reasonably untroubled fashion that seldom attracts the attention of others. At the same time, because this person is likely to be experiencing some dissatisfaction with himself or his life, he is more likely than most people to feel a need to change and to be receptive to interventions designed to reduce his level of subjectively felt distress. In treatment, such individuals benefit most not from efforts to reduce the stressors in their lives, but instead from help to improve their coping skills and to learn effective strategies for stress management. The specific sources of stress in his life appear to involve ongoing concerns and issues rather than merely situational or transient problems and worries. The test data identify the following possibilities in this regard, each of which is discussed elsewhere in this narrative report. He shows a level of emotional stress that appears to be interfering with pleasurable modulation of affect and that may make him susceptible to becoming depressed. His level of stress is probably due in part to self-critical attitudes that may be provoked by feelings of guilt and remorse or by regrets for ill-advised actions.

Affect

					Blends
☐ DEPI	=	4	EBPer = N/A	M.FD	
EB	=	2 : 1.0	FC:CF+C = 2 : 0	FM.m	
eb	=	4 : 4	Pure C = 0		
			SumC':WSumC = 0 : 1.0		
C' = 0	T = 1		Afr = 0.47		
V = 1	Y = 2		2AB+Art+Ay = 2		
		S	= 2		
			(S to I, II, and III = 0)		
			Blends/R = 2 : 22		
			CP = 0		

2. He is showing some emotional stress that probably derives in part from negative feelings he is experiencing toward himself in relation to personal characteristics he regards as undesirable, decisions he regards as badly made, or actions he regards as ill-advised.

3. He shows a potentially maladaptive style of experiencing and expressing affect in which he exerts more stringent control over his feelings than most adults. He appears capable of processing emotion in a

RIAP™ Interpretive Report
Client Name: Hypothetical
Client ID: 123456789

relatively well-modulated and reserved manner in which feelings emerge and dissipate slowly and are deeply felt but mild to moderate in their intensity. However, he gives little evidence of capacity for relatively unmodulated and spontaneous processing of emotion, in which feelings come and go quickly and tend to be superficial, yet sometimes intense, while they last. As a consequence, he is likely to be an emotionally reserved person who has difficulty relaxing emotionally, being spontaneous, showing his feelings, and relating to others on a casual and informal basis. This emotional inhibition may place him at risk for adjustment difficulties in his interpersonal relationships.

Self-Perception

R = 22	☐ OBS = No	☐ HVI = No		
3r+(2)/R = 0.32	FD = 1	MOR = 0	Hx = 0	An+Xy = 4
Fr+rF = 0	V = 1	T = 1	Sx = 0	
H : (H)+Hd+(Hd) = 1 : 1				

Responses to be read

MOR Responses	FQ- Responses	M Responses	FM Responses	m Responses
None	9, 17, 20, 22	4, 10	8, 16, 21	16

4. This person is not paying sufficient attention to himself and may even be purposefully avoiding self-focusing. An inclination to ignore oneself in this way often derives from a low estimate of one's personal worth. Accordingly, he may be comparing himself unfavorably to other people, whom he regards as being more able, more attractive, more talented, and generally more worthwhile than he is. If so, then he is likely to experience low self-esteem and may lack confidence in himself. Additionally, his tendency to judge himself unfavorably may result in feelings of futility and contribute to episodes of depression.

5. When this person is paying attention to himself, he tends to engage more often than most people in critical self-examination of his attitudes and motivations. Reflecting on oneself in this way often contributes to being (a) cognizant of how best to meet one's needs, (b) sensitive to how one's behavior affects other people, and (c) open to reconsidering one's self-image and impression of oneself. This capacity for introspection and self-awareness typically facilitates effective participation and positive personality change in psychotherapy. In this person's case, however, self-examination appears to include rumination about aspects of himself or his actions that he regards as undesirable. He may experience chronic self-criticism and poor self-regard, and his negative attitudes toward himself are probably promoting a sense of personal dissatisfaction that can range from mild displeasure to self-disgust or even self-loathing. Therefore his view of himself is likely to be generating emotional pain and may render him vulnerable to episodes of depression.

6. This person appears unusually preoccupied with and/or concerned about his body and bodily functions. People who have real or imagined physical handicaps or health problems often show such preoccupation and concern. In the absence of indications that he is currently experiencing somatic distress or diminished physical capacity, his bodily preoccupation probably reflects an image of himself as a fragile or vulnerable person.

7. Distorted form responses (FQ-) usually involve some projection of a person's underlying attitudes and concerns. Responses 9, 17, 20, and 22 are perceptually inaccurate and should be examined for the possible implications of their thematic imagery.

8. Movement responses often contain projected self- and object-representations that provide clues to people's underlying concepts of themselves and other people. Responses 4 and 10 in this record include M; responses 8, 16, and 21 include FM; and response 16 includes m. The imagery in these responses should be examined for the possible implications of its thematic content.

Client Name: Hypothetical
Client ID: 123456789

Interpersonal Perception

☑ CDI = 5	a:p = 4 : 2	T = 1	EA = 3.0	EB = 2 : 10	
☐ HVI = No	Food = 0	PER = 2	COP = 1	AG = 0	S = 2
Sum H = 2	H:(H)+Hd+(Hd) = 1 : 1		Pure H = 1		
GHR:PHR = 2 : 0					
Afr = 0.47		Isolate/R = 0.27		C'+T+V+Y = 4	

Responses to be read

M with Pair	FM with Pair	m with Pair	Human Contents
4	8, 16, 21	16	4, 10

9. This person appears to have limited ability to manage interpersonal relationships in a comfortable and rewarding manner. He may conduct himself appropriately in social situations and at times, even make an initially favorable impression on other people. Nevertheless, as a consequence of inadequate social skills that may not be readily apparent, he tends to opt for superficial and transient relationships with others and to back away from involved or prolonged relationships out of concern that they will make more demands on him than he can handle. In addition, his social ineptness may make him vulnerable to experiencing embarrassment and failure in social situations and to being ignored or rejected by others who see him as a distant, guarded, and ineffective person. Individuals with this pattern of deficient coping can frequently benefit from treatment focused on interpersonal anxiety reduction and social skills training.

10. This person gives evidence of adaptive capacity to anticipate and establish close, intimate, and mutually supportive relationships with other people. Ordinarily, this adequate basic capacity to form interpersonal attachments contributes to people needing, wanting, enjoying, and reaching out for physical and/or emotional closeness to others. However, being capable of forming attachments to others does not guarantee numerous and pleasurable interpersonal relationships, especially in people who lack good social skills or who for various reasons become socially fearful, isolated, or withdrawn.

11. He shows less interest in other people than most adults do. As a consequence, he may be indifferent to being around people and inattentive to what they are saying and doing. Such limited interpersonal interest constitutes a personality liability and is likely to be associated with his having infrequent or mostly superficial relationships with others. This likelihood is increased by other data suggesting that he is somewhat emotionally withdrawn.

12. This person shows little interest in or expectation of engaging in collaborative or competitive relationships with other people. Because of his seeming indifference or aversion to interpersonal involvement, he is likely to strike others as distant and aloof. Although he may not be actively disliked by members of social groups to which he belongs, he has limited prospects for becoming socially popular or well-liked. His personality characteristics in this regard will not necessarily prevent him from forming close relationships on an individual basis, but they are likely to result in his often hovering on the periphery of group interactions rather than seeking or finding a place at their core.

13. He tends to be less involved than most people in social interactions with others, and regardless of how much interest he may show in what people are doing, he gives evidence of being a socially withdrawn individual who is interpersonally isolated. Even people who enjoy and have an adequate capacity to form interpersonal attachments may for various reasons be avoiding social interactions or be in circumstances that allow few opportunities for interpersonal contact. As a consequence, there may not be many people who are playing an important part in his life, even if he appears to have the company of an ample number of friends and relatives. Whatever isolation he shows is probably related to his previously noted indifference to being around other people.

14. Movement responses that include a pair often contain projected object representations that provide clues to an individual's underlying concepts of people and how they are likely to interact. Response 4 in this record involves M with a pair; responses 8, 16, and 21 involve FM with a pair; and response 16 involves m with a pair. The imagery in these responses should be examined for the possible implications of its thematic content.

15. The nouns that are used to identify human content and the adjectives that are used to describe human or human-like figures often reveal underlying aspects of an individual's concepts of and attitudes toward

people. Responses 4 and 10 in this record involve human content and should be examined for the possible implications of their thematic imagery.

Information Processing

R	= 22	L	= 1.00			
EB	= 2 : 1.0	W:D:Dd	= 9 : 13 : 0	Zd	= -3.5	DQ+ = 4
Zf	= 12	W:M	= 9 : 2	PSV	= 1	DQv/+ = 1
☐ HVI	= No	☐ OBS	= No			DQv = 1

16. This person lacks adequate openness to experience and has an avoidant style in which he tends to view himself and his world with an overly narrow focus of attention. Such people frequently overlook the subtle nuances of social and interpersonal situations, arrive at decisions without having given them much thought, and select courses of action in which they have little emotional investment. Because of his narrow frame of reference, he is likely to have little tolerance for uncertainty and ambiguity, to feel most comfortable in clearly defined and well-structured situations, and to favor simple solutions, even to complex problems. Insensitivity to subtlety and simplistic problem solving may result in his failing to recognize the kinds of behaviors that are expected or required in various situations, which will in turn put him at risk for behaving in ways that offend others and get him into trouble.

17. In attending to his experience, he tends to take in too little information and to examine his experience less thoroughly than most people would consider adequate. As a consequence, he is at risk for coming to conclusions hastily, after only cursory attention to relevant considerations; for working carelessly and feeling satisfied with final products that do not reflect the full measure of his ability; and for scanning situations in a cursory manner that takes insufficient account of considerations he should notice. This predilection for seeking out and being satisfied with only minimal amounts of information defines a pattern of underincorporation that promotes rapid decision making and speedy completion of tasks, but often at the expense of ill-considered conclusions and inferior products. By taking inadequate account of information he could easily process, this person is at risk for errors of oversight in what he chooses to think and do and for lack of accomplishment in what he attempts to achieve.

18. The quality of his efforts to focus his attention with precision and to synthesize aspects of his experience falls below that of most people. This finding is not uncommon among individuals whose cognitive capacities are limited. In the presence of average intellectual ability and otherwise unimpaired cognitive capacities, however, it suggests a simplistic way of looking at the world in which little energy is devoted to seeking out or recognizing complex relationships between events. His preference for maintaining a narrow frame of reference and his tendency to oversimplify his experience are probably contributing to the below average quality of his information processing.

19. This person has given a Perseveration response which should be examined to determine whether it is a *Within card* Perseveration. If so, he appears to have some occasional difficulty in shifting his attention from one matter to another. He does not have a substantial problem in this regard and it seems to occur as a result of his preferring not to shift set, rather than his being unable to do so. Nevertheless, his lack of mental flexibility may detract from his ability to pay attention to events.

Cognitive Mediation

				Minus Responses
R = 22				9, 17, 20, 22
Lambda = 1.00	P = 7	☐ OBS = No		
FQx+ = 0		WDA% = 0.82		
FQxo = 14		XA% = 0.82		
FQxu = 4		X+% = 0.64		
FQx- = 4		F+% = 0.64		
FQx none = 0		X-% = 0.18		
		S-% = 0.00		
		Xu% = 0.18		
Pure C = 0	Pure Y = 0	M- = 0		
Pure C' = 0	Pure T = 0	M none = 0		

20. He is about as capable as most people of recognizing conventional modes of response. Although this ability and his willingness to recognize obvious aspects of reality constitute personality assets, they do not preclude the possibility of his distorting less obvious aspects of reality or choosing to see the world in unconventional ways.

21. He demonstrates generally good ability to form accurate impressions of himself and to interpret the actions and intentions of others without distortion. He is additionally capable of adequately anticipating the consequences of his own actions and of recognizing the boundaries of appropriate behavior in various situations. These indications of good reality testing and sound judgment identify a substantial personality strength that may not preclude his encountering adjustment difficulties, but that minimize their likelihood of occurrence and improve his prospects for overcoming them should they arise. His good grasp of reality is bolstered by his adequate ability to recognize and endorse obvious clues to conventional modes of response.

Ideation

R = 22	L = 1.00	PTI = 0	☐ DEPI = 4				
					Critical Special Scores		
EB	=	2 : 1.0	EBPer	= N/A	DV	= 0	DV2	= 0
eb	=	4 : 4	MOR	= 0	INC	= 0	INC2	= 0
FM	=	3	m	= 1	DR	= 0	DR2	= 0
a:p	=	4 : 2	M-	= 0	FAB	= 2	FAB2	= 0
Ma:Mp	=	1 : 1	M none	= 0	ALOG	= 0		
			2AB+Art+Ay	= 2	CONTAM	= 0	Raw Sum6	= 2
							Wgtd Sum6	= 8

Responses with Critical Special Scores:
4, 8

22. He appears to be experiencing a modest amount of intrusive ideation over which he has little control and that involves (a) disconcerting awareness of needs that are not being met and/or (b) worrisome thoughts about being unable to prevent other people or events from determining his destiny. The level of his intrusive ideation is within normal limits, however, consistent with harboring some unfulfilled wants and wishes, and it does not ordinarily impair his abilities to attend and concentrate.

23. He appears capable of thinking in a flexible manner that facilitates his being able to contemplate alternative perspectives on his experience, to consider changing his point of view, and to keep his mind open to new information and previously unfamiliar ideas, no matter how long or firmly he has held his present opinions and beliefs. Such flexibility is a personality asset that promotes good adjustment and contributes to progress in psychotherapy, although it does not ensure that a person will always think logically and coherently.

Overview

This person has produced a valid record that should ordinarily provide reliable information about his personality functioning.

This person lacks openness to experience and has an avoidant style in which he tends to view the world with an overly narrow frame of reference. As a consequence, he is likely to have little tolerance for uncertainty and ambiguity, to feel most comfortable in clearly defined and well-structured situations, and to favor simple solutions to even complex problems.

He demonstrates generally good abilities to perceive events conventionally without sacrificing his individuality, to form accurate impressions about himself, to interpret the actions and intentions of others without distortion, to adequately anticipate the consequences of his own actions, and to correctly construe what constitutes appropriate behavior in various kinds of situations. His good reality testing constitutes a substantial personality strength.

This person is inclined to examine his experience in a cursory manner and to take inadequate account of information he should consider. He is consequently at risk for being hasty and careless in the way he makes decisions and works on tasks.

Client Name: Hypothetical
Client ID: 123456789

He shows a potentially maladaptive style of experiencing and expressing affect in which he exerts more stringent control over his feelings than most people. Consequently, he is likely to be an emotionally reserved individual who has difficulty relaxing, being spontaneous, showing his feelings, and relating to others on a casual and informal basis.

This person appears to compare himself unfavorably to other people and consequently to suffer from low self-esteem and limited self-confidence.

This person appears to be less capable than most people of dealing effectively with everyday experience, especially with respect to social situations. His limited social skills are likely to be contributing to awkward, inept, or inappropriate management of interpersonal relationships.

This person gives evidence of adaptive capacity to anticipate and establish close, intimate, and mutually supportive relationships with other people. Nevertheless, given his limited social skills, he may have difficulty sustaining and enjoying interpersonal attachments.

He shows less interest in other people than ordinarily would be expected. Such limited interpersonal interest constitutes a personality liability and is likely to be associated with his having infrequent or mostly superficial relationships with other people.

End of Report

Rorschach Interpretation Assistance Program™ Client Report

by

Irving B. Weiner, PhD
and
PAR Staff

Client Information

Name: Hypothetical
Test Date: 12/15/2006

The following report is based on the responses you gave to the Rorschach Inkblot Method and should be discussed with the clinician who examined you. The report describes how you appear to pay attention to your surroundings, think about your experiences, express your feelings, manage your stress, think about yourself, and relate to other people. These descriptions are based on Rorschach findings among people in general who give responses similar to yours. The descriptions do not necessarily apply in every respect to each individual person. For this reason, some of the statements in the report may describe you more accurately than others. In addition, the report may identify some aspects of yourself that have previously escaped your notice or of which you have not been fully aware. Discussing these Rorschach results with your clinician, particularly with regard to understanding them in the context of your past and present life circumstances, will help you get the maximum benefit from the information provided by the test.

You gave enough responses to provide reliable information and to support sound conclusions about yourself.

The test findings suggest that you have above average capacities to manage stress. However, you appear to have been dealing with chronic demands in your life that exceed your ability to cope with them comfortably. You have been and continue to be at risk for episodes of anxiety, tension, nervousness, and irritability. You may have a limited tolerance for frustration and a tendency toward emotional outbursts and impulsive actions. Because your stress overload is only mild, you may be able to function in a reasonably effective manner in situations in which you know what is expected of you. However, in unfamiliar or challenging situations, your persistent concerns may interfere with your comfort level and with your ability to exercise adequate control over what you think, say, and do.

You are showing some possible problems with experiencing and expressing emotions in which you are exerting more control over your feelings than most adults. Your test responses suggest that you are an emotionally reserved person who has difficulty relaxing emotionally, being spontaneous, showing your feelings, and relating to others on a casual and informal basis.

You appear to be paying less attention to yourself than most people, which often results from having a poor opinion of oneself. Your test responses suggest that you tend to compare yourself unfavorably to other people. You may suffer from low self-esteem and lack self-confidence because of this tendency.

Your test responses suggest that you are more likely than most people to worry about aspects of yourself or your behavior that you view as undesirable. Your self-awareness should help you to recognize how you can have your needs met and how your behavior affects other people. At the same time, you may be inclined to be self-critical and to feel dissatisfied with yourself.

Your test responses suggest that you are very concerned about your body and bodily functions. You may be having some physical ailment or incapacity that accounts for this concern. If not, you may see yourself as a fragile person who is vulnerable to being harmed or becoming ill.

Your test responses suggest that you have difficulty managing relationships with other people in a comfortable and rewarding manner. This may be a result of limited social skills. You may be inclined to avoid getting involved with people because of concerns you have about not being able to meet their expectations.

You appear capable of forming close and mutually supportive relationships with other people. This capacity does not guarantee a pleasurable social life, but it is a valuable personality strength.

Your test responses suggest that you do not have much interest in or expectation of acting in cooperation with other people. Because of your apparent indifference to cooperating with others, you may seem distant and aloof to other people. This characteristic may not prevent you from forming close relationships on an individual basis, but it is likely to result in your not seeking or finding a place at the center of group activities.

You tend to be less involved than most people in social interactions. You give some evidence of being isolated from people who play an important role in your life.

Your test responses suggest that you are a practical kind of person who prefers to keep your life simple and to deal with situations in a direct manner. You may arrive at decisions without giving them much thought, and you may respond to situations without becoming fully involved in their emotional aspects. You probably do not have much tolerance for uncertainty or ambiguity, and you are likely to feel most comfortable in clearly defined and well-structured situations where you know exactly what is expected of you.

Your manner of responding to this test suggests that you are inclined to examine situations less thoroughly than most people, perhaps taking in less information than you need for solving problems or arriving at decisions. As a result, you may be at risk for making decisions hastily, working on tasks carelessly, and sacrificing accuracy for speed.

You appear to be about as capable as most people of being conventional. You are likely to behave in socially expected ways and to show respect for rules and regulations, but not to the extent of rigid conformity.

You generally show a good ability to form accurate impressions of yourself and to clearly see the actions and intentions of others. You seem capable of correctly anticipating the consequences of your actions and of recognizing what is appropriate behavior in various kinds of situations.

You appear to be capable of thinking about things in a flexible manner. This flexibility allows you to consider changing your opinions and your point of view. You tend to keep your mind open to new information and to previously unfamiliar ideas.

End of Report

Author Index

Subject Index

Aberrant Experiences scale [*RC8abx*], 102, 136, 192

Access to testing materials, 83, 89

Accuracy of interpretations, 71

Addiction Admission Scale [*AAS*], 102, 137, 192, 193, 194, 243

Addiction Potential Scale [*APS*], 102, 137, 193, 194

Additional Global Indices, 380–382

Aggression scale [*AGG*] 285, 301, 302
  Aggressive Attitude [*AGG-A*], 285
  Physical Aggression [*AGG-P*], 285, 307, 309, 311
  Verbal Aggression [*AGG-V*], 285, 311

Aggression scale [*AGGR*], 102, 136, 206

Agreeableness [*A*], 315, 316, 317, 319, 326, 331, 336, 338, 339, 340, 341
  Altruism [*A3*], 316, 332
  Compliance [*A4*], 316, 332
  Modesty [*A5*], 316, 332
  Straightforwardness [*A2*], 316, 332
  Tender-Mindedness [*A6*], 316, 333
  Trust [*A1*], 316, 332

Alcohol Dependence, 57, 60, 63, 103, 252, 278, 297, 300, 301

Alcohol/Drug Problem Acknowledgment scale [*ACK*], 102, 206, 243, 249

Alcohol/Drug Problem Proneness scale [*PRO*], 102, 243

Alcohol problems, 61, 62, 63, 65, 72

Alcohol Problems [ALC] scale, 104, 105

Alienation scale (MMPI-A [A-aln]), 101, 206, 238, 241, 242, 243

Anger scale:
  MMPI-2 [*ANG*], 101, 136
  MMPI-A [*A-ang*], 101, 206

Answering the Referral Questions, 40

Anticipating Interpersonal Intimacy and Security (SumT, HVI), 379–380

Antisocial Behavior scale:
  MMPI-2 [*RC4asb*], 102, 136, 169, 190, 192
  PAI [*ANT*], 284, 307, 311

Antisocial Features [*ANT*] scale, 104, 284–311
  Antisocial Behaviors [*ANT-A*], 284, 307, 311
  Egocentricity [*ANT-E*], 284, 307, 309
  Stimulus-Seeking [*ANT-S*], 284, 307, 311

Antisocial Personality Disorder, 113, 157, 169, 173, 175, 180, 300, 301, 302, 469, 515

Antisocial Practices scale (*ASP*), 101, 137, 140, 187, 190, 195, 461

Anxiety Related Disorders scale (*ARD*), 103, 284–307
  Obsessive-Compulsive [*ARD-O*], 284, 304
  Phobias [*ARD-P*], 284, 304
  Traumatic Stress [ARD-T], 284, 298, 304, 307, 309

Anxiety scale:
  MMPI-2 (*ANX*), 101, 103, 136
  MMPI-A (*A-anx*), 101, 206
  PAI (*ANX*), 284–303

665